Invitation to Corrections

with Built-in Study Guide

Clemens Bartollas
University of Northern Iowa

Allyn and Bacon
Boston ■ London ■ Toronto ■ Sydney ■ Tokyo ■ Singapore

Editor in Chief, Social Sciences: Karen Hanson
Series Editor: Jennifer Jacobson
Senior Development Editor: Mary Ellen Lepionka
Editorial Assistant: Thomas Jefferies
Marketing Manager: Judeth Hall
Editorial-Production Service: Omegatype Typography, Inc.
Composition and Prepress Buyer: Linda Cox
Manufacturing Buyer: JoAnne Sweeney
Cover Administrator: Linda Knowles
Electronic Composition: Omegatype Typography, Inc.
Photo Researcher: Katharine S. Cook
Text Designer: Carol Somberg Design

Library of Congress Cataloging-in-Publication Data

Bartollas, Clemens.
    Invitation to corrections : with built-in study guide / Clemens Bartollas.
        p. cm.
    Includes bibliographical references and index.
    ISBN 0-205-31412-0
        1. Corrections—United States—History. 2. Corrections—Study and Teaching—United
States. 3. Corrections—Government policy—United States I. Title.

HV9304 .B37 2002
365'.973—dc21   2001045803

Printed in the United States of America
10   9   8   7   6   CIN   11 10 09 08 07

Photo credits appear on page 510, which constitutes a continuation of this copyright page.

To Jacob Ethan Polatty,
A beautiful grandson

Brief Contents

Contents

chapter three

The Development of Corrections in the United States   44

chapter four

The Punishment of Offenders   68

PART 2   Community-Based Corrections   94

chapter five

The Rise of Community-Based Corrections   94

chapter six

Probation   120

PART 4   Prisoners   330

chapter fourteen

The Male Prisoner   330

chapter fifteen

The Female Prisoner   352

Preface

Some people say that the correctional system in the United States has never been in worse shape. Both inmates and corrections staff suffer the effects of overcrowding at levels not even imaginable two or three decades before. In the 1990s, there was wide support among policymakers that the purpose of prisons was to make inmates suffer. The inmate population is racially and ethnically polarized, and communal warfare is sometimes just a spark away. Correctional administrators face the problems of prison gangs, drug and alcohol abuse, and an increasing population of inmates with AIDS. Special offenders groups—prisoners with mental-health problems, prisoners over age 55, prisoners with physical impairments, sex violators, and a rapidly increasing population of female prisoners—pose additional challenges.

This is a good time to study corrections. The blueprint of the corrections system emerging in the twenty-first century will be somewhat different than it is now. This blueprint will probably indicate a declining emphasis on treatment and rehabilitation, as well as declining court involvement in prisoners' rights issues, and increasing emphasis on efficient and cost-effective management. Many of the old prisons and jails of the past have been replaced; indeed, 50 percent of prisons have been built within the past twenty years. Most of the recently constructed jails are "New Generation" jails, and they are a great improvement over traditional jail construction and supervision. During the 1990s, a new model of correctional administration was emerging throughout the United States, and the wardens who espouse this model promise both humane care of inmates and control in their institutions. There are increasingly better trained corrections staff, men and women who are committed to corrections as a career.

I wrote *Invitation to Corrections,* keeping three basic purposes in mind: (1) to engage students in the exciting study of corrections, (2) to present the material and insights that undergraduate students need to learn in a course in corrections, and (3) to prepare students to work in corrections and even to pursue corrections as a career.

Invitation to Corrections places a major emphasis on the historical and social contexts of corrections. This approach helps students understand reasons for changing ideas about how corrections functions in society. This text also has the unique feature of presenting the various lenses through which corrections is viewed. The perspectives of victims, prison reformers, wardens, correctional officers, conservative politicians, probation and parole officers, civil rights groups, and others are presented. In addition, this text provides an insider view of how the corrections system actually functions. The major participants' role expectations and challenges are developed. In taking the student inside the role behavior of the probation officer, jail officer, warden, correctional officer, and others, an underlying question guides the discussion: What does it mean to do an effective and satisfying job? Salary and other information are further presented that will interest anyone considering a corrections career.

The text considers the consequences of the bureaucratic movement in probation and parole in the 1990s and the means by which inmate gangs are presently handled. Students are asked to ponder the future of probation and parole, the use of intermediate sanctions, and the treatment of and services for inmates. The efforts of wardens of the 1990s are described, examining the new style of prisons management, with systematic classification, high-technology methods of maintaining security, and better use of human resources in understanding and controlling prisoners.

Each chapter, except for Chapter 1, has a "hero," someone who has made an outstanding contribution to the field and, in many instances, kindly agreed to share his or her thoughts about the profession (one notable exception is the hero of Chapter 2; John Howard [1726–1790], an English prison reformer). In statements often provided specifically for readers of this book, some of these individuals talk about the excitement of their jobs as the director of the Federal Bureau of Prisons (Kathleen Hawk Sawyer), as commissioners and directors of the California and Minnesota departments of corrections, as institutional superintendents and wardens, as a U.S. probation officer, as administrator of a large jail, as court monitor of several state correctional systems, and as director of the Fortune Society. Other "heroes" are recognized scholars in the field, such as Norval Morris, Michael Tonry, James B. Jacobs, Coramae Richey Mann, Mark Colvin, Doris L. MacKenzie, Jerome Miller, and Sister Helen Prejean.

Other helpful features for the student are the Within the Walls and Outside the Walls boxes in each chapter. In addition, the Web Destinations lists provide guidance where material in the chapter can be found on the Internet. Furthermore, the text has a built-in study guide.

Chapter 1 provides the background for the study of corrections and invites students to explore this changing field. Chapters 2 and 3 survey the history of corrections from ancient times to the present. Chapter 4 focuses on the goals of punishment and the changes introduced in sentencing legislation. Chapters 5 through 8 take readers through the gamut of community corrections, including probation, parole, and intermediate sanctions. Chapters 9 and 10 describe the changing structure and programs of jails and prisons. Chapters 11 through 13 deal with prison management, security and violence, and programs and services. Chapters 14 through 16 examine male and female prisoners and juvenile corrections. Chapters 17 through 20 focus on the death penalty; the relationship among race, gender, class, age, and incarceration rates; prison crowding; and prisoners' rights.

ACKNOWLEDGMENTS

As always, my wife, Linda Dippold Bartollas, has been a great source of support. My colleagues Joe Gorton and Keith Crew generously supplied materials and insights.

I am grateful to the "heroes" who were willing to be interviewed or to submit statements for this book: Coramae Richey Mann, Michael Tonry, Norval Morris, Sister Helen Prejean, Kenneth F. Schoen, Samantha J. O'Hara, Doris L. MacKenzie, Joanne Page, Donald Fatherree, Kathleen Hawk Sawyer, Frank Wood, Dr. Martin Groder, James B. Jacobs, Elaine A. Lord, Jerome Miller, and Vincent M. Nathan. I also want to thank W. L. Kautzky, John Hurley, Ellis C. MacDougall, William H. Dallman, Scott Dolan, Sara Carter, Donald L. Eckerman, Ernest F. Walters, Chris LeGear, Antoine Johnson, Herron Lewiel, Rebecca Hasenclever Saice, Barry Holman, Robert Martinas, Michael D. Bradbury, William M. DiMascio, Denny Fitzpatrick, and Walter Sheets for providing oral or written material.

I thank Betty Heine for all that she and her staff did to keep the manuscript moving into final form. Jamie Donaldson, Carrie Thompson, and Tim Boorom were of enormous help. Finally, I am grateful to Mary Ellen Lepionka, Senior Development Editor, who guided this project from beginning to end. Her help was indispensable.

I am grateful to this book's reviewers: Cheryl Banachowski-Fuller, University of Wisconsin; Christopher J. Drew, Montclair State University; Harold A. Frossard, Salt Lake Community College; James W. Marquart, Sam Houston State University; Daniel R. Miller, Bethune-Cookman College; Elena Natalizia, Mount Wachusett Community College; Michael Perna, Nassau Community College; Lynda J. Pintrich, Middlesex Community College; John C. Quicker, California State University, Dominquez Hills; and Debra L. Stanley, Central Connecticut State University.

Invitation to Corrections

Invitation to Corrections

Ellis C. MacDougall, former director of five correctional departments in the United States and professor of criminal justice at the University of South Carolina, argues that significant positive changes took place in corrections in the 1960s and 1970s. He spoke with some sadness about what he considers to be regression in correctional policy in the 1990s:

> You first have to realize where corrections has come. It's only in the last few years that corrections has come out of the Dark Ages. We still have a lot of problems in corrections, but we have come a long way. Let me illustrate by my experience.
>
> When I became commissioner of the South Carolina Department of Corrections in 1962, we fed inmates on 29 cents a day. There was open gambling on the yard. We weren't able to turn the system around until we started to get federal help in the late 1960s. Then we were able to develop training programs and hire qualified staff.
>
> In 1968 when I became commissioner of corrections in Connecticut, the jails—which were built in 1830—still had buckets in the cells. It is now a very good system. In 1971 when I went to Georgia as director, the deputy director of that major system had been a political appointee. He was a former disc jockey and a car salesman. Political patronage had reduced that system to a shambles.
>
> When I went to Mississippi in the early 1970s to become director, they did not have a Department of Corrections. I was asked to set up the legislation to establish a department and to stay and get it organized. At Parchment the Mississippi State Prison was a plantation with some nineteen camps scattered over 10,000 acres. The buildings were ramshackle, and most of the inmates worked on the vast farm. The place was rampant with disorder. The inmates ran the system.

In 1978, when I was asked by then Governor Bruce Babbitt to take over the Arizona Department of Corrections, they had had five directors in a year. At the Arizona State Prison they had three gangs, the Black Guerrilla Army, the Mexican Mafia, and the Aryan Brotherhood, and they were at war. They were having a stabbing a week and a killing a month. With management changes and introduction of meaningful programs, we had one stabbing the first year and then four years without another serious assault.

I felt, after completing the changes made in these five states, we had turned the corner and corrections was moving toward reform. My goal was a system that would incarcerate the hard-core inmate humanely but offer opportunity to the balance of the population to complete their education or learn a marketable skill followed by a release program that would assimilate them back into society. Unfortunately, since that time some systems have regressed.[1]

CRITICAL THINKING QUESTIONS

What do you think Ellis MacDougall means when he says that corrections recently emerged from the Dark Ages? What does he mean when he says that some systems have regressed?

MacDougall told the interviewer that he sees corrections as a system that varies from state to state. According to MacDougall, politics has immense influence on what takes place in corrections. His remarks convey a sense of excitement about corrections as a field of study and as a profession or career. In this part of the interview he recognizes regression in the 1990s, but later in the interview he said that the standards of the American Corrections Accreditation Program offer "not only a roadmap but also the main hope for enlightened corrections."

The title of this book and of this chapter mentions an "invitation" to corrections. What does that mean? How can anyone feel "invited" to such a complex field riddled with critical issues and deeply disturbing realities and focusing as it does on human tragedy and failure? How can anyone feel "invited" to a field so shaped by its social context that political and economic realities at times seem impossible either to maintain or to change? The answer is that corrections also is inspirational and change is always possible, though not always predictable. In corrections there are opportunities to make a positive difference in people's lives and in correctional institutions at different levels of the system, in ways ranging from common decency and kindness to penal reform.

The premise of this text is that it is possible to view corrections through more than one lens and willingness to take different perspectives leads to understanding. Each chapter offers perspectives from within the walls of correctional institutions as well as outside the walls, perspectives of people who are in the system, perspectives of people who have been professionally involved in corrections, and perspectives of critics, researchers, and reformers. Especially, this text encourages you to consider career options in corrections and allied fields, for there are heroes in corrections, and you could be among them.

This textbook is written to inform you about **corrections**—the institutions and methods that society uses to punish, control, and change the behavior of convicted offenders. Throughout, four major themes are developed. First, corrections is a system that functions as a subsystem of the criminal justice system. Second, corrections takes place in particular social contexts—environments and situations that influence people's responses to events. A sociological approach sheds light on how corrections functions in various social settings. Third, all the participants in the corrections process are important—victims, reformers, individuals who work within the system, offenders who are sentenced to the system, and others. Fourth, and last, the field of corrections offers many opportunities for a challenging, satisfying career.

HOW DOES THE CORRECTIONAL SYSTEM FUNCTION?

The traditional purpose of corrections is to provide sufficient punishment to individuals convicted by the courts for violating the law so that the public will be protected, the public's fear of crime will be reduced, and offenders will learn that crime does not pay. Corrections in the United States has developed as part of the larger criminal justice system, of which the police, the court system, and corrections are the three components, or subsystems. Law enforcement and the courts are at the front end of the justice process; corrections and communities are at the receiving end. The police arrest, the courts convict and sentence, and the correctional system punishes. Jails and police lockups, correctional institutions, probation and parole departments, residential facilities, and community agencies are components of the corrections subsystem.

The Purpose of Corrections

The preservation of order requires that people conform to society's rules. But establishing the purpose of punishment and the proper methods for dealing with lawbreakers has been a perplexing problem since the birth of the United States. In the colonial period, criminals were variously put in stocks, fined, forced to pay restitution for the harm they committed, banished, tortured, and executed. Periodically, reformers have tried to improve conditions and to rehabilitate rather than punish offenders. In the last quarter-century, the United States returned to hard-line solutions—punishment and incarceration.

Émile Durkheim (1858–1917), a French sociologist, stated that crime is functional for a society because it helps unite citizens against lawbreakers. He contended that people react to crime by increasing their social contacts and pulling together, thereby enhancing the solidarity of the community. "Crime is, then, necessary; it is bound up with the fundamental conditions of all social life," Durkheim asserted, "and by that very fact is useful, because these conditions of which it is a part are themselves indispensable to the normal evolution of morality and law."[2] Not surprisingly, the idea that the disorder of crime is necessary for the smooth functioning of society has little support today. In the 1970s, catchphrases such as "the crime problem," "law and order," and "crime in the streets" came to symbolize the public's fear of the disorder of crime.

Social contexts have a major influence on the types of punishable behavior and the punishments that are acceptable at a given time. **Social contexts** include historical developments and economic and political climates. Today, corrections is operating in a political context that encourages a conservative, hard-line approach to crime and punishment. This approach affects the numbers of offenders sent to correctional agencies and institutions and the duration and severity of their punishments. Thus the purpose of corrections has been narrowly defined. As another example of social contexts,

Sociologist Émile Durkheim said that crime and punishment are a necessary part of social life. What did he mean by that statement? How does it reflect the functionalist perspective in sociological approaches to corrections?

consider that some analysts have referred to corrections as a "prison–industrial complex" or "correctional–industrial complex." This "complex" is made up of private industrialists, governmental bureaucrats, and politicians who shape criminal justice policy, and it is fueled by interests that have a stake in it. For example, the money to be made in jail and prison construction "gives many companies and organizations a vested interest in assuring the continued expansion of the industry."[3]

Corrections and the Criminal Justice System

A system consists of a group of interacting, independent elements—subsystems— whose functioning is under the influence of a coordinated body of methods, plans, or procedures. The components of the **criminal justice system** function together to apprehend, prosecute, convict, sentence, and punish criminals. The **penal system** consists of local jails and police lockups; state and federal correctional institutions; state, county, and federal probation; state parole departments; and community-based agencies. Systematic approaches to handling society's criminals promise a coordinated flow of people from one subsystem to the next, along with a continuum of services.

Political control of the justice system is evident on all levels. Legislatures define criminal behavior and establish criminal penalties. They also pass laws involving criminal procedures, including rules and regulations regarding the laws of arrest, search warrants, bail, trial court procedures, and sentencing. In addition, legislatures are responsible for allocating financial support for criminal justice agencies and programs.

The judicial branch of government, especially the appellate, or appeal, courts, has primary responsibility for interpreting laws and presiding over court procedures. Both federal and state appellate courts interpret the law in light of precedents and constitutional standards. The U.S. Supreme Court is particularly important in deciding how the U.S. Constitution should be applied to cases.

The executive branch, represented by public officials such as the president (federal), state governor (state), and city mayor (local), has the power to appoint and dismiss executive directors of criminal justice agencies in their respective jurisdictions. On the federal and state levels, the president and governors have the power to grant pardons for crimes. See Figure 1.1 for the numbers of offenders on probation and parole and in jail and in prison in 1998.

The **systems approach** to criminal justice rests on the assumption that effective handling of the crime problem depends on the coordination and cooperation of all components of the criminal justice system. According to the systems approach, criminal justice agencies are inherently interdependent, and change in any one of them will affect the others. Proponents of a systems approach emphasize coordination and cooperation, mutual goal-setting, the sharing of resources, and systematic planning among the police, the courts, and corrections. However, the interdependence and cooperation needed among the police, courts, and corrections are sometimes so little in evidence that critics say the criminal justice system is a "nonsystem." The reality is that there are numerous criminal justice systems—one federal system, fifty state systems, and nearly countless local systems—all of which change over time.

The "nonsystem" aspects of the criminal justice system are signs of conflict and even hostility between jurisdictions and agencies because of competition for attention, power, and resources. Police, courts, and corrections are independent jurisdictions administered

Figure 1.1 **Number of Offenders Involved in the Main Components of the Corrections System**

Source: Bureau of Justice Statistics, *Prisoners in 1999* (Washington, D.C.: U.S. Department of Justice, 2000), and Bureau of Justice Statistics, *Probation and Parole* (Washington, D.C.: U.S. Department of Justice, 1999).

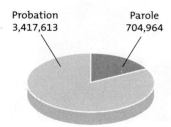

Probation
3,417,613

Parole
704,964

Prison Inmates
1,254,577

Jail Inmates
605,943

by separate agencies, and each has separate powers or authority, lines of communication, and accountabilities. Each subsystem sets its own goals. In addition, laws and philosophies of justice vary from state to state and even from jurisdiction to jurisdiction within a state. These factors contribute to noncooperation, failures in communication, and distrust among different components of the criminal justice system.

Corrections as a System

Corrections is charged with providing care in community and institutional settings to sentenced offenders. Corrections officials must ensure that offenders comply with the conditions of probation and avoid additional criminal behavior while on parole. Departments of corrections are expected to protect society against escapees from correctional institutions. Formerly, these departments were expected to rehabilitate offenders, but today in most states the courts require only that corrections departments maintain humane standards of care and grant prisoners their constitutional rights. Probation and parole officers have caseloads and must report to the court offenders who have violated the law. Parolees who violate the conditions of their paroles or commit additional crimes may be returned to prison. Juvenile and adult corrections offer nine correctional services:

1. Juvenile detention
2. Juvenile probation
3. Administration of juvenile institutions
4. Juvenile aftercare (parole)
5. Adult misdemeanor and felony probation
6. Jails
7. County workhouses
8. Adult institutions for felons
9. Parole

Corrections is extremely expensive for federal, state, and local governments. In 1996, state governments spent $25,294,111,000 for correctional activities; this was more than six times the $4,257,509,000 that state governments spent for correctional activities in 1980.[4] Corrections expenditures have risen more than for any other state function. In 1998, state legislatures increased appropriations for corrections by 6.6 percent, which excluded construction costs, compared to 4.1 percent increase for Medicaid and 5.1 percent increase for higher education.[5] Figure 1.2 shows the comparison between corrections costs and other agencies of the justice system between 1985 and 1995.

One of the major challenges affecting the ability of corrections to function as a system is system overload, which makes the handling of caseloads and jail and prison populations difficult. With record numbers sentenced to probation and placed on parole,

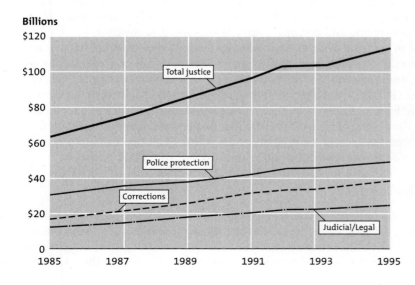

Figure 1.2 Federal, State, and Local Expenditure for the Criminal and Civil Justice System, 1985–1995 (in 1995 constant dollars)

Source: Bureau of Justice Statistics, *Justice Expenditure and Employment in the United States, 1995* (Washington, D.C.: U.S. Department of Justice, 1999), p. 1.

This is an adult correctional institution for felons. What other types of correctional services are part of the corrections system in the United States? In what sense is corrections a system? In what sense is it a non-system? What factors affect the ability of corrections to operate as a system in fulfilling the goals of criminal justice?

and with nearly 2 million defendants in jail or in long-term institutions, the capacity of the system is stretched more than ever before. The ongoing stress of dealing with mammoth caseloads and institutional overcrowding affects nearly all corrections workers who have direct contact with offenders. Problems arising from overcrowding challenge correctional administrators attempting to provide humane confinement for prisoners.

System overload places pressure on the system in other ways besides personnel fatigue, administrative frustration, and quality of life issues. Prison crowding leads to increased inmate defiance and makes prisons (especially maximum-security ones) more dangerous places in which to work. Correctional officers commonly complain that they have neither the control nor the respect they used to have. Some even report feeling that they are at the inmates' mercy (see Chapter 11).

WHAT ARE THE THREE DOMINANT PERSPECTIVES IN CORRECTIONS TODAY?

Throughout the history of corrections in the United States, reform and repression have alternated in gaining the support of the public and policymakers. Then, late in the twentieth century, the two lenses of reform and repression were joined by another reform lens. Ellis MacDougall articulates the older reform viewpoint at the beginning of this chapter: Corrections is evolving and becoming more professional. Some observers looking through the lens of reform have recently added that corrections must be humane and reflect the fact that it takes place in a civilized society—a society that accepts the notion that human progress is marked by "'the evolving standards of decency,' from the less civilized to the more civilized, from the more restrictive to the less restrictive, from tyranny to expanding freedom."[6] Observers looking through the lens of repression have has little tolerance for the notion of reform. They believe that it is necessary to "get tough" on criminals, that inmates have too many rights and privileges, and that troublesome prisoners should be placed in high-security units and isolated from other prisoners.

Emergence from the Dark Ages

To indicate how far corrections has come, observers from the becoming-more-professional perspective look to the past, to the so-called Dark Ages of corrections. During this period, discipline in American prisons was rough and physical, and public flogging was not unusual. One famous warden allowed himself to be photographed in the act of flogging a misbehaving prisoner, explaining to the watching press that "These men aren't here for playing hooky from Sunday School."[7]

Until 1966, when the federal courts outlawed the practice, the strap was used to punish prisoners in Mississippi and Arkansas. This strap was made of leather, 3½ to 5½ feet in length about 4 inches wide, with a wooden handle 8 to 12 inches long. Arkansas had an informal requirement that strapping be limited to ten blows on the buttocks at a time for any single offense. Sometimes, though not always, the prisoner's posterior might be bare.[8] Southern prisons employed convict guards for perimeter security and to maintain order in the fields and cellblocks. Their methods were straightforward and rough. Convicts working as guards were not supposed to administer the strap, but the federal courts found that this rule was sometimes breached.[9]

Condemned to Hard Labor.   Prison work traditionally was miserable and punitive. Pay, if any, was in pennies. Some states had coal mines in which prisoners were required to labor regardless of their skill or experience in mining. The danger of work in such conditions was great, but concern for the safety of convicts was not a priority. Depending on demand, most prisons had some sort of hard labor for convicts to do. A long-standing example of hard and unpleasant labor was the jute mill at California's largest prison, San Quentin (see Within the Walls 1.1).

Until the 1980s, all prisoners in Texas did their first six months of imprisonment "on the line," breaking soil, planting cotton, hoeing weeds and gathering cotton. The state's prison system was endowed with 100,000 acres of arable land, nearly all of which was put to productive agricultural use. Men working for nothing made it possible for the Texas Department of Corrections to be nearly self-supporting.

within the walls 1.1

The San Quentin Jute Mill

At San Quentin all able-bodied prisoners were required to work for a year in an antiquated jute mill, making burlap sacks for sale to California farmers, whose demand for burlap always exceeded the productive capacity of the mill. The looms and spinners were so old that replacements for worn-out parts had to be fabricated at the prison. The mill was dark and crowded. The noise from spinners and looms was deafening. The air was thick with dust and jute fiber. The danger from the rickety machinery was considerable. In this gloomy atmosphere it was easy for a convict to hurl objects at an adversary, or sometimes at a guard, without detection.

Assignment to the mill was for a year. During that time prisoners had to complete a daily task—so many spools of yarn, so many yards of burlap sacking—to the satisfaction of the foreman; otherwise, the day did not count toward the fulfillment of the required year. With heavy irony, the assignment lieutenant would explain to prisoners that it was for their benefit to learn to work in an industry in which measured performance would qualify them for the demands of industrial employment in free society. At the end of the mandatory year, convicts could be assigned to more constructive activ-

> The air was thick with dust and jute fiber.

ities, to school, to vocational training, or to less miserable work such as the manufacture of spare parts for the looms. Return to the mill was a dreaded sanction for prisoners who had been found guilty of serious disciplinary infractions.

In 1953, after the mill had been in service for eighty years, a fire of mysterious origin destroyed the plant. Arson was thought to have been the cause, but no arsonist was ever found. The wonder was that it took so many years for the demolition of this fire trap to be accomplished. It was replaced by a cotton mill with modern machinery with which fabrics were produced to manufacture clothing for inmates in all California institutions. Employment there was not the most prized assignment for San Quentin prisoners, but veterans of the jute mill saw little reason to complain.

CRITICAL THINKING QUESTIONS

What attitudes toward corrections did the jute mill reflect? Are these attitudes still present in corrections?

Source: Lore reported by correctional personnel at San Quentin.

The "line" was long and manned by scores of convicts, all dressed in white, working from dawn to dusk. Keeping them in an orderly row were guards on horseback who were not reluctant to administer physical discipline on recalcitrant or slow workers. The men were paid in time rather than in money (so many days of good time for so many days on the line). When the allotted introductory period was over, convicts might be reassigned to less exhausting or unpleasant work, usually paid at higher rates of "good time" but still not in money. As at San Quentin, men who ran afoul of prison discipline were subject to reassignment to the line.

Emergence of More Enlightened Care.   Having made their case about the brutality of the past, observers from the becoming-more-professional position then point with pride to progressive changes in corrections. Gone are breaking on the wheel; public hangings, disemboweling, and quartering; flogging; the sweatbox; the lock step; and convicts in striped suits splitting blocks of stone with sledgehammers. In addition, the quality and service of institutional food have improved. Vocational and educational programs have been expanded and improved in most institutions. Inmates often are employed by free-world enterprises that pay them wages at or near free-world levels. Minimum- and medium-security prisons provide humane alternatives to idle confinement.

As you will read in later chapters, throughout the history of corrections, admirable individuals and groups have stepped forward to eliminate abuses and make useful innovations. An eighteenth-century example is John Howard, who dedicated his life to the reform of the jails and prisons in England and throughout Europe. In the nineteenth century, Captain Alexander Maconochie's mark system brought reform for inmates transported to Norfolk Island in Australia, and Dorothea Dix sought improvement in the confinement for women prisoners.

"Heroes" featured throughout this text highlight reformers of the twentieth century. Richard A. McGee, for example, changed the nature of corrections in California by upgrading the physical plants and staffing patterns, by instituting research, and by developing alternatives to imprisonment. Kenneth Stoneman closed Vermont's only maximum-security prison in the 1970s. Lloyd McCorkle, instead of building more prisons, developed a network of satellites at other human services institutions. Kenneth F. Schoen was instrumental in laying out the principles of Minnesota's groundbreaking Community Corrections Act. James V. Bennett closed Alcatraz, opened Marion, planned Morgantown, and created a professional bureaucracy at the U.S. Bureau of Prisons. Elayn Hunt, before her death, was leading Louisiana corrections out of its dark ages.

The Necessity of Humane Care

Those who view corrections through this lens of reform are quick to say that lawbreakers must be treated with decency in the United States. The United States is a free and democratic society governed by elected representatives whose responsibility is to comply with the wishes of the people who elected them. U.S. society values both human rights and the freedom of the individual. What this means is that the government must strike a balance between individual rights and collective needs. This balance, reflecting a long history of constitutional government, is weighed on the side of individual rights.

The constitutional order established early in the history of this nation rests on several key principles. The U.S. Constitution, say observers from the humane-care perspective, is shaped by classical definitions of humankind that rest on the assumption that citizens are rational beings who prefer pleasure over pain and who are willing to sacrifice a portion of their freedom so that the larger society may enjoy security and peace. This view of law presumes that people are willing to play by the rules, and thus, it leads to a reform-oriented approach to criminal sanctions. Furthermore, the Constitution and Bill of Rights were designed to protect the individual against coercive government action. This protection of the rights of the individual places a heavy burden on the state to prove the guilt of individuals suspected of criminal behavior.

Proponents of humane care frequently quote the Russian novelist Fyodor Dostoyevsky, who once said, "The degree of civilization in a society can be judged by entering the prisons."[10] Dostoyevsky, who did hard time in a Russian prison, was suggesting that the quality of maturity or decency of a society can be measured not by how the finest citizens are treated but by how the worst are treated. In 1910 Winston Churchill stated that "The mood and temper of the public in regard to the treatment of crime and criminals is one of the most unfailing tests of the civilization of any country."[11] In 1984 Chief Justice Burger of the U.S. Supreme Court in the case of *Hudson v. Palmer* made this same point: "The way a society treats those who have transgressed against it is evidence of the essential character of that society."[12] A decent society, these statements are arguing, offers humane care and social justice to all of its citizens.

Does the standard of humane care apply today in the American correctional system?

Let Them "Break Rocks"

The third lens through which corrections is viewed reveals a get-tough perspective. These observers believe that society needs to "get even" with those who do social harm. They express the opinion that the longer people are incarcerated and the worse their conditions of confinement are, the less likely they will be to commit another crime. The popularity of this repressive perspective is evident in the reinstatement of chain gangs and striped convict uniforms in some jurisdictions. In other jurisdictions, air conditioners and televisions have been removed from facilities. In still other jurisdictions, incentives for good behavior have been eliminated, visiting rules revised, and educational and vocational programs abolished.[13] Congress passed the Zimmer Amendment in 1996, which forbade the replacing or repairing of weight-training equipment in federal prisons. This amendment will eventually remove weight lifting from federal facilities. Mississippi, Alabama, and South Carolina are states that have eliminated weight-training equipment from their prisons, and others are considering the policy.[14]

The policy of maximizing punishment was bluntly stated by former Massachusetts Governor William Weld, who said in April 1998 that life in prison should be "akin to a walk through the fires of hell."[15] Michigan state representative Mike Goschka also reflected this attitude during a debate on prisoner conditions when he said, "Prisoners have it too easy now. They got color TV's, weight lifting equipment, libraries. . . . We need to return to the concept that prison is not fun."[16] A spokesperson for then California Gov-

Forced hard labor was a characteristic of the Dark Ages of corrections. What were some other characteristics of that time, and how did more enlightened care emerge? Through what three lenses, or perspectives, is corrections viewed today?

ernor Pete Wilson said in February 1998 that prisoners are "there to be punished, and hopefully rehabilitated. . . . They're not there to be entertained and catered to."[13]

These statements suggest that the most effective way to prevent crime is to make the punishment so harsh and severe that individuals considering a life of crime will decide that the risk is not worth taking. Thus, "make 'em break rocks" is not only viewed by a large segment of the public as an effective and appropriate means of fighting crime but has become a cornerstone in the correctional agenda of many public officials.[18]

Do you agree?

WHAT DOES IT MEAN TO HAVE A SOCIOLOGICAL APPROACH TO CORRECTIONS?

Sociology can be defined as "the scientific study of human society and social behavior."[19] Sociology, then, offers an examination of how social life shapes us as human beings.[20] According to Michael Schwalbe, "being **sociologically mindful** . . . is a way to see more deeply into the process of world-making and to appreciate the nature of the social world as a human accomplishment."[21]

A sociological approach also looks at **social construction.** Corrections, for example, is a social construct—a human creation rather than a natural phenomenon, a human creation based on people's expectations of social life. Social construction takes place through people's interactions and relationships, such as between staff and inmates, among staff members at various levels of an organization, and within inmate populations. The purpose of a sociological approach to corrections is to place the study of community-based corrections and prison life firmly in the context of American society.

Social Forces and the Correctional System

Being sociologically mindful includes examining social forces that impinge on social systems such as corrections. What the public and policymakers want has a fundamental influence on the philosophy of punishment, the mission of corrections, and correctional programs. In Within the Walls 1.2, Gresham Sykes in his classic study,

within the walls   1.2

Corrections and the External Environment

The Prison is not an autonomous system of power; rather, it is an instrument of the State, shaped by its social environment, and we must keep this simple truth in mind if we are to understand the prison. It reacts to and is acted upon by the free community as various groups struggle to advance their interests. At certain times, as in the case of riots, the inmates can capture the attention of the public; and indeed, disturbances within the walls must often be viewed as highly dramatic efforts to communicate with the outside world; efforts in which confined criminals pass over the heads of their captors to appeal to a new audience. At other times the flow of communication is reversed and the prison authorities find themselves receiving demands raised by a variety of business, political, religious, ethnic, and welfare interest groups.

> . . . inmates can capture the attention of the public . . .

In addition, both the inmates and the custodians are drawn from the free community, whether voluntarily or involuntarily, and they bring with them the attitudes, beliefs, and values of this larger world. The prison as a social system does not exist in isolation any more than the criminal within the prison exists in isolation as an individual; and the institution and its setting are inextricably mixed despite the definite boundary of the wall.

CRITICAL THINKING QUESTIONS

In what ways is the prison "not an autonomous system"? What social forces impinge on prison life?

Source: Reprinted from Gresham Sykes, *The Society of Captives* (Princeton, N.J.: Princeton University Press, 1958), p. 7.

The Society of Captives, points out how the external social environment influences what goes on within the walls.

Sociological Perspectives on the Correctional System

The functionalist perspective, the conflict perspective, and the interactionist perspective are three broad theoretical paradigms in sociology. Functionalists and conflict theorists take a broad view, looking at "macro" or institutional issues of social life. Interactionist sociologists focus on "micro" or interpersonal issues. An integrated or balanced sociological approach draws from all three perspectives.

Émile Durkheim, one of the originators of the **functionalist perspective,** argued that societies are held together by their members' shared beliefs and values. He wanted to know what function in the social system a given behavior or institution has. He also wanted to establish how the various subsystems of society contribute to the maintenance of the whole.[22] Functionalist theory, through its more recent spokespersons Talcott Parsons and Robert K. Merton, continues to view society as being made up of organized, stable, and well-integrated systems. An example of the application of a functionalist perspective in corrections is Gresham M. Sykes and Sheldon L. Messinger's examination of the inmates' unwritten code, showing that it is ultimately functional both to prison administrators and to prisoners.[23]

The **conflict perspective** derives its inspiration from Karl Marx, who saw the struggle between social classes as the main source of change. Defining conflict as tension, hostility, competition, and disagreement over goals and values, present-day conflict theorists assume that conflict is a permanent feature of society. The source of conflict is the unequal distribution of the things that people most desire, such as wealth, power, and prestige; demand for them exceeds supply. Those who gain control of scarce resources protect their own interests at other people's expense. Consequently, social order is maintained by force or by the implied threat of force rather than by consensus. According to conflict theory, social inequality exists because the people who wield political and economic power are able to pass on their advantages to their descendants.[24] An example of the application of the conflict perspective to corrections is Georg Rusche and Otto Kirchheimer's classic interpretation of the function of punishment as a means of supporting one class's interests against another's.[25]

The **interactionist perspective** relies on the notion of social construction. The social world is a human invention. The corrections system is made up of people who socially construct meaning and purpose. Social actors act on these meanings, sharing ideas, maintaining structures, and creating process. For example, inmates within an institution construct the role behaviors that inmates expect of each other.[22] Not everyone has an equal say in this constructed social world of inmates, however, because some have more power over others.

WHO ARE THE PARTICIPANTS IN THE CORRECTIONS SYSTEM?

Victims of wrongdoing, offenders, prison reformers, probation and parole officers, residential staff, and institutional staff ranging from wardens to custody staff are all participants in the correctional process. This text emphasizes the role behaviors of participants. You are taken behind the scenes and into the institutions and agencies so that you can better appreciate the opportunities and constraints that affect the quality of corrections in local communities and institutional settings. This approach emphasizes the human side of the corrections system as the participants strive to achieve personal and organizational goals. Institutional pressures and objectives are very important in this approach, as are the inevitable tendencies of systems to seek and maintain an equilibrium, internally and with other institutions.

How do participants in corrections actually perform their jobs?

Informal, unwritten codes of behavior that tell participants what they should or should not do emerge on site in response to the pressures of the job. These codes may

the walls   1.3

within

Standards of Employee Conduct

- The Bureau of Prisons emphasizes employee ethics, responsibility, and standards of conduct.

- The Bureau of Prisons expects its employees to conduct themselves in a manner that creates and maintains respect for the agency, the Department of Justice, the Federal Government, and the law.

- The Bureau of Prisons recognizes the inherent dignity of all human beings and their potential for change.

- An employee may not show favoritism or give preferential treatment to one inmate, or a group of inmates, over another.

- An employee may not use physical violence, threats or intimidation toward fellow employees, family members of employees, or any visitor to a Bureau work site.

> The Bureau of Prisons recognizes the inherent dignity of all human beings and their potential for change.

- An employee may not use profane, obscene, or otherwise abusive language when communicating with inmates, fellow employees, or others. Employees shall conduct themselves in a manner which will not be demeaning to inmates, fellow employees, or others. . . .

- Illegal activities on the part of any employee, in addition to being unlawful, reflect on the integrity of the Bureau and betray the trust and confidence placed in it by the public.

CRITICAL THINKING QUESTIONS

What provisions would you find most difficult to meet? Which do you think you would find easiest to meet? Are there any provisions that you might add?

Source: Materials received from the Federal Bureau of Prisons, October 2000.

survive for decades. They are made up of beliefs based on both fact and fantasy and are passed on to each newcomer. They are established as a result of participants communicating with one another, trying to define their roles, and deciding how they should act. When informal codes are violated, the offending actor may be subjected to punishment ranging from verbal teasing to physical assault to dismissal from his or her job.

Formal codes spell out official standards that the organization expects employees to meet. Within the Walls 1.3 presents the standards of employee conduct of the Federal Bureau of Prisons.

WHAT ARE THE CHALLENGES OF CORRECTIONS WORK?

Participants who work directly with offenders face the challenges posed by overloaded systems plagued by the scarcity of resources. They may work in systems that are increasingly finding new ways to punish prisoners. Also not likely to diminish anytime soon are the volume of paperwork, the constant influx and outgo of offenders, issues concerning the rights of offenders, and the perennial problems of violence, drugs, inmate gangs, and civil suits.

In discussing the challenges of corrections work, this text focuses on the qualities that promote effectiveness in corrections workers. Although it is important to recognize those who fail on their jobs, especially those who are involved in brutal and corrupt behaviors or who compromise human rights, for readers who might consider a career in corrections it is more helpful to develop as clearly as possible the characteristics and profiles of those who do an outstanding job. The ultimate challenge of a corrections career is to feel good about your job and to believe that you are making a difference.

SUMMARY

There is great variation in opinions about how criminals should be treated. Expressions of what reform and repression mean tend to vary from one period to another. Today, they focus on the hope of continued progress in corrections, on the necessity of treating people in a humane and decent way, and on the desirability of giving inmates more severe punishments for the criminal acts they have committed.

Throughout this text four major themes are developed. What readers need to know to understand the field of adult corrections today has guided the construction of these themes: (1) Corrections functions as a system.

(2) An understanding of corrections through a sociological approach promotes understanding of the complexity of the correctional system, the behavior of people in the system, and the social contexts of crime and punishment. (3) People who participate in the corrections process are perhaps the most important parts of the system. The job behaviors of those who are performing effectively receive special emphasis. (4) A career in corrections can be both challenging and satisfying. Professional insights and an insider view are provided for anyone who is considering a career in corrections.

KEY TERMS

conflict perspective, p. 13
corrections, p. 4
criminal justice system, p. 6
functionalist perspective, p. 13
interactionist perspective, p. 13

penal system, p. 6
social construction, p. 12
social contexts, p. 5
sociologically mindful, p. 12
systems approach, p. 6

CRITICAL THINKING QUESTIONS

1. Why do some people say that the present is the best of times and also the worst of times for corrections?
2. What do you think contributed to the "let them break rocks" treatment of inmates in the 1990s in some prisons in the United States?
3. What limitations, if any, do you think should be placed on the humane perspective? Should all lawbreakers benefit from it, even child molesters?
4. How does the sociological perspective promote an understanding of corrections?
5. Why is corrections not a career for the faint of heart?

WEB DESTINATIONS

The National Institute of Corrections of the U.S. Department of Justice provides information and assistance to federal, state, and local corrections agencies working with adult offenders.
http://www.nicic.org/

Follow links on this SocioSite page for sociological perspectives on deviance and crime.
http://www.pscw.uva.nl/sociosite/TOPICS/right.html

This site presents a basic overview of the components and functioning of the criminal justice system in the United States.
http://www.ncvc.org/infolink/Info11.htm

Explore San Quentin State Prison in depth and read about its colorful history, including the administration of "The Big House" reformer, Clinton T. Duffy.
http://www.cdc.state.ca.us/facility/instsq.htm

http://www.theweboftime.com/Issue-5/sanquentin.htm

Read about the implementation of the Minnesota Community Corrections Act of 1973 at this site for participating counties.
http://www.maccac.org/

FOR FURTHER READING

Evans, Jeff, ed. *Undoing Time*. Boston: Northeastern Press, 2001. A number of fascinating stories written by U.S. prisoners. Provides a very good description of life within correctional institutions and of the problems prisoners face with current correctional policy.

Gray, Tara. *Exploring Corrections: A Book of Readings*. Boston, Allyn and Bacon, 2002. Readings describe what prison life is like for adults and juvenile inmates and what prison work is like for guards and administrators. The key debates and issues in corrections are also contained in this book of readings.

May, John P., ed., *Building Violence: How America's Rush to Incarcerate Creates More Violence*. Thousand Oaks, Calif.: Sage Publications, 2000. Questions the policies of incarceration that are being implemented today.

Rideau, Wilbert, and Ron Wikberg, eds. *Life Sentences: Rage and Survival behind Bars*. New York: Times Books, 1992. A well-crafted group of essays, mostly written by prisoners, that presents the lens through which long-term inmates view imprisonment at Angola State Prison in Louisiana.

Schwalbe, Michael. *The Sociologically Examined Life: Pieces of the Conversation*. Mountain View, Calif.: Mayfield, 1998. Schwalbe's presentation of the importance of social constructionism and its application to social life is an important work in making us sociologically mindful.

NOTES

1. Interviewed by the author in January 1979 and November 2000.
2. Émile Durkheim, *The Rules of Sociological Method,* trans. Sarah A. Solovay and John H. Mueller, ed. George E. G. Catlin (New York: Free Press, 1938), pp. 67–69; originally published as *Règles de la méthode sociologique* (1895).
3. Elizabeth Alexander, "The Care and Feeding of the Correctional–Industrial Complex," in *Building Violence,* ed. John P. May (Thousand Oaks, Calif.: Sage Publications, 2000), p. 52.
4. Bureau of Justice Statistics, *Justice Expenditure and Employment in the United States, 1995* (Washington, D.C.: U.S. Department of Justice, 1999), p. 1.
5. Stan C. Proband, "State Correctional Budgets Up 5.1 Percent in 1998," *Overcrowded Times,* 9 April 1998, p. 3.
6. Mumia Abu-Jamal, *Live from Death Row* (Reading, Mass.: Addison-Wesley, 1995), p. 31. For quotation of "evolving standards of decency," see *Trop v. Dulles* 356 U.S. S.Ct., 86 101, 78 S.Ct. 590, 598, 2 L.Ed.2d. 630 (1958).
7. Elam Lynds, warden of the New York State Prison at Auburn, made this statement. Cited in W. David Lewis, *From Newgate to Dannemora: The Rise of the Penitentiary in New York, 1796–1848* (Ithaca, N.Y.: Cornell University Press, 1965), p. 51.
8. See *Jackson v. Bishop,* 404 F2d 571 (8th Cir. 1968).
9. Ibid.
10. Fyodor Dostoyevsky, *The House of the Dead* (1861; reprint, London: Oxford University Press, 1956).
11. Spoken before the House of Commons in 1910 after witnessing Jean Galsworthy's play *Justice,* quoted by Evelyn Ruggles-Brise in *The English Prison System* (London: Macmillan, 1910).
12. *Hudson v. Palmer,* 468 U.S. 517 (1984).
13. Stephen J. Ingley, "Corrections without Correction," in *Building Violence,* p. 20.
14. Cited in Jon Marc Taylor, "The Prison Pump," in *Undoing Time,* ed. Jeff Evans (Boston: Northeaster University Press, 2001), p. 196.
15. Keynote speech, United States Attorney General's Summit on Corrections, 27 April 1998, quoted in Kenneth L. McGinnis, "Make 'Em Break Rocks," in *Building Violence,* p. 35.
16. Quoted in T. Gest, "Crime and Punishment: Politicians Are Vowing to Get Tough, but Will More Prisons and Fewer Perks Really Cut Crime? *U.S. News & World Report,* 3 July 1995, pp. 24–26.
17. Quoted in D. Morain, "More Inmate Privileges Fail in Get-Tough Drive," *The Los Angeles Times,* 9 February 1998.
18. McGinnis, "Make 'Em Break Rocks," p. 35.
19. Ian Robertson, *Sociology,* 2nd ed. (New York: Worth, 1981).
20. Michael Schwalbe, *The Sociologically Examined Life: Pieces of the Conversation* (Mountain View, Calif.: Mayfield, 1998), p. 79.
21. Ibid., p. 25.
22. Durkheim, *The Rules of Sociological Method.*
23. Gresham M. Sykes and Sheldon L. Messinger, "The Inmate Social System," in *Theoretical Studies in the Social Organization of the Prison,* ed. Richard A. Cloward et al. (New York: Social Science Research Council, 1960), pp. 6–8.
24. Robertson, *Sociology,* pp. 19–20.
25. Georg Rusche and Otto Kirchheimer, *Punishment and Social Structure* (New York: Columbia University Press, 1939).
26. Schwalbe, *The Sociologically Examined Life,* p. 25.

CHAPTER 1 / BUILT-IN STUDY GUIDE

Multiple Choice Questions

1. Currently the corrections system operates in a political context that encourages which of the following approaches to crime and punishment?
   A. Rehabilitative
   B. Liberal
   C. Due process
   D. Conservative

2. Which branch of government defines criminal behavior, establishes criminal penalties, passes laws involving criminal procedure, and is responsible for allocating financial support for criminal justice agencies and programs?
   A. Legislative
   B. Judicial
   C. Executive
   D. Federal

3. Which branch of government has the responsibility of interpreting laws and presiding over court proceedings?
   A. Legislative
   B. Judicial
   C. Executive
   D. Federal

4. Which branch of government has the power to appoint and dismiss top officials of criminal justice agencies, such as a superintendent of a prison?
   A. Legislative
   B. Judicial
   C. Executive
   D. Federal

5. What is one of the major challenges affecting the ability of corrections to function as a system?
   A. Systems overload
   B. Prisoner's rights groups
   C. Medical care for inmates
   D. Managing mentally ill offenders

6. What is the traditional purpose of corrections?
   A. To provide rehabilitation to those convicted of violating the law
   B. To provide punishment for those who are convicted of violating the law
   C. To provide reintegration for those who have served a criminal sentence
   D. To provide humane conditions for inmates

7. Identify the three components that make up the criminal justice system.
   A. Police, courts, corrections
   B. Police, prosecution, prisons
   C. Police, courts, penal institutions
   D. None of the above

8. How many individuals were incarcerated in correctional institutions as of 1998?
   A. Over 500,000
   B. Nearly 1,000,000
   C. Nearly 1,500,000
   D. Nearly 2,000,000

9. What are the three dominant perspectives of corrections?
   A. Hands on period; hands off period; one hand on, one hand off period
   B. Prison guard, correctional officer, corrections professional
   C. Professional, humane, get tougher
   D. Jails, reformatories, institutions

10. Ellis C. MacDougall's goal for a correctional system included which of the following?
    A. A system that incarcerated hard-core offenders humanely, while offering education and a program that enhanced assimilation back into society for the remainder of the inmate population
    B. A system that was based on the warehousing concept of corrections and operated in an economically efficient manner
    C. A system that operated through the use of a military management model with work furlough programs, based on merit available to qualified inmates near their release date.
    D. A system based on "truth in sentencing laws"

11. Identify the approach required to analyze and understand correctional functions in various environments and situations that influence people's responses to events.
    A. Systems
    B. Sociological
    C. Organizational
    D. Economic

12. In colonial America, which of the following methods punished criminal behavior?
    A. Counseling
    B. Indeterminate sentencing
    C. Banishment
    D. Boot camps

True/False Questions

T F 1. There is one criminal justice system in operation throughout all levels of government in this country.

T F 2. Corrections functions as a separate system outside the influence of the criminal justice system.

T F 3. According to Émile Durkheim, crime brings conflict to society because people will respond to criminal events by engaging in vigilante justice against the perpetrators of the offense.

T F 4. Law enforcement and the courts are at the front end of the criminal justice process.

T F 5. Corrections is a system that varies from state to state.

T F 6. Punishment in the form of imprisonment increased with the development of postindustrial society.

T F 7. Over the last twenty-five years in this country methods of punishing offenders have moved from incarceration to a rehabilitative approach.

T F 8. Police lockups are not included in the category of a penal system.

T F 9. A conservative approach to punishment has no impact on the number of offenders sent to correctional institutions and the length of their sentences.

T F 10. Analysts who refer to corrections as a "prison-industrial complex" believe that those who shape criminal justice policy are motivated by selfish interests and have a stake in the continued growth in the corrections system. For example, as the number of incarcerated individuals increases, more institutions will need to be constructed and more jobs created. As a result, there is money to be made from the enhanced growth of the correctional system.

T F 11. Corrections only provides care and supervision for individuals in institutional settings.

T F 12. The prison is an instrument of punishment, separate and apart from any influence from the state or federal government.

Fill-in-the-Blank Questions   (based on key terms)

1. _____ is made up of the institutions and methods that society now uses to punish, control, and change the behavior of convicted offenders.

2. The _____ is an integrated process that is concerned with the apprehension, prosecution, conviction, sentencing, and correction of criminals.

3. Jails, prisons, probation, and parole systems make up the _____.

4. A perspective that supports the position that all components of the criminal justice system must cooperate and work together to effectively address the crime problem is based on the _____.

5. With regard to crime, during the 1970s phrases such as "the crime problem," "law and order," and "crime in the streets" made up the political climate of the times. This political climate is part of the _____ that has a great impact on determining what behaviors are criminal as well as their acceptable punishment during a specific time in history.

6. An analytical perspective that analyzes crime as being useful for uniting the members of society against lawbreakers is known as the _____.

7. An analytical perspective that views competition for scarce resources as a main source of change is known as the _____.

8. The _____ explains the operation of the prison social system through human relationships. For example, interactions between staff and inmates or within the inmate population would be of value using this perspective.

9. According to Michael Schwalbe, someone who is concerned with how the prison social system shapes the life of an inmate or a correctional officer is being _____.

10. _____ views corrections as a human creation based on the expectations of social life.

Essay Questions

1. Identify each branch of government and define its purpose. Additionally, explain how the function of each branch influences the corrections system.

2. Identify and completely explain the three dominant perspectives in corrections.

3. Using a sociological approach, identify at least four social forces and explain how each influences the corrections system.

4. Why is it necessary to use a systematic approach to understand the functions of corrections and its relationship to the criminal justice system?

5. Explain the concept of social contexts and discuss why they have a major influence on the types of punishable behavior and methods of punishments that are acceptable at a certain period in time?

Critical Thinking Questions

1. The famous warden photographed in the act of flogging a misbehaving prisoner stated to the press, "These men aren't here for playing hooky from Sunday School." What do you think the warden's behavior and statement say about the purpose, methods, and desired outcomes of punishment?

2. In February 1998, a spokesperson for California Governor Pete Wilson said prisoners are "there to be punished, and hopefully rehabilitated. . . . They're not there to be entertained and catered to." Do you think the spokesperson's statement supports the premise that punishment will lead to rehabilitation? Provide a rationale for your response.

ANSWERS

Multiple Choice Questions

1. D	7. A
2. A	8. D
3. B	9. C
4. C	10. A
5. A	11. B
6. B	12. C

True/False Questions

1. F	7. F
2. F	8. F
3. F	9. F
4. T	10. T
5. T	11. F
6. T	12. F

Fill-in-the-Blank Questions

1. Corrections
2. Criminal Justice system
3. Penal system
4. Systems approach
5. Social context
6. Functional perspective
7. Conflict perspective
8. Interactionist perspective
9. Sociologically mindful
10. Social construction

From Vengeance to Reform:
A Historical Perspective

Repression and reform have been the basic strategies for dealing with law violators since the dawn of history. At one period, repression may have been the dominant method, but the failure of repression usually led to a period of reform. Early on, repressive measures against criminals carried the day. The notion of draconian measures as demonstrating the ultimate in severity refers to the laws of Draco, an Athenian lawgiver of the seventh century B.C.E. (before the Common Era).

Several centuries later, Plutarch, a Greek biographer, described how discriminately harsh Draco had been:

> death was the punishment for almost every offence, so that even men convicted of idleness were executed, and those who stole pot-herbs or fruits suffered just like sacrilegious robbers and murders. . . . It is said that Draco himself, when asked why he had fixed the punishment of death for most offences, answered that he considered these lesser crimes to deserve it, and he had no greater punishment for more important ones.[1]

CRITICAL THINKING QUESTIONS

How much would such an extensive use of the death penalty be a deterrent to crime?

In nearly every age some people cry out for draconian punishments against criminals. They urge the punishment of offenders, sometimes administered with horrifying brutality. In the nineteenth century, Sydney Smith, an English clergyman otherwise noted for his altruism, wrote:

> [A prison] should be a place of punishment, from which men recoil with horror—a place of real suffering painful to the memory, terrible to the imagination. [It should be] . . . a place of sorrow and wailing, which should be entered with horror and quitted with earnest resolution never to return to such misery; with that impression, in short, of the evil which breaks out in perpetual warning and exhortation to others.[2]

But we are getting ahead of ourselves. Let us start at the beginning. *How were individuals who violated society's norms or laws treated at the beginning of recorded history?*

WHAT WERE THE LEGAL CODES OF THE ANCIENT WORLD?

The development of agriculture led to increases in large, permanently settled populations. Work became specialized among farmers, merchants, artisans, and soldiers, who protected the territory from marauders or expanded it to put more land under cultivation. Kings, prophets, and priests ruled. Property owners gained property interests not only in their land but in slaves who worked the land. Those interests had to be protected, and the first laws concerned property rights. These laws enabled property owners to depend on the community to protect them and their property rather than having to rely on their own defenses. Punishments for property offenses often were as severe as punishment for murder, rape, assault, and other violent crimes against persons.

As states, kingdoms, and empires superseded clan and tribal societies, the state assumed the role of punishing violators of societal norms. For the state to take over private vengeance, it was necessary to formalize the system of government, and written laws accomplished this purpose. The written laws embodied the customs by which organized societies dealt with violators of the norms of conduct. The kings and prophets who were the early lawgivers intended that the state or other legitimate authority replace the individual in exacting restitution or revenge. Today, the modern state assumes the exclusive right to respond to criminals; it denies the victims of crime the liberty of taking the law into their own hands. Thus, throughout history the state's retribution has officially replaced private vengeance.

Prophets and priests interpreted the early laws that were based on religious beliefs and values. Kings codified these laws, and their armies enforced them. As societies became more complex, more laws were required to protect public safety and private interests. Rulers of kingdoms around the Fertile Crescent, site of Babylon and other early civilizations, created systems of law to govern human behavior. Later, the Greeks examined the nature of justice in the legal codes that they passed, and the Romans developed a system of law that continues to influence the criminal law of present-day nations.

Laws of Early Civilizations

The first codifier of whom we have records was Hammurabi, who reigned for forty-three years as king of Babylon during the eighteenth century B.C.E.[3] He used military means to expand the authority of Babylon throughout Mesopotamia. Written laws had the effect of stabilizing his kingdom as well as standardizing custom and tradition. Like other early kings, Hammurabi was the unchallengeable chief executive, sole legislator, and supreme judge.

The **Code of Hammurabi** (see Outside the Walls 2.1) provides the first example of written laws issued by a nation-state.[4] Hammurabi's Code was issued in about 1752 B.C.E. Its influence throughout the Fertile Crescent was enormous. Fragments of later codes in other kingdoms have been found that clearly derive from Hammurabi's laws.

Hammurabi's Code called for compensation to the victim of a robbery by the authorities of the city in which the robbery occurred, if the thief was not caught. In such a case, the victim "shall declare his loss in the presence of a god" to the mayor of the city and certify the amount of his loss. Thereupon the authorities were required to provide compensation because they had failed to maintain law and order. By making the state directly responsible for restitution, Babylonian law reduced intergenerational feuds and blood vengeance between families. This idea of justice has been characteristic of all criminal codes since that time.

outside the walls 2.1

Hammurabi's Code

Hammurabi's Code was carved in stone. When discovered by French archaeologists in 1901, the slab was taken to the Louvre in Paris, where it remains.

Hammurabi's Code contains 282 clauses or sections, most having to do with matters that modern systems of law assign to civil law. But more than fifty sections deal with crimes and the punishments for committing them. The punishments are severe. Fines were considered inappropriate for the most serious crimes. Robbery, theft, false testimony, and even poor workmanship, such as building a house that collapses on its owner, were punishable by death.

The **law of talion,** or the principle of "an eye for an eye" (today most often associated with Mosaic law), is the basis of punishment of criminals. Punishment is the same as the harm inflicted on the victim. In the example of poor workmanship, for instance, the law required that if the house collapsed and killed the owner's son, the son of the builder—not the builder himself—would be executed. For the crime of knocking out the tooth of a free man, the offender would have one of his teeth knocked out. For striking the cheek of a ranking free man, the assaulter would be "scourged" in the city's assembly. If a victim's bone was broken during an assault, the same bone in the assailant's body would be broken.

Penalties differed according to rank. For fatally injuring a free man, a payment of one-half menah of silver would be exacted. The penalty for the same injury to a slave would be only one-third menah of silver. These payments were equivalent to civil damages payable today to a victim or his or her family in addition to any criminal punishment imposed.

> Robbery, theft, false testimony, and even poor workmanship . . . were punishable by death.

CRITICAL THINKING QUESTIONS

In the modern world are there nations that attempt to practice the law of talion? Why is making the punishment fit the crime an elusive goal?

Source: G. Driver and John C. Miles, 2 vols. *The Babylonian Laws* (London: Oxford University Press, 1952).

Laws of the Greeks

Greek philosophers had a great deal to say about the nature of justice, and one, Plato, wrote extensively on the punishment of criminals. Laws in ancient Greece reflected the belief that obtaining justice is a private matter between individuals. Initially the Greeks relied on customs to deal with wrongdoing. The victim's family even dealt with murder and rape. Sometimes negotiations between the offender and the victim's family would result in compensation. The bargain might be that the killer or rapist would pay the aggrieved family a sum of money in return for an agreement that the family would not exact further vengeance.

As Greek society became organized into city-states, judgment in criminal matters passed into the hands of kings and elders. Because no lawyers represented clients, it was up to victims or their families to prosecute. Defendants had to depend on their own resourcefulness to present their cases. Although a king in early Athens might decide what should be done, interested bystanders could influence the judgment. The disputing parties would state their cases, and the public was free to cheer or deride them as they found the speakers convincing or unconvincing. A long period of time separates the Greek marketplace (the *agora*), where trials were conducted, from the modern courtroom, but the jury system in wide use for centuries throughout the West traces its beginnings to the participation of the Greek public in legal proceedings.

The Code of Draco.   The Athenian ruler Draco was known to be tough-minded but perhaps not as harsh as the quotation from Plutarch at the beginning of this chapter suggests. The **Code of Draco,** adopted in 621 B.C.E., was severe enough that Solon, Draco's successor, repealed all Draco's criminal laws except the law on homicide.

In 1843, a stone slab was discovered on which part of Draco's law on homicide was inscribed. The slab was badly deteriorated, but eventually most of the inscription was deciphered.[5] The law sets forth the cases of unintentional or unpremeditated killing for which the killer would not be punished. Nothing is written about the penalties for other kinds of homicide or about how they were to be punished. Murderers could avoid execution by going into exile. They were automatically convicted, because their choice of exile was taken as an admission of guilt. A convicted exile who returned to Athens could be killed by a citizen, and such a killing was not considered a crime. Life in exile was full of hardships, and the very survival of anyone who chose exile was in jeopardy.

The death penalty in ancient Greece was administered with great brutality. A convicted offender—not necessarily a murderer—might be thrown off a cliff or fastened with metal restraints to a board and left to die of exposure, starvation, or predation. Poisoning by a draught of hemlock was another method of execution. Socrates, the great philosopher, drank hemlock for corrupting the minds of youth and believing in new gods instead of the gods recognized by the city.

Early Athenians regarded homicide as a pollution of the city. Ceremonies of purification had to take place to remove the curse of the gods. Before trial, accused murderers were forbidden to approach the temple or public buildings lest they enrage the gods by polluting sacred places. The trial itself had to take place in the open agora to ensure that no building would be contaminated by the presence of murderers. Because of the danger of pollution, even persons charged with unintentional homicide were exiled unless they could obtain a pardon from the victim's family.

The Laws of Solon.   The twenty-seven years following the issuing of the Code of Draco were years of discontent and economic hardship. The Athenian aristocracy was enriching itself at the expense of the city's merchants and the farmers in the surrounding countryside. The appointment of Solon, an aristocrat and a respected merchant, took place at a time in which there was the imminence of revolution if measures were not taken to relieve the misery of the poor. Solon's vigorous administration did much to correct economic inequity. Solon also undertook a thorough revision of the criminal laws of Athens.

When elected archon of Athens, Solon was given legislative powers primarily to reconcile the nobility with the peasants, most of whom had fallen deeply into debt.[6] Criminal law reform became a necessary part of his job, because people deep in debt were stealing in order to survive. In 594 B.C.E., the **Laws of Solon** were issued. Solon repealed all but the law on homicide and substituted fines and banishment wherever such lesser penalties could be substituted for capital punishment. Disenfranchisement—the denial of civil rights (citizen's rights) for the offender and sometimes the offender's family—was often imposed. A disenfranchised person could neither vote in the agora nor enter the temples or public buildings.

Under Solon's laws, a thief was required to return stolen property and pay the victim a sum equal to twice its value. The thief could also be confined in the public stocks for five days and nights. For the crime of temple robbery, the penalty was death. For the rape of a free woman, the penalty was a fine of 100 drachmas. Seduction was considered a more heinous offense because it constituted the corruption of a woman's mind as well as her body. In such a case the aggrieved husband could propose any punishment short of bloodshed. The woman seduced was excluded from religious ceremonies and could be sold as a slave.[7]

Reviewing his accomplishments, Solon said, "Laws I wrote, alike for nobleman and commoner, awarding straight justice to everybody."[8] Solon believed that a lawgiver had to make laws that applied equally to all citizens (other than women). He also believed that punishment had to be proportionate to the severity of the crime.

Criminal Law in Ancient Rome

Roman law began with the **Twelve Tables,** written around 451 B.C.E., when Rome was changing from a kingdom to a republic. Brutal methods of punishment similar to those spelled out in the Code of Draco were described in the Twelve Tables. In the sixth century C.E., the emperor Justinian appointed a commission of experts to review and revise Roman law. The result of this enormous undertaking was the **Justinian Code.**

The Twelve Tables. Before the Twelve Tables were legislated by a ten-member commission of both patricians (members of the nobility) and plebeians (common people), justice was based on custom, administered by patricians. The demands of commoners for greater fairness in the administration of justice led to the translation of customs into written laws.[9] So far as can be determined, Roman civil and criminal law was not influenced by Greek precedent or practice.

Throughout Roman history, the Twelve Tables were the foundation of all law. Some statutes remained in force until the end of the Roman Empire, more than a thousand years after the special commission had drafted them. The tables setting forth the laws of property and contract—civil law—are regarded as a significant legacy of Rome.

Roman criminal law required the death penalty in nine of the twenty-seven sections on criminal law in the Twelve Tables. For example, "whoever shall publish a libel—that is to say, shall write verses imputing crime or immorality to anyone—shall be beaten to death with clubs." Arson of a house or a stack of corn was punishable by being tortured to death: "He shall be bound, scourged, and burned alive." Nocturnal meetings for any purpose were prohibited under pain of death. Judges who accepted bribes and judges who offered bribes were subject to execution. Any act of treason was punishable by scourging and crucifixion.[10]

The Romans inflicted the death penalty with terrible brutality. A man who killed a relative was convicted of parricide and was subjected to a punishment that began with scourging and ended with being "sewn into a leather sack with a dog, a cock, a viper, and an ape, and then to be thrown into the sea." A person guilty of false witness was "hurled from the Tarpeian rock."[11] A vestal virgin who violated her vow of chastity was buried alive.[12]

The Justinian Code.   In 527 C.E. Emperor Justinian succeeded to the throne of a declining Roman Empire, the capital of which had been moved from Rome to Constantinople. Justinian wanted to restore the empire to its former glory and undertook a review and revision of Roman law, which had become a huge and confusing mass of laws passed by the Roman senate, imperial edicts, judges' decisions, and the opinions of lawyers and legal scholars. This enormous task was accomplished from 529 to 565. The result, now known as *Corpus Juris Civilis,* became the necessary textbook of legal education in Europe.

The Justinian Code consisted of four books: (1) *Codex Constitutionum,* (2) *Digesta* or *Pandectae,* (3) *Institutiones,* and (4) *Novellae Constitutiones Post Codicem.*[13] The *Institutiones* (*Institutes*) retained the brutal laws from the Twelve Tables without significant amendment. Parricide continued to be punishable by shrouding the offender in a sack with a cock, a dog, a viper, and an ape and flinging the sack into the ocean. We have no record of how often this sentence was pronounced and carried out, or what effect, if any, it had on deterrence.

After the fall of Rome, Justinian's Code disappeared, only to be rediscovered in the twelfth century at the University of Bologna in Italy. Scholars from all over Europe flocked to Bologna to study Roman law, which was the law of the land throughout most of the Middle Ages. Its principles still profoundly influence law in Europe.[14] See the Timeline for the development of corrections from ancient times to the nineteenth century.

timeline
Development of Corrections from the Ancient Times to the Nineteenth Century

Date	Event
1752 B.C.E.	Code of Hammurabi
621	Code of Draco
594	Laws of Solon
450	Twelve Tables
529 to 565 C.E.	Justinian's Code
1750	Montesquieu's *On the Spirit of the Laws*
1757	Execution of Damiens
1764	Beccaria's *Of Crimes and Punishment*
1776	Transportation of criminals to the American colonies ends
1777	Howard's *The State of the Prisons in England and Wales*
1857	Transportation of criminals to Australia ends

WHAT IS THE RELATIONSHIP BETWEEN SOCIAL CONTEXTS AND JUSTIFICATIONS FOR PUNISHMENT?

During the early Middle Ages and extending to the modern era, punishment has been justified in a variety of social contexts. The justifications range from punishment as natural revenge, punishment as social control, punishment as deterrence, punishment as a source of labor, and punishment as exile, to punishment as moral justice. These justifications vividly demonstrate that types of punishment vary from one period to another and that punishment is interrelated with the social order.[15] To understand the historical development and present-day operation of punishment, David Garland would add that punishment, or penalty, must be viewed "as an institution" and, "in its relatedness, as a social institution."[16]

Punishment as Natural Revenge

An ongoing theme throughout history is the desire for revenge. Some people argue that vengeance, a desire to hurt those who hurt you, is fundamental to human nature. Supporters of this position would add that the vengefulness of punishment has solid roots in European correctional history and was transplanted to the United States. Others retort that ascribing a desire for revenge to human nature is problematic, and to support their position, they might point to individuals such as Bishop Desmond Tutu in South Africa, Dr. Martin Luther King Jr. in the United States, and Mahatma Gandhi in India.

It is easy to understand why, in ancient times, a wronged family would react with horrifying brutality toward an offender who had slain a loved one. What is more difficult to understand is why punishment as natural revenge continued to receive support when the state had replaced families and individuals in administering punishment to offenders. Indeed, it can be argued that the brutality of the state's punishments often exceeded the brutality of crimes committed by offenders.

The justification of punishment as natural revenge was often one attempt by the ruling class to maintain the existing social order. For example, after the fall of Rome in the fifth century c.e., law and order were mostly in the hands of the nobles and bishops ruling the towns and principalities into which the empire fragmented. Rulers decided the fates of offenders according to what seemed best to them. Criminals were seen as menaces to the community. Punishments of appalling cruelty were administered to make certain that the contrast between the riches of the few and the miseries of the many did not diminish.[17]

The justification of punishment as natural revenge can also be explained by the fact that the Middle Ages were violent centuries during which life was insecure, justice was uncertain, and danger was everywhere. Those who increased misery by their criminal acts were perceived to deserve severe punishment and even torture. Distinctions between right and wrong were sharply drawn. No one hesitated over questions such as whether guilt might be mitigated by poverty, or over the possibility that the people believed to be offenders might be innocent, or over the prospect that offenders could be reformed if good influences were brought to bear.

Furthermore, punishment as natural revenge was justified when it was perceived that an individual had committed an offense against what was understood as the true expression of faith. The Crusades of the eleventh through thirteenth centuries provide countless examples of how the blood of Christians and Muslims was shed to avenge the God of the Christians and Allah, the God of Islam. Later, as religious conflicts divided Roman Catholics and Protestants in the sixteenth and seventeenth centuries, and as European nations fought religious wars in the seventeenth century, little tolerance was shown individuals who were defined as heretics. They were burned at the stake, hanged, decapitated, and tortured.

These English thieves received capital punishment for their crimes during the reign of Elizabeth I. Which of the purposes of punishment do you think the practice in this illustration best expresses: natural revenge, social control of the dangerous poor, deterrence from crime by example, acquisition of a labor supply, exile of dangerous offenders, or moral justice?

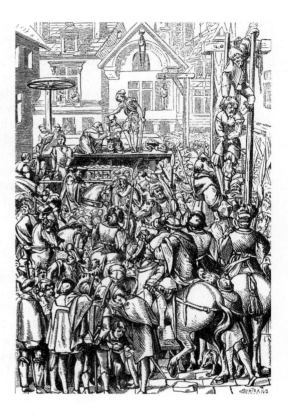

Punishment as Social Control

Feudalism, the economic system that developed in Europe during the ninth century and endured until the fourteenth century, provides one of the best examples of the use of punishment for social control. During the feudal period, almost all the rural land was divided into large estates owned by absentee lords or nobles, managed by landlords, and farmed by peasants. The obligation of the landlord was to protect the peasants, their families, and their possessions.[18] The ability to repress dissent among the peasants, considered the "inferior" and "wicked" class, was one of the chief reasons feudal society survived so long. The isolated and self-sufficient society of the fief prevented peasants from being "corrupted" by processes of social change or by revolutionary ideas. Religious beliefs and pressures helped the peasants to accept the misery of their lives, but the peasants also knew that if they broke the rules (and the rules were very clear) they would be severely punished.[19]

One scholar places the development of punishment in the context of a changing balance of freedom and dependence in feudal society. Punishment was a means of keeping serfs in their place at a time when the feudal system was beginning to break down. This study also observes that punishment was not enforced in feudal society (nor is it enforced in the present) unless the person on whom the penalty is inflicted is subordinate to the person imposing the penal act.[20]

Punishment as Deterrence from Crime

One of the chief justifications of punishment in any age is its deterrence effect—that is, its ability to discourage some people from committing crime. Penalties frequently were severe because it was presumed that they had greater deterrence value than milder forms of punishment. It was not unusual for a king or queen who felt that the nation was under attack by internal dissidents to order mass executions to deter additional civil discord. Mass executions also could be used when particular crimes seemed to be a problem. For example, during the reign of Henry VIII in England (r. 1509–1547), more than seventy-two thousand thieves were hanged. During the reign of his daughter Elizabeth I (r. 1558–1603), "vagabonds were strung up in rows, as many as three or four hundred at a time."[21]

The supposed deterrence value of cruel punishment is exemplified by the execution of Robert François Damiens in Paris in 1757. Damiens had been convicted of the attempted murder of King Louis XV (r. 1715–1774), of whose dissolute conduct the strait-laced Damiens disapproved. He managed to stab the king, inflicting a slight wound. For that attempt he paid a terrible price (see Outside the Walls 2.2).

Louis XV believed in the divine right of kings, so an attempt on his life not only threatened the state but was an affront to God. Undoubtedly Damiens's fate was intended to be a deterrent example to the restive French populace. That example, however, did not deter the French from guillotining Louis's successor, King Louis XVI, thirty-six years later, as well as thousands of the French nobility.

Public viewing of criminals about to be executed for their crimes was intended to be another form of deterrence. In the eighteenth century, about two hundred crimes were lawfully punishable by death. These crimes ranged from murder to stealing from a shopkeeper objects valued at 5 shillings or more. Hangings were public and usually conducted like theatrical performances. Critical attention was paid to how the hangman, the chaplain, and the condemned played their roles. The hangman's part was played without words but had to be performed deftly and without mistakes. The chaplain had a sermon to preach to the person who was about to die and to the attending crowd, to impress on all the wages of sin. The condemned person was at liberty to say anything he or she pleased, including a protestation of innocence. If the demeanor of the condemned at this awful time was marked by contrition and courage, he or she would be applauded but nevertheless would swing from the gallows.[22]

outside the walls 2.2

The Execution of Robert Damiens

On 2 March 1757 Damiens the regicide was condemned to "make the amende honorable before the main door of the Church of Paris," where he was to be "taken and conveyed in a cart, wearing nothing but a shirt, holding a torch of burning wax weighing two pounds"; then "in the said cart, to the Place de Grave, where, on a scaffold that will be erected there, the flesh will be torn from his breasts, arms, thighs and calves with red-hot pincers, his right hand, holding the knife with which he committed the said parricide, burnt with sulphur, and, on those places where the flesh will be torn away, poured molten lead, boiling oil, burning resin, wax and sulphur melted together and then his body drawn and quartered by four horses and his limbs and body consumed by fire, reduced to ashes and his ashes thrown to the winds."

"Finally, he was quartered," recounts the *Gazette d'Amsterdam* of 1 April 1757. "This operation was very long, because the horses used were not accustomed to drawing; consequently, instead of four, six were needed, and when

> . . . excessive pain made him utter horrible cries . . .

that did not suffice, they were forced, in order to cut off the wretch's thighs, to sever the sinews and hack at the joints.

It is said that, although he was always a great swearer, no blasphemy escaped his lips, but the excessive pain made him utter horrible cries, and he often repeated: 'My God, have pity on me! Jesus, help me!' The spectators were all edified by the solicitude of the parish priest of St. Paul's who despite his great age did not spare himself in offering consolation to the patient."

CRITICAL THINKING QUESTIONS

What did this horrible public torture say about the times? What do you think Foucault means when he says that "the spectators were all edified?"

Source: Reprinted from Michel Foucault, *Discipline and Punish: The Birth of the Prison*, trans. Alan Sheridan (New York: Pantheon Books, 1977), pp. 3–6, quoting an article in the *Gazette d'Amsterdam*, 1 April 1757.

Punishment as a Source of Labor

Punishment has also been used as a source of labor. One of the best examples of this justification of punishment is **galley service.** Naval vessels called galleys were propelled by oars manned by galley slaves. As many as two hundred might be required to propel a ship. The conditions of galley service were harsh. Slaves were chained to their benches, four men to an oar.

In England and France in the sixteenth century, the galley oarsmen were criminals convicted of less-than-capital crimes. Queen Elizabeth I proclaimed in 1602 that prisoners, "except when convicted of willful Murther, Rape and Burglarye," might be reprieved from execution and sent to the galleys, "where in, as in all things, our desire is that justice may be tempered with clemency & mercy . . . and the offenders to be in such sort corrected and punished that even in their punishments they may yield some profitable service to the Commonwealth."[23] In France the courts were instructed to refrain from executing, torturing, or even fining criminals so that the king's galleys would be filled with oarsmen.

Galley service was not soft justice. It usually was a lifetime assignment. There was little concern about the oarsmen's well-being because there always were more recruits in the jails. By the end of the seventeenth century, the development of man-of-war ships under sail gradually put an end to galley service.[24]

Punishment as Exile and Banishment

Punishment also has been used to justify exiling and banishing offenders from one country to another. Throughout the eighteenth century and far into the nineteenth century, England sent convicted criminals to colonies abroad, first to North America and then, after the American Revolution, to Australia. This sentence was referred to as **transportation.**[25] Men and women transported to America were indentured to planters and tradesmen for five to ten years. Their condition was little better than slavery. They were forbidden to return to England before the expiration of their sentences, and they were hanged if caught in the attempt.[26] Transportation to North America ended in 1776.

The supply of convicted offenders continued to be plentiful. In London, they were assigned to work projects such as clearing gravel from the Thames riverbed. The prisoners lived in "hulks," decommissioned naval vessels, and were ill fed and kept in unsanitary, overcrowded quarters. The jails of England, hitherto mostly used for the detention of accused offenders before trial, received unprecedented numbers of men and women who could not be accommodated in the hulks. Practical politicians knew that the gallows, hulks, and antiquated jails did not add up to a solution to the crime problem.[27]

The discovery of Australia provided the solution. From 1787 to 1857, when the British Parliament abolished the transportation system, between 130,000 and 160,000 men, women, boys, and girls were transported to various locations in Australia. The first shipment from England to New South Wales consisted of 983 prisoners on embarkation; 273 of them died during the ten-month voyage, and 486 were too sick to disembark under their own power.[28]

Convicts who survived the voyage to Australia and lived inoffensively under the harsh regimen of the military and naval officers in charge could work under reasonable conditions. Skilled and semiskilled men and women could obtain paid employment either from the settlement or from employment by free immigrants. Unskilled men would work in chain gangs. Good behavior could entitle a convict to a **ticket of leave,** freedom to seek paid employment anywhere in the colony, subject to restrictions and the possibility of revocation. Tickets of leave were a precursor of the modern system of parole. Many transportees, when their sentences ended, became settlers with farms or shops of their own.

outside the walls 2.3

Life on Norfolk Island

Norfolk Island is in the South Pacific Ocean 930 miles northeast of Sydney, Australia. It is 5 miles long and 2½ miles wide. It has no harbor, and landings are difficult except in very calm water. About two thousand convicts were settled there under the government's order that "the felon who is sent there is forever excluded from hope of return." Prisoners on Norfolk Island were "doubly convicted," first of felonies committed in England and then of new crimes committed in Australia. Accounts of Norfolk Island describe conditions of depravity and brutality seldom matched in human history. A chaplain reported that so terrible were the conditions of existence that when he went into a cell in which condemned men were awaiting execution to announce the results of the governor's review of their sentences, the men who were reprieved "wept bitterly, and each man who heard of his condemnation to death went down on his knees and thanked God."

> ...conditions of depravity and brutality ... seldom matched in human history.

CRITICAL THINKING QUESTIONS

How much pain in the course of punishment is too much? How do people handle incarceration when no hope is present?

Source: John Howard, *Prisons and Lazarettos,* vol. 1, *The State of the Prisons in England and Wales* (1777; reprint, Montclair, N.J.: Patterson Smith, 1973), p. 165.

Australian discipline was severe and began with flogging, as many as a thousand lashes administered with the cat-'o-nine-tails. For the most serious offenders, reassignment to one of four penal settlements was the dreaded punishment.[29] Outside the Walls 2.3 gives a brief description of the most infamous of these settlements.

Punishment as Moral Justice

Punishment has also been justified as moral justice. One moral justice rationalization is the idea that humans are wicked and require punishment. John Calvin, one of the guiding lights of the Protestant Reformation, focused on the sinfulness of humans, whose "insolence and wickedness" is so great that they "can scarcely be restrained by extremely severe laws."[30] In the seventeenth century the English philosopher Thomas Hobbes argued that the defective nature of human beings requires repressive social controls by the state to avoid widespread social disruption. Hobbes's support of an all-powerful state was based on his belief that, without strict controls, social life would collapse into ongoing warfare between individuals with conflicting interests and humankind might end up destroying itself.[31] Three hundred years later James Q. Wilson remarked that "wicked people exist" and "nothing avails but to set them apart from innocent people."[32] This "humans are naturally wicked" argument is a functionalist one, suggesting that punishment is necessary to control those who are dysfunctional to the social order.

Another functionalist argument justifies punishment as social justice because human nature is hedonistic or pleasure seeking. In the eighteenth century the French political philosopher Jean-Jacques Rousseau contended that each individual possesses an irrational and unceasing drive for more of everything and anything, a drive that will generate massive social conflict unless it is checked. In other words, the more one has, the more one wants.[33] In this regard, Rousseau asked: "If, in order to fall heir to the property of a rich mandarin living at the farthest confines of China, whom one has never seen or heard spoken of, it were enough to push a button to make him die, which of us would not push that button?"[34]

In summary, this section presented several explanations of why punishment has had such an alluring appeal throughout history. Perhaps the most persuasive explanation is that less coercive means of correcting human behavior simply have not been trusted. Thus, punishment is a human invention that is designed to protect society from the chaos that it is believed would erupt if strong forces of social control were not used on those prone to evil and destructive behavior. Furthermore, this section proposed that methods of punishment tend to vary from one period to the next. Sometimes, punishment shapes its social environment; at other times, it is shaped by that environment. Punishment, as David Garland suggested, became "a social institution" with the spectacle of public executions and the transportation of prisoners and especially with the rise of imprisonment.[35]

WHAT IS THE ROLE OF IMPRISONMENT IN THE DEVELOPMENT OF CORRECTIONS?

Imprisonment goes back to the early history of corrections, is used more extensively during medieval times, and becomes the social institution that increasingly replaces the role of executions in more contemporary times.

Early Prisons

Prisons can be traced to the ancient Greeks. In 399 B.C.E., Socrates was condemned by a jury of five hundred members in a trial that lasted a single day. Socrates had the right to propose his penalty, and he chose the death penalty rather than imprisonment. He was confined in prison because of a delay imposed by the Athenian religious calendar, and it was there that he drank poison.[36]

The only instance of imprisonment in the Twelve Tables took place in the laws concerning debt. Debtors could be held in private confinement by their creditors for sixty days. Then, they were to have their debts publicly announced on three successive market days. It they were still unable or unwilling to pay on the third day, they could be executed or sold into slavery outside the city.[37]

The Romans later used the prison more extensively, both in and outside of Rome. The quarry prisons in Rome were known as *latumiae*, which were part of a prison complex located on the southern slope of the Capitoline Hill. They were adjacent to an underground chamber called the *Tullianum*; this lower chamber was used as a place of confinement as well as an execution chamber.

The influential jurist Ulpian stated in what came to be understood (erroneously) as the doctrine of imprisonment in Roman law: "Governors are in the habit of condemning men to be kept in prison or in chain, but they ought not to do this, for punishments of this type are forbidden. Prison indeed ought to be employed for confining men, not for punishing them."[38]

Medieval Prisons

The development of canon law led to an entirely new function for the prison. From around the sixth century on, delinquent monks and nuns were confined in an *ergastulum*, which was a disciplinary cell within the monastery. These individuals were not only separated from their fellows but also were required to do labor. This penitential confinement might in severe cases be a confinement for life.[39]

Some church councils in the eighth and ninth centuries began to insist on punitive incarceration for the laity that were involved in particularly offensive acts, such as incest and magic. The role of the church in prisons increased significantly following the period of the Inquisition. For those who were to deviate from orthodoxy, it was decided to construct special inquisitorial prisons. The inquisitors' frequent use of imprisonment brought attention to their disrepair, and from the fourteenth century on, inquisitors' prisons were the best-maintained prisons in Europe.[40]

Contemporary European Prisons

In sixteenth-century England, minor offenders were sent to local prisons managed by county sheriffs. These **bridewells,** or houses of corrections, were established under local authorities to teach habits of industry to vagrants and idlers. There were also debtors' prisons, to which individuals who were unable or unwilling to pay their creditors were sent. Laws established the standards of treatment of prisoners that sheriffs and magistrates were supposed to meet, but local authorities everywhere ignored those laws with impunity. The conditions in bridewells called for radical reform, and John Howard, a pious county sheriff who is discussed later in this chapter began that process.

A version of the houses of corrections was constructed in 1773 at Ghent (later to become Belgium) and was called the *Maison de Force.* What was different about this facility was the notion that labor could be a positive technique to reform the offender. The Maison de Force's first director, Jean Jacques Philippe Vilain, saw labor and vocational training as important means to put prisoners in a position that they could earn an honest living on their release.[41]

HOW DID THE IDEAS OF ENLIGHTENMENT THINKERS INFLUENCE THE DEVELOPMENT OF CORRECTIONS?

The Enlightenment was an eighteenth-century European philosophical movement characterized by rationalism, skepticism in social and political thought, an impetus toward learning, and moderation in punishment.[42] During the Enlightenment, the explanations of crime based on sin and demons were being replaced by explanations focusing on rationality, individual responsibility, and free choice. Philosophers were advocating the primacy of the rights of the individual over those of the state. Enlightenment thinkers were particularly indignant at the injustice of the criminal law in its widespread use of torture, corporal punishment, and the death penalty. They blamed these brutal measures on authorities' lack of regard for human life.[43]

The philosophical ideas that underlie modern corrections can be traced to three Enlightenment philosophers: Charles de Secondat, Baron de Montesquieu; Cesare Bonesana Beccaria; and Jeremy Bentham. Montesquieu wrote about the need to moderate punishment. Beccaria and Bentham believed that offenders are responsible for their behavior and should be punished, but they also believed that the goal of the state should be deterrence, not revenge.

Montesquieu's and Beccaria's Calls for Reform

Montesquieu (1689–1755), one of the leaders of the Enlightenment, was concerned with government's proper role in the punishment of criminals. In *On the Spirit of the Laws,* he argued that "the severity of punishments is fitter for despotic governments whose principle is terror, than for a monarchy or a republic whose strength is honor and virtue. In moderate governments the love of one's country, shame and the fear of blame, are restraining motives, capable of preventing a great multitude of crimes." Montesquieu added that in a moderate and lenient government, "the greatest punishment of a bad action is conviction. The civil laws have therefore a softer way of correcting, and do not require so much force and severity."[44] His book was a literary success; twenty-two editions were published in less than two years.[45] But many readers of his time, used to the ghastly punishments inflicted in England and France, considered Montesquieu's ideas of moderation in punishment nothing less than sedition.

Another great influence propelling the movement to reform the savage criminal laws of the eighteenth century was the short treatise *Of Crimes and Punishment,* published in 1764 by Cesare Bonesana Beccaria (1738–1794), a Milanese aristocrat.[46] It was written under unusual circumstances. Recently qualified as a lawyer, Beccaria found himself with nothing urgent to do. He was invited to join a reading club, the Academy of Fists, so named because the intellectual disputes that the reading aroused sometimes led to fisticuffs. It was a small group of not more than a dozen young men, meeting nightly to read and discuss well-known French and English authors of the Enlightenment.

The work of Montesquieu had been widely read in Italy, and the terrible execution of Robert Damiens had been discussed and condemned as unacceptably harsh. The time had come for a serious consideration of criminal justice reform, and that was an appropriate topic for the Academy of Fists. Pietro Verri, the organizer of the Academy, suggested to Beccaria that he look into the state of criminal justice. Accepting the assignment, Beccaria amassed a great deal of information about how crimes were punished in Italy and in other countries. There was much discussion within the Academy about his ideas, and, after a year of research and discourse, *Of Crimes and Punishments* was published. It is a classic of criminological literature, still read by scholars and jurists.

Beccaria based the legitimacy of criminal sanctions on the social contract. The authority to make laws rested with the legislator, who should have only one view in sight: "the greatest happiness of the greatest number." Beccaria considered punishment as a necessary evil and suggested that "it should be public, immediate, and necessary; the least possible in the case given; proportioned to the crime; and determined by the laws."[47] He defined the purpose and consequences of punishment as being "to deter persons from the commission of crime and not to provide social revenge. Not severity, but certainty and swiftness in punishment best secure this result."[48]

Beccaria's treatise rejected justifications of torture, the indiscriminate application of capital punishment to hundreds of crimes, many of them petty, and the emphasis on retribution rather than prevention of crime. To this day the U.S. corrections system has been unable to comply with Beccaria's admonition that punishment be swift and certain as well as moderate.

Bentham's Utilitarian Model

Jeremy Bentham (1748–1832) believed that the law should accomplish some utilitarian purpose, and this social desirable outcome from criminal sanctions was the protection of society. He contended that punishment would deter criminal behavior if it was made appropriate to the crime. He stated that punishment has four objectives: (1) to prevent all offenses if possible, (2) to persuade a person who has decided to commit an offense to commit a less rather than a more serious one, (3) "to dispose [a person who has resolved upon a particular offense] to do no more mischief than is necessary to his purpose," and (4) to prevent the crime at as cheap a cost to society as possible.[49]

Bentham believed that human beings are governed by "twin masters": pleasure and pain. If an offender was to be punished, Bentham wrote, the pain inflicted should exceed the pleasure of the crime,[50] but the differential must not be more than absolutely necessary under the circumstances. Bentham believed in a "hedonic calculus" by which the amount of pleasure and the amount of pain could be calculated, compared, and adjusted so that punishment would be no more than sufficient and always just.[51]

The Panopticon

As a solution to challenges posed by crime, the care of the insane, the education of the young, and the rehabilitation of paupers, Bentham proposed a factory design that his brother had invented. He modified the factory design to create the Panopticon—a prison consisting of a circular building with tiers of prison cells rising around the circumference and in the center a towerlike structure from which inspectors could observe the inmates in their cells at hard labor. The prisoners would work twelve to fourteen

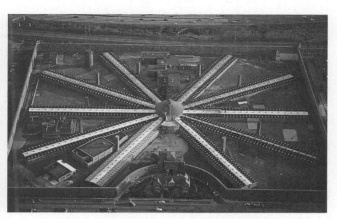

What was Jeremy Bentham's theory of crime and punishment? How did this theory reflect ideas of the Age of Enlightenment? How was the architecture of Bentham's Panopticon an expression of his theory? How did Enlightenment thinkers such as Bentham inspire early prison reformers?

hours a day and would sleep on hammocks.[52] The Panopticon would hold as many as two thousand offenders serving terms ranging from a few months to many years.[46]

Bentham proposed that he manage the Panopticon under contract with the government. Profits from the prisoners' labor would go to the manager, who would divide one-sixth of the proceeds among the prisoner workers. The prisoners would learn trades and receive education. Although Bentham had no experience whatsoever in the management of factories or prisons, he confidently volunteered to manage Panopticons personally and even engaged to insure the lives of the inmates, to provide for annuities for their old age, and to pay the government a sum for each escape.

The twentieth-century French philosopher and historian Michel Foucault observed that, in contrast to the old ways of punishment, the Panopticon focused on the personality of the prisoner. The success of the Panopticon depended on the achievement of its objective: knowledge of prisoners as individuals. Inmates were to be observed so that the warden would know them and could with knowledge control their minds and actions.[53]

Bentham's Panopticon embodies the essence of modern penology. Today, the prison warden exercises control by organizing information about each convict. Prisoners are classified and assigned to housing and programs in which the information can be used and augmented by further observation. In the Stateville Penitentiary in Illinois, the Panopticon form itself survives.

WHO WERE THE EARLY PRISON REFORMERS?

Three early prison reformers had their own ideas about what reforms were needed to make the incarceration experience more humane. John Howard and Captain Alexander Maconochie were British; Walter Crofton was Irish. Howard spent his career trying to improve jails. He inspected jails in England and on the European continent and wrote an influential book on the need for jail reform. On Norfolk Island, in the South Pacific, Maconochie developed a mark system, allowing graduated release from incarceration. Crofton developed the Irish mark system, which was implemented in a prison in Ireland. Later, his mark system was brought to Britain's North American colonies and become what we now know as parole.

John Howard Reforms the Bridewells

In 1773, John Howard (1726–1790) was appointed High Sheriff of Bedfordshire, England. He was a well-to-do and pious country squire. As a young man he had traveled to Europe, hoping to help in the relief of Lisbon after the disastrous earthquake of 1755. On the way, the French, with whom England was at war, captured him and held him prisoner for two months in conditions of great barbarity. He was returned to England on a prisoner exchange. His biographers do not tell us to what extent his experiences

h e r o e s

John Howard

Jail Reformer

When Howard became a sheriff—then mainly a ceremonial office with responsibility for the county's jails and bridewells—he took the post seriously, as practically no other holder of the office ever had. When he inspected the jail under his control, he was shocked to discover several penniless prisoners who had been acquitted of the offenses for which they had been charged and were eligible for release but were being detained until they paid "sundry fees" to the jailer and the clerk of the court. This practice was not legal, but jailers' only source of income was the fees paid by their prisoners.

Howard proposed that jailers be paid salaries. The county magistrates, however, asked the sheriff to find out what other counties were doing to pay jail personnel. Howard's county-by-county survey revealed that jailers and clerks everywhere extorted their income from prisoners living in horrible conditions. Howard decided to devote the rest of his life to the reform of prisons and jails. Explaining his motives, he wrote: "I was prompted by the sorrows of the sufferers and love to my country. The work grew on me insensibly: I could not enjoy my ease and leisure in the neglect of any opportunity, offered me by Providence, of attempting the relief of the miserable."

Jail fever, or typhus, was endemic in most prisons, spread by rats and lice, and from prisoner to prisoner. Numerous prisoners, as well as jailers, judges, and court officers, died of it. In addition to typhus, many prisoners suffered from active cases of smallpox. Howard called for attention to cleaning up the dangerously unsanitary conditions in English prisons. He died of typhus after inspecting a prison in southern Russia.

CRITICAL THINKING QUESTIONS

What motivated Howard to try to improve conditions in jails and prisons? How likely are individuals, such as Howard, to make a real difference in corrections? In what ways can individuals make a difference?

Source: John Howard, *Prisons and Lazarettos,* vol. 1, *The State of the Prisons in England and Wales* (1777; reprint, Montclair, N.J.: Patterson Smith, 1973), p. 1.

as a prisoner of war influenced his later single-minded determination to reform all the prisons of Europe. His book *The State of the Prisons in England and Wales,* published after his initial survey, made him a celebrity.[48] His name is still associated with prison reform in Britain and the United States, where Howard Leagues have long been established to maintain vigilance over the standards set for prison operations. John Howard is acknowledged as one of the real heroes of the development of corrections.

Between 1774 and 1791 Parliament enacted a series of statutes embodying Howard's recommendations. Unfortunately, the legislation permitted local magistrates to decide whether to put the recommendations into practice. Local authorities resisted raising taxes to provide salaries to jailers and to make life healthier for prisoners. As a result, the conditions of neglect and abuse in jails continued long after the death of John Howard.

Captain Alexander Maconochie Reforms Norfolk Island

Captain Alexander Maconochie (1787–1860) was a retired naval officer brought to Australia by Sir John Franklin, a friend and fellow naval officer who had been appointed lieutenant governor of Van Diemen's Land (present-day Tasmania), a British colony populated mostly by transported convicts. Maconochie, a strict Scottish Presbyterian, was shocked by the treatment of the convicts. He developed proposals for drastic changes, but Franklin was so disturbed by the criticisms that he dismissed him.[55] Nevertheless, the proposals, advanced by Maconochie in several long memoranda to the Colonial Office in London, received a sympathetic review that ended with the recommendation that he be appointed to superintend a penal settlement where he could try out his ideas.

Maconochie's proposals were based on two beliefs. First, "brutality and cruelty debase not only the person subjected to them, but also the society which deliberately uses them or tolerates them for purposes of social control." Second, "the treatment of the wrongdoer during his sentence of imprisonment should be designed to make him fit to be released into society again, purged of the tendencies that led to his offense, and strengthened in his ability to withstand temptation to offend again."[56]

Sir George Gipps, the governor of New South Wales, decided that Norfolk Island would be a good place for the experiment. In 1840 Maconochie became superintendent of the prison there. About eight hundred ordinary convicts—men not "doubly convicted"— were to be sent to the island. Sir George's idea was that the new convicts would be kept separate from the old. Given the size of the island and the limited facilities for housing prisoners, this plan was impractical. From the first, Maconochie expressed his reservations about it but went ahead with the hope that something positive would emerge.

On arrival at the island, he told the prisoners what he intended to do and why. A **mark system** would be established whereby prisoners would receive a fixed number of "marks of commendation" for completing assigned tasks. They could use the marks to purchase food and clothing. Prisoners who accumulated enough marks would receive a ticket of leave.[57] Those who earned 6,000 marks would discharge a seven-year sentence; 8,000 marks would free a man from a life sentence. Prisoners guilty of disciplinary infractions were be fined a certain number of marks.

Maconochie decided that the "doubly convicted" and the new men had to be treated alike. This decision got him into trouble with Sir George Gipps. From that time on, Maconochie operated under constraints, and his mark system was limited to offenders with sentences of three years or less. The experiment ended in 1844 with Maconochie's recall to England.[58]

Maconochie returned to England and waged a long and seemingly unsuccessful campaign to reform the British prison system. He wrote and published pamphlets explaining how his ideas would not only humanize penology but also save the taxpayers a great deal of money. His campaign, to which he devoted the rest of his life, attracted many followers as well as the skepticism and derision of hard-liners. His followers were responsible for sweeping reforms of the penal system in the second half of the nineteenth century.

Walter Crofton Invents the Irish Mark System

In the 1850s the British Parliament passed a succession of Penal Servitude Acts, anticipating the gradual end of the transportation system. Under Sir Joshua Jebb, a "Progressive Stage System" of convict management was developed. From the beginning, the influence of Maconochie's mark system could be seen. After some experimentation, the Act of 1857 required convicts to serve nine months in solitary confinement for the first stage of their sentences. During the second stage they would receive pay for work done and privileges of movement and association with other prisoners. The third stage was release on license for the rest of the sentence to be served.[53]

Walter Crofton, a retired army officer, had worked with Jebb in the prison administration. In 1854 Crofton was sent to introduce the Progressive Stage System at a new prison at Mountjoy, near Dublin. The basic plan was Jebb's, but Crofton soon developed innovations. The complete program became known as the "Irish mark system" and made Crofton a celebrity in international penology circles.[54]

The system applied to convicts serving terms of three years or more. It was separated into three stages. The first stage lasted eight or nine months, depending on the man's conduct. The first three months were spent in solitary confinement (no work) and on reduced rations (no meat). When finally eligible for the second stage, the prisoner would be moved to Spike Island, off the southern coast of Ireland, or, if he happened to be skilled at a craft, to a construction site at Philipstown, where convicts were building a new prison. The second stage included four classes: third, second, first, and "advanced." In each class, a prisoner had to earn marks for a maximum of 9 a month: 3 for good conduct, 3 for good work on an assigned job, and 3 for diligence in school. Prisoners were punished for rule violations by the loss of marks. Although all classes worked together, they were distinguished from one another by badges, gratuities that increased from class to class, and progress toward the third stage. The third stage was spent at Lusk Common, 15 miles from Dublin, where convicts were housed in dormitories, worked at land reclamation, and were given vocational training to fit them for employment when finally released.[61]

The Irish mark system was based on the contention that prisoners should be so changed in attitude and behavior that when released they would be unlikely to return to crime. Just to be sure, when they were finally released on license (or ticket of leave) from Lusk Common, they were required to report periodically to the police. The license expired at the conclusion of the sentence. The released men were made to understand that if there were signs of a relapse into criminal ways, they would be hustled back to Mountjoy in disgrace.

In 1862 illness forced Crofton to retire. After his retirement, his mark system came under attack from many influential quarters. During the debate that ensued, Crofton was persuaded to return to the Irish prison system in 1877. He retired again the following year. Aided by widespread foreign interest, his system became the standard in England.[62]

SUMMARY

The Code of Hammurabi, the laws of the Greeks, and criminal law in ancient Rome marked the transition from vengeance as a private matter to punishment being handled by the state against wrongdoers. In these early societies, punishment became a social institution when executions became public events intended to deter criminal acts.

In Europe, from the early Middle Ages to the end of the nineteenth century, a variety of reasons were used to explain and justify punishments. Philosophical justifications linked punishment with vengeance, deterrence, social control, and moral justice. Punishments such as public executions, transportation, and imprisonment in jails and long-term institutions also came to be viewed as social institutions serving a public purpose.

During the Enlightenment, Montesquieu, Beccaria, and Bentham articulated ideas that contributed to the moderation of punishment. A number of their ideas

were instrumental in the development of modern corrections, such as their opinions that punishment should be swift and certain as well as moderate, that the purpose of punishment is to prevent and deter the commission of crime, and that the reform of punishment meant the rejection of torture and the end of the indiscriminate application of capital punishment to hundreds of crimes.

John Howard, Captain Alexander Maconochie, and Walter Crofton were widely hailed for the reforms they attempted to bring to punishment during the eighteenth and nineteenth centuries. Howard attacked the abuses in jails in England and on the European continent. Maconochie attempted to improve the treatment of convicts in Australia by installing the mark system in Norfolk Island. Crofton adapted the mark system to a prison setting in Ireland. In the next chapter, the ongoing debate between advocates of repression and advocates of reform moves to the United States.

KEY TERMS

bridewells, p. 33
Code of Draco, p. 24
Code of Hammurabi, p. 23
galley service, p. 30
Justinian Code, p. 25
law of talion, p. 23

Laws of Solon, p. 25
mark system, p. 37
ticket of leave, p. 30
transportation, p. 30
Twelve Tables, p. 25

CRITICAL THINKING QUESTIONS

1. When the state took over the punishment of offenders, why do you think its punishments were no less brutal than private vengeance?
2. How can the cruelty of punishment in the Middle Ages be explained? Does the explanation have some relevance for our time?
3. In what ways do the ideas of Beccaria and Bentham still influence criminal justice?

4. Suppose that you are the director of corrections in your state. Would Crofton's Irish mark system be an appropriate basis for programming adult prisoners? What further elements would you add for maximum effectiveness?
5. How does the social context influence the justification for punishment? Illustrate your answer with examples from this chapter.
6. Do you think there is still a place for prison reformers today? Why or why not?

WEB DESTINATIONS

Read in more depth on the topic of Roman law, on which the British and American systems of justice are based.
http://www.britannica.com/bcom/eb/article/2/0,5716,115342+1+108633,00.html

This page describes the life and contributions of the eighteenth-century political and moral philosopher Cesare Beccaria, whose ideas influenced the development of correctional systems in Europe.
http://www.utm.edu/research/iep/b/beccaria.htm

Access a virtual tour of Jeremy Bentham's Panopticon that explains the philosophy behind this architecture and puts you inside the prison.
http://is.gseis.ucla.edu/impact/f96/Projects/dengberg/

Learn more about corrections reformer John Howard through the site of the John Howard Society of Canada.
http://www.johnhoward.ca

Read about the history of inmate incentive programs, such as the mark system introduced in the nineteenth century by Alexander Maconochie at Norfolk Island prison.
http://www.penlex.org.uk/pages/prtiep.html

FOR FURTHER READING

Drapkin, Israel. *Crime and Punishment in the Ancient World.* Lexington, Mass.: Lexington Books, 1989. A scholarly and comprehensive account of crime and justice.

Garland, David. *Punishment and Modern Society: A Study in Social Theory.* Chicago: University of Chicago Press, 1990. A classic study in the sociology of punishment.

Garland, David, "Penal Modernism and Postmodernism." In *Punishment and Social Control: Essays in Honor of Sheldon L. Messinger,* edited by Thomas G. Blomberg and Stanley Cohen, pp. 181–209. New York: Aldine de Gruyter, 1995. Garland projects what punishment or penalty will look like in the postmodern future.

Howard, John. *Prisons and Lazarettos.* 2 vols. 1777. Reprint, Montclair, N.J.: Patterson Smith, 1973. The first volume focuses on conditions in prisons in England and Wales and constitutes the report that Howard made to Parliament on his survey of English prisons. The second volume covers the lazarettos (hospitals for the diseased poor) and the prisons in foreign countries that Howard surveyed after his earlier report on English prisons had made him a celebrity.

Ignatieff, Michael. *A Just Measure of Pain: The Penitentiary in the Industrial Society, 1750–1850.* New York: Pantheon Books, 1978. The author locates the genesis of modern punishment within the history of ideas and intellectual movements.

NOTES

1. Plutarch, *Plutarch's Lives* XVII, trans. Aubrey Steward and George Long, vol. 1 (London: Bell, 1906), pp. 144–145. Some historians believe that Plutarch exaggerated Draco's harshness.
2. Sydney Smith, *On the Management of Prisons* (London: Warde Locke & Co., n.d.), pp. 226, 232.
3. This account draws from the definitive study of the Code of Hammurabi in G. Driver and John C. Miles, *The Babylonian Laws,* 2 vols. (London: Oxford University Press, 1952).
4. C. H. W. Johns, *The Oldest Code of Laws in the World* (Edinburgh: T & T. Clark, 1905).
5. Ronald S. Stroud, *Dracon's Law on Homicide* (Berkeley: University of California Press, 1968).
6. Archon of Athens was an elective office that was held for one year. The archon acted as chief magistrate. As archon, Solon was specially empowered to repeal old laws and make new ones.
7. For an adequate summary of what is known about punishment in Athens, see Douglas M. MacDowell, *The Law in Classical* Athens (Ithaca, N.Y.: Cornell University Press, 1978), pp. 120–132.
8. Victor Ehrenberg, *From Solon to Socrates* (London: Methuen, 1968), p. 70.
9. For a text of the Twelve Tables, see W. A. Hunter, *A Systematic and Historical Exposition of Roman Law* (London: Sweet and Maxwell, 1897).
10. Cicero, *De Legibus,* 11.23.
11. The Tarpeian rock was a steep rock face on one of the Roman hills. No one thrown from its height could possibly survive.
12. H. F. Jolowicz, *Historical Introduction to the Study of Roman Law* (Cambridge: Cambridge University Press, 1954), pp. 321–331.
13. "Justinian, Code of," *Encyclopedia Britannica Online.*
14. Jolowicz, *Historical Introduction to the Study of Roman Law.*
15. David Garland, *Punishment and Modern Society: A Study in Social Theory* (Chicago: University of Chicago Press, 1990), p. 284.
16. Ibid.
17. Johan Huizinga, *The Waning of the Middle Ages* (London: Edward Arnold, 1924), p. 1.
18. Charles Seingnobos, *The Feudal Regime* (New York: Holt, 1908), pp. 3–4.

19. Ibid.

20. Cited in Pieter Spierenburg, *The Spectacle of Suffering: Executions and the Evolution of Repression* (Cambridge: Cambridge University Press, 1984).

21. Georg Rusche and Otto Kirchheimer, *Punishment and the Social Structure* (New York: Columbia University Press, 1939).

22. Leon Radzinowicz, *A History of the English Criminal Law,* 4 vols. (London: Stevens, 1948–1969).

23. Quoted in George Ives, *A History of Penal Methods* (London: Stanley Paul, 1914), pp. 101–107.

24. Ibid.

25. See Robert Hughes, *The Fatal Shore* (New York: Knopf, 1987).

26. Ibid.

27. Ibid.

28. Ibid.

29. John Howard, *Prisons and Lazarettos,* vol. 1, *The State of the Prisons in England and Wales* (1777; reprint, Montclair, N.J.: Patterson Smith, 1973), p. 3.

30. John Calvin, *Institutes of the Christian Religion,* trans. John McNeil (Philadelphia: Westminister Press, 1958); originally published as *Christianae religionis Institutio* (Basel, 1536).

31. Thomas Hobbes, *Leviathan* (1651; reprint, New York: Columbia University Press, 1983), p. 81.

32. James Q. Wilson, *Thinking about Crime,* rev. ed. (New York: Basic Books, 1983), p. 260.

33. Quoted in William Bonger, *Criminality and Economic Conditions* (Bloomington: Indiana University Press, 1969), pp. 126–127.

34. Thomas J. Bernard, *The Consensus–Conflict Debate: Form and Content in Social Theories* (New York: Columbia University Press, 1983), p. 81.

35. Garland, *Punishment and Modern Society,* p. 282.

36. Edward M. Peters, "Prison before the Prison: The Ancient and Medieval Worlds," in *The Oxford History of the Prison: The Practice of Punishment in Western Society,* edited by Norval Morris and David J. Rothman (New York: Oxford University Press, 1995), p. 6.

37. Ibid., p. 15.

38. Cited in Ibid., p. 21.

39. For an extensive examination of monastic prisons, see Ralph B. Pugh, *Imprisonment in Medieval England* (London: Cambridge University Press, 1968), chapter 18.

40. Peters, "Prison before the Prison," p. 31.

41. H. E. Barnes and N. K. Teeters, *New Horizons in Criminology,* 3rd ed. (Englewood Cliffs, N.J.: Prentice-Hall, 1943).

42. *Webster's New Twentieth Century Dictionary of the English Language,* 2nd ed. (New York: Simon and Schuster, 1983).

43. Philip Jenkins, "Varieties of Enlightenment Criminology," *British Journal of Criminology* 24 (April 1984), p. 112.

44. Montesquieu, *On the Spirit of the Laws,* trans. Thomas Nugent, ed. David W. Carithers (Berkeley: University of California Press, 1977), p. 158; originally published as *L'Esprit des lois* (1747).

45. Ibid., p. 158.

46. Cesare Beccaria, *Of Crimes and Punishment,* trans. Fr. Kenelm Foster and Jane Grigson (New York: Oxford University, 1964), p. 13; originally published as *Dei deletti e delle pene* (1764).

47. Ibid.

48. Ibid.

49. Ysabel Rennie, *The Search for Criminal Man: A Conceptual History of the Dangerous Offender* (Lexington, Mass.: Lexington Books, 1978), p. 15.

50. Jeremy Bentham, *An Introduction to the Principles of Morals and Legislation* (1823; reprint, New York: Hafner, 1948).

51. Ibid.

52. In 1830, Bentham published a pamphlet entitled *History of the War between Jeremy Bentham and George the Third, by One of the Belligerents.* It contains an account of Bentham's plan for the Panopticon.

53. Michel Foucault, *Discipline and Punish: The Birth of the Prison,* trans. Alan Sheridan (New York: Pantheon Books, 1977), p. 202.

54. Howard, *The State of the Prisons in England and Wales.*

55. John Vincent Barry, *Alexander Maconochie of Norfolk Island* (Melbourne: Oxford University Press, 1958).

56. Ibid., p. 75.

57. Sean McConville, *A History of English Prison Administration* (London: Routledge & Kegan Paul, 1981).

58. Ibid.

59. Mary Carpenter, *Reformatory Prison Discipline, as Developed by the Rt. Hon. Sir Walter Crofton* (London: Longmans, Green, Reader and Dyer, 1872), pp. 5–22.

60. Ibid.

61. Ibid.

62. Ibid.

CHAPTER 2 / BUILT-IN STUDY GUIDE

Multiple Choice Questions

1. What type of prison design consisted of a circular building with the prison cells rising around the circumference?

    A. The big house
    B. Bridewell house
    C. Panopticon
    D. Reformatory

2. What event signified the beginning of the state's assuming the role of punishing offenders?

    A. A formalized system of government and written laws
    B. The development of bridewell houses and written laws
    C. A formalized system of government and bridewell houses
    D. Private citizens engaging in acts of vengeance and written laws

3. Which of the following concepts is consistent with Jeremy Bentham's philosophy of punishment?

    A. Pain will not deter offenders from engaging in future criminal behavior
    B. The pain inflicted on the offender should exceed the pleasure of the crime
    C. The pain inflicted on offenders will promote future criminal behavior
    D. Certainty and swiftness, not the severity, of punishment will deter offenders from engaging in future crime

4. Which of the following is the first known set of recorded laws?

    A. Code of Draco
    B. Law of Solon
    C. Twelve Tables
    D. Code of Hammurabi

5. Identify the set of Greek laws adopted in 621 B.C.E. that was so severe that all of them, except the law on homicide, had to be replaced.

    A. Code of Draco
    B. Law of Solon
    C. Twelve Tables
    D. Code of Hammurabi

6. All of the following are books that make up the *Corpus Juris Civilis* except:

    A. *Codex Constitutionum*
    B. *Digesta*
    C. *Institutuiones*
    D. *Codex Romania*

7. Which dominant, European economic system that was prominent from the ninth to the fourteenth century signified an example of punishment used as social control?

    A. Feudalism
    B. Monarchism
    C. Socialism
    D. Parliamentary

8. The chief justification of punishment throughout history has been:

    A. Deterrence
    B. Incapacitation
    C. Rehabilitation
    D. Reintegration

9. What was the origin of the modern parole system?

    A. Mark system
    B. Ticket of leave
    C. Bridewell system
    D. House of corrections

10. Throughout history all of the following have been justifications of punishment except:

    A. Punishment as natural revenge
    B. Punishment as social control
    C. Punishment as education
    D. Punishment as labor supply

11. What event ended the transportation of criminal offenders from England to the colonies?

    A. The end of the feudal system
    B. The constitutional convention
    C. The end of England's system of parliament
    D. The American Revolution

12. According to Beccaria, to deter offenders from committing future crime punishment has to be:

    A. Severe and certain
    B. Severe and swift
    C. Swift and certain
    D. Punitive and rehabilitative

True/False Questions

T F 1. The first known laws in history were concerned with property rights.

T F 2. Rehabilitation and reintegration have been the basic strategies for dealing with law violators since the dawn of history.

T F 3. The Panopticon focused on warehousing offenders.

T F 4. Throughout history the state has assumed the role of punishing violators of societal norms.

T F 5. Throughout the history of Rome, the Twelve Tables were the foundation of all laws.

T F 6. Throughout the majority of history the human desire for revenge against wrongdoers is continuous.

T F 7. The philosophical ideas that modern corrections is based on can be traced to Roman law.

T F 8. The conditions in bridewell houses served as a model that prison reformer John Howard implemented in jails.

T F 9. Enlightenment philosophers supported the criminal law and its widespread use of the death penalty and other forms of torturous punishment.

T F 10. The Code of Hammurabi proscribed capital punishment for all unlawful offenses.

T F 11. Solon advocated punishment that was proportional to the severity of the crime.

T F 12. The seventeenth-century philosopher Thomas Hobbes supported state-mandated social control as necessary to suppress the inherently evil nature of humans.

Fill-in-the-Blank Questions

(based on key terms)

1. Written in 451 B.C.E., the _____ signified the beginning of Roman law.

2. _____ were established under local authorities to teach habits of industry to vagrants and idlers.

3. _____ was a form of punishment used in the sixteenth century that required criminals convicted of less than capital crimes to row naval vessels.

4. The _____ issued in about 1752 B.C.E. was the first known set of codified laws on record.

5. During the eighteenth century, England used a sentence called _____ that sent convicted criminals to America and Australia.

6. The _____ developed by Alexander Maconochie and used on Norfolk Island allowed prisoners to earn rewards and privileges based on labor and good behavior.

7. Originally developed by Walter Crofton, the _____ entitled convicts who maintained good behavior the freedom to seek paid employment anywhere in the colony, subject to restrictions on behavior and the possibility of revocation.

8. The _____ issued in 594 B.C.E. was a significant revision of the criminal laws of Athens.

9. Twelve experts were appointed to review and organize Roman law into a digest at the _____.

10. On the appointment of Solon, all of the laws except for the one addressing homicide from the code of laws known as the _____ were repealed.

Essay Questions

1. Explain the transition of punishment as being a form of vengeance carried out by a private individual to punishment being administered by the state against wrongdoers. In your response include factors that influenced this transition.

2. Explain how the social contexts and the economic means of production during certain periods of history influenced the forms and justifications of punishment during those periods.

3. Explain how the ideas that come from the Enlightenment influenced the development of corrections.

4. Identify the three early prison reformers noted in your textbook and explain how their ideas for reform made for a more humane incarceration experience.

5. Compare the philosophies of punishment under Greek law, Roman law, and the Enlightenment. Which period was the most punitive and which was the most liberal?

ANSWERS

Multiple Choice Questions

1.	C	7.	A
2.	A	8.	A
3.	B	9.	B
4.	D	10.	C
5.	A	11.	D
6.	D	12.	C

True/False Questions

1.	T	7.	F
2.	F	8.	F
3.	F	9.	F
4.	F	10.	F
5.	T	11.	T
6.	T	12.	T

Fill-in-the-Blank Questions

1. Twelve Tables
2. Bridewell
3. Galley service
4. Code of Hammurabi
5. Transportation
6. Mark system
7. Ticket of leave
8. Law of Solon
9. Institute of Justinian
10. Code of Draco

chapter **three**

The Development of Corrections in the United States

When the English novelist Charles Dickens visited the United States in 1842, he visited the Cherry Hill Prison in Philadelphia. What he saw during his two-hour visit gave him enough ammunition to denounce the solitary confinement system. Dickens's denunciation began with these words: "The system here is rigid, strict and hopeless solitary confinement," and "I believe it, in its effect, to be cruel and wrong." His next comments were even harsher:

> In its intention, I am well convinced that it is kind, humane and meant for reformation but I am persuaded that those who devised the system and those benevolent gentlemen who carry it into execution, do not know what it is that they are doing. I believe that very

few men are capable of establishing the immense amount of torture and agony which this dreadful punishment, prolonged for years, inflicts upon its sufferers. . . . I hold this slow and daily tampering with the mysteries of the brain to be immeasurably worse than any torture of the body; and because its ghastly signs and tokens are not so palpable to the eye and sense of touch as scars upon the flesh; because its wounds are not on the surface, and it extorts few cries that human ears can hear; therefore I denounce it as a secret punishment which slumbering humanity is not roused up to stay.[1]

CRITICAL THINKING QUESTIONS

Do you believe that Dickens overstated the case against solitary confinement? How long do you think you could handle solitary confinement before losing your mind?

Dickens's charges, whatever their accuracy might be, are a vivid reminder of the unintended consequences of human actions. The Pennsylvania reformers chose a rehabilitative model because they believed that a penitent offender could use solitude to become a God-fearing and law-abiding citizen. Their justification for solitary confinement also rested on the belief that it was an effective punishment. These reformers seemed not to be aware of the devastating effects of solitary confinement on the mind.[2]

In our own time, solitary confinement has made a comeback with the construction of super-max prisons and high-security units. Some inmates are housed in complete solitary confinement today, but the objective is no longer, as it was with the Pennsylvania model, to rehabilitate the inmates.[3]

WHAT WAS DISTINCTIVE ABOUT THE EARLY HISTORY OF CORRECTIONS IN THE COLONIES?

The American experience with corrections was shaped by what took place in Europe. Other than the Quaker-inspired "Great Law" of Pennsylvania, brutal punishments derived from European methods of punishing criminals were common throughout the colonies. Initially, the colonies used the harsh criminal codes of England, but the idealism and social activism of the colonists led to the development of distinctly American legal practices, such as the penitentiary.

Colonial Punishment

The Puritans in New England used correctional punishment as a means to enforce their strict Puritan codes. They viewed the deviant as willful, a sinner, and a captive of the devil. Informal community pressures, such as gossip, ridicule, and ostracism, were found to be effective in keeping most citizens in line. Mutilations, hangings, burnings, and brandings were used to punish serious crimes. Fines, confinement in the stocks and the public cage, banishment, and whippings were other frequently used methods of control, and any citizen who was not a respected property owner was rejected from the town. The jail, which was brought to the colonies soon after the settlers arrived from England, was used to detain individuals awaiting trial and those awaiting punishment.[4]

The East Jersey codes of 1668 and 1675 called for first-time burglary offenders to be branded with a *T* on the hand; the second offense was punished by the branding of a *T* on the forehead. In Maryland, those who were found guilty of blasphemy were branded on the forehead with the letter *B*. An adulteress, like Hester Prynne, in Nathaniel Hawthorne's novel *The Scarlet Letter*, was forced to wear a scarlet letter *A* in Puritan-controlled New England. Stocks held sitting prisoners, with their feet and hands fastened in a locked frame, and pillories held standing prisoners with their hands similarly locked.[5]

The Quakers and Criminal Law

The Quaker colonies of Pennsylvania and West Jersey at first rejected English criminal law. Legislation enacted in 1682 by the first assembly in Pennsylvania provided that only murderers were subject to the gallows.[6] The other traditional felonies were punishable by hard labor. William Penn, the founder of the colony, drafted these comparatively mild statutes expressing the Quaker aversion to cruelty and bloodshed. In addition to the pillory, the stocks, and the whipping post, Pennsylvania's law of 1682 required the first prisons and specified the care of inmates:

> All prisons shall be workhouses for felons, thiefs, vagrants, and loose, abusive, and idle persons, whereof one shall be in every county.
>
> Gaolers [jailers] shall not oppress their prisoners, and all prisons shall be free as to room, and all prisoners shall have liberty to provide themselves bedding, food and other necessaries, during their imprisonment, except those whose punishment by law, will not admit of that liberty.[7]

In 1721, however, the Pennsylvania legislature repealed the Quaker criminal code and adopted the criminal laws of England. In addition to murder, twelve other crimes became capital offenses: manslaughter by stabbing, treason, maiming, highway robbery, burglary, arson, sodomy, buggery, rape, concealing the death of an illegitimate child, advising the killing of such a child, and witchcraft.[8] As the condemned stood on the scaffold awaiting the noose, clergymen preached sermons to the witnessing crowds about the wickedness of the condemned and the righteousness of ending his or her life. Those who swung from the gallows were warnings to others who might be inclined to commit similar crimes.

Larceny and the less serious crimes, especially fornication and giving birth to an illegitimate child, became punishable by whipping, branding, or mutilation. The pillory and the stocks were used to make examples of drunkards, swearers, public gamblers, and other petty offenders.

After the adoption of the Declaration of Independence, the Pennsylvania legislature repealed the British laws that the colony had enacted. A series of statutes abolished capital punishment for all crimes other than first-degree murder.[9] For the major felonies, terms of imprisonment were provided. Fines or jail terms replaced the whipping post, the pillory, and the stocks. A system of state prisons was established to accommodate felons avoiding the gallows under the terms of the new laws. It has been argued that "a more thorough transformation in the character of a penal code, by peaceful legislation, is not recorded in the world's history than that which took place in Pennsylvania during the eighteen years immediately succeeding the Declaration of Independence."[10]

In sum, advocates of repression and of reform were in conflict in Pennsylvania, as they would continue to be throughout the history of corrections in the United States. Reformers came to an early conclusion that incarceration in jails or state prisons was preferable to such forms of punishment as the whipping posts and the stocks and much preferable to the frequent use of the death penalty. One impetus for reform was the influence of religion.

The Influence of Religion on Penal Policy

Throughout the history of corrections, the influence of religion on the treatment of offenders has been significant. As Émile Durkheim pointed out, ancient societies and primitive people often assigned a religious meaning to the penal process, and punishment was perceived as a required sacrifice to an aggrieved deity. In such cultures, crime was associated with sin, guilt, and impurity; therefore, the act of punishment involved expiation as well as a ritual cleansing of polluting elements in society.[11]

During the Middle Ages the Roman Catholic Church developed penal techniques later used by rulers of the European states. Ecclesiastical courts (church courts) developed their own institutions of imprisonment, and the spiritual exercises of the monastic orders gave rise to the practices of penitential discipline and cellular confinement. The Vatican prison served as a model of prison design in both America and Europe.

The Protestant Reformation influenced the development of state, or secular, imprisonment. Protestant influence is evident in the Dutch houses of correction of the sixteenth century and in the Quaker penitentiaries of the early nineteenth century. Protestant theology favored solitary confinement, the penitence model, and productive work, which were supposed to lead to spiritual redemption.[12] Mark Colvin notes "that during the seventeenth, eighteenth, and nineteenth centuries [in America], religion became a powerful force in forming individual and societal views of the world." He adds "that these religious perspectives and tensions were to play a major role in shaping the penitentiary."[13]

In the past two centuries, evangelical Christians were in the vanguard of reform movements in both Britain and the United States. They helped to ameliorate conditions and captivity and to aid prisoners upon their release, and they helped to develop alternatives to imprisonment, such as probation, which began as a form of missionary work funded by church-based temperance societies.[14]

WHAT WAS PENNSYLVANIA'S INNOVATION IN PENAL REFORM?

The **penitentiary,** Pennsylvania's innovation in penal reform, did not spring out of nowhere in the 1780s. The penitentiary "had existed in people's minds," Adam Jay Hirsch notes, "long before it took shape as a physical construct of stone and mortar."[15] The word *penitentiary*, according to Hirsch, was first used in the English Penitentiary Act of 1779. Yet financial difficulties, arising from wars in the colonies and with France and from the cost of transporting criminals to Australia, delayed England's entry into penitentiary building.[16] The American version of the penitentiary was designed to isolate persons found guilty of a felony from normal society. It was believed that penitence, pastoral counseling, and reasonable discipline would correct criminal behavior.[17]

The Penitentiary

A significant influence in the development of the penitentiary was the Philadelphia Society for Alleviating the Miseries of Public Prisons, the first prison reform organization in the United States.[18] In 1788, the Society petitioned the Pennsylvania Legislature for a statute providing for solitary confinement at hard labor in the privacy of the penitentiary. The Society's report also urged that the existing Walnut Street Jail no longer be used for long-term prisoners. In 1803, the legislature authorized a new prison, for the detention of debtors, which solved the problem of placing debtors with felons. Not until 1818, however, did the legislature authorize construction of two new penitentiaries: one near Pittsburgh and the Eastern State Penitentiary in Philadelphia.[19]

Eastern State Penitentiary was finished in 1829 and became a model for prisons in several European countries. It has a **radial design.** Seven wings, each containing 76 cells, radiated from a central hub, where control personnel were stationed (see Figure 3.1). Each cell was 12 feet long, 8 feet wide, and 10 feet high, designed for single occupancy.[20] A separate exercise yard, in which the prisoner was allowed to be in the open air for an hour a day, was provided adjacent to the cell. Cells were separated by stone partitions 18 inches thick, which effectively prevented communication from prisoner to prisoner. Solitude was the goal, and prisoners spent their days alone. Even at compulsory chapel services they could not see one another, because they were seated in chairs resembling up-ended coffins. The building was a massive fortress, resembling a medieval castle, intended to deter would-be offenders.

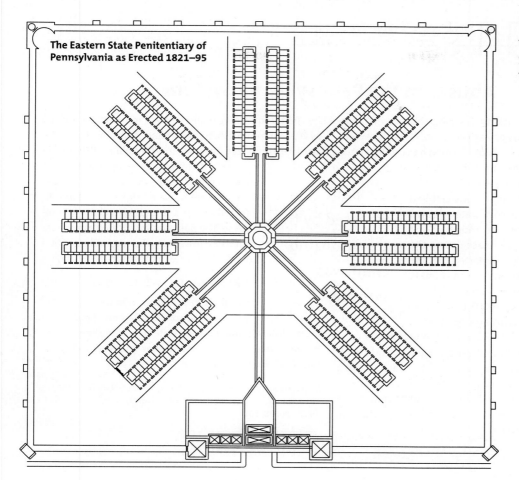

Figure 3.1
The Layout of Eastern
State Penitentiary
in Philadelphia

The **Pennsylvania model** was a penal system based on the belief that most prisoners would benefit from the experience of incarceration. According to the first warden, Samuel Wood:

> When a convict first arrives, he is placed in a cell, and left alone, without any work and without any book. His mind can only operate on itself; generally but a few hours pass before he petitions for something to do and for a Bible. No instance has occurred in which such a petition has been delayed beyond a day or two. If the prisoner have [sic] a trade that can be pursued in his cell, he is put to work as a favour; as a reward for good behaviour, and as a favour, a Bible is allowed him. If he has no trade, or one that cannot be pursued in his cell, he is allowed to choose one that can, and he is instructed by one of the overseers, all of whom are master workmen in the trades they respectively superintend and teach. Thus work and moral and religious books are regarded and received as favours, and are withheld as punishment.[21]

The system was costly to run. Within a few years crowding became a problem, prisoners were doubled up in cells, and solitude was no longer possible. By the end of the Civil War, the penitentiary's population had reached 1,117 prisoners.[22] Within the Walls 3.1 describes some of the abuses that took place inside Eastern State Penitentiary.

The Pennsylvania penitentiary, with its solitary confinement and **penitence model**, was widely hailed, both in the United States and in Europe. Yet, as some critics realized at the time, forcing inmates to reform in repressive conditions (solitary confinement for extended periods) was far more likely to result in insanity rather than rehabilitation.

the walls   3.1

within

Abuses in the Pennsylvania System

Serious charges of brutality were launched against Eastern State Penitentiary as early as 1834. A legislative minority report alleged that the warden had ordered cruel and unusual punishment of inmates. In one incident, an inmate who was tied by his wrists to a wall outside his cell had buckets of extremely cold water thrown on him. This torture was known as the "shower bath" and took place during the middle of winter. It was reported that the water froze on his body. Another inmate had an iron bar that was used to gag inmates for attempting to talk to other inmates fastened so tightly around his head that blood suffused into his brain, killing him instantly. Other forms of punishment used at Eastern State Penitentiary were being ducked under water, restraint in a straitjacket, severe deprivation of food, and restraint in the tranquilizing chair. Hidden from public view, these punishments took place on a regular basis inside the walls of the penitentiary.

> . . . pain inflicted by the tranquilizing chair was intense.

The tranquilizing chair was used frequently. Invented by Dr. Benjamin Rush, this chair had straps for the hands, arms, legs, and feet, an apparatus for holding the head in a fixed position, and a receptacle beneath the seat to catch excrement. When the straps were fastened tightly, the pain inflicted by the tranquilizing chair was intense. The pain was intensified even more for those prisoners who received a beating while they were in the chair.

CRITICAL THINKING QUESTIONS

How did the Quakers, who were pacifists, justify the use of brutal forms of punishment? When do you think the state crosses the line between necessary forms of discipline and cruel and unusual forms of punishment?

Source: Negley K. Teeters and John D. Shearer, *The Prison at Philadelphia: Cherry Hill* (New York: Columbia University Press, 1957), pp. 98, 101.

HOW DID THE NEW YORK PENAL SYSTEM DIFFER FROM THE PENNSYLVANIA MODEL?

The New York penal system eventually replaced the Pennsylvania system. Its influence on both the design of prisons and the philosophy of imprisonment is still evident.

In 1796 New York enacted legislation abolishing capital punishment for all offenses other than first-degree murder and treason. To accommodate felons who would now do time rather than be subjected to flogging or the gallows, Newgate Prison was built in 1797 in what is now Greenwich Village in Manhattan. A crime wave at the end of the War of 1812 led to overcrowding at Newgate Prison, and in 1816 the legislature authorized a new prison at the western New York town of Auburn. It became a model for maximum-custody prisons. When Auburn filled up in 1825, the legislature authorized the building of Sing Sing Prison at Ossining on the Hudson River. Sing Sing was built in three years by convict labor, except for three civilians—a master carpenter, a blacksmith, and a mason.[23]

The Auburn Silent System

Two years after the completion of the prison at Auburn, a new wing was built that became famous as the "Auburn cellblock." At its center was an island of cells five tiers high and 20 cells long, surrounded by 11 feet of vacant space on all four sides. It was built for long-term solitary confinement, from which inmates would not emerge until the end of their terms. The cells were 7 feet long, 3½ feet wide—24½ square feet. Each tier consisted of two rows of cells, back to back.[24]

Prisoners assigned to this block, first occupied on Christmas Day in 1821, were not allowed to work, nor were they permitted to lie down during daylight hours.[25] The rationale for this austere program was simple: "[The penitentiary system could not be preserved] unless the convicts are made to endure great suffering, and that applied, as much as possible, to the mind."[26] Suicides, attempted suicides, and various mental and physical infirmities attributed to the requirement that men be on their feet all day became so prevalent that this regimen was ended in 1825.

Auburn officials were committed to the idea that solitude is essential to prison discipline. The challenge was to maintain solitude while large numbers of prisoners were eating together, working together, and moving together through the prison. An ingenious deputy warden, John D. Cray, found a solution, which became known as the **Auburn Silent System.** It was the successful alternative to the Pennsylvania model and, like the Auburn cellblock, was the basis of practical penology until the mid-twentieth century. This system demanded silence from all convicts at all times. They marched in lockstep from the cellblock to the mess hall and to the factory. With right hand on the right shoulder of the person immediately ahead, face turned toward the watching guards, each convict in this platoon of silent offenders was watched for any attempt to communicate.[27]

Within the Walls 3.2 reveals the philosophy and procedures of Captain Elam Lynds, who for many years was in charge of the Auburn Silent System. Lynds became a prison superintendent at a time in which prison officials enjoyed great latitude in the methods they could use to inflict punishment on criminals. Corporal punishment was an accepted

within the walls 3.2

Captain Elam Lynds

Captain Elam Lynds (1784–1855) is a memorable figure in American penological history. An army captain in the War of 1812, he returned to Auburn, his hometown, when he was demobilized, and he joined the staff of the new prison as warden—or, to use the terminology of the time, as agent and principal keeper.

Lynds would not stand for individual treatment of convicts. Each was to be treated exactly like all the others. Inmates were known only by number. Good behavior was not to be rewarded in any way. In Lynds's opinion and in the opinion of the Auburn Board of Inspectors, executive clemency or pardons mocked justice. According to Lynds, a prisoner's good behavior was no sign of a change of character: "Men of the most artful, desperate, and dangerous character are the most orderly, submissive, and industrious when confined." No one should be offered an incentive to behave according to penitentiary rules, he believed.

Every effort was made systematically to divest prisoners of self-respect and personality. They were dressed in black-and-white-striped uniforms, and no visitors were permitted. Prisoners were not allowed to send or receive letters; indeed, they could read nothing but the Bible. To add to the prisoners' humiliation, citizens could pay admission to look them over, as if the prison were a zoo. Punishment for rule infractions was immediate and administered with the lash on the spot. Captain Lynds's

> Inmates were known only by number.

discipline was criticized for severity, but flogging was standard in the military, and Lynds believed that convicts were not entitled to better treatment than defenders of the nation.

When Lynds was asked whether he thought flogging might be dispensed with, he was forthright: "I consider chastisement by the whip the most efficient, and at the same time, the most humane that exists. . . . I consider it impossible to govern a large prison without a whip. Those who know human nature from books only, may say the contrary." Lynds insisted that flogging "was necessary to begin with curbing the spirit of the prisoner, and convincing him of his weakness. This point attained, everything becomes easy, whatever may be the construction of the prison or the place of labor."

CRITICAL THINKING QUESTIONS

Why might a person like Elam Lynds want to work in corrections? Why were Lynds's critics, who were well aware of his abusive treatment of prisoners, unable to remove him from office?

Source: W. David Lewis, *From Newgate to Dannemora: The Rise of the Penitentiary in New York, 1796–1848* (Ithaca, N. Y.: Cornell University Press, 1965) and Gustave de Beaumont and Alexis de Tocqueville, *On the Penitentiary System in the United States and Its Application in France,* trans. Francis Lieber (1833; reprint, Carbondale: Southern Illinois University Press, 1964).

component of inmate control, but Lynds, in the opinion of increasing numbers of people, seemed, to carry it to extremes.

Sing Sing

Elam Lynds remained warden of Sing Sing after he finished building it with convict labor. The prison, designed for 800 prisoners, almost immediately housed 1,000. More than 100,000 inmates were sentenced to Sing Sing during the next hundred years. Lynds continued as warden until 1830, when he resigned amid controversy over his abuses of power. He was charged with starving the convicts, defrauding the state on contracts, appropriating penitentiary supplies for his own use, and making personal trips at state expense. There was a legislative investigation, but the only possible witnesses were his subordinates, none of whom was inclined to testify against him, so Lynds was cleared of wrongdoing.[28]

After Lynds retired, his deputy, Robert Wiltse, took over as warden and continued using Lynds's regimen for the next decade. In 1840 Wiltse's administration was discredited by the exposure of serious abuses and brutality culminating in the deaths of two prisoners. Wiltse was dismissed, and a new warden, David Seymour, was installed with instructions to rehabilitate, not to punish. As a result, prisoners were allowed to read books, and the use of the lash became infrequent. Families could visit, and correspondence was permitted.[29]

WHAT DOES IT MEAN THAT PRISONS ARE PLACES FOR REHABILITATION?

In 1870, a group of reformers, unhappy with the Auburn system, convened the leading figures in penology to hear proposals for change in the management of prisons. These reformers brought together the tough-minded wardens and keepers of America's prisons and persuaded them to agree to a radical, new Declaration of Principles to guide the reformation of the nation's prisons. Wardens were challenged to accept the principle that the rehabilitation of offenders must be their goal. No longer should managers of prisons be satisfied with mere repression.[30]

The thirty-seven principles for reform set forth in the Declaration were applied to the new reformatory in Elmira, New York, in 1876. But reformers soon became disillusioned with that reform model, and during the Progressive era, (1890–1920) a new, medical model of individualized treatment of offenders was proposed. Proponents wanted to treat inmates as though they were sick and to diagnose and treat them.

The 1870 Declaration of Principles in Cincinnati

The First Correctional Congress, held in Cincinnati in 1870, was carefully planned and chaired by Ohio's Governor Rutherford B. Hayes, who was later to become the nineteenth president of the United States. Speakers from the United States and abroad were invited to present new and progressive ideas, such as giving prisoners educational opportunities and religious instruction. Practical prison men from twenty-two states, Canada, and Latin American nations enthusiastically "rose above the monotony of four gray walls, men in stripes shuffling in lock-step, sullen faces staring through the bars, coarse mush and coffee made of bread crusts, armed sentries stalking the walls. They forgot it all and voted for their remarkable declaration of principles."[31]

The **Declaration of Principles** passed by this Correctional Congress emphasized that the reformation of prisoners should be the goal of corrections. To achieve it, prisoners should be classified on the basis of a mark system, rewards should be provided for good behavior, and indeterminate sentences should be substituted for fixed sentences. The prison's aim should be to create industrious free men, rather than orderly and obedient prisoners. Prisons should be small, and separate institutions should exist for different types of offenders.[32]

The Reformatory Model at Elmira

Attending the Cincinnati Congress of 1870 was Zebulon Brockway, warden of the Detroit House of Correction. In his paper "The Ideal Prison System for a State," he urged that the very word *prison* be stricken from the statutes: "The true attitude of government is that of guardian; its true function to shelter, shield, help, heal."[33] In 1876, Brockway became superintendent of Elmira Reformatory, where his proposals for a model reformatory were to have full rein.

Brockway felt strongly about the merits of what has been called the **reformatory model.** He advocated indeterminate sentencing as "quite indispensable to the ideal of a true prison system" and an essential part of his rehabilitative model.[34] The Elmira Reformatory was originally designed for 500 prisoners, but later additions increased its capacity to 1,700. Admission was restricted to first offenders between the ages of 16 and 30. All would receive an indeterminate sentence—no minimum sentence but a statutory maximum. The program would aim at changing the prisoner's character. The superintendent would decide when the change in the convict's character justified release. All releases were conditional, and discharge would depend on conduct while under supervision in the community over a period of six months.

Elmira was the first correctional institution to pay wages to prisoners as a reward for diligence and productivity. From their wages they paid for room and board, clothing and other necessities, and medical care. The economics of the system were arranged so that at the time of discharge there would be some money to the prisoners' credit. The Elmira program was being emulated in twelve other states by the turn of the twentieth century and in eleven more by 1933, despite growing doubts about the success of the system.[35]

The reformatory model borrowed from the Irish mark system the notion of assigning convicts to grades. New prisoners entered the second grade, with minimum privileges, where they were to remain until their behavior and diligence qualified them for promotion to the first grade. Well-behaved prisoners would remain in the first grade. Prisoners demoted for disciplinary infractions landed in the third grade. They occupied starkly austere cells, marched to and from work in the demeaning lockstep, and could neither correspond with family and friends nor receive visitors. The plan somehow broke down. As time went on, nearly everybody was in the first grade, except those in the third and new arrivals in the second, who were soon promoted.[36]

Word of the Elmira innovations spread fast. European penologists made the pilgrimage to New York and returned home with generally enthusiastic accounts. But it was not long before Brockway's methods came under fire. In 1894, allegations against him prompted the governor to order a special investigation, in which it was found that he had reserved the worse whippings for those who suffered from mental or physical disability. In 1900, Brockway resigned as superintendent, as bruised as Lynds had been before him.[37]

Alexander W. Pisciotta's recent evaluation of reformatories characterizes Elmira and other early reformatories as "ineffective and brutal prisons which did not provide kindly reform or 'Christian treatment.'"[38] According to Pisciotta, the reformatories "had an enormous impact on Americans' approach to thinking about crime and treating criminals." Among the products of this movement are the designation of youthful offenders as a dangerous criminal class, the policy of indeterminate sentencing, the professionalization of penology, and the creation of "scientific criminology." Pisciotta is especially critical of Elmira for its "repressive class control agenda," which "was aimed at controlling the lower classes."[39]

Pisciotta also expresses a less positive view of Brockway as superintendent of Elmira Reformatory than is usually found in the prison literature. He quotes Brockway to show that he did not hold criminals in high regard. He also presents examples of Brockway's brutal and inhumane punishments—for example, "Brockway admitted that he whipped inmates, punched them in the face, struck them with the club-like handle of his whip, chained them for months in rest cure cells on a diet of bread and water, used corporal punishment to extract confessions, and sent threatening notes to terrorize offenders into compliance."[40]

Brockway's proposals for an ideal prison clearly did not work well in practice. It can be argued that he was no better than other prison superintendents at the time and that Elmira and other reformatories were no better than Auburn-style penitentiaries across the nation. Nevertheless, the reformatory model, as established in Elmira and other prisons, made some lasting contributions to corrections—the system of indeterminate sentencing, the payment of inmates for work, the supervision of inmates released into the community, a system of behavior modification, and the development of what later came to be parole.

The Medical Model of Rehabilitation

During the Progressive era, optimism fueled the search for new answers to old problems and led to an emphasis on individualized treatment of offenders. The result was the medical model of rehabilitation.[41]

The reformers' optimism can be traced to three influences. First, the new social sciences assured them that, through the approach of **positivism**, problems could be solved. The first step was to gather all the "facts." Equipped with the data, reformers would be able to analyze the issue in "scientific" fashion and discover the correct solution. Reformers also believed that the data would provide them with all the arguments they would need to win approval of remedial programs from state legislatures. Second, the Progressives had full confidence in the ultimate benefits of the American system. The Progressives' basic social goal was for all Americans to abandon Old World vices, accumulate private property, and become hard-working, respectable middle-class citizens. Third, the reformers believed that the state could exercise its authority to correct imbalances, to bring about equality, and to realize the common good.[42]

Armed with these beliefs, reformers focused on the problem of criminality in American society. They were confident that they knew how to analyze the causes of criminality. The Progressives looked first to environmental factors—poverty—as the most important cause of crime and concluded that no one raised in poverty could be held strictly accountable for his or her actions. Progressives with some knowledge of eugenics argued that hereditary factors predisposed some people to criminal behavior. Eventually, however, psychological factors outweighed either environmental or hereditary factors as sources of criminal behavior.

Psychiatrists, the first proponents of the psychological roots of crime, contended that criminals were sick, rather than bad, and that their sickness drove them to crime. Proponents of the **medical model** had little patience with the concept of the personal responsibility, or culpability, of offenders; they were more concerned with finding cures than assigning blame. They believed that they could cure the disease of criminality by prescribing the proper kind of treatment and by implementing the ideal treatment plan.

Under the leadership of psychiatrists, who were well established in prisons by the 1920s, the medical model was implemented in correctional institutions throughout the United States. Many correctional authorities looked forward to a time when the diagnosis and treatment of criminals would match the successes of modern medicine. The prison would become an analogue to the hospital. Cures would be found for most if not all forms of criminal behavior.

One of the earliest advocates of the treatment-prison was Howard B. Gill (1889–1989).[43] Gill proposed that the Norfolk Prison Colony in Virginia rehabilitate offenders by curing criminals of the disease of crime. Gill was explicit about the prison's function to cure criminals:

> Sometimes I liken a prison to a great social hospital in which there are men with all manner of diseases—the seriously sick, the men with minor ailments, the men who will get well in a short time, the men who will never get well. . . . The things which the hospital considers elementary we look upon as revolutionary.[44]

He carried the hospital metaphor even farther. Hospitals had to diagnose before treatment could be initiated, so he devised a classification system for sorting out the "mental diseases" from which his inmates suffered. This was the "Scamp" system, which was to become briefly famous. "Scamp" was an acronym for five categories of convicts, ranging from those who have medical and psychological problems, to those who are old and senile, to those who are antisocial.[45] Gill thought that rehabilitation would be the goal for all the inmates except those who were old and senile. The hitch was that treatment modalities had yet to be formulated for the four classes for whom social restoration would be the goal. Gill was convinced that most of them could be helped with social casework methods of diagnosis and therapy. Physicians would treat the medical cases, psychiatrists would administer therapy to the personality cases, teachers would be responsible for the asocials, social workers would help the situationals, and police and "caretakers" would control the custodials.[46]

It did not take Gill long to realize that the prison was not a hospital. After a year of difficulties and disappointments, he became disillusioned. In the aftermath of an escape attempt by a team of inmates, a successful escape by two inmates, and increasing institutional disorders, Gill was dismissed.

The Present Status of Rehabilitation in Prison

In the mid-1970s, correctional rehabilitation received a biting attack. In 1974, Robert Martinson stunned correctional personnel and the public in general by announcing that "With few and isolated exceptions, the rehabilitative efforts that have been reported so far have had no appreciable effect on recidivism."[47] This statement was quickly translated into the conclusion that "nothing works" in correctional treatment. Martinson's pronouncement, supplemented by his coauthored book, *The Effectiveness of Correctional Treatment,* persuaded many that the time had come to bury the rehabilitation model and to move on to more fruitful endeavors.[48]

In the 1980s and 1990s, studies supporting the effectiveness of correctional treatment were published about as quickly as studies challenging the efficacy of correctional treatment. The massive attack on treatment that surfaced in the 1970s forced proponents of rehabilitation to devise models that were more effective than the medical model and to develop better treatment techniques in adult corrections.

In sum, the history of efforts to achieve reform in the penitentiary reveals one disappointing story after another. The Pennsylvania system reflected Bentham's goals of reforming and deterring the offender. The Auburn system was a pragmatic effort to administer punishment as thriftily as possible. The reformatory model turned out to be even more repressive than the Pennsylvania and Auburn models. Brockway's brutal and inhumane punishment of prisoners at Elmira illustrated how difficult it was to translate rhetoric at prison conferences into policies and programs within prison walls. Nor did it take reformers long to realize that the medical model was incompatible with the harsh realities of prison settings. Whatever the prison, there was common agreement that it was not a hospital to treat the disease of criminality.

HOW DID THE PUNISHMENT OF WOMEN DIFFER FROM THE PUNISHMENT OF MEN?

Another important aspect of the development of corrections concerns the rise of women's prisons and the treatment of women in correctional settings. In the early days of prison history in the United States, both women and men suffered in filth, overcrowding, and harsh conditions. Women were confined in separate quarters in men's prisons.[49]

In the nineteenth century, women's prisons became testing grounds for new ideas about penology: Prison reformers regarded females as good candidates for rehabilitation, probably because they were considered less dangerous than their male counterparts. On becoming matron of the women's prison at Sing Sing in 1844, Eliza Farnham stirred

Mrs. Conway, a jailor from San Angelo, Texas, was one of the few women working in corrections in the mid-nineteenth century.

up controversy with the new rehabilitative techniques that she implemented and with her articulate defense of them. Farnham strove in many ways to brighten the tone of inmate life during her tenure.[50]

Typical women's prisons during the nineteenth century were harsh and disciplinary institutions in which the reformatory tradition was ignored and little concern was shown for the incarcerated women. In 1844 New York prison authorities expressed their disdain for women prisoners and the hopelessness of efforts to rehabilitate them: "The opinion seems to have been entertained, that the female convicts were beyond the reach of reformation, and it seems to have been regarded as a sufficient performance of the object of punishment, to turn them loose within the pen of the prison and there leave them to feed upon and destroy each other."[51]

After 1920, many of the occupants of women's reformatories were prostitutes and women with venereal diseases, as well as felons. In growing numbers, African Americans and descendants of immigrants from southern and eastern Europe filled women's institutions.[52] They were defined as "depraved women" who had violated the ideal of "true womanhood." In the 1980s and 1990s, especially, women of color were adversely affected by new, mandatory drug-sentencing laws for using or selling crack cocaine. The sentencing of women of color for drug offenses contributed largely to the rising numbers of women in prison during the 1990s.

HOW DID CRIMINAL PUNISHMENT IN THE SOUTH DIFFER FROM PUNISHMENT ELSEWHERE?

From slavery and its legacy emerged one of the most brutal systems of punishments in the history of the United States.[53] The Civil War demolished the Old South and its institution of slavery. But the interconnected issues of race and labor transformed criminal punishment in the South into a system of chain gangs and convict leasing. There was a strong need for a controlled agricultural force after the abolishment of slavery. The disruption of white political solidarity led to a period of lynching in the late nineteenth and early twentieth centuries.[54]

Chain Gangs and Field Labor

Colvin argues that white southerners were convinced that force was required to keep blacks tied to agricultural production. Planters looked to the states to provide this labor for them, and black codes in Mississippi and South Carolina were created to restore the system of plantation slavery. These codes generated considerable national controversy and were eventually repealed. Nevertheless, with no direct reference to race, southern courts sent increasing numbers of blacks to prison.[55]

Beginning in Georgia in 1866, chain gangs were organized throughout the South.[56] Long lines of offenders chained together while working on southern roads provided enduring images of southern punishment.[57]

The development of field labor on prison farms in several southern states also dates from the days of plantation slavery. In the morning, inmates were taken to the fields. Guarded by officers on horseback, the inmates performed manual field labor. Bruce Jackson gives a sense of what this work was like in Texas:

> The Line does manual farm work. It picks cotton, cleans the banks of the turnrows, weeds, chops. The pace isn't difficult, but the work is dull. Every so often, the boss calls a water break and the members of the Line walk to the water wagon, take a quick drink, and then go back to the field. The sun moves across the sky, the boss calls out orders, the convicts ask and get permission to roll a cigarette, to urinate, to ask a question.[58]

Today in the South, inmates are still engaged in backbreading field labor. The Southern chain gangs, which disappeared in the early twentieth century after much criticism, have reemerged in several states across the nation. In 1995, Alabama reinstated chain gangs before it was necessary to drop them for financial reasons in 1999. Arizona, Florida, Iowa, Maine, and Massachusetts have added chain gangs to their corrections practices.[59]

Convict Leasing

Convict leasing was a system in the South in which state prisons leased inmates to planters and businesses. A driving force in the expansion of convict leasing was the profit motive of both governmental officials and private businesses.

Convicts leased to planters and businesses experienced horrible conditions. They were cruelly treated, and the sick were often neglected.[60] A Mississippi grand jury found extremely brutal treatment of convicts: "Most of them have their backs cut in great wales, scars, and blisters, some with skin peeling off in pieces as the result of severe beatings. . . . They were lying there dying . . . [with] live vermin crawling over their faces."[61] The death rate was alarmingly high during the years in which convict leasing was used. In 1870, 41 percent of Alabama's convicts died.[62] In 1883, an Alabama doctor estimated that most convicts died within three years. Overall, the average death rate in prisons in southern states was nearly three times the rate in northern states.[63] Not until the 1920s did the convict-leasing system decline in importance in South and elsewhere.

In the twentieth century, corrections in the South began to resemble what was taking place elsewhere in the nation. Penitentiaries were built, and executions within prison walls increasingly took place. At the beginning of the twenty-first century, the South leads the nation in rates of incarceration and in the numbers of executions per year. See the Timeline for the history of American prisons.

timeline

History of American Prisons (through 1876)

Date	Event
1773	Establishment of Newgate Prison (Simsbury, Connecticut)
1776	Walnut Street Jail (Philadelphia, Pennsylvania)
1865	Castle Island (Boston, Massachusetts)
1792	Walnut Street Jail's Penitentiary House
1800	Virginia and Kentucky Prisons (Richmond, Virginia, and Frankfort, Kentucky)
1817	Auburn Prison (Auburn, New York)
1825	Auburn Prison's Women's Unit (Auburn, New York)
1826	Western State Penitentiary (Pittsburgh, Pennsylvania)
1828	Sing Sing (Ossining, New York)
1829	Eastern State Penitentiary (Philadelphia, Pennsylvania)
1831	Vermont State Prison
1831	Tennessee State Prison (Nashville)
1832	New Hampshire State Prison
1833	Illinois State Prison (Alton)
1834	Ohio Penitentiary (Columbus)
1835	Louisiana Penitentiary (Baton Rouge)
1836	Missouri State Penitentiary (Jefferson City)
1837	New Jersey State Prison (Trenton)
1838	Rhode Island State Prison (Providence)
1838	Southern Michigan State Prison (Jackson)
1840	Iowa State Penitentiary (Ft. Madison)
1841	Georgia State Prison
1842	Indiana State Prison (Jeffersonville)
1842	Mississippi State Prison (Jackson)
1845	Maine State Prison (Thomaston)
1845	New York State Prison (Clinton)
1848	Texas State Prison (Huntsville)
1851	Minnesota State Prison (Stillwater)
1852	California State Prison (San Quentin)
1852	Wisconsin State Prison (Waupun)
1858	Illinois State Penitentiary (Joliet)

1860	Indiana State Prison (Michigan City)
1864	Kansas State Prison (Lansing)
1864	Nevada State Prison (Carson City)
1865	South Carolina State Penitentiary (Columbia)
1866	West Virginia State Penitentiary (Moundsville)
1869	Nebraska State Prison (Lincoln)
1873	Indiana Reformatory Institution for Women and Girls (Indianapolis, Indiana)
1876	Elmira Reformatory (Elmira, New York)

WHAT WAS DISTINCTIVE ABOUT CORRECTIONS IN THE TWENTIETH CENTURY?

Two major movements in corrections in the twentieth century were the rise of community-based corrections and the development of modern management.

Community-based corrections arose with the development of probation and parole. Probation began in the 1840s and 1850s with the volunteer services of John Augustus; the word itself was coined by Augustus. In 1879, the Massachusetts legislature passed a law institutionalizing probation, and the city of Boston appointed the first full-time, publicly paid probation officer. In 1891, Massachusetts law required the criminal courts to appoint probation officers. Parole originated in the United States when inmates were released from the Elmira Reformatory and received supervision in the community. From this beginning, community-based corrections slowly developed during the first six decades of the twentieth century. Then, in the 1960s and 1970s, there was an explosion of interest in community correctional programs.

Before 1930, prison wardens exercised almost total authority in their own institutions. As long as they kept in favor with the governor's office and avoided institutional violence and inmate escapes, their word was unquestioned law. Things began to change in 1930 when Congress enacted legislation creating a central Bureau of Prisons to administer the expanding network of federal penitentiaries and reformatories. The bureaucratization of corrections took longer at the state level. It did not begin until after World War II, when governors and state legislators demanded the creation of management systems that would ensure their control of prison through accountability. The result was the development of statewide correctional systems made up of both institutional and community facilities and programs.

In the midst of the rise of community-based corrections and modern management, the final decades of the twentieth century brought a variety of institutional problems. The most serious was prison crowding. Other institutional problems were prison riots, inmate gangs, violent racial conflicts, and drug trafficking. In addition, increasing numbers of prisons were under court order.

Rise of Community-Based Corrections

With the waning of interest in rehabilitation in correctional institutions, there was increased interest in rehabilitation in community-based programs, especially in the late 1960s and early 1970s. This plan is known as the **reintegration model**. One of its basic assumptions is that offenders' problems must be solved in the communities in which they occur. Another basic assumption is that society has a responsibility for its own problems and can partly fulfill this responsibility by helping law violators reintegrate themselves back into the social order.[64]

Community-based programs sprouted in nearly every state in the early 1970s. Before the decade was over, community-based corrections was made up of pretrial release and diversion, probation, residential and reentry programs, and parole. Among some, there was even the feeling that eventually it would be possible to phase out correctional institutions and to place all offenders in community-based corrections programs. But in the mid-1970s, the anti-institutional feelings lessened as the mood of the public changed to favor a "get-tough with criminals" approach. Publications of official statistics and media coverage of street crime were major factors convincing the public that the crime problem had gotten out of hand.

Community-based corrections still held promise during the final three decades of the twentieth century. Twenty-five states passed community corrections acts.[65] Several counties developed a continuum of services and a coordinated correctional effort, so that a comprehensive program including several subsystems of the correctional system was under local administration.[66] In addition, privately administered community-based programs were providing an increased variety of services to offenders sentenced to community-based corrections.

In the 1980s and 1990s, the focus of community-based corrections changed to surveillance models. These risk control and crime reduction strategies used tactics such as intensive supervision in probation and parole, house arrest, electronic monitoring, and increased surveillance of substance abusers.

Modern Management

Since World War II the administration of state correctional systems has been centralized. Most states assign the prisons to departments of corrections in which a director or commissioner is responsible for budgets, policy, and personnel selection. In five small states the prisons are administered under "umbrella" departments of human services, along with juvenile institutions, mental health, and public health.

In Chapter 11, on correctional administration, we trace the causes of these structural changes and discuss their significance. Here it must suffice to say that their importance to the understanding of corrections cannot be overstated. Central staff services make possible the coordination of functions such as the recruitment of personnel, the supervision of technical operations, and the classification of prisoners. Most important of all, the creation of single-headed administration has made possible accountability and coherent policy. Rules and regulations, manuals of standards, and uniform enforcement of laws and policy have replaced the autocratic decisions of wardens. Correctional leadership is now vested in the directors or commissioners of corrections.

The hero in this chapter is Richard A. McGee, former director of the California, New York City, and Washington State Departments of Corrections. From 1944 to 1967, McGee became one of the most widely respected leaders in corrections in the United States. As the Heroes box reflects, he totally changed the nature of Corrections in California.

WHAT CAN WE LEARN FROM THE PAST?

One insight we can learn from a study of correctional history is that past penal systems greatly influence punishment practices today. Super-max prisons are contemporary versions of the solitary confinement in the Pennsylvania model of the 1830s. Boot camps incorporate military-style discipline used in the Auburn penitentiary. Proposals for paddling, whipping, or caning considered by at least six state legislatures in 1995 go

h e r o e s

Richard A. McGee

Former Director of Corrections in California

In his foreword to McGee's *Prisons and Politics,* John P. Conrad writes:

"In this book you will read a few reflections and predictions of Richard McGee, who made Californian corrections a byword for decency and order, a model for emulation throughout the world, and a laboratory for change in prison and parole administration. . . .

"It is hard to recapture the excitement of those days. We worked for a restless, perpetually dissatisfied leader who exacted superior performances from his subordinates. His intellectual curiosity swept in ideas from every point of the compass; our job was to translate these ideas into programs. It was inconceivable that a year could pass without a new experiment in the improvement of the system, a new study commissioned to find out what more could be done to make sense out of prison, or a new program to train people to do more than they had previously thought possible. Bureaucrats that we were, there was plenty of paper to shuffle, and it had to be shuffled right, but there were always task-force meetings to prepare for the memorandums to draw up the refinement of an innovating plan. It is an exhilarating experience to engage in an enterprise in which all participants are convinced that they are leading the world to great improvements in the established order

of things. We knew that that was the case; we could see the improvements and their effects, and we heard the acclaim from travelers who came from all over the world to see for themselves. The grumblers changed their tunes.

"In most prison systems the only excitement in humdrum routines occurs when something goes seriously wrong: an escape from maximum custody, a riot, the taking of hostages. For those of us who worked with McGee, the excitement was of a different quality—a new program that proved its worth, new legislation to solve an old problem, or a new procedure that simplified operations. There were mistakes and disappointments, but it was unthinkable that we could be allowed to subside into the management of drift. . . . Even our failures during McGee's regime had at least the benefit that something important was under trial; there was hope for a system in which optimists were in control."

CRITICAL THINKING QUESTIONS

Why do you think Conrad respected McGee so much? Does the type of leadership that McGee demonstrated have a place in corrections today?

Source: Richard McGee, *Prisons and Politics* (Lexington, Mass.: D. C. Heath, 1981), pp. ix–x.

---

back to practices of the colonial period. The recent enthusiasm for reintroducing chain gangs goes back to the predominating form of punishment in the South in the late nineteenth and early twentieth centuries. It can be argued that the only thing that is actually new is the massive scale to which corrections has grown.[67]

Another insight we can learn is that the history of corrections in the United States has been a history of good intentions.[68] Reformers attempted a variety of ways to bring reform to the prison, beginning with the penitence model of the Pennsylvania system. Other strategies for reform were the reformatory model and the medical model. The persistence of the reformers' zeal was matched only by their disappointment when their results failed. No matter what they tried, the penitentiary failed to rehabilitate prisoners. Inmates, for the most part, differed little when they left from the way they had been when they arrived.

Another insight is that repression and reform have had the support of policymakers at different times in the history of U.S. corrections. The failure of one seems to lead to support for the other. The mood of society, affected by political, economic, and religious influences, also affects decisions about how prisoners should be treated in correctional institutions.

The final, and perhaps the most important, insight is that the fascination of Americans with the prison has prevailed, regardless of the continued failure with institutionalization. In 1865, Samuel Gridley Howe, a leading American philanthropist and prison reformer, rightly predicted: "Institutions . . . so strongly built, so richly endowed . . . cannot be got rid of so easily."[69] Norval Morris has even proposed that "the irony is that the less effective the prisons are in reducing crime, the higher the demand for still more imprisonment."[70]

SUMMARY

Reformers, seeking a humane alternative to the whipping post and the gallows, invented the penitentiary, an innovation in both concept and architecture. The Pennsylvania's penitence model emphasized the reformation of the offender and was based on the belief that prisoners would benefit from their enforced isolation. The cost of this model, as well as growing skepticism about the value of solitary confinement, led to the adoption of the Auburn Silent System. This system also demanded silence but was more economical because prisoners worked together and did not need cells as large as those required by the Pennsylvania model. The Auburn Silence System left its mark on American corrections through the Auburn cellblock and prisoners' marching in lockstep. The reformatory movement quickly discovered that the high hopes of reformers were swallowed up in prisons that continue to be similar in many ways to prisons of the past.

The rise of community-based corrections and the development of modern management techniques were the most influential developments during the twentieth century. Alson, during that century systems of corrections were established in the Bureau of Prisons and in the fifty states.

KEY TERMS

Auburn Silent System, p. 51
Declaration of Principles, p. 52
Eastern State Penitentiary, p. 48
medical model, p. 54
penitence model, p. 49
penitentiary, p. 48

Pennsylvania model, p. 49
positivism, p. 54
radial design, p. 48
reformatory model, p. 53
reintegration model, p. 59

CRITICAL THINKING QUESTIONS

1. Some writers argue that although Eastern State Penitentiary was organized around an absurdly impractical set of principles, it represents an important advance in corrections. In what respects is this statement true?
2. Did the 1870 Declaration of Principles bring about any immediate improvements in the prison? What was its significance in the long run?
3. Captain Elam Lynds believed that flogging criminals was a necessary step toward breaking their wills and thereby achieving their reform. Even if we now consider corporal punishment unacceptable, would you allow that perhaps this idea has some validity? If so, what?
4. From all accounts, Crofton's Irish plan was an outstanding success. Brockway, who tried to emulate it, had to admit failure. What did he do wrong?
5. What are the essential elements of the medical model of corrections? What serious flaws, if any, do you see in the concept?

WEB DESTINATIONS

Read a comprehensive definition and some background on the field of penology.
http://www.britannica.com/bcom/eb/article/5/0,5716,60585+1+59103,00.html

Visit the Eastern State Penitentiary historical site and museum in Philadelphia, Pennsylvania.
http://www.easternstate.com/

Tour New York's Auburn Prison through historical photographs, and learn more about the development of solitary confinement in the United States.

http://co.cayuga.ny.us/history/cayugahistory/prison.html

Read an article on the history of Sing Sing Prison and the "hard labor" system.
http://www.hudsonriver.com/halfmoonpress/stories/0500sing.htm

Read about the history of Elmira Reformatory and Zebulon Brockway's ideas about prison reform.
http://www.geocities.com/MotorCity/Downs/3548/facility/elmira.html

FOR FURTHER READING

Beaumont, Gustave de, and Alexis de Tocqueville. *On the Penitentiary System in the United States and Its Application in France.* Trans. Francis Lieber. 1833. Reprint, Carbondale: Southern Illinois University Press, 1964. In this volume the Pennsylvania model and the Auburn Silent System are described by two young French visitors, one of whom, Tocqueville, was to become famous for his study of democracy in America.

Colvin, Mark. *Penitentiaries, Reformatories, and Chain Gangs: Social Theory and the History of Punishment in Nineteenth-Century America.* New York: St. Martin's Press, 2000. Colvin examines the rise of penitentiaries in the Northeast, changes in treatment of women offenders in the North, and the transformation of punishment in the South after the Civil War.

Hirsch, Adam Jay. *The Rise of the Penitentiary: Prisons and Punishment in Early America.* New Haven: Yale University Press, 1992. An important book tracing the rise of the penitentiary in early American society.

Lewis, W. David. *From Newgate to Dannemora; The Rise of the Penitentiary in New York, 1796–1848.* Ithaca, N.Y.: Cornell University Press, 1965. A detailed and authoritative account of the development of the New York prison system up to the time of major revisions of the Auburn Silent System. Particularly good on the evaluation of Captain Elam Lynds.

McKelvey, Blake. *American Prisons: A History of Good Intentions.* Montclair, N.J.: Patterson Smith, 1977. The standard history of American prisons is still a reliable source on the development of penological practice.

Pisciotta, Alexander W. *Benevolent Repression: Social Control and the American Reformatory-Prison Movement.* New York: New York University Press, 1994. Pisciotta's book is an insightful study of the reformatory movement, especially Elmira. He viewed this movement as part of a repressive class control agenda aimed at controlling the lower classes.

Rothman, David. *The Discovery of the Asylum: Social Order and Disorder in the New Republic.* Boston: Little, Brown, 1971. Rothman, a historian, examines the history of the institutionalization of social deviants, including criminal offenders. There are excellent chapters on the invention of the penitentiary and on Gill's attempted innovations at Norfolk.

NOTES

1. The Dickens quotations are found in Negley K. Teeters and John D. Shearer, *The Prison at Philadelphia: Cherry Hill: The Separate System of Penal Discipline, 1829–1913* (New York: Columbia University Press, 1957), pp. 114–115.

2. Ibid.

3. Mark Colvin, *Penitentiaries, Reformatories, and Chain Gangs: Social Theory and the History of Punishment in Nineteenth-Century America* (New York: St. Martin's Press, 2000), p. 106.

4. David J. Rothman, *The Discovery of the Asylum* (Boston: Little, Brown, 1971), pp. 46–52.

5. Ibid.

6. In West Jersey the death penalty applied only to first-degree murder and treason.

7. From the *Charter and Laws of Pennsylvania, 1682–1700,* p. 121, as quoted in Harry Elmer Barnes, *Evolution of Penology in Pennsylvania* (Indianapolis: Bobbs-Merrill, 1927), p. 56.

8. For a full account of this preposterous trade-off see ibid., pp. 31–48. Barnes quotes at length contemporary narratives describing the brutal corporal punishments administered to petty thieves and fornicators.

9. One reformer, Dr. Benjamin Rush, the leading physician of Philadelphia, argued vigorously but unsuccessfully against the death penalty even in cases of murder.

10. Barnes, *Evolution of Penology in Pennsylvania,* p. 73, quoting from Pennsylvania Prison Society, *A Sketch of the Principal Transactions of the Philadelphia Society for Alleviating the Miseries of Public Prisons* (Philadelphia: Merrihew and Thompson, 1859), p. 5.

11. Émile Durkheim, *The Elementary Forms of the Religious Life* (London: Allen and Unwin, 1976); originally published as *Les Formes élémentaires de la vie religieuse* (1912).

12. David Garland, *Punishment and Modern Society: A Study in Social Theory* (Chicago: University of Chicago Press, 1990), p. 204.

13. Colvin, *Penitentiaries, Reformatories, and Chain Gangs,* p. 43.

14. Garland, *Punishment and Modern Society,* pp. 203–204.

15. Adam Jay Hirsch, *The Rise of the Penitentiary: Prisons and Punishment in Early America* (New Haven: Yale University Press, 1992), p. 32.

16. Ibid., p. 232.

17. It was the penitence model that was to make the American version of the penitentiary unique.

18. It continues to thrive but under a more prosaic name, the Pennsylvania Prison Society.

19. Hirsh, *The Rise of the Penitentiary,* p. 83.

20. Note that at 96 square feet, these cells far exceeded the 60 square feet called for in the present Standards of the American Correctional Association.

21. Barnes, *Evolution of Penology in Pennsylvania,* pp. 159–160.

22. For an expansive treatment of this prison, see Teeters and Shearer, *The Prison at Philadelphia: Cherry Hill.*

23. Ibid.

24. W. David Lewis, *From Newgate to Dannemora: The Rise of the Penitentiary in New York, 1796–1848* (Ithaca, N.Y.: Cornell University Press, 1965).

25. Ibid. The Auburn officials were an unsentimental lot.

26. Ibid. p. 68. Lewis is quoting from the *Journal of the State Assembly* (1822), p. 218.

27. Blake McKelvey, *American Prisons: A Study in American Society History Prior to 1915* (Montclair, N.J.: Patterson Smith, 1977).

28. Lewis, *From Newgate to Dannemora*.

29. Ibid. pp. 161–165.

30. McKelvey, *American Prisons*.

31. Ibid., p. 71.

32. Ibid.

33. For a condensed version of this landmark speech, see Zebulon Brockway, *Fifty Years of Prison Service* (Montclair, N.J.: Patterson Smith 1969), pp. 389–408.

34. Ibid.

35. McKelvey, *American Prisons*.

36. Ibid.

37. Scott Christianson, *With Liberty for Some: 500 Years of Imprisonment in America* (Boston: Northeastern University Press, 1998), p. 181.

38. Alexander W. Pisciotta, *Benevolent Repression: Social Control and the American Reformatory-Prison Movement* (New York: New York University Press, 1994), pp. 4–5.

39. Ibid., 7.

40. Ibid., p. 53.

41. This section on the Progressive era is largely adapted from David J. Rothman, *Conscience and Convenience: The Asylum and Its Alternatives in Progressive America* (Boston: Little, Brown, 1980), pp. 32–60.

42. Ibid.

43. Ibid.

44. Ibid., pp. 386–387.

45. Ibid., pp. 391–392.

46. Ibid.

47. Robert Martinson, "What Works?—Questions and Answers about Prison Reform," *Public Interest* 35 (Spring 1974), pp. 22–54.

48. Douglas Lipton, Robert Martinson, and Judith Wilks, *The Effectiveness of Correctional Treatment: A Survey of Treatment Evaluation Studies* (New York: Praeger, 1975).

49. N. Kurshan, "Behind the Walls: The History and Current Reality of Women's Imprisonment," in *Criminal Justice: Confronting the Prison Crisis* (Boston: South End Press, 1996).

50. Lewis, *From Newgate to Dannemora*, pp. 230–255.

51. Ibid., p. 159.

52. Colvin, *Penitentiaries, Reformatories, and Chain Gangs*, p. 181.

53. Ibid., p. 199.

54. Ibid., p. 200.

55. Ibid., p. 220.

56. See Edward L. Ayers, *Vengeance and Justice: Crime and Punishment in the Nineteenth Century American South* (New York: Oxford University Press, 1984).

57. Colvin, *Pententiaries, Reformatories, and Chain Gangs*, p. 220.

58. Bruce Jackson, "Ellis," unpublished manuscript, State University of New York at Buffalo.

59. Y. Zipp, "Chain Gangs Arrive—Yankee Country," *Christian Science Monitor*, 25 June 1999, p. 1.

60. Colvin, *Penitentiaries, Reformatories, and Chain Gangs*, pp. 246–247.

61. Quoted in C. Vann Woodward, *The Origins of the New South, 1877–1913* (Baton Rouge: Louisiana State University Press, 1971), p. 214.

62. Ayers, *Vengeance and Justice*, p. 200.

63. Colvin, *Penitentiaries, Reformatories, and Chain Gangs*, p. 247.

64. The National Advisory Commission on Criminal Justice Standards and Goals developed the reintegration model in this publication, *Corrections* (Washington, D.C.: U.S. Government Printing Office, 1973).

65. See Michael C. Musheno et al., "Community Corrections as an Organizational Innovation: What Works and Why," *Journal of Research in Crime and Delinquency* 26 (May 1989), p. 139.

66. See David E. Duffee and Edmund F. McGarrell, *Community Corrections: A Community Field Approach* (Cincinnati: Anderson, 1990).

67. Colvin, *Penitentiaries, Reformatories, and Chain Gangs*, p. 267.

68. This is a basic theme of McKelvey's *American Prisons*.

69. Quoted in Edgardo Rotman, "The Failure of Reform: United States, 1865–1965," in *The Oxford History of the Prison: The Practice of Punishment in Western Society*, edited by Norval Morris and David J. Rothman (New York: Oxford University Press, 1995), p. 194.

70. Norval Morris, "The Contemporary Prison 1965–Present," in Ibid., p. 257.

CHAPTER 3 / BUILT-IN STUDY GUIDE

Multiple Choice Questions

1. Which of the following had the most influence on the American correctional experience?

    A. The European approach to punishment
    B. The Asian approach to punishment
    C. The Canadian approach to punishment
    D. The Australian approach to punishment

2. How did the Puritans view the criminal and deviant offender?

    A. As a product of a dysfunctional family
    B. As a captive of the devil
    C. As a mentally ill person
    D. As a person with a biological abnormality

3. What was the function of the jail in colonial American society?

    A. To be used as a form of punishment
    B. To punish offenders who refused to pay fines
    C. To be used as a poor house for vagrants
    D. To detain individuals awaiting trial

4. During colonial America, what event marked the termination of British laws by the Pennsylvania legislature?

    A. Adoption of the U.S. Constitution
    B. Adoption of the Declaration of Independence
    C. Adoption of the Articles of Confederation
    D. The Philadelphia National Convention

5. According to Mark Colvin, which of the following factors played a major role in the development of the penitentiary?

    A. Politics
    B. Economics
    C. Religion
    D. Society

6. All of the following describe how inmates at the Auburn prison were treated except:

    A. Inmates were not allowed to read anything
    B. Inmates were dressed in black-and-white striped uniforms
    C. Inmates were not allowed to have visitors
    D. Inmates were not allowed to send or receive letters

7. The overcrowding and unsanitary conditions that were present from the beginning of the Newgate Prison raised concern about:

    A. Escapes
    B. Inmate suicides
    C. Inmate strikes
    D. Danger of epidemic diseases

8. The Declaration of Principles emphasized all of the following to attain the reformation of prisoners except:

    A. Classification of inmates based on the mark system
    B. A system of rewards for good behavior
    C. The use of indeterminate sentencing
    D. A prison environment that promotes obedience among inmates

9. Who decided when an inmate was ready to be released at the Elmira Reformatory?

    A. Judge
    B. Parole board
    C. Superintendent
    D. Prison psychologist

10. What happened during the 1970s that marked the demise of correctional rehabilitation?

    A. The end of prison industry
    B. The Martinson Report
    C. Rockefeller drug laws
    D. Parole being abolished

11. Which of the following factors largely contributed to the rising numbers of women in prison during the 1990s?

    A. The baby boom generation coming into its high crime years
    B. Increase in violent crime by white women
    C. Increase in the number of women of color who were single-parent mothers
    D. The sentencing of women of color for drug offenses

12. Which of the following was the most serious problem correctional institutions had to confront during the final decades of the twentieth century?

    A. Prison crowding
    B. Inmate gangs
    C. Drug trafficking
    D. Demands made by special masters

True/False Questions

T F   1. Captain Elam Lynds supported the use of corporal punishment to maintain inmate control.

T F   2. Male and female prisoners have always been confined in separate correctional institutions.

T F   3. Under the reformatory model, all inmates started off their period of confinement with the same privileges and ended their period of confinement with the same privileges.

T F   4. According to Alexander W. Pisciotta, Zebulon Brockway used brutal and inhumane punishments toward inmates while he was superintendent of the Elmira Reformatory.

T F   5. The Progressive approach to analyzing criminal behavior viewed crime as a product of environmental, biological, and psychological factors beyond the control of the individual.

T F   6. The Elmira Reformatory was the first correctional institution to grant pay wages to prisoners according to diligence and productivity.

T F   7. The Pennsylvania legislature repealed the Quaker criminal codes and adopted the criminal laws of England in 1821.

T F   8. Over the past one hundred years, female prisons have abandoned the warehousing approach in favor of a rehabilitative approach.

T F   9. The northeast region of the United States has the highest incarceration rate.

T F 10. The rise of community-based corrections and the development of modern management strategies to operate correctional institutions are the two key movements in corrections during the twentieth century.

T F 11. The administration of state correctional systems has been centralized since World War II.

Fill-in-the-Blank Questions   (based on key terms)

1. The _____ was a correctional institution designed to isolate persons found guilty of a felony from society and punish them through pastoral counseling and reasonable discipline.

2. The _____ required prisoners to remain silent while eating together, working together, and moving through the prison together.

3. During the Progressive era, the _____ was proposed, with a focus on individualized diagnosis and treatment of prisoners.

4. The _____ was based on the belief that solitary confinement was beneficial for prisoners.

5. The _____ was a guide designed to provide assistance to the nation's prisons.

6. Correctional institutions that focused on changing a prisoner's character through the use of various programs as well as the implementation of indeterminate sentencing were based on the _____.

7. The _____ was costly to operate because it was originally designed for prisoners to be detained in a cell by themselves; after a few years overcrowding became a problem.

Essay Questions

1. Explain the influence religion has had on the way offenders have been treated throughout the history of corrections.

2. Describe the Eastern State Penitentiary and the Auburn prison system. How were they similar and how were they different? Which system eventually prevailed and became influential in the design of later prisons? Explain why this system prevailed.

3. How did the First Correctional Congress, held in 1870, influence the future of prison operation?

4. How has the treatment of female inmates differed from the treatment of male inmates throughout the history of corrections?

5. Explain how slavery influenced punishment in the southern region of the United States.

ANSWERS

Multiple Choice Questions

1.	A	7.	B
2.	B	8.	D
3.	D	9.	C
4.	B	10.	B
5.	C	11.	D
6.	A	12.	A

True/False Questions

1.	T	7.	F
2.	F	8.	F
3.	F	9.	F
4.	T	10.	T
5.	T	11.	T
6.	T		

Fill-in-the-Blank Questions

1. Penitentiary
2. Auburn Silent System
3. Medical model
4. Eastern State Penitentiary
5. Declaration of Principles
6. Reformatory model
7. Pennsylvania model

The Punishment
of Offenders

The late John P. Conrad, noted corrections critic and author, writes about an offender he once knew:

> Billy was one of a fairly large family of Appalachian antecedents living on the margins of the economy. His parents had been more often on welfare than not. Poor managers, they had been unable to provide their children with more than subsistence. Violence, rather than love and harmony, were constantly manifested in their home. Billy recalled having been beaten with electric cords, straps, belts, sticks, broom handles, and boards from early childhood. This type of discipline went on until one day, when he was 14, his mother came at him in a fury, armed with a plank with which she was going to beat him. He knocked her out. For the next three years, he was mostly on his own.
>
> School had been an arena of defeat. He had great difficulty in reading and was eventually found to be dyslexic—neurologically impaired so that letters did not arrive in his brain in intelligible order for words to be made out of them. He learned to think of

himself as a dummy, the word that other kids applied to him. He dropped out of school soon after the assault on his mother.

He took to hanging around, sometimes in the company of an uncle 14 years older who introduced him to homosexual practices. It was not long before he was earning 20 dollars a trick as a prostitute. A large portion of his earnings was spent on various uppers and downers and marijuana. He does not seem to have used "heavy stuff."

One of his customers was the old man who was the victim in this offense. It is hard to be sure about the events that took place on the Fourth of July weekend. Billy and his uncle spent the holiday at the old man's apartment. They drank heavily and smoked pot. As they became more and more drunk, conviviality turned into acrimony. They ran out of beer, and the old man told Billy to go out and get some more, calling him a dummy and a punk as he issued the order. The police account alleged that in a rage Billy attacked him with his fists, knocked him flat, and then stomped him until the old man succumbed. The pathologist's report showed that the alcoholic content of his blood was so high that death would have been imminent anyway.[1]

CRITICAL THINKING QUESTIONS

Given what is said in this account, what would be a just punishment for this 17-year-old offender? If you had been the juvenile judge, would you have transferred Billy to the adult court?

Billy stood accused of the most serious of offenses, murder. Billy's background and personal situation inspired no confidence in his ability to change. To make the case that he was not dangerous was to dismiss the horrible affair on the Fourth of July and his record of violent family relations.[2]

The public defender was concerned about whether this youthful offender, a slight youngster with chestnut blond hair, could survive in prison. He had scored above average on an IQ test but spoke haltingly and seemed painfully childish. If he could get out of his trouble, he intended to go to Florida and find work as a deep-sea fisherman. But his dreams of being a fisherman were never realized. The juvenile court decided to transfer Billy over for trial in the adult court. Three weeks later, Billy hanged himself with a sheet in his cell.[3]

On the chalkboard the differing goals of criminal justice are easy to comprehend, if not always easy to reconcile. In the courtroom as a conscientious judge struggles to make a reasoned disposition of a tormented offender, too often there seems to be no good answer. Billy was a real defendant caught in the grip of the justice system. His seventeen years were a tragic story of neglect, abuse, and violence. His decisions to make money from sex and to use drugs eventually led him to the final decision, to end his life. Billy was like many other offenders who come into contact with the adult and juvenile justice systems. Their lives reflect many tragic dimensions that make simple answers hard to find. Nor is it always a simple matter to decide what punishment is appropriate for an offender.

Punishment is a social institution that came into existence in a particular social context and performs specific social functions. Chapters 2 and 3 analyze in part how the philosophies and forms of punishment have related to each other and how punishment has contributed to social order, state power, or class domination.[4] In contrast to that broad historical survey of punishment, this chapter examines several critical questions: *What are the goals of punishment? How do the forms of punishment differ? How is punishment related to the social system? How is sentencing related to the correctional process? How do the various sentencing systems differ?*

WHAT ARE THE GOALS OF PUNISHMENT?

A number of different punishment goals can be recognized today during the sentencing processes across the United States: classical retribution, deterrence, rehabilitation, incapacitation, just deserts, and restorative justice. For centuries, **retribution** was the dominant motive in punishing criminals. In the eighteenth century, Jeremy Bentham, introduced **deterrence** as the purpose of the criminal law. Bentham proposed that acts and laws be judged by their consequences and that punishment be useful in deterring criminals from future law-violating behavior.

Rehabilitation was a major goal of punishing criminals for most of the history of U.S. corrections. Only in the late twentieth century did attacks on rehabilitation reduce its appeal as a means of punishing criminals. **Incapacitation** as a purpose of sentencing refers to the isolation of offenders from the general community in order to protect society.[5] Incapacitation was a common goal in the late eighteenth and early nineteenth centuries. With the attacks on rehabilitation in the late 1960s and early 1970s, incapacitation became increasingly acceptable as a justification for imprisonment.

The popularity of incapacitation in the past three decades was accompanied by the rise of two other goals of punishment: **just deserts** and **restorative justice.** The justice model of corrections developed by David Fogel and others emphasizes offenders' receiving the punishment they deserve—their just deserts. It rests on the assumption that individuals are punished because they deserve to be punished. Rooted in the concept of reparation, restorative justice, the most recent goal of punishment, requires the offender to make amends.

Retribution

Throughout much of history, there has been general cultural acceptance of retribution as a proper response to crime. Grotesque tortures were devised and accepted as necessary to the public safety. Ingenious instruments for the infliction of slow and painful death aroused no serious objection from religious leaders or anyone else.

To understand why reasonable and humane men and women were willing to accept such severe punishments, it is necessary to consider the context of the times. Society was divided between a small ruling aristocracy and a vastly larger class of peasants and artisans. For both classes life was precarious. The state could provide the rulers little protection for their lives and property beyond the intimidation of the laws and the force to make intimidation real. Even in good times the peasantry and urban workers led lives in which misery was never distant, and in bad times they might starve. The desperation of the poor was obvious to the comfortable rich. Brigands and bandits were common. The terror of the criminal law protected the aristocracy and its property. The governing class viewed the inferior classes as truly inferior people who required great severity if they were not to endanger the state. Sympathy for their suffering would be wasted.

For the state, intimidation was a necessary means of social control. There was no organized police. There were many law violators, and punishments had to be capital or corporal or sometimes both. There were no prisons in the modern sense. Confinement in the Tower of London or the Bastille in Paris was reserved for defeated rivals for the throne, for those who had incurred royal displeasure, and for political malcontents. Common criminals, when caught and convicted, would be expedited to the gallows.[6] By handing out retributive punishment, society seeks to "get even" with the offender for violating the social contract on which the law is based. Society takes revenge on the criminal. The criminal pays his or her debt to society by suffering the pain of punishment.[7] Outside the Walls 4.1 presents the viewpoint that corporal punishment represents an effective means of inflicting retribution on offenders.

outside
outside

the walls   4.1

Should We Return to Corporal Punishment?

Corporal punishment relates to any punishment or pain inflicted on the body. Traditionally, this has meant branding, whipping, or amputation. Branding was sometimes used in the early history of this nation, and whipping was extensively used as a means of punishment in the nineteenth-century prison. The state of Delaware has held onto corporal punishment longer than other states; indeed, it did not even have a state prison until the twentieth century. A noticeable decline of whippings in Delaware took place after petty larceny was removed in 1941 from the list of crimes punishable by whippings.

The prevailing position, both among policymakers and the courts, is that corporal punishment is unacceptable because it is cruel and unusual punishment. However, there are signs that corporal punishment may be gaining more support than it has had for some time. In 1994, when Michael Fay was convicted in Singapore of vandalism, possession of stolen property, and criminal mischief, he was punished with four strikes of a rattan cane and twelve weeks in jail. There was widespread support among the U.S. public for the caning of Fay as an acceptable sanction.

Graeme Newman's *Just and Painful: A Case for the Corporal Punishment of Criminals* (1995) argues that corporal punishment (whippings and especially electric shock) is a reasonable alternative to imprisonment. He contends that corporal punishment may cause pain and hurt but is not cruel and unusual punishment because it does not cause any lasting damage to the body. He acknowledges that corporal punishment, as with any form of punishment, is subject to abuse. Yet, compared with prison violence, men-

> . . . greater equability can be attained through punishment relying on acute pain . . .

tal torture, harsh diet, and neglect, Newman still sees corporal punishment as more humane than imprisonment.

Hannah Long's recent article (1998) first dismisses incarceration for its inequable severity. She defines the severity of prison conditions arising from the prison's sexual violence and humiliating prison conditions and from the damage that imprisonment does to an inmate's HIV status, mental health, and life expectancy. She then argues that greater equability can be attained through punishment relying on acute pain rather than long-term imprisonment. This form of punishment is justified as long as it "does not result in permanent physical damage, is of brief duration, and the offender is fully informed of these facts and the approximate intensity of the pain he will feel." Long proposes that possible equable techniques of imposing pain would be radiant heat, cold pressure (placing an offender's hand or limb in ice water), chemical ingestations, or electricity.

CRITICAL THINKING QUESTIONS

What is your evaluation of the return of use of corporal punishment? If you had the choice between a severe beating that left no permanent injuries and ten years in prison, which would you choose?

Source: H. T. S. Long, "The 'Inequability' of Incarceration," *Columbia Journal of Law and Social Problems* 31, (1998), pp. 321–353; Graeme Newman, *Just and Painful: A Case for the Corporal Punishment of Criminals* (Albany, N.Y.: Harrow and Heston, 1995).

Criticism of retribution refers to incidents of callous brutality and to the indifference of retribution-oriented correctional systems to the maintenance of standards of decency. In the United States, federal courts have consistently ruled that although prison officials are not obligated to rehabilitate the offenders committed to them, they may not administer their institutions in such a way that inmates have no opportunities to improve themselves. Modern criminal justice looks back at what the offender did and mandates a punishment that fits the crime, not the criminal. It also looks forward and demands that punishment make it possible for the criminal to become, in Plato's formulation, "a better man, or, failing this, at least less of a wretch."

What is the most attractive feature of retribution? For which offenders does it make the most sense? For which offenders does it make the least sense?

Deterrence

Deterrence theory sees punishment not as an end in itself but as a means to accomplish some socially beneficial outcome. It is commonly agreed that criminals deserve punishment, but most citizens would like the punishment to serve some useful purpose, such as to deter crime and protect the social order.

Two types of deterrence are general deterrence and special deterrence. The basic idea behind **general deterrence** is that punishing one person for his or her criminal acts will discourage others from committing similar acts. The notion of **special deterrence** holds that an individual offender will decide against repeating an offense after experiencing the painfulness of punishment for that offense.[8]

Because conclusions vary from study to study, the research evidence on general deterrence is extremely difficult to evaluate.[9] The results typically show that jurisdictions with higher sanction rates appear to have lower crime rates, but there is uncertainty as to why this is so. There is consistent evidence that the certainty of the sentence (as measured by the probability that a sentence will be imposed if a criminal act is committed) has greater effect than does the severity of the sentence (as measured by the length of the sentence).[10]

According to Bentham and Beccaria, for punishment to deter, it must have *celerity, certainty,* and some measure of *severity.* Celerity has to do with the swiftness of justice. Bentham suggested that a punishment that follows closely after the offense will result in greater pain to the offender and thus offer deterrence.[11] Several theorists have concurred that swifter punishment offers a greater deterrent effect than punishment that is delayed, but they question whether, in practical terms, it is possible to achieve swift punishment.[12]

Another constraint on deterrence is the limited ability of the criminal justice system to identify, apprehend, and punish criminals with certainty. To be an effective de-

Why might this crime be seen as having high deterrent effects? According to research, how does punishment relate to deterrence? What are the three other principal goals of punishment other than deterrence? Theoretically, how might each goal be applied in the case of this shoplifter?

terrent, a perceived certainty factor must attain a specific level. Researchers contend that general deterrence policy has little value unless the lawbreaker regards the certainty of identification, apprehension, and punishment to be in the 30 to 50 percent range.[13] A punishment has enough severity to serve as a deterrent if an offender believes that the cost of sanction outweighs the pleasure or the benefit of the criminal act.

Deterrent effects appear to be greater with some crimes than others. Typically, the more serious the crime is, the lower the rates of deterrent effects that sanctions have. For example, driving while intoxicated, shoplifting, and parking violations are crimes for which studies have found a high rate of deterrent effects. Drug violations and murder are crimes that generally have low rates of deterrent effects.

Daniel S. Nagin's evaluation of deterrence research at the end of the twentieth century concludes that recent studies of criminal offending found greater deterrent effects than had been apparent in the 1970s and 1980s. Negin goes on to say that improvements in the future depend on making progress in several areas. It is necessary to go beyond estimating only short-term consequences to determining long-term effects of punishment and to come to a better understanding of how and why responses of offenders vary from one period to another and from one place to another.[14]

Why do the rates of deterrence vary from crime to crime?

Rehabilitation

The goal of rehabilitation is to change an offender's character, attitudes, or behavior so as to diminish his or her criminal propensities.[15] **Indeterminate sentencing** has been an integral part of rehabilitation efforts since the final decades of the nineteenth century. The parole board is charged with determining when an offender is rehabilitated and thus ready to return to the community.

The quest for rehabilitation, like the quests for the Holy Grail and the Fountain of Youth, has preoccupied members of society throughout history. One reason for the appeal of rehabilitation is that it seems so much more attractive and humane than retributive forms of punishment. One study drew this conclusion: "It would be difficult to overstate the degree to which the concepts and vocabulary of rehabilitation have dominated discourse about the purposes and functions of imprisonment in modern American history."[16]

The most widely accepted statement of the rehabilitative purpose of sentencing is contained in the Model Penal Code of the American Law Institute. This code, which was approved by the Institute in 1962, has been a model for state laws and sentencing practices throughout the United States. In Section 1.02(2), titled "Purposes Concerning Sentencing and Treatment," the purposes of criminal sentences are listed as follows:

a. to prevent the commission of offenses;
b. to promote the correction and rehabilitation of offenders;
c. to effect individualized treatment; and
d. to advance the use of generally accepted scientific methods and knowledge in the sentencing and treatment of offenders.

Support for indeterminate sentencing began to erode when reformers began to raise questions about the ethics of the rehabilitation model. The erosion accelerated after Robert Martinson and his associates failed to find any systematic evidence that indeterminate sentencing actually worked and prison programs actually rehabilitated inmates.[17] It was also charged at the time that parole boards were unable to determine when inmates eligible for release had been cured of their criminal propensities. The combined evidence made a mockery of the term "correctional institution." It also raised fundamental "questions about the wisdom of maintaining a sentencing policy that was not only failing to achieve its primary objective but doing so in a manner that lacked coherence and evenhandedness."[18] Francis A. Allen articulates why he feels the goal of rehabilitation is unattainable:

First, the rehabilitate ideal constitutes a threat to the political values of free societies. Second, a distinct but closely related point—the rehabilitative ideal has revealed itself in practice to be peculiarly vulnerable to debasement and the serving of unintended and unexpressed social ends. Third, either because of scientific ignorance or institutional incapacities, a rehabilitative technique is lacking; we do not know how to prevent criminal recidivism by changing the characters and behavior of offenders.[19]

The sudden collapse of the rehabilitation ideal in the early 1970s as the principal justification for imprisonment left a void. It was a void that the goal of incapacitation was soon to fulfill. Yet rehabilitation has made something of a comeback in the 1980s and 1990s. A number of meta-analyses, which are comprehensive reviews of research on the effectiveness of correctional treatment, have found that some treatment programs do have positive outcomes in improving the attitudes of offenders and in reducing recidivism.[20] The challenge is to identify which program will work with what offenders in what setting.

Incapacitation

Incapacitation has become the chief justification for imprisonment in the United States. Offenders are imprisoned to restrain them physically from offending again while they are confined. The rise of incapacitation occurred at a time in which "get tough" with crime proposals were beginning to gain momentum. Incapacitation gained the approval of both liberals and conservatives in the 1970s. According to liberals, prison was to be reserved for a group of especially dangerous repeat offenders who required an incapacitation strategy. The conservative view was that general incapacitation "would achieve large aggregate crime prevention gains by imprisoning substantial numbers of run-of-the-mill felons."[21]

Obviously, the death penalty is the most severe means of protecting society; to take the life of an individual is to ensure that he or she will bring no further harm to society. The placement of an offender in a prison setting is the second most severe sanction; the offender who is "out of sight and out of mind" has no further chance to harm society until released. A jail sentence protects society only for a brief period, because most jail inmates are quickly back on the streets. Imprisonment in a long-term correctional institution is the most widely used means of incapacitation. Although considerable research has been done on the effects of incapacitation in reducing crime, the results are inconclusive and do not substantiate the claim that incapacitation reduces recidivism.[22]

The concept of **selective incapacitation** arose from the predictive research done by Peter Greenwood of the Rand Corporation. Greenwood noted that previous Rand research, particularly surveys of prisoners in California, Michigan, and Texas, had found that a relatively small number of offenders were responsible for a very large number of serious crimes. These surveys had collected self-report questionnaires from 2,100 male prison and jail inmates. Greenwood reasoned that with prediction methods it should be possible to identify the "high-rate" robbers and burglars and provide for their long-term incarceration.[23] The advantage of selective incapacitation, according to Greenwood, is that targeting these high-risk offenders for incarceration will reduce the rates of crime.

The effectiveness of selective incapacitation has been extensively examined. Steven Van Dine, Simon Dinitz, and John P. Conrad's study of the dangerous offender in Ohio raised the question: "How many actual offenses might have been prevented by sentencing policies which are designed for the purpose of incapacitating the dangerous offender?" These authors concluded that using the most stringent option would have prevented no more than 4 percent of the violent crime in Franklin County in 1973.[24] Although their study received much criticism, there has been little consensus on the value of selective incapacitation. Some argue that the incapacitative effects are negligible, but others claim that major impacts on crime are possible through increases in the use of imprisonment.[25]

What is most troubling about the concept of selective incapacitation?

Just Deserts: The Justice Model

Retribution, deterrence, rehabilitation, and incapacitation are sometimes called *consequentialist* strategies because they are based on the position that the justification of any action, practice, or policy depends on its expected overall consequences.[26] A *nonconsequentialist* strategy, according to R. A. Duff, is based on the belief that "actions and practices may be right or wrong by virtue of their *intrinsic* character, independently of their consequences."[27] A central retributionist position is that punishment can be justified if and only if it is deserved because of a past crime. The different ideas about retribution that have arisen in recent decades can be seen as attempts to explain and articulate this claim.[28]

J. D. Mabbott's seminal 1939 essay, "Punishment," was the first step in the development of the view of punishment as just deserts. Mabbott argued that it is unfair to deprive a person of liberty as a consequence of that person's committing a criminal act for any reason other than that the act "deserves" to be punished and that person committed that act.[29] The presumption that an offender deserves to be punished simply because of what he or she has done rather than for any social reasons was sharply debated by philosophers in the decades following publication of Mabbott's essay. One of the positive outcomes of this debate was the development of constructs of just deserts.

In the 1970s David Fogel and others developed the **justice model** of corrections, and it has become one of the most popular retributionist positions. Fogel believes that individuals have free will and are responsible for their decisions and thus deserve to be punished if they violate the law. The punishment that offenders receive should not be based on their needs; instead, it should be proportionate to the damage the crime inflicted on society.[29] Fogel's view of punishment is nonutilitarian. The goal of punishment, he believes, is not to achieve social benefits or advantages, such as deterrence or rehabilitation; rather, the goal of punishment is to give offenders what they deserve—their just deserts. However, the punishment must be fair, commensurate with the seriousness of the offense or the harm done.[30]

In 1976, a report from the Committee for the Study of Incarceration was published under the title *Doing Justice: The Choice of Punishment*. Andrew von Hirsch, the Committee's executive director, drafted the report. The Committee called for sentences to be administered on the basis of just deserts: *The severity of punishment should be commensurate with the seriousness of the wrong.*[32] Neither deterrence, nor incapacitation, nor rehabilitation should enter into the sentencing decision. Furthermore, the committee, as Fogel does, recommends determinate sentencing, dismantling of rehabilitative procedures, limited use of confinement, and reduced lengths of sentences.[33]

The justice model has been incorporated into the sentencing systems of many states' statutes. What proponents of the justice model regret is that state legislatures, in their revisions of criminal codes, frequently transform the just-deserts philosophy of correction into a more repressive system by lengthening offenders' sentences.

What is the fairness of the justice model of corrections? Why does the justice model result in more repressive criminal sentences?

Restorative Justice

Restorative justice demands that the offender compensate the victim or society for the harm resulting from a criminal offense. Restorative justice has roots in the concept of **reparation**, something done or paid to make amends for harm or loss. In victim-oriented reparation, the offender returns to the rightful owner either what has been taken away or its equivalent, usually in money or service. In community-oriented reparation, the offender either pays a fine or renders community service; the community thus functions as a substitute victim. In offender-oriented reparation, the rehabilitative effect on the offender becomes the focus: Providing compensation for the social harm done is supposed to provide healing for the criminal. Offender-oriented reparation also provides offenders who cannot pay compensation to their victims the opportunity to render useful public service.

Restorative justice has expanded the concept of reparation and become a major focus of criminology.[33] Its emphasis, as with reparation, is to restore victims, offenders, and communities to their precrime state. Tony Marshall has defined restorative justice as "a process whereby all the parties with a stake in a particular offense come together to resolve collectively how to deal with the aftermath of the offense and its implications for the future."[35] John Braithwaite adds that restorative justice restores property loss, restores injury, restores a sense of security, restores dignity, restores a sense of empowerment, restores deliberative democracy, restores harmony based on a feeling that justice has been done, and restores social support.[36]

Restorative justice is grounded in the concept that the government should surrender its control over responses to crime to those who are most directly affected—the victim, the offender, and the community. This expression of punishment is based on the premise that communities will be strengthened if local citizens participate in the response to crime, and this response is tailored to the needs and preferences of victims, communities, and offenders.[36] For an example of a state that has advanced the concept of restorative justice, see Outside the Walls 4.2.

outside the walls 4.2
outside

Minnesota, a Pioneer in Restorative Justice

Minnesota has been a groundbreaker in restorative justice. Its Department of Corrections created the "Restorative Justice Initiative" in 1992, hiring Kay Pranis as a full-time Restorative Justice Planner in 1994—the first such position in the country. The initiative offers training in restorative justice principles and practices, provides technical assistance to communities in designing and implementing practices, and creates networks of professionals and activists to share knowledge and provide support.

Sentencing Circles

Besides promoting victim–offender mediation, family group conferencing, and neighborhood conferencing, the department has introduced sentencing circles. Citizen volunteers and criminal justice officials from Minnesota have participated in training in the Yukon Territory, where peacemaking circles have been held since the late 1980s. In Minnesota, the circles process is used by the Mille Lacs Indian Reservation and in other communities in several counties.

The Circle Process

The circle process usually has several phases. First the Community Justice Committee conducts an intake interview with offenders who want to participate. Then, separate healing circles are held for the victim (and others who feel harmed) and the offender. The committee tries to cultivate a close personal relationship with victims and offenders and to create support networks for them. In the end, a sentencing circle, open to the community, meets to work out a sentencing plan. In the towns of Milaca and Princeton, followup circles monitor and discuss the offender's progress.

> The committee tries to cultivate a close personal relationship with victims and offenders and to create support networks for them.

CRITICAL THINKING QUESTIONS

How appealing do you believe the concept of restorative justice is to the American public? Is the appeal of this goal of punishment likely to increase in the twenty-first century?

Source: Reprinted from Leena Kurki, "Incorporating Restorative and Community Justice into American Sentencing and Corrections," *Sentencing and Corrections: Issues for the 21st Century* (Washington, D.C.: U.S. Department of Justice, 1999), p. 5.

Table 4.1

Characteristics of Punishment Philosophies

Policy	Retribution	Deterrence	Rehabilitation
Approach to the Offender	Free will based on the classical school	Free will based on classical school	Deterministic or positivistic approach
Focus on Act or Actor	Act	Act	Actor
Type of Sentencing Advocated	Determinate	Determinate	Indeterminate
Purpose of Punishment	Pay for what an offender has done	Prevent future antisocial behavior	Change an offender
Role of Treatment	Ineffective and coddles criminals	Reduces chances of future antisocial behavior	Basic goal of correctional process
Reactive or Proactive Punishment	Basically reactive	Basically reactive	Intended to be proactive
Crime Control Strategy	Get-tough policies	Protect society	Eliminate factors causing crime through therapeutic intervention

Restorative justice's emphases on accountability and victims' rights have gained for it the acceptance of hard-liners. Restoration of offenders, dignity of both offenders and victims, and conflict resolution strategies draw applause from liberals. Another reason for the popularity of restorative justice is that it can be used with other forms of punishment.

There are similarities and differences among these punishment philosophies (see Table 4.1). Retribution is the punishment philosophy that has been around the longest, but the numbers of those in jail and prison show the popularity of incapacitation. Just deserts is a contemporary version of retribution philosophy; its influence is seen in the revision of sentencing structures in legislatures across the nation. For those offenders whose offenses are minor or who are sentenced to community-based corrections, restorative justice and its emphasis on victims' rights is receiving increased attention in this nation's court systems.

According to the justice model of punishment, in what circumstances might a longer prison sentence for this incarcerated felon be seen as fair? How is restorative justice different? In general, how would you describe the range of punishments from least to most severe?

Incapacitation	Just Deserts	Restorative Justice
Free will based on the classical school	Free will based on the classical school	Free will based on the classical school
Act	Act	Actor and victim
Determinate	Determinate	Determinate
Protect society	Doing justice	Restoring balance that offender has upset
Reduces prison tension and violence	Voluntary but necessary in a humane system	Reconciliation among offender, victim, and community
Basically reactive	Reactive and proactive	Reactive and proactive
Get-tough policies	Justice as fairness for offenders, for practitioners in the justice system, and for victims	Restoration for offenders, for victims, and for the community

HOW DO THE FORMS OF PUNISHMENT DIFFER?

The forms of punishment, or sanctions, available to judges vary from jurisdiction to jurisdiction but generally include diversionary programs, fines, probation, intermediate sanctions, confinement in jail, incarceration in a state or federal prison, and the death penalty. The responsibility of the judge is to weigh the costs and benefits to the defendant and to society in arriving at the appropriate disposition. The judge also has the responsibility to escalate the punishment to fit the crime. Each form of punishment described in this section increases the costs of criminal behavior. In later chapters, these forms of punishment are discussed more extensively.

Diversionary Programs

Placement of a defendant in a **diversionary program** usually occurs early in the court process, although a drug addict or an alcoholic may be given a choice between a prison sentence or placement in a therapeutic community. The use of alternatives to the formal justice system decreased in the 1970s and 1980s. Then, in the 1990s, the development of drug courts increased the use of diversionary programs for drug offenders.

Fines

The court may fine a defendant if a monetary sanction appears to be the best method of discouraging future unlawful behavior. A fine is frequently imposed in misdemeanor cases, with jail as an alternative if the offender cannot or will not pay. Fines are also commonly a condition of probation. They are sometimes imposed in felony cases, especially if the offender gained money or property by committing the offense. Day fines are increasingly a part of intermediate sentencing sanctions. Some defendants, such as white-collar criminals, are persons of means and can easily pay a fine, but for a poor defendant a fine is often an unbearable burden. Installment payments are frequently used to help defendants pay their fines.

Probation

Probation permits a convicted offender to remain in the community, under the supervision of a probation officer and subject to certain conditions set by the court. Most states have statutes that restrict the use of probation with some offenders, especially those who have committed serious crimes. Reacting to the criticism of hard-liners that probation is soft on crime, judges began to give split sentences (an offender must spend time in jail before being placed on probation) and to place more probationers on house arrest and electronic monitoring. Prison overcrowding has also meant that offenders who otherwise might be sentenced to prison must be placed on probation and be given intensive probation services.

Intermediate Sanctions

Intermediate sanctions are imposed on offenders who are perceived to require more serious sanctions than traditional probation services would require. They include intensive probation and parole services, residential facilities, boot camp experiences, house arrest, electronic monitoring, community service, and day reporting centers.[38]

Confinement in Jail

Offenders who in the opinion of the judge do not merit probation may be sent to jail for up to a year in most jurisdictions. Sentenced offenders, in some instances, are placed on work release, a plan under which they spend every night in jail but then work during the day in the community. Convicted offenders are sometimes permitted to stay at home with their families and work on their jobs during the week, but they must report to the jail on Friday evening and remain there until Sunday evening.

Incarceration in a State or Federal Prison

Judges are using imprisonment as a disposition more than ever before, as the crowded conditions of nearly every prison in the United States testify. Defendants who have committed serious crimes are usually the ones sent to prison, but nearly half of those currently sentenced to prison have not committed violent offenses. A judge may feel that an offender does not deserve a prison sentence but may have no other alternative available except traditional probation to select from in that jurisdiction. The judge may order that terms of imprisonment be served concurrently or consecutively. **Concurrent sentences** are served simultaneously. **Consecutive sentences** must be served one after the other.

Death Penalty

The ultimate disposition, of course, is the decision by the court to take the life of a convicted defendant. The general trend in the twentieth century was a decline in executions, from 1,667 in the 1930s to 191 in the 1960s. In 1972, the death penalty was struck down by the U.S. Supreme Court in the *Furman v. Georgia* decision, which declared the arbitrary nature of the death penalty as the chief reason for declaring it unconstitutional.[39]

On 2 July 1976, five cases involving death penalty laws were heard by the Supreme Court. The death penalty statutes in Texas, Florida, and Georgia were affirmed, while the statutes of North Carolina and Louisiana were struck down. The Supreme Court, in the *Gregg v. Georgia* decision, cited the review procedure before the state supreme court as a model for such statutes.[40]

Thirty-eight states permit the death penalty, and, as of 9 June 2001, 712 convicted murderers have been put to death since 1976. On Monday 11 June, Timothy McVeigh became the thirtieth prisoner executed in 2001 and the first federal prisoner in thirty-eight years. For the past two years, increased numbers of people have questioned whether the death penalty is administered fairly. That has been largely because wider availability of DNA testing has cleared about 100 U.S. prisoners convicted of serious crimes, including at least 10 on death row.[41]

WHAT ARE THE MAIN THEORETICAL POSITIONS ABOUT PUNISHMENT AND THE SOCIAL SYSTEM?

To understand the philosophy of punishment at a particular time, it is necessary to locate this philosophy in time and place and to understand what the relationship of punishment is to the functioning of the social system. Émile Durkheim wrote at a particular time of social crisis, as did Karl Marx. Their interpretation of the role of punishment is related to the functions of punishment in the social systems of which they were a part. Similarly, Michel Foucault examined the role of power and its relationship to punishment in the late twentieth century.

Émile Durkheim and Punishment in Support of Social Solidarity

The development of sociology brought about a new perspective on the justification for punishment. One of its founders, the French sociologist Émile Durkheim (1858–1917), saw that punishment is above all a moral process that functions to preserve the shared values and normative conventions on which social life is based.[42]

Durkheim contends that for the most part the criminal law of society is an embodiment of the basic moral values that society holds sacred. Accordingly, crimes violating this "collective conscience" will tend to provoke collective moral outrage and a passionate desire for vengeance. The rituals of punishment are directed less at the individual offender than at the impassioned onlookers whose cherished values and security have been undermined by the offender's actions. Thus, punishment's significance is best conceived as social and moral rather than penological.[43]

Durkheim's theory of punishment returns its justification to the idea of retribution. When criminals are not caught and punished, the social consensus about values is eroded. Indeed, for Durkheim crime is normal, necessary, and, in a way, desirable. When a criminal is found guilty, the public is reminded of the importance of the value that the offender violated. In Durkheim's view, both crime and punishment build the solidarity of the community.

This Durkheimian description of punishment has some severe limitations. Primarily concerned to explain punishment's moral content and moral consequences and to trace punishment's role in the maintenance of moral order, it is very much a one-dimensional account. Durkheim places minor emphasis on the other characteristics, sources, and effects of punishment. Nor does Durkheim offer much analysis of the actual apparatus and instrumentalities of punishment or the ways in which penal institutions are influenced by social forces, such as economics and politics, that are totally unrelated to moral passions or a collective conscience.[44]

Karl Marx and Conflict Criminology

Karl Marx (1818–1883) wrote primarily about the historical forces that created bourgeois capitalism, about the economics of surplus value, and about the empowerment of the proletariat through revolutionary means. He had little to say about crime and punishment. In his view, crime was one of the consequences of the capitalist system and would doubtless play a much less significant part in the socialist system of the future. Perhaps his most significant remark about the problem of crime in nineteenth-century society was contained in an article written for the *New York Daily Tribune* on the topic of capital punishment: "[I]s there not a necessity for deeply reflecting upon the alteration of a system that breeds these crimes, instead of glorifying the hangman who executes a lot of criminals to make room only for the supply of new ones?"[45]

Marx held that the miseries of the proletariat, of which the "tatterdemalion" segment is only the most miserable, would continue until capitalism is overthrown and the nations of the world become classless societies. Hence there is no reason to suppose that crime will diminish while capitalism survives.

From this sketchy account of crime, Marxist criminologists have moved on to a theory that crime is the natural and inevitable result of the conflict of classes. If society is engaged in a class war, then criminals are casualties of the war. Marxist criminology reached its heyday in the 1960s and the 1970s. The explanation of crime lies in the economics of capitalism. The victims of oppression are motivated by hardship, and their status is analogous to that of political prisoners in totalitarian, or dictator-ruled, countries.

Marxists' efforts to explain penal practice by reference to class struggle and economic relations are open to criticism. They overestimate the explanatory power of economic factors, and they fail to recognize the ways in which economic concerns are always tempered by other social forces. Marxist contentions that criminal justice is a kind of class instrument used to regulate and control the working classes are also challenged by the fact that the criminal law commands broad support among the working classes, who perceive it as protecting their interests as well as those of the ruling class.[46]

Michel Foucault and the Power of Modern Punishment

In *Discipline and Punish: The Birth of the Prison,* Michel Foucault examines an ongoing debate about the uses of the prison in a modern society.[47] Foucault focuses on explaining the disappearance of public spectacle and of bodily violence and the emergence of another style of punishment in which the prison comes to be the standard penal method. He selects this problem because he wants to examine the theme of how power is exercised and individuals are governed in the contemporary world. Thus, for the most part, Foucault analyzes the apparatus of power that the prison deploys and the forms of technology, knowledge, and social relationship on which this apparatus depends.[48]

Foucault's work takes us to the internal workings of the penal apparatus, as it focuses on the specific technologies of penal power and their model of operation. He analyzes in detail the mechanisms whereby modern penal sanctions exert their specific forms of control, the principles of inspection, surveillance, and discipline on which they rely, and the penological knowledge and rationalities that inform these modes of exercising power. He goes on to show the detailed ways in which the "microphysics of power" come into contact with the bodies of those subjected to it.[49]

A major limitation of this account of punishment is that in focusing on the relations of power and knowledge structuring modern punishments, Foucault neglects such issues as moral values, the sensibilities, and emotional forces that form the cultural framework in which penal power takes place. An even more critical limitation of Foucault's work is that although he may describe very well the power–knowledge relations within treatment-oriented prisons, such strategies are no longer characteristic of penal policy.[50]

heroes | *Norval Morris*

Professor of Law at the University of Chicago Law School

"I just yesterday signed a contract and finished a book which examines the issue of punishment in this country. It is a fictional account, with a series of commentaries on the implications of the fiction. We are still debating its title; it is either going to be *Maconochie's Prison* or *Maconochie's Gentlemen*. It is the story of Norfolk Island and the roots of modern prison reform.

"I have done my best in this fiction to capture the readers' imagination. I pose such questions as: 'Why should America for identical nonviolent crimes with identical nonviolent crime rates hand out punishments in bucketfuls when Western Europe hands out punishments in spoonfuls? Why are we so excessive in our punishment?' I am not sure how these questions should be answered. There is no simple answer, and I am suspicious of those who think they know the answer.

"In this country, we have relied excessively on the prison for punishment. I have given a good deal of thought to the prison over my career. I think the mission of prisons is very simple and very easy to state. It seems to me that when you state it, most prison authorities will accept it. It's a mistake to send anyone to prison for his or her own good. You send people to prison for what they have done to others. But having said that, it seems to make good sense to provide all reasonable self-generating possibilities for personality changes and vocational or educational development that we can afford in such facilities. Some people can change and want to help themselves; we should help them to do so.

"What I don't care for is what is called the 'humane warehousing model.' It is a necessary but not a sufficient condition for the decent prison to protect the weak from the strong, the victims from the predators. We do have obligations to minimize brutality and violence and to respect minimum human rights. We do want to create a situation in which we don't have to be ashamed of our prisons. This all refers to the necessary but not sufficient condition of imprisonment.

"I wish to add the next step, which I'm not sure the humane warehousing has as a further requirement. It seems to me that we should help the illiterate to read, should help the vocationally untrained to learn a trade if they wish, and we should help those who want to do so to develop themselves educationally, culturally, and personally. We should help them to lead a more law-abiding life.

"What astonishes me is that many of the people who oppose prison self-improvement programs as futile, work in universities. They must believe in the capacity of people to change themselves; otherwise, they wouldn't take either state or private money as educators because they would be stealing. In that sense, I don't see any difference between a law school professor and a prison governor. If we are not helping people in the University of Chicago Law School to develop their integrity, their capacity to practice law, and their cultural understanding of the law, then we shouldn't get what little salary we get. Prisoners also have the capacity to change and to be helped.

"Our harshness toward crime is related at least in part to a combination of misleading statements by the media and to politicians seeking for votes. This started with the Goldwater campaign in the 1960s and is now voiced by both parties. I don't think there are many differences between the two parties when it comes to the crime issue. I mean it was fascinating to me how both candidates running for president avoided the issue of race and crime. I think they know what ought to be done, but they are not prepared to do it. I don't think there is difficulty in knowing what ought to be done.

"I don't know what the future has in store for us. There are more and more people with a greater understanding of all issues, including crime. But there are also an over-abundance of people who simply shout slogans. If you do no more than mouth slogans, you will have what we have today with candidates for public office."

CRITICAL THINKING QUESTIONS

Professor Morris developed a model prison for the federal Bureau of Prisons. Given what he says here, what do you think would be some of the features of this prison? Why do you think the United States punishes "in bucketfuls" and Western Europe "in spoonfuls"?

Our hero in this chapter is Norval Morris, a widely esteemed criminologist who is also a law professor and former dean of the University of Chicago Law School. Professor Morris has written a number of books, ranging in content from insanity and the criminal law, to imprisonment, to social policy and criminal law, and to intermediate sentencing. His authored or coauthored books that are particularly helpful to the corrections student are *The Honest Politician's Guide to Crime Control, The Future of Imprisonment,* and *Between Prison and Probation.* The Heroes box provides his comments for *Invitation to Corrections* in 2000.

HOW IS SENTENCING RELATED TO THE CORRECTIONAL PROCESS?

Sentencing is the beginning of the correctional process. Criminal sentencing and the sanctions imposed by it represent society's most powerful means to discourage repeated unlawful behavior. Society expects sentences that are appropriate to the seriousness of the criminal act, that incarcerate violent criminals, and that prevent innocent people from becoming victims of crime. The sentencing of convicted offenders is being transformed in a number of ways today. The discretion available to judges has decreased in the past decade, as many states have experimented with one or more types of sentencing reform—sentencing guidelines, determinate sentencing, mandatory sentences, and alternative forms of punishment. The purposes of sentencing have shifted from an emphasis on utilitarian aims, especially rehabilitation, toward a greater focus on appropriate punishment proportionate to the harm done.[51]

Determinate versus Indeterminate Sentencing

The sentencing system in the United States no longer has a standard approach. As of 1999, more than thirty states retained some form of indeterminate sentencing, which permits early release from a correctional institution after the offender has served a required minimum portion of his or her sentence. The remainder of the states have some form of "structured sentencing." Eight or nine operate with "presumptive" sentencing guidelines, another eight to ten have "voluntary" guidelines, and two jurisdictions in one state have "mandatory" guidelines. Five states have statutory determinate sentencing systems. These numbers are somewhat misleading because systems differ so much that there is wide disagreement over which label best characterizes a particular system. In addition, all jurisdictions are affected by recently enacted three-strikes, mandatory minimum, or truth-in-sentencing laws. Figure 4.1 indicates which states had three-strikes mandatory sentencing laws as of 1997.[50]

The Bureau of Justice Assistance (BJA) published two surveys that attempt to make sense of this hodgepodge of sentencing. The most recent sentencing survey, published in 1998, reports that thirty-six states and the District of Columbia have indeterminate sentencing systems. The remainder of the states employ **determinate sentencing,** which imposes a sentence for a definite term. The factor that the BJA used to distinguish one system from the other was whether parole release remained available for a sizable fraction of cases. The fourteen states with determinate sentencing had basically eliminated parole release.[53]

Sentencing Guidelines

Sentencing guidelines had their beginning in October 1984, when Congress passed the Comprehensive Crime Control Act, which among other things abolished parole as of November 1987.[54] The United States Sentencing Commission was created in a companion Sentencing Reform Act of 1984. The Sentencing Reform Act spelled out three objectives for the Commission. First, the Commission was to "reduce crime through an effective, fair sentencing system." To accomplish this goal, the system had to be *honest*—that is, there was to be no more reduction of terms in prison by grants of parole. The sentence in months or year, whatever it was, would be served. Second, the Commission was to ensure *uniformity* in sentencing so that persons committing similar crimes would serve similar terms. Third, the Commission was to ensure *proportionality* by imposing "appropriately different sentences for criminal conduct of different severity."[55]

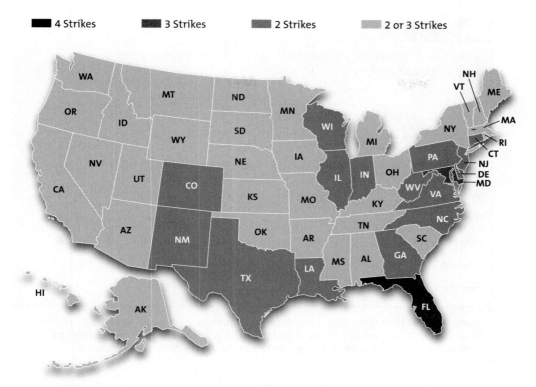

Figure 4.1 States with Three-Strikes Mandatory Sentencing Laws

Note: Imposition of the mandatory sentence in the two- or three-strikes states depends on the circumstances of the crime and the prior record of the offender.

Source: Michael Vitiello, "Three Strikes: Can We Return to Rationality?" *Journal of Criminal Law and Criminology* 87 (Winter 1997), p. 395.

Forty-three levels of offenses were specified, and most federal crimes were assigned to a defined level. Petty offenses were not included, and the Commission did not get around to assigning levels for rarely committed felonies. Departures by the sentencing judges from the guidelines were discouraged. If a judge believed he or she had to depart from the guidelines, the judge was expected to justify that departure in writing and expect that it would be appealed. Table 4.2 shows federal guidelines for months of incarceration before release on parole.

The federal sentencing guidelines have been criticized on several fronts. Judges complain about their complexity and difficulty of use along with the fact that they limited the exercise of judicial discretion. Defense counselors have little use for them because of their harshness and because they shift sentencing authority from judges to prosecutors and are based on prior record and offense elements rather than on conviction charges. Many federal officials also dislike the guidelines because of their dissimilarity to the prior system of sentencing and because of the disruption they brought to a system that was working well enough before the change. The most disturbing of the criticisms of the federal guidelines is that they were developed with insufficient attention being paid to either ethical considerations of basic justice or basic concerns about their effects on prison populations.[56]

About twenty states established sentencing guidelines in the final two decades of the twentieth century. Twelve are still in existence. Sentencing guidelines have been particularly

Table 4.2

U.S. Parole Guidelines: Recommended Months of Incarceration before Release on Parole for Adults

Offense Severity	Offender Characteristics			
	Very Good 10–8	**Good** 7–6	**Fair** 5–4	**Poor** 3–0
Low	0–6	6–9	9–12	12–16
Low moderate	0–8	8–12	12–16	16–22
Moderate	10–14	14–18	18–24	24–32
High	14–20	20–26	26–34	34–44
Very high	24–36	36–48	48–60	60–72
Greatest I	40–52	52–64	64–78	78–100
Greatest II	52+	64+	78+	100+

Source: Adapted from National Research Council, *Research on Sentencing, The Search for Reform* (Washington, D.C.: National Academy Press, 1983), vol. I, p. 171. Reprinted from "Research on Sentencing," 1983, with permission from the National Academy Press, Washington, D.C.

well received in Delaware, Minnesota, Oregon, Pennsylvania, and Washington.[57] A good many other states have rejected guidelines because they perceive them as an improper interference with the role of the judiciary, or because respected judges have been vocal in their opposition.

The guidelines that are probably most admired by criminal justice sentencing scholars are those in force in Minnesota since 1978.[58] Like the federal guidelines, the Minnesota guidelines are based on a grid—the vertical axis with 10 levels of severity, the horizontal axis providing for 6 scores for criminal history (see Figure 4.2). One special feature of the Minnesota guidelines is that the sentencing commission is legally required to adjust the application of the guidelines in order to avoid prison crowding.

Lisa Stolzenberg and Stewart J. D'Alessio evaluated the Minnesota guidelines and found that initially they reduced disparity for the prison/no prison decision but that inequality gradually reverted to pre-guideline levels as time passed. Stolzenberg and D'Alessio also found that the guidelines had a permanent effect on reducing disparities in decisions on the length of prison sentence. Indeed, there was a 60 percent reduction in inequality for the judicial decision concerning the length of prison sentences.[59]

As Michael Tonry pointed out, Delaware, Oregon, Pennsylvania, and Washington also produced sentencing guidelines that appear to reduce unwarranted disparities, including gender and racial discrimination, without deeply upsetting judges and policymakers. The key to the success of those states' guidelines is careful crafting, which prevents the guidelines from swelling the prison population and insulates them from political pressures to get forever tougher on offenders.[60]

Sentencing guidelines have evolved from simple guidelines for prison terms in Minnesota, Pennsylvania, and Washington to much more comprehensive guidelines incorporating community and intermediate punishments and relating state programs for funding county initiatives. The best known example is North Carolina's comprehensive structured sentencing system, but Ohio and Pennsylvania also have pursued more comprehensive sentencing systems. The significant and distinctive aspect of these sentencing systems is that they establish sentencing standards for felonies and misdemeanors as well as for intermediate and community, jail, and prison punishments.[61]

Presumptive Sentence Lengths in Months

Italicized numbers within the grid denote the range within which a judge may sentence without the sentence being deemed a departure.

Offenders with nonimprisonment felony sentences are subject to jail time according to law.

CRIMINAL HISTORY SCORE

SEVERITY LEVELS OF CONVICTION OFFENSE		0	1	2	3	4	5	6 or more
Unauthorized Use of Motor Vehicle Possession of Marijuana	I	12*	12*	12*	13	15	17	19 *18–20*
Theft Related Crimes ($250–$2500) Aggravated Forgery ($250–$2500)	II	12*	12*	13	15	17	19	21 *20–22*
Theft Crimes ($250–$2500)	III	12*	13	15	17	19 *18–20*	22 *21–23*	25 *24–26*
Nonresidential Burglary Theft Crimes (over $2500)	IV	12*	15	18	21	25 *24–26*	32 *30–34*	41 *37–45*
Residential Burglary Simple Robbery	V	18	23	27	30 *29–31*	38 *36–40*	46 *43–49*	54 *50–58*
Criminal Sexual Conduct, 2nd Degree (a) & (b) Intrafamilial Sexual Abuse, 2nd Degree subd. 1(1)	VI	21	26	30	34 *33–35*	44 *42–46*	54 *50–58*	65 *60–70*
Aggravated Robbery	VII	24 *23–25*	32 *30–34*	41 *38–44*	49 *45–53*	65 *60–70*	81 *75–87*	97 *90–104*
Criminal Sexual Conduct, 1st Degree Assault, 1st Degree	VIII	43 *41–45*	54 *50–58*	65 *60–70*	76 *71–81*	95 *89–101*	113 *106–120*	132 *124–140*
Murder, 3rd Degree Murder, 2nd Degree (felony murder)	IX	105 *102–108*	119 *116–122*	127 *124–130*	149 *143–155*	176 *168–184*	205 *195–215*	230 *218–242*
Murder, 2nd Degree (with intent)	X	120 *116–124*	140 *133–147*	162 *153–171*	203 *192–214*	243 *231–255*	284 *270–298*	324 *309–339*

1st Degree Murder is excluded from the guidelines by law and continues to have a mandatory life sentence.

▨ At the discretion of the judge, up to a year in jail and/or other non-jail sanctions can be imposed as conditions of probation.

☐ Presumptive commitment to state imprisonment.

Figure 4.2 Minnesota Sentencing Guidelines Grid

Source: Minnesota Sentencing Guidelines Commission.

SUMMARY

This chapter examines the punishment of offenders, punishment and the social system, and the sentencing process. Retribution was the original goal of punishment and in the minds of many remains the primary goal of punishment. But in the past couple of centuries other goals have emerged, including deterring offenders from crime, rehabilitating them in correctional contexts, isolating them to protect society, and requiring them to make amends for their wrongful behaviors. In the 1970s and 1980s, retribution regained popularity with the rise of the justice model of corrections.

Most jurisdictions have a variety of forms of punishment, including diversion, fines, probation, confinement in jail, incarceration in a state or federal prison, and the death penalty. Diversion and fines have declined in judicial use at the sentencing stage; and jail and incarceration have increased. Even when probation is ordered by the court, more intensive forms of supervision are more widely used today than in the past. In the 38 states that have the death penalty, its use has increased in recent decades.

There are a variety of sentencing structures in the United States. More than thirty states still retain some form of indeterminate sentencing. The remainder have some form of "structured sentencing." Determinate sentencing remains popular in nearly one-third of the states. Beginning with the federal sentencing guidelines, about 20 states have adopted sentencing guidelines.

KEY TERMS

concurrent sentences, p. 80
consecutive sentences, p. 80
determinate sentencing, p. 84
deterrence, p. 71
diversionary program, p. 79
general deterrence, p. 73
incapacitation, p. 71
indeterminate sentencing, p. 74
intermediate sanctions, p. 80
just deserts, p. 71

justice model, p. 76
probation, p. 80
rehabilitation, p. 71
reparation, p. 76
restorative justice, p. 71
retribution, p. 71
selective incapacitation, p. 75
sentencing guidelines, p. 84
special deterrence, p. 73

CRITICAL THINKING QUESTIONS

1. Tomorrow you will appear before the judge. Are you hoping for an indeterminate or a determinate sentence? Why? Compare the two types of sentencing.
2. Rehabilitation, retribution, deterrence, incapacitation, and restorative justice are five goals of punishment. Which one do you favor? Why? Explain the dispositions suitable to your choice.
3. Do you believe the punishment should fit the crime or the needs of the offender? Explain your reasoning.
4. Do you think a just system of sentencing is possible? Why or why not?
5. Attend a criminal trial and describe the difficulties you would have in imposing a just and reasonable sentence.

WEB DESTINATIONS

Follow arguments in the debate about the effectiveness of capital punishment as a means of deterrence.
http://www.deathpenaltyinfo.org/deter.html

Read comprehensive definitions of the main theories of crime and punishment, including, for example, incapacitation.
http://www.britannica.com/bcom/eb/article/1/0,5716, 120711+4+111023,00.html

Gain an in-depth perspective on the concept of restorative justice at this site.
http://www.restorativejustice.com/

Follow links on this page to further explore the subject of crime and punishment.
http://crime.about.com/newsissues/crime/

Read about the work of the Sentencing Project to evaluate the use and effectiveness of punishment in the United States.
http://www.sentencingproject.org/

FOR FURTHER READING

Braithwaite, John. "Restorative Justice: Assessing Optimistic and Pessimistic Accounts." In *Crime and Justice: A Review of Research* 25, edited by Michael Tonry. Chicago: University of Chicago Press, 1999. In this and other writings Braithwaite provides a comprehensive summary of restorative justice.

Garland, David. "Sociological Perspectives on Punishment." In *Crime and Justice: A Review of Research* 14, edited by Michael Tonry. Chicago: University of Chicago Press, 1991. Garland's essay relating punishment to sociological perspectives is extremely well done and insightful.

Nagin, Daniel S. "Criminal Deterrence Research at the Outset of the Twenty-First Century." In *Crime and Justice: A Review of Research* 23, edited by Michael Tonry. Chicago: University of Chicago Press, 1998. An excellent overview of criminal deterrence.

Tonry, Michael. "Sentencing Commissions and Their Guidelines." In *Crime and Justice: A Review of Research* 17, edited by Michael Tonry. Chicago: University of Chicago Press, 1993. One of the most perceptive presentations of sentencing commissions.

Tonry, Michael. "Reconsidering Indeterminate and Structured Sentencing." *Sentencing and Corrections: Issues for the 21st Century.* Washington, D.C.: U.S. Department of Justice, 1999. Tonry sheds light on the complexity of sentencing in the United States.

Zimring, Franklin E., and Gordon Hawkins. *Incapacitation: Penal Confinement and the Restraint of Crime.* New York: Oxford University Press, 1995. A comprehensive examination of incapacitation.

NOTES

1. John P. Conrad, "The Hoodlum in the Helpless Society" (paper presented at the North Carolina Conference on Juvenile Justice, 1979), cited in Clemens Bartollas, *Juvenile Delinquency,* 5th ed. (Boston: Allyn & Bacon, 2000), pp. 71–72.

2. Ibid.

3. Ibid.

4. David Garland, "Sociological Perspectives on Punishment," in *Crime and Justice: A Review of Research* 14, ed. Michael Tonry (Chicago: University of Chicago Press, 1991), p. 119. See also David Garland, *Punishment and Modern Society: A Study in Social Theory* (New York: Oxford University Press, 1990).

5. For an examination of incapacitation as a punishment strategy, see Jacqueline Cohen, "Incapacitation as a Strategy for Crime Control: Possibilities and Pitfalls," *Crime and Justice: An Annual Review of Research* 5, ed. Michael Tonry and Norval Morris (Chicago: University of Chicago Press, 1983), pp. 1–84.

6. The executioner's indispensability to a well-ordered state was explicitly and vigorously argued by the French anti-Enlightenment philosopher Joseph de Maistre (1753–1821) in a panegyric to be found in the posthumously published *Les Soirées de Saint-Pétersbourg* (Paris: Garnier, 1821), Vol. 1, pp. 29–33; Vol. 2, pp. 4–5.

7. For an expansive treatment of retribution, see R. A. Duff, "Penal Communications: Recent Work in the Philosophy of Punishment," in *Crime and Justice: A Review of Research* 20, ed. Michael Tonry (Chicago: University of Chicago Press, 1996), pp. 1–97.

8. For descriptions of other types of deterrence—actual deterrence, perceptual deterrence, absolute deterrence, marginal deterrence, total deterrence, and partial deterrence—see Richard A. Wright, *In Defense of Prisons* (Westport, Conn.: Greenwood Press, 1994), pp. 63, 65.

9. For an overview of research on criminal deterrence, see Daniel S. Nagin, "Criminal Deterrence Research at the Outset of the Twenty-First Century," in *Crime and Justice: A Review of Research* 23, ed. Michael Tonry (Chicago: University of Chicago Press, 1998), pp. 1–42.

10. Albert Blumstein, "Sentencing Reforms: Impacts and Implications," *Judicature* 68 (October–November 1984), p. 36.

11. Jeremy Bentham, *An Introduction to the Principles of Morals Legislation* (1823; reprint, New York: Hafner, 1984).

12. Ernest van den Haag, "The Criminal Law as a Threat System," *Journal of Criminal Law and Criminology* 73 (1982), pp. 769–785.

13. See Charles Tittle and Allan Rowe, "Moral Appeal, Sanction Threat, and Deviance: An Experimental Test," *Social Problem* (1973), pp. 490–495; and William Bailey, "Certainty of Arrest and Crime Rates for Major Felonies: A Research Note," *Journal of Research in Crime and Delinquency* (July 1976), pp. 145–154.

14. Nagin, "Criminal Deterrence Research at the Onset of the Twenty-First Century," p. 36.

15. Andrew von Hirsh, *Doing Justice: The Choice of Punishment* (New York: Hill and Wang, 1976), p. 12.

16. Franklin E. Zimring and Gordon Hawkins, *Incapacitation: Penal Confinement and the Restraint of Crime* (New York: Oxford University Press, 1995), p. 6.

17. Robert Martinson, "What Works? Questions and Answers about Prison Reform," *Public Interest* 35 (Spring 1974), pp. 22–54.

18. Brian Forst, "Prosecution and Sentencing," *Crime,* ed. James Q. Wilson and Joan Petersilia (San Francisco: Institute for Contemporary Studies, 1995), p. 376.

19. Francis A. Allen, *The Decline of the Rehabilitation Ideal: Penal Policy and Social Purpose* (New Haven: Yale University Press, 1981), pp. 33–34.

20. Paul Gendreau and R. R. Ross, "Revivication of Rehabilitation: Evidence from the 1980s," *Justice Quarterly* 4 (1987), pp. 349–408; Paul Gendreau and M. A. Paporozzi, "Examining What Works in Community Corrections," *Corrections Today* (February 1995), pp. 28–30; Larry W. Sherman, Denise Gottfredson, Doris MacKenzie, John Eck, Peter Reuter, and Shawn Bushway, "Preventing Crime: What

Works, What Doesn't, What's Promising," *Research in Brief* (Washington, D.C.: National Institute of Justice, 1998).

21. Zimring and Hawkins, *Incapacitation,* p. 10.

22. Alfred Blumstein, Jacqueline Cohen, Susan E. Martin, and Michael Torny, eds., *Research on Sentencing: The Search for Reform,* 2 vols. (Washington, D.C.: National Academy Press, 1983).

23. Peter W. Greenwood with Alan Abrahamse, *Selective Incapacitation* (Santa Monica, Calif.: Rand, 1982).

24. Stephen Van Dine, John P. Conrad, and Simon Dinitz, "The Incapacitation of the Dangerous Offender: A Statistical Experiment," *Journal of Research in Crime and Delinquency* 14 (1977), pp. 22–35.

25. Alfred Blumstein, Jacqueline Cohen, and Daniel Nagin, *Deterrence and Incapacitation: Estimating the Effects of Criminal Sanctions on Crime Rates* (Washington, D.C.: National Academy of Sciences, 1978), pp. 66–67.

26. Duff, "Penal Communications," pp. 4–5.

27. Ibid., p. 6.

28. Ibid., p. 7.

29. J. D. Mabbott, "Punishment," in *Justice and Social Policy,* ed. Frederick A. Olafson (Englewood Cliffs, N.J.: Prentice-Hall, 1961), 39.

30. David Fogel, *"We Are the Living Proof . . . ": The Justice Model for Corrections* (Cincinnati: Anderson, 1975).

31. David Fogel and Joe Hudson, eds., *Justice as Fairness: Perspectives on the Justice Model* (Cincinnati: Anderson, 1981), p. 1.

32. von Hirsch, *Doing Justice,* pp. 132–140.

33. Andrew von Hirsch and Kathleen Hanrahan, *The Question of Parole* (Cambridge: Ballinger, 1979).

34. John Braithwaite, "Restorative Justice: Assessing Optimistic and Pessimistic Accounts," in *Crime and Justice: A Review of Research* 25, ed. Michael Tonry (Chicago: University of Chicago Press, 1999), p. 1.

35. Quoted ibid., p. 5.

36. John Braithwaite, "Restorative Justice and a Better Future," *Dalhousie Review* 76 (1996), pp. 9–32.

37. Leena Kurki, "Incorporating Restorative and Community Justice into American Sentencing and Corrections," *Sentencing and Corrections: Issues for the 21st Century* (Washington, D.C.: U.S. Department of Justice, 1999), p. 1.

38. Michael Tonry and Mary Lynch, "Intermediate Sanctions," in *Crime and Justice: A Review of Research* 20, ed. Michael Tonry (Chicago: University of Chicago Press, 1996), pp. 99–144.

39. *Furman v. Georgia,* 408 U.S. 238 (1972).

40. *Gregg v. Georgia,* 428 U.S. 153 (1976).

41. Emilie Lounsberry, "As McVeigh Execution Nears, Death Penalty Debate Rages," *Saint Paul Pioneer Press,* 10 June 2001, 1A.

42. David Garland, "Sociological Perspectives on Punishment," p. 122.

43. Ibid., p. 123.

44. Ibid., p. 124.

45. "On Capital Punishment," *New York Daily Tribune,* 18 February 1853; reprinted in *Crime and Capitalism,* ed. David F. Greenberg (Palo Alto, Calif.: Mayfield, 1981), pp. 55–56.

46. Garland, "Social Perspectives on Punishment," pp. 132–133.

47. Michel Foucault, *Discipline and Punish: The Birth of the Prison,* trans. Alan Sheridan (New York: Pantheon Books, 1977).

48. Garland, "Sociological Perspectives on Punishment," p. 135.

49. Ibid., p. 134.

50. Ibid., p. 140.

51. Blumstein, "Sentencing Reforms," p. 130.

52. Michael Tonry, "Reconsidering Indeterminate and Structured Sentencing," *Sentencing and Corrections: Issues for the 21st Century* (Washington, D.C.: U.S. Department of Justice, 1999), p. 1.

53. Bureau of Justice Assistance, *1996 Survey of State Sentencing Structures* (Washington, D.C.: U.S. Department of Justice, 1998).

54. Under Section 5.15 of the *Guidelines Manual,* the court must order a period of supervised release for any prisoner serving a term exceeding one year. See U.S. Sentencing Commission, *Guidelines Manual* (Washington, D.C.: U.S. Government Printing Office, 1988).

55. Ibid.

56. Forst, "Prosecution and Sentencing," p. 377.

57. Michael Tonry, "Sentencing Commissions and Their Guidelines," in *Crime and Justice: A Review of Research* 17, ed. Michael Tonry (Chicago: University of Chicago Press, 1993), p. 138.

58. See Lisa Stolzenberg and Stewart J. D'Alessio, "Sentencing and Unwarranted Disparity: An Empirical Assessment of the Long-Term Impact of Sentencing Guidelines in Minnesota," *Criminology* 32 (May 1994), pp. 301–310.

59. Ibid., pp. 301, 306.

60. Michael H. Tonry, "Structuring Sentencing," in *Crime and Justice: A Review of Research* 10, ed. Michael Tonry and Norval Morris (Chicago: University of Chicago Press, 1988), pp. 140–141.

61. Michael Tonry, "The Fragmentation of Sentencing and Corrections in America," *Sentencing and Corrections: Issues for the 21st Century* (Washinton, D.C.: U.S. Department of Justice, 1999), p. 4.

Multiple Choice Questions

1. According to your text, all of the following are goals of punishment in the United States except:
   A. Retribution
   B. Deterrence
   C. Incapacitation
   D. Due process

2. According to research, general deterrence policy has little value unless:
   A. Punishment is extremely rare and directed at certain cases
   B. The lawbreaker regards the certainty of identification, apprehension, and punishment to be in the 30 to 50 percent range
   C. The lawbreaker regards the certainty of punishment as extremely great
   D. The lawbreaker sees more police officers

3. What type of sentencing has been an important part of the rehabilitation philosophy?
   A. Indeterminate
   B. Determinate
   C. Mandatory
   D. Judicial

4. Identify the state that has been a groundbreaker in the use of restorative justice.
   A. New York
   B. Connecticut
   C. Minnesota
   D. Texas

5. Criminal defendants who have been convicted of felonies are usually sent to:
   A. Prison
   B. Jail
   C. Probation
   D. Boot camp

6. Which of the following signifies the beginning of the correctional process?
   A. Sentencing
   B. Jury verdict
   C. Presentence investigation report
   D. Jail

7. A judge sentences an offender who has been convicted of four counts of murder in the first degree to four life sentences. The sentences will be served one after the other. This is an example of:
   A. Concurrent sentence
   B. Consecutive sentence
   C. Legislative sentence
   D. Presumptive sentence

8. All of the following are sentences available to a judge except:
   A. Probation
   B. Prison
   C. Jail
   D. Parole

9. Identify the goal of punishment that places emphasis on accountability and victims' rights.
   A. Retribution
   B. Reintegration justice
   C. Justice as fairness
   D. Restorative justice

10. Who has the responsibility for determining when an offender has been rehabilitated and is ready to be released from prison with an indeterminate sentencing model?
    A. Judge
    B. Probation board
    C. Parole board
    D. Clemency committee

11. When a judge sentences someone to spend time in jail before being placed on probation is known as:
    A. Shock incarceration
    B. Intensive supervision probation
    C. Split sentencing
    D. Jail release

True/False Questions

T F   1. Deterrent effects are the same for all types of crime.

T F   2. Incapacitation has become the chief justification for imprisonment in the United States.

T F   3. Placement of a defendant in a diversionary program usually occurs early in the court process.

T F   4. Imprisonment is currently being used more as a sentence than at any other time in our country's history.

T F   5. The purpose of sentencing has shifted from an emphasis on appropriate punishment proportionate to the harm done toward a greater focus on rehabilitation.

T F   6. Currently, sentencing guidelines apply only to prison terms.

T F   7. According to Marx, crime will not diminish while capitalism survives.

T F   8. The Comprehensive Crime Control Act abolished parole on the federal level of government as of November 1987.

T F   9. According to Durkheim, both crime and punishment break down the solidarity of the community.

T F 10. A judge's discretion to sentence offenders has decreased over the past decade.

T F 11. Intensive probation services, residential facilities, and house arrest are examples of determinate sanctions.

T F 12. Considerable research on the effects of incapacitation in reducing crime conclude that incapacitation has a positive impact on reducing recidivism rates.

Fill-in-the-Blank Questions   (based on key terms)

1. The philosophy that supports the position that the punishment should fit the crime is referred to as _____.

2. The goal of punishment that mandates offenders to pay compensation to the victims or to society for the harm caused by a criminal offense is known as _____.

3. The main focus of _____ is to require that the offender's sentence be a fixed period of time.

4. A criticism of the _____ is that they limit judicial discretion.

5. The philosophy of _____ focuses on changing the offender's internal attitudes and behaviors in an attempt to limit his or her predisposition to commit crime.

6. The purpose of punishment that supports preventing future law-violating behavior is known as _____.

7. The _____ philosophy justifies punishing offenders because they deserve it, with the only criterion being that the punishment given to the offender must equal the seriousness of the offense.

8. The goal of punishment that focuses on isolating and controlling offenders for the purpose of community safety is known as _____.

9. The position that supports punishing someone for committing robberies by sending him or her to prison with the desire that this will prevent him or her from committing future robberies is an example of _____.

10. A strategy that is based on the use of a prediction mechanism to target high-risk, repeat offenders and provide for their long-term incarceration is known as _____.

11. The type of sentencing guidelines that is structured and has a sentencing range for particular categories of offenses as well as offenders is known as _____.

12. _____ were adopted by California, Colorado, and Connecticut during the final years of the twentieth century. These types of sentences vary in specificity and severity.

13. When a state punishes someone for committing a robbery by sending him or her to prison with the desire that this will prevent others from committing robberies is an example of _____.

Essay Questions

1. Explain why deciding how to punish an offender is not an easy process. What factors influence the punishment decision?

2. Describe the liberal and conservative approaches to the increased use of imprisonment as a form of incapacitation.

3. Identify and explain four different goals of punishment that reflect sentencing processes across the United States.

4. Explain how indeterminate sentencing and the use of the parole board are significant elements of the rehabilitation philosophy.

5. Identify and explain four different forms of punishment that are available to a judge. What goal of punishment is each form based on?

ANSWERS

Multiple Choice Questions

1.	D	7.	B
2.	B	8.	D
3.	A	9.	D
4.	C	10.	C
5.	A	11.	C
6.	A		

True/False Questions

1.	F	7.	T
2.	T	8.	T
3.	T	9.	F
4.	T	10.	T
5.	F	11.	F
6.	F	12.	F

Fill-in-the-Blank Questions

1. Retribution
2. Restorative justice
3. Determinate sentencing
4. Sentencing guideline system
5. Rehabilitation
6. Deterrence
7. Justice as fairness
8. Incapacitation
9. Special deterrence
10. Selective incapacitation
11. Presumptive sentencing guidelines
12. Statutory determinate sentencing laws
13. General deterrence

The Rise of Community-Based Corrections

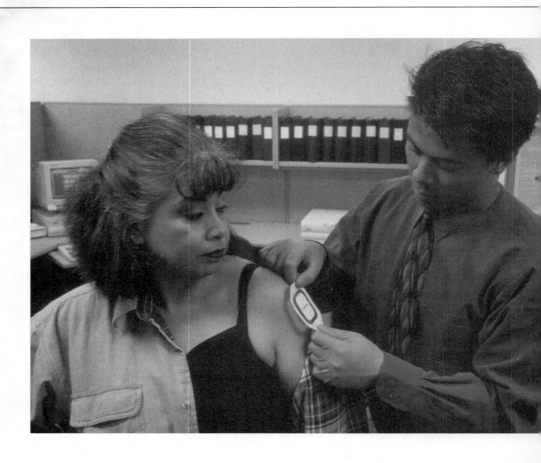

"Jennifer's story" reports the successful experience that a suburban housewife addicted to drugs had with Talbert House, a privately administered community-based treatment program.

Jennifer was a typical suburban wife—happily married with two children—except she was secretly addicted to drugs. As a nurse, she had begun stealing narcotics from the hospital where she worked. Throughout her six years of addiction, she began using more often and in heavier doses in order to get the same physical and emotional effects.

After being caught by hospital officials, Jennifer was sentenced by the Hamilton County Drug Court to the Talbert House Women's Adapt program for treatment. "I am horrified today that I was so out-of-control," states Jennifer.

Because Adapt is equipped for children to reside with their mothers, Jennifer's son was able to stay with her during residential treatment. "He was having such a difficult time with me being gone. This really helped him to understand what was going on," remembers Jennifer.

After completing the intensive outpatient and continuing care phases of treatment, Jennifer successfully graduated in June of 1999 from the Adapt program. "My life is much simpler and cleaner," states Jennifer. "I am thankful for the quality treatment that I received from Talbert House."[1]

CRITICAL THINKING QUESTIONS

How was Jennifer's stay in the Talbert House treatment program different from placement in a women's prison? What do you think Jennifer meant by "quality of treatment"?

Jennifer was not a typical correctional client. She was middle class, married, and living with her husband and two children in a suburban setting. She held a good job as a nurse in a hospital. She became addicted to drugs and eventually was caught stealing narcotics from the hospital where she worked. She appeared before a judge, who sentenced her to a residential program rather than to a prison setting. Permitted to have her son with her in this private residential placement, she used the therapeutic tools in this program to return home and put her life back together, without drugs.

Community-based corrections consists of probation, intermediate sanctions, parole, and reentry programs. Distinguishing features of community-based programs include the frequency, duration, and quality of community relationships. The quality of community relationships, however, is even more important than the frequency and duration of community contacts. A chain gang places inmates in the community outside the prison walls but scarcely yields the relationships that are needed for successful community-based programs.[2]

HOW IS COMMUNITY-BASED CORRECTIONS CHANGING?

Community-based corrections had its origins early in the history of this nation. The Puritans in New England attempted to punish deviants in the community, as a means to enforce their strict Puritan codes. Informal community pressures, such as gossip, ridicule, and ostracism, were found to be effective in keeping most citizens in line. Offenders might be confined in the stocks and the public cage, or for the most serious crimes, they might be whipped, branded, banished, or hanged.

The community nature of corrections receded in importance with the rise of the American version of the penitentiary. Yet, in the middle of the nineteenth century, probation began with the volunteer services of John Augustus in Massachusetts. In 1841, Augustus provided bail for a man charged with being a common drunkard, subject to the man's appearing in court three weeks later. From 1841 to 1851, Augustus provided bail for 1,102 males and females, some of them as young as 8 years old. Accustomed to a caseload of 125 to 150 probationers at a time, he had to give up shoemaking and seems to have depended on the contributions of friends and admirers for funds to put up bail. This was the beginning of probation; the word itself was Augustus's invention.[3]

Probation became the most common form of punishment during the twentieth century. Following its beginnings as a voluntary movement in the late nineteenth century, probation experienced rapid growth in the first decades of the twentieth century and in the 1960s. During the 1960s and 1970s, guided by reintegration philosophy, probation subsidy statutes were passed in a number of states, team probation was widely implemented, and experiments were conducted in California to determine whether intensive probation was as effective in reducing recidivism as commitments to institutions.

Parole in the United States was derived from Walter Crofton's Irish mark system of releasing rehabilitated inmates to the community. It was introduced into this country in 1863 by Gaylord Hubbell, warden of Sing Sing in New York. Franklin Sanburg, Enoch Wines, and Zebulon Brockway joined with Hubbell to form a humane and progressive movement of releasing inmates from imprisonment. Brockway developed this system of parole most fully at the Elmira Reformatory in the final decades of the nineteenth century.

Parole took longer than probation to gain widespread public acceptance. In the mid-1970s, Richard McGee, director of the California Department of Corrections, encouraged his staff to see whether a strong parole program could lessen prison overcrowding. Various experiments were conducted, leading to confidence that credible programs of control and professional assistance could shorten prison terms and eventually divert many offenders away from prison and into community-based corrections.

The emphasis on **diversionary programs** began in 1967, when the President's Commission on Law Enforcement and Administration of Justice recommended the establishment of alternatives to the juvenile justice system.[4] In the late 1960s and early 1970s, diversionary programs sprouted across the nation in both juvenile and adult justice. In the 1970s, resolution of citizen disputes, deferred prosecution, and Treatment Alternatives to Street Crime were the most widely used pretrial diversionary programs for adults. Therapeutic communities also were called on at the pre- and posttrial stages to divert drug addicts from the criminal justice system.

Residential programs were further developed during the late 1960s and 1970s. As part of the expansion of community-based corrections, residential facilities were designed to house probationers having difficulties with traditional probation and high-risk parolees being released from prison. Some communities were more receptive than others to the establishment of residential facilities in their neighborhoods.

Community Reintegration

What sparked the growth of community-based corrections during the late 1960s and 1970s was political support. As crime was emerging as a major social problem during the 1960s, President Lyndon B. Johnson appointed the President's Commission on Law Enforcement and Administration of Justice to study the problem and make recommendations. Recommendations of the Corrections Task Force, such as diversionary programs for juveniles, captured the imagination and support of American citizens in the late 1960s and early 1970s. The spirit of the times favored reform. Deinstitutionalization was the watchword in the treatment of the mentally ill in the 1960s. Increasing numbers of mental patients were kept in the community rather than placed in large mental institutions. The turbulence brought on by the Vietnam War, urban riots, and disturbances on college campuses, and the widespread questioning of traditional values by youth countercultures, fostered receptivity to new solutions. Bloody prison riots that erupted between 1971 and 1973 also helped support the conclusion that there must be a better way. It was thought that perhaps deinstitutionalization could be used by the criminal justice systems, too.

Federal funding provided the catalyst linking correctional reform with social and political realities and thereby creating an array of community-based corrections programs throughout the nation. For example, from the inception of the **Law Enforcement Assistance Administration (LEAA)** in 1967 to July 1975, $23,837,512 of Safe Street Act federal money was matched with $12,300,710 of state and local funds for grants devoted to residential **aftercare.**

According to the 1967 Corrections Task Force of the President's Commission on Law Enforcement and Administration of Justice, the new challenge of corrections was to keep offenders in the community and to help reintegrate them into community living.[5] In 1973, the National Advisory Commission on Criminal Justice Standards and

Goals—a blue-ribbon commission that focused on developing standards for criminal justice—explained why keeping offenders out of long-term institutions was a good idea:

> Prisons tend to dehumanize people. . . . Their weaknesses are made worse and their capacity for responsibility and self-government is eroded by regimentation. Add to these facts the physical and mental conditions resulting from overcrowding and from the various ways in which institutions ignore the rights of offenders, and the riots of the present time are hardly to be wondered at. Safety for society may be achieved for a limited time if offenders are kept out of circulation, but no real public protection is provided if confinement serves mainly to prepare men for more, and more skilled, criminality.[6]

Together, the President's Crime Commission and the National Advisory Commission developed the basic assumptions of **reintegrative philosophy**—the idea that every effort should be made to return offenders to the community as law-abiding citizens.

Proponents of reintegrative philosophy recommended community-based corrections for all but hard-core criminals. It was reasoned that because nearly all offenders eventually would return to their communities, they should receive help sooner rather than later. All the resources of the community were to be mobilized to help offenders restore family ties, obtain employment and education, and find their place in society. Thus, meaningful contacts within the community were required to assist offenders.

For offenders who had to be institutionalized, a wide variety of reentry programs would be available. Inmates would be able to choose their prison programs and receive services to help them restore family ties and obtain employment and education after their confinement ended.[7]

The Decline of Public Acceptance

Community-based corrections, however, declined in popularity even more rapidly than it had gained public approval. In the mid-1970s, the mood of the country suddenly changed to a get-tough-with-criminals approach. Publications of official statistics and media coverage of street crime convinced the public that crime had gotten out of hand. The seemingly permissive approach that kept offenders in the community became less and less acceptable. Supporters of the punishment model urged incarceration as a more fitting way of dealing with crime. Proponents of this model insisted that offenders should pay for their crimes in prison rather than in the community, where they could come and go more or less as they pleased. One result of the decline of support for community-based corrections was the growth of institutional populations to an all-time high.

Paradoxically, in spite of declining support for residential and diversionary programs in the 1970s, prison crowding actually brought about an expansion of community-based corrections in the 1980s. Federal court orders forced thirty-six states to take steps to relieve prison crowding. Prison construction offered a long-term solution, but immediate relief was clearly needed. Community-based corrections, particularly probation and parole, suddenly gained the favor of judges and politicians, and the numbers of offenders on probation skyrocketed.

In the 1980s and 1990s, a new mission for community-based corrections was defined, based on intensive surveillance. This new mission has given rise to a number of themes:

- It is commonly agreed that intensive supervision increases the number of offenders who can be left in the community without endangering the safety of citizens. Georgia's Intensive Probation Supervision program was begun in 1982, and within five years, the positive evaluation of this program encouraged thirty-nine other states to develop their own intensive probation projects.[8] In the 1980s and 1990s, intensive parole arose in several states as a means to release inmates early from overcrowded prisons.

- Intermediate sanctions are widely used throughout the United States and are supported by nearly all corrections interest groups. In particular, electronic monitoring and house arrest are increasingly used to supervise offenders without incarcerating them. **House arrest** is a sentence imposed by the court whereby offenders are ordered to remain confined in their own residences for the length or remainder of their sentence. They may be allowed to leave their homes for medical reasons, employment, and approved religious services. They also may be required to perform community service. Electronic monitoring equipment may be used to verify offenders' presence in the residence where they are required to remain.

- More attention has been paid to substance abusers, primarily because so many of these offenders have histories of substance abuse. Because of this focus on substance abusers, the work responsibilities of many probation officers and parole officers now include the regular collection of urine samples and the drafting of violation reports on individuals whose samples do not meet the required standard. Increasing numbers of parolees have been returned to prison for parole violations. Indeed, probationers' and parolees' use of drugs has been part of society's war on drugs.[9]

- Better screening and classification systems have been developed regarding the level of probation supervision.

- Greater emphasis has been placed on community restitution programs and work orders as part of the victims' rights movement. In many court systems, restitution is an almost inevitable condition of probation.

- Efficiency and accountability are being demanded of community-based programs. Probation and parole departments have developed new technologies of control in order to fashion a surveillance model based on risk management.

As we enter the first decade of the twenty-first century, liberal and conservative politicians support the position that substantially more offenders must be involved in community-based corrections than are confined in prisons. An increasingly widely accepted belief is that the state simply cannot afford the prohibitive costs of building more prisons. See the Timeline for the development of community-based corrections.

timeline

The Rise of Community-Based Corrections in the United States

Date	Event
1841	John Augustus provides bail to first client.
1863	Parole is introduced to the United States.
1876	Zebulon Brockway becomes superintendent at Elmira Reformatory and implements indeterminate sentencing and parole.
1967	President's Commission on Law Enforcement and Administration of Justice recommends diversionary programs for juveniles. Inception of Law Enforcement Assistance Administration, which over the next decade provides large amounts of money for community-based correctional programs.
1973	National Advisory Commission on Criminal Justice Standards and Goals recommends strategies to keep offenders out of prison and develops the basic assumptions of reintegrative philosophy. Enactment of Minnesota's Community-Based Corrections Act.
1990	New mission of community-based corrections emerges.

WHAT IS THE STRUCTURE OF COMMUNITY-BASED CORRECTIONS?

Comprehensive state-sponsored programs, locally sponsored (usually by the courts) programs, and privately administered programs are the three basic types of community-based corrections. States administer community-based corrections in several ways. Forty-five states administer probation. State departments of corrections also are responsible for reentry programs, such as work release, home furloughs, and study release. Moreover, parole supervision is administered by the state in every state that still allows parole. Community Corrections Acts are the means by which twenty-five states administer community-based corrections. A few communities across the nation have developed a continuum of community-based correctional services, in which several subsystems of the correctional system are administered under local jurisdiction. Privately administered programs offer contract services to both probationers and parolees. They include the operation of group homes, halfway houses, and work release centers.

State-Sponsored Community Corrections Acts

A **Community Corrections Act (CCA)** is a law passed by a state legislature in which a state grants funds to local units of government to plan, develop, and deliver corrections services and sanctions. One of the major purposes of Community Corrections Acts is to encourage local sentencing options in lieu of state imprisonment.[10] Figure 5.1 shows

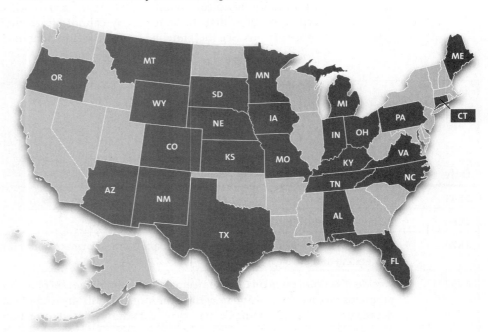

■ States with Community Corrections Legislation

Figure 5.1 States with Community Corrections Legislation, January 1994

Note: A number of other states have some form of community corrections policy or have initiated structured programs under existing administrative mechanisms.

Source: National Committee on Community Corrections.

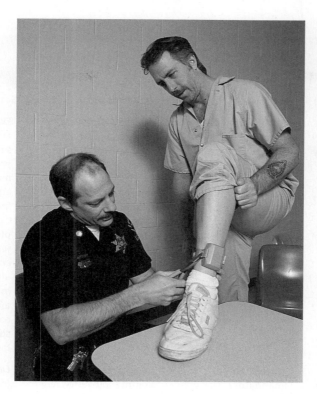

The intensive supervision models that became popular in the 1980s and 1990s included greater emphasis on electronic surveillance. What are some other goals and strategies used in intensive supervision models? How might state-sponsored Community Corrections Acts be involved in intensive supervision, and in what other correctional activities might CCAs be involved?

the states that have CCAs for adults. In analyzing Community Corrections Acts, Kay Harris found that the statutes have a number of characteristics in common. CCAs

- are legislatively authorized: Statutes provide the framework and authority for the other defining features of CCAs.
- are authorized statewide: CCAs mandate or authorize all localities, individually or in combination, to take advantage of the funds and authority granted.
- provide for citizen participation: CCAs provide for citizen involvement and specify roles that citizens may play.
- define an intergovernmental structure: CCAs delineate the roles to be performed and the power and authority to be exercised by involved state and local agencies or units of government.
- require local planning: CCAs provide that local planning will precede and serve as the basis for the development, implementation, and modification of local correctional sanctions and services.
- provide for state funding: CCAs provide for state subsidies to support local correctional programs and services.
- call for decentralized program design and delivery: CCAs provide for local control of the processes employed to assess local needs, to establish local priorities, and to plan local programs.
- endorse locally determined sanctions and services: CCAs provide resources and authority for sanctions and services to be developed and delivered at the local level.[11]

According to Harris, in the early 1970s, Minnesota, Iowa, and Colorado adopted CCAs that served as models for the CCAs developed in other states. Harris also describes a fourth model, which incorporates features of the Minnesota and Colorado CCAs but has unique elements that lead her to characterize it as a "Southern" model.[12] Table 5.1 presents a comparison of the defining features of the Minnesota, Colorado, Iowa, and "Southern" CCAs.

| Table 5.1 | | | | |

Defining Features of the Minnesota, Colorado, Iowa, and "Southern" Models of Community Corrections Acts (CCAs)

	Minnesota Model	Iowa Model	Colorado Model	"Southern" Model
Goals	• *Explicit:* Increase public safety and promote efficiency and economy • *Implicit:* Improve local programs, reduce state prison commitments, and contain state costs	• *Explicit:* Provide programs to meet needs of judicial districts • *Implicit:* Provide integrated range of programs for judicial districts	• *Explicit:* Promote state-local collaboration, provide flexibility and range of options, and increase public safety • *Implicit:* Encourage flexibility and use of local facilities and programs in lieu of state prison	• *Explicit:* Promote creativity and flexibility; increase sentencing options; reserve prison for violent felons/reduce use for nonviolent; address offender needs and reduce reoffending; provide close supervision; maintain public safety; promote restitution, efficiency, economy, and citizen and official involvement • *Implicit:* Reduce prison and jail commitments and contain state costs in ways consistent with need for local support
Nature and scope	• Decentralized/voluntary (county) • Discretionary programs • Comprehensive local sanctions	• Decentralized/mandatory (judicial districts) • Mandated categories of programs • Comprehensive local sanctions	• Decentralized/voluntary (county, community board, or program) • Residential program emphasis • Intermediate sanctions and transition (from prison)	• Decentralized/voluntary (county, city, combination, boards, private entities, state) • Discretionary programs • Front-end intermediate sanctions in lieu of prison/jail

Source: M. Kay Harris, "Key Differences among Community Corrections Acts in the United States: An Overview," *The Prison Journal* (June 1996), pp. 200–201.

The Iowa CCA is the only one that is mandatory for an entire state, and the "Southern" CCA is the only one that has a restricted target population. Each of the CCAs has a somewhat different base of funding, but the goals, though stated quite differently, have much in common.

Minnesota. The first step in the enactment of the broad and comprehensive Community Corrections Act in Minnesota was the formation in July 1972 of a study committee, whose task it was to review and assess the correctional systems in the state.[13] This group, composed of legislators and their staffs, police, judges, representatives of state and county agencies, local elected officials, and staff from the department of corrections, drafted the Community Corrections Act. After extensive review and revision, the draft legislation was presented to state legislature in February 1973. The act became law during that session, with an appropriation of $1.5 million for the first phase of implementation in three pilot areas. The 1975 legislature appropriated over $7 million to continue the program in the pilot areas and to expand it to include an additional eighteen counties during the next two years. The 1977 legislature continued its support by providing $13.6 million to maintain the program in all the counties where it had been implemented and to extend it into nine additional counties. As of 1 January 1998,

	Minnesota Model	**Iowa Model**	**Colorado Model**	**"Southern" Model**
Local structure	• Locally unified • Local advisory boards • Citizen role	• Locally unified • District boards and project advisory boards • Strong citizen role on boards	• Separate administration • Community corrections boards • Citizen case screening and policy roles	• Separate administration • Community corrections boards • Citizen role in obtaining local support, developing services
Funding	• Formula-based state subsidy • Funding to counties • "Chargeback" enforcement mechanism (in original act)	• State funding by district budget • Funding to judicial district corrections departments • State reviews and audits	• State funding by caseloads and per diems • Multiple funding recipients • State reviews and audits	• State grant funding • Multiple funding recipients • Continuation funding linked to diversionary effectiveness
Target population	• Target population not restricted • Diversionary, but not exclusively • Multiple CJ selection stages	• Target population not restricted • Diversionary, but not exclusively • Multiple CJ selection stages	• Broad target population • Diversionary • Selection at sentencing and release from prison	• Restricted target population • Diversionary • Selection at sentencing (including postsentence modifications)

thirty-one counties had elected to be part of the Minnesota Community Corrections Act. These counties organized into sixteen administrative service units and are known as the Minnesota Association of Community Corrections Act Counties.

The Community Corrections Act has four major purposes: (1) reduction of commitments to state prisons; (2) encouragement of local units of government to maintain responsibility for offenders whose crimes are not serious (those who would receive a sentence of less than five years in a state facility); (3) promotion of community corrections planning at the local level; and (4) improved coordination among local components of the criminal justice system.

The establishment of a local community advisory board is basic to the implementation of the plan in each new area. This board, which represents the criminal justice system and other community groups, develops a local comprehensive plan that identifies correctional needs and defines the programs and services necessary to meet these needs. After the comprehensive plan has been completed, it is submitted to the county board (or joint power board in multicounty units) for final approval. The plan is then sent to the commissioner of corrections thirty days before the expected starting date. When the commissioner has approved the comprehensive plan, the county or multicounty unit becomes eligible for a state financial subsidy. Figure 5.2 shows the organization of the Minnesota CCA.

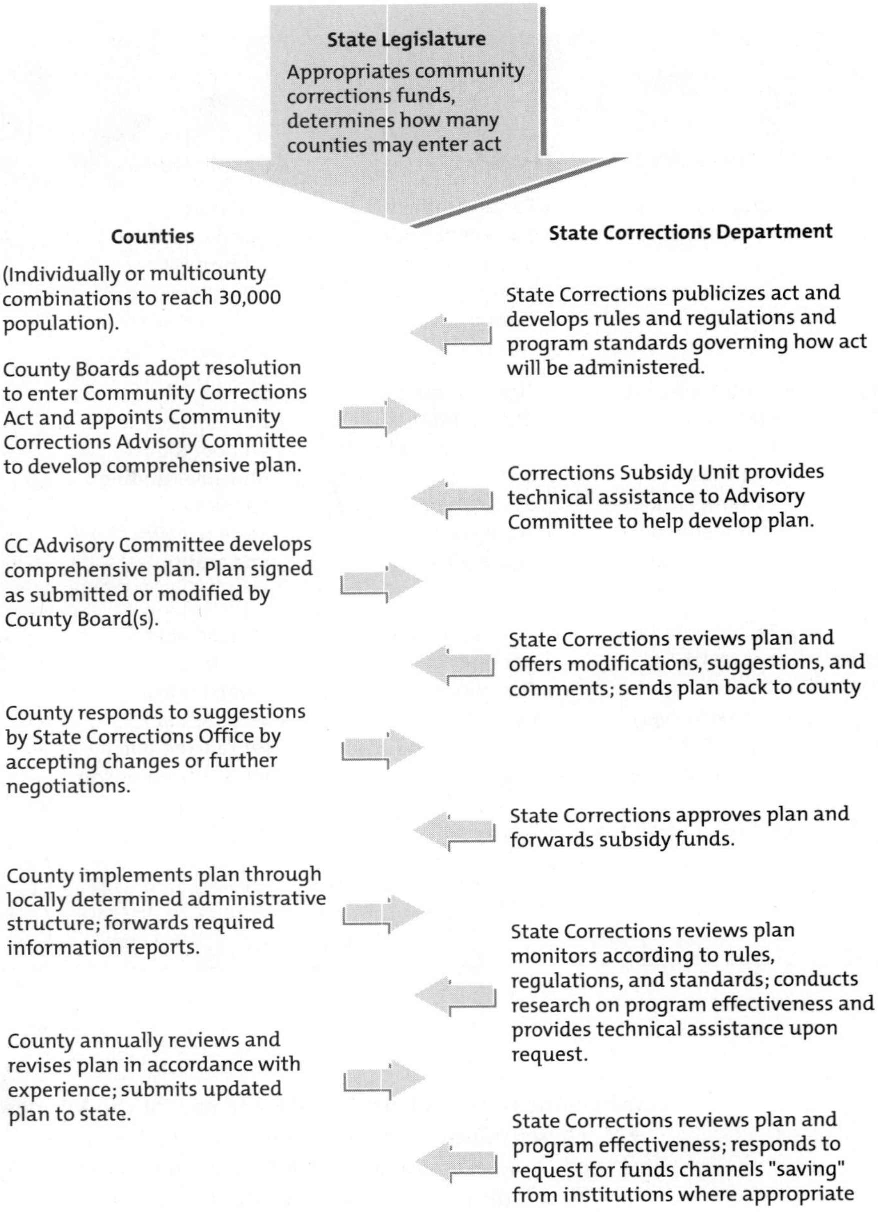

Figure 5.2
The Minnesota
Corrections Act

Source: E. Kim Nelson, Howard
Ohmart, and Nora Harlow,
*Promising Strategies in Proba-
tion and Parole* (Washington,
D.C.: U.S. Government Printing
Office, 1978), p. 61.

State Legislature
Appropriates community
corrections funds,
determines how many
counties may enter act

Counties

State Corrections Department

(Individually or multicounty
combinations to reach 30,000
population).

State Corrections publicizes act and
develops rules and regulations and
program standards governing how act
will be administered.

County Boards adopt resolution
to enter Community Corrections
Act and appoints Community
Corrections Advisory Committee
to develop comprehensive plan.

Corrections Subsidy Unit provides
technical assistance to Advisory
Committee to help develop plan.

CC Advisory Committee develops
comprehensive plan. Plan signed
as submitted or modified by
County Board(s).

State Corrections reviews plan and
offers modifications, suggestions, and
comments; sends plan back to county

County responds to suggestions
by State Corrections Office by
accepting changes or further
negotiations.

State Corrections approves plan and
forwards subsidy funds.

County implements plan through
locally determined administrative
structure; forwards required
information reports.

State Corrections reviews plan
monitors according to rules,
regulations, and standards; conducts
research on program effectiveness and
provides technical assistance upon
request.

County annually reviews and
revises plan in accordance with
experience; submits updated
plan to state.

State Corrections reviews plan and
program effectiveness; responds to
request for funds channels "saving"
from institutions where appropriate

In the 1980s and 1990s, the Community Corrections Act in Minnesota underwent
a significant change. The original act gave the counties a financial disincentive for sending short-term adult offenders (those sentenced to less than five years) to prison. If they
were sent to prison, the county was required to pay a per diem for their care. But if these
short-term offenders were kept in the community, the county was permitted to keep its
subsidy money. In 1981, when a sentencing guidelines law was passed, this financial disincentive was dropped. This new law basically told the courts whom to sentence and for
how long. Counties were no longer charged for anyone sent to prison, nor did they receive subsidy money for keeping offenders in the community.[14]

Our hero in this chapter is Kenneth F. Schoen, former commissioner of the Minnesota
Department of Corrections, director of the New York City Corrections Planning Project,
and director of the community corrections program of the Edna McConnell Clark Foun-

h e r o e s | *Kenneth F. Schoen*

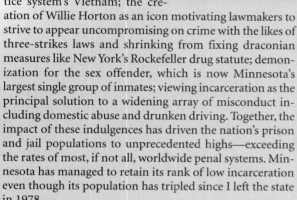

Former Commissioner of the Minnesota Department of Corrections

"Since we spoke almost twenty years ago, critical phenomena have emerged that have had a destructive and irrational impact on penal policy—the war on drugs, which has become the justice system's Vietnam; the creation of Willie Horton as an icon motivating lawmakers to strive to appear uncompromising on crime with the likes of three-strikes laws and shrinking from fixing draconian measures like New York's Rockefeller drug statute; demonization for the sex offender, which is now Minnesota's largest single group of inmates; viewing incarceration as the principal solution to a widening array of misconduct including domestic abuse and drunken driving. Together, the impact of these indulgences has driven the nation's prison and jail populations to unprecedented highs—exceeding the rates of most, if not all, worldwide penal systems. Minnesota has managed to retain its rank of low incarceration even though its population has tripled since I left the state in 1978.

"Nonetheless, during this period community corrections across the nation has considerably improved its ability to control offenders, providing better rehabilitation through electronic technology, enhanced risk and treat-

ment prediction models, specialized treatment programs and by offering an alternative and more fruitful paradigm for dispensing justice through the restorative justice model. However, the progress and capacity of community corrections has been thwarted by the lion's share of corrections budgets being devoted to prisons and jails. The huge expansion in use of incarceration has not been dampened by the exorbitant price tag when states and federal coffers are awash with funds. When this holiday from economic history ends, the burden of underwriting the cost of unnecessary imprisonment—the elderly, the drug user, the subjects of mindless mandatory sentences—will make policymakers look to community corrections as an attractive alternative for these people. We can then get back on track, providing just, safe and cost-effective programs for sentenced offenders."

CRITICAL THINKING QUESTIONS

Do you agree with Schoen that there is something irrational and destructive about this nation's penal policy at the present time? Do you agree with him when he says that community-based corrections will return to its popularity of the 1970s?

dation. His leadership was instrumental in the development and passage of the Minnesota Community Corrections Act. He wrote the text contained in the Heroes box for *Invitation to Corrections* in 2000.

Locally Sponsored Community-Based Programs

Community-based corrections programs that are sponsored by the local community have several forms of administration. In five states probation is administered by the courts and funded by the county. The judiciary or the prosecutor's office also frequently administers pretrial diversion programs. Some counties have established work-release centers. A few counties have developed a continuum of services and a coordinated correctional effort, so that a comprehensive program that includes several subsystems of the correctional system is administered under local jurisdiction. In these coordinated programs, fragmentation is reduced and services are improved. Model comprehensive programs have been developed in Polk County, Iowa (the Des Moines Program), and in Washington County, Oregon.

The Des Moines Program.   This program, which began in 1971, has four components that provide correctional services to defendants and convicted offenders at varying stages of the criminal justice process:

    Pretrial release

    Supervised release

    Probation/presentence investigation

    Community corrections facility

The pretrial release stage is modeled on the Vera-Manhattan Bail Reform Project of New York City, and it stipulates **release on** (the offender's) **own recognizance (ROR).** Immediately after being processed, each booked defendant is interviewed and evaluated according to objective criteria. If the defendant's scores indicate stable roots in the community, the staff recommends to the court that release on personal recognizance be granted.[15]

The supervised release program—the most innovative element—covers persons who do not qualify for ROR pretrial release. If defendants are willing to participate in a carefully structured program of supervision, counseling, and treatment, and appear likely to be able to profit from such an experience, they are recommended for release to the custody of the supervised-release staff. If the court approves the release, the defendant is assigned a counselor and, after taking a battery of tests, is assigned to a treatment plan. Job development assistance, marital and psychological counseling, and drug abuse therapy are common treatment areas.

Probation/presentence investigation is the third link in the chain of services provided to defendants and convicted offenders. Probation, a county responsibility in Polk County, is housed in the same building as the supervised-release staff, for the two programs complement one another. The intent of supervised release is to help defendants build a good track record that, if they are convicted, should ensure assignments to probation; the probation effort is then directed to continuation of the treatment objectives of supervised release. Problem solving rather than surveillance is the main thrust of the probation unit.

Up until the late 1980s, the community corrections facility, the fourth component, was a fifty-bed, nonsecure, renovated barracks at Fort Des Moines, a partially deactivated army base at the edge of the Des Moines city limits. This facility, predominantly for males, was by statute a jail used to retain sentenced offenders for the duration of their sentences. Work release, referral to community agencies, counseling within the facility, and overnight or weekend furloughs were all offered at Fort Des Moines.

The Des Moines Program is being used as a model in other Iowa cities and has been replicated in Clark County (Vancouver), Washington; San Mateo County, California; Salt Lake County, Utah; St. Louis County (Duluth), Minnesota; and Orange County (Orlando), Florida. In 1998, Iowa's community-based corrections provided services to 46,205 offenders through contact with eight judicial districts. Figure 5.3 shows the growth in the number of offenders served since fiscal year 1967. Iowa manages 76 percent of its adult offenders in community-based programs.[16]

Figure 5.3
Number of Offenders Receiving Community-Based Services in Iowa since 1967

Source: Iowa Community-Based Corrections, 2000.

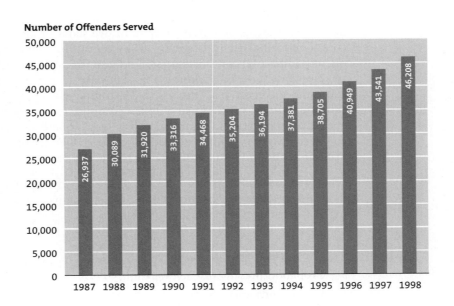

Number of Offenders Served

Year	Offenders
1987	26,937
1988	30,089
1989	31,920
1990	33,316
1991	34,468
1992	35,204
1993	36,194
1994	37,381
1995	38,705
1996	40,949
1997	43,541
1998	46,208

Washington County, Oregon.   The Probation and Parole Division supervised 3,800 offenders on 31 December 1997. The division is divided into seven teams, each providing specialized services or serving a specific population. The seven teams are Intake/Community Service, Sex Offender/Presentence Investigation, Female/Domestic Violence, Parole/Mental Health, General/Chemical Dependency, Multicultural/DUII, and Level II (low-limited risk) offenders. See Outside the Walls 5.1 for the services that these seven teams provide.

outside the walls   5.1

Services Provided by the Probation and Parole Division of Washington County, Oregon

Intake Team
- Receives all incoming supervision and investigation cases, assembles necessary background information, and assigns each case to the appropriate specialty team. . . .

Community Service
- Provides a sentencing alternative to the courts and a local intermediate sanction for Level I (high- and medium-risk) offenders who fail to comply with conditions of supervision. . . .

Day Reporting Center
- Provides intensive supervision and services to some of the county's highest-risk offenders (ages 18 to 34). . . .

DUII Supervision
- Assists offenders convicted of Driving Under the Influence of Intoxicants in successfully completing supervision through a combination of treatment services, supervision, and sanctions.

Female/Domestic Violence Supervision
- Provides specialized assessment and referral, supervision and sanctions to female offenders and batterers. . . .

General/Chemical Dependency Supervision
- Provides assessment and referral, supervision and sanctions to general caseload, a majority of whom have histories of substance abuse. . . .

General Supervision (Level II)
- Supervises a large caseload of "low" and "limited" risk offenders. There is emphasis on engaging the offender in needed services in the first three months, with lim-

ited compliance monitoring during the balance of supervision.

Multicultural Supervision (Level I)
- Provides bilingual/bicultural assessment and supervision to monolingual (Spanish) caseload of high- and medium-risk offenders. . . .

Multicultural Supervision (Level II)
- Provides bilingual/bicultural assessment to "low" and "limited" risk monolingual (Spanish) offenders. . . .

Parole/Mental Health Supervision
- Provides specialized assessment, supervision, and sanctions to offenders on parole/postprison supervision and offenders experiencing serious mental illness. There is close coordination with institution and community support services.

Presentence Investigation
- Provides background and offense information to assist the court in making sentencing decisions. . . .

(Sexual) Abuse Prevention Supervision
- Provides specialized supervision to offenders convicted of sex offenses. . . .

CRITICAL THINKING QUESTIONS

What are the advantages to the county of having such a broad range of services for offenders? Do you think coordinating so many teams and services would be a problem?

Source: Reprinted from the Washington County, Oregon, Webpage, 30 August 2000.

The Probation and Parole Division of Washington County Residential services further provide residential services. These services include a community corrections center, which operates a 219-bed facility for male and female offenders; intermediate sanctions; transitional housing; and intensive custodial home supervision.[17]

Privately Administered Community-Based Programs

Privately administered programs provide contract services to both probationers and parolees. Private vendors are beginning to offer probation services in some jurisdictions. The Salvation Army Misdemeanant Program (SAMP) up until the mid-1990s provided nearly all of the misdemeanant probation supervision in Florida,[18] and private firms are beginning to provide judges with presentence investigation reports.[19]

There has also been a significant increase in the number and types of services purchased from private vendors operating group homes, halfway houses, and work-release programs. In addition to residential services for probationers and parolees, they sometimes offer programs to assist drug abusers, ex-offenders, and victims. Private agencies profit from being smaller operations and thus escaping some of the bureaucratic red tape that affects state residential programs. These programs depend on a variety of funding sources, including federal, state, local, and private foundations. Dismas House and Talbert House are well known for the high-quality services they offer to offenders.

Dismas House. Named after the repentant criminal crucified with Jesus, Dismas House was founded by Reverend Jack Hickley, OP, a Vanderbilt University chaplain. The first Dismas House opened in 1974. Currently, there are eleven houses in five states (Indiana, Massachusetts, New Mexico, Tennessee, and Vermont). Each Dismas House provides a supportive residence for ex-offenders who have no family or who fear that a return to their former environment might result in a return to crime. Residents usually stay for three to six months and leave with a sense of self-worth, a stable income, and hope for the future. In addition, Dismas House is a residence for university students. They join with community volunteers to create a welcoming environment for offenders. Students generally remain in residence one or two semesters.[20]

Would you volunteer to live with ex-offenders for a semester or two in Dismas House? What do you think you would learn from such an experience?

Talbert House. Founded in 1965 in Cincinnati, Ohio, by a group of citizens who wanted to develop a better way of returning individuals to the community, Talbert House has expanded its services through the years. It now operates multiple service sites throughout Cincinnati for clients struggling with criminal victimization, chemical dependency, personal crisis, mental illness, and criminal justice issues.

The services include prevention services, adolescent treatment, outpatient services for adult substance abuse, residential treatment for drug abuse, mental health services, a community corrections center, and residential programs for women offenders.[21] Funding is typically a problem for private programs, but Talbert House receives support from agencies such as the Hamilton County Community Mental Health Board, Hamilton County Alcohol and Drug Addiction Services Board, Ohio Department of Rehabilitation and Corrections, Hamilton County Commissioners and Courts, United Way–Community Chest, and the City of Cincinnati–Neighborhood Services Division. Figure 5.4 shows the variety of services that Talbert House offers. In this figure, services are organized by cluster. Each circle represents a cluster, and the services and programs within that cluster are listed next to the appropriate circle. Core behavioral health centers and mental health services are now subsidiaries of Talbert House.

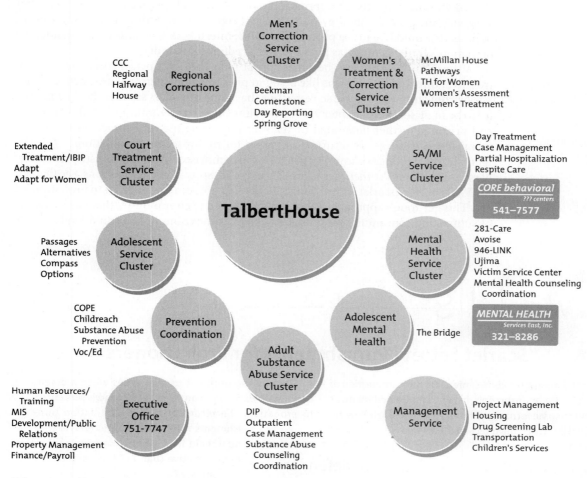

Figure 5.4 Services Offered by Talbert House

Source: Talbert House, Cincinnati, July 2000.

HOW DOES COMMUNITY-BASED CORRECTIONS FUNCTION?

Community corrections takes place in the midst of political, legal, and social mandates. The political mandate requires that a get-tough attitude be apparent in what takes place in community supervision and surveillance of offenders. The legal mandate specifies who can be placed in the community rather than sent to prison, what conditions of probation or parole offenders must meet, and when probation or parole may be revoked. The social mandate varies somewhat from community to community but ultimately mirrors a community's receptivity to community programs.

Community-based corrections provides a variety of services to those sentenced to this criminal sanction. In later chapters, the roles of probation officers and parole officers are examined. This chapter describes how residential staff perform their jobs in running residential programs.

Tough Enough Surveillance in the Community

Politicians base their get-tough approach on the public's fear and anger over crime. They justify this approach by saying privately and even publicly that they cannot get elected without a get-tough approach to crime. They take solace in the fact that they are giving the public what they want. When it comes to corrections in the community, politicians would like to see probation, parole, intermediate sanctions, and residential placements limit, as much as possible, the freedom of offenders.

Community corrections becomes appropriate, then, if it places strict enough controls over offenders so that it is like being in prison. Some intermediate sanctions, such as electronic monitoring, are so restrictive that some offenders say that they would prefer to be in prison (see Chapter 7). The thin line between community-based corrections and prison is further illustrated by the ever increasing use of technical violations. In many states, parolees are returned to prison for minor technical violations. With this mentality of making community programs like imprisonment, it is not surprising that harsh punishments sometimes take place in community-based corrections. See Outside the Walls 5.2 for "scarlet letter" punishments that are sometimes given to probationers.

This get-tough approach makes it difficult even in communities that have a history of supporting community programs. A violent crime committed by an offender under

outside the walls 5.2

"Scarlet Letter" Punishments for Probationers

One of the recent trends in sentencing is the imposition of "scarlet letter" punishments, in which the defendant must submit to some form of public humiliation. The following noteworthy cases have received national attention:

- In Illinois, a defendant convicted of criminal battery was placed on probation and ordered to post a sign on his driveway stating: "A violent felon lives here. Travel at your own risk."
- In Boston, men caught soliciting prostitutes were sentenced to clean the streets under the district attorney's "Operation John Sweep" program.
- A South Carolina judge ordered a 15-year-old adolescent female shackled to her mother for a month as punishment for various petty crimes.
- A thief in Texas was sentenced to shovel horse manure, and another was sentenced to carry a sign in front of a bookstore stating, "I stole from this store."
- In Milwaukee, a convicted drunk driver was offered a reduced jail sentenced if he agreed to walk through the business district wearing a sandwich board proclaiming his crime.
- In Houston, a man who was convicted of domestic violence was forced to apologize at the entrance to city hall.

> ...a defendant ... was...ordered to post a sign on his driveway stating: "A violent felon lives here. Travel at your own risk."

Shaming punishment usually arises when a defendant qualifies for a prison term but instead is sentenced to probation. The return of public humiliation punishments raises two questions: Will they be upheld in appellate courts? Are they more effective than existing methods of punishment?

There is some evidence that shaming sentences will survive legal challenge and will likely gain in popularity over the next several years. Little hard data supports the effectiveness of shaming sentences.

CRITICAL THINKING QUESTIONS

What is your reaction to humiliating offenders who have been sentenced to probation? Why have shaming punishments that were long ago relegated to the dustbin of history been revived in courtrooms across the United States? How would you like to be sentenced with a scarlet letter punishment? Would it be effective with you? Do you believe it would be effective with most offenders?

Source: Douglas Litowitz, "The Trouble with 'Scarlet Letter' Punishments," *Judicature* 81 (September–October 1997), pp. 52–53.

community-based supervision can spark instantaneous withdrawal of support for community-based interventions. The publicity of criminal offenses committed by offenders sentenced to community-based corrections in other jurisdictions can even erode the basis of long-standing support for community-based corrections.

Technocorrections and the Uncertain Threats

Electronic tracking and location systems, pharmacological treatments, and the possibility of genetic and neurobiological risk assessments are the technologies that are most likely to be found in corrections during the first few decades of the twenty-first century. The use of "technocorrections" appears to be on the rise as correctional bureaucrats involved in community-based corrections attempt to find more cost-effective ways to increase public safety.[22]

Electronic tracking has been used since the 1980s. Electronic monitoring with bracelets that communicate through a device connected to telephone lines or newer versions based on cellular or satellite technology are used in most states. Soon, the technology should be able to furnish to potential victims tracking devices that trigger alarms or warning notices on the approach of an offender. Tiny cameras could also be integrated into tracking devices to provide live video of offenders' locations and circumstances.[23]

Pharmacological treatments, including new drugs, are being developed to control behavior in correctional and noncorrectional settings. In 1996, California passed a law requiring chemical castration of repeat child offenders. This law provides that any person convicted twice of specified sexual offenses in which the victim is under 13 must receive medroxy progesterone actate (identified as Depo-Provera) treatment on being released on parole. Administered by injection, what the medication does is lower the testosterone level and blunt the sex drive. Georgia, Florida, Texas, and Wisconsin are other states that either allow or require chemical castration for sex offenders.

It is only a matter of time before research findings will lead to the development of drugs to control neurobiological processes, including the management of violence and the prevention of violence.

Gene management technologies, presently widely used in medicine, will probably be used in corrections in assessment tools using genetic or neurobiological profiles to identify children who have a propensity toward violence, sex offending, or addiction. Once under correctional control, "offenders could be identified, on the basis of such testing and risk assessment, as likely violent recidivists. The group so classified could be placed under closer surveillance or declared a danger to themselves and society and be civilly committed to special facilities for indeterminate periods."[24]

Although the rapid expansion of technocorrections may increase public safety, these technologies also pose a threat to a democratic society, for they may be used in ways inconsistent with constitutional or ethical standards. The challenge will be to make optimal use of them without losing essential freedoms, increasing regimentation, and building an apparatus of control for the state to abuse.[25] It would probably be wise to heed Charles Edgley and Dennis Brisset's warning: "The more we ask government to meddle into the lives of others, the closer we get to creating an apparatus that will in all likelihood eventually meddle into our own."[26]

Residential Staff in Community-Based Corrections

The line staff member of state, local, and private residential programs does not have an easy job.[27] Low pay, long hours, hectic work schedules, and lack of appreciation from

The staffs of residential programs, such as these correctional professionals at a halfway house for offenders, are among those who actually make community-based corrections work. What opportunities and challenges do these staffs face with their clients? What opportunities and challenges do they face with the communities in which they work?

clients are among the reasons for high staff turnover and burnout. In privately administered residential programs, line staff members are usually paid less well than they would be in state residential programs.

Line staff in residential programs face problems comparable to those of line staff in correctional institutions. They are, after all, running a 24-hour-a-day, 7-day-a-week operation. They also are charged with providing services to residents. Furthermore, like institutional staff, they face problems with the physical facility, as when the heating unit breaks down or when the pipes freeze. Residential and institutional line staffs both work with the losers of the system. The "cream of the crop" tends to remain on regular probation or receive parole; those placed in residential programs often have few resources and no employment history. Yet residential staff do not have the physical control over offenders that institutional staff have over their inmates. This leads to problems because residents usually have the freedom to leave the halfway house for part of the day and to be exposed to the temptations of the community. In probation referrals, the family and friends of residents are still in the immediate area, and they are often the source of the offenders' problems.

Unlike prison line staff, who work in an environment in which life is fairly predictable, residential staff must function daily on a very irregular routine. In small facilities they usually are alone after 5 to 6 o'clock in the evening, and even in larger ones, there are usually not more than two staff members on the premises after 6 o'clock.

Counselors also do not have easy jobs. The limited size of residential programs builds into the job an intensity that is usually not found in a prison job; nor do probation or parole officers face the intensity of working with the same small caseload on a daily basis. Moreover, residential counselors hear complaints from clients so frequently that it is sometimes difficult to recognize a legitimate complaint. The most important skill that counselors or caseworkers possess is the ability to listen to and communicate with residents.

Directors and assistant directors are the top-level staff responsible for administrative duties, supervision of staff, and making decisions concerning residents.[28] Administrative duties include preparing monthly, quarterly, and annual reports on program performance. Monthly billing reports must be submitted to various funding agencies; these reports are frequently sent to the executive offices for agencywide billing by the business manager. Other duties include liaison work with other criminal justice and mental health agencies and speaking engagements outside the facility. Budget planning and review are also important, although final approval usually comes from an executive director.

Staff supervision can sometimes be very frustrating and may cause more problems for the director than any other task. The director often must learn to adjust job descriptions to staff needs and abilities, which may mean that he or she must delegate some of his or her own responsibilities. The maintenance of the house is assigned to staff and residents, but ensuring that everything is clean, safe, and in good repair is a big job.

Making decisions concerning disciplinary action toward residents is the third major responsibility of top-level staff. These decisions will often affect a resident's freedom. For example, a bad disciplinary report to a probation officer may result in the revocation of probation and the imposition of a prison sentence.

Nevertheless, directors and assistant directors usually like their jobs. They complain about the frustrations, the long hours, the dubious capability of line staff, and the way the job interferes with their lives. Still, there are many satisfactions in this work: The possibility for personal growth is unlimited. Considerable professional freedom is possible, because the job permits a casual lifestyle. Morale is enhanced because the director and assistant director can assume "ownership" of the program.

HOW HAS THE VICTIMS' RIGHTS MOVEMENT AFFECTED COMMUNITY-BASED CORRECTIONS?

The rights of victims is one of the most critical issues in corrections. The public has become incensed because victimization occurs so frequently in the United States; indeed, 31 million criminal victimizations took place in 1999: about 21.2 million property crimes (motor vehicle theft, burglary, and household theft), 7.4 million violent crimes (rape or sexual assault, aggravated assault, robbery, and simple assault), and about 0.2 million personal thefts (purse snatching and pocket picking). The 31 million victimizations in 1999 actually represented a decline from 35 million victimizations in 1997 and continued a downward trend that began in 1994.[29]

During the 1980s, a number of grassroots groups called attention to the needs and rights of victims. The women's movement brought national attention to the victims of rape and spouse abuse and was influential in developing rape crisis centers and domestic violence shelters for women and children. Established in 1978, Parents of Murdered Children focuses on the needs of the next-of-kin of murder victims and provides peer counseling. Mothers against Drunk Driving (MADD), founded in 1980, advocates stiff punishment for intoxicated drivers. As a result of these grassroots movements, as many as four thousand programs were helping crime victims cope with victimization and the complexities of criminal justice.[30]

The passage of the Crime Control Act of 1990 was a major gain for victims' rights. An important component of this act was the Victims' Rights and Restitution Act, which required specific actions and spelled out the responsibilities of federal employees dealing with crime victims.[31] A noteworthy feature of the Victims' Rights and

Restitution Act was the Crime Victims' Bill of Rights. It gives a crime victim the following rights:

1. The right to be treated with fairness and with respect for the victim's dignity and privacy
2. The right to be reasonably protected from the accused offender
3. The right to be notified of court proceedings
4. The right to be present at all public court proceedings related to the offense unless the court determines that testimony by the victim would be materially affected if the victim heard other testimony at trial
5. The right to confer with attorney for the government in the case
6. The right to restitution
7. The right to information about the conviction, sentencing, imprisonment, and release of the offender

In the 1990s, all fifty states adopted a victims' bill of rights that identified basic rights' and protections for victims of crime. Twenty-nine of the states went on to adopt a constitutional amendment for victims' rights.[32] The scope of these provisions varies but usually includes the following rights:

- Attendance at and participation in criminal justice proceedings
- Notification of the stages and proceedings in the criminal justice process
- Notification of other legal remedies
- Protection from harassment and intimidation
- Confidentiality of records
- Prompt return of victims' personal property seized as evidence in the criminal justice process
- Availability of offenders' profits from the sale of the stories of their crimes
- Victim compensation and restitution[33]

The **victims' rights movement** has impacted community-based corrections in several ways. Corrections departments are increasingly mandated to provide programs for victims. Financial restitution and community service projects are now commonly ordered by the court as a condition of probation and are becoming increasingly required at other points in the criminal justice process. Furthermore, the fear of victimization has made it more difficult to establish halfway houses, work-release centers, and diversionary projects in a community. Citizens are now more willing to mobilize against the establishment of such programs. In addition, victims are increasingly becoming part of criminal justice decision making. In some jurisdictions, when probation officers prepare presentence investigative reports (see Chapter 6), these reports may contain victim-impact statements as well as the defendant's version of what took place.

SUMMARY

Community-based corrections consists of probation, intermediate sanctions, parole, and reentry programs. In the early 1970s, reformers recommended that all but violent offenders receive corrections in the community. Some students of corrections even predicted that correctional institutions would soon be a relic of the past.

But the late 1970s were not good years for community-based corrections. Residential programs and parole were subjected to a great deal of criticism, and reentry programs were dramatically reduced in jurisdiction after jurisdiction across the nation. Probation and pretrial diversion programs held their own, but they, too, were under attack. A few states passed Community Corrections Acts and made the establishment of strong community-based programs one of their priorities. Sweeping offenders out of the way and into institutions was still the choice of many states.

The reality of community-based corrections in the 1990s was quite different from the 1970s rhetoric of the community-based movement. Community-based corrections in the 1990s developed a new mission based on intensive surveillance. It included an emphasis on intensive supervision, electronic monitoring and house arrest, substance abuse, screening and classification systems, intermediate sanctions, and bureaucratic efficiency and accountability. The implementation of its mission requires that community programs deal with crowded caseloads, programs, and facilities without sacrificing delivery of services; expand intermediate sanctions without sacrificing community safety; and respond to the rising demand for victims' rights without sacrificing needed programs.

KEY TERMS

aftercare, p. 97
Community Corrections Act, p. 100
diversionary programs, p. 97
house arrests, p. 99
**Law Enforcement Assistance Administrations
   (LEAA),** p. 97

parole, p. 96
probation, p. 96
reintegrative philosophy, p. 98
release on own recognizance (ROR), p. 106
residential programs, p. 97
victims' rights movement, p. 114

CRITICAL THINKING QUESTIONS

1. You have been elected to the state senate of the populous state of New Scotland, and you chair the Judiciary Committee. The commissioner of corrections will testify today on a bill to adopt a version of the Minnesota Community Corrections Act. New Scotland has a high rate of crime, and all the prisons are badly overcrowded. What questions will you and other committee members ask the commissioner to justify passage of this legislation?

2. Several states legislate and fund extensive community correctional programs. Would you favor payments to counties that send fewer offenders to state prisons?

3. What community-based corrections options are available in your county?

4. You are the administrator in charge of the new John Augustus House. Many neighbors do not want this halfway house nearby because they fear that such a concentration of criminals poses a threat to public safety. What steps will you take to reassure the public and gain better acceptance?

WEB DESTINATIONS

The National Institute of Community Corrections of the U.S. Department of Justice. This site reports on the activities, technical services, and publications of the NIC (National Institute of Corrections) Division.
http://www.nicic.org/inst/nicccd.htm

Explanation and assessment of the benefits of a successful county-administered community corrections program in Indiana.
http://www.county.tippecanoe.in.us/departments/cc/

Colorado Adult Criminal Justice System Research. This address to the Colorado General Assembly reports on the effectiveness of Colorado's community corrections programs.
**http://www.state.co.us/gov_dir/leg_dir/lcsstaff/research/
PRISON.html**

Vermont's program of core skills for correctional officers involved in community-based corrections. This site provides practical information about community-based correctional programs for adult and juvenile offenders and professional training for correctional officers.
http://www.neias.org/VTC00course.html

FOR FURTHER READING

Cohen, Stanley. *Visions of Social Control.* Cambridge, England: Polity Press, 1985. Cohen's analysis of social control is required reading for the corrections student. Cohen provides insights that are essential to an understanding of community-based and institutional corrections.

DiMascio, William M. *Seeking Justice: Crime and Punishment in America.* New York: Edna McConnell Clark Foundation, 1995. Long acknowledged as a supporter of community-based programs, this foundation provides one of the best overviews of community-based corrections.

Harris, M. Kay. "Key Differences among Community Corrections Acts in the United States: An Overview." *The Prison Journal* 76 (June 1996), pp. 192–234. An excellent overview of the origins and development of Community Corrections Acts across the nation.

Petersilia, Joan. "Probation in the United States." In *Crime and Justice: A Review of Research* 22, edited by Michael Tonry, pp. 149–200. Chicago: University of Chicago Press, 1997. Petersilia, who has established herself as one of the foremost authorities on community-based corrections, is particularly helpful in this chapter on charting out the unrealized potential in probation.

NOTES

1. "Jennifer's Story" is found in the Talbert House 1999 annual report (Cincinnati: Talbert House, 2000), p. 5.

2. Robert B. Coates, "A Working Paper on Community-Based Corrections: Concept, Historical Development, Impact, and Potential Dangers" (paper presented at the Massachusetts Standards and Goals Conference, November 1974), pp. 3–4.

3. John Augustus, *A Report of the Labors of John Augustus,* bicentennial ed., preface by Milton G. Rector, foreword to the 1939 ed. by Sheldon Glueck (Lexington, Ken.). American Probation and Parole Association, 1984; originally published in 1852.

4. President's Commission on Law Enforcement and Administration of Justice, *Task Force Report: Juvenile Delinquency* (Washington, D.C.: U.S. Government Printing Office, 1967), p. 2.

5. President's Commission on Law Enforcement and Administration of Justice, *Task Force Report: Corrections* (Washington, D.C.: U.S. Government Printing Office, 1967), p. 7.

6. National Advisory Commission on Criminal Justice Standards and Goals, *Corrections* (Washington, D.C.: U.S. Government Printing Office, 1973), p. 121.

7. President's Commission on Law Enforcement and Administration of Justice, *Task Force Report: Corrections;* National Advisory Commission on Criminal Justice Standards and Goals, *Corrections.*

8. For an excellent summary of intensive probation projects, house arrests, and electronic monitoring programs, see Joan Petersilia, *Expanding Options for Criminal Sentencing* (Santa Monica, Calif.: Rand, 1987).

9. Edward E. Rhine, William R. Smith, and Ronald W. Jackson, *Paroling Authorities and Current Practice: Recent History* (Waldorf, Md.: American Correctional Association, 1991), pp. 122–139.

10. Patrick D. McManus and Lynn Zeller Barclay, *Community Corrections Act: Technical Assistance Manual* (College Park, Md.: American Correctional Association, 1994), p. 12.

11. M. Kay Harris, "Key Differences among Community Corrections Acts in the United States: An Overview," *The Prison Journal* 76 (June 1996), p. 202.

12. Ibid., p. 199.

13. This account of the Community Corrections Act in Minnesota is adapted from "A State Report, April 1978, The Community Corrections Act" (St. Paul, Minn.), pp. 1–4.

14. Information received in a 1990 interview with Jeff Martin, coordinator of the Community Corrections Act in Minnesota.

15. David Boorkman, et al., *An Exemplary Project: Community-Based Corrections, in Des Moines* (Washington, D.C.: U.S. Department of Justice, 1976), pp. 1–4.

16. State of Iowa Webpage, 2000.

17. Washington County, Oregon, Webpage, 8 August 2000.

18. See "The Salvation Army Conquers Florida," *Corrections Magazine* (February 1983), pp. 40–41.

19. James S. Granelli, "Presentence Reports Go Private," *National Law Journal,* 2 May 1983, p. 9.

20. Dismas House Webpage, 26 August 2000.

21. Talbert House brochure, 2000.

22. This account of technocorrections is adapted from Tony Fabelo, " 'Technocorrections': The Promises, the Uncertain Threats," *Sentencing and Corrections: Issues for the 21st Century* (Washington, D.C.: U.S. Department of Justice, 2000).

23. Ibid., p. 2.

24. Ibid., p. 3.

25. Ibid., p. 6.

26. Cited ibid., p. 5, and found in Charles Edgley and Dennis Brisset, *A Nation of Meddlers* (Boulder, Colo.: Westview, 1999).

27. Stanley Swart, a former director of the Young Men's Fellowship of Lake County, Illinois, provided materials on line staff in residential settings.

28. Neil F. Tilow, president of Talbert House for Men, Cincinnati, Ohio, provided materials on top-level staff.

29. Bureau of Justice Statistics, *Criminal Victimization 1999: Changes 1998–1999 with Trends 1993–1999* (Washington, D.C.: U.S. Department of Justice; Bureau of Justice Statistics, 2000), p. 1.

30. Peter Finn and Beverly N. W. Lee, "Establishing and Expanding Victim-Assistance Programs" (Washington, D.C.: National Institute of Justice, 1988).

31. William G. Doerner and Steven P. Lab, *Victimology* (Cincinnati: Anderson, 1995), p. 215.

32. National Victim Center, *Rights of Crime Victims* (Washington, D.C.: U.S. Department of Justice, 1998).

33. Ibid.

CHAPTER 5 / BUILT-IN STUDY GUIDE

Multiple Choice Questions

1. Probation, intermediate sanctions, parole, and reentry programs make up:

    A. Community-based corrections
    B. Reintegrative approaches
    C. Community supervision project
    D. Diversion programs

2. What is the type of sentence that requires offenders to remain confined in their own residences for the length of their sentences?

    A. House conditions of probation
    B. House arrest
    C. Residential supervision
    D. Home detention

3. All of the following are components of correctional services provided by the Des Moines program except:

    A. Pretrial release
    B. Supervised release
    C. Community corrections facility
    D. Work furlough programs

4. Line staff in residential programs face problems:

    A. Related to the demographics of the community
    B. Comparable to those of line staff in correctional institutions
    C. Unique to the population they supervise
    D. Related to budgetary constraints

5. During 1999 how many criminal victimizations occurred in America?

    A. 31 million
    B. 21 million
    C. 25 million
    D. 35 million

6. What ignited the growth of community-based corrections during the late 1960s and 1970s?

    A. Vietnam War
    B. Prison overcrowding
    C. Civil Rights Movement
    D. Political support

7. All of the following mandates influenced the operation of community-based corrections except:

    A. Political mandate
    B. Legal mandate
    C. Social mandate
    D. Correctional mandate

8. Which of the following is the most important skill that counselors or caseworkers can possess?

    A. Ability to write reports on residents
    B. Ability to listen to and communicate with residents
    C. Ability to classify residents
    D. Ability to supervise residents

9. Which of the following pieces of legislation signified a major gain in victims' rights?

    A. Crime Control Act of 1990
    B. Community-Based Corrections Act of 1992
    C. Domestic Violence Act of 1990
    D. Mothers Against Drunk Drivers Act of 1990

10. In the 1970s, all of the following were widely used pretrial diversion programs for adults except:

    A. Mediation programs
    B. Deferred prosecution programs
    C. Treatment alternatives to street crime programs
    D. Day reporting centers

True/False Questions

T F   1. Electronic monitoring and house arrest are being used more frequently as ways to enhance supervision of offenders.

T F   2. Parole supervision is administered at the county level in every state that still conducts parole services.

T F   3. All community-based corrections programs that are sponsored by the community are administered by the court system and funded by the county.

T F   4. Electronic monitoring operates with bracelets that communicate through a device connected to a telephone line or more modern versions are used in most states.

T F   5. Currently, private vendors are not offering any probation services in the United States.

T F   6. Community-based corrections is an appropriate intervention when it places enough supervision and control on offenders to not jeopardize public safety.

T F   7. The Probation and Parole Division of Washington County, Oregon, is divided into seven teams that provide specialized services to specific populations of offenders.

T F   8. The most distinguishing feature of community-based correctional programs is the quality of staff that works in these facilities.

T F   9. Approaches to community-based corrections were the same in the 1990s as they were in the 1970s.

T F   10. Diversion programs fall into the category of community-based corrections.

Fill-in-the-Blank Questions

(based on key terms)

1. _____ has been the most frequently used punishment during the twentieth century.

2. The release of rehabilitated inmates from prison back into the community is known as _____.

3. During the late 1960s and 1970s, _____ were designed to provide community housing for probationers struggling to comply with traditional probation and high-risk parolees being released from prison.

4. A perspective that supports returning offenders to the community as law-abiding citizens is known as the _____.

5. As a result of increasing levels of criminal victimization occurring in this country, the _____ is one of the most critical issues in corrections.

6. When a state government grants funds to local units of government for planning, development, and delivery of corrections services and sanctions a _____ has occurred.

Essay Questions

1. Explain how community-based corrections changed from the late nineteenth century to the present.

2. What is the reintegrative philosophy? Explain how the reintegrative philosophy has influenced community-based corrections.

3. Identify and describe four of the major themes that form the new mission of community-based corrections.

4. Explain how political, legal, and social mandates influence the functions of community-based corrections.

5. Describe two significant events of the victim's rights movement. Also, explain how the victim's rights movement has influenced community-based corrections.

ANSWERS

Multiple Choice Questions

1. A
2. B
3. D
4. B
5. A
6. D
7. D
8. B
9. A
10. D

True/False Questions

1. T
2. F
3. F
4. T
5. F
6. T
7. T
8. F
9. F
10. T

Fill-in-the-Blank Questions

1. Probation
2. Parole
3. Residential programs
4. Reintegrative philosophy
5. Rights of victims
6. Community Corrections Act

Probation

A probation officer tells an account of probation that had a very positive outcome:

> One success story I remember is a 17-year-old black girl who had been arrested on first-degree robbery and prostitution. She had never been referred before. What it came down to was there were two juvenile girls with two adult males who were their boyfriends, and they were in a bar trying to shake down this white guy. The girls got him up to their apartment, and they were going to get it on with him. Then their boyfriends came up and were real mad because he was with their women. The white guy said, "Take anything," and they took some money he had in his car. The robbery charge was dropped, but there was a finding of fact on the prostitution charge. She was placed in supervision until her eighteenth birthday. When I got her, the first thing we did was go out to the hospital's family practice center to have her checked and placed on birth control. But she was already pregnant. The majority of time we spent together was concentrated on job, education, getting ready for the baby, and independent living skills. It wasn't a traditional probation case. We spent a lot of time together, getting ready for her future. Her mother was dead, and her father was in the Mental Health Institute. Several older sisters were already on ADC [Aid to Dependent Children], weren't married, and were not models by any means. So I felt like I'm the one she counted on. I took her to the hospital when she had her baby and was with her during delivery. It was a neat experience. She asked me to be the godmother for her baby. She's now very motivated to make something out of herself. She is now 19, has her own car, and keeps an apartment fairly well. She has either gone to school or worked since before she had the baby. With what she has had to work with, it's amazing she is doing so well."[1]

What was there about this experience that made the probation officer feel so good about it? How frequently do you think a probation officer becomes such a source of support for a probationer?

Probation is the same as, yet different from, the way it has always been. Probation continues to be a correctional service allowing an offender to remain in the community for the duration of a sentence under supervision by an officer of the court and requiring the offender to comply with whatever conditions the court imposes. Probation continues to be the most widely used correctional option. The goal and the benefit of probation have not changed. Its goal is to promote law-abiding behavior by the offender. Its benefit is

Table 6.1

Adults on Probation, 1999

Region and Jurisdiction	1/1/99	Probation Population 1999		12/31/99	Percent Change during 1999	Number on Probation on 12/31/99 per 100,000 Adult Residents
		Entries	Exits			
U.S. Total	3,670,591	1,819,403	1,714,630	3,773,624	2.8%	1,864
Federal	33,390	14,571	14,793	32,816	−1.7%	16
State	3,637,201	1,804,832	1,699,837	3,740,808	2.8	1,848
Northeast	572,832	195,038	187,977	575,270	0.4%	1,465
Connecticut	55,000	30,000	29,930	55,070	0.1	2,244
Maine	6,953	5,379	4,808	7,524	8.2	782
Massachusetts[a]	46,567	40,676	40,976	46,267	−0.6	983
New Hampshire	5,175	:	:	3,160	...	...
New Jersey[a]	129,377	58,500	59,543	128,634	−0.6	2,095
New York[a]	178,612	45,618	40,544	183,686	2.8	1,335
Pennsylvania[a,b]	121,094	1,072	623	118,635	−2.0	1,298
Rhode Island	21,049	7,972	7,268	21,753	3.3	2,902
Vermont	9,005	5,821	4,286	10,541	17.1	2,320
Midwest	849,703	458,923	436,681	871,319	2.5%	1,858
Illinois	131,850	58,695	56,275	134,270	1.8	1,501
Indiana[a]	104,624	87,517	86,270	105,871	1.2	2,399
Iowa[a]	18,447	18,863	17,635	19,675	6.7	915
Kansas	17,219	21,090	20,542	17,767	3.2	909
Michigan[a]	170,997	69,124	69,210	170,978	**	2,341
Minnesota	100,818	60,872	58,164	104,615	3.8	2,986
Missouri	49,992	26,037	23,536	52,493	5.0	1,290
Nebraska	16,527	19,095	15,160	20,462	...	1,674
North Dakota	2,726	1,620	1,617	2,729	0.1	576
Ohio[a,c]	178,830	68,480	60,661	184,867	5.2	2,198
South Dakota	3,441	3,064	3,044	3,461	0.6	647
Wisconsin	54,232	24,466	24,567	54,131	−0.2	1,387
South	1,503,679	837,091	783,397	1,556,507	3.5%	2,170
Alabama	40,379	15,835	14,457	41,757	3.4	1,264
Arkansas	28,698	8,537	6,755	30,840	6.2	1,612

Note: Because of nonresponse or incomplete data, the probation population for some jurisdictions on 31 December 1999, does not equal the population on 1 January, 1999, plus entries, minus exits. During 1999 an estimated 2,042,500 persons entered probation supervision, and 1,927,700 exited, based on imputations for agencies which did not provide data.

: Not known.

... Comparable percentage or rate could not be calculated.

**Between −0.05% and 0.05%.

[a]Data do not include cases in one or more of the following categories: absconder, out of state, inactive, intensive supervision, or electronic monitoring.

keeping the adjudicated individual in the community, out of prison. What has changed is the means of achieving the desired goal. Probation is more hard-line than it used to be in the past. Its current emphasis is on risk control and risk reduction. Probation is no longer "soft" on crime; instead, it is committed to public safety. Accordingly, probation officers who personally deliver valued services to clients are increasingly rare.

Another sign of the changing nature of probation is judges' increasing willingness to impose a jail term along with probation. In Minnesota, 60 percent of persons sentenced to probation are required to serve some jail time. In California, nearly 80 percent of felons who are granted probation must also do jail time.[2] This jail time may be served on weekends or at night, or a specified term in jail may be followed by a period of probation.

The Bureau of Justice Statistics reports that 3,773,600 adult men and women were on probation in the United States on 1 January 2000—a 41.3 percent increase of adults on probation since 1990.[3] An examination of Table 6.1 reveals that the South utilizes probation

| Region and Jurisdiction | Probation Population | | | | Percent Change During 1999 | Number on Probation on 12/31/99 per 100,000 Adult Residents |
| | 1/1/99 | 1999 | | 12/31/99 | | |
		Entries	Exits			
Delaware	20,030	11,015	10,069	20,976	4.7	3,673
District of Columbia	11,234	10,877	9,265	12,129	8.0	2,863
Florida[a]	283,965	194,529	189,140	292,399	3.0	2,533
Georgia[a]	278,669	183,322	154,944	307,653	. . .	5,368
Kentucky[a]	17,594	16,848	12,311	18,988	7.9	634
Louisiana	33,028	14,425	12,335	35,118	6.3	1,104
Maryland	78,051	41,117	37,882	81,286	4.1	2,105
Mississippi[a]	11,530	5,748	4,830	12,448	8.0	618
North Carolina	105,227	59,195	59,327	105,095	−0.1	1,841
Oklahoma	29,093	12,257	13,213	27,997	−3.8	1,131
South Carolina	46,482	15,244	16,797	44,929	−3.3	1,534
Tennessee[a,d]	38,924	23,289	22,153	40,060	2.9	967
Texas	443,688	198,573	195,161	447,100	0.8	3,121
Virginia	30,576	26,280	24,758	32,098	5.0	616
West Virginia	6,511	:	:	5,994	−7.9	427
West	710,987	313,780	291,782	737,712	3.8%	1,653
Alaska[a]	4,274	1,795	1,552	4,517	5.7	1,069
Arizona	51,329	32,611	26,864	57,076	11.2	1,657
California	324,427	162,543	152,604	332,414	2.5	1,372
Colorado[a]	45,502	26,601	26,613	45,339	−0.4	1,516
Hawaii	15,711	7,228	7,232	15,707	**	1,753
Idaho	31,172	2,970	3,033	36,705	17.7	4,073
Montana[a]	5,358	1,102	634	5,906	10.2	896
Nevada	12,561	:	:	11,787	−6.2	894
New Mexico[a]	10,397	8,850	7,956	11,291	8.6	907
Oregon	44,809	17,140	16,459	45,490	1.5	1,828
Utah	9,482	3,843	3,899	9,426	−0.6	663
Washington[a]	152,140	47,213	43,088	158,213	4.0	3,705
Wyoming	3,825	1,884	1,848	3,841	0.4	1,089

[b]Entries and exits do not include county data.

[c]Percent change in probation population during 1999 excludes 134 local probation agencies for which a single population estimate was obtained for 31 December 1999.

[d]Data are for the period beginning 1 May 1999, and ending 30 April 2000.

Source: Bureau of Justice Statistics, *Probation and Parole, 1999* (Washington, D.C.: U.S. Government Printing Office, 2000), p. 4.

more than the other regions of the nation. Texas's probation population of 447,100 led the nation, followed by California, 332,414; Georgia, 307,653; Florida, 292,399; New York, 183,686; Michigan, 170,978; and Washington, 158,213. Eight states registered a 10 percent or more increase in their adult probation population in 1998; Idaho had the largest increase at 17.7 percent, and Vermont was second with 17.1 percent. Eleven states reported a decrease in 1999, led by West Virginia, down 7.9 percent, and Nevada, down 6.2 percent.

HOW DID PROBATION ORIGINATE AND DEVELOP?

Probation in the United States began with the innovative work of John Augustus, a Boston cobbler. He spent considerable time in the courtroom, and in 1841 he asked the judge to defer sentencing for a man whose offenses were "yielding to his appetite for strong drink" for three weeks and release the man to his custody.[4] At the end of the three weeks, the offender convinced the judge of his reform and received a small fine.

From this first probation client, Augustus devoted the remainder of his life (he died in 1859) to the cause of probation. He became convinced that many lawbreakers needed only the interest and concern of another person to be able to straighten out their lives. Augustus worked with women and children as well as with men. He was willing to work with all types of offenders—drunkards, petty thieves, prostitutes, and felons—as long as he met a contrite heart. He bailed out over eighteen hundred individuals in the Boston courts, making himself liable to the sum of $243,234.[5] He also initiated such services as investigation and screening, supervision of probationers, interviewing, and arranging for relief, employment, and education—all of which are provided today. He further made impartial reports to the court.

The state of Massachusetts, much impressed with Augustus's work, established a system of visiting probation agents in 1869 to assist both youths and adults. The philosophy of this system was that first offenders showing definite promise should be released to probation. Probation was regulated by statute for the first time in 1878, when the mayor of Boston was authorized to appoint to the police force a paid probation officer to serve under the police chief. In 1880, the authority to appoint probation officers was extended to all cities and towns in Massachusetts. By 1890, probation had become statewide, and the authority to appoint rested with the courts rather than with municipal authorities. In 1901, New York passed the first statute authorizing probation for adult offenders. Soon thereafter, Vermont, Missouri, Illinois, Minnesota, Rhode Island, and New Jersey enacted probation statutes. By 1956, all states had adopted juvenile and adult probation laws.

In the twentieth century, probation developed haphazardly and with no real thought about its mission. From the start, there was tension between law enforcement and probation agencies because of the rehabilitation purposes of probation. Tasks were continually added to probation's responsibilities, even though funding remained the same or declined.[6] For example, a 1979 survey found that probation departments were responsible for more than fifty different activities, including court-related civil functions (minority-age marriage investigations and step-parent adoption investigations).[7] In the Timeline, Joan Petersilia reveals the significant events in the development of probation in the United States.

WHAT IS THE PRESENT LANDSCAPE OF PROBATION?

The conditions of probation vary from jurisdiction to jurisdiction and may also vary to meet the personal situation of particular offenders. The payment of fines, restitution to victims, community service assignments, random urine and alcohol testing, and regular

timeline

Significant Events in the Development of U.S. Probation

Date	Event
1841	John Augustus introduces probation in Boston.
1878	Massachusetts is the first state to adopt probation for juveniles.
1878–1938	Thirty-seven states, the District of Columbia, and the federal government pass juvenile and adult probation laws.
1927	All states but Wyoming have juvenile probation laws.
1954	All states have juvenile probation laws.
1956	All states have adult probation laws (Mississippi became the last state to pass authorizing legislation).
1973	National Advisory Commission on Criminal Justice Standards and Goals endorses more extensive use of probation.
1973	Minnesota became the first state to adopt a Community Corrections Act; 18 states followed by 1995.
1974	Martinson's widely publicized research purportedly proves that probation does not work.
1975	U.S. Department of Justice conducts the first census of U.S. probationers.
1975	Wisconsin implements first probation case classification system.
1976	U.S. Comptroller General's study of U.S. probation concludes it is a "system in crisis" due to inadequate funding.
1982	Georgia's intensive supervision probation program claims to reduce recidivism and costs.
1983	Electronic monitoring of offenders begins in New Mexico, followed by larger program in Florida.
1985	Rand Corporation releases study of felony probationers showing high failure rates; replications follow, showing that probation services and effectiveness vary widely across the nation.
1989	General Accounting Office survey shows all fifty states have adopted intensive probation and other intermediate sanction programs.
1991	U.S. Department of Justice funds nationwide intensive supervision demonstration and evaluation.
1993	Program evaluations show probation without adequate surveillance and treatment is ineffective, but well-managed and adequately funded programs reduce recidivism.

Source: Joan Petersilia, "Probation in the United States," in *Crime and Justice: A Review of Research* 21, ed. Michael Tonry (Chicago: University of Chicago Press, 1997), p. 158.

employment are common requirements. For special conditions imposed on adult felony and misdemeanor probationers, see Table 6.2. Fees/fines/costs and drug testing and treatment are particularly widely used special conditions by the courts. In addition, **financial restitution** and **community service** are also conditions placed on probationers by many courts. The use of restitution actually predates both incarceration and modern forms of community treatment; the current trend is toward a more purposeful and imaginative

Table 6.2

Special Conditions of Probations

| | Percent of Adults on Probation | | |
	Total	Felony	Misdemeanor
Total	100 %	100 %	100 %
Offense			
Violent	17.3%	19.5%	13.5%
Property	28.9	36.6	18.2
Drug	21.4	30.7	7.6
Public-order	31.1	12.1	59.6
Criminal history			
None	49.9%	49.2%	52.1%
Priors	50.1	50.8	47.9
Juvenile	9.0	10.3	5.6
Adult	45.1	45.1	44.3
Type of sentence			
Probation only	49.8%	45.7%	54.8%
Split	50.2	54.3	45.2
Jail	37.3	36.5	38.3
Prison	15.3	20.6	9.0
Special conditions			
Any	98.6%	98.4%	98.9%
Fees/fines/costs	84.3	84.2	85.1
Drug testing	32.5	43.0	17.1
Drug/alcohol treatment	41.0	37.5	45.7
Employment	34.7	40.9	27.3
Community service	25.7	27.3	24.0

Source: Bureau of Justice Statistics, *Characteristics of Adults on Probation, 1995* (Washington, D.C.: U.S. Department of Justice, 1997), p. 1.

use of restitution. At times, the victim is even involved with the offender in the development of restitution agreements.[8]

Probation orders usually put offenders under supervision for a set period of time. Probationers must report to a probation officer as often as required. They must keep him or her informed of changes in their circumstances, especially as to contacts with the police, employment, address, marital status, and income or indebtedness.

Some jurisdictions allow a **deferred sentence.** This variation delays conviction on a guilty plea until the completion of a term of probation, at which time the offender withdraws the guilty plea. The court dismisses the charge, thereby clearing the offender's record of a conviction. This procedure is not the same as pretrial diversion, because a probation officer supervises the offender when the deferred sentence is imposed by a judge; in pretrial diversion the offender is diverted from the system.

Other jurisdictions suspend a prison sentence ordered after formal conviction, allowing the offender to serve the sentence in the community while on probation. The judge actually pronounces the sentence but then suspends it and places the offender on probation. Shock probation calls for the shock of a few weeks in prison for a first-time offender followed by a standard term of probation.

In addition to these legal variations, two other types of probation are used in the United States. Some jurisdictions permit bench, or supervised probation, especially with misdemeanants (persons convicted of a misdemeanor). The **split sentence** is also used by some jurisdictions: Offenders spend a period of time in jail before being placed on probation in the community, or they are sentenced to so many weekends in jail while remaining in the community on probation status during the week. Under **intensive probation,** a probationer is supervised far more strictly than under standard services. The skyrocketing increase in the number of defendants placed on probation across the nation is partly explained by the fact that courts now are sentencing to probation many more convicted felons than they did in the past. Intensive probation receives more attention in Chapter 7, on intermediate sanctions.

Wide variability exists in the use of probation across the nation. One study of thirty-two jurisdictions found that the numbers receiving probation varied from 30 percent in New York County (Manhattan) to 75 percent in Hennepin County (Minneapolis). This study suggested that some of the variation is due to the sentencing laws under which these jurisdictions function. Courts in states with determinate sentencing (without a parole board) typically use probation more frequently than do courts in states with indeterminate sentencing (with a parole board). Judges may be less willing to sentence to prison when lengths of sentences are fixed.[9]

The variation in probation occurs in part because many probation departments supervise both probationers and parolees. The U.S. Probation Department supervises individuals placed on probation and those released from prison. Outside the Walls 6.1 is an account of a well-known computer criminal who was released from prison and placed on federal probation.

outside the walls 6.1

Kevin Mitnick and His Adjustment to Federal Probation

Federal authorities have ordered Kevin Mitnick to get off the lecture circuit or risk going back to prison. Mitnick previously served a five-year prison term for cyber crimes related to the theft of software and altering of computer information at technology companies and institutions across the country.

"They're saying I can no longer write or speak about technology issues," Mitnick said after federal authorities notified him through his probation officer to curtail the speaking engagements. "I think it is an abrogation of my First Amendment rights. . . . Probation is not supposed to be punitive."

Mitnick, 36, was one of the FBI's most wanted computer criminals when he was finally tracked to his Raleigh, N.C., apartment in 1995 after an exhaustive three-year manhunt. Under a plea bargain, he served time for only a fraction of the crimes he was accused of, but authorities believe he caused millions of dollars in damage to companies including Motorola, Novell, Nokia, and Sun Microsystems, and the University of Southern California.

Mitnick was released from prison in January under a plea bargaining agreement that bans him for three years from having any access to computers, cellular telephones, televisions, or any equipment that can be used for Internet access.

In ordering the ban, U.S. District Judge Mariana Pfaelzer said she thought Mitnick would be unable to earn anything above minimum wage.

> . . . Mitnick had $20,000 worth of speaking engagements scheduled through August

But the feds didn't count on Mitnick's status as a cyber world hero. A recent Internet report said Mitnick had $20,000 worth of speaking engagements scheduled through August [2000].

"They don't like the idea of my being like a celebrity," Mitnick said, "They're trying to chill my free speech in hopes that my notoriety will die down."

Mitnick said he has been trying to educate others about protecting themselves against cyberspace intrusions.

"This is good for the public and good for me because I feel productive," Mitnick said. "I recognize the errors of my past and I want to be productive."

Mitnick said probation officers have instructed him to find employment in a field totally unrelated to computers. He has refused.

"I'm not going to spend time and money educating myself in a new field when in two years I'll be off probation and can go back to computers," he said.

CRITICAL THINKING QUESTIONS

Does Mitnick have a case: Are his constitutional rights being violated? Is his statement that "Probation is not supposed to be punitive" correct?

Source: Reprinted from "Hacker Must Quit Lecturing or Face Return to Prison," *Fox News.Com.,* 28 April 2000.

Studies also reveal that judges seem to be more willing to place felons on probation when they perceive that the probation department is able to monitor the offender closely and that the resources of the community are able to address some of the offender's underlying problems. Arizona, Minnesota, and Washington, three states that widely use probation, are well known for delivering good probation supervision and for having the resources to provide adequate treatment and services.[10]

Joan Petersilia and Susan Turner's examination of felony probation in California revealed that in 75 percent of the cases individuals receiving probation could be distinguished from those receiving a prison sentence. They found that people sent to prison had two or more conviction counts (i.e., convicted on multiple charges), were on probation or parole at the time of the arrest, were drug addicts, or had seriously injured a victim or used a weapon during the commission of the offense.[11]

Risk Assessment and Increased Surveillance Models

In the 1980s and 1990s, probation came under criticism as a lenient measure that allowed offenders to escape their just deserts. In an attempt to convince the public, as well as policymakers, that probation could be "tougher" on criminals, probation administrators attempted to enter into a bureaucratic–managerial stage characterized by the effective control of probationers.[12] Malcolm Feeley and Jonathan Simon argue that the old penology goal of normalizing individual offenders has been replaced by new penology goals aimed at regulating groups of offenders.[13] This emerging bureaucratic–managerial stage of probation began to emphasize strategies that would better ensure public protection. The most widely used of these strategies have been the combination of probation and incarceration, intensive probation, and electronic monitoring and house arrest. Intensive probation and electronic monitoring and house arrest are examined in Chapter 7.

Considerations of public safety have also led most probation departments to develop classification systems for placing offenders under intensive, medium, or minimum supervision. Most of these instruments are modeled after the **Wisconsin classification system,** or the NIC Model Probation Client Classification and Case Management System.[14]

On the basis of an objectively scored, structured interview, the Wisconsin classification system assigns clients to appropriate casework groups. The classification interview covers 40 items dealing with probationers' attitudes toward their offense, the offense history, family and interpersonal relationships, current problems, and future plans. One or two open-ended questions are asked in each general area, followed by more specific questions designed to elicit detailed information. There are also 12 objective background and offense-history items, 5 behavior ratings (based on interview behavior), and 7 items calling for the agents' impressions of the probationers' most and least important problem areas.[15]

Probationers are assigned to one of four case-management treatment strategies: a selective intervention group, a casework/control group, an environmental structure group, and a limit-setting group.[16] The most prominent characteristic of probationers in the selective intervention group is that they tend to have relatively stable and prosocial lifestyles. The most prominent characteristic of probationers in the casework/control group is a general instability as evidenced by problems in the home, inability to hold a job, and a lack of goal-directedness. Probationers in the environmental structure group tend to allow themselves to be led by others because they are deficient in social and vocational skills. Probationers in the limit-setting group usually have had a long-term involvement in crime and, therefore, need ground rules, maximum supervision, and a redirection of their intellectual and social skills.

Under the Wisconsin system, each probationer is given a risk/needs assessment at regular intervals. The risk scale is derived from empirical studies that show certain factors to be good predictors of recidivism—such as prior arrest record, age at first conviction, the nature of the offense for which the probationer was convicted, and employment patterns.

The needs assessment focuses on indicators such as emotional stability, financial management, family relationships, and health. The scores derived from the risk/needs assessment are used to classify probationers by required level of supervision—intensive, medium, or minimum. These levels, in turn, impose corresponding restrictions on liberty and requirements for contact between offenders and probation staff. Reassessment of cases takes place at regular intervals, and the level of supervision may be increased or reduced.[17]

In October 1977, this classification system was first implemented in two probation and parole units in Wisconsin. The system has since received further modification and has been used in additional units throughout the state. The Wisconsin system is currently used in at least one hundred jurisdictions throughout the United States.[18]

HOW IS PROBATION ADMINISTERED?

How to administer probation has been a subject for debate for some time. Should the judicial or the executive branch of government administer probation? Should probation be within a state or a local administrative structure? Should probation and parole be administered separately, or should they be combined? Should states offer rewards in the form of revenue support or labor to local probation systems that comply with state standards?

The Organization of Probation

In about one-fourth of the states, probation is primarily a local responsibility, and the state is accountable only for providing financial support, setting standards, and arranging training courses. This locally based approach accounts for about two-thirds of all probationers supervised in the United States (see Figure 6.1 for the various probation

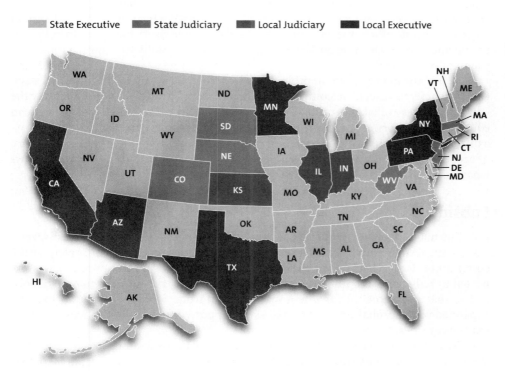

☐ State Executive   ■ State Judiciary   ■ Local Judiciary   ■ Local Executive

Figure 6.1
Administrative Structure of Adult and Juvenile Probation

Source: Source Book on Criminal Justice (Washington, D.C.: U.S. Department of Justice, 2000).

administrative structures in the states). District judges of the U.S. courts control federal probation services, but the probation division's administrative offices administer recruitment and training of personnel.

One of the most persuasive arguments for local administration of probation is that citizens and agencies of the community more readily support programs that are open to their participation and are responsive to local needs and problems. Another supporting argument is that small operations are more flexible, adjust more quickly to change, and are less encumbered by bureaucratic rigidity. Yet three arguments against local administration have won the support of many policymakers: (1) A state-administrated probation system can set standards of service, thereby ensuring uniformity of procedures, policies, and services. (2) A larger agency can make more effective use of funds and personnel. (3) Greater efficiency in the disposition of resources is possible when all probation officers are state employees.[19]

Those who favor judicial control of probation note that it is a service by which offenders are retained under the supervision of an officer of the court and subject to conditions imposed by the court. Revocation of probation and discharge from supervision are court functions. An important disadvantage to judicial control of probation is the widely varying tax base from county to county. An affluent metropolitan county will be able to support a competent probation department, but poor or rural counties will have trouble scraping up funds to support minimal services.

Assignment of probation to the executive branch on a statewide basis allows uniform standards of policymaking, recruitment, training, and personnel management. Coordination with the state department of corrections and with the parole service is also facilitated. The most significant disadvantage is the development of a large probation bureaucracy with echelons of decision makers shuffling memoranda from out-basket to in-basket with little contact with the real world of the streets. Firm leadership with a grasp of sound management procedures can prevent this dismal prospect.

Thirty states have executive branch agencies that provide both probation and parole services. Critics of the combined system argue that probationers, especially first-time offenders, should be kept separate from parolees and that probation is a service to judges and should be under their control. However, it is argued that a combined system conserves scarce resources and has greater public acceptance. A combined system requires only one office, one set of directives, and one supervisory hierarchy. In both probation and parole, the same goals are sought and the same skills are required for supervision of offenders.[20]

In sum, the management of probation and parole can be organized in several ways. On the whole, the executive control of probation probably utilizes more effectively the scarce resources available to probation systems. Yet decentralized services make sense in counties with a tradition of effective probation programming. In addition, statewide organization of combined probation and parole services seems to offer the best assurance of accountability and economy, given firm leadership by an administrator who knows what has to be done and how to do it.

Probation Subsidy

A California innovation, **probation subsidy** was initiated in the 1960s because several studies suggested that many juvenile and adult offenders could remain safely in the community if they had good probation supervision. The subsidy program was expected to reduce prison populations and to delay further prison construction, an objective that was achieved for a few years in California. Studies also found that the expanded use of probation necessitated state-supported financial incentives to participating counties.

Until it was replaced in 1978, California's probation subsidy program provided state funds to participating counties (most of the fifty-eight counties participated) that reduced the number of offenders they committed to state institutions. The more cases that were diverted from the prison system, the larger was the subsidy a county received. The level of subsidy was determined by comparing a county's actual commitment rate with an ideal normative commitment rate. If, within a given period, a county committed only one hundred persons when, according to the normative yardstick, it could reasonably have committed two hundred, the county achieved a 50 percent reduction. This reduction meant a savings to the state, and the county received a portion of the money saved.

Other states also have subsidy programs. The state of Washington has a history of compensating counties for reduced rates of commitment to state institutions. In New York State, a probation subsidy is given to local communities willing to follow state guidelines for staffing probation departments. These local units of government are reimbursed for up to 50 percent of their operating costs for probation services. Michigan assigns state-paid probation officers to work with local probation officers and makes direct payment to local units of government to defray part of probation services. In 1979, a probation subsidy law went into effect in Illinois. This law mandates officer training and minimum standards of operation, and in turn, participating counties receive $400 a month for each probation officer. In the 1980s and 1990s, probation systems under county or judicial control increasingly looked to the state for assistance in training, standard-setting, and financial subsidies.

WHAT ARE THE BASIC FUNCTIONS OF A PROBATION OFFICER?

The three basic functions of an adult probation officer are to manage a caseload, to supervise adult probationers, and to make presentence investigation and other reports to the courts. Probation officers function within bureaucratic organizations, and the resulting focus on control and accountability sometimes limits the satisfactions and increases the frustrations of the job. Nevertheless, effective probation officers find a way to deliver services to probationers.

Casework Management and Other Administrative Duties

The probation officer maintains a file on each probationer for whom he or she is responsible. Within this file are the court documents that spell out the requirements of probation, chronological entries of contacts between the officer and the probationer and others whose relationship with the probationer might be significant, items of correspondence, and periodic reports made to the courts or to officials of the agency.

Commonly, probation departments divide probationers into several categories, based on their needs or on the risk they pose to the community. Some offenders are placed on minimum-supervision status and are required only to mail in a report once a month or even less frequently. Offenders on medium-supervision status, must visit their probation officers at least once a month. Offenders on maximum- or intensive-supervision status must see their officers several times a month. Bureau of Justice statistics reveal that 95 percent of adult probationers in the United States are supervised on regular caseloads, about 4 percent are placed on intensive supervision, and about 1 percent constitute specialized caseloads of individuals subject to electronic monitoring or sent to boot camps.[21]

Probation officers' caseloads are so large that maintaining contact with probationers is difficult. In 1998, caseloads ranged from 352 cases per officer in Rhode Island to

60 cases per officer in West Virginia and in federal probation. Among probation officers who also had parolees on their caseloads, caseloads per officer ranged from 154 in Arkansas to 51 in Ohio and Wisconsin.[22] In 1998, probation officers had an average of 14 face-to-face contacts with probationers who were on regular supervision, 74 contacts with probationers on intensive supervision, and 73 contacts with probationers on electronic monitoring.[23]

Supervision, Investigation, and Surveillance

The majority of officers used to see themselves more in the helping or counseling role. Personal involvement in the supervision of offenders was emphasized. But during the 1970s, with the popularity of the reintegrative model, the majority of probation officers began to see themselves as resource managers or brokers, rather than as counselors. The role of community resource manager rested on the premise that "the probation officer will have primary responsibility for meshing a probationer's identified needs with a range of available services and for supervising the delivery of these services."[24] To fulfill this role effectively, the probation officer must assess the situation, be aware of available resources, contact the appropriate resources, assist a probationer in obtaining these services, and follow up the case. If it is necessary to purchase community services, the task, then, is to monitor and evaluate them.

This treatment hat has been replaced by viewing the role of the probation officer as one of enforcing public safety. This law enforcement hat complies with the current risk assessment and surveillance models that are popular in probation today.[25] The probation officer is expected to be "tough" on clients to ensure public probation. The officer is required to determine as much as possible whether a client is obeying the law and complying with the terms of probation. If a client fails to comply with the conditions or terms of probation, then violation is in order.

Even though personal involvement in the supervision of offenders is no longer emphasized, officers still must establish a relationship with the offender, establish supervision goals to comply with the conditions of probation, and decide how and when to terminate probation. The investigation and surveillance aspects of supervision call for at least periodic checks on probationers' employment, on the status of their restitution payments, on whether they are clean on their urine "drops," and on whether they are participating in required programs.

Presentence Investigation Reports

The main purposes of the **presentence investigation** (**PSI**) are to help the court decide whether to grant probation, to determine the condition of probation, to determine the length of the sentences, and to decide on community-based or institutional placement for the defendants. The PSI is the major report required of a probation officer and is used at the time of the sentencing hearing. The importance of the PSI report is demonstrated by studies that show that judges' sentencing decisions are consistent with the probation officer's recommendation about 95 percent of the time.[26]

PSI reports vary somewhat in form but usually have six categories:

1. Information about the offense and a description of its exact nature
2. The defendant's prior record, including juvenile adjudications
3. Background information on the defendant: upbringing, educational background, employment, marital situation, physical and emotional health, military service, financial situation

4. A statement by the prosecution about what the appropriate disposition should be
5. A summary of the foregoing information along with sentencing alternatives available to the court
6. The probation officer's recommendation on the most appropriate sentence, based on the information in the report

In most states a PSI report must be prepared regardless of whether the offender is eligible for probation. If he or she is sent to prison, the report will accompany the commitment document for the information of the prison authorities.

The long form of a PSI report may take up to twenty hours to complete. Probation officers must first interview the defendant, preferably more than once, in order to verify information. Officers then review the defendant's arrest record, reports concerning the current offense, previous presentence reports, and any available psychiatric or psychological reports. Occasionally they must interview the arresting officer and the defendant's employer, and they often talk with the defendant's family.

In a number of large departments, because of the increasing specialization of probation services, some officers spend most of their time preparing PSI reports. In Texas, in 1998, probation staff wrote 151,280 PSI reports, the most in any state. Also in 1998, probation staff in South Carolina wrote 26 reports, the fewest. In 39 of 47 responding agencies, probation officers were responsible both for writing PSI reports and for supervising probationers.[27]

Probation officers have the authority to file a notice of violation with the court when a probationer commits a violation of the conditions of probation or is arrested again. The prosecutor may decide to prosecute the new offense, especially if the penalty exceeds revocation itself and he or she has a solid case. If the prosecutor decides not to prosecute, the case is placed on the court calendar, and the probationer is directed to appear in court for a preliminary hearing. If a revocation hearing is scheduled after the preliminary hearing, the probation officer is charged before the hearing to present the judge a full violation-of-probation report documenting the charges and summarizing the probationer's degree of adjustment to supervision. See Outside the Walls 6.2 for a sample PSI.

Probation officers frequently prepare a presentence investigative report on a client. What is involved in preparing a PSI report? What information is contained in a PSI report, and what is the purpose of it?

outside
outside

the walls   6.2

Sample Presentence Investigation Report

FIRST JUDICIAL DISTRICT DEPARTMENT OF CORRECTIONAL SERVICES
Presentence Investigation Report
Ordered By: Honorable
Anticipated Sentence Date:
PSI Preparer:
County
Cause Number(s): FECR0

Offender Summary

Offender Number:
Full Name:

Birth Date:
SSN:

FBI Number:
DCI Number:
Race:
Ethnic Origin:

Sex:
Height: 5'3"
Weight: 108 Pounds
Hair Color:
Eye Color (L, R):   Brown, Brown

Address 1:
Address 2:
City:
State:
Zip Code:

Days In Jail: 2
Deferred Eligibility: The defendant is eligible for a deferred judgment.

> . . . a deferred judgment is recommended, however, probation supervision is recommended . . .

Aliases

Instant Offenses(s)

Charge Date	Cause Number
Crime Code	Year of Code
Offense Description	
Comment	
02/12/2001	FECR0
715A.2(2)(A)	1987
FORGERY	
—	

(continued)

Criminal History

Official Version

On ▓▓▓▓▓▓▓ allegedly forged ▓▓▓▓▓▓▓ signature on a $7500 Wells Fargo Draft and deposited it into her individual account and later withdrew the money. ▓▓▓▓▓▓▓ were separated at the time of this incident. ▓▓▓▓▓▓▓ did not give the defendant permission to sign this draft. Following an investigation into this matter, Defendant ▓▓▓▓▓▓▓ admitted to this offense and was arrested for Forgery.

Post-Arrest Information

Decision: Release on Bond   **Date:** 02/14/2001

Comment: Following the defendant's ▓▓▓▓▓▓▓ arrest, she remained in the custody of the ▓▓▓▓▓▓▓ for 2 days before posting $7500 bond. On ▓▓▓▓▓▓▓, a pre-plea pre-sentence investigation was ordered and further proceedings were set for ▓▓▓▓▓▓▓. To the best of this investigator's knowledge, Defendant ▓▓▓▓▓▓▓ has incurred no further criminal arrests.

Arrest History

Arrest Date	Arresting Authority	Offense
Disposition Date/Type		
Sentence Type	Start Date	End Date
Disposition		
Comment		

02/12/2001	Police Dept.	FORGERY
02/12/2001 — Arrested		
No Sentence Information		
No Penalty Information		
—		

Arrest History Comments

The defendant has no prior arrests as a juvenile or as an adult.

Employment History

Employer	Address (City, State)	Start Date	End Date
Job Status	Salary		
Comment			

		April 2001	06/19/2001
Spot Job	$6.50/Hourly		

At the time of her pre-sentence interview, Defendant ▓▓▓▓▓▓▓ reported working various jobs through ▓▓▓▓▓▓▓ for the past two months. She indicated she "checks in" at ▓▓▓▓▓▓▓ daily to be placed at a job, however, ▓▓▓▓▓▓▓ personnel report the defendant has not worked since 6/19/2001 and has been in "maybe a couple times" since that date.

		03/10/2001	04/21/2001
Part-Time	$4.00/Hourly		

Defendant ▓▓▓▓▓▓▓ reported the above employment dates stating she was paid cash and quit without notice because the "owner very rude."

Employment History Comments

The defendant is currently unemployed. Prior to the above-listed periods of employment, Defendant ▓▓▓▓▓▓▓ worked as a waitress at ▓▓▓▓▓▓▓ in ▓▓▓▓▓▓▓ for a short period of time but left due to the low pay. She also reports working as a paramedic for 4–5 years before being terminated after she refused to transfer a patient from ▓▓▓▓▓▓▓ to ▓▓▓▓▓▓▓. Releases of information were sent to all of the above employers, however, only ▓▓▓▓▓▓▓ responded prior to the writing of this report.

(continued)

the **walls** 6.2, *continued*

outside

Military History			
Branch		**Start Date**	**End Date**
Discharge Type	**Rank at Discharge**		
Comment			

Not Applicable

Military History Comments

The defendant has no military experience.

Education History		
School Name	**Start Date**	**End Date**
Address (City, State)	**Educational Level**	
Comment		

High School		1982
	High School Diploma	

The defendant graduated from high school in ▓▓▓▓▓▓▓. She reports she incurred a 3-day out-of-school suspension in jr. high for fighting. She states she was defending herself in this fight.

Community College	10/08/1990	10/12/1999
	Technical Training Completion	

HCC records reflect Defendant ▓▓▓▓▓▓▓ completed several EMT-related courses between October 1990 and October 1999 which led to her employment as a paramedic.

Education History Comments

The defendant has no immediate plans to further her education.

Financial	
Debts	
Description	**Value**
Comment	

credit card debt	$20,000.00

The defendant reportedly owes $20,000 in credit card debt.

delinquent child support	$0.00

The defendant admits she is approximately one-year delinquent on her court-ordered child support payments.

Assets	
Description	**Value**
Comment	

No Asset Information

Means Of Support	
Support	**Earnings/Interval**
Comment	

No Means of Support Information

Financial History Comments

The defendant reported during her employment with ▓▓▓▓▓▓▓ she was earning $700-$800/month. She listed $545 in monthly liabilities. She admits she is currently having financial problems and is contemplating filing for bankruptcy due to her credit card debt.

(continued)

Family Dynamics

Relationship	Name	Birth Date
Address 1	City, State	
Comment		

Mother-Natural   age 59

The defendant's mother is retired. According to the defendant, her mother has no reported history of prior criminal arrests, nor any mental, drug or alcohol problems, however ▓▓▓▓▓▓▓▓ records reflect during her June 2000 treatment, the defendant described her mother as an alcoholic.

Father-Natural   age 62

The defendant's father is retired from ▓▓▓▓▓▓▓. He has no reported history of prior criminal arrests, nor any mental, drug or alcohol problems. ▓▓▓▓▓▓▓▓ records reflect the defendant reported her father sexually abused her from ages 10–17.

Brother-Full   age 39

▓▓▓▓▓▓▓▓ is employed at a cable company. He has no reported history of prior criminal arrests, nor any mental, drug or alcohol problems. The defendant has contact with ▓▓▓▓▓▓▓ every couple of months.

Family Dynamics Comments

The defendant was raised by both of her parents. She described them as "good parents" and reported no history of abuse while growing up, however, as indicated above, ▓▓▓▓▓▓▓ records reflect the defendant admitted she was sexually abused by her father from ages 10–17. These records further reflect the defendant's mother is an alcoholic. The defendant reports both of her parents have been supportive throughout this matter. She maintains weekly phone contact with both her mother and father and has physical contact with them approximately once a month.

Marital/Relationship Dynamics

Relationship	Name	Birth Date
Address 1	City, State	
Comment		

Son-Biological   age 17

▓▓▓▓▓▓▓▓ is a student at ▓▓▓▓▓▓ High School. He resides with his father in ▓▓▓▓▓▓.

Son-Biological   age 11

▓▓▓▓▓▓▓ attends ▓▓▓▓▓▓ School and resides with his father.

Son-Biological   age 9

▓▓▓▓▓▓▓ is a student at ▓▓▓▓▓▓ School and resides with his father.

Marital/Relationship Comments

The defendant has been married three times. Her first marriage was to ▓▓▓▓▓▓ of ▓▓▓▓▓▓. They were married from 1982–1986 and had one child together, ▓▓▓▓▓▓ (age 17). The defendant reports ▓▓▓▓▓▓ drank a lot during their marriage but was not abusive. She reports she was simply too young to be married. Her second marriage was to ▓▓▓▓▓▓ of ▓▓▓▓▓▓. They were married from 1988–1994. Two children resulted from this marriage: ▓▓▓▓▓▓ (age 11) and ▓▓▓▓▓▓ (age 9). According to the defendant, this marriage ended as they grew apart while she was attending school. The defendant's third marriage was to ▓▓▓▓▓▓ currently of ▓▓▓▓▓▓. They were married in December 1997 but divorced in January 2001. The defendant reports they divorced because "he left me." No children were born to this marriage.

Presently, the defendant is involved in a relationship with ▓▓▓▓▓▓ is employed as a ▓▓▓▓▓▓. He has no reported history of prior criminal arrests, nor any mental, drug or alcohol problems. They have been together for the past 8 months.

(continued)

the walls 6.2, *continued*

outside

Living Arrangement History

Address	Start Date	End Date
City, State	Property Type	Monthly Cost
Comment		

| | April 2001 | |
| | Rent $100.00 | |

Defendant ▨▨▨▨▨ currently resides at the above address with her boy-friend, ▨▨▨▨▨. Mr. ▨▨▨▨▨ has lived at this location for approximately 6 years. The defendant plans to remain at this residence and reports such is in a good neighborhood.

| | February 2001 | April 2001 |

The defendant lived at the above address with ▨▨▨▨▨ for a couple of months. She left this residence due to ▨▨▨▨▨ abuse of alcohol.

| | January 2001 | February 2001 |

At the time of her arrest, Defendant ▨▨▨▨▨ was residing at the above address with a friend, ▨▨▨▨▨. She lived at this residence for one month.

Living Arrangement History Comments

The defendant was born and raised in ▨▨▨▨▨. At age 20 she moved to ▨▨▨▨▨ where she lived for 10 years. She then moved to ▨▨▨▨▨ for a couple of years before moving to ▨▨▨▨▨ where she has since remained.

Leisure/Recreation

The defendant has not belonged to any clubs or organizations in the past year. Among her hobbies/interests she likes outdoor activities, goes fishing 3–4 times a week during the summer months and goes bowling once a week.

Companions

Based on her past involvement with crack cocaine, Defendant ▨▨▨▨▨ admittedly has some criminal acquaintances and some criminal friends. She was able to name two pro-social acquaintances in her life but was unable to name two pro-social friends.

Alcohol Abuse

During her pre-sentence interview, the defendant denied any history of alcohol abuse, however, ▨▨▨▨▨ records reflect upon her admission into inpatient treatment, Defendant ▨▨▨▨▨ admitted to drinking daily and having many problems with her alcohol use in the past including blackouts, loss of control, and increased tolerance.

Drug Abuse

The defendant reports a history of crack cocaine and marijuana use. She reports she ▨▨▨▨▨ experimented with marijuana once as a "kid" and did not like this illicit drug. She denied any other illegal drug use until May 2000 when she and her friend, ▨▨▨▨▨ tried crack cocaine. She reports after her initial use of crack cocaine, she continued to use this addictive substance weekly. The defendant reports she told her husband, ▨▨▨▨▨ of her cocaine use and he threatened to divorce her if she continued to use cocaine. She did continued to use this drug and advised her husband of such and he then committed her into inpatient treatment and then filed divorce papers while she was in treatment. Defendant ▨▨▨▨▨ admits she completed inpatient substance abuse treatment in June 2000 but continued to use cocaine for two months following her discharge. She denies any illicit drug use since August 2000.

(continued)

Offender Interventions

Intervention
Eligibility   **Start Date**   **Completed**

No Offender Intervention Information

Offender Intervention Comments

On 6/9/2000, Defendant ▓▓▓▓▓ was committed to inpatient substance abuse treatment at Treatment Center in ▓▓▓▓▓ as a result of her addiction to crack cocaine. A past history of alcohol abuse was also mentioned, however, the time frame of this abuse was not mentioned. ▓▓▓▓▓ records reflect the defendant admits to going to work under the influence of alcohol and/or drugs. She completed inpatient treatment on 6/13/2000 and was transferred to day outpatient treatment on that date.

▓▓▓▓▓ records verified Defendant ▓▓▓▓▓ was admitted to ▓▓▓▓▓ intensive day outpatient treatment program on 6/14/2000 under court committal for continued treatment of chemical dependency. She was subsequently discharged on 6/27/2000 because of failure to comply and her court committal was dismissed. The defendant was recommended to attend growth group, along with individual counseling.

Emotional/Personal Health

Health Issue Type   **Occurrence Date**
Description
Medication
Comments

No Emotional/Personal Health Information

Emotional/Personal Health Comments

The defendant described her health as "good." She denies having any physical disabilities, nor any prior long-term illnesses or surgeries. She reports she is not taking any prescription medications.

Sexual History

Not applicable

Psychosexual Assessments
Assessed Date   **Submitted Date**   **Reason Assessed**
Comment

Not Applicable

Defendant's Version

Since this is a pre-plea pre-sentence investigation, the defendant did not provide her version of this offense. She does, however, believe her charge in this matter is fair and is willing to comply with the conditions of probation supervision. The defendant is hoping for a deferred judgment and probation in this matter and plans to make full restitution to the victim.

Victim Information

Victim's Version

The victim appears to agree with the above official version.

Victim Impact Statement

As in the writing of this report, a Victim Impact Statement has not been forwarded from the ▓▓▓▓▓ County Attorney's Office.

Restitution Information

As in the writing of this report the ▓▓▓▓▓ County Attorney's Office has provided no information regarding restitution owed in this matter. Court costs and court appointed attorney fees are yet to be determined.

(continued)

Offender Needs

Need Identified	Priority
Alcohol/Drug Problem 07/05/2001	1
Attitudes/Orientation 07/05/2001	2
Emotional/Personal 07/05/2001	3
Employment 07/05/2001	4
Financial 07/05/2001	5

Recommendations

In verifying information gathered for this investigation, it became apparent Defendant ▬▬▬▬▬▬ was dishonest about her family history, as well as her history of alcohol abuse and prior mental health treatment. She failed to report her mother's alcoholism, the sexual abuse she incurred by her father, as well as her documented history of alcohol abuse and mental health treatment. Despite her deceitfulness, based on the fact this Is her first criminal offense, a deferred judgment is recommended, however, probation supervision is recommended to hold the defendant accountable for her crime and to monitor her behavior including her employment, restitution payments, substance abuse and mental health. Hopefully the defendants recent criminal behavior is out-of-character for her and she will take this opportunity to prove to the Court such illicit acts will not be repeated.

IF ADJUDGED GUILTY:

The First Judicial District Department of Correctional Services respectfully recommends ▬▬▬▬▬▬ be granted a deferred judgment the crime of Forgery and be placed on probation supervision for 2 years. It is also recommended the defendant be placed in the Corrections Continuum and shall be assessed by the Department of Correctional Services to determine the appropriate level of supervision. While on probation, the defendant needs to obtain and maintain full-time employment, make full restitution in this matter, and abstain from all mood-altering substances.

HOW DOES THE PROBATION OFFICER DO HIS OR HER JOB?

This section examines three important questions: What satisfactions are there in working as a probation officer? What frustrations does this officer experience? What are the qualities or attributes of an effective probation officer?

Job Satisfactions and Frustrations

Probation officers experience pressure and role conflicts that may undermine their job commitment. Among the sources of pressure are feelings of being underpaid and overburdened, stressful encounters with probationers, and bureaucratic constraints.

Although salaries have risen in recent years, probation officers believe they are underpaid. On 1 January 1999, the average entry-level salary of probation officers who dealt only with probationers was $27,197. Entry-level probation officers received the highest pay in Connecticut ($37,314) and the lowest pay in West Virginia ($20,670). In departments that combined probation and parole services, the average entry-level salary was $25,662. Entry-level probation officers in combined departments were paid the most in California ($43,644) and the least in Tennessee ($20,412).[28] Although all states paid a starting probation officer $20,000 or more a year, this base salary was typically less than the salaries of parole and police officers in the same jurisdiction.

Large caseloads make probation officers feel overworked. Probation officers who handle only probation cases had a caseload averaging 124 clients during 1998. Those officers with both probation and parole cases had an average caseload of 94 clients during 1998.[29] The large caseloads, large numbers of PSI reports, other never-ending paperwork, the amount of time that must be spent in court, and the contacts that must be made in the community make the job seem overwhelming.

Another source of stress is the pressure of working with individuals who are constantly involved in crisis situations and failure. Probation officers often note that "a PO never gets the client very far away from the crisis line." Probationers are commonly resistant and sometimes hostile to probation officers. Officers face the risk of physical assault, including rape.[30] As a result of the increased risks posed by probationers—especially felony probationers—more probation officers are authorized to carry weapons than in the past. Camp and Camp's survey of probation and parole departments during 1999 found that 15 of 28 reporting probation agencies authorized officers to carry weapons and 25 of 29 responding probation and parole agencies authorized officers to carry weapons.[31]

Another source of frustration is that the emerging crime-control model frequently produces bureaucratic rigidity. The overall pattern of probation in the late 1980s and 1990s showed much defensiveness on the part of administrators and little tolerance for innovation. All too often, probation officers are told that the first commandment of working in the office is not to embarrass the agency. This inflexible, "play it safe" stance sometimes limits the delivery of services to clients.

The Effective Officer

The most effective probation officers have certain characteristics. They try to remain genuine in officer–client relationships; they will not play games. Effective officers are compassionate and respectful toward their clients; however, they are streetwise and will not be manipulated. The best probation officers have an uncanny ability to help others to achieve success. When a client fails, the officer can help him or her try again. Successful probation officers know themselves and keep their personal problems separate from their clients' problems. Most important, they are committed to their jobs, not just to receiving a paycheck. Their motivation remains constant and strengthens them against burnout. Many remain as involved in their work as they were on their first day on the job.

Probationers respect officers with those characteristics. Such officers can usually discipline offenders without alienating them. They develop a bank of successes to draw from when burnout threatens. Effective officers enjoy the respect of colleagues in the justice system and maintain good relationships within the office. Whether they are promoted or not (promotions are impossible in a one-person office), they are rewarded by an awareness of their reputations for fairness, genuineness, and commitment to their jobs. In short, their efforts do pay off, and they do make a difference in the lives of probationers.

Samantha J. O'Hara is the hero of this chapter. She is a U.S. probation officer in Des Moines, Iowa, and a Ph.D. student in criminal justice at the University of Nebraska at Omaha. Ever since her undergraduate days she has been making a difference in whatever she does. The Heroes box contains what she wrote for *Invitation to Corrections* in 2001.

heroes

Samantha J. O'Hara

U.S. Probation Officer

"After completing several internships and undergraduate and graduate degrees at the University of Northern Iowa, I was hired first as a residential officer and then a counselor at an Iowa Department of Correctional Services residential facility (a halfway house) in Marshalltown. Intrigued by the differences between state and federal offenses and criminals, I investigated various positions and was appointed as a U.S. probation officer in Des Moines, Iowa, a short time later. I have since been working at the U.S. Probation Office for the U.S. District Court in the Southern District of Iowa for nearly three years. I am a presentence investigation writer—that is, I investigate and prepare reports for the federal judges on individuals who have been found guilty or pled guilty to various federal criminal offenses.

"In the U.S. Probation Office in the Southern District of Iowa, officers comprise groups in the pretrial, presentence, and supervision units. Some officers monitor defendants awaiting trial or sentencing, while others provide supervision of those placed on probation or who are coming out of an institution on supervised release. In the presentence unit, my duties include interviewing of the defendant, conducting a thorough criminal and social history investigation, reviewing offense conduct materials provided by the U.S. Attorney's Office, calculating and applying the U.S. Sentencing Guidelines, working with both counsels, and conveying the finished product (the PSI report) to the district court judge. Since the implementation of the United States Sentencing Guidelines, the offense conduct and criminal history are the primary issues of concern.

"There are several differences between state (at least in Iowa) and federal probation. In the state of Iowa, probation officers have caseloads approaching 200, whereas federal probation officers typically carry between 50 to 75 supervisees. Salary ranges differ as well, partially based on educational/experience requirements of the U.S. Probation Office—the minimum educational requirement is a bachelor's degree, while the majority of the officers have master's degrees. Law degrees and doctorates of philosophy in related disciplines are not rare. Additionally, in Iowa, many of the state probation officers belong to a union, while in the federal system, officers are appointed by the District Court and work "at the pleasure of the Court."

"In presentence report writing, federal probation officers have a much more active role in the process, from answering objections to the PSI report from both counsels to contacting case agents with questions about the instant offense, than at the state level. Because of the implementation of the U.S. Sentencing Guidelines, the role of the officer has become much more legalistic and that of a "fact-finder" than in the days of pre-guidelines. These pre-guideline times more closely mirror the state of Iowa's current system.

"I enjoy my position as a U.S. probation officer writing PSI reports for several reasons: I like learning of people's stories and how they became involved in their offenses. The contact with a variety of people, including offenders, their families, assistant U.S. attorneys, defense counsel, case agents, and our bosses, the judges, makes for an extremely diverse mix. It is rewarding to see that the final product is helpful to the U.S. District Court judges, later possibly the Federal Bureau of Prisons, and eventually my colleagues in the Supervision Units nationwide. I relish reading, writing, listening, and talking to people (although not necessarily in that order), so for me, the position is a good fit. I feel these areas need to be in the repertoire of a good probation officer.

"Learning aspects of the federal criminal justice system made me desire more education. I enrolled part-time last year in the criminal justice doctoral program at the University of Nebraska at Omaha to be able to look more critically at the entire U.S. criminal justice system. With the encouragement and office hour flexibility of the chief probation officer, I travel to Omaha for my coursework. With the assistance of wonderful faculty and challenging courses there, I have been able to put my schooling and correctional experience to work. I feel that I am better able to critically examine specific policy areas, such as sentencing issues, as a Ph.D. graduate student who writes PSI reports. When judges ask for my opinion on an issue, or have questions, I believe I have an improved base with which to hold a discussion. This, I think, will improve as I continue with my coursework.

"Because, as we all know, the criminal justice system is a work in progress, we should all strive to make it better."

CRITICAL THINKING QUESTIONS

What does Samantha O'Hara say are some differences between a U.S. probation officer and a state probation officer? What does she like about her job? What does she see as the relationship between her job and her Ph.D. studies?

WHAT ROLE DOES A VOLUNTEER PLAY IN PROBATION?

Probation began with volunteers. Professional staff began appearing by the turn of the twentieth century. In the 1950s, Judge Keith J. Leenhouts initiated a court-sponsored volunteer program in Royal Oak, Michigan, that sparked the rebirth of the volunteer movement. Today, more than 2,000 court-sponsored volunteer programs are in operation in juvenile and adult probation. Volunteers assist probation officers in a variety of ways. Volunteers have become one of the most valuable resources to help offenders adjust to community life.

Many volunteers are matched one-on-one with probationers. After a period of training, each volunteer works with his or her probationer. Volunteers typically are involved in activities such as counseling, mentoring, and recreation. Outside the Walls 6.3 describe two success stories from a volunteer program run by the First Judicial District in Iowa.

outside the walls   6.3

Partners against Crime Mentoring Program

Sara Carter, an adult probation officer in the First Judicial District in Iowa, reports this success story:

"I matched an 18-year-old white male client in our youthful offender program with an African American 44-year-old male mentor in January 2000. They hit it off really well. The client came from a very chaotic home life. His father was abusive and his mother tried her best but couldn't provide everything. He did not have any positive male role models in his life and tended to hang out with the wrong crowds. He was on probation for burglary 3rd and possession of marijuana.

> . . . you could really see a positive change in [the client's] attitude.

"The client would stop in my office a lot and tell me how much he enjoyed meeting with his mentor. The mentor owned a construction company in town and after getting to know the client a little gave him a job at his office. The mentor helped the client to secure an apartment, as well as checking into going on to Hawkeye Community College after completing his high school equivalency diploma. When seeing the client, you could really see a positive change in his attitude. He was so excited that his mentor included him in his life and wanted to go out to do fun stuff with him. The client knew that if he needed someone to talk to he could call his mentor. Their match officially ended in August, but I believe they will always keep a connection."

Sara Carter reports another story:

"I matched a 39-year-old black female client on regular street probation with a 22-year-old white female mentor in December 1999. Despite the age difference they had a lot in common and got along really well. The client lived in a group home for mentally ill females. She suffered from bipolar disorder as well as having many physical problems. This is one match from which I believe the mentor really gained as much as the client in terms of cultural awareness and awareness to mental illness. They enjoyed going to church together as well as many other activities. The client wrote beautiful poetry and shared a lot of it with her mentor. The client had struggled with a substance abuse problem for some time so did not have many friends that did not use. She really was able to find a positive support through her mentor and find many positive things to do with her time. The client really treasured the times she was able to get out with her mentor. They continued to meet with each other after the six months was up. Her mentor recently moved out of the state, but I believe that they may continue to talk on the phone."

CRITICAL THINKING QUESTIONS

What values can a probationer learn from a mentor? Do you think you would like to be a volunteer and work with probationers? Why or why not?

Source: Sara Carter contributed these materials to *Invitation to Corrections,* 2001.

WHAT ARE PROBATIONERS' RIGHTS?

The most important cases concerning probation that have been litigated by the courts have involved disclosure of PSI reports and probation revocation. Defense attorneys prefer disclosure of the information on the PSI report compiled by the probation officer because they seek the opportunity to challenge any disputable statements in the reports.

The question of disclosure of the PSI report to defense counsel was first raised in *Williams v. New York* (1949).[32] In that case, the lower court convicted Williams of murder and recommended a life sentence. When the judge imposed the death sentence on the basis of the PSI report, Williams's lawyer appealed, arguing that the sentencing procedures violated due process rights "in that the sentence of death was based upon information supplied by witnesses with whom the accused had not been confronted and as to whom he had no opportunities for cross-examination or rebuttal." The U.S. Supreme Court rejected Williams's appeal, concluding that the disclosure to the defendant and counsel of the PSI report would prevent judges from obtaining information they needed to make a sentencing decision.[33]

In *Gardner v. Florida* (1977), a capital punishment case decided twenty-eight years after *Williams,* the sentence of death was pronounced by the trial court after consideration of a PSI report, some portions of which had been withheld from open court as confidential.[34] The jury had had no opportunity to review the report but had recommended that the court judge impose the death penalty. In delivering the opinion of the Supreme Court, Justice John Paul Stevens held that circumstances had changed since *Williams.* If the PSI report including the confidential information had been "the basis for a death sentence, the interest in reliability plainly outweighs the State's interest in preserving the availability of comparable information in other cases."[35]

In *Booth v. Maryland* (1987), still another death penalty case, the PSI report included a victim-impact statement.[36] The adult son and daughter of elderly victims of a murder committed in the course of a burglary made eloquent comments on the brutality of the offense, their grief and sorrow, the fears and depression that the murder of the parents had caused, and their parents' qualities as citizens. In a 5–4 decision, the Supreme Court ruled that such a statement was likely to inflame the jury against the defendants and therefore could not be allowed.[37]

The U.S. Supreme Court has ruled on three important cases concerning **revocation of probation**: *Mempa v. Rhay* (1967), *Gagnon v. Scarpelli* (1973), and *Beardon v. Georgia* (1983). In *Mempa,* the Court held that the right to counsel, guaranteed by the Sixth Amendment, applies to the sentencing hearing because the hearing is a crucial stage of criminal prosecution. Extending this reasoning to apply to deferred sentencing and probation revocation hearings, the Court ruled that because Mempa did not have counsel at his revocation hearings, the decision of the lower courts was reversed and Mempa was to be released from prison.[38]

In *Beardon v. Georgia,* the U.S. Supreme Court ruled that a judge cannot revoke a defendant's probation for failure to pay a fine and make restitution, unless the probation is somehow responsible for the failure or the alternative forms of punishment are inadequate to meet the state's interest in punishment and deterrence. *Beardon* involved a Georgia defendant who was unable to pay his restitution because he lost his job and could not find another. The trial court revoked probation, and the defendant was sent to prison. On appeal, the Supreme Court ruled that if a state determines a fine or restitution to be appropriate and an adequate penalty for the crime, it may not thereafter imprison a defendant solely because he or she lacks the resources to pay, because this would be a violation of a probationer's right to equal protection.[39]

Because the case-by-case approach for determining the right to counsel is arbitrary, considerable confusion still exists concerning the revocation of probation. A sound argument can be made for the position that counsel should be appointed in all revocation cases because the potential loss of liberty by the probationer outweighs any possible burden on the state in providing counsel.

IS PROBATION EFFECTIVE?

There are at least three story lines concerning the effectiveness of probation. First, in 1975, Douglas Lipton, Robert Martinson, and Judith Wilks found that recidivism rates with standard probation were lower than rates with most other types of working with offenders.[40] This finding continues to hold true.

Second, the effectiveness of probation varies by groups of probationers. Recidivism rates are low among those placed on probation for a misdemeanor: Data suggest that upwards of three-fourths of offenders placed on probation for a misdemeanor successfully complete their supervision.[41] But Rand researchers found that felon probationers typically have high rates of recidivism. These researchers tracked a sample of 1,672 felony probationers sentenced in Alameda and Los Angeles counties, California, in 1980 for a three-year period. During that time, 65 percent of the probationers were rearrested, 51 percent were reconvicted, and 34 percent were reincarcerated.[42] According to the Rand study, felons placed on probation had particularly high recidivism rates in areas where supervision was minimal and where probation was used extensively. However, other agencies replicating the Rand study found that recidivism rates for felon probationers varied from jurisdiction to jurisdiction, depending on the length of follow-up, the surveillance provided, and the seriousness of the underlying population characteristics.[43]

Third, adult probation is having increased success with drug offenders. Research at UCLA and elsewhere has found that drug abuse treatment is effective and that individuals coerced into treatment derive benefits similar to the benefits of those who enter voluntarily.[44] The largest study of drug treatment outcomes found that criminal justice system clients stayed in treatment longer than clients without involvement in the justice system and, consequently, had higher-than-average success rates.[45]

To improve the effectiveness of probation even more (what Petersilia calls "reforming, reinvesting, and restructuring"), several steps appear to be necessary.[46] More financial resources must be provided to implement quality programming for appropriate probation target groups. The credibility of probation with the public and the judiciary must be improved. Support is needed from a public that views the probation sanction as sufficiently punitive to make up for the harm of criminal behavior and from a judiciary that is convinced offenders will be held accountable for their behavior. More innovative programs in probation across the nation need to be implemented. For example, John Gorcyck, head of the Vermont Department of Corrections, has designed what he calls "Reparative Citizen Boards," in which community members interact with offenders to draw up contracts stipulating probation conditions.[47] In addition, probation must be made a priority research topic. Most of the research in probation has been on intermediate sanctions, but many other issues merit examination. For example, what purpose is served by revoking probation for technical violations? Is the benefit worth the cost? What groups in prison could safely be supervised in the community?[48]

SUMMARY

Adult probation is the most widely used correctional option. Probationers are permitted to remain in the community as long as they comply with the conditions of the court under supervision of a probation officer. Woefully underfunded, probation can have a positive impact on offenders, especially those who are misdemeanants. There is also evidence that drug treatment has a positive effect on some probationers with histories of drug abuse. Supporters strongly argue that probation is a sound policy for offenders who do not threaten the community.

In the 1980s and 1990s, probation was widely criticized by those who wanted to get tough on crime. As a result, probation has gotten tougher. More probationers are assigned to intensive supervision and other intermediate sanctions; more probationers do time in jail as part of the conditions of probation; and more time is spent on drug testing and other such means of surveillance. In the process of getting tougher, adult probation has developed a bureaucratic control model. The rigidity of this model is sometimes frustrating to line probation officers.

Still, effective probation officers continue to deliver valued services to probationers, often fostering their successful adjustment to community living.

KEY TERMS

community service, p. 125
deferred sentence, p. 126
financial restitution, p. 125
intensive probation, p. 127
presentence investigation, p. 132

probation subsidy, p. 130
revocation of probation, p. 144
split sentence, p. 126
Wisconsin classification system, p. 128

CRITICAL THINKING QUESTIONS

1. "I sentence you to eighteen months of probation," the judge said. What benefits do you expect from serving out your sentence in the community?
2. Probationers enjoy many of the same rights as unconvicted citizens. But a probationer's right to know on what information his or her sentence is based is a hotly debated issue. Why do many probation officers object to making PSI reports public?
3. You accepted a position in the X County Probation Department. You lack experience, and you want to be effective in your new job. Your supervisor hands you a casebook and tells you to do the best you can. She says she is swamped with reports to write and court appearances and cannot spend much time with you. What should you do first, second, and third?
4. During your first hours after settling into the job, six young men barge into your office. They are very belligerent. They want to know whether you are going to continue the racist actions of your predecessor, filing violation charges against members of their gang for wearing gang colors. What is the best way to respond to this confrontation?
5. Probation officers report feeling overburdened, underpaid, and lacking in community support. Surprisingly, some probation officers remain highly effective. What qualities make for success in the field?

WEB DESTINATIONS

Learn what information and resources are available from the American Probation and Parole Association.
http://www.appa-net.org/

Get details on the purpose and contents of presentence investigation reports.
http://www.appa-net.org/about%20appa/probatio1.htm

Read the code of ethics that probation officers and parole officers are expected to observe.
http://www.appa-net.org/about%20appa/codeof.htm

Read the American Probation and Parole Association position statement on electronic monitoring of offenders in the community.
http://www.appa-net.org/about%20appa/electron.htm

Compare job descriptions for probation officers and parole agents in different states—for example, Washington and North Carolina.
http://www.wa.gov/careerguide/career/jobs/job8422.html
http://www.osp.state.nc.us/jobs/08/by_name/jobfile44.html

FOR FURTHER READING

Augustus, John. *First Probation Officer*. New York: New York Probation Association, 1939. Originally published as *A Report of the Labors of John Augustus, for the Last Ten Years, in Aid of the Unfortunate*. Boston: Wright & Hasty, 1852. The first probation officer tells his story.

Clear, Todd, and Anthony A. Braga. "Community Corrections." In *Crime*, edited by James Q. Wilson and Joan Petersilia. San Francisco: Institute for Contemporary Studies, 1995. A helpful discussion of the effectiveness of probation.

Petersilia, Joan. "Probation in the United States," in *Crime and Justice: A Review of Research* 21, edited by Michael Tonry, 149–200. Chicago: University of Chicago Press, 1997. An excellent overview of probation in the United States.

Petersilia, Joan, Susan Turner, James Kahan, and Joyce Peterson. *Granting Felons Probation: Public Risks and Alternatives*. Santa Monica, Calif.: Rand, 1985. An examination of recidivism rates among a sample of felon probationers in California.

NOTES

1. Interview conducted in 1985 by Linda Dippold Bartollas and reprinted from Katherine Stuart van Wormer and Clemens Bartollas, *Women and the Criminal Justice System* (Boston: Allyn & Bacon, 2000), p. 211.

2. Minnesota Sentencing Guidelines Commission, *Sentencing Practices: Highlights and Statistics Tables* (St. Paul: Minnesota Sentencing Guidelines Commission, 1996); California Department of Justice, *Crime and Delinquency in California, 1994* (Sacramento: California Department of Justice, Bureau of Criminal Statistics and Special Services, 1995).

3. Bureau of Justice Statistics, *Probation and Parole in the United States, 1998* (Washington, D.C.: U.S. Department of Justice, 1999), p. 1.

4. *John Augustus: First Probation Officer* (Montclair, N.J.: Patterson Smith, 1972), pp. 4–5.

5. Joan Petersilia, "Probation in the United States," in *Crime and Justice: A Review of Research* 21, ed. Michael Tonry (Chicago: University of Chicago Press, 1997), p. 156.

6. Ibid., p. 157.

7. Timothy L. Fitzharris, *Probation in an Era of Diminishing Resources* (Sacramento: Foundation for Continuing Education in Corrections; California Probation, Parole, and Correctional Association, 1979).

8. E. K. Nelson, Howard Ohmart, and Nora Harlow, "Promising Strategies for Probation and Parole," in *Probation, Parole, and Community Corrections: A Reader,* 3rd ed., ed. Robert M. Carter, Daniel Glaser, and Leslie T. Wilkins (New York: Wiley, 1984), p. 410.

9. Petersilia cites a study by Mark Cunnif and Mary Shilton, *Variations on Felony Probation: Persons under Supervision in 32 Urban and Suburban Counties* (Washington, D.C.: U.S. Department of Justice, 1991, p. 176.

10. Ibid., p. 177.

11. Joan Petersilia and Susan Turner, Prison versus Probation in California: Implications for Crime and Offender Recidivism (Santa Monica, Calif.: Rand, 1986).

12. Carol Lucken, "Contemporary Penal Trends: Modern or Postmodern? *British Journal of Criminology* 38 (Winter 1998), p. 39. In a study that tests whether probation has entered into a bureaucratic–managerial stage, E. M. Lemert, from his examination of four counties in California, questions whether any revolutionary new form of social control has been implemented. See E. M. Lemert, "Visions of Social Control: Probation Considered," *Crime and Delinquency* 39 (1993), p. 460.

13. Malcolm M. Feeley and Jonathan Simon, "The New Penology: Notes on the Emerging Strategy of Corrections and Its Implications," *Criminology* 30 (1992), pp. 449–474.

14. Todd R. Clear and Kenneth W. Gallagher, "Probation and Parole Supervision: A Review of Current Classification Projects," *Crime and Delinquency* 31 (July 1985).

15. Department of Health and Social Services, *Project Report #7: Client-Management Classification Process* (Madison, Wis.: Bureau of Probation and Parole, August 1977), p. 2.

16. Ibid., pp. 3–5.

17. Ibid.

18. Joan Petersilia, *The Influence of Criminal Justice Research* (Santa Monica, Calif.: Rand, 1987).

19. National Advisory Commission on Criminal Justice Standards and Goals, *Corrections* (Washington, D.C.: U.S. Government Printing Office, 1973), pp. 313–316.

20. Jodi M. Brown, Darrell K. Gilliard, Tracy L. Snell, James J. Stephan, and Doris James Wilson, *Correctional Populations in the United States, 1994* (Washington, D.C.: Bureau of Justice Statistics, 1996).

21. Bureau of Justice Statistics, *Probation and Parole in the United States, 1998*, p. 4.

22. Camille Graham Camp and George M. Camp, *The Corrections Yearbook 1999 Adult Corrections* (Middletown, Conn.: Criminal Justice Institute, 1999), p. 176.

23. Ibid., p. 177

24. National Advisory Commission on Criminal Justice Standards and Goals, *Corrections* (Washington, D.C.: U.S. Government Printing Office, 1973), p. 322.

25. T. R. Clear and E. J. Latessa, "Probation Officer Roles in Intensive Supervision: Surveillance versus Treatment," *Justice Quarterly* 10 (1993), pp. 441–462.

26. Eugene H. Czajkoski, "Exposing the Quasi-Judicial Role of the Probation Officer," *Federal Probation* 37 (September 1973), pp. 9–10. See also Curtis Campbell, Candace McCoy, and Chimezie A. B. Osigweh, Yg, "The Influence of Probation Recommendations on Sentencing Decisions and Their Predictive Accuracy," *Federal Probation* 54 (December 1990), pp. 13–20.

27. Camp and Camp, *The Corrections Yearbook 1999,* p. 202.

28. Ibid., p. 206.

29. Ibid., p. 176.

30. For an examination of job burnout in probation, see J. T. Whitehead, "Job Burnout in Probation and Parole: Its Extent and Intervention Implications," *Criminal Justice and Behavior* 12 (1985), pp. 91–110.

31. Camp and Camp, *The Corrections Yearbook 1999,* p. 184.

32. *Williams v. New York State* (337 U.S. 241, 69 S. Ct. 1949).

33. Ibid.

34. *Gardner v. Florida,* 430 U.S. 349 (1977).

35. Ibid.

36. *Booth v. Maryland,* 482 U.S. 496 (1987).

37. Ibid.

38. *Mempa v. Rhay,* 389 U.S. 128 (1967).

39. *Beardon v. Georgia,* 33 CrL 3101 (1983).

40. Douglas Lipton, Robert Martinson, and Judith Wilks, *The Effectiveness of Correctional Treatment: A Survey of Treatment Evaluation Studies* (New York: Praeger, 1975), pp. 26–61.

41. Petersilia, "Probation in the United States," pp. 180–181.

42. Joan Petersilia, Susan Turner, James Kahan, and Joyce Peterson, *Granting Felons Probation: Public Risks and Alternatives* (Santa Monica, Calif.: Rand, 1985.

43. Petersilia, "Probation in the United States," p. 181.

44. Douglas Anglin and Yih-Ing Hser, "Treatment of Drug Abuse," in *Drugs and Crime,* ed. Michael Tonry and

James Q. Wilson, vol. 13 of *Crime and Justice: A Review of Research,* ed. Michael Tonry and Norval Morris (Chicago: University of Chicago Press, 1990).

45. Institute of Medicine, Committee for the Substance Abuse Coverage Study, "A Study of the Evolution, Effectiveness, and Financing of Public and Private Drug Treatment Systems," in *Treating Drug Problems,* vol. 1, ed. D. R. Gerstein and H. J. Harwood (Washington, D.C.: National Academy Press, 1990).

46. Petersilia, "Probation in the United States," p. 185.

47. Vermont Reparative Probation, "Program Overview" (n.p., 1999); Vermont Reparative Probation, "Fact Sheet" (n.p., 1999).

48. Petersilia, "Probation in the United States," p. 193.

CHAPTER 6 / BUILT-IN STUDY GUIDE

Multiple Choice Questions

1. Who is generally considered to be the founder of probation?
   A. Walter Crofton
   B. Alexander Maconochie
   C. Zebulon Brockway
   D. John Augustus

2. When an offender is taken out of the formal criminal justice process prior to trial and directed to participate in a treatment program with the possibility that successful completion of the program will result in criminal charges being dropped, this is known as:
   A. Deferred sentence
   B. Pretrial diversion
   C. Adjournment in contemplation of dismissal
   D. Suspended sentence

3. All of the following are basic functions of an adult probation officer except:
   A. Managing a caseload
   B. Supervision of probationers
   C. Developing a presentence investigation report
   D. Working in community residential centers

4. What have the most important legal cases concerning probation involved?
   A. Disclosure of information related to the PSI and probation revocation
   B. Constitutionality of general conditions of probation
   C. Constitutionality of special conditions of probation
   D. Disclosure of information justifying the early release of an individual on probation

5. All of the following factors make the job of probation officer seem overwhelming except:
   A. Large caseloads
   B. Number of PSIs
   C. Time spent in court
   D. Drug testing of probationers

6. The basic purpose of the presentence investigation report is:
   A. To provide a tool for classifying offenders in jail
   B. To provide a tool for classifying offenders in prison
   C. To assist the judge in making an appropriate sentence
   D. To assist the parole board in evaluating the offender's progress while in prison

7. A type of sentencing strategy in which a judge orders a prison sentence for an offender and cancels it, allowing the offender to serve the sentence in the community while on probation is known as:
   A. Deferred sentence
   B. Suspended sentence
   C. Alternative sentence
   D. Presumptive sentence

8. According to the study of thirty-two jurisdictions noted in the text, what accounts for the variation in the use of probation across the country?
   A. Sentencing laws
   B. Judicial discretion
   C. Prosecutorial discretion
   D. Prison overcrowding

9. What is the basic role conflict present in the occupation of a probation officer?
   A. Enforcing the law and supervising offenders
   B. Helping offenders and supervising offenders
   C. Enforcing the law and helping offenders
   D. Acting as treatment agent and referral agent

10. Which of the following U.S. Supreme Court cases held that the Sixth Amendment right to counsel applies to sentencing hearing because it is a critical stage of the criminal prosecution as well as extending this right to the probation revocation hearing?
    A. *Mempa v. Rhay*
    B. *Beardon v. Georgia*
    C. *Booth v. Maryland*
    D. *Gagnon v. Scarpelli*

11. In 1998 what was the average caseload size for probation officers who carried only probationers on their caseload?
    A. 114
    B. 124
    C. 134
    D. 144

True/False Questions

T F   1. The current emphasis of probation is on rehabilitation and reintegration of the offender.

T F   2. The North utilizes probation more than any
other region in this country.

T F   3. Frequently, probation departments use classification systems to categorize probationers
based on their treatment needs or the risk they
present to the community

T F   4. Currently probation caseloads are manageable
and so it is easy for probation officers to maintain contact with probationers.

T F   5. Judges' sentencing decisions are consistent with
the probation officers' recommendation about
95 percent of the time.

T F   6. The use of volunteers has become one of the
most valuable resources to help offenders adjust to community life.

T F   7. By 1926 all states had juvenile and adult probation laws.

T F   8. A deferred sentence occurs when an offender
plea-bargains to a less serious offense.

T F   9. The effective use of funds and manpower is an
argument against local administration of probation services.

T F 10. The major report required of the probation
officer is a motion for a violation of probation
report.

T F 11. The ruling in *Beardon v. Georgia* allows the
state to imprison a defendant if he or she lacks
resources to pay a fine.

Fill-in-the-Blank Questions

(based on key terms)

1. A type of sentence in which an offender spends a period of time in jail before being placed on probation in
the community is known as a _____.

2. Based on the findings of several studies that suggested
that many juvenile and adult offenders could remain
safely in the community if they had good probation supervision, _____ were developed.

3. A form of probation with increased supervision and
more restrictions on the offender is referred to as
_____.

4. A _____ delays conviction on a guilty plea
until the completion of a term of probation, at which
time the defendant withdraws the guilty plea.

Essay Questions

1. What factors influenced the development of probation in America? How is probation different today
from its early history and how is it similar?

2. Describe the arguments for the judicial and executive
branches of government to administer probation. Describe the positions that form the arguments for state or
local administration of probation. Once these tasks are
completed, take a position and provide a justification.

3. Identify and explain the basic functions of the adult
probation officer.

4. How have volunteer programs affected the operation
of probation?

5. Explain the results of court litigation involving disclosure of presentence investigation information and issues surrounding probation revocation proceedings.

ANSWERS

Multiple Choice Questions

1.	D	7.	B
2.	B	8.	A
3.	D	9.	C
4.	A	10.	A
5.	D	11.	B
6.	C		

Fill-in-the-Blank Questions

1. Split sentence
2. Subsidy programs
3. Intensive probation
4. Deferred sentence

True/False Questions

1.	F	7.	F
2.	F	8.	F
3.	T	9.	T
4.	F	10.	F
5.	T	11.	F
6.	T		

Intermediate
Sanctions

Dav99id C. Anderson's book about intermediate sanctions begins with these words:

> I met the man I will call Mal some years ago in the course of reporting about a judge who sentenced young offenders to do odd jobs for public agencies instead of spending time in jail or prison.
>
> Mal was no stranger to the judge. For several years, he had committed burglaries and robberies in order to support his taste for alcohol and drugs. Repeatedly arrested, he repeatedly accepted work assignments. Though he completed them successfully, he then soon returned to substance abuse and crime. The judge, exasperated, finally gave up and sent him to the state penitentiary.
>
> While there, Mal overcame his addictions. Released, he took up carpentry, stayed away from alcohol and drugs and become a successful contractor. But he remained a familiar face around the courthouse; I sought him out for an interview as he arrived for one of the rap sessions he conducted weekly with juvenile offenders.

Here is the gist of our conversation, which began when I asked him what he thought of the judge's jobs programs:

"Pretty good stuff," Mal said. "It's a good deal for kids. It can work to help kids."

"But did it help you?" I asked.

"Oh, no," Mal replied. "I must have painted the courthouse fence a dozen times. But I kept going back to the booze and drugs. The judge, he finally just got fed up with me and sent me away."

"So how did you get straightened out?"

"I did that by myself. I'd had a wife, and we had a little girl. But after I got sent away she was so mad at me she never wanted to see me again. She left and took my daughter with her. And sitting in prison one day, I realized how much I had lost. I either had to turn myself around or kill myself. And I decided to turn myself around."

"So as far as you were concerned, then, the jobs program here was pretty much a failure."

"Oh, no, not at all. Sure, I rehabilitated myself. But I never forgot how the judge was willing to try to help me all those times. And I think he was trying to help me even when he finally sent me away. That meant an awful lot to me. Because he showed me how much he cared."[1]

CRITICAL THINKING QUESTIONS

Why was Mal so positive about the judge's job program? Is he saying that people who care can make a difference, even in the lives of the most difficult offenders?

It is an inspiration to see offenders who are making wrong and destructive decisions turn their lives around. Another inspiration is to observe participants in the justice system take a chance on those offenders who deserve a break. When questioned, they are likely to say, "You have to take a chance on people." They work as police officers, judges, probation and parole officers, residential staff in community-based facilities, and institutional staff.

Taking a chance on people is the main focus of this chapter. Providing justice through a continuum of sanctions is one of the exciting innovations in corrections today. The basic assumption behind a continuum of sanctions, or **intermediate sanctions,** is to escalate punishments to fit the crime. Judges are able to exercise discretion by selecting from a range of sentencing options the punishment that best fits the circumstances of the crime and the offender. Prisons, then, are treated as backstops, rather than backbones, of the corrections system.[2]

How do you know which offenders deserve a break? Can you think of an example of what it would mean to take a chance on an offender?

WHAT IS THE CONTINUUM OF SANCTIONS?

Advocates for more effective sentencing are increasingly calling for a range of punishment options, providing graduated levels of supervision in the community. Intermediate sanctions are said to allow judges to match the severity of punishment with the severity of the crime.[3] Probation is at one end of the continuum, traditional incarceration at the other. A variety of community-based corrections, such as intensive probation, community service, electronic monitoring and house arrest, and placement in a boot camp, bridge the middle ground[4] (see Figure 7.1).

Escalating Punishments to Fit the Crime

This includes generalized descriptions of many of the sentencing options that are in use in jurisdictions across the country.

Jail

More serious offenders serve their terms at state or federal prisons, while county jails are usually designed to hold inmates for shorter periods.

Boot Camp

Rigorous military-style regiment for younger offenders, designed to accelerate punishment while instilling discipline, often with and educational component.

Halfway House

Residential settings for selected inmates as a supplement to probation for those completing prison programs and for some probation or parole violators. Usually coupled with community service work and/or substance abuse treatment.

House Arrest and Electronic Monitoring

Used in conjunction with intensive supervision and restricts offender to home except when at work, school, or treatment.

Day Reporting

Clients report to a central location every day, where they file daily schedules with their supervision officer showing how each hour will be spent—at work, in class, at support group meetings, etc.

Substance Abuse Treatment

Evaluation and referral services provided by private outside agencies and used alone or in conjunction with either simple probation or intensive supervision.

Community Service

Used alone or in conjunction with probation or intensive supervision and requires completion of hours of work in and for the community.

Restitution and Fees

Used alone or in conjunction with probation or intensive supervision and requires regular payments to crime victims or to the courts.

An expanded range of sentencing options gives judges greater latitude to exercise discretion in selecting punishments that more closely fit the circumstances of the crime and the offender. The approach treats prisons as the backstop, rather than the backbone, of the corrections system.

Intensive Supervision Probation

Offender sees probation officer three to five times a week. Probation officer also makes unscheduled visits to offender's home or workplace.

Probation

Offender reports to probation officer periodically, depending on the offense sometimes as frequently as several times a month or as infrequently as once as year.

Figure 7.1 A Continuum of Sanctions

Source: William M. DiMascio, *Seeking Justice: Crime and Punishment in America* (New York: Edna McConnell Clark Foundation, 1995), pp. 32–33.

outside
outside

the walls   7.1

The Best of Times and the Worst of Times for Intermediate Sanctions

Our plea is for neither increased leniency nor increased severity; our program, if implemented, would tend toward increased reliance on punishments more severe than probation and less severe than protracted imprisonment. At present, too many criminals are in prison and too few are the subjects of enforced controls in the community. We are both too lenient and too severe; too lenient with many on probation who should be subject to tighter controls in the community, and too severe with many in prison who would present no serious threat to community safety if they were under control in the community. . . .

These are the best of times and the worst of times for intermediate punishments. Prison crowding and fiscal concerns have forced attention on the development of punishments that do not require provision of more prison beds. Across the country, many jurisdictions are responding by creating sentencing programs aimed at preventing or reducing crowding by keeping newly convicted criminals out and by releasing previously sentenced prisoners. From the perspective of institution-building, narrowly conceived, these are good times for intermediate punishments. They are bad times,

> . . . too many criminals are in prison and too few are the subjects of enforced controls in community.

though, because the crowding impetus gives only a negative reason for new programs—to avoid prison crowding and the resulting court orders—rather than positive reasons; programs aimed at avoiding something are less likely to endure than are programs aimed at achieving something. We wish to make our case for a substantial expansion of intermediate punishments independent of the fact that our prisons have become crowded beyond capacity of control. Quite apart from the availability of cells, far too many criminals are sentenced to prison and to jail as punishments—too many felons and too many misdemeanants.

CRITICAL THINKING QUESTIONS

Do you agree with Morris and Tonry that society is both too lenient and too severe in punishment? What is your reaction to their notion of the best of times and worst of times for intermediate sanctions?

Source: Reprinted from Norval Morris and Michael Tonry, *Between Prison and Probation* (New York: Oxford University Press, 1990), pp. 3, 34.

In Outside the Walls 7.1, Norval Morris and Michael Tonry provide one of the clearest statements justifying the need for intermediate sanctions.

WHAT IS A FAIR ASSESSMENT OF INTENSIVE SUPERVISION OF PROBATION?

Intensive supervision of probation (ISP) permits probationers to live at home but under relatively strict restrictions. ISP offenders usually are required to perform community service, work, attend school or treatment program, meet with a probation officer or a team of two officers as often as five times a week, and submit to tests for drug and alcohol use, curfews, and employment checks.[5] A fairly new but already widely used program, ISP seems especially useful with high-risk probationers. This type of program, initiated in Georgia in 1982, is based on the belief that increased contact and referral result in more positive adjustment—as evidenced, for example, by a higher employment rate and lower rate of involvement in crime.[6] By 1990, ISP programs had been implemented in one or more jurisdictions in every state.[7]

Georgia's Intensive Probation Supervision program is the strictest form of intensive probation in the United States. Thirteen teams across the state—each composed of a probation officer and a "surveillance officer"—watch over no more than twenty-five probationers at a time. They see their clients at least five times a week, sometimes more often. Probationers have a curfew that is checked on frequently.[8] A 1987 evaluation showed that offenders placed in Georgia's program had rates of recidivism lower than the rates of comparison groups of offenders released from prison and supervised on regular probation. The same evaluation also showed that the majority of those who committed new crimes were involved in less serious forms of criminal behavior.[9]

Felons sentenced to probation commit a considerable amount of crime. It is commonly agreed that ISP programs have a particularly important role to play with these more serious offenders. Joan Petersilia and Susan Turner evaluated three counties in California (Contra Costa, Ventura, and Los Angeles) that participated in the ISP demonstration project in fourteen sites in nine states.[10] They found that at the end of the one-year follow-up period, about one-fourth of the ISP offenders in each site had no new incidents (technical violations or new arrests), about 40 percent had only technical violations (violations of probation conditions), and about a third had new arrests. Furthermore, they found that there were no significant differences in the severity of the arrest offenses among experimental (ISP) and (non-ISP) offenders.[11] Evaluation of the ISP project at the other eleven sites revealed that the programs usually did not reduce recidivism but recidivism among ISP participants was related more often to technical violations than to new crimes. These technical violations were more often caught simply because of the increased supervision of intensive probation.[12] A 1993 evaluation of intensive supervision of probation in Florida found that carefully designed and managed programs yielded better-than-average results. Graduates of this program committed new crimes at a lower rate than a comparable group of offenders released from prison.[13]

Joan Petersilia has identified nine conditions for implementing successful ISP programs:

1. The project must address a pressing local problem.
2. The project must have clearly articulated goals that reflect goals that reflect the needs and desires of the community.
3. The project must have a receptive environment in both the "parent" organization and the larger system.
4. The organization must have a leader who is vitally committed to the objectives, values, and implementation of the project and who can devise practical strategies to motivate and effect change.
5. The project must have a director who shares the leader's ideas and values and uses them to guide the implementation process and operation of the project.
6. Practitioners must make the project their own, rather than being coerced into it. They must participate in its development and have incentives to maintain its integrity during the change process.
7. The project must have clear lines of authority and no ambiguity about "who is in charge."
8. The change and its implementation must not be complex or sweeping.
9. The organization must have secure administration, low staff turnover, and plentiful resources.[14]

In sum, the studies on ISP suggest that there is value in this intermediate sanction. Its value increases when there is careful targeting of who is eligible for intensive probation, and when there is a range of responses to technical violations in order to avoid the use of incarceration when violations occur.[15]

HOW ABOUT RESTITUTION, FINES, COMMUNITY SERVICE, AND FORFEITURE?

Fines, financial restitution, community service, and forfeiture have become widely used conditions of probation in recent years. Interest in these programs, according to Joan Petersilia, "has recently increased due to growing interest in the rights of victims and the search for alternatives to incarceration."[16]

Financial Restitution

Financial restitution is payment of a sum of money by the offender either to the victim or to a public fund for victims of crime. The amount is usually based on the crime and, in some instances, on the offender's ability to pay. The purposes of financial restitution are to compensate victims for their losses and to teach offenders financial responsibility. Offenders who do not have the resources to make their restitution payments may be confined to a correctional facility at night while they are employed elsewhere during the day to earn money for their payments. About thirty states now operate restitution centers.[17] R. C. Davis and colleagues' study of seventy-five restitution programs in the United States found that these programs reported an average of 67 percent of offenders paid their restitution sum in full. However, when these researchers examined the case records at four sites, they learned that 42 percent of offenders paying off their restitution was a more accurate figure. Those offenders, they found, who were more willing to make full compliance with their restitution were the ones having strong community ties and were employed or in school.[18]

Fines

Day fines, which are used more frequently in Europe than in the United States, are fines that approximate an offender's daily wages. The purpose of the day fine is to equalize the financial impact of sentences on offenders. Day fines address the concern that fines are unduly harsh on poor offenders but permit affluent offenders to buy their way out of more punitive sanctions.[19]

Judges in Phoenix now use a form of day fine called FARE (Financial Assessment Related to Employability) probation. Under a FARE probation sentence, a certain number of units are assigned to a particular offense based on its seriousness. For example, 30 units for credit card forgery and 160 units for a burglary. Each unit is given a dollar value based on an offender's income. The penalty amounts range widely—from $180 for a laborer with six children who was convicted of making a false statement in an unemployment claim, to $22,000 for a restaurant owner who was convicted of money-laundering.[20]

Community Service

A **community service order** is a court order that requires an offender to work a certain number of hours at a private nonprofit or government agency. Two general patterns have emerged for structuring community obligations: (1) referring offenders to community agencies that handle the work placement and supervise completion of the community service obligation and (2) assigning a group of offenders to provide a community service. The number of hours of community service to be completed is generally determined by the court or sometimes by program staff.[20] Commonly assigned public service projects include cleanup work on the local streets or in city parks, volunteer service in hospitals or in nursing homes, and repair jobs in rundown housing.

In an examination of fourteen community service programs across the nation, Joe Hudson and Burt Galaway developed a model of the structure and logic of community service program inputs, activities, and outcomes. They indicate the resources necessary to support community service activities, the immediate results of program activities, and the socially beneficial outcomes.[22] See Figure 7.2 for a schematic representation of this model.

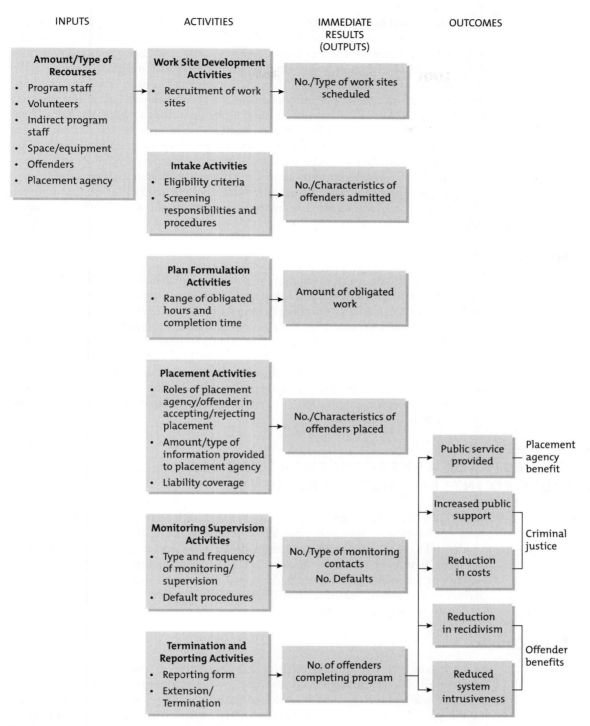

Figure 7.2 The Community Service System

Source: Joe Hudson and Burt Galaway, "Community Service: Toward Program Definitions," *Federal Probation* (June 1990).

In the early 1980s, the Vera Institute of Justice designed a community service sentencing project in three New York City boroughs. The Vera project focused on persistent property offenders who were housed in jail, and it was quite clear in its objectives: "The community service sentence was to be first and foremost a punishment."[23] Vera decided to set up and operate its own program, with its staff supervising work assignments. All persons sentenced to community service in this project are required to perform seventy hours of unpaid labor even though they have committed different acts. About 85 percent of the offenders in the three Vera projects completed their community service obligations. Most of those who fail are brought back to court and given a jail term.[24]

Since the mid-1960s, community service sentencing has been growing more popular. At first, it was used to permit misdemeanants, traffic defendants, minor property offenders, and other offenders, who could not pay their fines to work off their obligation by working without pay for the community. Community service sentences were considered a rehabilitative alternative to jail sentences.[25] Today, community service has new advocates because it can relieve jail and prison crowding by diverting certain kinds of offenders. However, community service programs are difficult to design, implement, and manage. A program must appear punitive enough to satisfy the public that justice is being served. A sizable staff is also needed to keep track of convicted offenders' community service.[26]

Forfeiture

Congress restored the criminal sanction of forfeiture, which had not been used since the American Revolution, with the passage of the Racketeer Influence and Corrupt Organization Act (RICO) and the Continuing Criminal Enterprise Act (CCE). Through amendments in 1984 and 1986, Congress was able to improve the implementation of forfeiture.

Forfeiture involves the government's seizing property that was derived from or used in criminal activity. In civil law, property used in criminal activity can be seized without a finding of guilt. Under criminal law, forfeiture takes place following conviction and requires that offenders relinquish assets related to the crime. In the 1990s, state and federal law enforcement officers confiscated an estimated $1 billion worth of assets from drug dealers.[27]

HOW DO SUBSTANCE ABUSE TREATMENT PROGRAMS CONTRIBUTE TO INTERMEDIATE SANCTIONS?

Judges have frequently been left with prison as their only sentencing option for nonviolent offenders who have substance abuse problems. Drug courts are now growing rapidly and have become one of the most widely used sources of intermediate sanctions. The Drug Treatment Alternative to Prison (DTAP) program, initiated by the district attorney's office in Brooklyn, New York, targets nonviolent defendants in drug cases charged with a second felony offense. They ordinarily would be sent to prison in New York State, because of the mandatory sentencing law.[28]

Drug Courts

In the 1980s, with the number of drug cases escalating dramatically, petty drug offenders were recycled through the justice system at an alarming rate. Courts everywhere began to seek sentencing alternatives for addicted offenders.[29] At the same time, treatment began to be seen as a means to reduce drug use by criminally involved addicts as well as their tendency to commit crime.[30] Research was further proving that coerced treatment was as effective as voluntary treatment.[31]

The social setting was conducive to the growth of drug courts, and the first drug court was established in 1989. When the National Association of Drug Court Professionals (NADCP) was established in 1994, the founding drug court judges numbered fewer than fifteen. In 1999, the NADCP's annual training meeting drew 3,000 participants. By the end of 1999, there were more than 400 drug courts that were found in nearly every state and the District of Columbia.[32]

Three Drug Court Mentor Sites (in New Haven, Connecticut; San Diego, California; and Seattle, Washington) presently provide multijurisdictional and agency training.

The National Association of Drug Court Professionals in Alexandria, Virginia, works closely with the U.S. Department of Justice to develop, coordinate, and implement standardized training and linkages among the various programs and community policing partnerships. Federal discretionary grants are available under the Violent Crime Control and Law Enforcement Act of 1994, Title V. [33]

The NADCP and the U.S. Department of Justice identifies that a drug court has the following key elements:

- Integration of substance abuse treatment with justice system case processing
- Use of the nonadversarial approach, in which prosecution and defense promote public safety while protecting the right of the accused to due process
- Early identification and prompt placement of eligible participants
- Access to a continuum of treatment, rehabilitation, and related services
- Frequent testing for alcohol and illicit drugs
- A coordinated strategy among judge, prosecution, defense, and treatment providers to govern offender compliance
- Ongoing judicial interaction with each participant
- Monitoring and evaluation to measure achievement of program goals and to gauge effectiveness
- Continuing interdisciplinary education to promote effective planning, implementation, and operation
- Partnerships with public agencies and community-based organizations to generate local support and enhance drug courteffectiveness [34]

Drug courts are designed for nonviolent offenders with substance abuse problems who require integrated sanctions and services including (1) mandatory periodic testing for the use of controlled substances; (2) substance abuse treatment; (3) diversion, probation, or other supervised release; and (4) aftercare services such as relapse prevention, health care, education, vocational training, job placement, housing placement, and child care. According to a federal survey in 1996, 65,921 people had been admitted to drug court programs in the United States since 1989. About 31 percent (20,594) had completed programs, and about 24 percent (16,051) had failed to complete programs because they were terminated, had voluntarily withdrawn or had died.[35]

What have been the outcomes of the drug court movement? Where does substance abuse treatment fit in the continuum of sanctions? How might the criteria for effective intensive supervision probation (ISP) programs be applied to community-based drug treatment programs? What are the pros and cons of diversion programs and other intermediate sanctions for offenders? For communities? For the criminal justice system?

On 22 June 2000, the drug court movement spread throughout New York State, which became the first state to require nearly all nonviolent criminals who are drug addicts to be offered treatment instead of jail time. Chief Judge Judith S. Kaye ordered the state courts to start phasing in the drug court program immediately. It is projected to be fully in place by 2003. Judge Kaye indicated that the initiative would divert up to ten thousand nonviolent criminals a year to addiction treatment. But this initiative would not apply to nonviolent offenders convicted under the state's Rockerfeller-era drug laws, which sometimes result in longer sentences for offenders arrested with drugs than for murderers and rapists. The chief judge said the plan would deal not only with a justice system but with "ruined lives, broken families, neglected children, ravaged communities." Instead of going to jail, drug defendants will enter a rigorous program that usually will last two years. They will submit to strict monitoring by specially trained judges, including continued drug tests.[36] For the relationship between drug courts and community-oriented policing, see Outside the Walls 7.2.

outside the walls   7.2

Eliminating the Revolving Door— Community Policing and Drug Courts

"After 12 years of working the streets, I was beginning to think that the day would never come. I mean, for years I had worked with and watched my fellow officers as we all became increasingly frustrated by the revolving door of the criminal justice system. Day after day, I would have to try and explain, to the citizens of the community that I served, why the criminal who had been arrested the night before was released before the morning sun lifted into the sky. It was getting pretty hard to come up with reasonable answers for the concerns of citizens who approached me at the local Neighborhood Watch programs. How could I allay their fears of increasing crime in their communities? How could I convince them that justice would be served on the suspects whom I had arrested, if I was having the same feelings of helplessness and hopelessness that they were having? . . .

"What was a surprise to me was learning that a solution to AOD- [alcohol and other drug] related crimes had been quietly sweeping its way across the country. Developed from the concepts and the philosophy of community-oriented policing, new linkages are now being forged which offer hope to communities plagued by AOD crime. The problem-solving solution, the drug court program, started only a short time ago, in 1994. It has already proven successful in such places as San Diego, CA, Miami, FL, New Haven, CT, and Seattle, WA. This is a solution that works. . . .

> . . . the drug court program works to break the cycle of recidivism . . .

"Drug court handles cases involving less serious drug-using offenders through an intensive supervised treatment program. Drug court programs bring the full weight of all interveners (e.g., the judge, probation officers, correction and law enforcement personnel, prosecutors, defense council, treatment specialist, and other service personnel) to bear, forcing the offender to deal with his or her substance abuse problem. If offenders fail, they suffer the consequences and punishment does come swiftly in the drug court program.

"Drug courts provide a unified system, which serves to coordinate a wide range of antidrug strategies. Utilizing a combination of parole and probation, rehabilitative and treatment services, education and training, and corrections and police services, the drug court program works to break the cycle of recidivism in the offender. By removing the single most disruptive factor in offenders today (AOD addictions), the drug court program works together with law enforcement in achieving the goals and objectives of community policing."

CRITICAL THINKING QUESTIONS

What is your evaluation of the drug court movement? What criticism, if any, would you make of this movement?

Source: Statement by Jon Gamson found at the Webpage of the National Criminal Justice Reference Service, 2000.

Drug Treatment Programs

The Drug Treatment Alternative to Prison (DTAP) program offers pretrial defendants in drug cases charged with a second felony offense an opportunity to enter residential treatment centers. Those offenders who successfully complete the program have their charges dismissed by the district attorney's office, and the offender avoids a prison sentence. As of 1995, the program had achieved a 60 percent retention rate, a significant level because retention is the best predictor of successful drug treatment.[37]

Another of the emerging drug treatment programs is El Rio in the South Bronx (New York City). This intensive outpatient center treats addicts in their own community as an alternative to pretrial detention or incarceration. Clients spend an average of six months at El Rio, as they work with staff, learn new skills, and participate in a variety of group activities and individual counseling. They also undergo frequent drug testing and receive acupuncture for detoxification and sobriety maintenance.[38]

Drug courts are currently riding a wave of success. They are being established throughout the nation, and the initial evaluations have been favorable. The wide claims for success of drug courts may not be sustained once more sophisticated evaluations become available. There is every reason to believe that as less treatable groups participate, rates of compliance and graduation will decline and recidivism will increase.[39]

HOW ABOUT DAY REPORTING SANCTIONS?

Day reporting is another form of intermediate sanction. The offender is assigned to a facility where he or she must report on a regular basis at a specific time every day to participate in activities such as counseling, social skill training, and employment training.[40] The goals of the **day reporting center** are to provide punishment in a cost-effective way,

This director of a day reporting center is tracking parolees using a GPS tracking system. What are the goals of day reporting programs, and how do day reporting centers operate? What is known about the effectiveness of this type of sanction? How might their performance be explained? How is day reporting different from restitution, fines, and community service? How are house arrest and boot camp different from day reporting?

to ensure community safety, and to rehabilitate the offender through intensive programming. A day reporting center usually requires the offender to be supervised by a probation officer.

The old Hampden County jailhouse in Springfield, Massachusetts, houses one of the most widely hailed day reporting centers. Participants in the program are allowed to live at home but report to the center at least once a day in person. They are required either to work or to spend time looking for employment, to perform community service, and to participate in counseling groups. About half of the 150 or so enrolled in this program on a given day would otherwise be in jail.[41]

A 1989 survey identified 13 day reporting programs in the United States; by 1994, 114 centers had spread across twenty-two states. A 1994 study of these 114 centers found that 87 percent enrolled probationers, 73 percent included probation or parole violators, and 42 percent took parolees from prison. In addition, 37 percent enrolled pretrial detainees from county jails, and 25 percent accepted offenders released early from jail sentences. Finally, 20 percent enrolled state inmates on furlough or administrative release.[42]

This 1994 evaluation of day reporting programs found that offenders failed to complete them at a high rate. The figures vary widely (from 14 to 86 percent), but on average 50 percent of offenders are terminated for negative reasons. Programs offering more social services tended to have higher termination rates, perhaps because these programs subject offenders to more rules and responsibilities and thereby create more ways for them to fail. The study acknowledged that day reporting programs are in a state of transition but acknowledged their potential as a form of intermediate sanctions providing both rigorous supervision and diverse services.[43]

HOW ABOUT RESIDENTIAL AND INSTITUTIONAL SANCTIONS?

House arrest and electronic monitoring and placement in halfway houses and boot camps are all residential or institutional sanctions. **House arrest** is a court-imposed sentence that orders an offender to remain confined in his or her own residence for a specific amount of time. **Electronic monitoring** allows corrections staff to verify that an offender is at home or in a community correctional center during specified hours.[44] A **halfway house** is a residential center in which offenders are placed. Offenders frequently leave the halfway house during the day for employment, school, or therapy and on weekends to visit families. **Boot camps,** styled after the military model for basic training, are used as an alternative to prison in order to deal with the problem of prison crowding and public demands for severe treatment.[45] Boot camps usually resemble an institutional rather than a residential facility.

House Arrest and Electronic Monitoring

The concept of house arrest, or home confinement, tends to vary from one jurisdiction to another and to produce varying degrees of offender control. Home confinement rages from evening curfew to detention during all nonworking hours to continuous confinement at home. The most severe form of home confinement, or house arrest, requires offenders to remain in their home, other than when they have permission to leave for employment, religious services, and medical reasons. The sanction of house arrest can stand alone, or it can be coupled with electronic monitoring, fines, community service, and other obligations. Monitoring techniques, a widely used sanction with home confinement, range from periodic visits or telephone calls to continuous monitoring

outside the walls   7.3

Does Money Make a Difference in House Arrest?

In 1988, in Addison County, Vermont, the Honorable Frances McCaffrey stunned an already cynical public when he imposed an innovative but controversial sentencing sanction on a convicted cocaine peddler who stood before him for punishment. The defendant, at 26, had been a student at Middlebury College and was known on campus as the "pharmacist" in view of his drug dispensing capabilities. What made this defendant unique was that John Zaccaro Jr. was the son of the 1984 Democratic vice presidential candidate, Geraldine A. Ferraro, and the product of an affluent, influential background. With his defense lawyers at his side, defendant Zaccaro was sentenced to serve four months of a one- to five-year suspended prison term under house arrest rather than behind bars.

> ... Zaccaro was ... not being punished but grounded for ninety days.

Within a short time, the media discovered that Zaccaro was serving his period of house arrest in a $1,500-a-month luxury apartment in Burlington, Vermont, which included cable television, maid services, and privileges at the neighboring YMCA. When interviewed, the prosecutor John Quinn stated that house arrest was a joke and concluded that Zaccaro was, for the most part, not being punished but grounded for ninety days. Expressing the view that Zaccaro's incarceration in an experimental program was making a mockery of the jail sentence, a spokesperson for Vermont's then governor, Madeline M. Kunin, stated, "We will take a look and maybe we will make some changes." In spite of the protestations, Zaccaro successfully completed the program without incident.

CRITICAL THINKING QUESTIONS

What is your reaction to this sentencing sanction? Do you believe Zaccaro's wealthy parents affected the sanction he was given?

Source: Reprinted from Stephen J. Rackmill, "An Analysis of Home Confinement as a Sanction," *Federal Probation* 58 (March 1994), p. 45.

using electronic equipment. House arrest can last from several days to several years.[46] Home confinement is a sanction that sometimes finds itself in the midst of considerable controversy. See Outside the Walls 7.3.

Electronic monitoring can be traced back to 1964 when an electronic telemetry system based on a triangulation process using radio signals to locate vessels was adapted for possible criminal justice application. During the mid-1960s, electronic monitoring systems were used to determine the location of mental patients, research volunteers, and parolees in Boston, Massachusetts. The initial systems used multiple receivers to trace movement throughout specified areas. The number of receivers used and transmission characteristics of the environment depended on the size of the monitored area.[47]

More current monitoring systems require telephone lines to communicate between offenders' residences and a central location. One type is an active system, consisting of a transmitter, a receiver-dialer unit, and a central computer or receiver. The transmitter is strapped to the offender and broadcasts an encoded signal to a receiver in the offender's home. The receiver is connected by telephone to the receiving unit or central computer. A second type uses telephone lines and consists of a central office computer, and encoder device, and a verifier box. Referred to as a passive system, the offender wears the encoded device on either the wrist or ankle. A remote computer is programmed to generate random telephone calls to the offender, who must provide voice indentification and then insert the encoder device into the verifier box to confirm the offender's indentity.[48]

The National Institute of Justice reports that, on average, 45,000 offenders in all fifty states were electronically monitored every day in 1992—a considerable increase from the 95 offenders, on average, monitored everyday in 1986.[49] In 1995, Florida had over 14,000 offenders under house arrest, many of whom were also electronically monitored.[50]

The application of high technology to the field of corrections has raised a number of controversies that have yet to be resolved by research. On the positive side, to the limited extent that it can provide a genuine alternative to incarceration and its destructive consequences, electronic monitoring is beneficial to the offenders who avoid the jails and to society, which can defer building more institutions. Furthermore, keeping the offender in the community facilitates the task of resocialization.

On the negative side, electronic monitoring is subject to three serious criticisms. First, it depersonalizes the relationship between the correctional agency and offenders even more than the maintenance of bureaucratic control does. Absent from the electronic model of control is any person—bureaucrat or not—to whom offenders might turn for help. There is no one who is interested in helping them. Their only contact with the corrections system is the anklet or bracelet and telephone.

Second, the move toward technological supervision could undermine the professional standing of probation officers. Electronic monitoring calls for the routine, straightforward clerical function of checking and responding to computer printouts. Electronic monitoring programs not only de-skill but change the nature of probation work and re-define the tasks to be carried out by probation officers. For example, new probation officer training in Florida—one of the first states to embark on an electronic monitoring program—stresses officer safety, self-defense, surveillance techniques, and search-and-seizure law.[51]

Third, the fact that electronic monitoring intrudes into the home by monitoring the activities of one inhabitant challenges the idea of "home" as a refuge, a sanctuary, and a bulwark. "What next?" is a question that anyone concerned about civil liberties might ask. The sociologist Gary Marx warns that electronic monitoring has the potential for turning every home into a prison and every bedroom into a cell, and suggests that we would do well to consider whether we want to take that risk.[52]

In sum, a real worry is the possible dangers resulting from electronic monitoring. Aware of the damage this system might do, a staff of probation officers can keep in touch with offenders providing help as needed and reassurance throughout the experience.

Placement in a Halfway House

Probation centers, restitution centers, county work-release centers, and therapeutic communities are the main types of halfway houses for probationers. These programs usually are reserved for the probationer who is making a marginal adjustment to community supervision. These "halfway-in houses" offer a last chance before a person is sentenced to a correctional institution.

Oregon, Florida, and Minnesota are among the states that have developed live-in probation centers in the community as an alternative to imprisonment. Court-imposed restitution has long been a part of probation, but recent efforts now emphasize restitution as a tool of corrections. Residential restitution programs include the Restitution Shelters developed by Georgia's Department of Offender Rehabilitation, the Probation in Restitution Experiment of the Polk County (Des Moines) Iowa Court Services, the Mississippi Restitution Corrections Center, the Florida Restitution Centers, and the Offender Restitution Program in Orleans Parish, Louisiana. Some counties have established work-release facilities to provide more intensive services for offenders who need more than probation but less than prison. Finally, some therapeutic communities, especially in Minnesota, are reserved for offenders who have committed serious crimes. They are characterized by almost total reliance on in-house resources and confrontation groups (encounter groups and intensive attack therapies).

Placement in a Boot Camp

Shock probation was a widely used option in which the judge sentenced a defendant to prison and then released this person on probation supervision after a period of time (frequently ninety days). It was used under various names and forms in Ohio, Kentucky, North Carolina, Texas, Indiana, Idaho, and Maine. In the 1980s, shock incarceration replaced shock probation in many states. The major difference between the earlier shock probation and shock incarceration programs relates to the required participation in drills and physical training in "boot camps," prison settings that are components of the recent shock incarceration model.[53]

Offenders sentenced to boot camps live in military-style barracks. They are usually first-time offenders in their late teens or early twenties, who undergo rigorous physical and behavioral training for three to six months. Boot camps are designed to give offenders a sense of responsibility and accomplishment while improving self-discipline.[54] In a survey of boot camp programs, it was found that the typical pattern was the use of strict discipline, physical training, drill and ceremony, military bearing and courtesy, physical labor, and summary punishment for minor violations of rules.[55] Boot camps originated in Georgia and Oklahoma in 1983 and are now in more than thirty states and the Federal Bureau of Prisons. Boot camps have also been opened for juvenile offenders.[56] Douglas Martin writes about a New York boot camp:

> Days are 16 hours long, and two-mile runs and calisthenics on cold asphalt are daily staples. Work is chopping down trees or worse. The discipline recalls Paris Island. . . . Those who err may be given what is genteelly termed "a learning experience, something like carrying large logs around with them everywhere they go or, perhaps, wearing baby bottles around their necks.[57]

Critics are quick to say that this new panacea raises a number of disturbing issues. First, journalistic accounts of boot camp celebrate a popular image of a dehumanizing experience marked by hard, often meaningless, physical labor. The inmate is portrayed as deficient and requiring something akin to being clubbed over the head to become "a man." This imagery is particularly troubling when it is remembered that the inmates are disproportionately minorities and underclass members. Second, why would a facility developed to prepare people to go into war be considered to have much potential in deterring or rehabilitating offenders? Third, how do the aggressive treatment of residents and the insistence on unquestioning obedience to authority foster prosocial behavior?[58]

The rearrest rates of boot camp graduates are similar to those of prison inmates.[59] Some corrections experts argue that the boot camp experience does not have a lasting impact because boot camps do not do enough to meet the needs of offenders. There has been some interest in developing aftercare services for boot camp graduates to reduce the recidivism rates. For example, a boot camp in New York combines a military regimen with substance abuse counseling, community services, and high school equivalency classes. Upon release, the men and women in this program are required to participate in an intensive six-month aftercare program that provides them with a job and helps them stay employed. It is hoped that such aftercare services will improve their chances of success.[60]

Our hero in this chapter is Doris L. MacKenzie, a professor of criminal justice at the University of Maryland. Dr. MacKenzie was one of the first researchers to examine boot camps, and her research findings have been helpful in identifying the various characteristics, strengths, and shortcomings of this form of intermediate sentencing.

theh e r o e s   *Doris L. MacKenzie*

Professor of Criminal Justice at the University of Maryland

"I've been studying boot camps since about 1987. The way I got started is that I was teaching at Louisiana State University, and a friend in the corrections department, a psychologist, called me and said, 'Look, we have this new program starting here, and you might be interested in examining it. I really have some questions on what this agency is trying to do.'

"This happened to be one of the early boot camps. It was a program for the state dealing with adult males. So I went and visited the program. The more I examined this particular site, the more I heard of the differences among boot camps emerging elsewhere. Some of them had a lot of treatment components, and others emphasized the military aspects.

"As I was in the process of completing the study for Louisiana, I applied for a larger NIJ [National Institute of Justice] grant to pull together researchers in eight different states, to get a multisite study going to examine whether our results would be generalized to other boot camps. NIJ had been hearing about these programs and was interested in trying to support some research. So I applied and got funding. Then what happened was that I became involved in this network of people who were developing and evaluating boot camps. In the 1990s, we decided to conduct a large study of juvenile boot camps and compare them to traditional facilities where the kids would spend time if they weren't in the boot camp. I started out really feeling that there was not much to them at all. It just seemed to be a "get tough" on offenders' punishment model. As soon as I started working with the corrections system, people who were developing the programs, I had more sympathy for what they did. I thought that there might be some positive aspects to the boot camps. What worried me the whole time, though, was that there are some staff who just cannot adjust. They see it as a power trip where they're really going to be abusive to in-

mates. It takes a lot of supervision to minimize the damage of the staff.

"We started getting results from the program, but there just wasn't strong enough evidence that they had any impact on recidivism. However, when I walked into juvenile and adult boot camps, I saw a positive atmosphere and positive inmates' attitudes. We asked the kids in both boot camps and other types of juvenile facilities how they felt about their experience. Overall, we found that the juveniles in the boot camps came out much more positive about their experiences. They also thought they were safer. We thought that the juveniles might be getting more treatment in boot camps than in juvenile facilities, but we found that juveniles in boot camps spent no more time in treatment than juveniles in other juvenile facilities. We also considered that it might have to do with the fact that the kids were more positive about boot camp because of the type of kids who were permitted to enter the boot camps. We are still left with the problem of seeing positive things going on in boot camps, but nobody to date has seen any impact on recidivism.

"In boot camps, we see a philosophy that has come and gone in correctional programs and corrections, where great attention is given on keeping people physically active in a very structured environment. We did this with the wilderness camps. I think there seems to be something positive about a very structured environment that keeps people wanting to stay active. I think we can do more with treatment in the boot camp experience, but it is the aftercare component that is so critical. We cannot expect to see a difference if we send boot camp participants back into the community without any aftercare follow-up and support."

CRITICAL THINKING QUESTIONS

What surprises did Doris MacKenzie find in studying boot camps? Why is aftercare support in the community so important for graduates of boot camps?

WHAT IS A FAIR EVALUATION OF INTERMEDIATE SANCTIONS?

Agreement is widespread that **graduated sanctions** hold promise for increasing compliance to the conditions of the courts.[61] For example, the experiences of drug courts, which emphasize the concept of graduated sanctions, have revealed that this approach reduces rates of substance abuse.[62]

A number of benefits have been attributed to graduated sanctions:

■ *Certainty* because infractions of the behavioral contract are quickly discovered and sanctioned

- *Celerity* because the response to violations is swift

- *Consistency* because there is a structured sanctions menu to deal with violations of the behavioral contract

- *Parsimony* because the structured sanctions menu is designed to make certain that no more punishment is imposed than is necessary

- *Proportionality* because the structured sanction menu is designed to ensure that the level of punishment is commensurate with the severity of the criminal behavior

- *Progressiveness* because the structured sanctions menu is designed to result in increasingly stringent responses to continued violations[63]

In the midst of the wide praise that intermediate sanctions is receiving today, there has been criticism. Stanley Cohen and others are concerned that intermediate sanctions are expanding the net of the criminal justice system. Instead of reducing the number of those sentenced to prison, it is argued that intermediate sanctions are resulting in an expansion of the overall system.[64] Michael Tonry and Mary Lynch contend that few programs have diverted large numbers of offenders from prison, saved the public money on prison beds, or reduced recidivism rates. They feel that the most serious problems with intermediate sanctions are the 40 to 50 percent rates of revocation and subsequent incarceration and the assignment of less serious offenders than program developers anticipated to these programs.[65]

SUMMARY

Intermediate sanctions had widespread approval in the 1990s. There are those who support these sanctions because they serve as a means to reduce prison crowding. Others support them because graduated sanctions reduce the leniency of the system toward those who continue to fail time after time. There are also those who support intermediate punishment because they believe it is the right thing to do.

Types of intermediate sanctions include intensive supervision of probation, restitution and fines, community service orders, day reporting centers, house arrest and electronic monitoring, halfway houses, drug courts, and boot camps. Some sanctions are much older than the others. The halfway house movement goes back to early in the twentieth century. Some—intensive supervision of probation, restitution and community service orders, house arrest and electronic monitoring, drug courts, and boot camps—are more widely used than others. Reviews of these sanctions are mixed, but there seems to be general agreement that they are preferable to returning offenders to prison for technical violations of probation and that some offenders, especially drug offenders, appear to profit from these programs.

KEY TERMS

boot camps, p. 164

community service order, p. 158

day fines, p. 158

day reporting center, p. 163

drug courts, p. 161

electronic monitoring, p. 164

financial restitution, p. 158

graduated sanctions, p. 168

halfway house, p. 164

house arrest, p. 164

intensive supervision of probation (ISP), p. 156

intermediate sanctions, p. 154

CRITICAL THINKING QUESTIONS

1. Why is it that intermediate sanctions are one form of punishment about which individuals with competing views can reach some agreement?
2. Of the various types of intermediate punishments, which one makes the most sense to you? How would you recommend expanding it?
3. Of the various types of intermediate punishments, which makes the least sense to you? What do you feel is needed to make it more acceptable?
4. You have received a grant to develop a novel intermediate sanction specifically for your community. How will your intermediate punishment operate?

WEB DESTINATIONS

Read a paper on the concept and forms of intermediated sanctioning.
http://www.csc-scc.gc.ca/text/forum/bprisons/english/usa2e.html

Read a Department of Justice report on the use of fines in intermediate sanctioning.
http://www.ncjrs.org/txtfiles/156242.txt

Visit a day reporting center in Salt Lake City, Utah.
http://www.slcocjs.org/html/aventext.html

Read an article on youth boot camps and shock incarceration in New York State, and read a paper comparing the cost of boot camp to the cost of incarceration and the effects of boot camp on recidivism.

http://www.uncg.edu/edu/ericcass/bootcamp/DOCS/bcamps03.htm

http://www.ncsc.dni.us/is/MEMOS/Archives/S95–1798.HTM

Read the current federal policy and guidelines on shock incarceration.
http://www.ussc.gov/1998guid/5f1_7.htm

Utah's drug courts. In addition to describing Utah's programs, this site includes links to initiatives, research, and statistics at the national level relating to use of drug courts in community-based corrections.
http://www.hsdsa.state.ut.us/Drug_Court.htm

FOR FURTHER READING

Anderson, David C. *Sensible Justice.* New York: Free Press, 1998. Anderson describes a variety of intermediate sanctions in an arresting way.

DiMascio, William M. *Seeking Justice: Crime and Punishment in America.* New York: Edna McConnell Clark Foundation, 1995. DiMascio examines many of the issues of imprisonment, including the various intermediate sanctions.

Gebelein, Richard S. *The Rebirth of Rehabilitation: Promise and Perils of Drug Courts.* Washington, D.C: U.S. Government Printing Office, 2000. Provides a good overview of the development and present status of drug courts.

Morris, Norval and Michael Tonry. *Between Prison and Probation.* New York: Oxford University Press, 1990. Morris and Tonry place intermediate punishment in the context of a rational sentencing system.

Taxman, Faye, S. and Adam Gelb. "Graduated Sanctions: Stepping Into Accountable Systems and Offenders." *The Prison Journal* 79, 1999: 182–204. Article presents a procedural justice theory for graduate sanctions and defines the critical components of this model.

Tonry, Michael and Mary Lynch. "Intermediate Sanctions." In *Crime and Justice: A Review of Research.* Edited by Michael Tonry. Chicago: University of Chicago Press, 1999: 99–144. An astute and critical statement concerning the practice of intermediate sanctions in the United States today.

NOTES

1. David C. Anderson, *Sensible Justice* (New York: New Press, 1998), pp. 1–2.
2. William M. DiMascio, *Seeking Justice: Crime and Punishment in America* (New York: The Edna McConnell Clark Foundation, 1995), p. 33.
3. Rebecca D. Petersen and Dennis J. Palumbo, "The Social Construction of Intermediate Punishments," *The Prison Journal* 77 (March 1997), p. 77.
4. DiMascio, *Seeking Justice,* p. 34.
5. DiMascio, *Seeking Justice,* p. 35.

6. Billie S. Ervin, *Evaluation of Intensive Probation in Georgia* (Atlanta: Georgia Department of Offender Rehabilitation, Office of Evaluation, 1984).

7. DiMascio, *Seeking Justice*, p. 35; Faye S. Taxman, David Soule, and Adam Gelb, "Graduated Sanctions: Stepping into Accountable Systems and Offenders," *The Prison Journal* 79 (June 1999), p. 183.

8. Ervin, *Evaluation of Intensive Probation in Georgia.*

9. Billie Erwin and Lawrence Bennett, "New Dimensions in Probation: Georgia's Experience with Intensive Probation Supervision (IPS)," in *Research in Brief* (Washington, D.C.: National Institute of Justice, 1987).

10. Joan Petersilia and Susan Turner, *Intensive Supervision for High-Risk Probationers* (Santa Monica, Calif.: Rand, 1990), p. vi.

11. Ibid., p. ix.

12. Joan Petersilia and Susan Turner, "Evaluating Intensive Supervision Probation and Parole," in *Intermediate Sanctions in Overcrowded Times*, ed. Michael Tonry and Kate Hamilton (Boston: Northeastern University Press, 1995).

13. Dennis Wagner and Christopher Baird, "Evaluation of the Florida Community Control Program" (Washington, D.C.: National Institute of Corrections, 1993).

14. Joan Petersilia, "Conditions for Implementing Successful Intensive Supervision Programs" (Santa Monica, Calif.: Rand, 1988), p. 8.

15. DiMascio, *Seeking Justice*, p. 35.

16. Joan M. Petersilia, *Expanding Options for Criminal Sentencing* (Santa Monica, Calif.: Rand, 1987), p. 70.

17. Joe Hudson and Burt Galaway, "Community Service: Toward Program Definition," *Federal Probation* (June 1990), p. 6.

18. R. C. Davis, C. Smith, and S. Hillenbrand, "Increasing Offender Compliance with Restitution Orders," *Judicature* 74 (1991), pp. 245–248.

19. DiMascio, *Seeking Justice*, p. 36.

20. Ibid.

21. Hudson and Galaway, "Community Service." p. 60.

22. Ibid.

23. Center for Alternative Sentencing and Employment Services. Cited in DiMascio, *Seeking Justice*, p. 37.

24. Ibid.

25. Douglas C. McDonald, *Punishment without Walls* (New Brunswick, N.J.: Rutgers University Press, 1986).

26. Petersilia, *Expanding Options for Criminal Sentencing*, pp. 73–74.

27. Todd R. Clear and George F. Cole, *American Corrections*, 5th ed. (Belmont, Calif.: Thompson Publishing Co., 2000), p. 206.

28. DiMascio, *Seeking Justice*, p. 37.

29. Richard S. Gebelein, *The Rebirth of Rehabilitation: Promise and Perils of Drug Courts* (Washington, D.C.: U.S. Department of Justice, 2000), p. 3.

30. See Robert L. Hubbard et al., "Criminal Justice Client in Drug Abuse Treatment," in *Compulsory Treatment of Drug Abuse: Research and Clinical Practice*, ed. C. G. Leukefeld and F. M. Tims (Washington, D.C.: U.S. Department of Health and Human Services, 1988), p. 66.

31. See D. Farabee, M. Prendergast, and M. D. Angin, "Effectiveness of Coerced Treatment of Drug-Abusing Offenders," *Federal Probation* 62 (June 1998), pp. 3–10.

32. Petersilia, *Expanding Options for Criminal Sentencing*, p. 73.

33. Ibid.

34. Gebelein, *The Rebirth of Rehabilitation*, p. 3.

35. Petersilia, *Expanding Options for Criminal Sentencing*, p. 73.

36. Katherine E. Finkelstein, "New York to Offer Addicts Treatment instead of Prison," *New York Times*, 23 June 2000, p. A23.

37. DiMascio, *Seeking Justice*, p. 37.

38. Ibid.

39. Gebelin, *The Rebirth of Rehabilitation*, p. 5.

40. Liz Marie Marciniak, "The Use of Day Reporting as an Intermediate Sanction: A Study of Offender Targeting and Program Termination," *The Prison Journal* 79 (June 1999), p. 205.

41. Anderson, *Sensible Justice*, p. 55.

42. Ibid.

43. Ibid., p. 57.

44. Daniel and Annesley K. Schmidt, "Electronically Monitoring Home Confinement," in *NIJ Reports* (Washington, D.C.: U.S. Department of Justice, 1985), p. 2.

45. See Merry Morash and Lisa Rucker, "A Critical Look at the Idea of Boot Camp as a Correctional Reform," *Crime and Delinquency* 36 (April 1990), pp. 204–222.

46. Stephen J. Rackmill, "An Analysis of Home Confinement as a Sanction," *Federal Probation* 58 (March 1994), p. 46.

47. Ibid.

48. Ibid.

49. National Institute of Justice, *25 years of Criminal Justice Research* (Washington, D.C.: U.S. Department of Justice, 1994).

50. Florida Department of Probation and Parole, "Probation and Parole Fact Sheet (Jasper Fl.: Florida State Department of Probation and Parole Office, 1995).

51. Ronald Corbett Jr., "Electronic Monitoring," *Corrections Magazine* (October 1989), p. 80.

52. Doris Mackenzie, et al., "Shock Incarceration: Rehabilitation or Retribution," *Journal of Offender Services and Rehabilitation* 14 (1989), p. 26.

53. Gary T. Marx, "The Maximum Security Society" (paper presented at the 38th International Criminology Congress, Montreal, Canada, 1987).

54. Corbett, "Electronic Monitoring," p. 80.

55. DiMascio, *Seeking Justice*, p. 40.

56. DiMascio, *Seeking Justice*, p. 41.

57. Douglas Martin, "New York Tests a Boot Camp for Inmates," *New York Times,* 4 March 1988, p. 15.

58. Morash and Rucker, "A Critical Look at the Idea of Boot Camp as a Correctional Reform," p. 206.

59. Ibid.

60. DiMascio, *Seeking Justice,* p. 41.

61. Ibid.

62. Taxman et al., "Graduated Sanctions."

63. Ibid., p. 188.

64. Stanley Cohen, *Vision of Social Control* (Cambridge: Polity Press, 1985), pp. 43, 49, 69.

65. Michael Tonry and Mary Lynch, "Intermediate Sanctions," in *Crime and Justice: A Review of Research,* ed. Michael Tonry (Chicago: The University of Chicago Press, 1999), pp. 99–144.

CHAPTER 7 / BUILT-IN STUDY GUIDE

Multiple Choice Questions

1. A continuum of sanctions between traditional probation and prison designed to provide judges with more sentencing options so that they can more effectively match the sentence with the severity of the crime is known as:
   A. Intermediate sanctions
   B. Middle sanctions
   C. Alternative sanctions
   D. Qualitative sanctions

2. Which of the following states has the strictest form of intensive probation in the United States?
   A. Texas
   B. New York
   C. Georgia
   D. California

3. Identify the type of sanction that requires the offender to perform a certain number of work hours at a private, nonprofit, or government agency.
   A. Work camp
   B. Work furlough
   C. Community furlough
   D. Community service

4. The purpose of this type of sanction is to equalize the financial impact of the sentence on the offender's financial earnings.
   A. Day fines
   B. Offender fines
   C. Income fines
   D. Income garnishment

5. Identify one of the most widely used forms of intermediate sanctions for nonviolent offenders who have substance abuse problems.
   A. Methadone maintenance tanks
   B. Community residential centers
   C. Drug courts
   D. Work furloughs

6. All of the following are goals of the day reporting center except:
   A. Providing punishment in a cost-effective manner
   B. Ensuring community safety
   C. Rehabilitating the defendant through intensive programming
   D. Supervising of offenders by parole officers

7. All of the following are true about the drug treatment alternative to prison program except:
   A. Offenders who successfully complete the program have their charges dismissed by the district attorney's office
   B. They are not cost-effective compared to incarceration
   C. As of 1995, the program had achieved a 60 percent retention rate
   D. Offenders who successfully complete the program avoid a prison sentence

8. Which of the following states was the first to require that nearly all nonviolent criminals who were drug addicts be offered treatment instead of jail time?
   A. New York
   B. Connecticut
   C. Pennsylvania
   D. Vermont

9. All of the following are the main types of halfway houses for probationers except:
   A. Probation centers
   B. County work-release centers
   C. Therapeutic communities
   D. Day-fine centers

10. Boot camps are designed to do all of the following except:
    A. Give offenders a sense of responsibility
    B. Give offenders a sense of accomplishment
    C. Give offenders an extremely severe punishment
    D. Improve offenders' self-discipline

11. According to Petersilia, all of the following are necessary conditions for implementing successful intensive probation supervision programs except:
    A. Project must address a pressing local problem
    B. Project must have clear lines of authority
    C. Project must have clearly stated goals separate from the community goals
    D. The change and its implementation must not be complex or sweeping

True/False Questions

T F 1. Intermediate sanctions are needed to deal with the problem of prison crowding.

T F 2. The studies of intensive probation supervision suggest that there is no value in this intermediate sanction.

T F 3. Since the mid 1960s, community service as a sentence has been increasing in popularity.

T F 4. Community service programs are easy to design, implement, and manage.

T F 5. Drug courts handle cases involving less serious drug-using offenders through an intensive supervised treatment program.

T F 6. Fines, financial restitution, and community service have been used less frequently as conditions of probation in recent years.

T F 7. A day reporting center is a type of pretrial diversion program.

T F 8. Offenders cannot be sentenced to house arrest for more than one year.

T F 9. Electronic monitoring devices must be used when an offender is sentenced to house arrest.

T F 10. The rearrest rate of boot camp graduates is similar to those of prison inmates.

T F 11. Halfway house programs represent a last chance before a person is sentenced to a correctional institution.

Fill-in-the-Blank Questions

(based on key terms)

1. The sanction that establishes a sum of money that the offender must pay either to the victim or to a public fund for victims of crime is known as _____ .

2. The _____ has provided an innovative sentencing option for nonviolent offenders who have substance abuse problems.

3. A _____ is a community-based facility where offenders live but can leave to participate in various community programs, employment, therapy, or family visits.

4. Structured like military basic training, _____ satisfy the public demand for severe punishment as well as address the problem of prison crowding.

5. Intermediate sanctions, also referred to as _____ , are designed to ensure that the level of punishment is equal to the severity of the criminal behavior.

6. The amount of a financial sanction that is determined by the offender's daily income is known as a _____ .

7. An offender has been sentenced to _____ when the court orders him/her to remain confined in their own residence for the length of their sentence.

8. Correctional staff use _____ equipment to verify that offenders are at their residence or at a community correctional center at a specific time.

Essay Questions

1. Identify and describe the continuum of sentencing options that make up intermediate sanctions. How will the use of intermediate sanctions benefit the corrections system?

2. Describe the drug court movement of the 1990s. What factors influenced the initiation of this movement? How has the drug court movement affected prison crowding? What services do drug courts provide?

3. Identify and explain three perspectives that support the use of intermediate sanctions in corrections.

4. What are some of the positive and negative controversies when the field of corrections uses high technology?

5. Describe how boot camps operate and the typical offender that gets sent to one. Discuss the criticisms of boot camps.

ANSWERS

Multiple Choice Questions

1.	A	7.	B
2.	C	8.	A
3.	D	9.	D
4.	A	10.	C
5.	C	11.	C
6.	D		

True/False Questions

1.	T	7.	F
2.	F	8.	F
3.	T	9.	F
4.	F	10.	T
5.	T	11.	T
6.	F		

Fill-in-the-Blank Questions

1. Financial restitution
2. Drug court movement
3. Halfway house
4. Boot camp
5. Graduated sanctions
6. Day fines
7. House arrest
8. Electronic monitoring

chapter **eight**

Parole, Surveillance, and Reentry Programs

Walter, an ex-offender who has stayed out of trouble for more than twenty-five years, talks about his experiences on parole and his adjustment to community living.

I was out of prison for four months when I got busted for heroin. I went back to jail for two years, and when I came out, I realized to make it on parole I had to stay away from drugs and live like a Boy Scout. I also had to follow the parole rules and my special stipulations. Then, I had to set myself a program.

My program was to go to school, which I did. I took the responsibility of carrying a good grade average to show that I was serious about getting off parole and being responsible. I got off parole in six months. I got married after that, but it did not work out. I still took her two children by her first marriage and a baby girl we had, and I decided to raise them. I went to school full-time, including summer terms, and raised the three kids. I got a four-year degree in three years. I did my homework during the day and raised the kids at night.

I can't say that I haven't been tempted. For a while I was tempted all the time. I remember one time when money was tight and I was outside the registrar's office. The women collecting money went into another office for a minute, and there was all that money sitting there, ready to be taken. I looked at it and decided that I was not going back to where I was before. I did twenty-six years in youth and adult facilities. I was not going back.

After college, I worked in a private facility for juveniles. I couldn't get a job in a state facility because of my felony record. I hurt my back in this private facility, and I had to go on disability. Since that time, I have been baking for restaurants and special orders from individuals. My cakes are known all over the area.[1]

CRITICAL THINKING QUESTIONS

Why do you think Walter made it while so many others do not? What were the key decisions he made that led to his staying out of trouble?

Release is the prime goal of individuals who are incarcerated. The days, weeks, months, years, and sometimes decades are occupied by thoughts and fantasies of release or even escape. Even those who have a life sentence without parole or a death sentence speculate about how they might win a new trial and be released. The "lifer" tells other inmates who have a life sentence not to think about the time they have to serve, but it is hard not to fantasize about returning to the free world. For many, those thoughts and desires become all-consuming passions and govern every action.

Then comes the big day when they leave the prison. In addition to their surge of excitement as they burst forth from their cage, there is a feeling of fear or anxiety. To those who have been locked up for a long time, the world seems completely changed. After fifteen or twenty years, nothing seems familiar. The pace of life sometimes startles them. Some may feel like outsiders in the communities in which they grew up. Others may find themselves alone because their loved ones have died and their friends are either dead or in prison.

Release from prison takes place in several ways: conditional or mandatory release, pardon, commutation of sentence, involvement in a reentry program, or parole. Offenders must be freed on conditional or mandatory release once they have served their sentence minus "good time." In a state that grants ten days of "good time" for each thirty days earned, a prisoner serving a six-year sentence would be released in four years. Governors and the president of the United States have the power to grant pardons or executive clemency, an act of grace toward a convicted offender. Commutation of sentence reduces the time an inmate must serve. Inmates who assist the staff during a prison riot or who are terminally ill are most likely to have their sentences commuted. Inmates can participate in a reentry program, in the course of which they are gradually reintegrated into the community. Finally, inmates can be granted parole, in which case they return to the community and are supervised by a parole officer.

Parole can be defined as releasing offenders from a correctional institution, after they have served a portion of their sentence, under the continued custody of the state and under conditions that permit their reincarceration in the event of a violation. Parole is based on the following legalities. The state extends to offenders a privilege by releasing them from prison before their full sentence is served. The state also enters a release contract with offenders in exchange for their promise to abide by certain conditions. Offenders who violate the law or the conditions of parole can be returned to prison to complete their sentences. The state retains control of parolees until they are dismissed from parole.[2]

Parolees do not easily walk away from the prison experience. They face a number of difficulties when they first return home. Occasionally, as they attempt to orient themselves to outside society, they may find themselves using the coping strategies they used within the institution. Some of their institutional "flashbacks" may simply provide a good laugh for others and for themselves. But some of their learned behaviors may be costly in terms of employment, friendship, marriage, and children. Years of institutional restrictions make it difficult for them to adapt to unfamiliar parole rules and regulations. Another difficulty is that the lack of meaningful employment and meager pay increase the temptation to return to crime and, for a brief time, to enjoy the pleasures denied by their years in prison.

On 31 December 1999, those on parole numbered 712,713, a record population.[3] (See Table 8.1 for the adults on parole on 1 January 1999.) The parole population grew

Table 8.1

Adults on Parole, 1999

Region and Jurisdiction	Parole Population					Number on Probation on 12/31/99 per 100,000 Adult Residents
	1/1/99	1999		12/31/99	Percent Change during 1999	
		Entries	Exits			
U.S. Total	696,385	429,172	412,167	712,713	2.3%	352
Federal	67,169	26,653	22,575	71,020	5.7%	35
State	629,216	402,519	389,592	641,693	2.0	317
Northeast	162,006	49,962	51,023	162,840	0.5%	415
Connecticut	1,396	1,338	1,208	1,526	9.3	62
Maine	33	0	2	31	−6.1	3
Massachusetts*	4,489	4,033	3,689	4,304	−4.1	91
New Hampshire	1,141	:	:	1,146	0.4	128
New Jersey	13,218	10,394	10,644	12,968	−1.9	211
New York	59,548	25,200	26,792	57,956	−2.7	421
Pennsylvania	81,001	8,199	7,917	83,702	3.3	916
Rhode Island	432	515	534	413	−4.4	55
Vermont*	748	283	237	794	6.1	175
Midwest	94,110	77,648	71,737	100,021	6.3%	213
Illinois	30,432	25,422	25,370	30,484	0.2	341
Indiana*	4,258	4,898	4,617	4,539	6.6	103
Iowa*	2,194	2,805	2,485	2,514	14.6	117
Kansas	6,025	5,352	5,468	5,909	−1.9	302
Michigan	15,331	9,681	9,471	15,541	1.4	213
Minnesota	2,995	3,464	3,308	3,151	5.2	90
Missouri	10,366	8,501	7,419	11,448	10.4	281
Nebraska*	624	687	699	612	−1.9	50
North Dakota	174	370	387	157	−9.8	33
Ohio	11,304	11,237	6,765	15,776	39.6	188
South Dakota*	1,125	964	729	1,360	20.9	254
Wisconsin	9,282	4,267	5,019	8,530	−8.1	219
South	223,922	96,430	94,250	223,469	−0.2%	312
Alabama*	5,221	1,861	2,170	5,005	−4.1	151
Arkansas	6,979	5,519	4,853	7,645	9.5	404
Delaware*	572	268	206	634	10.8	111
District of Columbia	7,055	:	:	5,103	. . .	1,204
Florida*	6,487	4,780	4,413	6,418	−1.1	56
Georgia	20,482	12,149	10,290	22,003	7.4	384
Kentucky*	4,508	3,117	2,757	4,868	8.0	163
Louisiana	18,759	14,185	11,040	21,904	16.8	688
Maryland*	15,528	8,059	8,580	15,007	−3.4	389
Mississippi	1,489	688	821	1,356	−8.9	67
North Carolina	5,806	5,603	7,020	4,389	−24.4	77
Oklahoma	1,532	610	615	1,527	−0.3	62
South Carolina	4,404	786	1,246	3,944	−10.4	135
Tennessee	7,605	3,288	3,555	7,338	−3.5	177
Texas	109,820	30,316	30,826	109,310	−0.5	763
Virginia	6,700	4,357	5,197	5,860	−12.5	113
West Virginia	975	844	661	1,158	18.8	83
West	149,178	178,479	172,582	155,363	4.1%	348
Alaska*	478	321	306	493	3.1	117
Arizona*	3,742	6,490	6,517	3,715	−0.7	108
California*	108,424	153,571	148,303	114,046	5.2	471
Colorado*	5,204	3,979	3,920	5,263	1.1	176
Hawaii*	2,009	1,058	911	2,252	12.1	251
Idaho*	1,309	873	872	1,310	0.1	145
Montana*	667	500	618	549	−17.7	83
Nevada	4,055	:	:	3,893	−4.0	295
New Mexico	1,773	1,710	1,561	1,922	8.4	154
Oregon	17,270	7,485	6,881	17,874	3.5	718
Utah	3,424	2,249	2,285	3,388	−1.1	238
Washington	375	15	190	200	−46.7	5
Wyoming	448	228	218	458	2.2	130

Note: Because of nonresponse or incomplete data, the probation population for some jurisdictions on 31 December 1999, does not equal the population on 1 January 1999, plus entries, minus exits. During 1999 an estimated 451,600 persons entered parole supervision, and 434,300 exited, based on imputations for agencies that did not provide data.

. . . Comparable percentage could not be calculated.

: Not known.

*Data do not include parolees in one or more of the following categories: absconder, out of state, inactive, intensive supervision, or electronic monitoring.

Source: Bureau of Justice Statistics, *Probation and Parole in the United States, 1999* (Washington, D.C.: U.S. Department of Justice, 2000), p. 5.

179

2.3 percent during 1999, less than the average annual increase of 3.3 percent since 1990. Eight states reported a parole population increase of 10 percent or more in 1999: Ohio, 39.6 percent; South Dakota, 20.9 percent; West Virginia, 18.8 percent; Louisiana, 16.8 percent; and Iowa, 14.6 percent. Twenty-four states in 1999 reported a declining parole population, led by Washington, down 46.7 percent and North Carolina, down 24.4 percent. At the end of 1999, California had 114,046 on parole supervision, the largest number of persons under parole supervision. Texas maintained 109,310 on parole, the second largest parole population.[4]

HOW DID PAROLE DEVELOP IN THE TWENTIETH CENTURY?

Parole began in the nineteenth century and had a rapid growth in the early decades of the twentieth century, as part of the overall movement for reform during the Progressive era. Parole statutes were passed in nearly every state and jurisdiction across the nation. By 1922, forty-four states had a parole system; by 1927, only Florida, Mississippi, and Virginia were without a parole system.[5] What is striking about the rapid development of parole is that state after state enacted parole legislation with minimum debate.[6] According to David Rothman, parole's broad-based support included concerned citizens, settlement house workers, social workers, psychologists, psychiatrists, judges, district attorneys, and institutional administrators.[7]

Parole became the principal means of releasing inmates from state prisons and reformatories by the second decade of the twentieth century. In 1927, of the 44,208 inmates released from prison, 49 percent were paroled, 42 percent were released upon expiration of their maximum sentence, and 9 percent were released by other means.[8]

In 1931, the National Commission on Law Observance and Enforcement (better known as the Wickersham Report) evaluated the status of parole and concluded that the most serious deficiency was in the quality of supervision provided to parolees after release. In fourteen states, the only contact with parolees was through correspondence. Written reports were required, but there was little attempt to verify their accuracy.[9] The 1930s and 1940s were decades in which discretionary parole release was one of the key features of the rehabilitative ideal. Under indeterminate sentencing, parole boards were given broad discretion to set release dates. Yet in most jurisdictions, parole hearings were informal and relatively unstructured, and parole boards' membership was part-time or ex-officio.[10]

During the 1960s the status of parole reached its highest level. The President's Commission on Law Enforcement and Administration of Justice's *Task Force Report: Corrections* gave parole its stamp of approval, saying that when parole is used appropriately, it accomplishes the goals of public protection and offender reintegration.[11]

What is ironic is that soon after this endorsement, parole was seriously challenged by both liberals and conservatives. Attacks on parole seemed to center on the following criticisms.[12] Little scientific evidence was available that suggested parole release and supervision reduced subsequent recidivism.[13] Parole and indeterminate sentencing also were challenged as unjust and inhumane, especially when imposed on unwilling participants. Research showed little relationship between participation in rehabilitation programs and postrelease recidivism.[14] Furthermore, indeterminate sentencing permitted the parole board and other decision makers to use a great deal of uncontrolled discretion in release decisions. It was argued that these decisions were often discriminatory and inconsistent.

The survivability of parole was further challenged during the late 1970s and 1980s when all fifty states, the federal government, and the District of Columbia revised or considered replacing indeterminate with determinate sentencing codes. Although a majority of jurisdictions ultimately retained their indeterminate sentencing codes, fifteen states between 1976 and 1982 passed determinate sentencing legislation.[15] But even in states that retained indeterminate sentencing, mandatory sentencing laws were passed, and habitual or repeat offender laws were either passed or strengthened.[16]

The response that parole made to this political and legal pressure was to reshape itself along the lines of a new "managerial model."[17] This "managerial model," according to Jonathan Simon, involved "a diminishing role for discretion" and individual judgment, "increased integration of production functions and functions that monitor performance, and a tendency to transform substantive evaluation (Is he dangerous?) into formal procedures (Is his drug test positive?)."[18]

WHAT DO PAROLE PRACTICES CONSIST OF TODAY?

The movement to abolish parole peaked by the mid-1980s, but significant limits already had been placed on the discretion of paroling authorities in many states, particularly concerning the release and supervision of offenders. The parole board has been abolished in eleven states and the federal government.[19] Twenty-one other states severely limit the use of the parole board. The proportion of inmates released by parole boards has declined for more than a decade. Dramatic examples of this are New York and Texas.[20] In New York, the parole board granted parole to 66.7 percent of inmates who applied when their minimum sentences were up in 1991. By 1995, the rate was 63.5 percent and by 1999, it had dropped to 46.6 percent. In Texas, 57 percent of all cases considered for parole release in 1988 were approved, but only 20 percent were approved in 1998.

Community supervision for individuals released from prison is required in every state except Maine and Virginia. Inmates enter supervision either by a parole board decision or by mandatory release. In indeterminate-sentencing systems, the parole board releases inmates to conditional supervision in the community based on statutory or administrative determination of eligibility. Inmates usually must serve some fraction of the minimum or maximum before becoming eligible for parole. But in determinate-sentencing systems, inmates are conditionally released from prison when they have served their original sentence minus time off for good behavior, a type of release that is referred to as **supervisory mandatory release.**[21]

In contrast, **unconditional prison releases** are those that occur when the offender's obligation to serve a sentence has been satisfied. For example, "expiration of term" refers to a release from prison after a sentence has been fully served or after earned credits have been reduced. When this happens, no further conditional supervision in the community is required. About one in five state inmates leaves prison with no postrelease supervision.[22]

By the end of the twentieth century, parole continued to symbolize the leniency of a system in which inmates are "let out" early. The public is quick to call for abolishing parole when a parolee commits a particularly heinous crime, such as the kidnapping and murder of 13-year-old Polly Klass by California parolee Richard Allen Davis or the rape and murder of 7-year-old Megan Kanka in New Jersey by a released sex offender, Jesse Timmendequas. See Outside the Walls 8.1.

Polly Klass was kidnapped at knifepoint from her bedroom slumber party on 1 October 1993. The community of Petaluma, California, as well as the entire San Francisco Bay Area, responded with a spontaneous effort to find her. Thousands of volunteers joined in what became an international search to find the missing child. The Polly Klass Foundation was formed 23 October 1993, to continue the search for Polly. When her murder was discovered, the Foundation adopted a new mission: "Make America Safe for Children." The Polly Klass Foundation perceives Polly as truly "America's Child." It is

outside the walls 8.1

The Murder of Megan Kanka and the Passing of Megan's Law

In 1994, Jesse Timmendequas, age 36, murdered 7-year old Megan Kanka of Hamilton Township, New Jersey. He lived across the street from the Kankas, but they were unaware that Timmendequas was a convicted child molester. During Timmendequas's trial, Richard Kanka described his daughter to the jury as "Mom's little homemaker," a gentle girl who held tea parties for her dolls while also playing in the mud with her brother's trucks.

The tragedy of the death of this child led to New Jersey passing the legislation commonly called "Megan's Law." This law, as well as a 1994 federal crime measure, allows states to inform a community when a convicted sex offender moves into the area. In 1996, Congress passed a tougher version of Megan's Law, which requires states to inform the public when a convicted sex offender considered a danger to the public is released from prison and settles in the neighborhood. On 17 May 1996, President Clinton signed Megan's Law legislation. States were required to establish a warning system by September 1997 or lose some federal anticrime funds. A National Sex Offender Registry became fully operational in 1999.

> Each state's Sex Offender Registry makes it possible for citizens to make inquiries...

Some states subject sex offenders who are on parole or probation to regular polygraph tests to determine whether they have experienced the urge to commit new sex offenses. Some support is given to chemical castration as an appropriate form of punishment. Each state's Sex Offender Registry makes it possible for citizens to make inquiries to the sheriff or police departments about "at risk" sex offenders. Some states' Sex Offender Registries are online or on CD-ROM and provide photos of offenders.

CRITICAL THINKING QUESTIONS

The purpose of Megan's Law is to protect children. Can a sex offender have his name legitimately removed from the Sex Offender Registry? What more can be done to protect children against predators?

Sources: Jeremy Travis, "But They All Come Back: Rethinking Prisoner Reentry," *Sentencing and Corrections: Issues for the 21st Century* (Washington, D.C.: U.S. Department of Justice, 2000), p. 5.

committed to turning the tragedy of her death into a force of positive change for the protection of children.[23]

Parole at the end of the twentieth century was being altered by new technologies of control aimed at risk management. These technologies had emerged from the earlier managerial model developed during the 1970s. Prediction and classification, computerized databases, drug testing, and a no-nonsense approach were the basic parameters of the new control model.[24] The emergence of these technologies was driven by their ability to fit into the new ideological and organization environment left by the breakdown of the rehabilitation model.[25]

HOW DOES THE PAROLE BOARD FUNCTION?

The **parole board** is administered either by an independent agency (autonomous model) or by a board that is part of a single large department that runs all state correctional programs (consolidated model). The parole board is an independent agency in all but five states (Maryland, Michigan, Minnesota, Ohio, and Texas), but parole field services are administered by the department of corrections in two-thirds of the states (see Table 8.2).[26]

Table 8.2

Parole Service Providers

State	Number Board Members	Adult Paroling Authorities	Adult Parole Services
Alabama	3	Bd Pardons & Paroles	Bd Pardons and Paroles
Arkansas	5 (PT)	Bd Parole	Dept. Corrections
Arizona	7	Bd Exec Clemency	Bd Exec Clemency
California	7 (PT)	Post-Prison Transfer Board	Bd C & Cmty Pun/Dept County Pun
Colorado	9	Bd Prison Terms	YAC/DOC/Par & County Svcs Div
Connecticut	7	Bd Parole	DOC/Div Adult Parole Supv
Delaware	11 (PT)	Bd Parole	DOC/Div Op/Cmty Svcs
District of Columbia	5 (PT)	Bd Parole	DOC/Div Cmty Svcs
Florida	5	Parole Commission	DOC/Prob & Parole Svcs
Georgia	7	Bd Pardons & Paroles	Bd Pardons and Paroles
Hawaii	5	Paroling Authority	Paroling Authority/Field Svcs
Idaho	3 (PT)	Cmsn for Pardons and Parole	DOC/Div Field & Cmty Svcs
Illinois	5 (PT)	Prisoner Review Bd	DOC/Cmty Svcs Div
Indiana	12	Parole Bd	DOC/Parole Svcs Section
Iowa	5 (PT)	Parole Bd	DOC/Div Cmty Corr Svcs
Kansas	5	Parole Bd	DOC/Cmty Field Svcs
Louisiana	7	Parole Bd	DPSC/Div Prob & Parole
Maine	5 (PT)	Parole Bd	DOC/Div Prob & Parole
Maryland	8	Parole Commission	DPSCS/Div Parole & Prob
Massachusetts	8	Parole Bd	Parole Bd
Michigan	10	Parole Bd	DOC/Field Op Admin
Minnesota	4 (PT)	DOC/Office Adult Release	DOC/Prob Par Supv Rel/Co Cts or Cra
Mississippi	5	Parole Bd	DOC/Cmty Svcs Div
Missouri	5	Bd Prob & Parole	DOC/Bd Prob & Parole
Montana	3 (PT)	Bd Pardons	DCHS/CD/Prob & Parole Bureau
Nebraska	5	Bd Parole	DCS/Adult Parole Admin
Nevada	6	Bd Parole Commission	DMV/Div Parole & Prob
New Hampshire	5 (PT)	Bd Parole	DOC/Div Field Svcs
New Jersey	9	Parole Bd	DOC/Bureau Parole
New Mexico	4	Adult Parole Bd	CD/Prob & Parole Div
New York	19	Bd Parole	Div Parole
North Carolina	5	Parole Commission	DOC/Div Adult Prob & Parole
North Dakota	3 (PT)	Parole Bd	DCR/Div Parole & Prob
Ohio	11	DRC/Prob & Parole Field Svcs Ad Parole Auth & Parole Bd	DCR/Prob & Parole Field Svcs
Oklahoma	5 (PT)	Pardon & Parole Bd	DOC/Prob & Parole Svcs
Oregon	4	Bd Parole & Pos Prison Supv	DOC/Cmty Corrections
Pennsylvania	5	Bd Parole & Parole & Co Cts	Bd Prob & Parole & Co Cts
Rhode Island	6 (PT)	Parole Bd	DOC/Div Rehab Svcs
South Carolina	7 (PT)	Bd Pardons & Paroles	Dept Prob, Parole & Prob Svcs
South Dakota	6 (PT)	Bd Pardons & Paroles	DOC
Tennessee	7	Bd Paroles	BP/Parole Field Svcs
Texas	18	Bd Pardons & Paroles	TDC/PPD/Parole Supv
Utah	5	Bd Pardons	DOC/Div Field Operations
Vermont	5 (PT)	Bd Parole	AHS/DOC
Virginia	5	Parole Bd	DOC/Div Cmty Corr
Washington	3	Indeterminate Serv Review Bd	DOC/Div Cmty Corr
West Virginia	3	Parole Bd	DFS/Div Corrections
Wisconsin	5	Parole Commission	DOC/Div Prob & Parole
Wyoming	7 (PT)	Bd Parole	DOC/Div Field Svcs
United States	9	Parole Commission	Admin Ofc of U.S. Courts

Source: American Correctional Association, *Probation and Parole Directory* (Laurel, Md.: American Correctional Association, 1998).

The majority of states have a full-time parole board. As Table 8.2 reveals, the membership of state parole boards varies from 3 to 19. New York has the largest parole board, with 19 members. Eighteen jurisdictions have 5-member boards; six have 3-member boards. In nineteen states, the governor appoints the parole board. Wisconsin and Ohio are the only states in which members are appointed from a civil service list. Very few states have specific professional qualifications for board members.[27]

Parole decisions are made in a number of ways. In some jurisdictions the entire board interviews eligible inmates. In other jurisdictions, only part of the board conducts interviews. A few jurisdictions use hearing examiners to interview inmates. In some states, inmates are not interviewed at all; the parole board make its decisions from written reports.

Most states have recently taken steps to ensure due process at release hearings. For example, about half of the states now permit counsel to be present and witnesses to be called. Verbatim transcripts are frequently made of the hearings. Inmates are typically provided both a written and an oral explanation of the parole decision. Yet inmates continue to be denied access to their files, so they are unable to determine why their cases are decided as they are.

Eligibility for parole is determined in different ways across the nation. The common procedure is to make an inmate eligible for parole when he or she has served the minimum sentence minus credits for "good time." But some states make an inmate eligible for parole at the parole board's discretion or at the completion of one-third or one-half of the inmate's maximum sentence. See Table 8.3 for the status of parole release in 1998.[28]

The new federal guidelines are based on the abolition of parole for federal prisoners received after 1989. The U.S. Parole Commission, then, has jurisdiction only over prisoners received before 1989. The U.S. Parole Commission does not have jurisdiction over inmates released from prison, because the Federal Probation Service administers both probation and parole.

Twenty-seven states and the District of Columbia have established truth-in-sentencing laws, which require individuals convicted of selected violent crimes to serve at least 85 percent of the announced prison sentence. To satisfy the 85 percent test (and thus qualify for federal funds for prison construction), states have limited the powers of parole boards to set release dates or prison staff to award "good time" and "gain time" (time off for good behavior or for participation in treatment or work programs) or both. Truth-in-sentencing laws nearly eliminate not only parole but also most "good time" statutes.[29]

The majority of the fifteen jurisdictions that give parole authorities the discretion to release still use parole guidelines, or risk prediction instruments, to assist in parole decision making. **Parole guidelines** are actuarial devices predicting the risk of recidivism

This hearing is in a state that gives the parole board full discretionary powers to release convicts from prison. Is this common? In what other ways is parole organized? Who is on a parole board and what is its traditional role? How is eligibility for parole determined? What issues have affected the development of parole policies and practices in the United States?

Table 8.3

Parole Boards and Release Powers

	Parole Board Has Full Release Powers	Parole Board Has Limited Release Powers	If Parole Board Powers Are Limited, Crimes Ineligible for Discretionary Release	Discretionary Parole Abolished (Year Abolished)
Alabama	x			
Alaska		x		
Arizona				x (1994)
Arkansas		x		
California		x	Only for indeterminate life sentences	
Colorado	x			
Connecticut		x	Murders, capital felonies	
Delaware				x (1990)
Florida		x	Certain capital/life felonies	
Georgia		x	Several felonies	
Hawaii	x		Punishment by life without parole	
Idaho	x			
Illinois				x (1978)
Indiana				x (1977)
Iowa		x	Murder 1, kidnap, sex abuse	
Kansas				x (1993)
Kentucky	x			
Louisiana		x	Several felonies	
Maine				x (1975)
Maryland		x	Violent, or death penalty sought	
Massachusetts		x	Murder 1	
Michigan		x	Murder 1, 650+ grams cocaine	
Minnesota				x (1980)
Mississippi				x (1995)
Missouri		x	Several felonies	
Montana	x			
Nebraska		x	Murder 1/life, kidnap/life	
Nevada	x			
New Hampshire		x	Murder 1	
New Jersey	x			
New Mexico				x (1979)
New York		x	"Violent felony offenders"	
North Carolina				x (1994)
North Dakota	x			
Ohio				x (1996)
Oklahoma	x			
Oregon				x (1989)
Pennsylvania	x			
Rhode Island	x			
South Carolina	x			
South Dakota		x	None with life sentence	
Tennessee		x	Murder 1/life, rapes	
Texas		x	None on death row	
Utah	x			
Vermont	x			
Virginia				x (1995)
Washington				x (1984)
West Virginia		x	No life without mercy	
Wisconsin		x	No life without parole	*
Wyoming	x			
Total	15	21		14

*Wisconsin abolished discretionary parole release in 1999, to go into effect on 1 January 2000, for crimes committed on or after that date.

Source: Joan Petersilia, "Parole and Prisoner Reentry in the United States," *Prisons: Crime and Justice: A Review of Research* 26, ed. Michael Tonry and Joan Petersilia (Chicago: University of Chicago Press, 1999), p. 496. Petersilia compiled this table from National Institute of Corrections, *Status Report on Parole, 1996. Results from an NIC Survey* (Washington, D.C., 1997).

Table 8.4

Tennessee's Parole Risk Assessment Instrument

Risk Factor	Category	Score	
Number of previous paroles on this sentence	None One or more	2 5	_____
Maximum sentence length at time of release	5 years or less 6–9 years 10 years or more	0 2 5	_____
Age at first juvenile adjudication	No juvenile record 13 or younger 14 or over	0 1 3	_____
Number of previous felony incarcerations	None 1 or more	0 4	_____
Instant offense was burglary, forgery, or fraud	No Yes	0 4	_____
Living arrangement with spouse or parents	Yes No	0 3	_____
Age at incarceration on current offense	32 or older 22–31 21 or younger	0 1 3	_____
Employment status at first parole contact	Employed Unemployed	0 2	_____
Parole officer assessment of attitude	Positive Generally positive Generally negative Negative	0 2 5 7	_____
Parole officer assessment of risk	Minimum Medium Maximum	0 1 2	
		Total Score:	_____

Score ranges: 0–10 minimum, 11–17 medium, 18–24 maximum, 25+ intensive supervision.

Source: Tennessee Department of Corrections, 1986.

based on background information about the offender and the crime. Such instruments have been shown to be better predictors of recidivism than release decisions based on individual assessments or on case studies. One-half of the jurisdictions in the United States presently use formal risk assessment instruments in relation to parole release.[30] Table 8.4 shows the parole risk assessment instrument used in Tennessee.

HOW DOES THE PAROLE OFFICER FUNCTION TODAY?

Parole officers usually wear a law enforcement hat, but there is a new movement in parole among officers who understand that service remains an important part of the job. They regard parolees as assets to be managed rather than liabilities to be supervised.[31]

Parole officers are seen as community corrections officers with community policing responsibilities (Boston, Massachusetts), as community outreach workers (Spokane, Washington), and as job and service brokers (Deschutes County, Oregon).[32]

Parole officers have much in common with probation officers. Both perform duties that are investigatory and regulatory. They face similar role conflicts and frustrations. Both cope with excessive caseloads, both lack community resources, and both are inadequately trained.

In the vast majority of states a bachelor's degree is required for entry-level parole officer positions. Some states that require a bachelor's degree also specify that the degree must be in an allied field, such as sociology, psychology, social work, or administration of justice. States not requiring a bachelor's degree (Idaho, Indiana, Iowa, Kansas, Maine, Massachusetts, Minnesota, Nevada, and Wisconsin) generally substitute several years of experience as an entry requirement.[33]

In 1998, the number of parole officers in a state ranged from 2,598 in California, 2,659 in Texas, and 2,640 in New York to 37 in South Dakota and 30 in Nebraska. The minimum annual starting salary, as of 1 January 1999, ranged from $43,644 in California, $38,068 in Massachusetts, $36,444 in New Jersey, to $21,902 in South Dakota, $20,452 in West Virginia, and $20,412 in Tennessee. In the eighteen states that have parole agencies, the average entry-level salary is $28,491, the average salary is $37,319, and the average highest-level salary is $45,185.[34]

The average regular caseload of parole officers in 1998 was 67 clients, less than the average caseload of probation officers (124) or the combined probation and parole department caseload (94). The largest regular caseload (105) was found in Minnesota, the smallest in Nebraska (40). Parole officers' caseloads, like those of probation officers, also include intensive cases, electronic cases, and special cases.[35]

In many states and the federal government, the same officer provides both probation and parole services. In separated departments, state-administered parole services usually pay officers somewhat better than do county-funded probation services. Parole officers also tend to be older and more experienced in the criminal justice system than are probation officers.

Surveillance and Constraint

Parole agents are powerful legal actors. They are equipped with legal authority to carry and use firearms. In 1998, 17 of 25 state parole agencies across the nation authorized their officers to carry firearms; 25 out of 29 combined probation and parole agencies authorized their officers to carry firearms.[36] Parole agents have legal authority to search persons, places, and property without fulfilling the requirements imposed by the Fourth Amendment. They are able to order arrests without probable cause and to confine without bail. Parole agents also are able to recommend revocation of parole for new crimes or for technical violations of the conditions of parole. Agents' authority extends into the wider community. Their power to search applies to households where a parolee is living and to businesses where a parolee is working.[37]

Parolees are required to sign an agreement stating that they will abide by certain regulations—standard conditions applicable to all parolees and special conditions tailored to particular parolees. Specific conditions for substance abusers almost always include periodic drug testing. Common general conditions include reporting to a parole officer within twenty-four hours of release; reporting changes of address and employment; seeking and maintaining employment; obeying the law; submitting to search by police and parole officers; and avoiding carrying a weapon, leaving the county for more than forty-eight hours without prior approval from the parole agent, or traveling more than fifty miles from home.[38]

The relationship that develops between parole officer and parolee is much more adversarial than supportive. Parolees see the officers' weapons and handcuffs and know the officers can have them returned to prison. Indeed, parole officers sometimes personally escort inmates back to prison. In turn, parole officers know that some parolees are dangerous and require little provocation for assault. In explaining why parolees are so dangerous now, a veteran supervisor described the differences between heroin addicts in the past and cocaine abusers now:

> Rehabilitation is less workable now than in the old days. Now we have more violent parolees. Heroin users in the old days were our main concern. They committed property crimes but they were not particularly violent. They also had more of a will to try to change. The emphasis on self-help is not there anymore. We have younger, more aggressive offenders who abuse cocaine. Their potential for violence is truly frightening.[39]

An examination of a large district parole office in Illinois (a 1978 study and a 1992 update) and a study of parole agents in a midwestern state found that bureaucratic, or organizational, constraints greatly influenced officers' supervision of parolees.[40] Another study found that the decisions of parole officers, especially about revoking parole, are affected in part by their perceptions of their supervisors' likely response.[41]

Parole Revocation and Parolees' Rights

The types of parole violations that justify the return of a parolee to prison have attracted the interest of policymakers. If a state is too quick to return parolees to prison for minor violations of parole conditions, parolees may conclude that parole sets them up for failure. If too many parolees are returned to prison, prison overcrowding worsens and politicians issue warnings about being "too tough" on criminals. Outside the Walls 8.2 describes the incidents that landed one parolee back in prison for a technical violation.

outside the walls 8.2

"I Made a Mistake, but I Haven't Committed Any Crimes"

An inmate released from a prison in Oregon received an interstate transfer to his parents' home in the Midwest. Tom found a job doing heavy construction, lived at home, and made an excellent initial adjustment to the community. The company transferred him to a western state for a road construction job. His parole officer had no problem with his working out West. Several months later, Tom broke his hand and returned home while his hand healed.

When Tom was able to work again, the construction company put him on a local job. It was here that he met a woman who was working in the office and had separated from her husband. It was not long before they began a relationship. Although the county where she lived was not the county where Tom was on parole, he decided to move in with her. Her estranged husband called Tom's parole officer, who had Tom arrested and put in jail for violating his parole.

> Tom had changed residences without telling his parole officer . . .

Tom had changed residences without telling his parole officer; he was living outside the county without his parole officer's permission; and he was interfering in a still legally intact marriage. The decision was made to return him to Oregon, where he would receive a parole revocation hearing. At the hearing, parole was revoked, and Tom was returned to prison.

CRITICAL THINKING QUESTIONS

Do you think that Tom gave parole authorities sufficient reason to revoke his parole and return him to prison? If not, what would have been a more appropriate punishment? What technical violations of parole do you believe would justify returning a parolee to prison?

Source: This incident was reported to the author in 2000 by the parolee.

Technical violations of parole have become such a serious problem in recent years that they constitute over half of parole violations. In 1991, about 140,000 parole violators were returned to prison; in 1998, more than 200,000 parole violators were returned, an increase of 45 percent.[42]

In *Morrissey v. Brewer* (1972), the U.S. Supreme Court first ruled on procedures for **revocation of parole.** Morrissey was a check writer who had been paroled from the Iowa State Penitentiary. Seven months after his release, his parole was revoked for a technical violation, and he was returned to prison. At about the same time, a second petitioner, Booher, was returned to prison on a technical parole violation. Both men petitioned for habeas corpus on the ground that they had been denied **due process** of the law and returned to prison without opportunities to defend themselves at an open hearing. The two cases were consolidated for appeal and eventually reached the U.S. Supreme Court.

In his opinion, Chief Justice Warren Burger laid down the essential elements of due process for parole revocation. The first requirement was a hearing before an "uninvolved" hearing officer, who might be another parole officer or perhaps an "independent decision maker," who would determine whether there was reasonable cause to believe that a parole violation had taken place. If so, the parolee might be returned to prison, subject to a full revocation hearing before the parole board. Due process in such a proceeding was outlined as follows:

> Our task is limited to deciding the minimum requirements of due process. They include: (a) written notice of the claimed violation of parole; (b) disclosure to the parolee of evidence against him; (c) opportunity to be heard in person and to present witnesses and documentary evidence; (d) the right to confront and cross-examine adverse witnesses (unless the hearing officer specifically finds good cause for not allowing confrontation); (e) a "neutral and detached" hearing body such as a traditional parole board, members of which need not be judicial officers or lawyers; and (f) a written statement by the fact finders as to the evidence relied on and reasons for revoking parole.[43]

The importance of this decision to the administration of parole cannot be exaggerated. Before *Morrissey,* parole boards and parole officers were free to administer summary justice to parolees for technical violations of parole of little significance. The following justification was made for this treatment: Parole was an extension of confinement; parolees were prisoners serving part of their sentences outside the prison. Like other convicts, they were subject to changes in the program at the discretion of the system's officials. Due process of the law was irrelevant; at the time of conviction prisoners had received all the due process to which they were entitled. The *Morrissey* decision, by imposing strict requirements before the paroling authorities could inflict the "grievous loss" of freedom, drastically revised the whole concept of parole.

Several other issues were ruled on around the time of *Morrissey.* It was held that parolees have no legal right to bail pending a revocation hearing.[44] The courts also ruled that all that is needed to satisfy the parole board at the revocation hearing is demonstration that the parolee failed to meet the conditions of parole.[45] In other words, the standard of proof need not be "beyond a reasonable doubt."

The actual revocation procedures begin when the parole officer requests a warrant based on an alleged violation of parole. A parole officer, a warrant officer, or a police officer can issue a warrant. Once parolees are in custody, they are given a list of the charges against them. The next step in this process, which tends to vary from state to state, gives prisoners an opportunity to challenge at a preliminary hearing the allegation of violation and to confront adverse witnesses, including parole officers. The hearing officer is usually a senior officer, whose chief task is to determine whether there are reasonable grounds for believing that parolees have violated one or more of the conditions of parole—that is, whether there is "probable cause." If probable cause exists, parolees are held in custody for a revocation hearing. If probable cause is not found, parolees are returned to supervision.

A more comprehensive revocation hearing is held to determine whether the violation of parole is serious enough to justify returning parolees to prison. If parole is not revoked, parolees are returned to supervision. Jurisdictions vary greatly in determining how much time revoked parolees should spend in prison. They also vary in their decisions on whether parolees should receive credit for the time they spend under parole supervision.[46]

In complying with the requirements of due process imposed in *Morrissey v. Brewer,* parole officers and parole boards have focused their attention on the processing of violating cases. However, instead of receiving praise from the political system for its get-tough approach, the parole system has received criticism for its high return rates, because of the ongoing problem of prison overcrowding and its fiscal implications. Jonathan Simon has described this no-win situation: "Parole has been successful in transforming itself from a system of rehabilitative discipline to one of risk management and now finds itself criticized for that accomplishment."[47]

WHY IS RELEASE FROM PRISON TRAUMATIC?

Persons released to the community generally go through several stages before and after release from incarceration: prerelease stress, the frustrations of the early days at home, and struggles to uphold the commitment made in prison to "go straight."

Prerelease Stress

The problems that newly released men and women encounter have been recognized almost since the invention of the prison. As early as 1817, a commission of the Massachusetts legislature recommended the construction of a halfway house to ease the difficulties of readjustment.[48]

The stress and problems of the reintegration period actually begin as prisoners' release dates near. The "short time" syndrome—also known as "getting short," "shortitis," and "gate fever"—is quite real. According to one study, signs of this syndrome include irritability, anxiety, restlessness, and a variety of psychophysiological symptoms.[49]

The Frustrations of the Early Days at Home

The euphoria of release often gives way to a letdown. This is particularly true for individuals who return after several years away. Friends from the past have moved away or perhaps no longer want to be friends. Families, too, are not the same as they were when the offender was sent to prison. The attempt to restore old ties and establish new ones may be a threatening experience and may make the ex-offender feel like a stranger or an outsider. Moreover, the slow pace of prison life is replaced by hundreds of people shoving and crowding on streets and in shopping malls. Returned felons soon discover that the way to gain acceptance in prison does not work in the community. Trust in prison is problematic in a world where everyone is looking out for himself or herself. In the community, the failure to trust leads to social isolation.

The first forty-eight hours are critical. The ex-offender must report to a parole officer and face the initial temptations of the streets. Alcohol and drugs will probably be available. It is at this time that the person begins to reassess resolutions made in prison about staying off drugs, obeying the rules, and getting a job.

One of ex-offenders' major sources of frustration is finding a job. As one parolee said in a NBC documentary on parole, "An ex-con isn't exactly a résumé builder."[50] Without

What are the duties of a parole officer? What are the rights and responsibilities of a parolee? Under what circumstances could this parolee have his parole revoked and be returned to prison? How common is parole revocation? What does research suggest about the effectiveness of parole for the purpose for which it is intended?

jobs, ex-offenders cannot provide for their own needs or make financial contributions to their families. A midwestern parolee expressed his frustration with the job search:

> I think the hardest thing about coming out of prison to the free world is finding a job. I was born with two strikes, being black and male. Then once a man gets a criminal record, that is the third strike. They say they want you to make it, but everywhere you go—state agency, job interview with private employer—you are met with the same look. It's the look that says you're unwanted, and no matter how many help-wanted signs are in the window, it always seems they want everyone's help but mine. What makes it even more difficult is that while we were in prison we gained very few viable skills, nothing that can really help you out in society. So that when we get out, most of us are unequipped to make it.[51]

Another major frustration is related to housing. The parolee is given only a bus ticket and a limited amount of money when leaving prison. Parents may not want the parolee back in the house because their son or daughter was so disruptive before. The parolee may not like the living arrangements proposed by the parole officer but lacks money to pay for more desirable housing.

Another challenge is maintaining the commitment made in prison to stay away from negative influences. Old friends come around and want the parolee to do this and that, and it is not easy to turn them down. They may be the only friends the ex-offender has. What makes it so hard to say no is that negative peer influence was one of the reasons the parolee got into trouble in the first place.[52]

An additional frustration results from the civil disabilities imposed on convicted felons. The get-tough movement of the 1980s increased the statutory restrictions placed on parolees.[53] Ex-offenders confront legal and social barriers that stand between them and job opportunities. Examinations of statutory barriers indicate that as many as three hundred occupations require licenses that are unobtainable by persons with felony convictions. Felons are not likely to find work as nurses, barbers or beauticians, real estate

outside the walls 8.3

Why So Many Go Back

"Those who go back [to prison] are going back into that world. What happens is that world is developed within you while you are in prison and that world you left behind will creep up on you. It becomes a little monster inside of you that tells you that you would be better off in prison. When things start to fall apart, it is easy to go back into that world.

"In a real sense, those who go back can't handle the free world. They can't handle the fact that every day we are free it is a challenge. They aren't strong enough to say, 'I would rather be a bum living on skid row than be back in the confines of the prison experience.' Those who go back are those who give up on the hope that something good will happen to them in the free world."

> ... those who go back can't handle the real world.

CRITICAL THINKING QUESTIONS

In the opinion of this ex-offender, why do so many parolees return to prison? What theoretical explanation of crime does this explanation support?

salespersons, or cashiers, or to work in a place where alcoholic beverages are sold. Limited work experience, lack of training, difficulty in accepting supervision, and unrealistic expectations about income and promotion also put ex-offenders seeking jobs at a disadvantage. Also, dealing with the public and with coworkers is not a skill learned in prison, so ex-offenders are unlikely candidates for any job calling for interaction with strangers.

The disenfranchisement laws or civil disabilities extend into many other areas of the convicted felon's life. Fourteen states permanently deny convicted felons the right to vote (most other states restrict this right until felons fulfill their sentences). Their criminal records may preclude them from retaining parental rights, may be grounds for divorce, and may bar them from serving on a jury, holding public office, and owning firearms. Eight jurisdictions require ex-offenders to register with a police department on release from prison.[54]

Those Who Are Successful in "Making It" in the Community

Several factors appear to be crucial to success in the community. A support system is one of the most important. As one individual on parole put it, "If you come out of prison without a real support system of family and friends, nine times out of ten you won't make it."[55] Ex-offenders frequently claim that their "turning point" was the support they received from their spouses, parents, or religious faith. Determination is another important factor, but such determination must go on and on and on. Ex-offenders are aware that they are never out of the woods because it is so easy to go back.[56] Some individuals "make it" simply because they are fed up with spending their lives in prison.[57] One parolee expressed this feeling explicitly: "I have had enough of this. I want to go out and have a decent life."[58] In Outside the Walls 8.3 a parolee explains why so many ex-offenders return to prison.

WHAT ARE THE VARIOUS REENTRY PROGRAMS?

Various reentry programs, especially programs designed to help ex-offenders find jobs, have been established in recent decades to ease the transition from life in prison to living in the community. Some of these programs are associated with parole departments;

others are adjuncts of state employment services. Many other groups, too, are committed to helping ex-offenders. Reentry programs offered by these buffering agencies often make the difference between a parolee's success and return to prison.

Prerelease Instruction

A few institutions offer formal **prerelease instruction,** and inmates are excused from work in prison industries or from academic or vocational programs in order to attend. The purpose of some drug treatment programs attended in prison by inmates who are a year or so away from release is to prepare participants for community living. One such program is Delaware's Key-Crest therapeutic community program, which also includes postrelease supervision.[59]

Some prisons transfer inmates ready for prerelease programs to facilities outside the main prison compound. In other correctional systems, inmates ready to be released are transferred to prerelease guidance centers in the community; there they receive the benefit of work release, home furloughs, and formalized prerelease instruction. These programs typically provide information and instruction about on-the-job safety practices, loyalty to the employer, the importance of being on time, the development of needed skills for business and industry, job opportunities and employment aids, insurance, legal problems and contracts, basic financial management, personal health practices and proper diet, Social Security and Medicare benefits, perspectives on family responsibilities, and human relations.

Work-Release Programs

The generally agreed-upon objectives of **work release** are to place offenders in jobs they can retain after their release, give inmates a means of financial support, help them support their families, enable correctional officials to ascertain their readiness for parole, and preserve family and community ties.

Work-release programs are conducted in jails, prisons, and residential facilities. Inmates in a jail- or prison-based work-release program leave the facility in the morning, usually with lunch and enough money for transportation, and return at the end of the workday. Some inmates are provided transportation to and from work; others depend on public transportation. Commonly, it is the minimum-security facilities that sponsor work-release programs. Community work-release programs are usually held in halfway-house facilities called work-release centers, prerelease guidance centers, or community treatment centers.

All but a few states have laws permitting work-release programs, but states vary in their commitment to work release. In 1998, 37,950 inmates were placed on work release in thirty-six agencies. The states that placed the most inmates on work release were New York (9,085), Illinois (4,394), and Florida (3,690). Arizona, California, Connecticut, Mississippi, Montana, Nevada, New Hampshire, Wyoming, and the Federal Bureau of Prisons placed no inmates on work release during 1998.[60]

Study-Release Programs

Study release gives inmates the opportunity to attend school in the community. Forty states, the District of Columbia, and the Federal Bureau of Prisons have had study-release programs. Instructors who have taught inmates in prison or in the community tend to be quite positive about their academic performance. Inmates themselves usually regard study release as a worthwhile program.

Study release now takes place infrequently in U.S. corrections. In 1998, 103 inmates were placed in study-release programs in seven states: 35 in West Virginia, 20 in New Mexico, 20 in North Carolina, 7 in Massachusetts, 6 in Wisconsin, 5 in Hawaii, and 4 in Indiana.[61]

Home-Furlough Programs

Home furloughs, also called home visits, temporary leaves, and temporary community releases, usually last from forty-eight to seventy-two hours and are given on weekends. Half or more of all such visits are awarded to residents of halfway houses. To qualify for a home furlough, an inmate usually must have minimum-security status and a clean disciplinary record and be near the end of confinement.

Home furloughs have been hit hard by the get-tough approach. California, for example, granted fourteen thousand furloughs in the early 1970s but granted none in 1998. Several serious incidents, including the fatal shooting of a Los Angeles police officer by an offender on furlough, hastened the withdrawal of the furlough program there. Willie Horton, a Massachusetts prisoner who also committed murder while on furlough, became a political issue during the 1988 presidential campaign. Reacting to the adverse publicity given Horton's crime and the tolerant furlough policy of the Massachusetts Department of Corrections, the Bureau of Prisons reduced federal furloughs by one-half.

In 1998, thirty-one states and the Bureau of Prisons permitted furloughs, and 8,681 inmates were permitted to take 95,079 furloughs. New York was the jurisdiction that permitted the most inmates to take furloughs (2,360), but the Bureau of Prisons (2,761) and Texas (1,042) also had active furlough programs. Florida granted the most furloughs (67,790) but did not report the number of inmates involved in this reentry program.[62]

Halfway Houses

Halfway houses for parolees are known by different names in various jurisdictions. They may be called halfway houses, residential centers, work release centers, or **community treatment centers.** They range in size from fewer than ten residents to more than one hundred residents. These facilities typically provide a security-oriented environment in which rules and regulations are enforced. Treatment services may or may not be provided, but the stated purpose of these facilities is to provide an environment that will facilitate a parolee's reentry into the community. Fifty-five halfway houses were operated by ten state agencies on 1 January 1999. There were 19,381 inmates in these residential facilities. On 1 January 1999, twenty-seven states and the Bureau of Prisons had inmates in 573 community treatment centers. These community treatment centers provided services for 16,210 inmates during 1998.[63]

Community-Based Assistance Programs

In the late 1970s, 257 **community-based assistance programs** offered a variety of services to ex-offenders in the United States.[64] These services usually included vocational counseling and job development and placement. But the numbers of programs substantially declined in the 1980s and 1990s. One that has a long history is the Fortune Society in New York City, widely praised for its efforts in helping ex-offenders adjust to community living. This organization serves the largest group of ex-offenders in the nation. It has about twenty thousand names on its mailing list and provides services to about two thousand ex-offenders a year.

The Fortune Society offers counseling services, career development and educational services, substance abuse treatment, HIV services, acupuncture and massage therapy, and a drug-free social environment. In addition, the Fortune Society answers inmates' questions and provides information for inmates all over the country who are in need of services.[65]

The hero in this chapter is Joanne Page, the executive director of the Fortune Society. Since 1990, she has committed herself and her organization to offering helpful services to ex-offenders. Read what she said for *Invitation to Corrections* in 2000.

In sum, community-based assistance programs, like the other reentry programs, provide support and services essential for "making it" in the free world.

h e r o e s

Joanne Page

Executive Director of the Fortune Society

"I started in 1972, when I was in high school and volunteered my services at a program called 'Thresholds.' This program helped teach individuals decision-making skills in a prison setting. I grew up as a child of a concentration camp survivor. I found that working in programs dealing with prisons helped me deal with my history. Because of my background, I have very strong feeling about institutions and do what I can to fight the damage that prisons do to people.

"I felt I was meant for this profession, so I went to law school at Yale University. I graduated in 1980, and started practicing criminal defense law at the Legal Aid Society in Brooklyn, New York. I felt my career was like pushing people through a revolving door. The better job I did, the faster the individuals would come back to me. I got really frustrated working in an atmosphere that was not able to support individual change.

"I left there and went on to the Court Employment Project. Here is where I developed an alternative-to-incarceration program model targeted toward felony cases including robberies and burglaries. The program provided vigorous court advocacy coupled with close supervision and intensive services. We worked to help our clients to change their lives rather than simply getting them out of their cases. I worked there for about six years.

"I wanted to become more involved with system change. I had volunteered at the Fortune Society as a tutor. I loved the atmosphere, the commitment to hiring ex-offenders, and the ability to work with individuals who walked right in the door. That was eleven years ago, and I have been there ever since. The job keeps growing and changing before me and so I keep learning and growing from this job and its environment.

"What I love the most is that I get to watch people change their lives around. When I came to this organization, there were about 22 or 23 employees. Today there are around 110. We have grown tremendously with new programs as we have worked to create a one-stop shopping program model. When people come in, they don't have just one set of issues. If you can handle a variety of problems under one roof, you really increase the chances of getting the help the person needs. So we expanded education, career development, and incarceration services. We added substance abuse treatment and HIV services. Next year, we will be opening up a housing facility for our homeless clients in a building in West Harlem known as "the Castle."

"We serve about three thousand prisoners every year at Fortune. Maybe two-thirds of these at Fortune are new clients. The remaining ones are working on ongoing self-development such as attending our in-house education facility. We are just trying to make a difference. The people who come here are very hopeful for the future, but don't know how to make it happen, and need a supportive community and services to succeed. The greatest risk here is right after release. People come to us, and we help them survive this hardship and work toward their dreams. We do a lot of work around discharge planning to increase people's chances when they get out.

"The work that we are doing is work that is desperately needed, because 500,000 to 600,000 people come out of prison each year. Will they come out dangerous, or will they become people who build their families and their communities? We see people coming out who want to do better, but there are terrible odds against them. With services and a supportive community, role-modeling by successful ex-offender staff, and a lot of love, we work to tip the odds a little more in their favor. Then they have to do the rest, and so many build new and hopeful lives right before our eyes. I feel privileged to be able to do this work."

CRITICAL THINKING QUESTIONS

What does Joanne Page like about her job? Why does she feel the Fortune Society is making a difference?

WHY DOES PAROLE NEED REINVENTING?

Joan Petersilia quotes from a letter written to her by Joe Lehman, currently commissioner of the Washington State Department of Corrections: "We have a broken parole system. Part of the problem is that parole can't do it alone, and we have misled the public in thinking that we can. The public becomes frustrated and cries to abolish parole. We don't need to abolish parole, but a new model is sorely needed."[66]

Petersilia herself writes about the need to "reinvent" parole. Here are the four pillars of her "new model" of parole: (1) Top priority goes to the identification of dangerous and violent parolees, who require surveillance through human and technological means. (2) It is necessary to deliver quality treatment services, especially substance abuse and job-training programs, to the subgroup of offenders who research shows could benefit from them. (3) Intermediate sanctions and other means should be established and used to divert technical parole violators to community-based alternatives and away from imprisonment. (4) A commitment needs to be made to manage offender risk in the neighborhoods where parolees live and to form active partnerships—sometimes called "neighborhood parole"[67]—with local police, offenders' families, and community members.

SUMMARY

Parole makes it possible for some inmates to be released from prison. From a peak of popularity in the 1960s, parole has been under attack for the last three decades. One consequence of the criticisms of parole is that significant limitations have been placed on the exercise of discretion by paroling authorities. In fourteen states and the federal government, the parole board has been abolished. Another consequence of the criticism has been the development of a managerial model of parole calling for the use of new technologies of control based on risk management. A third consequence is the high rates of technical violations and revocations of parole that result from the new surveillance and control model adopted by the majority of parole departments.

Reentry programs have been established throughout the United States. A few years ago they were looked to as a vehicle for significant correctional reform, but people have been less than enthusiastic about the placement of these programs in their communities. Inmates look forward to the programs because they offer an escape from fortress-like prisons. Inmates' families also look forward to these programs. They provide opportunities for family members to spend some time with a son or a daughter, a husband or a wife, a mother or a father. Also, if the inmate is on work release, the family may receive some financial assistance. For some offenders, the fact that these programs ease community adjustment may make the difference between success and reincarceration.

KEY TERMS

community-based assistance program, p. 194
community treatment center, p. 194
due process, p. 189
halfway house, p. 194
home furlough, p. 194
parole board, p. 182
parole guidelines, p. 184

prerelease program, p. 193
revocation of parole, p. 189
study release, p. 193
supervisory mandatory release, p. 181
unconditional prison release, p. 181
work release, p. 193

CRITICAL THINKING QUESTIONS

1. "Parole boards are arbitrary and discriminatory, and they ought to be abolished," says John Q. Liberal. "Yes, but so is the whole criminal justice system," says Sally Middle. "At least the boards are trying to remedy inequities." What are likely to be the reasons behind each opinion?

2. Inmates on work release combine working at a job with serving the last months of their prison sentence, either in a prison facility or in a work-release center. What is your evaluation of work-release programs?

3. Some states place inmate release information on the Internet. Do you believe that an ex-offender's previous record should be made public? Does an ex-offender have any rights of privacy?

4. Technical violations of parole are filling our prisons and aggravating problems related to prison crowding.

What is your evaluation of technical violations of parole? For example, if a parolee moves in with his girlfriend and does not tell his parole officer, is this justification for returning him to prison?

5. How strong is your state's commitment to reentry programs? Which programs do you feel have the most value?

6. Suppose that you have been convicted of a felony and have served thirty months in your state's penitentiary. You will be released on parole next week. How will your parents, husband or wife, children, and friends receive you? What will you do about getting a job? Will the university readmit you without any special processing? How are you going to discuss the last thirty months with your former friends, some of whom do not know that you were in prison?

7. You are a parole officer, and you have been assigned to an area where narcotics are being freely used. One of your parolees comes up with dirty urine on a surprise test. His conduct has been otherwise satisfactory, and he has a steady job—no problems except for a positive test for "crack." He says he can take the stuff or leave it alone. You have to make a report to the parole board, with recommendations. What will your report say—and why?

WEB DESTINATIONS

See the Bureau of Justice Statistics probation and parole statistics.
http://www.ojp.usdoj.gov/bjs/pandp.htm

Explore this site for career probation and parole officers in New York and persons interested in careers in community corrections.
http://www.nyspoa.com/

Read an article on the use of probation and parole officers in public schools in Maryland.
http://www.mbhs.edu/silverchips/news/2000/dec99/13news.html

Find out about the work of the U.S. Parole Commission.
http://www.usdoj.gov/uspc/

APB Online offers links to state parole boards nationwide.
http://www.apbonline.com/resourcecenter/parole/

Read about work-release programs for offenders in states such as Pennsylvania and California.
http://www.ojp.usdoj.gov/bjs/pandp.htm

http://www.csc-scc.gc.ca/text/plcy/cdshtm/740-cde.shtml

FOR FURTHER READING

Lynch, Mona. "Waste Managers? New Penology, Crime Fighting, and the Parole Agent Identity." *Law and Society Review* 32 (1998), pp. 839–869. This excellent ethnographic study of parole officers in California reveals how the focus of parole services is on control-oriented activities.

McCleary, Richard. *Dangerous Men: The Sociology of Parole.* Albany, N.Y.: Harrow & Heston, 1992. This examination of a large district parole office shows the bureaucratic constraints on parole.

Petersilia, Joan. "Parole and Prisoner Reentry in the United States." In *Prisons: Crime and Justice: A Review of Research* 26, edited by Michael Tonry and Joan Petersilia, pp. 479–529. Chicago: University of Chicago Press, 1999. This is a comprehensive and insightful review of the parole process.

Rhine, Edward E., William R. Smith, and Ronald W. Jackson. *Paroling Authorities: Recent History and Current Practice.* Laurel, Md.: American Correctional Association,1991. Though a little dated, this publication provides an examination of parole practices in the United States.

Simon, Jonathan. *Poor Discipline: Parole and the Social Control of the Underclass: 1890–1990.* Chicago: University of Chicago Press, 1993. Simon provides a helpful review of the development of parole from a clinical service–oriented agency to a crime-control bureaucratic agency focusing on revocations.

Travis, Jeremy. "But They All Come Back: Rethinking Prisoner Reentry." *Sentencing and Corrections; Issues for the 21st Century.* Washington, D.C.: U.S. Department of Justice, 2000. Travis identifies parole projects across the nation that are attempting to reshape parole in a number of ways, including providing services to parolees.

NOTES

1. Interviewed in August 2000.
2. James L. Galvin et al., *Parole in the United States, 1976 and 1977* (Washington, D.C.: U.S. Government Printing Office, 1978), p. 13.
3. Bureau of Justice Statistics, *Probation and Parole in the United States, 1999* (Washington, D.C.: U.S. Department of Justice, 2000), pp. 1 and 5.
4. Ibid., p. 1.
5. National Commission on Law Observance and Enforcement, *Report on Penal Institutions, Probation, and Parole* (Washington, D.C.: U.S. Government Printing Office, 1931), p. 127.
6. Ibid.
7. David J. Rothman, *Conscience and Convenience: The Asylum and Its Alternatives in Progressive America* (Boston: Little, Brown, 1980), p. 44.
8. Ibid., pp. 44–45.
9. National Commission on Law Observance and Enforcement, *Report on Penal Institutions, Probation, and Parole.*
10. Edward E. Rhine, William R. Smith, and Ronald W. Jackson, *Paroling Authorities: Recent History and Current Practice* (Laurel, Md.: American Correctional Association, 1991), p. 19.
11. President's Commission on Law Enforcement and Administration of Justice, *Task Force Report: Corrections* (Washington, D.C.: U.S. Government Printing Office, 1967), p. 62.

12. These three criticisms of parole are found in Joan Petersilia, "Parole and Prisoner Reentry in the United States," in *Prisons: Crime and Justice: A Review of Research* 26, ed. Michael Tonry and Joan Petersilia (Chicago: University of Chicago Press, 1999), pp. 492–493.

13. Douglas Lipton, Robert Martinson, and Judith Wilks, *The Effectiveness of Correctional Treatment and What Works: A Survey of Treatment Evaluation Studies* (New York: Praeger, 1975).

14. Daniel Glaser, *The Effectiveness of a Prison and Parole System* (Indianapolis: Bobbs-Merrill, 1969).

15. Sandra Shane-DuBow, Alice P. Brown, and Erik Olson, *Sentencing Reform in the United States: History, Content, and Effect* (Washington, D.C.: National Institute of Justice, 1985).

16. Rhine, Smith, and Jackson, *Paroling Authorities*, p. 25.

17. Jonathan Simon, *Poor Discipline: Parole and the Social Control* (Chicago: University of Chicago Press, 1993), p. 106.

18. Ibid., p. 109.

19. Smith, Rhine, and Jackson, *Paroling Authorities*, pp. 24–25.

20. John Sullivan, "In New York and Nation, Chances for Early Parole Shrink," *The New York Times*, 23 April 2000, p. 29; and Petersilia, "Parole and Prisoner Reentery in the United States," pp. 479–480.

21. Ibid., p. 479.

22. Ibid. See also Jeremy Travis, "But They All Come Back: Rethinking Prisoner Reentry," *Sentencing and Corrections: Issues for the 21st Century* (Washington, D.C.: U.S. Department of Justice, 2000), p. 1.

23. See the Polly Klass Foundation Website.

24. Simon, *Poor Discipline*, p. 169.

25. Ibid., p. 171.

26. American Correctional Association, *1997 Directory of Juvenile and Adult Correctional Departments, Institutions, Agencies and Paroling Authorities* (Laurel, Md.: American Correctional Association, 1998).

27. Ibid.

28. Petersilia, "A Parole and Prisoner Reentry in the United States," p. 497.

29. Ibid.

30. Ibid.

31. Travis, "But They All Come Back," p. 7.

32. Ibid., pp. 6–7.

33. Petersilia, "Parole and Prisoner Reentry in the United States," p. 37.

34. Camille Graham Camp and George M. Camp, *The Corrections Yearbook, 1999: Adult Corrections* (Middletown, Conn.: Criminal Justice Institute, 1999), p. 206.

35. Ibid., p. 176.

36. Ibid., p. 184.

37. Simon, *Poor Discipline*, p. 193.

38. Petersilia, "Parole and Prisoner Reentry in the United States," p. 503.

39. Interview contained in Simon, *Poor Discipline*, pp. 185–186.

40. Richard McCleery, *Dangerous Men: A Sociology of Parole* (Beverly Hills, Calif.: Sage, 1978); *Dangerous Men: A Sociology of Parole*, 2nd ed. (Albany, N. Y.: Harrow & Heston, 1992); and Robert C. Prus and John R. Stratton, "Parole Revocation Decisionmaking: Private Typings and Official Designations," *Federal Probation* 40 (1976), pp. 48–73.

41. Paul Takagi and James O. Robison, "The Parole Violator and Organizational Reject," *Journal of Research in Crime and Delinquency* 5 (1969), pp. 78–86.

42. Travis, "But They All Come Back," p. 7.

43. *Morrissey v. Brewer*, 408 U.S. 1971, 92s. (1972).

44. *In re Whitney*, 421 F.2d 337, 1st Cir. (1970).

45. *United States v. Strada*, 503 f.2d 1081, 87th Cir. (1974).

46. Howard Abadinsky, *Probation and Parole: Theory and Practice*, 6th ed. (Upper Saddle River, N.J.: Prentice-Hall, 1997).

47. Simon, *Poor Discipline*, pp. 228–229.

48. Elmer H. Johnson, *Crime, Correction, and Society* (Homewood, Ill: Dorsey, 1968), p. 331.

49. B. N. Cormier, M. Kennedy, and M. Senduehler, "Cell Breakage and Gate Fever," *British Journal of Criminology* 7 (July 1967), pp. 317–324.

50. NBC, *Dateline*, 25 August 2000.

51. Interviewed in August 2000.

52. A parole officer contributed this point in an August 2000 interview.

53. Petersilia, "Parole and Prisoner Reentry in the United States," p. 509.

54. Ibid., p. 511.

55. Interviewed in August 2000.

56. Ex-offenders have made this statement to the author on a number of occasions.

57. See Robert J. Sampson and John H. Laub, *Crime in the Making: Pathways and Turning Points through Life* (Cambridge: Harvard University Press, 1993); and John H. Laub and Robert J. Sampson, "Turning Points in the Life Course: Why Change Matters to the Study of Crime," *Criminology* 31 (August 1993), pp. 301–320.

58. Quoted on NBC, *Dateline*, 25 August 2000.

59. Travis, "But They All Come Back," p. 4.

60. Camp and Camp, *The Corrections Yearbook 1999: Adult Corrections*, p. 126. For an evaluation of work release in the state of Washington, see Susan Turner and Joan Petersilia, "Work Release in Washington: Effects on Recidivism and Corrections Costs," *The Prison Journal* 76 (June 1996), pp. 138–164.

61. Ibid.

62. Ibid., p. 128.

63. Ibid., p. 124.

64. Mary A. Toborg, *The Transition from Prison to Employment: An Assessment of Community-Based Assistance Programs* (Washington, D.C.: U.S. Government Printing Office, 1978), p. 3.

65. The Fortune Society Webpage.

66. Quoted in Petersilia, "Parole and Prisoner Reentry in the United States," p. 515.

67. Ibid., p. 517.

CHAPTER 8 / BUILT-IN STUDY GUIDE

Multiple Choice Questions

1. All of the following are ways that release can occur from prison except:

   A. Conditional release
   B. Pardon
   C. Commutation of sentence
   D. Placed on probation

2. In a state that grants one-third time off a prison sentence for good behavior, an offender serving a sentence of twelve years sentence will be released in:

   A. 10 years
   B. 8 years
   C. 6 years
   D. 9 years

3. Which of the following individuals has the power to grant pardons or executive clemency?

   A. President of the United States
   B. Vice President of the United States
   C. Chief Justice of the U.S. Supreme Court
   D. Speaker of the House of Representatives

4. Approximately how many individuals were on parole, as of 31 December 1999?

   A. 700,000
   B. More than 400,000
   C. More than 200,000
   D. 100,000

5. Parole release is most closely associated with which goal of punishment?

   A. Retribution
   B. Incapacitation
   C. Deterrence
   D. Rehabilitation

6. Who makes the decision to release offenders who are serving an indeterminate prison sentence?

   A. Judge
   B. Correctional facility
   C. Parole board
   D. Governor's board

7. Identify the type of laws that not only greatly eliminate parole but also most good-time statutes.

   A. Truth-in-sentencing laws
   B. Three-strikes laws

   C. Mandatory sentencing laws
   D. Determinate sentencing laws

8. All of the following are minimum requirements of due process during a parole revocation proceeding except:

   A. Written notice of the claimed violation of parole
   B. Proof beyond a reasonable doubt that a violation occurred
   C. Disclosure to the parolee of evidence against him or her
   D. Opportunity to be heard in person and to present documentary evidence

9. All of the following are examples of reentry programs designed to assist offenders in making the transition from the institution to the community except:

   A. Work-release
   B. Home furloughs
   C. Prerelease instruction
   D. Diversion programs

10. Which of the following types of sentences is parole release linked to?

    A. Indeterminate
    B. Determinate
    C. Mandatory
    D. Presumptive

11. The release of an offender after he or she has served a period of the sentence in a correctional facility to the community where the offender must follow conditions and is under the custody of the state refers to:

    A. Probation
    B. Parole
    C. Pardon
    D. Executive clemency

12. All of the following signify elements of the parole officer's duties that are similar to the probation officer's except:

    A. Both have excessive caseloads
    B. Both have duties that involve investigation of offenders
    C. Both have duties that involve regulation of offenders
    D. Both write PSI reports for courts

True/False Questions

T F   1. A state governor may not grant pardons or executive clemency to state inmates.

T F   2. A commutation of an offender's sentence will terminate the sentence.

T F   3. Parolees have few problems when they first return home from prison.

T F   4. The proportion of inmates released by parole boards has been increasing over the past decade.

T F   5. New technologies of control based on risk management characterized parole at the end of the twentieth century.

T F   6. In making parole release decisions several jurisdictions use hearing examiners to interview inmates.

T F   7. In recent years technical violations have amounted to over one-half of parole violations in this country.

T F   8. Parole officers have legal authority to search parolees, without the requirements imposed by the Fourth Amendment of the Constitution.

T F   9. Currently, the federal level of government offers parole to inmates who are serving time in federal prisons.

T F 10. A support system is the most important factor that characterizes offenders who succeed in the community.

T F 11. The parole board must interview the inmate prior to making the parole release decision.

T F 12. Offenders regain all of their legal rights when they are on parole release.

Fill-in-the-Blank Questions
(based on key terms)

1. _____ occurs when inmates are conditionally released from prison when their original sentence has been served minus time off for good behavior.

2. The _____ is responsible for determining the eligibility of inmates for parole release.

3. When _____ occurs no further conditional supervision in the community is required.

4. _____ are designed to find jobs for ex-offenders.

5. The ruling in *Morrisey v. Brewer* imposed _____, which jurisdictions have to follow when a parolee is suspected of violating parole and may be sent back to prison.

6. _____ are designed to prepare inmates for community living.

7. One of the main purposes of _____ programs is to place offenders in jobs they can retain following release.

8. Inmates who are near the end of their confinement, have a clean disciplinary record, and have a minimum security status may qualify for brief periods of release usually forty-eight to seventy-two hours. This is known as _____.

9. A type of program that allows inmates to attend school in the community is known as _____.

Essay Questions

1. Describe the origins and development of parole in the twentieth century. Also, explain how parole practices have changed and what they consist of today.

2. Why is prison release so traumatic? Identify and explain the challenges and frustrations confronting newly released inmates. What are some factors that will determine whether an inmate will make it on release?

3. What are the various roles and responsibilities of the contemporary parole officer? How do the functions of the parole officer compare with those of the probation officer?

4. Explain how the parole board functions. Also, describe how decisions are made to determine if a prisoner is eligible for parole.

5. Identify and describe three different types of programs that are designed to assist offenders in making the transition from the institution to the community.

ANSWERS

Multiple Choice Questions

1.	D	7.	A
2.	B	8.	B
3.	A	9.	D
4.	A	10.	A
5.	D	11.	B
6.	C	12.	D

True/False Questions

1.	F	7.	T
2.	F	8.	T
3.	F	9.	F
4.	T	10.	T
5.	T	11.	F
6.	T	12.	F

Fill-in-the-Blank Questions

1. Supervised mandatory release
2. Parole board
3. Unconditional prison release
4. Community-based assistance programs
5. Parole revocation procedures
6. Prerelease programs
7. Work-release
8. Home furloughs
9. Study-release

Local Institutions

Richard A. Clark, a Florida correctional officer, provides a brief overview of what it is like to work in a jail:

> As a correctional officer, when I enter the jail every night, I never know what kind of problems I am going to be faced with. Entering the jail is like entering a different world. It is very difficult to explain to other people what it is like working in a jail environment.
>
> To understand what types of inmates we have in our jail population, you have to think of the jail population as a microcosm of our troubled society. To be an effective line officer, you must be able to deal with inmates who are from different ethnic and economic class backgrounds than what you are. This can appear to be an impossible task to do at times.
>
> Most Americans have grown up with a value system where we are taught the difference between right and wrong, but people in jail seem to have a different set of ethics. In a jail or prison environment, inmates have to play by a different set of rules in order to survive. In other words, inmates have to become "jail wise."
>
> As a line officer, you have to also become "jail wise" if you want to keep your sanity and live to receive your pension some day. As a line officer, you can learn a lot by observing how inmates handle different jail situations they are confronted with each day.

To make it in a modern correctional environment, a correctional officer must have good insight into human behavior. A good officer must also keep his or her sense of humor in such a negative environment as a jail. The average officer and staff member must be able to deal with inmates who have very serious emotional problems.

From my own personal experience, most of the serious problems are handled by the floor officer or a sergeant. As a jail officer, if you are assigned to a certain area for a long period of time, you soon learn to sense problems in your work area. After a while, I have been able to tell when there is a growing race conflict or when a gang fight is about to take place.[1]

CRITICAL THINKING QUESTIONS

If you went to work in a jail as a correctional officer, how would you become "jail wise"? How long do you think it would take?

Richard A. Clark says "Entering the jail is like entering a different world." It is a multicultural world that is difficult for an outsider to understand. Yet the underlying theme of this interview is that it is possible to make working in the jail environment a positive work experience. According to Clark, a correctional officer who is effective must have "good insight into human behavior," must be able to deal with inmates who have emotional problems, and must sense problems building up.

Jails, lockups, workhouses, and houses of corrections are the main types of local institutions. Jails have the authority to detain individuals for periods of forty-eight hours or longer; they also hold convicted inmates sentenced to short terms (generally a year or less). Jails are usually administered by the county sheriff but are sometimes managed on a regional basis or, in a few cases, by the state government. Lockups, sometimes called temporary holding facilities or police lockups, are generally found in city police stations or precinct houses, and they hold persons for periods of less than forty-eight hours. The primary function of workhouses and houses of corrections—operated by cities and counties and sometimes known as county prisons—is to hold convicted inmates sentenced to short terms.

The jail is a pivotal institution that touches the lives of more people than does any other correctional institution. Most people in jail stay there for short periods of time, then are replaced by more people of the same kind. A key difference between jails and state and federal institutions is that jails handle nonconvicted individuals, many of whom are first-time offenders. In addition to being an intake center for the entire criminal justice system, jails also serve as a place of first or last resort for individuals who belong in public health, welfare, and social service agencies.

HOW DID JAILS ORIGINATE?

The jail had its origin in medieval England. County correctional institutions spread through England in 1166, when Henry II (r. 1154–1189) ordered that the sheriff in each county (shire) establish a jail.[2] Although initially conceived as a place for detaining suspected offenders until they could be tried, jails gradually came to serve the dual purposes of detention and punishment. The English jail became an expression of the dominant authority of the county, which maintained control over the jails because the state had not developed its own institutions. Lack of adequate transportation to other county towns also made it necessary to hold suspected offenders within the counties until they could be tried.

An estimated two hundred jails existed in England throughout the sixteenth, seventeenth, and eighteenth centuries. Several different authorities operated these jails: The sheriff operated the county jail; corporation officers ran the town jails; and church and political leaders maintained private jails. The keeper of the jail ordinarily did not draw a salary, but a system of fees made it a very profitable job. Indeed, some sheriffs charged a fee to prisoners about to be released before they could actually leave; this was the practice that first interested John Howard in the jail. Although the fee system varied from jail to jail, inmates usually paid for every service they received. Rates varied by the class of the inmates; upper-class prisoners paid more for their beds, mattresses, bedclothes, and so forth. If a prisoner had enough money, he could live with his wife and family in a private suite outside the jail.[3]

The concept of the English jail was brought to Britain's colonies in North America soon after the settlers arrived from the Old World. The jail was used to detain individuals awaiting trial and those awaiting punishment. The stocks and pillory, and sometimes the whipping post, were usually located nearby. Instead of cells, the early colonial jails consisted of small rooms that housed up to thirty prisoners. An example of these early colonial facilities is the jail (gaol) at Williamsburg, Virginia, built in 1703–1704 (see Figure 9.1). Prisoners in each county were placed under the jurisdiction of the sheriff, who fed and lodged them. The fee system was also used in the colonies.

Virginia established the first colonial jail, but it was the Pennsylvania jails that became the model for other states. The Walnut Street Jail in Philadelphia (see Chapter 3) gave birth to the modern penitentiary when a separate wing was constructed in 1790 for the purpose of reforming convicted offenders. The penal law and codes of Massachusetts in 1699, New Jersey in 1754, South Carolina in 1770, and Maryland in 1811 also established jail systems. At the beginning of the nineteenth century, children, debtors, slaves, the mentally ill, and the physically ill all were housed in jails, but as the century progressed, children and the mentally ill were more often sent to other institutions. Jails began to house both pretrial and posttrial prisoners; some jails also held felons as well as misdemeanants.[4]

Public outrage and official condemnation have characterized the history of the jail in the United States. In 1831, a Protestant clergyman in an eastern state wrote, "In regards to our county prisons nothing has been done in the way of reform."[5] In 1911, penologist E. C. Wines warned the National Conference on Charities and Corrections that

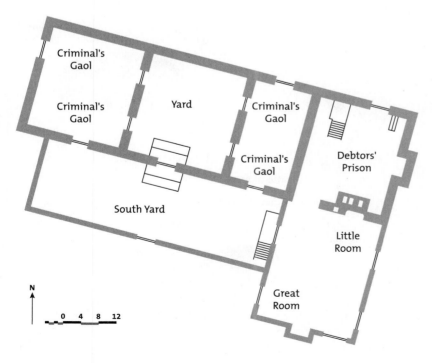

Figure 9.1 The Plan of the Reconstructed Jail at Williamsburg, Virginia

Source: Marcus Whiffen, *The Public Buildings of Williamsburg* (Williamsburg, Va.: The Colonial Williamsburg Foundation, 1958). Courtesy, the Colonial Williamsburg Foundation.

the only hope was "overthrow of the county jail system."[6] In the early 1930s, the Wickersham Report referred to jails as "dirty, unhealthy, unsanitary, and ill-fitted to produce either a stabilizing or beneficial effect on inmates."[7] A speaker informed the 1934 Attorney General's Conference on Crime that jail conditions were "so medieval, and barbarous, and so contrary to the ordinary tenets of democracy and social justice that [he was] shocked beyond experience."[8]

Jails continued to draw criticism throughout the next three decades, culminating in the report of the Corrections Task Force of the National Advisory Commission on Criminal Justice Standards and Goals in 1973: "Outmoded and archaic, lacking the most basic comfort, totally inadequate for any program encouraging socialization, jails perpetuate a destructive rather than reintegrative process."[9] The Task Force on Prisoner Rehabilitation described the jail as "the most glaringly inadequate institution on the American correctional scene."[10]

WHO IS IN JAIL?

During the fiscal year ending 30 June 1999, there were 19 million jail admissions and releases. On 30 June 1999, county jails housed 605,943 inmates. Nonconvicted inmates (those on trial or awaiting arraignment) made up 52 percent of the adults in jail.[11] The occupants of jails continue to be predominantly men, but women account for a larger percentage than they did in the past. The percentage of African American and Hispanic jail inmates in 1996 had not changed substantially from 1989 after increasing between 1983 and 1989.[12]

The percentage charged with a drug offense rose from 9 percent in 1983 to 23 percent in 1989 but remained at 22 percent in 1996. The percentage of inmates in jail for a violent offense went up slightly from 23 percent in 1989 to 26 percent in 1996. See Figure 9.2. In both 1989 and 1996, nearly 25 percent of the inmates were charged with a

Figure 9.2 Criminal History of Jail Inmates

Source: Bureau of Justice Statistics, *Correctional Populations in the United States, 1996* (Washington, D.C.: U.S. Government Printing Office, 1999), p. 3.

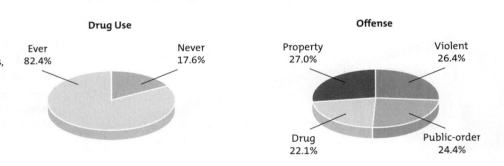

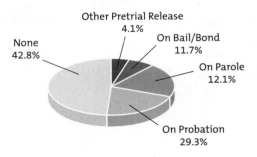

public-order offense: 7 to 9 percent were being held for driving while intoxicated (DWI) and 2 percent for a weapons violation. The most common offense among white inmates was DWI; an estimated 13 percent of white inmates, 7 percent of Hispanics, and 2 percent of African Americans were in jail for DWI.[13]

Nearly 1 in every 3 inmates was on probation at the time of his or her most recent arrest; 1 in 8 was on parole; and 1 in 8 was on bail or prerelease bond. The criminal records of jail inmates in 1996 were longer than those of inmates in 1989. Nearly a third of all inmates in 1996, compared to 23 percent in 1989, said that they had served three or more terms in jail, prison, or other correctional settings.[14]

There are twelve kinds of inmate populations in jail:

- Pretrial detainees, who cannot afford or were denied bail and who are held until their trial or disposition of their case
- Convicted offenders, who are housed in jail for periods of less than one year
- Convicted offenders awaiting sentences. These offenders may be federal, state, or local prisoners
- Misdemeanants, drunks, and the mentally ill
- Mandatory arrests for drunken driving, known across the nation as DWI, DUI (driving under the influence), and OMVI (operating motor vehicle while intoxicated)
- Inmates being held on detainer warrants from other states
- Probation, parole, and bail-bond violators and absconders
- Temporarily detained juveniles pending transfer to juvenile authorities
- Witnesses who are in protective custody or who are being held as witnesses prior to trial
- State and federal inmate prison overflow
- Military police detainees
- Those held for contempt of court[15]

John Irwin contends that, more than anything else, jails are "dumping grounds for the poor" and catchalls for uneducated, unemployed, homeless, and impoverished offenders. After spending more than a year of observation at the San Francisco jail and shorter periods of observation at several other jails, Irwin concluded that the occupants of jail were primarily offenders deemed disreputable or offensive to the larger society. He refers to these disorderly and disorganized persons as "rabble" and contends that the jail was invented and continues to be operated in order to manage society's rabble. Irwin found that the offensiveness of acts of the felony prisoners in the San Francisco jail was a more important factor in leading to their arrests than was the severity of their crimes.[16]

One study tested the rabble thesis by examining all bookings at the Multnomah County Jail (Portland, Oregon) for a period of time during the 1980s and all bookings in Skamania County, Washington, for one week in 1991. This study concluded that Irwin, using the San Francisco and other local jails as a sample group, overstated his case, but that some support existed for the idea that many jail bookings involve marginal and nonserious offenders.[17] These investigators did find that the majority of the bookings in these two jails involved individuals charged with or convicted of serious offenses.

HOW DOES ONE ADJUST TO JAIL?

Pretrial confinement is disruptive and traumatic, especially to a person who has not been to jail before. In Within the Walls 9.1, an inmate recently released after serving a number of years in California state prisons as well as the final three years of his imprisonment in

the walls   9.1

within

"You're in Jail"

"When I was arrested, the police said, 'We're going to lock you up.' In reality, it was lock me 'away.' Incarceration cuts a person off from the sensory experiences that bring texture to life. Separated from family and friends, each day is a grinding regimen, a battle to survive emotionally and physically. The feeling of isolation is profound—the sense of rejection is devastating. To survive, I disciplined myself to forget what I left behind on the outside.

"I quickly learned the culture behind bars is void of the basic moral tenets, both sectarian and secular, that guide society. It is a primitive life—force and violence the determining factors. You learn the rules of survival fast, or you become a victim. A man is respected for one thing and one thing only: his ability to stand his ground. To be a convict, that is to be an inmate respected amongst the prison population, you teach yourself to stop feeling—and learn how to fight. You have no need for a companion. A convict doesn't forgive or forget. Nothing is free inside. Your sole focus is on the present—to stay strong. The more violent and unpredictable you become, the more respect you earn. Fear and respect are synonymous on the inside. There are two animals on the inside: predators and prey. Then one day the powers-that-be decide to give you a release date. And after 5, 10, 20 or more years behind bars, all that you learned and have been required to do for survival, you must forget. Society demands a parolee to be a rational animal with compassion. Where's the logic?

"Nor was my time in jail any better. I was in the largest jail lockup in the United States, the Los Angeles

> ... culture behind bars is void of the basic moral tenets ... that guide society.

County Jail. This jail is a cement monolith that houses in excess of 11,000 men on any given day. Over 50 percent of the 150,000-plus inmates in California's thirty-three prisons originated from Los Angeles County. The jail is affectionately known throughout the state as the 'Concrete Jungle.' It houses the most dangerous lockups in the state, if not the country. LA County is a training ground for young LA gang members. It's where they earn their 'bones.' That is, it is where they stab rival gang members and show their 'Homies' that they are 'down' and willing to die for the 'click,' the gang. For the unaffiliated, inmates that are not in gangs, LA County is a treacherous maze. Civility is taken as weakness. Like prison, the use of violence is the only way to gain respect. You either learn to fight and defend your person, or become a victim that is mentally and physically abused. There is no middle ground. The culture is primitive. Rehabilitation or redemption doesn't figure into the equation. Life in the Concrete Jungle is all about survival."

CRITICAL THINKING QUESTIONS

What does this inmate suggest is the only way to survive in prison or in the Los Angeles County Jail? If you were in a large urban jail, how would you avoid becoming prey?

Source: Statement provided by Christopher Lynch, who was released from the Los Angeles County Jail in August 2000, and used with permission.

the Los Angeles County Jail speaks about the difficulties of jail adjustment. He focuses on the prison but is quick to say that his time in the Los Angeles County Jail was in many ways like doing prison time.

This inmate is suggesting that survival is a major problem in the large urban jail. In this culture, the strong prey on the weak, and an adequate adjustment to jail requires that inmates have the ability to protect themselves. Self-protection becomes particularly challenging if an inmate is not connected to a gang.

The average jail has a much less frightening inmate culture than does an urban jail, and other forms of adjustment become more important. Most detained prisoners live in an uncertain world. The uncertainties of jail include questions about the length of confinement, chances of obtaining pretrial release, and the results of the court process. Jail inmates also must deal with inactivity and boredom. The collective impact of the

For what reasons are people in jail? How is being in jail different from being in prison? What are some common social characteristics of people in jails? Is there any truth to the claim that the poor and indigent make up a disproportionate number of persons in jail? How do people get out of jail?

jail environment can lead to tension, anxiety, alienation, and guilt. If not handled in constructive ways, the stress of jail confinement can escalate to crisis proportions, resulting in psychological breakdowns.[18]

HOW DO PEOPLE GET OUT OF JAIL?

The vast majority of criminal defendants are released prior to jail. For example, about 85 percent of all state-level criminal defendants and 82 percent of federal criminal defendants are released prior to trial.[19] The defendants who receive bail or pretrial release will be given an opportunity to post bail. **Bail bonds** are generally cash deposits but may also consist of property or other valuables. For those defendants unable to make cash bail, pretrial alternatives to jail include **release on (the offender's) own recognizance (ROR)**, unsecured bail, percentage bail, third-party custody, signature bail, and supervised release.

Defendants who receive **pretrial release** are spared weeks or months of jail confinement. They also have the advantages of continuing their jobs, of being free to collect evidence in the community, of benefiting from the financial and emotional support of their families, and of coming into court as free citizens rather than being brought in handcuffed and in custody. Defendants accepted for pretrial release are also free to continue criminal activities, often with the objective of paying the expenses of trial. There is some evidence that sentencing judges are usually more reluctant to imprison defendants who stand before them as free men and women, holding a job and supporting a family, than to imprison defendants who are already in jail.

Those defendants who are charged with serious crimes or are thought likely to escape are generally held in jail until trial. Public concern about crimes committed by those who have been granted pretrial release has given rise to a preventive detention movement. The objective of **preventive detention** is to retain in jail defendants who are deemed dangerous or likely to commit crimes while awaiting trial. This concern for public safety became so strong that by the mid-1980s well over half of the states had enacted preventive detention laws.[20] Several studies have challenged the need for preventive detention. One study that examined pretrial detention in California jails found that most inmates do not need pretrial detention because they are arrested for relatively minor offenses and do not have extensive criminal histories.[21] General Accounting Office[22] and Bureau of Justice Statistics[23] evaluations of the new federal pretrial detention law both concluded that this law has lengthened periods of pretrial confinement and worsened jail crowding without resulting in a decrease in pretrial crime.[24]

Pretrial Release

Defendants who are released on their own recognizance (ROR) are put on their own honor to report when scheduled. A ROR staff member interviews arrestees and then verifies data about each defendant. A defendant who scores the required number of verified points, as determined by established criteria, is recommended for ROR (see Figure 9.3 for the pretrial release criteria used in the judicial districts of Iowa). After signing a promise to appear in court, the defendant is released, if the presiding judge of the criminal court agrees with the ROR recommendation and the district attorney decides not to contest it in court.

Unsecured bail allows release without a deposit or bail arranged through a bondsman. It differs from ROR in that the defendant is obligated to pay an established fee upon default. But, because the full bond amount is rarely collected, this program is basically the same as ROR. In percentage bail, the defendant deposits a portion of the bail amount, usually 10 percent, with the court clerk. In Illinois, where percentage bail is the most common form of pretrial release, only the defendant is permitted to execute the bond; thus, no professional bail bondsman or fidelity company can pay the bail. In Kentucky and Oregon, defendants who fail to receive ROR or conditional release have a right to be released under percentage bail, if they can afford the deposit. The defendant is released from custody once the specified percentage is paid, and when the defendant appears in court, 90 percent of the original 10 percent is refunded. Third-party custody occurs when the court assigns custody of the defendant to an individual or agency that promises to ensure his or her later appearance in court. A signature bond is usually given for minor offenses, such as minor traffic offenses, and is based on the defendant's written promise to appear in court.

Supervised release programs require more frequent contact with a pretrial officer, including phone calls and office interviews. Although the main purpose of supervision is to enforce the conditions imposed, the defendants also receive assistance with housing, finances, health problems, employment, and alcohol- or drug-related problems. Percentage bond, cash bail, or unsecured bail may be part of supervised release; in high-risk cases, intensive supervision may be used, requiring several contacts a week with a pretrial release officer.

Home detention with electronic monitoring is also beginning to be used with pretrial defendants to relieve jail crowding. Such a program was established in Marion County, Indiana, in 1988. Defendants were screened for pretrial release on home detention only after they had been denied other forms of pretrial release. Clients who were accepted into this program were fitted with a coded wristlet matching a base unit attached to their home telephone. Successes in the program whose cases had not reached disposition by the courts after 90 days typically were recommended for release on their own recognizance.[25]

Interview by _____

Date _____

Interview	Verified	
		Residence
3	3	Present residence 1 year or more or owns dwelling
2	2	Present residence 6 months or more or present and prior 1 year
1	1	Present residence 3 months or more or present and prior 6 months
0	0	Present residence 3 months or less
		Family Ties
3	3	Lives with family (spouse or dependents)
2	2	Lives with relatives or lives w/non-family individual 1 year or more
1	1	Lives with non-family individual
1	1	Lives alone and has sufficient support and/or family contact in the area
0	0	Lives alone
		Time in Area
2	2	Five years or more continuous, recent
		Employment/Support
4	4	Present local job 1 year or more
3	3	Present local job 6 months or present and prior 1 year
2	2	Social Services or Social Security income or full-time student for 6 months
1	1	Unemployment Compensations, family support
1	1	New student status, new job, part-time job
0	0	Unemployed, not sufficient support
		Alcohol/Drug Abuse
−1	−1	Present involvement
−2	−2	Present involvement and history of abuse
		Criminal Record
2	2	No convictions
1	1	One simple/serious misdemeanor conviction within last 5 years
0	0	One felony/aggravated misdemeanor or 2 simple/serious within last 5 years
−1	−1	Two or more felony convictions or 3 or more simple/serious convictions
−1	−1	Six months or more jail term or 3 or more jail sentences
−2	−2	Served prison term
		Current Offense Charge
−3	−3	Forcible felony/mandatory sentences
−2	−2	Present on probation or parole
−1	−1	Other criminal charges pending of aggravated misdemeanor or felony nature
		Miscellaneous (more than one may apply)
−2	−2	Previous Pre-Trial/Probation/Parole violations
−2	−2	Failure to appear or contempt of court charges
−3	−3	Flight to avoid prosecution or AWOL
		Health/Psychiatric (indicate if applicable)

_____ _____

Comments: _____

Figure 9.3 Pretrial Services Release Criteria in Iowa

Source: First Judicial District, State of Iowa.

HOW ARE JAILS RUN?

The type of jail administration, variation in size or other characteristics, supervision of inmates, and commitment to programs are the most important features defining how jails are run. County sheriffs usually have operational responsibility for the jails. There have been three generations of jail supervision: the linear-intermittent surveillance of inmates, the indirect or podular/remove surveillance of inmates, and the direct or podular/direct supervision of inmates. In some jails, the programs that are offered are quite impressive; in other jails, especially small ones, programs may be few or nearly nonexistent.

Administration of the Jail

In more than three thousand counties in the United States, the sheriff runs the jail.[26] A major problem with this means of jail administration is that sheriffs are politically accountable to county voters, so jails are one of the most political institutions in adult corrections.[27] Sheriffs receive a lot of criticism for jail administration. Some of it is deserved, but they also are criticized for things over which they have little control. For example, some jails continue to be real dungeons, but the sheriff is unable to get enough money to repair or build a new facility. A major contribution that sheriffs have made to jail administration is implementation of the minimum standards for local jails and detention facilities developed by the National Sheriffs Association.[28]

There are at least four alternatives to local control of jails: state-run jails, cooperative (regional) arrangements, state subsidy programs, and private services. Four states—Connecticut, Delaware, Rhode Island, and Vermont—currently have full operational responsibility for jails. Except for five locally operated jails, Alaska, too has a state-operated jail system.[29] Although state-run jails offer greater operational efficiency than locally operated jails, political opposition by the counties is one important reason why more states are not likely to select this approach.[30]

A widely used alternative to local or state control is regional or multicounty arrangements. Kentucky, Virginia, West Virginia, North Dakota, South Dakota, Nebraska, and Kansas were the first states to adopt regional jails.[31] This arrangement typically takes place when a jurisdiction with an adequate jail is willing to contract with neighboring cities and counties to house prisoners on a per diem basis. It also takes place when a group of local governments decide that no existing facility is adequate and then decide to build a new regional jail or "detention center." Furthermore, local governments may decide to specialize and house different populations, such as juveniles, females, pretrial detainees, or convicted felons awaiting transportation to state prisons. Transportation problems, multijurisdiction funding problems, and turf disputes limit or prohibit the even wider use of cooperative arrangements among local governments.[32]

State subsidies provide a third way to reach beyond locally operated jails, with their politics and financial constraints. Almost 60 percent of the states provide technical assistance to local governments having jail problems, and about 50 percent provide training for jail personnel. In addition, some subsidy programs assist jails in complying with state standards and in making capital improvements ordered by courts.[33]

Finally, jails, like other components of the correctional systems, utilize private services to some degree in the areas of medical and mental health care, food service, jail work programs, community-based inmate programs, facility financing, architectural services, and facility construction. Privatization is increasing, as reflected by the fact that 47 of the nation's 3,365 jails, housing 13,814 inmates, are privately owned or operated.[34] An argument can be made that a public–private partnership offers more advantages to local governments than does private agencies' running jails. Private-sector involvement seems to be more desirable for providing jail services and programs, including medical and mental health care, food service, and alcohol and drug treatment programs.[35]

Physical Characteristics

Most jails are small. The 1994 American Jail Association's directory listed 1,739 jails with 1 to 50 beds, 1,108 jails with 51 to 250 beds, 199 jails with 251 to 500 beds, 67 jails with 1,001 to 3,000 beds, and 8 jails with 3,001-plus beds. These figures suggest that only 75 jails have over 1,000 inmates in the United States and only 8 jail systems have over 3,000 beds.[36] The largest facilities are New York City's Rikers Island, Los Angeles County's Men Central Jail, the Cook County Jail at Chicago, the New Orleans Parish Prison, and Houston's Harris County Central Jail.

Jails range from old, dilapidated dungeons to modern, attractive facilities. Fortunately, only a few of the cagelike facilities of the nineteenth century are still in use. In those facilities, inflexible cells face inflexible day rooms. Prisoners spend most of the day in large cages or bullpens. Alcoholics, drug abusers, psychotics, and others with serious medical and behavioral problems are placed in isolation cells, or "drunk tanks"—generally unfurnished cubes of steel and concrete, many of which contain only a hole-in-the-floor toilet. Health problems are created by the shortage of items such as towels, soap, toothbrushes, clean bedding, and toilet paper.

Overcrowding has led to makeshift jails. These "temporary" facilities are simply conversions of existing structures or old buildings and provide a convenient and economical way to continue the rate of detention and incarceration. Some counties have converted old school buildings into minimum-security detention centers. An abandoned gas station in Denton, Texas, was converted into a makeshift jail. Maricopa County, Arizona, built a tent city outside Phoenix to relieve overcrowding in the county jail.[37] The Bibby Venture, a floating barge moored at New York City's waterfront, was used to ease crowding in the late 1980s and early 1990s at Rikers Island. The barge was purchased in 1987 for $19 million under a lease/purchase arrangement. With a capacity for 396 inmates, the barge was used to house detention and minimum-security prisoners. It has since been returned to England, where Her Majesty's Prison Service is using it.[38]

Supervision of Inmates

First-generation jails are designed to provide linear-intermittent surveillance of inmates. Staff–inmate interaction usually takes place through bars. The layout is similar to that of a hospital in which long rows of rooms open onto a corridor. Electronic surveillance has been used to compensate for the weakness of the linear design, but officers monitoring banks of video screens find it difficult to maintain effective watchfulness because of preoccupation with other activities, having to view too many cameras, and fatigue. Linear supervision jails have been faulted for their inability to protect vulnerable inmates. These facilities are known for high rates of inmate sexual assaults, fights, suicides, accidents, and unexpected medical emergencies.[39]

Second-generation jails are designed to provide indirect or podular/remove surveillance. The design is "indirect" because the officers' station is separated from the inmates' living area, or pod. The officers' station is inside a secure room. Observation is enabled through protective windows in front of a console/desk. Microphones and speakers inside the living unit permit officers to hear and communicate with inmates. This approach gives rise to several problems:

- If a problem occurs in a pod, the officer has to call "out front" for assistance.
- The flow of information between officers and inmates is drastically reduced.
- On-duty staff often overlook minor infractions because they believe it is not worth the trouble to call for assistance.
- Staff lacks knowledge of individual inmates and thus has to make guesses about levels of stress when trouble seems to be brewing in the pod.[40]

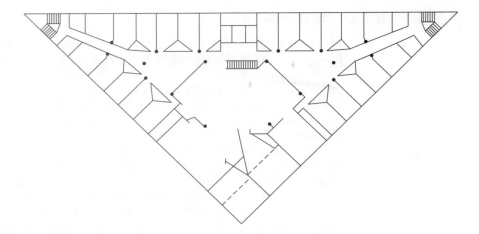

Figure 9.4 Direct Supervision Jail

Source: W. Raymond Nelson, *Cost Savings in New Generation Jails: The Direct Supervision Approach* (Washington, DC: U.S. Department of Justice, 1988), p. 3.

Third-generation jails—also known as **"New Generation" jails**—are praised because they allow direct or podular/direct supervision of inmates (see Figure 9.4). The New Generation, or direct supervision jail, attempts to use the physical plant to manage the jail population. Of the five hundred new jails either recently completed or under construction in the summer of 2000, about half were New Generation jails, using direct supervision.[41]

Direct supervision places the correctional officers' station within the inmates' living area, or pod, which means the officer can see and speak to inmates. During the day, inmates stay in the open area (day room). Generally, they are not permitted to go into their rooms except with permission. If they do so, they must quickly return. The officer controls door locks to cells from the control panel. A small radio worn on the front of the officer's shirt permits immediate communication with other jail staff if the need arises. In addition, the day room is covered by a video camera monitored in the central control room.

Direct supervision offers many advantages: effective control and supervision of inmates; improved communication between staff and inmates; safety of staff and inmates; manageable and cost-effective operations; improved classification and orientation of inmates, especially programming for specialized offender groups; staff ownership of operations; and the ability to shut a pod down when populations are low. Disadvantages include the difficulty of "selling" the jail to a public that tends to see the layout as a means of "coddling" prisoners; the amount of training needed to make the transition to the new style of supervision; and the fact that the overcrowding issue makes this design hard to implement.[42]

Several studies support the efficacy of New Generation jails. For example, one study found that correctional officers assigned to New Generation jails were more satisfied with their jobs, were more positive about the organizational climate, and experienced more job enrichment than did officers in traditional jails.[43] Another study found that inmates in direct supervision facilities were significantly more positive in their evaluations of the jail climate, the physical environment, and officers and experienced less psychological and physical stress than inmates in traditional jails.[44] A third study concluded that inmates in direct supervision jails are less likely to be assaulted and sexually victimized and to commit suicide than inmates in traditional jail settings.[45]

This is the Fairfax Country Adult Detention Center, a "New Generation" jail in Viginia, How is a New Generation jail different from first-generation linear supervision jails? How is a New Generation jail different from second-generation podular surveillance jails? What are some advantages of direct supervision in local correctional institutions?

The Fairfax County Adult Detention Center (Virginia) and the Metropolitan Correctional Centers (New York, Chicago, San Diego, Tucson, Miami, Houston, and Honolulu) of the Bureau of Prisons have been praised as innovative New Generation jails. The Fairfax County Adult Detention Center (ADC) opened in 1978 with a capacity of 254 beds. In 1984, the basement was renovated into a 72-bed intake center for receiving and evaluating new inmates. In 1987, a 200-bed maximum-custody unit and a 100-bed work-release center were opened. In the winter of 2001, a 750-bed medium-security, direct supervision jail was opened—one of the most innovative jail facilities in the nation.[46] One of the reasons for building the 750-bed medium-security jail was to deal with jail overcrowding.

The Fairfax County facility is fully accredited by the Virginia Department of Corrections, the American Correctional Association, and the National Commission of Correctional Health Care. With the direct supervision in the new medium-security unit, the ADC has all three types of supervision: linear, podular, and direct. The facility has shatter- and bulletproof glass rather than bars. Each modern cell has a stainless steel commode, a bed, and a small writing table. The hooks in the cells are designed to give way under more than 5 pounds of pressure in order to prevent suicides. Deputies in a central control room use cameras to monitor problem areas of the jail. In some cases, medium-security prisoners can open and shut the doors to their cells and go back and forth to an adjoining day room. Cameras monitor the day rooms of the maximum-security sections. Meals are prepared by civilian employees and planned by the state board of corrections. This jail also has an outdoor recreation yard, an indoor gymnasium, and one hundred program classes each week covering such areas as religion, Adult Basic Education (ABE), the general equivalency diploma (GED), substance abuse, forensic group sessions, and English as a second language (ESL). Educational technology already in place includes a closed-circuit cable TV system and fifteen computer workstations for inmate education programs. In 1990, the National Institute of Corrections designated the ADC's classification system as a national model. There is a work-release program for prisoners during the last 120 days of their sentences.[47]

The first federal Metropolitan Correctional Centers in New York City, Chicago, and San Diego were designed to provide an environment in which safe and secure detention would be assured. Inmates were divided into groups of forty to fifty for housing purposes. Living units were arranged to ensure that corrections officers could observe all areas within the unit, and every effort was made to minimize blind spots. No bars were used in the living units. Windows were provided in every prisoner's room. Carpets, colorful wall coverings, and padded and moveable furniture were used to reduce the trauma of institutionalization. The living units were designed with areas of open and unrestricted space. The most important design requirements were single cells for inmates, direct staff supervision, and "functional inmate living units." Functional units, as will be discussed later, place all housing, food, and hygiene facilities in one self-contained, multilevel space. A corrections officer is assigned to each unit to ensure continuous and direct supervision of inmates.[48]

The Metropolitan Correctional Center in Chicago is a 26-floor triangular structure that was completed in June 1975. This institution in August 2000 housed 700 inmates in nine separate living units. The security system is largely electronic. Doors, elevators, TV monitors, alarms, intercoms, and telephones are centrally controlled with the assistance of a computer. Most units consist of two floors, with a split-level design. The outside rows of 44 individual inmate rooms are divided into four 11-room modules, each with its own lounge area. Midway between the two floors is a multipurpose area with kitchenette, dining room, recreation and exercise areas, and visitors' lounge. The individual rooms provide both privacy and security for the inmate.[49]

Our hero in this chapter is Captain Don Fatherree, a twenty-five-year veteran of the Fairfax County Adult Detention Center in Virginia. He feels quite positive about the years he has spent in corrections and urges others to consider the corrections profession as a career. Read what he wrote for *Invitation to Corrections* in 2000.

Jail Programs

The lack of programs has long been a criticism of jails. It is difficult for small jails to develop a variety of programs because they lack space, staff, and fiscal resources. They are frequently dependent on volunteers. Large jails have more programs, but overcrowding makes it difficult to offer adequate programming for each inmate. Nevertheless, more programming exists now than was present a generation ago.[50]

Larger jails usually provide GED and Adult Basic Education programs, drug and alcohol treatment programs, counseling, work release, and jail industries, including inmate work programs and inmate vocational programs. Jails also are required to provide religious services, some exercise equipment, and access to a law library for long-term convicted inmates. Jails are constitutionally mandated to make available adequate health care delivery systems.

Some jails have exemplary health care delivery systems; others offer nearly no health care. The chief medical officer of the Los Angeles County sheriff's department listed the following crucial health care issues confronting individuals in the jail setting:

- Communicable diseases: tuberculosis, HIV disease, sexually transmitted disease, hepatitis, and measles
- Chronic diseases: hypertension, cardiovascular disease, diabetes, renal/liver disease, and lung diseases
- Chemical/substance abuse
- Prenatal care
- Smoking
- Mental health: homeless, mentally incompetent, and suicide[51]

Even the exemplary systems find it difficult to manage the serious health issues confronting jails today.

h e r o e s | *Captain Don Fatherree*

Corrections Professional at Fairfax County (Virginia) Adult Detention Center

"I got into corrections as a direct result of my temporary career in the Air Force. I enlisted when I was 19 and was chosen by the Air Force to be a police officer. At the time that was a tremendous disappointment to me. I spent six and a half years as a law enforcement specialist in the Air Force and enjoyed it much more than I thought. So much so, when I got out of the Air Force, I began going to school at Northern Virginia Community College and got my associate's degree in police science. Subsequently, I applied to several police departments and sheriff's offices. Fairfax County's sheriff office was the first to come through with a job offer, and I immediately took it and have enjoyed a successful career since. As soon as I graduated from the academy, I started working as a confinement officer in 1975. I began working in a very old, non–air conditioned environment, and as soon I completed my B.S. degree three years down the road, I was transferred from a confinement officer to a classification specialist. I worked in classification for three to four years, after which I was transferred to the prerelease center (PRC), which houses our medium-security work-release prisoners, weekend prisoners, and community service prisoners. I worked at the PRC for about nine years. I thoroughly enjoyed the job, eventually making lieutenant there. I was then transferred to the police academy, where I was in charge of all the in-service training for police jurisdictions that participated in the academy for Fairfax County. I was there for a little over a year, and then was promoted to captain and was named the first human resource branch chief. I held that position for about four years, hiring people and dealing with work issues and training issues. From there, I was transferred to law enforcement and the road deputies. Very recently, the sheriff has established a community relations branch. That particular branch handles all of the community activities that we participate in, either on our own or in conjunction with other local law enforcement agencies. I was made the branch chief of this branch and that is my present job now. I enjoy my job so much that I'm going to stick around for another five years and have a thirty-year career.

"I do want to make the point that the New Generation jail is much different from the traditional jail. In the old jail where I went to work in 1975, the typical picture looking down the hallways was the arms extended out of the bars. It was very easy to communicate with inmates in this linear design, but it was very hard to protect inmates against predators. We had an external walkway around the floor blocks that occupied each of the three floors in the old jail. In the podular system, the officer is locked up in the central control booth. With this system, there is no communication going on between the deputies and inmates. We are fortunate here in Fairfax County that we have a 750-bed expansion to the present facility that has direct supervision. It is inexpensive or less expensive to build than a maximum-security prison or jail. It is designed to hold medium-security inmates. The idea is that a deputy sheriff over a period of time can get to know the inmates and have more control over their behavior, since he or she spends between sixty and ninety days working the same unit inside the day room with the inmates.

"I would like to encourage students reading this book to consider working in a New Generation jail. I believe that it is a very positive career move. First off, you are not simply watching people. There is a challenge of getting to know inmates and earning their respect. The challenge comes from being consistent and treating them fairly, as individuals. Over time you will develop communication, decision-making, and problem-solving skills. There is much more to the job than simply being on the floor with the inmates. That is just the beginning. Once you indicate to your superiors that you have talent in other areas, you will be used in those areas and assume very interesting responsibilities within the facility. We have opportunities for communication specialists, computer program specialists, budget systems specialists, and other specialists, just like any other $53 million business. We are looking for good people."

CRITICAL THINKING QUESTIONS

Why is Captain Fatherree so positive about his job? What can he teach others who want to make corrections a career?

IS THE ROLE OF THE JAIL OFFICER CHANGING?

In the past, training for jail officers (also known as deputies or jailors) was frequently inadequate or nonexistent. Salaries were always low and sometimes incredibly low. Motivation was usually a problem, especially when sheriffs' deputies were used as jail personnel in place of career corrections officers.

Today, jail officers receive both introductory training and in-service training. According to a 1998 national survey, jails required an average of 271 hours of introductory training for new officers. Clark County, Washington, required the most: 1,120 hours; Jefferson County, Colorado, the least: 14 hours. On average, jails required 33 hours of in-service training each year. Sarasota, Florida, required the most: 160 hours; King County, Washington, the least: 14 hours.[52]

Jail officers' salaries also have significantly increased. According to a 1998 national survey, the average starting salary of officers was $25,593; the average salary was $30,439;

and the average highest salary was $37,536. The highest salary for a jail officer was $44,448, paid by Contra Costa, California. The lowest salary was $12,376, paid by Decatur County, Georgia.[53]

Jail officers have responsibilities for handling intake procedures, for ensuring that inmates receive their constitutional rights, for referring inmates to medical services when needed, and for providing supervision of inmates. Intake procedures include checking the arrest form and determining whether medical attention is needed, then patting-down or frisk-searching the inmates. Valuables are carefully recorded and placed in an envelope, and the inmate signs a property receipt. Basic information is collected. The inmate is photographed and fingerprinted, and a complete set of prints is sent to the FBI to check for outstanding warrants. The inmate is given a shower and may be given a uniform or permitted to remain in civilian clothes.[54]

Inmates must be given opportunities to make arrangements for bail and to contact an attorney. No inmate can be denied access to counsel. Incoming packages must be checked for drugs, alcohol, weapons, and other **contraband.** Medicines must be controlled carefully and taken in the presence of officers. In most jails, activities are provided that occupy time, offer educational courses, or promote jail skills or personal development.

The jail officer is also expected to maintain a secure and safe environment. It is necessary to keep a close watch on inmates who show signs of mental illness, display suicidal signs and symptoms, have serious medical problems, are predators of weaker inmates, or are inciting problems on their cellblocks. The direct supervision jail makes it much easier to detect the victimization of other inmates and sudden behavioral changes in inmates vulnerable to suicide.

WHAT ARE THE ISSUES OF JAIL CONFINEMENT?

The most serious issues facing the jail involve crowding, court orders and civil suits, mental health placements, and violence. Like other correctional institutions in the United States, jails have not escaped the skyrocketing influx of prisoners. Lawsuits are increasingly filed to effect a change in conditions in jails and to obtain punitive damages. Mental hospitals have traditionally provided for the mentally ill. But as shrinking budgets have caused many state hospitals to close their doors, the mentally ill now circulate between mental health clinics, homelessness, and jail.[55] Violence, especially in large facilities with linear supervision, continues to be a way of life in the jail. Overcrowding and idleness among heterogeneous populations provide an ideal setting for the strong to take advantage of the weak.

Jail Crowding

Jail crowding has grown progressively worse in the past two decades. Jail populations more than doubled from 1985 to 1999 (see Table 9.1). Table 9.2 lists the number of inmates on June 30, 1999, and includes the percentage of rated capacity that is occupied.

Table 9.1							
Inmates Held in Local Jails							
Year	**Number**	**Year**	**Number**	**Year**	**Number**	**Year**	**Number**
1985	265,615	1992	444,584	1995	507,044	1998	592,462
1990	405,320	1993	459,804	1996	518,492	1999	605,943
1991	426,479	1994	486,474	1997	567,079		

Source: Bureau of Justice Statistics, "Prison and Jail Inmates at Midyear 1996" (Washington, D.C.: U.S. Department of Justice, 1997), p. 2; Bureau of Justice Statistics, *Prisoners in 1998* (Washington, D.C.: U.S. Department of Justice, 1999), p. 1; and Bureau of Justice Statistics, *Prisoners in 1999* (Washington, D.C.: U.S. Department of Justice, 2000), p. 2.

Table 9.2

Number of Jail Inmates; Rated Capacity; Percentage of Capacity Occupied; Jail Incarceration Rate, by Jurisdiction, 30 June 1999

Region and Jurisdiction	Number of Jail Inmates 6/30/99	Rated Capacity[a]	Percent of Capacity Occupied	Jail Incarceration Rate 6/30/99[b]
U.S. Total	605,943	652,321	93%	222
Northeast	90,716	97,794	93%	193
Maine	1,113	1,220	91	89
Massachusetts	10,774	9,978	108	174
New Hampshire	1,592	1,812	88	133
New Jersey	16,830	15,349	110	206
New York	33,411	39,904	84	184
Pennsylvania	26,996	29,531	91	225
Midwest	97,652	108,261	90%	155
Illinois	16,880	19,069	89	139
Indiana	12,787	12,553	102	216
Iowa	2,998	3,125	96	104
Kansas	4,378	5,565	79	165
Michigan	15,629	16,661	94	159
Minnesota	5,002	5,970	84	105
Missouri	6,940	8,924	78	127
Nebraska	2,189	2,728	80	131
North Dakota	588	918	64	92
Ohio	16,638	17,219	97	148
South Dakota	1,064	1,623	66	144
Wisconsin	12,559	13,906	90	239
South	284,742	308,234	92%	297
Alabama	11,418	11,600	98	261
Arkansas	4,832	6,122	79	189
District of Columbia	1,653	1,378	120	320
Florida	51,080	55,493	92	337
Georgia	32,835	36,213	91	421
Kentucky	10,373	9,915	105	262
Louisiana	25,631	27,544	93	585
Maryland	10,945	11,821	93	211
Mississippi	8,886	9,778	91	320
North Carolina	13,279	15,456	86	173
Oklahoma	6,743	7,663	88	200
South Carolina	8,780	9,115	96	226
Tennessee	19,629	21,572	91	358
Texas	57,930	66,521	87	288
Virginia	18,235	15,514	118	266
West Virginia	2,493	2,529	99	138
West	132,833	138,032	96%	224
Alaska[c]	68	160	43	—
Arizona	10,320	12,629	82	216
California	77,142	75,088	103	233
Colorado	9,004	9,151	98	222
Idaho	2,809	3,203	88	225
Montana	1,521	1,791	85	172
Nevada	4,898	5,436	90	270
New Mexico	5,217	6,258	83	298
Oregon	6,283	7,210	87	189
Utah	4,024	5,904	68	188
Washington	10,542	10,004	105	183
Wyoming	1,005	1,198	84	209

Note: Prisons and jails form an integrated system in Alaska (except for fifteen locally operated facilities). Connecticut, Delaware, Hawaii, Rhode Island, and Vermont: All inmates in these states are counted as state prisoners.

—Not calculated

[a]Rated capacity is the number of beds or inmates assigned by a rating official to facilities within each jail jurisdiction.

[b]The number of jail inmates per 100,000 U.S. residents on 1 July 1999. Regional calculations exclude resident populations in States with integrated prison and jail systems.

[c]Based on fifteen locally operated facilities only.

Source: Bureau of Justice Statistics, *Prison and Jail Inmates at Midyear 1999* (Washington, D.C.: U.S. Government Printing Office, 2000), p. 8.

In seven states and the District of Columbia, the total jail population exceeded jail capacity. Some jails have reached the point where crowding makes it impossible to accept more prisoners. Other jails, under court order, must find ways to reduce the number of prisoners.

A contributing factor to jail crowding in 1999 was that 63,635 state prisoners were being held in local jails. The South held 46,585 of these prisoners. Louisiana's jails housed 14,892 state prisoners; Texas's jails, 7,131 prisoners; and Tennessee's jails, 5,716 prisoners.[56] The Edna McConnell Clark Foundation reported that a frustrated county sheriff in Arkansas attempted to get rid of the state inmates confined in his jail by chaining them to the state prison fence. However, state officials confronted the sheriff with shotguns and a court order to return the inmates to the county jail.[57]

What makes jail crowding such a serious problem is that jails have even fewer alternatives for dealing with overcrowded facilities than do state and federal institutions. States and the Federal Bureau of Prisons can transfer inmates from one facility to another. Parole boards in some overcrowded states release prisoners early. Such options are not usually available to jail administrators, who are dependent on bail-reform acts, speedy trials, and the benevolence of judges to alleviate overcrowded jail conditions.

Overcrowding is particularly acute in large urban jails, which hold more than 50 percent of the U.S. jail population. In the 1970s and the 1980s, the Tombs in New York City, the Cook County Jail in Chicago, the old District of Columbia jail, and the jails in Atlanta, Dallas, and Houston suffered from scandalously overcrowded conditions.

One of the problems resulting from overcrowding is inmate idleness. A long-accepted adage is that busy inmates create fewer problems than idle inmates. A few jails run work farms, and the city workhouses usually have labor gangs. But the existent jail programs, makeshift work, and maintenance tasks simply are not adequate. The endless empty hours in day rooms, accompanied by the usual restricted movement within the jail, result in restless prisoners. In first- and second-generation jails, idleness was one of the factors contributing to high rates of physical and sexual assaults among inmates.

Civil Suits and Court Orders

Jail administrators, as well as jail officers, are sensitive to the possibility of being sued by inmates. The National Prison Project of the American Civil Liberties Union (ACLU) and the Prisoners Rights Project of the Legal Aid Society of the City of New York are among the nonprofit law firms that file many of these suits. To stem the growing tide of lawsuits, Congress enacted and President Clinton signed the Prison Litigation Reform Act in the spring of 1996. It places limitations on population caps and limits the time periods of injunctions and consent degrees placed on institutions, forces solvent inmates to pay part of the filing fee, and requires judges to screen prisoner claims to eliminate frivolous lawsuits.[58]

Whether this law will have any impact or not, civil and class-action suits are a real headache for most jail administrators. In a survey of 125 jail systems reporting on litigation, 19 respondents indicated that one or more of the jail facilities that they operated were under a court order concerning conditions of confinement on 1 January 1999. The larger the jail, the more likely it was to be under a court order. For example, among the 21 largest jail systems, 9 (42.9 percent) were under a condition of confinement.[59]

A landmark case involving jail overcrowding was *Bell v. Wolfish* (1979), which attacked the double-bunking policies of the Metropolitan Correctional Center in New York City. A dramatic rise in pretrial detainees resulted in the Bureau of Prisons' double-bunking sentenced and nonsentenced inmates in single-occupancy accommodations. The *Bell* class-action suit alleged other constitutional rights violations, such as undue length of confinement, improper searches, and inadequate employment, recreational, and educational opportunities. The U.S. Supreme Court rejected all allegations as not violating inmates' constitutional rights. Significantly, the policy of double-bunking inmates was ruled constitutional because nearly all pretrial detainees would be released within 60 days.[60]

Sheriffs and wardens are concerned because the courts can hold them, as they have held other jail administrators, personally liable for damages. The courts have awarded civil damages and legal fees in excess of $1 million. Sheriffs can also lose their jobs and expend a great deal of time dealing with lawsuits.

Mental Health Placements

Approximately 670,000 mentally ill people are admitted to jails in the United States each year.[61] It is estimated that nearly 6 to 8 percent of annual commitments to jails are individuals with severe mental illnesses.[62] For example, a study in Santa Clara County, California, concluded that 10 to 15 percent of the county jail's 4,500 inmates were mentally ill. The study recommended diverting all nonviolent mentally ill inmates to community treatment.[63] In San Diego County, California, one out of four females and one out of seven males took psychotropic drugs to treat mental illness. The increased number of mentally ill inmates made it necessary to move them from two-person cells into two large dormitories.[64]

Mentally ill offenders are often arrested because community-based treatment programs do not exist, are filled to capacity, or are inconveniently located. Jail officials affirm that persons with severe mental illness are commonly jailed for such minor breaches of the law as vagrancy, trespassing, alcohol-related charges, disorderly conduct, or failing to pay for a meal.[65]

The mentally ill prisoner poses a special problem for the jail. Officers' lack of training, and insufficient intervention for mentally ill prisoners, make them high risks for jail confinement. Ideally, the mentally ill prisoner would be transferred to a psychiatric facility, but these facilities are often reluctant to accept troublesome prisoners with criminal histories.[66]

One does not have to be around a jail very long to discover the inability of mentally ill individuals to adjust to this environment. They may slump in a corner of their cell in a fetal position; they may be severely withdrawn and appear to be out of touch with what is happening to them. They may spend a good part of the day moaning or groaning in a loud voice. They may have conversations with imaginary partners or protectors. Or they may make ongoing attempts to injure themselves or commit suicide (suicide in jail and prisons is examined in Chapter 12).

Violence

Physical assaults, including rapes, are the most frequent types of violence, but mass disturbances sometimes erupt among jail populations. In Chapter 12, an analytical framework is developed to explain violence by incarcerated people. The good news is that physical and sexual assaults take place less frequently in newer jails, with direct supervision of inmates. The bad news is that assaults continue to be a problem in older jails, especially large urban jails. In these jails, women and first-offending males are the most likely victims.

In the 1970s, southern rural jails gained a reputation as places where women were sexually abused by their jailers. The trial of Joan Little, who fatally stabbed jailer Clarence Alligood in the Beaufort County Jail in North Carolina, spotlighted this accusation. Recent studies have documented the widespread sexual victimization of females by male guards in women's prisons. A few studies in the 1990s examined the sexual victimization of women in U.S. jails.[67] See Within the Walls 9.2.

the walls 9.2

Jails Wracked by Sexual Abuse Scandals

In two adult prisons, a juvenile facility, and a work-release center, Wackenhut Corrections has been under criticism for abusive treatment of inmates, inadequate and ill-prepared staff earning Wal-Mart wages, and sex with prisoners. But the biggest scandal erupted in the Wackenhut's operated jail in Texas, where eleven former officers and a manager were indicted for sexually assaulting or harassing sixteen female prisoners at the 1,033-bed Travis County Community Justice Center in 1998 and 1999.

One former female inmate said that sex was routinely traded for shampoo and underwear. She said that she was doped up on psychiatric medication late one night when a guard entered her cell and raped her. She said that over

> . . . sex was routinely traded for shampoo and underwear.

the next three months officers hit her to keep her from reporting the assault.

The criminal case could grow bigger. The district attorney is looking into the possibility of bringing sexual charges against twenty more officers and into whether Wackenhut impeded the investigation by shredding documents.

CRITICAL THINKING QUESTIONS

What can be done to eliminate the sexual victimization of female inmates by male guards in jails?

Source: Ron Young, "Wackenhut Wracked by Sexual Abuse Scandals," *Prison Legal News* 11 (August 2000), pp. 1–2.

WHAT TRENDS ARE SHAPING THE JAIL?

In recent years, a number of promising proposals for jail reform have been recommended and implemented.[68] The direct supervision of inmates that is found in the New Generation jail is becoming increasingly common across the nation. Indeed, nearly half or more of the recently constructed jails provide direct supervision. National jail expert Ken Kerle defines the direct supervision phenomenon as "the most significant event to impact jails in the twentieth century."[69]

The Commission on Accreditation for Corrections, the National Sheriff's Association, and the federal government are proposing minimum standards for the construction and operation of jails. Thirty-two states have established standards for jails, and in twenty-five states these standards are mandatory.[70] In addition, seven states in recent years have enacted legislation that transfers control of local jails to state government, and many more states have established procedures for state inspection of local jails. Furthermore, regional jails, serving multiple cities or counties, have become a large part of the landscape of American jails. In some jails, programming has been expanded to include drug treatment, jail industries, boot camps, and self-help programs. Finally, more extensive in-service training, as well as college-educated officers, are being used to improve jail operations.

SUMMARY

The traditional jail, an institution reserved for a variety of short-term convicted and nonconvicted inmates, has been wracked with problems—overcrowding, staff morale, inadequate programs, archaic physical facilities, and a violent environment. Much similarity exists between the culture of inmates in this traditional jail and that found within prison settings. There is little question that this jail is inadequately equipped to do its job. The traditional jail has frequently been accused of being one of the most inadequate institutions in American society.

In recent years, a third-generation jail has increasingly replaced the traditional linear-design jail. New Generation jails still often must deal with problems of over-crowding, but direct supervision of inmates, increased programming, and improved staff morale make this jail a more desirable placement for inmates. Another of the positive consequences of the direct supervision jails is that fewer physical assaults and sexual victimizations of inmates take place than in traditional jails. Voluntary and state-required jail standards, as well as regional or multi-county arrangements of jails, are other hopeful signs that the jails of the twenty-first century will be improved over those of the nineteenth and twentieth centuries.

KEY TERMS

bail bonds, p. 209
contraband, p. 218
direct supervision, p. 214
jail crowding, p. 218

New Generation jail, p. 214
pretrial release, p. 209
preventive detention, p. 210
release on own recognizance (ROR), p. 209

CRITICAL THINKING QUESTIONS

1. You are the undersheriff (in charge) at the Y County Jail. The rated capacity is 350, but the population for the last six months has exceeded 500. No relief is in sight. The budget is tight, and the food is meager and unappetizing. The captain reports that there is a lot of grumbling, and he fears that some inmates may be instigating an insurrection. What preventive measures will you put into effect? What recommendations would you make to the sheriff?

2. You are still at the Y County Jail, which is still over-crowded. An 18-year-old man asks for an interview with you. He is a handsome young man. He tells you that the older men in the task to which he was assigned committed a gangbang on him last night. He wants protection. He is serving a year and a day for auto theft and has nearly all of it left to serve. What are you going to do about his situation?

3. The traffic in cocaine and marijuana in Y County is heavy and poorly controlled by the police. A lot of stuff is coming into the jail. A study by the district attorney's investigative staff finds that officers are bringing much of it in for sale to inmate gang leaders. The investigators recommend that all officers be routinely frisked when they arrive at work. Is this a good idea? You know that many officers will protest that this is unfair to the law-abiding majority of the staff. Will you adopt the district attorney's recommendation anyway? If so how will you deal with the protest? If not, what other measures can you use to eliminate traffic in drugs?

4. Jails have been called "brutal, filthy cesspools." Why was that description frequently accurate in the past? Why is it less likely to be accurate in the present?

5. Direct supervision jails seem so much better than linear-design jails. What problems do you see in direct supervision jails? How much is the New Generation jail likely to improve the overall quality of jails in the United States?

6. Is there such a thing as a good jail? Imagine yourself inside a good one and describe it.

WEB DESTINATIONS

Read in depth about county and local corrections in Ohio and in Alaska.
http://www.state.oh.us/dys/CountyLocal.html
http://www.uaa.alaska.edu/just/links/corr.html

Follow links to compare and contrast local corrections in your state and nearby states in your region.
http://www.oletc.org/law/links2.html

Read a Human Rights Watch report on the controversial use of jails to detain immigrants.
http://www.hrw.org/reports98/us-immig/

The National Institute of Corrections has many resources on jails. Visit the Jails Division. See, for example, a study on podular direct supervision jails.
http://www.nicic.org/inst/nicjails.htm
http://199.117.52.250/pubs/jails.htm

Read a research brief on the issue of incarcerating the mentally ill in jails, calling for the diversion of nonviolent low-level offenders with mental health problems.
http://www.soros.org/crime/research_brief_1.html

FOR FURTHER READING

Goldfarb, Ronald. *Jails: The Ultimate Ghetto of the Criminal Justice System.* Garden City, N.Y.: Doubleday, 1976. The author discusses the shortcomings of the jail and its negative impact on offenders placed within.

Irwin, John. *The Jail: Managing the Underclass in American Society.* Berkeley: University of California Press, 1985. The underclass, or "rabble," thesis proposed in this book merits consideration by society's policymakers.

Kerle, Kenneth E. *American Jails: Looking to the Future.* Boston: Butterworth-Heinemann, 1995. Kerle provides a useful overview of the past, present, and future of the American jail.

Metz, Andrew. "Life on the Inside: The Jailers," *Newsday,* 21 March 1999, pp. A5, A50, A52. Presents the daily life of correctional officers in the Nassau County Correctional Center. One of the largest county lockups in the nation, the facility employs 1,100 corrections officers supervising about 1,800 inmates.

Thompson, Joel A., and G. Larry Mays, eds. *American Jails: Public Policy Issues.* Chicago: Nelson-Hall, 1991. The authors provide an excellent examination of the jail.

NOTES

1. Richard A. Clark was interviewed in January 1991.
2. For a more extensive history of the jail, see J. M. Moynahan and Earle K. Stewart, "The Origin of the American Jail," *Federal Probation* 42 (December 1978), pp. 41–50.
3. Henry Burns Jr., *Corrections: Organization and Administration* (St. Paul, Minn.: West, 1975), pp. 147–148.
4. Moynahan and Stewart, "The Origin of the American Jail," p. 45.
5. Orlando F. Lewis, *The Development of American Prisons and Prison Customs, 1776–1845,* Reprint Series in Criminology, Law Enforcement and Social Problems, no. 1 (Montclair, N.J.: Patterson Smith, 1967), p. 278.
6. Ibid., p. 269.
7. National Commission on Law Observance and Enforcement, *Report of the Advisory Committee on Penal Institutions, Probation and Parole* (Washington, D.C.: U.S. Government Printing Office, 1931), p. 272.
8. Joseph C. Hutcheson, "The Local Jail," *Proceedings of the Attorney General's Conference on Crime, December 10–13, 1934* (Washington, D.C.: Bureau of Prisons, Department of Justice, 1936), p. 233.
9. National Advisory Commission on Criminal Justice Standards and Goals, *Corrections* (Washington, D.C.: U.S. Government Printing Office, 1973), p. 4.
10. President's Commission on Law Enforcement and Administration of Justice, *Task Force Report: Prisoner Rehabilitation* (Washington, D.C.: U.S. Government Printing Office, 1967).
11. Bureau of Justice Statistics, *Prisoners in 1999* (Washington, D.C.: U.S. Department of Justice, 2000), p. 1.
12. Bureau of Justice Statistics, *Correctional Populations in the United States, 1996* (Washington, D.C.: U.S. Department of Justice, 1999), p. 3.
13. Ibid.
14. Ibid.
15. Dean J. Champion, *Corrections in the United States: A Contemporary Perspective* (Upper Saddle River, N.J.: Prentice-Hall, 1998), pp. 187–192.
16. John Irwin, *The Jail: Managing the Underclass in American Society* (Berkeley: University of California Press, 1985), pp. 26–38.

17. John A. Backstrand, Don C. Gibbons, and Joseph P. Jones, "What Is in Jail? An Examination of the Rabble Hypothesis," *Crime and Delinquency* 38 (1992), pp. 219–229.
18. See John H. Gibbs, "The First Cut Is the Deepest: Psychological Breakdown and Survival in the Detention Setting," in *The Pains of Imprisonment,* ed. Robert Johnson and Hans Toch (Beverly Hills, Calif.: Sage, 1982), p. 114.
19. Bureau of Justice Statistics, *Report to the Nation on Crime and Justice,* 2d ed. (Washington, D.C.: U.S. Department of Justice, 1988), p. 77.
20. Ibid.
21. Patrick G. Jackson, "The Uses of Jail Confinement in Three Counties," *Policy Studies Review* 7 (1988), pp. 592–606.
22. U.S. General Accounting Office, *Criminal Bail: How Bail Reform Is Working in Selected District Courts* (Washington, D.C.: U.S. Government Printing Office, 1988).
23. Bureau of Justice Statistics, *Pretrial Release and Detention: The Bail Reform Act of 1984* (Washington, D.C.: U.S. Government Printing Office, 1988).
24. Patrick G. Jackson, "Competing Ideologies of Jail Confinement," in *American Jails: Public Policy Issues,* ed. Joel A. Thompson and G. Larry Mays (Chicago: Nelson-Hall, 1991), p. 28.
25. Michael G. Maxfield and Terry L. Baumer, "Home Detention with Electronic Monitoring: Comparing Pretrial and Postconviction Programs," *Crimes and Delinquency* 36 (October 1990), pp. 522–528.
26. G. Larry Mays and Francis P. Bernat, "Jail Reform Litigation: The Issue of Rights and Remedies," *American Journal of Criminal Justice* 12 (1988), pp. 254–273.
27. G. Larry Mays and Joel A. Thompson, "The Political and Organizational Context of American Jails," in *American Jails: Public Policy Issues,* p. 11.
28. Kenneth E. Kerle, *American Jails: Looking to the Future* (Boston: Butterworth-Heinemann, 1975), pp. 32–33.
29. Ibid., p. 34.
30. Ibid., p. 35.
31. Ibid.
32. Advisory Commission on Intergovernmental Relations, *Jails: Intergovernmental Dimensions of a Local Problem* (Washington, D.C.: Advisory Commission, 1984).

33. Ibid., p. 170.

34. Bureau of Justice Statistics, *Prison and Jail Inmates at Midyear 1999* (Washington, D.C.: U.S. Department of Justice, 2000), p. 7.

35. Norman R. Cox Jr., and William E. Osterhoff, "Managing the Crisis in Local Corrections: A Public–Private Partnership Approach," in *American Jails: Public Policy Issues*, p. 228.

36. Cited in Kerle, *American Jails*, p. 11.

37. Carol J. Casteneda, "Arizona Sheriff Walking Tall, but Some Don't Like His Style," *USA Today*, 25 May 1995, p. 7A.

38. Kerle, *American Jails*, p. xvii.

39. For the three generations of jails, see William "Ray" Nelson, "New Generation Jails," Webpage of the National Institute of Corrections, Boulder, Colo.; Allen R. Beck, "Deciding on a New Jail Design," Webpage of Justice Concepts Incorporated; and Kerle, *American Jails*, pp. 190, 192.

40. Beck, "Deciding on a New Jail Design."

41. Nelson, "New Generation Jails."

42. Nelson, "New Generation Jails."

43. Linda L. Zupan and Ben A. Menke, "Implementing Organizational Change: From Traditional to New Generation Jail Operations," *Policy Studies Review* 7 (1988), pp. 615–625.

44. L. L. Zupan and M. Stohr-Gillmore, "Doing Time in the New Generation Jail: Inmate Perceptions of Gains and Losses," *Policy Studies Review* 7 (1988), pp. 626–640.

45. Robert Conroy, Wantland J. Smith, and Linda L. Zupan, "Officer Stress in the Direct Supervision Jail: A Preliminary Case Study," *American Jails* (November–December 1991), p. 36.

46. Information on the Fairfax County ADC was gained from the Webpage of the Fairfax County Adult Detention Center, 10 August 2000, and from a phone call with Captain Donald Fatherree of the ADC staff.

47. Fairfax County ADC Webpage.

48. Linda L. Zupan, *Jails: Reform and the New Generation Philosophy* (Cincinnati: Anderson, 1990), p. 67.

49. Federal Prison System, "Metropolitan Correctional Center," n.d., pp. 1–2. This information was updated in August 2000 by corrections staff at the Metropolitan Correctional Center in Chicago.

50. Kerle, *American Jails*, p. 146.

51. Cited ibid., p. 122.

52. Camille Graham Camp and George M. Camp, *The Corrections Yearbook 1999: Jails* (Middletown, Conn.: Criminal Justice Institute, 1999), p. 66.

53. Ibid., p. 84.

54. This material on staff responsibilities is adapted from Jeanne B. Stinchcomb and Vernon B. Fox, *Introduction to Corrections*, 5th ed. (Upper Saddle River, N.J.: Prentice-Hall, 1999), pp. 197–199.

55. Leslie Lunney, "Nowhere Else to Go: Mentally Ill and in Jail," *Jail Suicide/Mental Health Update* (Washington, D.C.: National Center on Institutions and Alternatives and the National Institute of Corrections, 2000), p. 13.

56. Bureau of Justice Statistics, *Prisoners in 1999* (Washington, D.C.: U.S. Department of Justice, 2000), p. 7.

57. Clark Foundation, *Overcrowded Time: Why Our Prisons Are So Overcrowded and What Can Be Done* (New York: Edna McConnell Clark Foundation, 1982).

58. See Sarah B. Vandenbraak, "Summary of Prison Litigation Reform Act (PLRA)," *American Jails* (July/August 1996), pp. 104–105.

59. Camp and Camp, *The Corrections Yearbook 1999*, p. 38.

60. *Bell v. Wolfish*, 441 U.S. 520 (1979).

61. H. J. Steadman, H. J. Morris, and D. L. Dennis, "The Diversion of Mentally Ill Persons from Jails to Community-Based Services: A Profile of Programs," *American Journal of Public Health* 85 (1995), p. 1634.

62. Jails Division, *Jail Mental Health Services Initiative from the National Institute of Corrections* (Washington, D.C.: National Institute of Corrections, 2000), p. 13.

63. Pretrial Resources Center, *The Pretrial Reporter* (Washington, D.C.: Pretrial Resources Center, December 1995), p. 5.

64. Kerle, *American Jails*, p. 19.

65. "Mental Illness in U.S. Jails: Diverting the Nonviolent, Low-Level Offender," *Research Brief* (November 1996), p. 2.

66. For discussion of mental health services in jail, see David Kalinich, Paul Embert, and Jeffrey Senesa, "Mental Health Services for Jail Inmates: Imprecise Standards, Traditional Philosophies, and the Need for Change," in *American Jails: Public Policy Issues*, pp. 79–99; E. Fuller Torrey, Joan Stieber, Jonathan Eziekial, Sidney M. Wolfe, Joshua Sharfstein, John H. Noble, and Laurie M. Flynn, *Criminalizing the Seriously Mentally Ill: The Abuse of Jails as Mental Hospitals* (Washington, D.C.: National Alliance for the Mentally Ill and Public Citizen's Health Research Group, 1992), pp. 137–139.

67. David W. Chen, "After Abuse Charges, Westchester Bars Male Guards from Women's Jail, Westchester County, New York," *New York Times*, 1 March 2000, p. B4.

68. Kerle, *American Jails*, p. 220.

69. Ibid.

70. Tom Rosazza, "Jail Standards: Focus on Change," *American Jails* (November/December 1990), pp. 84–87.

CHAPTER 9 / BUILT-IN STUDY GUIDE

Multiple Choice Questions

1. Which of the following type of correctional facilities is not operated on the local or county level of government?

    A. Lockups
    B. Jails
    C. Workhouses
    D. Prisons

2. The jail originated in:

    A. England
    B. France
    C. Sweden
    D. United States

3. Which of the following type of jail design provides the correctional officer with direct supervision of inmates?

    A. First generation
    B. Second generation
    C. Third generation
    D. Fourth generation

4. Which of the following is the most frequently used method of jail administration?

    A. State responsibility for operating a jail
    B. Private responsibility for operating a jail
    C. City responsibility for operating a jail
    D. County responsibility for operating a jail

5. Which of the following pretrial release options requires the defendant to pay an established fee if he or she fails to appear for trial?

    A. Unsecured bail
    B. Partially secured bail
    C. Bail
    D. Privately secured bail

6. All of the following are responsibilities of jail officers except:

    A. Handling intake procedures
    B. Ensuring inmates receive their constitutional rights
    C. Referring inmates to medical services
    D. Providing mental health counseling for inmates

7. What is the estimated percentage of annual commitments to jail that have severe mental illness?

    A. 8% to 10%
    B. 10% to 12%
    C. 6% to 8%
    D. 4% to 6%

8. The modern penitentiary was based on:

    A. Separate wing of the Virginia Street Jail
    B. Separate wing of the Walnut Street Jail
    C. Separate wing of the Chestnut Street Jail
    D. Separate wing of the Olive Street Jail

9. Which of the following is not a category of inmates who belong in jail?

    A. Pretrial detainees
    B. Probation violators
    C. Individuals convicted of misdemeanors
    D. Offenders serving a life sentence

10. All of the following are benefits of being released prior to trial except:

    A. Defendants can continue working at their job
    B. Defendants can receive emotional support of their family
    C. Defendants can continue their criminal activities
    D. Defendants come into court as free men or women

11. What form of pretrial release occurs when a defendant is released on a promise that he or she will return for trial?

    A. Conditional release
    B. Release on recognizance
    C. Honor release
    D. Unsecured bail

12. All of the following are alternatives to local control of the jail except:

    A. State-run jails
    B. Private service jails
    C. State subsidy programs
    D. National jail programs

True/False Questions

T F   1. In the early history of jails inmates usually paid a fee for every service they received.

T F   2. Jails are correctional facilities that can hold sentenced inmates for up to one year.

T F   3. The majority of jails in the United States have over 1,000 beds.

T F   4. First-generation jails provide for direct supervision of all inmates.

T F   5. The jail touches the lives of more individuals than any other correctional facility.

T F   6. The New Generation jail is more expensive to build than a maximum-security jail.

T F 7. The lack of programming has long been a problem of the jail.

T F 8. State and federal correctional institutions have more strategies to address overcrowding than jails.

T F 9. Large urban jails hold more than 50 percent of the U.S. jail population.

T F 10. Correctional officers report lower levels of job satisfaction while working in New Gen-eration jails than in traditional first-genera-tion jails.

T F 11. According to the Chief Medical Officer of the Los Angles County Sheriff's Department in-mates with cancer present a crucial health care issue confronting staff in a jail setting.

T F 12. Suspected parole violators wait for their parole revocation hearing in jail.

Fill-in-the-Blank Questions

(based on key terms)

1. A form of pretrial release, which generally involves cash deposits, property, or other valuables, is referred to as _____.

2. Defendants who are determined to be dangerous may be ordered to _____ in jail until their trial date to maintain public safety.

3. Physical assaults of inmates occur less frequently in _____ jails than in traditional jails.

4. _____ has become such a problem that some jails are under a court order to find ways to re-duce the number of inmates in their facilities.

5. A defendant who is accused of a crime and has re-ceived some form of _____ may collect evi-dence in his or her defense prior to trial.

6. _____ jails make it less difficult for the cor-rectional officer to detect sudden behavioral changes among inmates vulnerable to suicide.

Essay Questions

1. What are the three main types of local correctional in-stitutions?

2. Describe the historical development of the jail. When did the jail originate? What was its original purpose? How was it financed? How was it used in colonial America?

3. Identify and specifically describe six types of offenders that make up the inmate population in a jail.

4. Identify and explain three ways a defendant can avoid going to jail prior to trial.

5. Describe the architectural designs for the first-, second- and third-generation jails. How do they differ? How does the physical design of each influence the behav-ior of inmates as well as correctional officers?

ANSWERS

Multiple Choice Questions

1. D	7. C
2. A	8. B
3. C	9. D
4. D	10. C
5. A	11. B
6. D	12. D

True/False Questions

1. T	5. T
2. F	6. F
3. F	7. T
4. F	8. T

9. T	11. F
10. F	12. T

Fill-in-the-Blank Questions

1. Bail bonds
2. Preventive detention
3. Direct supervision
4. Jail crowding
5. Pretrial release
6. New Generation

Federal, State, and Private Institutions

William DiMascio, executive director of the Pennsylvania Prison Society, has this to say about prison reform:

> Prison reform was a serious matter to the early Quakers and others. They came together with strong convictions regarding corporal and capital punishment. As significant as prison reform was in those days, I believe that it is equally as important today.
>
> The most important part of our effort is our work with human beings; that equation is the same in the present as it was in the past. But our world today has become so much more materialistic and secular. There seems to be an incessant drumbeat to get more, attain more, and achieve more. It has the effect of leaving behind those who have started from disadvantaged positions. Those who are left behind are marginalized. We put them in institutions where they are walled off. We don't have to look at them anymore; we don't have to hear from them; and that is the end of that.
>
> The only time we are really concerned about them is when one of us gets caught up in it, or when that one of us is a rising star in the community. We have a local politician who

was such a "rising star" and is about to enter prison. When that happens, we are reminded that anyone of us or our children could be in the same situation, and then we get concerned.[1]

CRITICAL THINKING QUESTIONS

Do you agree with William DiMascio that prison reform is as important today as it was in the early days of corrections in this nation? What are the possible consequences of keeping people who are locked up out of sight and out of mind?

William DiMascio focuses on the quality of correctional care in institutional settings. He is concerned that increasing numbers of inmates are being ignored. As other leaders of the Pennsylvania Prison Society have urged for over two hundred years, he believes that the task of prison reform is to maintain constant vigilance over those placed in long-term institutions, especially those from disadvantaged backgrounds.

Prison reform has never had an easy time, for several reasons. First, the United States has a long and persistent belief in the value of the prison. Second, the get-tough mood of the present is at odds with the notion of making the prison more pleasant to inmates; indeed, advocates of toughness want to reduce privileges, not increase reform. Third, present-day prisons are so much better than prisons in the past that some people see no need for improvement. It is claimed that prisons are no longer dark, dingy, deteriorating dungeons where inmates suffer sensory deprivation and the human spirit is destroyed by monotony and regimentation.

Prison reformers see things differently. They charge that the denial of basic human rights remains one of prisons' least defensible attributes. They state that prisons are too frequently places of brutality, violence, and racial unrest. Furthermore, reformers remind us that although these institutions purport to cure offenders of crime, their record has not been encouraging.[2] They add that few would share the vision of Reverend James Finley, chaplain at Ohio Penitentiary in 1851:

> Could we all be put on prison-fare for the space of two or three generations, the world would ultimately be the better for it. Indeed, should society change places with prisoners . . . taking to itself the regularity, temperance, and sobriety of a good prison, the goals of peace, light, and Christianity would be furthered . . . taking this world and the next together . . . the prisoner has the advantage.[3]

WHAT DO PRISONS LOOK LIKE TODAY?

The four most widely used architectural designs in American prisons are the radial design, the telephone-pole design, the courtyard style, and the campus style (see Figure 10.1). The 1980s and 1990s were years of constant prison construction, and facilities built in those decades—mostly medium- and minimum-security prisons—have affected what prisons look like. What this means is that the maximum-security prisons depicted in 1930s movies—the prototype of prisons in the past—are no longer the dominant form of long-term institution for adults. During the late twentieth century, technological innovations, usually to promote security, altered the appearance of prisons.

Architectural Design for Today's Prisons

The structural design of early prisons was intended to produce a specific outcome: moral reformation. The isolated cells were intended to facilitate contemplation, industry, and penitence. Since with Jeremy Bentham's circular Panopticon in the nine-

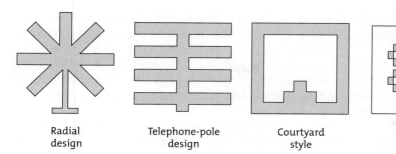

Radial
design

Telephone-pole
design

Courtyard
style

Campus
style

Figure 10.1
Prison Designs Used
in the United States

teenth century (see Chapter 2), institutional security or control, rather than reformation, has been the basic function of prison architecture.

Eastern State Penitentiary in Philadelphia was the first prison to utilize the **radial design.** In this wheel-shaped configuration, corridors radiate like spokes from a control center at the hub. The Federal Penitentiary at Leavenworth, Kansas, and state penitentiaries at Rahway and Trenton, New Jersey, are examples of radial design. In an examination of prison architecture, William G. Nagel found that radial design is rarely used anymore.[4]

A prison utilizing the **telephone-pole design** has a long central corridor serving as the means for prisoners to go from one part of the prison to another. Extending out from the corridor are cross-arms containing housing, school, shops, and recreation areas. This design, the most widely used for maximum-security prisons in the United States, was used for the Federal Penitentiary in Marion, Illinois, and state correctional institutions at Graterford, Pennsylvania; Somers, Connecticut; and Jackson, Georgia. This telephone-pole design makes it possible to house prisoners by classification levels. A major disadvantage of this layout is that militant convicts can barricade the corridor. In the event of a riot or a hostage-taking situation, it is easy for convicts to take control and difficult for guards to recapture control of the prison.

The **courtyard style,** likely to be found in newer prisons, has a corridor surrounding a courtyard. Housing units, as well as educational, vocational, recreational, prison industry, and dining areas, face the courtyard. The Women's Treatment Center at Purdy, Washington, has become a showplace among women's prisons and is built around multilevel and beautifully landscaped courtyards. The attractive buildings provided security without fences, until a number of escapes in the mid-1970s resulted in the construction of eight-foot fences. Small housing units with pleasant living rooms reflect the expectation that the women will behave like human beings, and, imply that they will be treated as such. The education, recreation, and training areas are ample and roomy. A short distance away are attractive apartments, each containing a living room, kitchen, dining space, two bedrooms, and a bath. Women who are close to release and are on work or educational release occupy these apartments.[5]

The **campus style,** found in minimum-security and a few medium-security prisons, utilizes an open design that allows some freedom of movement. Small housing units are scattered among the educational, vocational, recreational, and dining units of the prison. Women's prisons frequently use the campus design. Living units are grouped in cottages scattered around the institutional grounds, which are surrounded by a fence. The campus-like design is likely to be found in showplace institutions that have more generous visiting policies, than do typical institutions, allow more furloughs, offer better services and programs, and provide a safer environment for both staff and inmates.

Changing Form of the Prison

More than half of the prisons today are less than twenty years old. The 1990s, especially, were a decade of enormous prison construction. Between 1990 and 1998, 405 new prisons were constructed, an average of 45 a year. During 1998, 35 new correctional institutions were opened by 19 agencies. Of the 21,353 beds for which security levels were reported, 61.9 percent were medium security, 19.5 percent were minimum security, and 18.6 percent were maximum security. In addition, 28 agencies completed additions or renovations in 79 institutions during 1998.[6] As of 1 January 1999, 29 new institutions in 29 agencies were under construction, and 66 institutions in 17 agencies were undergoing additions or renovations.[7]

One of the disadvantages of prison construction and renovation is the expense that it brings to the state and federal governments. During 1998, the average cost of the 35 new prisons that were opened was $28,912,516. Nineteen agencies spent $716,552,096 during 1998 for their new correctional facilities. Illinois spent $75,900,000; Missouri, $68,868,500; and Pennsylvania, $61,580,000. During 1998, the 28 agencies that completed renovations or additions spent $539,601,802. New York spent the most, $160,000,000, on renovations and additions.[8]

A major advantage of the new prisons constructed across the nation is that the new facilities permit the tearing down or closing of many of the old, dungeon-like prisons. In Within the Walls, 10.1, in interviews from 1978 and 2000, William D. Leeke, former commissioner of the South Carolina Department of Corrections, recalls the notorious Cellhouse One in the Central Correctional Institution at Columbia, South Carolina.

Some of the newly constructed prisons across the nation do not look like prisons. The Minnesota Correctional (Facility) in Stillwater—Oak Park Heights—is one of the

within the walls   10.1

The Notorious Cellhouse One

In a 1978 interview, Commissioner Leeke said, "I am extremely concerned about that structure [Cellhouse One] and will remain dedicated to abolishing its use or seeing it removed, no matter what it takes to accomplish this goal. The building was constructed in the 1860s as the original cellblock for the state penitentiary. I have been trying since I became commissioner to do something about that place. The state legislature has even authorized our agency to do away with the Central Correctional Institution completely, in favor of smaller, regional facilities, but our tremendous growth in the number of inmates has forced us to continue utilizing the old building. In addition, I feel a great deal of concern for the inmates who live in Cellblock One and our employees who have to work there. I've personally been in that building in the midst of a disturbance, and it is extremely dangerous. It is a blight on our state and is a terrible situation. If our inmate population stabilizes, as it appears to be doing, we hope to be able to shut down that building forever."

> I have been trying since I became commissioner to do something about that place.

Twenty-two years later, in 2000, Leeke recalled the time in 1998 when Central Correctional Institution, including Cellhouse One, was demolished, "I have a big plaque on the wall in my office that a former secretary did for me that has a large crane and bar, and it says, 'And the wall came tumbling down.' It was such a relief to see it come tumbling down. But that has been accomplished, and the institution is closed. The city of Columbia is working toward the development of the waterfront there. Mainly, I think there were economic reasons for closing the prison and the city buying it. It was simply too valuable a piece of land to have a prison on it."

CRITICAL THINKING QUESTIONS

Why have correctional departments found it difficult to demolish or close old, dungeon-like prisons? When old prisons no longer house inmates, what do you think of converting them, as was done with Alcatraz, into a tourist attraction?

The Oak Park Heights correctional facility in Minnesota is one of the more technologically advanced and secure prisons in the nation. How has technology affected the development of penal institutions? How does prison construction reflect relationships with the community and wider society?

more technologically advanced and secure prisons in the nation. This three-story facility has some walls below ground level, and living space facing out on a sunken central courtyard. The subterranean design saves energy, and the prison has a heat-reclaiming unit. Within this innovative facility, inmates' freedom of movement decreases as they approach the institution's security perimeters. This restriction makes it possible to minimize guard-tower surveillance and thereby reduce costs. At Oak Park Heights, a sophisticated computer monitors the opening and closing of doors and other routine events. Any deviation must be cleared with security staff to avoid triggering alarms. The system also monitors perimeter security and fire safety and controls the heating and ventilation systems. Other security elements at Oak Park Heights include a closed circuit television monitoring system and an electronic alarm network on the roof of the facility and on the perimeter's double security fence.[9]

TO WHAT EXTENT DO PRISONS MIRROR THE LARGER SOCIETY?

An important consideration in corrections is the relationship between the prison and the wider society. James Jacobs's classic analysis of the Stateville Penitentiary in Illinois concludes that the social organization and moral values, as well as the major societal changes, of the larger society are found in the micro society within the walls.[10] Donald Clemmer's classic study of the prison community at Menard Correctional Center in Illinois also notes the existence of numerous parallels between the prison and the free world. Clemmer writes, "In a sense the prison culture reflects the American culture, for it is a culture within it."[11] Furthermore, James Fox observes that "the same civil rights issues, religious issues, and other social issues appear in prison as also appear in the city. The prison reflects the society it serves."[12]

There are those who argue that rather than the prison being a microcosm of the larger society, it is a distorted image of the larger society that is found within the prison walls. In its analysis of the 1971 Attica rebellion, the New York State Special Commission on Attica stated: "While it is a microcosm reflecting the forces and emotions of the larger society, the prison actually magnifies and intensifies these forces, because it is so enclosed."[13] Raymond Michalowski, in comparing the class divisions, organizational conflicts, sexual subjugation, and racial conflict in the prison and in free society, states:

> Prisons in America exist as a kind of distorted mirror image of American society. Like the mirrors in a carnival fun-house, prisons exaggerate and expand some of the characteristics of the society they reflect. Yet, like fun-house mirrors, what they show is based on the very real object they are reflecting. The parallel between free society and prisons exists at both the organizational and the social level.[14]

A closer examination of the relationship between the prison and society reveals that poverty, racial and gender discrimination, violent crime, and mental illness are found in more exaggerated forms within the prison. The vast majority of prisoners come from pockets of poverty. They have grown up in disorganized communities, have been victims of racial and sexual discrimination, have varying degrees of emotional disturbance, and have victimized others. As these individuals come into the prison, they must deal with the deprivations of confinement in an environment full of racial unrest and division. Predators in the outside world may become the victims in this enclosed world. For those who have emotional problems, the world of the prison is even more chaotic.

WHO HAS JURISDICTION OVER PRISON SYSTEMS IN THE UNITED STATES?

The Federal Bureau of Prisons, state departments of corrections, and prisons funded and administered by private corporations have jurisdiction over prisons in the United States. The Federal Bureau of Prisons was established in 1930 to ensure the administration of the eleven federal prisons in operation at that time. The Bureau of Prisons presently consist of nearly one hundred institutions, staff training centers, and community corrections officers. There are fifty separate state departments of corrections as well as the one in the District of Columbia. Correctional institutions vary tremendously from state to state. Some states have a few correctional facilities and other states have many. The prison populations of states correspond highly with the number of institutions. The private sector is now providing prisoners' work programs and medical, educational, and psychological services; financing for prison or jail construction; and managing and operating prisons or jails.

Federal Bureau of Prisons

Today, the Federal Bureau of Prisons (BOP) consist of 95 correctional institutions, 6 regional offices, a Central Office, 3 staff training centers, and 29 community corrections offices. BOP is responsible for the custody and care of 141,000 federal offenders; approximately 122,000 of these inmates are confined in Bureau-operated correctional institutions or detention centers. The remaining offenders are confined through agreements with state and local governments and through contracts with privately operated community corrections centers, detention centers, and juvenile facilities.[15] Figure 10.2 shows the placement of the Bureau of Prisons' correctional institutions.

The Bureau of Prisons has several strengths that facilitate the achievement of its mission and the delivery of correctional services. Both management and nonmanagement staff typically view themselves as members of a professional management team. Staff at all levels, from the director's office down, feel that the BOP offers excellent career op-

Figure 10.2 Federal Bureau of Prisons Correctional Institutions

Source: Federal Bureau of Prisons, *Annual Report, 1999* (Washington, D.C.: U.S. Government Printing Office, 2000)

portunities, providing up-to-date and skilled management and staff training for people who want to make a difference. Among administrators, there seems to be a fundamental belief that the BOP has talented employees who can be trained and groomed for the top jobs in the agency.[16] Correctional officers also tend to view themselves as professionals who have the possibility of upward career mobility in the agency.

The federal training centers do a superior job of creating esprit de corps among institutional personnel. The neatly attired correctional officers of the federal system stand in sharp contrast to the officers of some state systems. Rotating top administrative staff every two or three years also seems to help maintain a high level of professionalism and to avoid the stagnation and burnout often found among administrators in state institutions.

The Bureau of Prisons offers a variety of inmate programs that are a cut above what is found in most state correctional institutions. Nearly 50,000 inmates have completed their residential drug treatment programs since 1990. An interim report from an ongoing evaluation of this drug abuse program showed that those individuals who have been released to the community for at least six months after completing the program were 73 percent less likely to be arrested for a new offense and 44 percent less likely to test positive for drug use, as compared to inmates who did not complete the program. In 1999, nearly 6,000 inmates obtained a general equivalency diploma (GED), and many others completed vocational training and other educational programs. In addition, the BOP has developed a number of new life skills programs in recent years.[17]

The Federal Prison Industries (FPI) is the standard or goal for states' prisons to attempt to match. FPI employs nearly 21,000 inmates, or about 25 percent of the sentenced and medically eligible federal inmate population. FPI has up-to-date equipment, develops a strong work ethic, and pays considerably more than state prisoners receive from prison industry.[18]

The Bureau of Prisons further deserves praise because it has been willing to receive the most hard-to-control inmates from state prisons, thereby making the inmate population more manageable in state facilities. With the construction of super-max areas in many state facilities across the nation, states may become more willing to place these difficult inmates in their own high-security housing units.

In the midst of these accolades, the correctional institutions of the Bureau of Prisons have some troubling issues and limitations. Prison crowding is as least as serious a problem in BOP facilities as it is in state institutions.[19] Federal penitentiaries, such as Marion, Atlanta, and Leavenworth, also have serious problems generated by violence, homosexuality, inmate defiance, and drug traffic. Thus, daily existence for the federal prisoners in federal penitentiaries is not greatly different from life in a maximum-security state prison. Boredom, regimentation, personal indignities, the deprivations of imprisonment, and the difficulty of daily survival are found in both state and federal institutions.[20]

Furthermore, it is argued that BOP began one of the most destructive trends in the history of U.S. corrections when it developed a super-max prison at the federal penitentiary at Marion, Illinois. On 22 October 1983, Thomas Silverstein, an inmate at Marion, stabbed a corrections officer forty times, precipitating a total lockdown of the prison. The officer was one of two officers to die that day in separate incidents. The Bureau reacted by converting Marion into a permanent lockdown control unit to confine prisoners considered especially dangerous or escape risks. The now familiar routine for inmates at super-max prisons was established: solitary confinement, in-cell meals, and 23-hour lockup.[21] Supported by federal courts in a pivotal court case, *Bruscino v. Carlson* (1987), Marion became the model of super-max prisons in forty-one states.[22] "Marionization" is the term that a Human Rights Watch report coined for the constructing of super-max prisons and placing inmates in permanent 23-hours-a-day locked-up status.[23]

Overall, the Federal Bureau of Prisons has become a professional bureaucracy, living up to the vision of its first director, James V. Bennett. As part of the federal bureaucracy, the Bureau of Prisons has far more resources than do the states to build institutions, implement programs, and pay staff adequate compensation. The Bureau does have its limitations, but it still provides a quality of correctional care that far exceeds that found in state facilities.

Our hero in this chapter is Dr. Kathleen Hawk Sawyer, director of the Federal Bureau of Prisons. In 1973, she began her BOP career as a psychologist at the Federal Correctional Institution in Morgantown, West Virginia. During the 1980s and early 1990s, she was chief of staff training at the Staff Training Academy; an associate warden for programs at the Federal Correctional Institution in Fort Worth, Texas; warden at the Federal Correctional Institution in Butner, North Carolina; and the BOP's assistant director for program review. On 4 December 1992, she was appointed to serve as the Bureau of Prisons' sixth director. Read her statement for *Invitation to Corrections* in 2000.

States Departments of Corrections

The correctional systems of the fifty states and the District of Columbia are hard to compare and evaluate because of differences in ideology, structure, and programs. The quality of previous corrections leaders, the resources available, and the volume of inmates have largely shaped what takes place in corrections within a state.

h e r o e s

Kathleen Hawk Sawyer

Director of the Federal Bureau of Prisons

"My career choice was influenced by two things I learned from early work experiences at the Sargus Juvenile Facility in St. Clairsville, Ohio, and the Federal Correctional Institution (FCI) in Morgantown, West Virginia. I learned that the familiar prison stereotypes I and others had were erroneous and that working in a prison could offer a rich environment and exciting opportunities for anyone, especially a psychologist, eager to work with people and to attempt to make a difference in the lives of others. My experience as an intern at FCI Morgantown persuaded me to make corrections my life's work.

"A priority for the Bureau of Prisons is to effectively manage the increasing federal inmate population and our institutions that are operating above their intended capacity. We are especially attuned to securing the funds necessary to construct and operate prisons to handle the population increase, being able to recruit and retain a diverse workforce to manage a diverse inmate population, and being able to provide meaningful work and other self-improvement opportunities for inmates to increase their chances for a crime-free return to society. We have been putting a lot of energy into constructing new institutions, expanding existing facilities, changing institution security levels and missions, converting military property, and contracting for appropriate lower-security segments of the population.

"As the Bureau was growing rapidly in the 1980s and in anticipation of future growth, we realized that planning was becoming more and more important. We had developed a formal, structured, and ongoing planning process to review our mission, develop goals and objectives and prepare our budget. As our planning process evolved, we quickly realized that planning and monitoring go hand-in-hand. We monitor the operations, programs, and services within our institutions through comprehensive program reviews, or internal audits, and more-limited operational reviews. These reviews assess program performance and compliance with our policies and procedures, federal laws and regulations, and standards of correctional practice. In addition, our institutions and our health services programs seek accreditation from nationally recognized accrediting organizations. The Bureau also uses aggressive management techniques to identify and implement opportunities for improvement in programs and procedures, to enhance the efficiency and effectiveness of our operations.

"Our growth has also resulted in our increasing visibility, external scrutiny, and constituency interests. Our increased need for fiscal resources and staff resources has, in turn, led to more congressional oversight. With increased visibility, we have a heightened need to educate external groups about our agency and our successes at meeting our correctional goals. Many times, the public's concerns with how we manage inmates and what programs we offer conflict with the sound judgement of experienced correctional practitioners. Our correctional programs not only help to meet the societal goals of public safety and crime prevention through reduced recidivism, these programs also help us maintain the security of our institutions by keeping inmates constructively occupied. We know the importance of programs, especially industrial and institution work programs, education programs, vocational training, substance abuse treatment, pastoral care, psychology programs, life skills programs, and release preparation programs. We continue to defend programs that have been shown to meet demonstrable goals through sound and rigorous research. We also will continue to augment, expand, and develop offshoots from programs that work well.

"In light of our growth and the changing nature of the federal inmate population, we have placed a greater emphasis on basic inmate management. While we have always encouraged frequent communication between staff and inmates, the challenges posed by overcrowded institutions have focused our attention on our basic inmate management practices and the ongoing availability of staff to the inmates. Our ongoing review of inmate characteristics has revealed that the Bureau is confining a greater number of inmates who are younger, more impulsive and more confrontational, and have significant histories of violence and gang activity. We have placed greater emphasis on frequent and constructive interaction and communication between staff and all inmates and a heightened responsiveness to inmate concerns.

"To help us manage the increasing presence of quick-tempered, dangerous inmates, we have developed programs that focus on their emotional and behavioral responses to difficult situations. These 'cognitive restructuring' programs emphasize life skills and the development of prosocial values, respect for self and others, responsibility for personal actions, and tolerance.

"With the increasing federal inmate population comes the need for more staff at all levels of the organization. We have placed tremendous efforts into recruitment, employee development, succession planning, and the development of mid-level and executive-level managers. We have also been using preference profiles and other mechanisms to gain employees' input into their career aspirations. Our goal is to have a workforce that is satisfied with the workplace, their jobs, and their career opportunities.

"I think anyone who chooses a career with the Bureau of Prisons will discover a multitude of rewards that come from a career in public service and from working in an outstanding correctional agency. The approximately thirty-one thousand employees of the Bureau of Prisons are dedicated to their profession, to protecting public safety, and to carrying out the numerous responsibilities we have to the Department of Justice, the courts, and the citizens of this county. The wide variety of occupations, the locations, and our growth mean there are tremendous opportunities for advancement and for a varied and rewarding career in the Bureau of Prisons."

CRITICAL THINKING QUESTIONS

Does this statement make a job with the Bureau of Prisons attractive to you? Why or why not? How does the Bureau of Prisons attempt to manage difficult inmates?

Table 10.1

Number of Inmates in Custody of State or Federal Prisons or Local Jails, 31 December 1999

Region and Jurisdiction	Total Advance 1999	1998	Percent Change, 1998–99	Sentenced to More Than 1 Year Advance 1999	1998	Percent Change, 1998–99	Incarceration Rate, 1999[a]
U.S. Total	1,336,721	1,300,573	3.4%	1,305,393	1,245,402	3.2%	476
Federal	135,246	123,041	9.9	114,275	103,682	10.2	42
State	1,231,475	1,177,532	2.7	1,191,118	1,141,720	2.5	434
Northeast	179,758	175,681	1.5%	171,234	167,376	1.5%	330
Connecticut[b]	18,639	17,605	5.9	13,032	12,193	6.9	397
Maine	1,716	1,691	1.5	1,663	1,641	1.3	133
Massachusetts[c]	11,356	11,799	−3.8	10,282	10,744	−4.3	266
New Hampshire	2,257	2,169	4.1	2,257	2,169	4.1	187
New Jersey[d]	31,493	31,121	1.2	31,493	31,121	1.2	384
New York[e]	73,233	70,001	2.6	72,896	70,001	2.1	400
Pennsylvania	36,525	36,377	0.4	36,525	36,373	0.4	305
Rhode Island[b]	3,003	3,445	−12.8	1,908	2,175	−12.3	193
Vermont[b]	1,536	1,473	4.3	1,178	959	22.8	198
Midwest	232,905	228,116	2.1%	231,961	227,270	2.1%	367
Illinois[d,f]	44,660	43,051	3.7	44,660	43,051	3.7	368
Indiana	19,309	19,197	0.6	19,260	19,016	1.3	324
Iowa[d,f]	7,232	7,394	−2.2	7,232	7,394	−2.2	252
Kansas[d]	8,567	8,183	4.7	8,567	8,183	4.7	321
Michigan[f]	46,617	45,879	1.6	46,617	45,879	1.6	472
Minnesota	5,969	5,572	7.1	5,955	5,557	7.2	125
Missouri	26,155	24,974	4.7	26,133	24,950	4.7	477
Nebraska	3,688	3,676	0.3	3,632	3,588	1.2	217
North Dakota	943	915	3.1	866	834	3.8	137
Ohio[d]	46,842	48,450	−3.3	46,842	48,450	−3.3	417
South Dakota	2,506	2,422	3.5	2,498	2,417	3.4	339
Wisconsin	20,417	18,403	10.9	19,699	17,951	9.7	375
South	551,284	512,271	3.7%	528,377	493,488	3.4%	543
Alabama	24,658	22,676	8.7	24,109	22,214	8.5	549
Arkansas	11,415	10,638	7.3	11,336	10,561	7.3	443

—Not calculated.
[a]The number of prisoners with sentences of more than 1 year per 100,000 U.S. residents.
[b]Prisons and jails form one integrated system. Data include total jail and prison population.
[c]The incarceration rate includes an estimated 6,200 inmates sentenced to more than 1 year but held in local jails or houses of corrections.

Some states have few correctional institutions (New Hampshire, 6; Utah, 5; and Wyoming, 4). Other states have many (Texas, 107; North Carolina, 88; and Florida, 85.)[24] Texas had the largest number of inmates in state correctional agencies on 31 December 1999 (163, 190), followed closely by California (163,067); further back was the Federal Bureau of Prisons (135, 246).[25] Table 10.1 shows the number of inmates in state correctional agencies as of 31 December 1999. Furthermore, the 1998 adult correctional budgets of the states ranged dramatically from the highs of California ($4,024,313,000), Texas ($1,849,936,355), New York ($1,656,094,900), Michigan ($1,441,935,000), and Florida ($1,420,796,382), to the lows of North Dakota ($18,345,577), Vermont ($52,300,000), and West Virginia ($68,557,360).[26]

Region and Jurisdiction	Total			Sentenced to More Than 1 Year			
	Advance 1999	1998	Percent Change, 1998–99	Advance 1999	1998	Percent Change, 1998–99	Incarceration Rate, 1999[a]
Delaware[b]	6,983	5,558	—	3,730	3,211	—	493
District of Columbia[b]	8,652	9,829	−12.0	6,730	8,144	−17.4	1,314
Florida[f]	69,596	67,224	3.5	69,594	67,193	3.6	456
Georgia[f]	42,091	39,262	7.2	42,008	38,758	8.4	532
Kentucky	15,317	14,987	2.2	15,317	14,987	2.2	385
Louisiana	34,066	32,228	5.7	34,066	32,228	5.7	776
Maryland	23,095	22,572	2.3	22,184	21,540	3.0	427
Mississippi	18,247	16,678	9.4	17,410	15,855	9.8	626
North Carolina	31,086	31,961	−2.7	26,635	27,244	−2.2	345
Oklahoma[d]	22,393	20,892	7.2	22,393	20,892	7.2	662
South Carolina	22,008	21,764	1.1	21,228	20,910	1.5	543
Tennessee[d,e]	22,502	17,738	4.5	22,502	17,738	4.5	408
Texas[e]	163,190	144,510	1.9	154,865	139,863	0.7	762
Virginia	32,453	30,276	7.2	30,738	28,672	7.2	447
West Virginia	3,532	3,478	1.6	3,532	3,478	1.6	196
West	267,528	261,464	1.9%	259,546	253,586	2.0%	21
Alaska[b]	3,949	4,097	−3.6	2,325	2,541	−8.5	374
Arizona[f]	25,986	25,515	1.8	23,944	23,500	1.9	495
California	13,067	161,904	0.7	160,517	159,201	0.8	481
Colorado	15,670	14,312	9.5	15,670	14,312	9.5	383
Hawaii[b]	4,903	4,924	−0.4	3,817	3,670	4.0	320
Idaho[e]	4,842	4,083	12.9	4,842	4,083	12.9	385
Montana	2,954	2,734	8.0	2,954	2,734	8.0	335
Nevada	9,494	9,651	−1.6	9,413	9,651	−2.5	509
New Mexico	5,124	5,078	0.9	4,730	4,825	−2.0	270
Oregon	9,810	8,981	9.2	9,792	8,935	9.6	293
Utah[e]	5,426	4,453	4.2	5,271	4,402	4.3	245
Washington	14,590	14,161	3.0	14,558	14,161	2.8	251
Wyoming	1,713	1,571	9.0	1,713	1,571	9.0	355

[d]"Sentenced to more than 1 year" includes some inmates "sentenced to 1 year or less."
[e]Reporting changed in 1999; percents calculated on counts adjusted for comparable reporting.
[f]Population figures are based on custody counts.
Source: Bureau of Justice Statistics, *Prisoners in 1999* (Washington, D.C.: U.S. Department of Justice, 2000), p. 3.

Usually, within each state there is considerable variation in the quality of institutions. Typically, there is an old maximum security prison resembling an old castle, and a new minimum-security facility with an innovative and perhaps campus-style design. In visiting these facilities, it is hard to believe that both are under the same state's jurisdiction.

There are several ways in which state correctional institutions are better than they were in the past. State departments of corrections have become concerned about improving institutional standards. By the 1970s, state correctional administrators had begun to apply to the Commission on Accreditation of the American Correctional Association for accreditation of their institutions. Inspectors from the Commission would visit each institution to determine whether a particular prison was in compliance with the standards. If it was, the institution would receive accreditation. By October 2000, nearly all of the fifty states had participated in this accreditation process, and five-hundred correctional institutions had been accredited or were in the process of accreditation.[27]

In addition, most state departments of corrections have begun to emphasize preservice and in-service training. What this means is that newly hired correctional officers are likely to receive some type of training before they begin work in the institution. This training may take place at a state corrections academy, at the institution, or at some other location. Top institutional administrators and correctional counselors are also increasingly receiving in-service training.

Another feature of the majority of state departments of corrections is improved administrative leadership at the director's level as well as by institutional wardens and superintendents. It was not that long ago that a governor's appointee as director or commissioner had no background in corrections and the word of wardens was unquestioned. Today, with the rise of statewide bureaucracy, the head of the corrections department is accountable to the governor and the legislature and in turn expects accountability from wardens and superintendents.

Another admirable characteristic of many corrections departments is their receptivity to institutional research and evaluation. In addition, directors and commissioners of state systems and wardens and superintendents of state prisons are usually open and honest about institutional problems.[28]

State departments of corrections have many of the same problems that BOP institutions have. They are overcrowded and are filled with too much violence. But in contrast to most federal facilities, state institutions often have underdeveloped programming, insufficient prison industries for inmates, and insufficient resources for anything other than prison construction.

Overall, state correctional institutions are much better than they were in the past. The central office has more control of what is taking place in facilities across the state. The new state prisons that have sprouted up across the nation have replaced many of the old dungeons. Great strides have been made in professionalism. Nevertheless, the quality of corrections varies from state to state and from one time period to another within states.

Private Prisons

The private sector's involvement in corrections is not new. Private industry used prison labor in several ways during the late nineteenth century. Under the contract labor system, prisoners' labor was used to manufacture goods for private contractors who furnished tools and materials and supervised the work in prison. Under the piece-price system, contractors furnished raw materials and paid prisoners for the completed goods on a per piece basis. Under the lease system, prisoners "on loan" worked in farming, construction, and mining and on plantations, under the complete control of the lessee.[29]

Private operators contend that they can run prisons more efficiently and at less cost than public agencies.[30] In addition to saving money, proponents say, privatization would (1) increase the capacity of prisons by building facilities more quickly, (2) respond with greater flexibility to correctional needs by cutting red tape, (3) attract employees who are younger and more enthusiastic than public employees, and (4) bring fresh ideas into the correctional system.[31]

The impetus for privatization of corrections began in 1979 when the Immigration and Naturalization Service contracted with private firms to detain illegal immigrants.[32] By 1994, privately managed prisons were operating in thirteen states, and thirty-six states permitted them. Although inmates in these facilities represented only 2 percent of the total inmate population in U.S. prisons, the *Wall Street Journal* reported in 1994 that numbers of prisoners in privately run correctional institutions were growing four times faster than the rate of the general prison population.[33] The Corrections Corporation of America (CCA), a private contractor based in Nashville, had begun contracting with local and state governments to operate jail and prison systems in the mid-1980s. By 1994,

NOBODY HAS A GREATER CONCERN
FOR PUBLIC SAFETY
THAN THOSE WHO RISK
THEIR OWN EVERY DAY.

The face is one of courage, integrity and dedication. It represents just one of the 15,000 men and women who work at prisons and jails managed by Corrections Corporation of America throughout the country. They work as correctional officers, teachers, counselors, and nurses. While you may not know them, you need them. Because they are committed to making our tax dollars go as far as possible in the facilities managed by CCA in partnership with government. These are the men and women who've chosen to risk their lives to protect the community where you live because it's also the community where they live. They have families, children and homes here. And they are as concerned about public safety as you are. Perhaps even more.

CCA
CORRECTIONS CORPORATION OF AMERICA

QUIETLY GOING ABOUT THE BUSINESS OF PUBLIC SAFETY.

How widespread are private prisons? What is the trend in the involvement of the private sector in corrections, and what factors contribute to that trend? What are some advantages, disadvantages, and issues concerning the privatization of corrections?

CCA was the largest private prison contractor, operating twenty-seven facilities in the United States, with fifteen-thousand inmates.[34]

David Shichor's evaluation of private correctional facilities reveals "a somewhat lower cost and higher quality of services in private facilities."[35] Shichor warns that because these studies often focused on juvenile institutions and small facilities for special adult populations, some question must be raised about how applicable their findings are for "regular" adult prisons.[36] Increasing the involvement of private enterprise in corrections raises a number of important legal, financial, and moral questions that have not been adequately addressed. A state that surrenders its power of punishment to the lowest corporate bidder will seal off prisons from constitutional and popular controls. It also will sever any connection between justice and punishment, transforming the terms of the debate over the social objectives of incarceration from retribution, deterrence, and rehabilitation to productivity and profit.

In sum, there are many issues still open to debate about the privatization of corrections, especially the private sector's ability to manage large male prisons. Yet the recent growth in the privatization of corrections is a reminder that it is playing an increasingly important role in corrections and that it will likely continue to expand in the twenty-first century.

WHAT ARE THE MAIN TYPES
OF CORRECTIONAL INSTITUTIONS?

Correctional institutions have been traditionally designated as minimum-, medium-, and maximum-security facilities. Maximum-security prisons have been further divided into reformatories, state penitentiaries, and state prisons. In the 1990s, super-max prisons for men were built around the nation. Women's prisons usually provide all levels of security within the same facility. There are also special institutions for special offenders.

Table 10.2

Women under the Jurisdiction of State or Federal Correctional Authorities, 1990–1999

	Number of Female Inmates		Percentage Change		Incarceration Rate, 1999[b]
	1999	1990	1998–99	Average 1990–99[a]	
U.S. Total	90,668	44,065	4.4%	8.3%	59
Federal	9,913	5,011	7.9%	7.9%	6
State	80,755	39,054	3.9	8.4	53
Northeast	9,754	6,293	4.3%	5.0%	32
Connecticut	1,459	683	7.5	8.8	48
Maine	65	44	−7.1	4.4	9
Massachusetts[c]	742	582	−0.5	2.7	13
New Hampshire	117	44	0.9	11.5	19
New Jersey	1,862	1,041	12.6	6.7	44
New York	3,644	2,691	0.9	3.4	38
Pennsylvania	1,618	1,006	6.7	5.4	26
Rhode Island	188	166	−20.0	1.4	11
Vermont	59	36	13.5	5.6	14
Midwest	14,143	7,521	3.4%	7.3%	43
Illinois	2,802	1,183	5.9	10.1	45
Indiana[c]	1,222	681	2.0	6.7	40
Iowa	539	212	9.8	10.9	37
Kansas	570	284	9.0	8.0	42
Michigan[c]	2,027	1,688	−1.2	2.1	40
Minnesota	355	159	23.3	9.3	15
Missouri	1,891	777	0.6	10.4	67
Nebraska	251	145	0.8	6.3	28
North Dakota	70	20	1.4	14.9	20
Ohio	2,841	1,947	−2.4	4.3	49
South Dakota	189	77	−6.9	10.5	51
Wisconsin	1,386	348	18.7	—	51
South	37,525	15,366	5.6%	10.4%	67
Alabama	1,668	955	14.2	6.4	70
Arkansas	788	435	13.2	6.8	59

. . . Not calculated because of changes in reporting procedures.
[a]The average annual percentage increase from 1990 to 1999.
[b]The number of female prisoners with sentences of more than 1 year per 100,000 U.S. residents
[c]Growth from 1990 to 1999 may be slightly overestimated due to a change in reporting from custody to jurisdiction counts.

Women's Prisons

The first prison for women opened in 1863, and by the 1960s there were twenty-nine separate institutions for women. By the 1990s, the number of women sentenced to prison had increased in most states, and women's prisons began to be crowded. Table 10.2 shows the number of female prisoners under the jurisdiction of state and federal correctional authorities.[37]

During 1999, the number of female prisoners increased 4.4 percent, outpacing the rise in the number of male prisoners for the fourth straight year. Since 1990, the annual rate of growth of female prisoners has averaged 8.3 percent, higher than the 6.4 percent

	Number of Female Inmates		Percentage Change		
	1999	**1990**	**1998–99**	**Average 1990–99[a]**	**Incarceration Rate, 1999[b]**
Delaware	612	226	—	—	56
District of Columbia[c]	276	606	−23.1	−8.4	31
Florida	3,820	2,664	8.3	4.1	49
Georgia	2,607	1,243	5.4	8.6	64
Kentucky	1,097	479	4.9	9.6	54
Louisiana	2,268	775	4.0	12.7	100
Maryland	1,113	877	−2.4	2.7	37
Mississippi	1,405	448	15.8	13.5	89
North Carolina[c]	1,880	945	−3.0	7.9	34
Oklahoma	2,316	1,071	10.8	8.9	134
South Carolina	1,447	1,053	4.6	3.6	65
Tennessee[c,d]	1,368	390	11.7	15.0	48
Texas[d]	12,502	2,196	1.1	—	100
Virginia	2,119	927	14.1	10.2	57
West Virginia	239	76	13.3	13.6	26
West	**19,333**	**9,874**	**1.3%**	**7.8%**	**59**
Alaska	288	128	−4.6	9.4	45
Arizona	1,855	835	3.2	9.3	64
California[c]	11,368	6,502	−2.8	6.4	65
Colorado	1,213	433	13.4	12.1	59
Hawaii	553	171	28.6	13.9	80
Idaho	399	120	16.8	14.3	63
Montana	262	76	5.6	14.7	59
Nevada	731	406	−1.6	6.8	81
New Mexico	460	193	2.2	10.1	44
Oregon	583	362	11.3	5.4	35
Utah	368	125	9.6	12.7	33
Washington	1,111	435	9.1	11.0	38
Wyoming[c]	142	88	8.4	5.5	59

[d]Excludes an unknown number of female inmates in 1990 who were "paper-ready" state inmates held in local jails.

Source: Bureau of Justice Statistics, *Prisons in 1999* (Washington, D.C.: U.S. Department of Justice, 2000), p. 6.

average increase in the number of male prisoners. The total number of male prisoners has grown 75 percent since 1990, but the number of female prisoners increased 106 percent. On 31 December 1999, there were 59 sentenced female prisoners per 100,000 women, compared to 913 sentenced male prisoners per 100,000 men.[38]

Women's prisons usually do not look as foreboding as do men's prisons. They typically have the complex, campus, single-building, or cottage architectural design. Several buildings cluster around a central administration building at Goree Unit (Texas), Bedford Hills (New York), the Minnesota Correctional Institution for Women, and the Nebraska State Center for Women. A single building houses all functions at the Georgia

Rehabilitation Center for Women and the Colorado Women's Correctional Center. The campus design is used at the Women's Treatment Center at Purdy, Washington, the California Institution for Women, the Florida Correctional Institution, the North Carolina Correctional Center for Women, and the Massachusetts Correctional Institution (Framingham). The Detroit House of Corrections uses the cottage design, which consists of self-sufficient living units.[39]

Some states house women on the grounds of prisons for men, just off the main area of the institution, or in county institutions in which the states rent space. Fifteen states place women only in open institutions, and six states confine women in maximum-security facilities.[40] Thus, women prisoners are housed in a variety of settings, and instead of being sent to the most appropriate institution, they go to whatever the state has available.

Women's institutions that are attached to, or are satellites of, men's institutions typically are more security oriented than those that are not. The staff–inmate ratio in women's prisons is normally higher than in men's prisons, and the staff is more sexually mixed than in men's prisons. Inmates in treatment-oriented institutions tend to be less negative toward staff than those in custody-oriented institutions.

Women's prisons are generally smaller, more attractive, and more homelike than men's prisons. Some women's prisons seem overly programmed. For example, the California Institution for Women had so many programs that some women complained that they did not have time to do their time. The majority of women's prisons, however, offer fewer recreational programs and facilities than do men's prisons. The real difficulty in programming women's prisons is the traditional assumption that a paroled woman is limited to factory work in textiles, cosmetology, and typing.

In 1990 the task force of Corrections Canada developed a new women-sensitive correctional model. This task force proposed that women's prisons be characterized by five guiding principles: empowerment, meaningful and responsible choices, respect and dignity, supportive environment, and shared responsibility. The task force attributed the disempowerment of women to the structural arrangements of society and to women's lack of self-esteem. The task force defined meaningful choices as "choices which relate to their [women's] needs and make sense in terms of their past experiences, their culture, their morality, their spirituality, their abilities or skills, and their future realities of possibilities." The third principle, respect and dignity, is grounded "on the assumption that mutuality of respect is needed among prisoners, among staff, and between prisoners and staff if women are to gain the self-respect and respect for others necessary to take responsibility for their future." The fourth principle, supportive environment, is understood in terms of "the constellation of many types of environments . . . political, physical, financial, emotional/psychological, and spiritual, especially for Aboriginal women." Finally, shared responsibility emphasizes the responsibility of the inmate, the government, and the community.[41]

Minimum-Security Prisons for Men

Minimum-security prisons, in contrast to other men's prisons, have far more relaxed perimeter security, sometimes without fences or any means of external security. Minimum-security prisons for men that have abandoned the old fortress-type structure include Leesburg in New Jersey, Allenwood (a federal institution) in Pennsylvania, Fox Lake in Wisconsin, Jean in Nevada, and Vienna in Illinois. They all demonstrate that a more humane philosophy of imprisonment is possible. Openness sets these apart from other prisons. Jean resembles a condominium. Vienna and Leesburg are built around an open courtyard with a campus-like plan. Generous visiting policies, frequent home furloughs, better programs and services, and safer environments for both staff and inmates distinguish these facilities from others.

For the first two decades of its existence, the Vienna Correctional Center in Illinois was probably the most innovative correctional facility in the country. No riots and few escapes have occurred in its nearly thirty-year history. Vienna offers a variety of exciting community-based and institutional programs. Inmates provide round-the-clock emergency paramedical care to surrounding counties, teach cardiopulmonary resuscitation to local citizens, umpire Little League games on a baseball field that they built and maintain, and assist firefighters in nearby communities with labor and a fire truck. Southern Illinois University and Shawnee Community College formerly offered vocational and educational courses at the prison, which were also open to citizens of nearby communities. Local high schools, too, have started to use the prison recreational and vocational equipment. Most importantly, the residents are quite involved in both institution-based and community programs.

Medium-Security Prisons for Men

Medium-security prisons typically have single or double fencing, guarded towers or closed-circuit television monitoring, sally-port entrances, and zonal security systems to control inmate movement within the institution. In medium-security prisons, the emphasis is on controlled access to programs. Prisoners assigned to medium custody are under a lot of control and can be locked down in emergencies, but it is expected that they will participate in industrial or educational activities. Many maximum-security prisons, perhaps most of them, are in reality medium-custody facilities with units provided to house inmates who cannot be allowed any freedom of movement. In effect, we are moving away from the old dungeon thinking, providing for a programmed prison that allows a good deal of freedom of movement within a technologically secured perimeter. Oak Park Heights is an excellent example of this kind of planning. Sensors on the fences at Oak Park Heights warn the central control room of any approach to the fence, so that officers can be dispatched to apprehend anybody with escape on his mind.

Maximum-Security Prisons for Men

The assumption underlying **maximum-security prisons** is that the physical characteristics of the prison will be such that complete control of any and all prisoners can be applied at any time. Whether so many prisoners require this degree of control is irrelevant; this is the governing principle of maximum security. Designated by such names as correctional centers, penitentiaries, state prisons, and reformatories, maximum-security prisons for men have been bombarded with criticism.

Ancient, large, rurally located fortresses still exist. Like the pyramids, they were built to stand forever: Thick stone walls, massive gates, tall gun towers and steel doors bear testimony to their permanence. Their age and years of shoddy maintenance have resulted in dilapidated conditions, but the crowding of prisons, the need for maximum-security facilities, and the costliness of building new fortress-like prisons ensure their survival. The deficiencies of the old fortresses from the standpoint of economy in management and safety of personnel and prisoners, however, mandate that they be replaced as soon as possible. For example, if manned twenty-four hours a day, each tower would cost about $100,000 a year to maintain. Most of these relics from the nineteenth century were built without any thought of economy. The builders seemed to think that the more gun towers they installed, the better.

Most maximum-security prisons are large physical plants. The State Prison of Southern Michigan at Jackson has held as many as 6,500 prisoners. The San Quentin State Prison in California, the Stateville Correctional Center in Illinois, and the Ohio Penitentiary in Columbus (now closed) have each held over 4,000 inmates in the recent past. The Florida State Prison in Raiford and the Missouri Penitentiary in Jefferson City have each housed over 3,000 prisoners. The prison at Jackson is so big that more than 57 acres are enclosed within its walls.

Super-Max Prisons for Men

Forty-one states have embraced the idea of lockdown for their problem prisoners: Some states have constructed new high-tech super-max prisons; others have added high-security units to existing facilities. The newer prisons have totally automated the traditional jobs of correctional officers, such as opening cell doors, listening to complaints, and surveillance.[42] Whether these facilities are called super-max, security housing units, control units, or punitive or administrative segregation units, the conditions of confinement usually remain the same. Difficult-to-manage prisoners are housed in solitary confinement. They eat and exercise alone and are never allowed contact visits. They are entitled to a few hours a week of solitary recreation in an outdoor exercise cage, usually surrounded by a chain-link fence. They are permitted few, if any, in-cell vocational or educational programs.

These facilities are needed, say their supporters, to control those inmates whose behavior is so disruptive that they are unmanageable when housed with the general inmate population or placed in administrative segregation. Some inmates, these advocates, add, are simply too dangerous for the average prison setting. Gang leaders, disruptive inmates from other institutions, and inmates inciting riots are those most likely to be placed in super-max facilities or units.

Opponents speaking from the humane perspective question whether there is any justification for these institutions in a free and democratic society. They inflict unacceptable levels of pain and harm. Mentally ill prisoners are disproportionately represented in super-max prisons, because they have difficulty controlling their disruptive behavior. In addition, say the super-max opponents, inmates from these units who are released directly to the street are especially dangerous to society because of the harsh treatment they have received. Also, placement in super-max prisons is racist because 80 percent or more of the inmates are African Americans.[43]

In the late 1980s and 1990s, three long-term disciplinary units called security housing units (SHUs, prounounced "shoes") brought the California Department of Corrections considerable adverse publicity. Corcoran State Prison opened in 1988 and houses 1,400 men. Pelican Bay State Prison opened the next year and was touted as the prison of the future. Valley State Prison for Women, which opened in 1995, has its own SHU, which houses 52 women. Within the Walls 10.2, examines the Pelican Bay super-max unit.

At Corcoran's SHU, staff violence reached unbelievable levels. Under an "integrated yard policy," rival groups and known enemies were routinely brought together to fight in the small group exercise yards. For nine years, inmates were used as pawns in these setup fights. Correctional officers promoted their champions and even wagered on the fights for entertainment. An estimated eight thousand of these "gladiator fights" took place between 1988 and 1997.[44]

Officers in Corcoran used guns to control the yards, and more than two thousand shooting incidents took place. Hundreds were wounded and five were killed. An independent analysis of the five lethal shootings revealed that none was justified by the department of corrections' own criteria; yet, the "Shooting Review Board" routinely justified every shot ever fired in the SHU yards. In a wrongful-death lawsuit brought on behalf of the last inmate gunned down on the yards, former California corrections director Dan McCarthy testified that "The rate of violence in the Corcoran SHU in its first year of operation was absolutely the highest rate I have ever seen in any institution anywhere in the country."[45]

Special Institutions for Special Populations

Correctional institutions are sometimes catchalls for any lawbreaker who, in the opinion of the prosecutor and the judge, should be removed from society. In the past, offenders labeled psychotic, severely neurotic, and mentally defective; sexual offenders; defective delinquents (another name for sociopathic offenders); alcoholics, and drug

the walls   10.2

within

Pelican Bay Prison

Pelican Bay Prison, located in Crescent City, California, has a special housing unit for sixteen hundred inmates. They live in an X-shaped, windowless bunker. According to *Madrid v. Gomez* (1995), excessive and unnecessary force and abuse were common in the special housing unit.

Inmates were left naked in outdoor holding cages during inclement weather. Beatings occurred even after inmates had been restrained, and verbal harassment and racial taunting were commonplace. Inmates were shot for fistfights both on the outdoor recreation yards and inside the cellblocks. One mentally ill inmate suffered second- and third-degree burns over a third of his body when he was given a bath in scalding water in the prison infirmary a week after he had bitten an officer.

An inmate who refused to relinquish his dinner tray was brutally punished. At the time of the incident, he was unarmed, locked securely in his cell, and weighed around 130 pounds. A cell extraction team of five officers and a sergeant arrived on the scene. Prior to entering the cell, they discharged two multiple baton rounds, hitting the inmate in the groin, dispensed two bursts of mace, and then fired two taser cartridges. The team then entered the cell and restrained the inmate.

> "Dry words on paper cannot adequately capture the senseless suffering and sometimes wretched misery . . ."

Charles E. Fenton, ex-warden of the federal Marion Correctional Center, during court testimony openly criticized Pelican, describing a record of injuries and deaths due to guards' routine use of excessive force. "They [guards] either absolutely don't know what they're doing," he testified, "or they're deliberately inflicting pain."

The judge agreed with the prisoners in this class-action suit and ruled in their favor in 1995, stating, "Dry words on paper cannot adequately capture the senseless suffering and sometimes wretched misery that defendants' [prison staff and administration] unconstitutional practices leave in their wake."

CRITICAL THINKING QUESTIONS

Does the judge's statement seem biased? If it does not, how do you suppose California, with the most progressive departments of corrections in the nation, would end up with a facility like Pelican Bay?

Source: Madrid v. Gomez, 889 F. Supp. 1146 (N. D. Cal. 1995); Steve J. Martin, "Sanctioned Violence in American Prisons," in *Building Violence: How America's Rush to Incarcerate Creates More Violence*, ed. John P. May and Khalid R. Pitts (Thousand Oaks, Calif.: Sage, 2000), p. 116; and Corey Weinstein, "Even Dogs Confined to Cages for Long Periods of Time Go Berserk," in *Building Violence*, pp. 120, 123.

addicts were sent to specialized facilities, such as for the criminally insane. Today, they are typically placed with other inmates in the general population of prisons. For example, in 1996, 76 sex-offender programs existed in prisons across the nation.[46] Nevertheless, there still are correctional facilities designed for specialized groups or functions. Most states have diagnostic and reception centers, some independent of other institutions and some affiliated with other facilities. A few states have medical facilities. California has a facility reserved for drug treatment and a number of forestry camps and prison farms. North Carolina was one of the first states to develop youthful offenders camps for 16- to 18-year-old males. In the 1990s, Colorado, Florida, New Mexico, Minnesota, and Texas also developed intermediate systems between the juvenile and adult systems.[47]

There also are military correctional facilities. In December 1998, the U.S. military authorities held 2,426 prisoners in 69 facilities. Fifty percent of the inmates (1,377) had sentences of a year or more. The Army Disciplinary Barracks at Fort Leavenworth, Kansas, and five other local or regional Army facilities held nearly half (48 percent) of all prisoners under military jurisdiction.[48]

WHAT ARE THE INGREDIENTS OF A HUMANE PRISON?

People with a human view of corrections claim that a worthwhile goal is to create institutions that simulate as closely as possible the conditions of the real world. The simulation of the real world can be accomplished only when prisons are lawful, safe, industrious, and hopeful.[49]

The Lawful Prison

The lawful prison would prevent proscribed actions and conduct and provide inmates with all the rights granted by case law. Violators within the prison would be punished appropriately under conditions in which due-process procedures prevail. If prison administrators tolerate unlawful conduct by staff or prisoners, such as freely flowing drugs, thriving gambling rackets, and prostitution rings, nothing that they attempt will succeed.[50]

The Safe Prison

Both prisoners and staff must be assured of their safety in prison. Physical attacks on staff and inmates do take place in minimum-security institutions, but medium- and maximum-security prisons are the most likely settings for physical and sexual victimization, stabbings, and homicides. Guards across the nation express a common complaint: They have neither the control nor the respect they used to have. Nor do inmates feel any safer. The new breed of inmates brings with it the criminal expertise of street gang sophistication, the mechanics of narcotics distribution, and an inclination to mayhem at a level previously unknown in American prisons.

To ensure inmate and staff safety, changes are needed in the design and administration of prisons. Small prisons holding no more than four hundred inmates should be built. The physical design of the prison and its operations must ensure that adequately trained guards are in close contact with inmates in living quarters and at work assignments. Guards can best serve the interests of order and safety when they are competent in human relations, so that information can flow freely between prisoners and guards without fear that it will be misused, without expectation of special favor, and under conditions of respect and responsibility.

The Industrious Prison

Idleness is one of the real problems of prison life today. What work there is to be done in overcrowded facilities is spread so thin that it is no longer work. The yards and cell-blocks are full of boxed inmates. Some inmates engage in weight lifting and other physical activities, but too many inmates scheme during idle hours about drug drop-offs, prostitution rings, and "hitting" (stabbing) inmates in competing gangs.

Inmates need to be provided with more work and to have the work they do valued. Workers in prison are denied the value of their labor when they are paid at the low rates allowed in most correctional systems. Although to pay inmates the rates prevailing in the free market may be unrealistic, higher pay would produce benefits more than commensurate with the increased cost. Finally, work that is more marketable must be found. The useless and menial work characteristic of most prison industries is inappropriate because it fails to equip inmates for employment in the free community.

The 1980s and 1990s saw the revival of prison industries. This trend has emerged as a result of the pioneering involvement of a few private corporations and the driving force of former Supreme Court Chief Justice Warren E. Burger. Burger formulated the "factories with fences" concept and began promoting it with great energy. One of Burger's widely quoted observations is "To put people behind walls and bars and do little or nothing to change them is to win a battle but lose a war. It is wrong. It is expensive. It is stupid."[51]

The Hopeful Prison

Prisons should renew hope. Loss of hope is one of the consequences of a criminal career. To renew hope, prisons should offer inmates programs such as remedial elementary education, vocational training, individual and group therapy, and self-help techniques. No penalty should be levied against an inmate for failure to participate in a program, but there must be some incentive to engage in treatment. In the hopeful prison, inmates would feel that they have some say about their own lives. There is strong evidence that the freedom to make some decisions is needed to build a sense of responsibility. Finally, in the hopeful prison, prisoners would feel that they will receive acceptance in the outside community. Otherwise, the only reality for the inmate is the cellblock, the yard, and the prison industrial plant.[52]

SUMMARY

A belief in the value of incarceration has been one of the enduring aspects of correctional policy in the United States. Throughout American history, the public and policymakers have been willing to try various ways to reform or rehabilitate prisoners in long-term confinement.

The popularity of an approach to imprisonment at a given time is directly related to the social context. The mixing of solitary confinement and the discipline of work in order to achieve penitence and reform reflected the religious culture of Pennsylvania in the early decades of the nineteenth century. The imposing nature and miniature size of the Auburn-type cells in New York during the final decades of the nineteenth century indicated that the public wanted prisoners to receive sufficient punishment and to be isolated from law-abiding citizens. Today, prison cells are still very small, prison keepers are required to keep prisoners docile if they want to keep their jobs, and solitary confinement has again become a way of life in the most secure prisons across the nation.

This chapter focuses on federal, state, and private jurisdictions and describes the basic types of correctional institutions. The Federal Bureau of Prisons has many advantages over state prison systems, including better-trained staff, higher salaries, and more adequately funded programs and operations. No state is recognized today as a correctional leader, one that other states should emulate in providing correctional care. Private prisons are gaining in number and popularity, but there are still serious questions about the services they deliver. In considering the reform of the prison, it is suggested that prisons need to be lawful, safe, industrious, and hopeful.

KEY TERMS

campus design, p. 231
courtyard style, p. 231
maximum-security prison, p. 245
medium-security prison, p. 245

minimum-security prison, p. 244
radial design, p. 231
telephone-pole design, p. 231

CRITICAL THINKING QUESTIONS

1. Are all prisons like the "Big House" in movies of the 1930s? Explain your position using examples from your reading.

2. If you have not visited a prison, make arrangements to do so. Compare what you see with what you have read.

3. You wake up one morning and find yourself in prison. Based on your reading of this chapter, describe the sort of prison you hope it will be.

4. Why is the issue of humane care of prisoners so important?

5. Why did the popularity of super-max prisons increase in the 1990s?

6. Governor MacGregor requests your opinion about a proposal received from the well-known and respected Penal Corporation of America, which is offering to privatize the New Scotland prisons and guarantees substantial savings to the state. The governor suggests that if the state proceeds with this plan, you, the commissioner, will be responsible for oversight to ensure the maintenance of standards. He asks for your advice. You tell him that this is a complex problem and you will submit a memorandum within a few days. Outline the contents of your memorandum.

WEB DESTINATIONS

Explore resources on this home page for the U.S. Federal Bureau of Prisons.
http://www.bop.gov/

Use Web links or URLs at these sites to access state departments of corrections.
http://www.excite.com/lifestyle/politics_and_society/crime_and_justice/prisons_and_sentencing/departments_by_state/

http://www.cdc.gov/nchstp/od/cccwg/State_Departments_of_Corrections.htm

Take a virtual tour through Florida's state prisons.
http://www.dc.state.fl.us/oth/vtour/opendorm.html

Sample resources at this site to learn more about private prisons and prison privatization initiatives.

http://www.ucc.uconn.edu/~logan/

Read this article from the National Center for Policy Analysis tracing the growth and success of private prisons.
http://www.public-policy.org/~ncpa/ba/ba191.html

Read articles on controversies surrounding the treatment of dangerous offenders in super-max prisons.
http://www.isthmus.com/features/docfeed/archive/2000/65/

Read about an innovative special offenders unit for persons with mental retardation or mental illness who are involved in the criminal justice system.
http://www.co.lancaster.pa.us/soshome.htm

FOR FURTHER READING

Abu-Jamal, Mumia. *Live from Death Row.* Reading, Mass.: Addison-Wesley, 1995. An examination of prison life, especially death row, by a prisoner who views himself as a political prisoner.

Earley, Pete. *The Hot House: Life inside Leavenworth Prison.* New York: Bantam Books, 1992. Earley, a journalist, captures accurately a slice of life inside a federal maximum security prison.

May, John P., and Khalid R. Pitts, eds. *Building Violence: How America's Rush to Incarcerate Creates More Violence.* Thousand Oaks, Calif.: Sage, 2000. This edited volume has a number of insightful articles about the policy of incarceration.

Nagel, William G. *The New Red Barn: A Critical Look at the Modern American Prison.* New York: Walker, 1973. Nagel's examination of the architectural designs, programs, and problems of prisons in the United States is dated but fascinating.

Shichor, David. *Punishment for Profit: Private Prisons/Public Concerns.* Thousand Oaks, Calif.: Sage, 1995. This is the most up-to-date, balanced, and comprehensive treatment of private prisons.

Tonry, Michael, and Joan Petersilia, eds. *Prisons.* Vol. 26. Chicago: University of Chicago Press, 1999. This volume has a number of insightful articles on the functions and operations of present-day prisons.

NOTES

1. Interviewed in September 2000.

2. Norval Morris, *The Future of Imprisonment* (Chicago: University of Chicago Press, 1974), p. ix.

3. William G. Nagel, "An American Archipelago: The United States Bureau of Prisons" (Hackensack, N.J.: National Council on Crime and Delinquency, 1974), p. 1.

4. William G. Nagel, *The New Red Barn: A Critical Look at the Modern American Prison* (New York: Walker, 1973), p. 36.

5. Joan Potter, "In Prison, Women Are Different," *Corrections Magazine* 4 (December 1978), pp. 14–24.

6. Camille Graham Camp and George M. Camp, *The Corrections Yearbook 1999: Adult Corrections* (Middletown, Conn.: Criminal Justice Institute, 1999), p. 74.

7. Ibid., p. 75.

8. Ibid., pp. 74–75.

9. Minnesota Department of Corrections, "A New High Security Facility for Minnesota" (St. Paul, Minn.: Department of Corrections, n.d.), p. 2.

10. James B. Jacobs, *Stateville: The Penitentiary in Modern Society* (Chicago: University of Chicago Press, 1977).

11. Donald Clemmer, *The Prison Community* (New York: Holt, Rinehart & Winston, 1966), p. 298.

12. Cited in Charles Reasons, "Racism, Prison, and Prisoners' Rights," *Issues in Criminology* 9 (1974), p. 7.

13. *Attica: The Official Report of the New York State Special Commission on Attica* (New York: Praeger, 1972), p. 82.

14. Raymond Michalowski, *Order, Law and Crime* (New York: Random House, 1984).

15. Federal Bureau of Prisons Webpage.

16. In interviews, two former directors and the current director of the Bureau of Prisons—Norm Carlson, Michael Quinlin, and Kathleen Hawk Sawyer—all made this point.

17. Federal Bureau of Prisons Webpage.

18. Ibid.

19. See the statement that Kathleen Hawk Sawyer made before the Subcommittee on Criminal Justice of the Senate Judiciary Committee, 6 April 2000, and her remarks in the Heroes feature in this chapter.

20. For a vivid picture of life within a federal penitentiary, see Pete Earley, *The Hot House: Life inside Leavenworth Prison* (New York: Bantam Books, 1992).

21. Spencer P. M. Harrington, "Caging the Crazy: 'Supermax' Confinement under Attack," *The Humanist* (January–February, 1997), p. 18.

22. *Brusino v. Carlson* (Civil Action No. 84–4320), D.C.S.D. 34II (1987).

23. Mumia Abu-Jamal, *Live from Death Row* (Reading, Mass.: Addison-Wesley, 1995), p. 89.

24. Camp and Camp, *The Corrections Yearbook 1999*, pp. 66–67.

25. Bureau of Justice Statistics, *Prisoners in 1999* (Washington, D.C.: U.S. Department of Justice, 2000), p. 3.

26. Camp and Camp, *The Corrections Yearbook 1999*, pp. 84–85.

27. Information provided by the American Correctional Association, October 2000.

28. Impressions gained from interviewing top administrators of state departments of corrections and the Federal Bureau of Corrections.

29. See Mark Colvin, *Penitentiaries, Reformatories, and Chain Gangs: Social Theory and the History of Punishment in Nineteenth-Century America* (New York: St. Martin's Press, 2000), pp. 243–246.

30. Joan Mullen, *Corrections and the Private Sector* (Washington, D.C.: U.S. Department of Justice, National Institute of Justice, 1985).

31. This overview of privatization in corrections is adapted from William M. DiMascio, *Seeking Justice: Crime and Punishment in America* (New York: Edna McConnell Clark Foundation, 1997), p. 10.

32. David Shichor, *Punishment for Profit: Private Prisons/Public Concerns* (Thousand Oaks, Calif.: Sage, 1995), pp. 15–16.

33. Paulette Thomas, "Making Crime Pay," *Wall Street Journal,* 12 May 1994.

34. Sam Vincent Meddis and Deborah Sharp, "As Spending Soars, So Do the Profits," *USA Today,* 13 December 1994.

35. Shichor, *Punishment for Profit,* p. 231.

36. Ibid.

37. Bureau of Justice Statistics, *Prisoners in 2000* (Washington, D.C.: U.S. Department of Justice, 1999), p. 6.

38. Ibid., p. 5.

39. Ruth M. Glick and Virginia V. Neto, *National Study of Women's Correctional Programs* (Washington, D.C.: U.S. Government Printing Office, LEAA, 1977), p. 20.

40. Ibid.

41. Kelly Hannah-Moffat, "Feminine Fortresses: Woman-Centered Prisons and Jails?" *Prison Journal* 75 (June 1995), pp. 135–140.

42. Corey Weinstein, "Even Dogs Confined to Cages for Long Periods of Time Go Berserk," *Building Violence: How America's Rush to Incarcerate Creates More Violence,* ed. John P. May and Khalid R. Pitts (Thousand Oaks, Calif.: Sage, 2000), p. 121.

43. Ibid.

44. Ibid., pp. 122–123.

45. Quoted ibid., p. 123.

46. Robert E. Freeman-Longo, David Burton, Jan Levins, and June A. Fiske, *1996 Nationwide Survey of Treatment Programs and Models* (Brandon, Vt.: Safer Society Foundation, 1999).

47. *Combatting Violence and Delinquency: The National Juvenile Justice Action Plan: Report* (Washington, D.C.: Coordinating Council on Juvenile Justice and Delinquency Prevention, 1996), p. 27.

48. Bureau of Justice Statistics, *Prisoners in 1998* (Washington, D.C.: U.S. Department of Justice, 1999).

49. This section on the humane prison is adapted from John P. Conrad and Simon Dinitz, "The State's Strongest Medicine," in *Justice and Consequences,* ed. John P. Conrad (Lexington, Mass.: Lexington Books, 1981).

50. Simon Dinitz, "Are Safe and Humane Prisons Possible?" *Australia and New Zealand Journal of Criminology* 14 (March 1981), p. 13.

51. Gail S. Funke, ed., *National Conference on Prison Industries: Discussion and Recommendations* (Washington, D.C.: National Center for Innovation in Corrections, 1986).

52. Introducing another dimension of hope, John P. Conrad says that the prison should be a school of citizenship. See John P. Conrad, "Where There's Hope There's Life," in *Justice as Fairness,* ed. David Fogel and Joe Hudson (Cincinnati: Anderson, 1981), pp. 16–19.

CHAPTER 10 / BUILT-IN STUDY GUIDE

Multiple Choice Questions

1. Which of the following is not one of the four most widely used architectural designs of American prisons?

   A. Radial design
   B. Telephone design
   C. Courtyard design
   D. Panopticon style

2. All of the following societal elements are found in enhanced forms in prison except:

   A. Poverty
   B. Violent crime
   C. Mental illness
   D. Elderly

3. As of 31 December 1999, which state had the highest inmate population?

   A. Texas
   B. Florida
   C. California
   D. North Carolina

4. All of the following are traditional security designations for correctional facilities except:

   A. Minimum
   B. Medium
   C. Maximum
   D. Extensive maximum

5. Female prisons are characterized by all of the following attributes except:

   A. Telephone architectural design
   B. Single buildings
   C. Cottage architectural design
   D. Campus style design

6. What shaped the appearance of prisons during the late twentieth century?

   A. Boot camp prisons
   B. Shock incarceration programs
   C. Technological innovations
   D. Staff innovations

7. Which of the following prison designs is the most widely used for maximum-security prisons in the United States?

   A. Radial design
   B. Telephone design
   C. Courtyard style
   D. Campus style

8. The campus-like design provides for all of the following except:

   A. Maximum security for inmates
   B. More generous visiting policies
   C. Safer environment for staff
   D. More and frequent furloughs

9. All of the following have control or jurisdiction over prisons in the United States except:

   A. Federal Bureau of Prisons
   B. State departments of corrections
   C. Private corporations
   D. Regional municipalities

10. All of the following are guiding principles proposed by the 1990 Task Force of Corrections Canada that should characterize female prisons except:

    A. Empowerment
    B. Respect
    C. Shared responsibility
    D. Authoritarian leadership

11. All of the following are attributes of a humane prison that simulate conditions of the real world except:

    A. Economical
    B. Lawful
    C. Safe
    D. Industrious

12. All of the following signify ways that state correctional institutions are better now than they were in the past except:

    A. More concern about improving institutional standards
    B. Building separate prisons for HIV and AIDS inmates
    C. Improved administrative leadership at the director's level
    D. More emphasis on pre-service and in-service training

True/False Questions

T F   1. A disadvantage of the telephone pole design is that it is impossible to house prisoners by classification levels.

T F   2. The 1990s were characterized by an extremely large amount of prison construction.

T F   3. Currently, fifty states have state department of corrections organizations.

T F   4. There are more inmates in federal prisons than in state prisons.

T F   5. The variety of inmate programs offered by the Federal Bureau of Prisons is a grade below what is found in state correctional institutions.

T F   6. Prison crowding is not as serious a problem in Federal Bureau of Prisons facilities as it is in state correctional facilities.

T F   7. Private contractors argue that they can construct and operate prisons at less cost than public agencies.

T F   8. Private sector involvement in corrections has occurred only in the last few years.

T F   9. Comparing and evaluating the administration and operation of state correctional systems is difficult due to the variations in correctional ideology and the structure of programs.

T F 10. Since 1990, the growth rate of female prisons has outpaced that of male prisons in the United States.

T F 11. Traditionally, female inmates have been housed in facilities with programs that meet their treatment needs.

T F 12. Prisoners that are difficult to manage are housed in solitary confinement.

Fill-in-the-Blank Questions   (based on key terms)

1. The dominant objective of _____ is the ability to apply complete control to all prisons at any time.

2. The type of prison design that allows for openness and freedom of movement is the _____.

3. The _____ of prisons has a control center at the hub and spokes that stem outward from it.

4. The type of prison that is characterized by a humane approach to imprisonment, a safe environment for staff and inmates and better programs is known as a _____.

5. The _____ is characterized by having housing, educational, vocational, and recreational units face out toward an open area.

6. _____ place an emphasis on controlled access to programs. Inmates in these facilities are controlled, but the expectation is that they will be engaged in industrial or educational activities.

7. Prisons that have a long, central corridor that serves as the means for prisoners to go from one part of the prison to another have a design known as the _____.

Essay Questions

1. Identify and describe the four most widely used architectural designs for constructing U.S. prisons. What security level of inmates does each architectural design address?

2. What did James Fox mean in his observation, "The prison reflects the society it serves"?

3. Explain the influence that privatization has had on corrections. Describe the arguments supporting privatization of correctional facilities.

4. From a historical perspective, describe the female inmate's prison experience. Compare male prisons with female prisons.

5. Identify and describe the four elements of a civilized prison that reflect the conditions of the real world.

ANSWERS

Multiple Choice Questions

1.	D	7.	B
2.	D	8.	A
3.	A	9.	D
4.	D	10.	D
5.	A	11.	A
6.	C	12.	B

True/False Questions

1.	F	7.	T
2.	T	8.	F
3.	T	9.	T
4.	F	10.	T
5.	F	11.	F
6.	F	12.	T

Fill-in-the-Blank Questions

1. Maximum-security prisons
2. Campus design
3. Radial design
4. Minimum-security prisons
5. Courtyard style prisons
6. Medium-security prisons
7. Telephone pole designs

chapter eleven

Correctional Managers and Officers

When William H. Dallman retired in 1994, he had been a warden for more than twenty-two years. Since 1994, he has worked as a consultant in matters related to prison litigation and has been involved in dozens of prisons in the United States and Puerto Rico:

> During my thirty-six years of correctional work, I have witnessed changes in the focus and role of a warden. In years past, wardens were quite autonomous, had more latitude to personalize their management styles, and performed their duties in an obscure environment veiled by walls, fences, and public and political indifference. Prisoners' rights, employee unions, frequent lawsuits from all concerned, and pesky media reporters were not regular issues. Wardens had more opportunity to structure their operations and programs in a manner that reflected their view of the etiology and nature of criminal behavior or rehabilitation and so forth. Today, much has changed. No longer do a warden's personal theories and beliefs significantly determine prison operations. Nor do the beliefs of criminologists or other behavior scientists. Nearly every prison activity and operation is currently defined, influenced, and regulated by decisions of state and federal courts.
>
> Lawyers and judges are the primary determiners of correctional methods. Political indifference has vanished. With 2 million Americans in prison, with prison budgets swelling, and with citizens being highly fearful of crime, political leaders have had to turn their attention

inward to prisons and other responses to crime. Also, political candidates learned that crime issues and punishment can be used effectively in elections, often trying to outdo one another with their alleged toughness. Today, wardens, instead of being aided in their duties by a legion of loyal correctional employees, sometimes spend more time struggling with self-interested employee unions than dealing with prisoners and prison programs.

In many ways, I was not affected by these changes as much as some of my colleagues. I think this is because I never really thought it was supposed to be my show or that I owned the prison. Also, many of the changes have been good. By any measure, we have much better prisons today than we did a generation ago. And I always knew that it was my job to manage problems and change. No one was going to pay me just to sit atop of an untroubled and severe fiefdom. Finally, let me say that I enjoyed my job as a warden to the end.[1]

CRITICAL THINKING QUESTIONS

What social context does Dallman suggest faces the contemporary warden? Why would it be easier to be a warden if you did not consider the prison to be yours?

Managing a prison is not an easy job. The job of a warden, as well as the jobs of other prison workers, is thankless and demands physical and emotional stamina. Some wardens are quick to say that the work is a struggle and that every decision they make takes a toll on them. If they make a mistake, they may not have a job tomorrow. If they make a mistake, the inmates may not let them forget it. One warden noted that he had ulcers at 28, heart problems at 39, and hypertension in his forties.[2]

Of course, some wardens thrive on their jobs. They are innovative, resourceful, fair, and resilient; indeed, they may remain ten, fifteen, or more years at the same facility. To them, correctional administration is interesting and challenging, and they speak with pride when they discuss their careers. They not only understand management theory but are effective managers within their institutions. They do their best to anticipate problems rather than constantly engaging in crisis-centered decision making.

In addition to wardens and other top administrators in the prison, this chapter examines the work of correctional officers. It is the correctional officer who is entrusted with managing inmates in the cellblocks, on the yard, and in other locations throughout the prison. Security is the number-one priority of a correctional institution, and it is the correctional officer who is responsible for enforcing the security measures devised by supervisors. The correctional officer also has the responsibility for defusing conflict within the prison. This custody staff member typically has a greater positive effect on inmates than do correctional counselors and other treatment staff.

This chapter considers several important questions:

How has correctional administration changed from the past?

What are characteristics of innovative wardens of the twenty-first century?

What are the challenges of correctional administration?

How do female correctional officers function in a prison for men?

How is it possible to enrich the job of the correctional officer?

WHAT ARE THE CHANGING ROLES OF INSTITUTIONAL WARDENS?

From the birth of the penitentiary until the years following World War II, the institutional warden was sovereign; as long as he kept in favor with the governor's office, his word was law. Believing that no one else could run their organizations, these **autocratic**

wardens took total responsibility for planning, staffing, and controlling. They refused to accept either staff or inmate resistance; indeed, the prisoners, like slaves, were denied nearly every human right beyond survival. Wardens mixed terror, incentives, and favoritism in order to keep their subjects "fearful but not desperate, hopeful but always uncertain." Guards were subject to the absolute power of the warden and were dependent on his favor for their security and promotion.[3]

Prison absolutism, the warden's total control over what took place in the institution, withstood many attacks: the opening of prisons to official inspection, the introduction of professionals, the adoption of the Principles of the National Prison Association in 1870, and commitment to the rehabilitation ideal. Its collapse finally occurred after World War II, when governors and legislators demanded the creation of management systems that would ensure their control of prisons through chains of accountability. The result was the **bureaucratization of corrections,** which produced statewide correctional systems, whose goals were greater efficiency, clear accountability, higher standards, more flexible programming, and better allocation of resources. Thus, the absolute authority of the autocratic warden was replaced by specific, limited, and delegated power. The czars who had ruled as they pleased became field officers whose performance and recommendations were reviewed in the central office; the sovereigns, in effect, became accountable bureaucrats.[4]

Autocratic Wardens

To protect his authority, the autocratic warden created disunity in the prison community in that the formation of groups of either prisoners or guards was never permitted. The warden's intelligence system ensured that neither guard nor prisoner could trust anyone. The **paramilitary model** of management, with its military terminology, downward flow of communication, rigid rules and regimentation, and impersonal relationships, further protected the warden's absolute power and helped maintain an orderly, neat, and secure institution. Bloody uprisings did take place, but they were dealt with harshly. Ringleaders especially felt the heavy hand of unregulated authority.

Joseph Ragen, warden of Stateville and Joliet penitentiaries in Illinois from 1936 to 1961, is the best-known autocratic warden. Sometimes called "Mr. Prison," Ragen ran the two penitentiaries by exercising personal control over every detail of prison life. He permitted no one to challenge him and had such control that there were no riots and escapes from within the walls during his twenty-five years as warden; only two guards and three inmates were killed during this time. Ragen demanded absolute loyalty; he kept outsiders out, and, within the walls, he maintained absolute power. Ragen recruited guards from southern Illinois, which in his time was a chronically depressed area. These men were just about totally dependent on him for their livelihoods. If they incurred his wrath, it was a catastrophe for them.[5]

State Bureaucrats

After World War II, corrections departments discovered, as did other departments of state government, that no organization, private or pubic, could survive without bureaucratization. Bureaucratization, however, has been a dubious blessing. The volume of paper generated in any professional bureaucracy far exceeds that of the simpler generations of management. All that paperwork must be read, initialed, and shuffled off to other desks or to accessible files. Many wardens complain that they spend far too much time in their offices, coping with memoranda and urgently required reports. They say that they are too busy to inspect their cellblocks from one week to the next.

Bureaucratization also led to the development of civil service. The director's or commissioner's responsibility is to make certain that there are no categories or decisions that are not governed by regulations. As an appointee of the governor, he or she is also responsible for supervising wardens of state institutions as well as for public relations, political contacts with the legislature, fiscal management, policy implementation, and long-range planning.

Directors may supervise wardens directly, or they may turn that responsibility over to a subordinate, who reports to the director. But managers other than the director also have ongoing contact with institutions. Headquarters staff involved in the inspection of institutions include the deputy director for operations, the deputy director for programs, the business manager and budget analysts, the supervisor of classification, the personnel officer, and the staff attorney.

Other changes have also limited the warden's power. Civil service rules set limits for hiring and firing. Professional associations hold the warden responsible for meeting their requirements. Unions and employee associations impose rules about working conditions and promotions by seniority for their members. Courts insist on inmate's due-process rights.

Today, top managers are more professional and more knowledgeable about managerial concepts. They are usually college graduates and may have advanced degrees; some have studied correctional administration. Correctional administrators appear to be younger than in the past. Associate wardens are now often appointed when they are in their early thirties, and they become wardens or superintendents before age 40. Although the percentage of women in top management has not significantly changed over the years, several women have been directors of state systems, and many are wardens or superintendents of state institutions. For more on the women who have served as superintendents or wardens in U.S. corrections, see Within the Walls 11.1.

the walls   11.1

within

Female Correctional Administrators

Mary Weed, who was named principal keeper of the Walnut Street Jail in Philadelphia in 1793, was the first female correctional administrator in the United States. Nineteenth-century leaders included Eliza W. B. Farnham, head matron at New York's Sing Sing Prison between 1844 and 1848, and Clara Barton, who served as superintendent of the Massachusetts Reformatory Prison for Women at Framingham in 1882.

In 1907, Kate Barnard was elected the first commissioner of charities and corrections in Oklahoma; she served for two terms. Katherine Davis was appointed superintendent of the Bedford Hills Prison from 1901 to 1914. Also in the early decades of the twentieth century, Mary Bell Harris became the first superintendent of the Federal Women's Prison at Alderson, West Virginia. Kate Richard O'Hare, first an inmate sentenced for violation of the Federal Espionage Act, eventually became assistant director of the California Department of Penology, after her pardon. Marble Walker Willebrandt oversaw the administration of federal prisons from 1921 to 1929, and Dr. Miriam van Waters served as superintendent of the Massachusetts Reformatory for Women from 1932 to 1957.

More recently, Elayn Hunt was appointed director of corrections in Louisiana in 1972; she died four years later before she could implement many of her reforms. In the 1980s, Ward Murphy in Maine, Ali Klein in New Jersey,

> Women have slowly made some administrative inroads in male institutions.

and Ruth L. Rushen in Califorinia became directors of state systems. In 1990, Alaska, North Dakota, South Dakota, and Puerto Rico had women commissioners of adult corrections—a record number. In 1992, Kathleen Hawk Sawyer was appointed director of the Federal Bureau of Prisons (see the Heroes feature in Chapter 10).

Women have slowly made some administrative inroads in male institutions. By 1997, women represented about 10 percent of wardens and superintendents of the nine hundred statewide correctional facilities for men. Camille Graham Camp was one such groundbreaker. In 1977, she became warden of the Maximum Security Center in South Carolina—the first woman to head such a facility, which housed the state's most violent inmates.

CRITICAL THINKING QUESTIONS

What does the increase in the number of female wardens, superintendents, and heads of state corrections systems say about corrections? How difficult would it be for a woman to become warden of a maximum-security prison for men?

Source: Katherine van Wormer and Clemens Bartollas, *Women and the Criminal Justice System* (Boston: Allyn & Bacon, 2000), pp. 214–215.

This warden is surveying damage after an inmate riot in 2001 at Western New Mexico Correctional Facility. During the twentieth century, the field of corrections saw a significant increase in the number and promotion of female correctional administrators. What other changes in correctional administration are reflected in the characteristics and roles of contemporary wardens, superintendents, and heads of state corrections systems? What social factors have contributed to those changes?

HOW HAS THE MANAGEMENT STYLE OF WARDENS CHANGED?

Wardens' management styles during the 1970s differed greatly from those of the 1980s and 1990s. The majority of bureaucratic wardens of the 1970s used participatory management. Many wardens of the 1980s chose the control, consensual, or responsibility model to manage their institutions. The wardens of the 1990s and first decade of the twenty-first century viewed themselves as professionals and team players dealing with institutional problems in innovative ways.

Participatory Management

Participatory management is a management style based on a team approach and on involving employees throughout the organization in decision making. Correctional administrators in the 1970s found themselves thrust into the center of a shifting and volatile field of forces. They not only had to relate to the staff and inmates of their institutions but also interact successfully with the director, the legislature, the press, labor unions, employee organizations, law-enforcement agencies, the courts, and the various special-interest groups in the community. They knew that their negotiations within this web of relationships had to protect and maintain the institution, yet at the same time it was necessary to generate needed internal development and change. The corporate management model, adapted from the private sector, and the shared-powers model were the two styles of participatory management developed to meet the challenges of running a correctional institution.

Corporate Management Model.   During the 1970s, correctional administrators turned to the private sector for management models. The **corporate management model** emphasizes modern management techniques and participant management. Lines of authority and accountability are clear; feedback and quantitative evaluations are widely used.

It did not take long for correctional administrators to discover that the new management theory did not solve the problems they faced in American prisons. By the 1980s, most of these correctional administrators saw that in spite of private-sector management theory, most prisons had more violence, worse living conditions, and fewer programming opportunities than they had had under the autocrats of old.

Shared-Powers Model. In the 1970s, inspired by the rehabilitative ideal, many correctional administrators turned to a **shared-powers model** of management. Wardens attempted to enhance the "respect," "dignity," and "status" of both staff and inmates by granting them some say in the governance of the prison. They wished to involve inmates, as well as staff and the central office, in institutional decision making.

Into the power vacuum created by the attempt at democratization rushed both prisoners and guards, eager to advance their respective interests. Specific groups, such as the Black Muslims, and inmate councils, were the two main types of inmate associations developed in the prison.[6]

The inmates' gain in power antagonized the prison guards, who, along with the warden, were losing power and authority. To regain what they had lost, correctional officers began to organize into unions so that they could demonstrate a united front when presenting their demands. In addition to the traditional bread-and-butter issues, guard unions expressed concern about personal safety and security within the walls. The effectiveness of the correctional officers' unions is seen in the fact that they now control work assignments and many other job-security decisions.

As a result of the shared-powers model, inmates became politicized, and prison guards and the warden lost power. This model hastened the erosion of authority and power of corrections staff and contributed significantly to the widening alienation between guards and institutional administrators.[7]

In the 1980s, nearly all correctional systems abandoned the shared-powers model. A few states, however, particularly California and Illinois, came close to sliding into an inmate control model. In these states, inmate gangs wielded such power within the walls that they attempted, sometimes successfully, to dictate prison policy.[8]

Philosophies of Control, Consensus, and Responsibility

John J. DiIulio Jr., in examining prison management during the 1980s, identified three main approaches: In the **Texas control model,** staff has total control of the institution. In the **Michigan responsibility model,** management tries to make inmates responsible for their own actions. In the **California consensual model,** as DiIulio presents it, gangs run the prisons and prison administrators attempt to consult and negotiate with them.

The differences in these approaches, according to DiIulio, are rooted in differences in correctional philosophy. He adds that the importance of prison management is that it determines the quality of prison life—the orderliness, the amenities, and the available services. Indeed, he claims that the prison disorders of the 1980s were the "simple tales of failed prison management."[10] Bert Useem and Peter Kimball's study of prison riots supports this viewpoint:

> If one accepts our thesis that the cause of prison riots is the disorganization of the state, then it follows that maintaining a strong, coherent prison administration is the crucial ingredient in avoiding disturbances. New Mexico and the other prison systems under study "blew," not because they chose the wrong style of management, but because their efforts were so thoroughly disorganized and incoherent. In short, good administration is the key.[11]

DiIulio is most supportive of the Texas control model, which was dismantled by the *Ruiz v. Estelle* (1987) decision. DiIulio strongly supports the order that the control model achieved, especially during the ten years (1962–1972) George Beto was director of the state corrections department. According to DiIulio, there was less overt violence under the control model, and infractions were less frequent and less severe. This meant that prisoners in Texas prisons were less at risk than prisoners in other institutions across the nation. Life within the prison system during the heyday of the control model was calm, stable, and predictable.[12]

DiIulio is far more critical of the Michigan and California approaches to correctional management. He believes that the Michigan responsibility model maximizes inmates' responsibility for their own actions. Prisons, according to this model, are to be run by imposing minimum constraints on inmates, an approach that supposedly fosters prison community. DiIulio charges that the major internal defect of this model is the alienation and lack of support from correctional officers.[13]

The California consensual model, concludes DiIulio, is even more of a disaster. This model "is a crazy-quilt pattern of correctional principles and practices."[14] He claims that the management of California prisons eventually evolved into the question of how to manage prison gangs. He charges that former directors Raymond Procunier, orginator of the consensual model, and J. J. Enomoto, his successor, consulted and negotiated with the gangs. Thus, because of California's preoccupation with gang organization and violence and the enduring instability this gang preoccupation brings to the institution, DiIulio believes that California has "given the store away" to the inmates.[15]

With some variations, DiIulio would like to see the return of the Texas control model. He seems to buy into Warden Ragen's adage that either the inmates or the staff are in control, and he believes that a paramilitary operation and unflagging discipline will recapture the prison from inmates. He adds that "to punish rule violators proportionately" is the key to prison discipline and control.[16]

Rational and Learning Management

Wardens of the twenty-first century appear to be divided into two groups: those who are disillusioned and overwhelmed and those who are innovative and in control of their facilities. Disillusioned wardens tend to feel that they have lost their reform ideology, because they no longer have the rehabilitation ideal, human relations model, participatory management philosophy, or shared-powers model to provide the hope that the present state of imprisonment could be changed. Faced with overwhelming problems, especially in maximum-security prisons, these wardens would agree that the pressure is heavy-duty and that they feel numb when they leave the institution at night. They question whether any warden can last three years in their institution.[17]

Innovative wardens are attempting to develop new approaches to correctional administration. They feel positive about their jobs and see themselves as proactive, rather than reactive, to the challenges of institutional leadership. These wardens differ in several ways from their disillusioned colleagues.[18]

- *They believe they can make a difference.* They believe they can have an impact and need not be limited by what others have done. They believe prisons can be run in such a way that inmates and staff have hope and have confidence in and respect for each other.

- *They have a hands-on approach.* They spend a good deal of time walking the cellblocks, visiting inmates in their cells, touring the yard, and talking with staff at their assignments. They believe that to reduce the frequency, scope, and seriousness of institutional problems, the top administrator must interact directly with inmates and all levels of staff on a regular basis. This system provides information that can be used to avoid or defuse pending problems.

- *They realize the importance of a supportive team.* A major concern of these wardens is to build a team of supportive staff—not only top management staff, including associate wardens and unit managers, but also captains, lieutenants, and sergeants who supervise correctional officers.

- *They are receptive to technological innovations.* The new breed of correctional administrator is quick to take advantage of technological advances. Today, innovations within the prison in combination with external supervision are enabling federal and some state corrections officials to shape a new prison environment based on accountability, functional integration, risk assessment, and institutional differentiation. Management information systems (MIS) have brought about systemwide changes. Inmates are tracked more effectively throughout the system, personnel have been upgraded, and population needs can be projected. Smaller and newer prisons, better classification systems, and unit management are helping to defuse institutional violence.

- *They are committed to reasonable or rational action.* There is a real commitment among these correctional administrators to administer institutions in a rational way. In *Organization in Action* J. D. Thompson suggests that organizations are expected to produce results, and, therefore, their actions must be reasonable or rational. Accordingly, managers must act rationally in a way that will produce the desired results.[19] One way to do this is by reducing uncertainty among inmates and staff.

- *They are receptive to improved means of supervising correctional institutions.* They welcome legislative task forces that examine everything from free time (recreation) on death row to training, industry, and education (TIE) vocational programs. They also are receptive to inmate grievance procedures. They do not resist court supervision of prisons.

- *They model the behaviors that they want to elicit from inmates and staff.* They believe that a crucial component of a human relations approach is their willingness to demonstrate to others what involvement in and understanding of others entails. They also affirm that before they can expect this response from staff, they must demonstrate to others their job commitment, trustworthiness, loyalty, and moral integrity. Also, as part of this modeling they attempt to show staff how to interact effectively with inmates without losing their respect and without being compromised, manipulated, or taken for a ride.

- *They seek CAC accreditation.* These wardens usually enthusiastically endorse the accreditation process of the Commission on Accreditation for Corrections (CAC) (formerly the American Correctional Association). An institution or a community-based program is accredited when it meets the minimum standards proposed by the CAC. Accreditation has been so widely supported because wardens feel that the standards of accreditation ensure the improvement of correctional institutions, that accreditation is an attainable goal, and that accreditation is a major step forward in the development of corrections.

Correctional administration by these individuals can be understood as an attempt to become "rational," which means to be receptive to information and knowledge, or learning, as the means of effecting organizational change. The purpose of rational action is to know the end to be achieved and the proper means to reach that goal.[20] These correctional administrators pursue a learning metaphor, rather than traditional prison metaphors. As Gareth Morgan describes it: "the whole process of learning hinges on an ability to remain open to changes occurring in the environment, and on an ability to challenge operating assumptions in a most fundamental way."[21]

Our hero in this chapter is Frank Wood, the former commissioner of corrections in Minnesota and the warden of Stillwater and Oak Park Heights Correctional Centers in Minnesota. When he retired, an editorial in the *Pioneer Press* (St. Paul, Minnesota) observed: "In a tough, often thankless vocation, Wood's thoughtfulness and professionalism have served Minnesota well for nearly four decades. He retires with the state's gratitude and good wishes."

h e r o e s

Frank Wood

Former Commissioner of Corrections and Warden in Minnesota

"I don't know if I can speak for all wardens, but I can go back and search my memory for things that I thought were helpful in preparing me to be a warden. A very important aspect of my background was the experience as an entry-level uniformed officer. This helps you to understand from the very ground level what is going on in the institution. I also believe it is helpful for anyone who is planning a professional career in corrections to get involved in the union movement when they're line officers. I think it's important to have this experience so that you can appreciate and understand the unique aspects of organized labor. There is a distinct advantage in having experience on both sides of the table. College-level academic education is important. I advocate having a broad-based and generalized college education that can be supplemented periodically in your career with specific courses that enhance your competence, effectiveness, leadership skills, and ultimately your promotability. I would also advise people not to be tempted to stay in a comfortable position, just because there are good working hours and good days off. I would advise that anyone aspiring to be a warden or director of corrections to exercise caution in their interactions with politicians. We need to have enough integrity, confidence, and conviction to tell public policy decision makers in a tactful, respectful, and diplomatic way things they may not want to hear. Corrections professionals and criminal justice experts must speak out.

"In sum, it's important to understand that in order to be an attractive candidate for an appointment as a warden, you have to be prepared experientially and academically. Your character, credibility, and integrity should be a matter of record. If you are not prepared, it is unlikely you will be asked to administer an institution. Prepare yourself in the event that you are in the right place and the right time in the future. I would encourage all those people who aspire to be a warden to remember that there are hundreds of important, influential, and high-impact positions in the corrections profession from which you can get a lot of personal and professional satisfaction, make lasting contributions, and grow to your full personal and professional potential without being a warden.

"Each of us has our own strengths and limitations, and what I look for to fill the positions that answer directly to the warden are those people who can fill in the gaps where I have limitations. I also look for people who have the following characteristics:

- Who challenge me to be my very best
- Who in their own right are confident and quite capable of running the institution as well as or better than I
- Who have knowledge, skills, experience, and personal characteristics that I don't exhibit as well as they do
- Who have differing perspectives and viewpoints than myself and can articulate those opposing views in a nonadversarial way, but yet are consistent with the ultimate philosophy and goals that I consider to be crucial to the pursuit of excellence in managing and operating an enlightening institution
- Who I believe will not only enhance my confidence and decision making but also will bring to the entire administrative team a higher level of review, deliberation and consideration to ensure that we, as a team, have explored all of the possibilities and options in making tough, very complex decisions
- Who are not easily provoked and have the capacity to be restrained even under extreme provocation
- Who demonstrate and have a track record of demonstrating maturity, good judgment, insight, and wisdom
- Who for the most part agree with my philosophy and can communicate that they believe in it with the same sincerity and intensity that I do
- Who are honest and have integrity so that they will take stands on issues after thoughtful analysis and deliberation and not be wetting their finger and holding it up to find which way the wind is blowing on a given day
- Who are tactful and are able to articulate things well so that they can be understand by staff at all levels and the inmate clientele
- Who have perseverance and tenacity and are in the profession for the long haul
- Who have the courage to tell the emperor that he's naked and do that appropriately, privately, and not to elevate themselves at the expense of others
- Who are not easily intimidated
- Who have the capacity to understand and relate to inmates
- Who are not arrogant, pompous, know-it-all, offensive, condescending, caustic, abrasive, and self-righteous
- Who have the intellectual depth to know that rarely will we find simplistic solutions to society's and humankind's very complex problems.

"In sum, I look for the best and the brightest. I look for people who don't just talk golden rule, but those who practice it. People who are loyal, and people who will be responsive to both the real and imagined concerns of inmates and staff. I look for staff who have commitment and are dedicated and able to convince other people that our profession is important and noble and that we can make a difference."

CRITICAL THINKING QUESTIONS

How do you think inmates responded to Frank Wood when he was warden? Would you have liked to have been one of his associate wardens? How does Wood exemplify the principles of innovative wardens?

WHAT ARE THE CHALLENGES OF ADMINISTRATION?

The warden or superintendent is ultimately responsible for everything that takes place within the prison. As the chief executive officers of prisons, wardens are well paid. On 1 January 1999, the average salary for a warden in U.S. prisons was $53,504; the lowest annual salary was in Tennessee ($31,104); and the highest amount paid to a warden was in the Federal Bureau of Prisons ($119,470).[22]

The warden delegates the responsibility for custodial services and for program services to assistant wardens (see Figure 11.1). In large correctional institutions, an assistant warden for management services and an associate warden for industrial and agricultural services are charged with the responsibility for those areas. The associate wardens, in turn, rely on middle managers and line staff to operate the various departments within their sphere of responsibility. Institutional administration encompasses establishment of policy, planning, civil suits, institutional monitoring, staff development, and fiscal management.[23]

Establishment of Policy

Wardens determine policy for their particular institutions, although major policy changes must be cleared with the central office. One of the challenges of determining policy stems from the number of groups that must be satisfied: the public, the inmates, the various levels of institutional staff, and the director of corrections.

Figure 11.1 Institutional Table of Organization

Source: Illinois Menard Correctional Center.

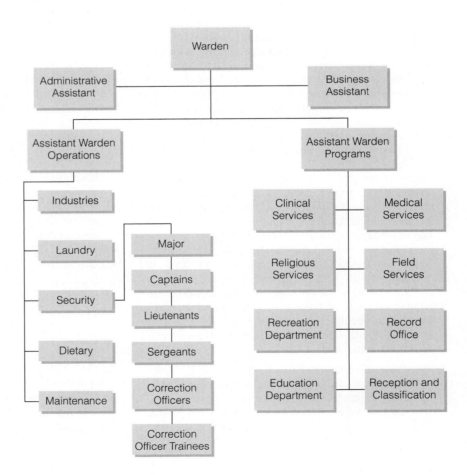

Planning

The warden is expected to develop goals and methods for achieving them. Some top administrators continue to find modern management principles to be helpful tools in the goal-setting process. If no long-range plan exists, most wardens know they will become involved in crisis-centered management and will have to face the same problems day after day. Staff burnout and inappropriate reactions to organizational problems are the consequences of crisis-centered management.

Dealing with Civil Suits

Civil lawsuits by inmates constitute another area in which planning is needed. Autocratic wardens used to stroll through the prison yard, priding themselves on their ability to relate to convicts. As inmates stood at attention, the warden would make friendly inquiries about how they were doing. Contemporary institutional administrators are faced with much more complex relations with inmates. Administrators who are sued by several prisoners each week must spend much of their time responding to charges, preparing affidavits, and testifying in court. This time-consuming process is not only frustrating and draining on administrative resources but also intimidating. Administrators may end up paying exorbitant attorney's fees or sustaining extensive damages, possibly losing everything they own. Court decisions that impose new procedures, standards, and personnel requirements on a state system can also be expensive, time-consuming, and full of problems for administrators. To deal effectively with civil suits, the wise administrator uses planning to eliminate any inhumane conditions exposed by these court actions, documents all decision making relating to inmates, develops expertise in correctional law, and swiftly complies with the orders of the court.

Institutional Monitoring

The effective institutional supervisor must have adequate information about what is taking place within the facility and must provide for special inmate needs. To keep informed, wardens must find ways to maintain good communication with prisoners. The day when a warden can act as an isolated autocrat is gone. Smart wardens now spend time in the yard relating with inmates. They insist that the assistant wardens also spend time working to maintain open relationships with inmates. Wardens can also improve rapport with inmates by "running a call line," extending an open invitation to inmates who wish to see them.

Because of the inmate gangs in many prisons, maintaining effective communication with inmates is more difficult than it was years ago. Gangs want prison administrators to recognize their existence and, if they can persuade them to do so, to negotiate with gang leaders. Another important aspect of institutional monitoring is providing for special inmate needs. Prisoners with special needs vary from youthful offenders, mentally restricted and emotional disturbed prisoners, to sexually deviant and long-term prisoners.

Staff Development

The warden is expected to develop training programs for new staff and to make changes in job assignments when necessary. The warden's style of leadership affects the way subordinates do their jobs. Most institutional administrators continue to believe that staff morale and job involvement are enhanced when all levels of personnel participate in decision making, but the degree of personnel involvement is a decision that the top manager must make.

Shared decision making can take many forms. One top administrator may sell an already formulated decision to the group. Another may present a tentative decision subject to change. Still another will describe the problem, take suggestions for its resolution, and make the final decision independently. Other administrators define the limits but allow the group to make the decision.[24]

Fiscal Management

"A good warden," as correctional administrators are fond of saying, "always has a handle on the budget." Fiscal management should be a year-long process. There should be periodic (perhaps monthly) staff meetings to keep abreast of developments and the status of the budget. The warden should maintain his or her own file on changes that will be needed and others that will be recommended for the next year's budget.

A successful warden is an individual who is able to meet these challenges of correctional administration. In Within the Walls 11.2, John Hurley, a former warden of the Federal Bureau of Prisons, talks about what it means to be a successful warden.

within the walls   11.2

Characteristics of Successful Wardens

"There are two characteristics that stand out in being a successful warden. First is that these wardens are always 'people persons.' They enjoy interaction with all types of people, even if they wear the label of inmate, staff, or community representative. The second is that these wardens understand the importance of visibility. They are people who are constantly visible at their facility. They want to be available so that staff or inmates can ask them questions or get clarification on some matter. They want inmates to realize, 'Hey, I don't have to worry about writing the warden. I am going to see him. He is either out here in the yard, or in the cellhouse, or in the program area.'

"These characteristics stand out regardless of the type of facility you are in or the mission of that facility. For example, I was warden of the administrative maximum facility of the Bureau of Prisons in Florence, Colorado. This facility was unique in terms of its mission and the type of population it housed. I was there when several infamous offenders came in, Timothy McVeigh and his codefendant of the Oklahoma City bombing; Ramsey Yuseff, the World Trade Center bomber; and Ted Kaczynski, the Unabomber.

"Even with the mission of 'security beyond anything else,' it was critical to be very visible and interact with both the inmate population and the staff. I would even say that it was more important for the interaction with staff at that facility because they had such a challenge every day. It was a dangerous experience every time they moved an inmate, because of the type of offender that was housed there and the propensity these offenders had toward violent and disruptive behavior. Even though the

> . . . it was critical to be very visible and interact with both the inmate population and the staff.

offenders were locked down, so your interaction was different than it would be in a typical open environment, you still had to walk the ranges and make sure that the offender saw you. If the offender wanted you to stop, they would let you know. If they didn't, they would just nod their head and you would keep on going.

"I received a lot of satisfaction from my years of working in corrections. One is the satisfaction I got out of doing the job and that came from my relationship with both the staff and the inmates. Even when I was a correctional officer, if I felt that I had impacted the safety and security of the facility, I felt good about that. Another source of satisfaction is that every day was different. The challenges were always new; the activities were always different. In the midst of the consistency of every day, there would be some unique circumstances that you had to figure out, 'How am I going to deal with this? How am I going to manage it? What am I going to learn from it? How am I going to take that with me to higher levels of responsibility and be better the next time?' Further, I received satisfaction from the people. I think that people who gravitate to law enforcement and corrections in general are great people and are fun to be around. They always want to be part of a team. There is a very good feeling to associate with those people."

CRITICAL THINKING QUESTIONS

Why is it so important to be a "people person"? How do you think it would feel to be warden of a super-max facility? Would it be difficult to stay positive in this environment?

WHO REALLY RUNS THE PRISON?

Historically, the paramilitary model has been used for security in most institutions. Custodial staff wear uniforms and badges; are assigned titles such as sergeant, lieutenant, captain, and major; use designations such as company, mess hall, drill, inspection, and gig list; and maintain a sharp division between lower- and higher-ranking officers. The procedures and organizational structures that control inmates are also militaristic in form. For many years, prisoners marched to the dining hall and to their various assignments. They removed their hats in the presence of a captain and stood at attention when the warden approached.

Although the prison has been stripped of the autocratic warden and some of the regimentation, the paramilitary model is alive and flourishing. Associate wardens of custody or operations are ultimately responsible for knowing the whereabouts of all inmates at all times. Guard captains, few in number, are usually assigned to full-time administrative responsibilities or to shift command. They often chair assignment and disciplinary committees. Guard lieutenants are known as troubleshooters. They roam the institution dealing with volatile incidents. "The lieutenant's job, is to be right there with his men. If a problem arises, the lieutenant goes in first."[25] The lieutenants take troublesome inmates out of their cells and walk them to segregation. Guard sergeants, like army sergeants, manage particular units, such as cellhouses or the hospital, and supervise several other officers.

Officers carry out their duties in several different areas:

- Housing Unit Officers: These officers are responsible for the security of the housing units. They open and close steel-barred doors, allowing entrance and exit; take inmate counts several times a day; distribute medicine, mail, and laundry; oversee maintenance activities; and supervise the showers of the inmates.

- Work Detail Supervisors: These officers monitor inmate behavior while they are working in the kitchen, laundry, or trash pick-up in the prison or outside details such as farming operation.

- Industrial Shop and School Officers: The responsibility of these officers is to monitor inmate activities at the various prison industry locations and in academic or vocational classes.

- Yard Officers: These officers maintain order and ensure security while inmates participate or watch recreation activities that take place within the prison.

- Perimeter Security Officers: In the traditional prison, perimeters officers are stationed in towers positioned along the high wall surrounding the prison. In more recently built prisons, perimeter officers typically walk and drive patrol outside the razor wire perimeter.[26]

The Changing Role of Correctional Officers

On 1 January 1999, 250,740 uniformed staff members (including majors, captains, lieutenants, sergeants, and correctional officers) were employed by the Federal Bureau of Prisons, state departments of corrections, and the District of Columbia's Department of Corrections. Of these uniformed staff, 21.6 percent were female and 33.5 percent were minority officers.[27]

Higher salaries, improved standards, greater training, and unionization are signs that the role of the correctional officer is undergoing change. Guards, now called correctional officers, are beginning in most states to make a living wage. On 1 January 1999, the average starting salary of an officer in the United States was $21,855 per year; starting salaries ranged from $34,070 in New Jersey to $15,324 in Louisiana. Maximum salaries for a correctional officer in 1999 ranged from $57,996 in Alaska to $22,839 in Maine.[28]

Over half of the states now require a high school diploma or a GED certificate as their minimum employment requirement. Many states have academy training programs for

What is the typical organizational structure of a prison as an institution? Within that structure, what are the roles of correctional officers? How do the roles of wardens interface with the work of correctional officers? How do wardens and correctional officers work together? What are some of the requirements, stresses, and rewards of becoming a correctional officer?

pre-service and in-service officers, which appear to be effective in ensuring that officers bring basic skills to their jobs. The Federal Bureau of Prisons requires three years of college for correctional officers.

The growth of unions among correctional officers has encouraged them to seek greater rights, more recognition, and higher pay. Correctional officers in the majority of states are now unionized. The unions that represent correctional officers include AFSCME (American Federation of State, County, and Municipal Employees), AFL-CIO, SEIU (Service Employees International Union), the International Brotherhood of Teamsters, and state employee associations. Officers in Connecticut, New Jersey, New York, and Ohio have gone on strike to protest low wages or poor working conditions. When correctional officers walk out, other personnel, the state police, and sometimes even the National Guard are forced to run the institution until the strike is settled.

Female Correctional Officers

Affirmative-action measures have increased the number of minority officers, so that in many states the percentage of racial minorities among officers is now equal to the percentage of the minority population within the state. But not until the enactment of equal employment legislation, specifically Title VII, which prohibited sex discrimination in hiring by state and local governments, did doors begin to open for women in men's prisons.

Women working as correctional officers in men's prisons have received three criticisms. It has been said that women are not fit for the job because they are not strong enough, are too easily corrupted by inmates, or are poor backups for officers in trouble. Women also have been criticized as being a disruptive influence because inmates refuse to follow their orders or compete for their attention. Critics also say that the presence of women violates inmates' privacy, especially when women are working in shower areas or conducting strip searches.

Dothard v. Rawlinson (1977) and *Gunther v. Iowa State Men's Reformatory* (1979) are the two most important U.S. Supreme Court cases examining whether women are qualified to work in men's prisons.[29] The former was an Alabama lawsuit filed by Diane Rawlinson, a recent college graduate in correctional psychology, who was denied a job as a correctional officer because she was five pounds below the minimum weight requirement. Her class-action suit challenged the state's height and weight requirements. The suit also charged that a department of corrections regulation preventing female officers from "continual close proximity" to prisoners in maximum-security prisons for men (known as the no-contact rule) was discriminatory. The U.S. Supreme Court, in a 5–4 decision, overturned a lower court decision that had invalidated the no-contact rule. The Supreme Court was unwilling to let women work in maximum-security prisons for men in Alabama because of the danger of sexual attack and because the vulnerability of women to attack would weaken security and endanger other prison employees.[30]

In the *Gunther* decision, however, the Court dismissed security issues as a reason for limiting women's employment as guards in Iowa. The *Gunther* decision said that job requirements to strip-search male inmates or witness male inmates in showers constituted an attempt to prevent women from working as correctional officers.[31]

Those and other cases indicate that the courts have generally tried to protect both women's right to employment and inmates' privacy as much as possible. In *Ford v. Ward* (1978), a circuit court held that "equal job opportunity must in some measure give way to the right of privacy."[32] The background of this case was that female inmates at the Bedford Hills Correctional Center in New York contended that their right to privacy was violated because male correctional officers were assigned to duties in hospitals and housing units. The inmates argued that male correctional officers were able to observe them while they were sleeping, showering, dressing, and using the toilet facilities.[33] In *Torres v. Wisconsin* (1988), prison officials used the bona fide occupational qualification (BFOQ) defense for restricting male correctional officers from working in the living units of a women's prison. The case went through two appeals processes, but eventually the rights of female inmates were determined to take precedence over the equal employment rights of male correctional officers.[34]

Those supporting the employment of female officers in male prisons argue that departments of corrections can achieve privacy by means of administrative policies preventing women from doing strip searches. The installation of modesty half-screens, fogged windows that permit figures to be seen, or privacy doors on toilet stalls offers another solution to privacy issues. Security does not have to be sacrificed, and these modifications can be made to the physical environment at little cost.

Several studies have compared male and female correctional officers.[35] They generally have found no differences in the quality of job performance, but this does not mean that they are equal in all tasks. Although men may be better able then women to handle a physical assault, women may more effectively defuse an incident before violence erupts.[36] Various studies have found that female correctional officers are more treatment oriented than their male counterparts.[37] Women also tend to supervise inmates with a more personal interaction style than men officers. For example, women frequently ask inmates to perform certain tasks, rather than commanding them to do so.[38] Lynn Zimmer adds that inmates claim that women officers explain orders more fully, while male officers tend to bark orders and resent any attempt by inmates to get a fuller explanation.[39]

A woman correctional officer in a men's prison usually finds that the stress of working in a violent environment is intensified by conflict with male coworkers. But even assuming that problems with male coworkers can be resolved, the role confusion or uncertainty of the job may cause a woman to seek out or be assigned low-contact positions.[40] This decision results in dead-end work assignments and limits promotional possibilities.[41]

WHAT PROBLEMS DO CORRECTIONAL OFFICERS FACE?

In most state systems, correctional officers have at least as many problems as the guards of yesteryear. Theirs can be dangerous, dead-end, low-status jobs with confusing role expectations. Hans Toch describes how guards are imprisoned in their roles:

> Prison guards are truly imprisoned. They are not physically confined but are locked into movie caricatures, into pejorative prophecies (sometimes self-fulfilling), into anachronistic supervision patterns, into unfair civil service definitions, into undeserved hostilities and prejudgments of their actions. Officers are imprisoned by our ignorance of who they are and what they do, which is the price they pay for working behind walls.[42]

A study at Stateville (Joliet, Illinois) supports the opinion that the behavior of correctional officers is a product of their organizational roles and is independent of variables such as education, age, race, and political orientation. This study compared African American and white correctional officers. Although the African American officers were typically younger, better educated, and more liberal than the white officers, they manifested no consistent differences in their attitudes toward jobs, correctional goals, other staff, and inmates.[43]

Conflicting Goals and Expectations

The skills acquired through guarding are usually transferable only to even lower-paying private security jobs. A few officers are promoted through the ranks, but these opportunities are likely to disappear early in an officer's career. Furthermore, professional training is increasingly required of prison managers, which reduces the availability of top administrative positions for officers.

The conflict of goals and expectations creates a new problem for officers. In the days of autocratic wardens, guards used to know what was expected of them, including the avoidance of undue familiarity with inmates. Prisons were custodial in nature. Today, requirements for shakedowns and counts seem to change with each new supervisor, and policies on relations with prisoners are often open to interpretation. The lack of predictability of officers' behavior, as well as the inconsistent rule-enforcement structure, has contributed to the creation of stress with inmates.[44]

In addition to the problems of low status, role confusion, and inmate defiance, correctional officers also must deal with the reality that they sometimes are treated no better than inmates. For example, occasionally they are subjected to strip searches, although many union chapters have become strong enough to resist this kind of control. Strip searches are necessitated by the fact that one route for illegal drugs into the prison is the officer whom prisoners have identified as a willing conduit. Officers view these searches as unjust because most officers have committed no crimes. Correctional officers also share the same environment and many of the same deprivations as inmates and, as a result, often see themselves as "doing time," although they are able to go home at night.

Increased inmate defiance makes prisons, especially maximum-security ones, dangerous and stressful places in which to work. Security staff across the nation express a common complaint—they have neither the control nor the respect they used to have. Officers often say, "If the inmates want you, they can get you." It is no wonder that the incidence of high blood pressure, heart disease, psychological problems, and alcoholism is high among the men and women who work in this violent atmosphere.[45]

Officers' Responses to Problems on the Job

Old-timers tell new correctional officers about acceptable behavior on the job. Experienced officers know that all will be punished severely for violations of security. A mistake that leads to an escape may cost them several weeks "in the streets" (suspension) or may even result in termination. Any erosion of security makes it more likely that inmates will initiate a disturbance and that the disturbance will mushroom into a full-scale riot. Moreover, experienced officers know that inmates cannot be given too much leeway or they will end up controlling the institution and abusing their keepers. These officers try to teach newly certified correctional officers how to strike a balance between rigidly enforcing all the rules and allowing the inmates to gain control. Finally, experienced officers know that the best hope for security is fair treatment of inmates. Simply put, an inmate who is treated fairly and with respect is much less likely to become a security problem than a prisoner who feels humiliated and abused by staff.[46]

Nevertheless, some correctional officers respond with inappropriate behaviors to their alienating roles. They take seriously the old prison saying "The first year, a guard can't do enough for an inmate; the second year, a guard can't do enough to a convict."[47] Hans Toch and John Klofas, in an examination of correctional officers in the Northeast, found that about a quarter of the guard force could be classified in this way.[48] Many officers believe that acting tough, dominating the weak, threatening violence, and putting inmates in their place will show the "captives" who is in control.[49] James Marquart found that the escalating strategies used by this group moved from "verbal assaults," to physically abusive "tune-ups," to overt violent "ass-whippings" and "severe beatings."[50] The code of silence that often exists in subcultures of correctional officers serves to protect those officers who brutalize inmates.

Moreover, there are always a few officers who become involved in corrupt and illegal behavior that jeopardizes security and violates the law. They may agree to bring contraband into the institution because they have been set up by inmates. This violation often occurs when a correctional officer agrees to do something against the rules in order to be well liked. For example, one correctional officer agreed to mail a birthday card to an inmate's daughter on his way home from work. Although this was against policy, it meant that the card would reach the child on her birthday. Subsequently, the inmate demanded that the officer comply with other requests, threatening to report the first violation to the captain.

Some officers carry contraband for profit. Inmates who are trafficking drugs in the institution or have a large drug appetite themselves seem to be able to raise large amounts of cash. According to offenders who have spent time in federal and state institutions, inmates watch and talk with each new officer and soon figure out who can be corrupted.[51] An example is a correctional officer in a midwestern state who was caught in a strip search with two large bags of marijuana taped across his chest. This particular individual apparently had been bringing drugs into the prison for some time and had been able to buy a Cadillac and expensive clothes with his additional tax-free income.[52]

Job Enrichment: A Challenge for Administrators

Perhaps the way to make the officer's role more attractive to individuals considering a career in corrections, as well as make it more meaningful to individuals already working as officers, is to offer incentives such as career development programs to reinforce and increase the number of officers who want to provide humane services to inmates. A number of studies appear to indicate that at least some officers enjoy providing such services.[53] These officers see correctional work as a worthwhile endeavor.[54] In *Hard Time,* Robert Johnson strongly emphasizes this point:

> It is by helping prisoners—by promoting secure and responsive prison regimes—that some officers rise above the limitation of their formal custodial role. They use their authority to help inmates cope with prison life; they provide human services rather than custodial repression. They do the best they can with the resources at their disposal to make the prison a better place in which to live and work.[55]

Female officers seem more likely than males to take a human relations view of the correctional officer's job. The "softening" effect that some women officers have in men's prisons seem to make these institutions more livable and less violent. Yet, as with any generalization, glaring exceptions exist; some women officers feel obligated to be brusque and impersonal with inmates.[56]

Daniel Glaser's examination of the prison over three decades ago found that officers who were fair and friendly and who related to inmates as human beings were liked and obeyed.[57] Stan Stojkovic's more recent examination of the prison found that officers themselves agreed that "consistency, fairness, and flexibility in the enforcement of rules were what made a good officer," and that "effective officers are able to develop a sense of respect with inmates by being fair and consistent."[58] John Hepburn's study similarly concluded that "the level of institutional authority appears to be greatest" among those correctional officers "who have a less punitive and custodial orientation, who maintain a lower degree of social distance from inmates, and who express a higher level of job satisfaction."[59]

Thus, the human relations approach leads not only to improved personal relationships with inmates but to a greater degree of correctional authority. It can also help calm the prison by officers providing needed goods and services to inmates, by their acting as referral agents or advocates, and by their helping inmates with institutional adjustment problems.[60]

SUMMARY

The warden's administrative role as it has evolved over the last two or three decades is outlined in this chapter. From a princely autocrat, lord of all he surveyed in the prisons of the nineteenth and most of the twentieth centuries, the warden has become a field manager for the state's department of corrections or the Bureau of Prisons.

The autocrats of the past were accountable to no one, unless a headline-making scandal or a radical political change upset their regime. Today, wardens are civil service bureaucrats, directly accountable to their superiors—a director or commissioner in the state capital. Their autocratic predecessors could ignore the outside world. They could exclude both the public and the press from their institution. The new wardens cannot fend off many intruders. Journalists, lawyers, union representatives, professional associations, and a host of other outsiders must be accommodated, people who would not have been given the time of day by the old autocrats.

Today, prisons have problems with violence and contraband that far exceed in danger and prevalence any similar problems in prisons in the nineteenth and most of the twentieth century. Exacerbating these conditions is the unprecedented overcrowding of the contemporary prison. Turnover rates among all staff, including top administrators, are high. Many are appointed without sufficient experience; others lack the stamina for a 24-hour-a-day job and the imagination to prepare for future contingencies. Nevertheless, a substantial number of wardens have developed the knack of penal administration to a high degree. Their secret is intelligent and continuous examination of experience.

The role of correctional officers' has changed in many ways. Yet they continue to face jobs that are dangerous, dead-end, and low status. Some correctional officers physically and emotionally abuse inmates and bring drugs into the institution, also bringing considerable disorder to the prison environment. Fortunately, most correctional officers try to be fair and decent in their treatment of inmates. Some officers even take a human relations approach, which seems to have the effect of calming the prison environment.

KEY TERMS

autocratic warden, p. 258
bureaucratization of corrections, p. 259
California consensual model, p. 262
corporate management model, p. 261
Michigan responsibility model, p. 262

paramilitary model, p. 259
participatory management, p. 261
shared-powers model, p. 262
Texas control model, p. 262

CRITICAL THINKING QUESTIONS

1. What were the advantages of the autocratic regime of prison management? To the staff? To the prisoners? To the political establishment?
2. Should prison wardens be selected by civil service procedures? Discuss the advantages of recruitment by civil service as contrasted with selection by the director from his or her knowledge of available candidates nationwide.
3. You have been assigned to the warden's office in a maximum security prison. In your initial conference with the associate warden in charge of custody, you are told that his most critical problem is violence between members of rival prison gangs. What questions will you ask him to inform yourself about the extent of the problem and the measures he has taken to control it?
4. To what extent should a warden involve himself or herself with the institutional budget? Why should budgeting not be done by the central office staff?
5. Do you believe that female correctional officers can work effectively in a maximum-security prison for males?

WEB DESTINATIONS

Read an Amnesty International criticism detailing allegations of abuse of inmates by prison guards in California in 2000 and a similar 1998 case in Florida.
http://www.web.amnesty.org/ai.nsf/index/AMR510982000

http://www.prisonlegalnews.org/Issues/1098/002.htm

This site gives details on the career of a correctional officer.
http://www.jobbankusa.com/ohb/ohb156.html

This California Correctional Officers Association site is for anyone considering a career as a correctional officer.
http://www.susanvillenews.com/co.html

Read an article on recent innovations in definitions of the attitudes and role behavior of prison guards.
http://www.oicj.org/public/story.cfm?story=9FD2986A-F6AC-11D3-AA9E-00C04F409AD4

This article reports on prison wardens' conclusions about the role of recreational amenities for inmates in prison management.
http://www.strengthtech.com/correct/issues/mediais/hartford.htm

FOR FURTHER READING

DiIulio, John J., Jr. *Governing Prisons: A Comparative Study of Correctional Management*. New York: Free Press, 1987. A controversial book because of the author's support for the Texas control model.

Jenne, D. L., and R. C. Kersting. "Aggression and Women Correctional Officers." *Prison Journal* 76 (1996), pp. 442–460. One of the better articles examining the role of women correctional officers in a male institution.

Johnson, Robert. *Hard Time: Understanding and Reforming the Prison*. Belmont, Calif.: Wadsworth, 1996. An excellent examination of the deprivations of confinement as well as a valuable account of the human services role of the correctional officer.

Lombardo, Lucien X. *Guards Imprisoned*. 2nd ed. Cincinnati: Anderson, 1989. Lombardo's study of the Auburn Prison in New York State is one of the most perceptive examinations of the correctional officer.

Morgan, Gareth. *Images of Organization*. Beverly Hills, Calif.: Sage, 1986. Develops the learning metaphor discussed in this chapter.

Riveland, Chase. "Prison Management Trends: 1975–2025," in *Prisons* ed. Michael Tonry and Joan Petersilia (Chicago: University of Chicago Press, 1999), pp. 163–203. Chase Riveland sketches out the changes that have taken place in correctional administration over the past twenty-five years and anticipates the challenges of the future.

Zimmer, Lynne. *Women Guarding Men*. Chicago: University of Chicago Press, 1986. Clearly describes the problems of women working as correctional officers in men's prisons.

NOTES

1. Statement supplied for *Invitation to Corrections* in September 2000.
2. Statements made by wardens during interviews during the 1970s, 1980s, and 1990s.
3. This section on the changing role of correctional administrators is adapted from John Conrad and Simon Dinitz, "Position Paper for the Seminar on the Isolated Prisoner" (paper presented at the Academy for Contemporary Problems, National Institute of Corrections, Columbus, Ohio, 8–9 December 1977), pp. 4–11.
4. James B. Jacobs, *Stateville: The Penitentiary in Modern Society* (Chicago: University of Chicago Press, 1977).
5. Conrad and Dinitz, "Position Paper for the Seminar on the Isolated Prisoner," pp. 4–11.
6. Israel L. Barak-Glantz, "Toward a Conceptual Schema of Prison Management Styles," *The Prison Journal* (1981), p. 49.
7. Ibid., p. 50.
8. Ibid., p. 51.
9. John J. DiIulio Jr., *Governing Prisons: A Comparative Study of Correctional Management* (New York: Free Press, 1987), p. 5.
10. Ibid., p. 30.
11. Bert Useem and Peter Kimball, *States of Siege: U.S. Prison Riots, 1971–1986* (New York: Oxford University Press, 1989), p. 227.
12. DiIulio, *Governing Prisons*, pp. 50–53.
13. Ibid., pp. 118–123.

14. Ibid., p. 128.

15. Ibid., pp. 128–134.

16. Ibid., p. 144.

17. Wardens have related such incidents to the author.

18. The assistance of Frank Woods, former warden of Oak Park Heights in Minnesota and commissioner of corrections in Minnesota, was invaluable in shaping this section.

19. J. D. Thompson, *Organization in Action* (New York: McGraw-Hill, 1967).

20. Ibid.

21. Gareth Morgan, *Images of Organization* (Beverly Hills, Calif.: Sage, 1986).

22. Camille Graham Camp and George M. Camp, *The Corrections Yearbook 1999: Adult Corrections* (Middletown, Conn.: Criminal Justice Institute, 1999), p. 131.

23. Richard Gramley, a former Illinois warden, defined these basic responsibilities of the correctional administrator and helped shape this discussion.

24. Robert Tannenbaum and Warren Schmidt, "How to Choose a Leadership Pattern," *Harvard Business Review* 51 (May–June 1973), p. 164.

25. Statement made to the author by a male lieutenant.

26. Philip L. Reichel, *Corrections: Philosophies, Practices, and Procedures* (Boston: Allyn & Bacon 2001), p. 353.

27. Camp and Camp, *The Corrections Yearbook 1999,* p. 135.

28. Ibid., p. 151.

29. *Dothard v. Rawlinson,* 433 U.S. 321 (1977); *Gunther v. Iowa State Men's Reformatory,* 612 F.2d 1079 (6th Circ. 1979).

30. *Dothard v. Rawlinson.*

31. *Gunther v. Iowa State Men's Reformatory.*

32. *Ford v. Ward,* 471 F. Supp. 1095(S.D.N.Y. 1978).

33. Ibid.

34. K. J. Maschke, "Gender in the Prison Setting: The Privacy–Equal Employment Dilemma," *Women and Criminal Justice* 7 (1996), pp. 23–42.

35. Geoffrey P. Alpert, "The Needs of the Judiciary and Misapplication of Social Research: The Case of Female Guards in Men's Prisons," *Criminology* 22 (1984), pp. 441–455; G. R. Gross, S. J. Larson, G. D. Urban, and L. P. Zupan, "Gender Differences in Occupational Stress among Correctional Officers," *American Journal of Criminal Justice* 18 (1994), pp. 219–234; D. L. Jenne and R. C. Kersting, "Aggression and Women Correctional Officers in Male Prisons," *Prison Journal* 76 (1996), pp. 442–460; N. C. Jurik, "An Officer and a Lady: Organizational Barriers to Women Working as Correctional Officers in Men's Prisons," *Social Problems* 32 (1985), pp. 375–388.

36. Cheryl Bowser Peterson, "Doing Time with the Boys: An Analysis of Women's Correctional Officers in All-Male Facilities," in *The Criminal Justice System and Women,* ed. B. R. Price and N. J. Sokoloff (New York: Clark Boardman, 1982), pp. 444–445.

37. N. J. Jurik and G. J. Halemba, "Gender, Working Conditions and the Job Satisfaction of Women in a Non-Traditional Occupation: Female Correctional Officers in Men's Prisons," *The Sociological Quarterly* 25 (1984), pp. 551–556.

38. J. M. Pollock, "Women in Corrections: Custody or the 'Caring Ethic,'" in *Women, Law and Social Control,* ed. A. V. Merlo and J. M. Pollock (Boston: Allyn & Bacon, 1995), pp. 97–116.

39. Lynne Zimmer, *Women Guarding Men* (Chicago: University of Chicago Press, 1986).

40. Ibid.

41. Jurik, "An Officer and a Lady," pp. 375–388.

42. Hans Toch, foreword to Lucien X. Lombardo, *Guards Imprisoned* (New York: Elsevier, 1981), p. xiv.

43. James B. Jacobs and Lawrence S. Kraft, "Integrating the Keepers: A Comparison of Black and White Prison Officers in Illinois," *Social Problems* 25 (February 1976).

44. Lucien X. Lombardo, "Alleviating Inmate Stress: Contributions from Correctional Officers," in *The Pains of Imprisonment,* ed. by Hans Toch and Robert Johnson (Beverly Hills, Calif.: Sage, 1982), p. 293.

45. F. E. Cheek and M. D. S. Miller, "The Experience of Stress for Corrections Officers: A Double-Bind Theory of Correctional Stress," *Journal of Criminal Justice* 11 (1983), pp. 105–120.

46. B. M. Crouch and J. W. Marquart, "On Becoming a Prison Guard," in *The Keepers: Prison Guards and Contemporary Corrections,* ed. B. M. Crouch (Springfield, Ill.: Charles C. Thomas, 1980), p. 61, and Lombardo, *Guards Imprisoned,* p. 63.

47. Found in Pete Earley, *The Hot House: Life inside Leavenworth Prison* (New York: Bantam Books, 1992), p. 221.

48. H. Toch and J. Klofas, "Alienation and Desire for Job Enrichment among Correctional Officers," *Federal Probation* 46 (1982), pp. 35–44.

49. Robert Johnson, *Hard Time: Understanding and Reforming the Prison* (Belmont, Calif: Wadsworth, 1996).

50. J. W. Marquart, "Prison Guards and the Use of Physical Coercion as a Mechanism of Prisoner Control" (paper presented at the annual meeting of the American Sociological Association, San Antonio, Tex., August 1984).

51. Conversations with inmates.

52. Incident reported to the author.

53. Charles A. Lindquist and John T. Whitehead, "Guards Released from Prison: A Natural Experiment in Job Enrichment," *Journal of Criminal Justice* 14 (1986), pp. 283–294.

54. N. C. Jurik, "Individual and Organizational Determinants of Correctional Officer Attitudes toward Inmates," *Criminology* 23 (1985), pp. 523–539.

55. Johnson, *Hard Time,* pp. 137–138.

56. P. J. Kissel and P. L. Katsampes, "The Impact of Women Corrections Officers on the Functioning of Institutions Housing Male Inmates," *Journal of Offender Counseling, Services and Rehabilitation* 4 (1980), pp. 213–231; B. A. Owen, "Race and Gender Relations among Prison Workers," *Crime and Delinquency* 31 (1985), pp. 147–159.

57. Daniel Glaser, *The Effectiveness of a Prison and Parole System* (Indianapolis: Bobbs-Merrill, 1969).

58. Stan Stojkovic, "An Examination of Compliance Structures in a Prison Organization: A Study of the Types of Correctional Power" (paper presented at the annual meeting of American Criminal Justices Sciences, Chicago, March 1984).

59. John R. Hepburn, "The Erosion of Authority and the Perceived Legitmacy of Inmate Social Protest: A Study of Prison Guards," *Journal of Criminal Justice* 12 (1984), pp. 579–590.

60. Lombardo, "Alleviating Inmate Stress," p. 287.

CHAPTER 11 / BUILT-IN STUDY GUIDE

Multiple Choice Questions

1. According to the text, the main priority of a correctional institution is:

   A. Security
   B. Treatment
   C. Punishment
   D. Drug counseling

2. Which of the following models of prison management does John J. DiIulio Jr. suggest is most effective?

   A. Michigan responsibility model
   B. California consensual model
   C. Texas control model
   D. Minnesota democratic model

3. All of the following signify changes in the role of the correctional officer except:

   A. Higher salaries
   B. Greater training
   C. Unionization
   D. Fewer civil suits

4. Identify the specific event that ended state and local discriminatory hiring practices of women in male prisons.

   A. Civil Rights Act
   B. Title VII
   C. Equal Employment Act
   D. State Hiring Act

5. Which of the following signify the two basic types of management philosophy found in correctional institutions in the United States?

   A. Autocratic and bureaucratic
   B. Total quality and problem solving
   C. Authoritarian and military
   D. Democratic and participatory

6. According to DiIulio, what is the key to prison discipline and control?

   A. Punish violators proportionately
   B. Have an extensive special housing unit
   C. Treatment programs
   D. Prison industry

7. Currently, innovations within the prison combined with external supervision are enabling federal and some state correctional officials to shape a new prison environment based on all of the following except:

   A. Accountability
   B. Risk assessment
   C. Functional integration
   D. Enhanced special housing units

8. What makes maintaining effective communication with inmates more difficult than it was in the past?

   A. Inmate codes
   B. Prisonization
   C. Inmate gangs
   D. Grievance boards

9. All of the following signify problems faced by the correctional officer except:

   A. Low status
   B. Unpredictable shift changes
   C. Inmate defiance
   D. Role confusion

10. In *Torres v. Wisconsin*, what defense did prison officials use for restricting male correctional officers from working in the living units of a female prison?

    A. Bono fide occupational qualification
    B. Gender discrimination
    C. Sexual discrimination
    D. Gender occupational qualification

11. What discovery did state correctional systems make after World War II?

    A. Bureaucracy killed private and public organizations
    B. Bureaucracy leads to lower productivity
    C. Bureaucracy works only in the private sector
    D. No organization can survive without bureaucracy

12. The result of the shared powers model to management resulted in:

    A. Enhancing the alienation between guards and institutional administration
    B. Enhancing the powers of correctional officers and administration
    C. Enhancing the powers of administrators and central corrections agencies
    D. Decreasing the power of inmates

True/False Questions

T   F   1. The development of inmate grievance systems probably represented the greatest gains for prisoners.

T   F   2. Wardens who are disillusioned usually enthusiastically endorse the accreditation process of the Commission on Accreditation for Corrections.

T   F   3. Affirmative action measures have resulted in equaling the percentage of minority correctional officers to that of the minority population of the state.

T   F   4. According to the text, female corrections officers may more effectively calm an incident before violence erupts.

T   F   5. Innovative wardens believe that a critical element of the human relations approach is their willingness to demonstrate to others the behaviors they want others to demonstrate.

T   F   6. Management styles of wardens in the 1980s and 1990s do not differ greatly from those of 1970s.

T   F   7. Prisoners' rights make communicating with inmates more difficult than it was in the past.

T   F   8. Unionization has changed the role of the correctional officer.

T   F   9. The main priority of a correctional institution is rehabilitation of inmates.

T   F   10. The Equal Employment Act ended discrimination in hiring practices of females in male prisons on the local and state level.

Fill-in-the-Blank Questions   (based on key terms)

1. Correctional systems that strive for clear accountability, higher standards, and better allocation of resources reflect the _____.

2. The _____ is characterized as having sovereign powers as well as having total responsibility for planning, staffing, and control.

3. Institutions where staff members have almost total control of the operation resemble the _____.

4. Correctional administrators who realize the importance of their negotiations with the press, labor unions, employee organizations, and the courts are practicing the _____ philosophy.

5. According to John J. DiIulio Jr., the _____ resulted in gangs operating the prison.

6. A management model that supported a democratic prison environment that would result in the enhanced respect, dignity, and status of both staff and inmates by granting them the same power in the governance of the prison is referred to as the _____.

7. Prisons that operate by imposing minimum constraints on inmates, designed to foster a prison community are using the _____.

8. Private-sector management models adopted by correctional administrators that place emphasis on accountability, feedback, and quantitative evaluations are characteristic of the _____.

Essay Questions

1. What events have influenced the role of the warden throughout the history of corrections?

2. Describe the five elements that make up the warden's administrative responsibilities.

3. Describe the Texas control model, Michigan responsibility model, and California consensual model. Explain what each model is based on.

4. How has the role of the correctional officer changed throughout history? What events have influenced this change? Additionally, what obstacles have female correctional officers had to overcome to find work in a male prison?

5. Identify and explain some of the problems correctional officers face. What has been the response to some of these problems?

ANSWERS

Multiple Choice Questions

1.	A	7.	D
2.	C	8.	C
3.	D	9.	B
4.	B	10.	A
5.	A	11.	D
6.	A	12.	A

True/False Questions

1.	T	6.	F
2.	F	7.	F
3.	T	8.	T
4.	T	9.	F
5.	T	10.	F

Fill-in-the-Blank Questions

1. Bureaucratization of corrections
2. Autocratic warden
3. Texas control model
4. Participatory management
5. California consensual model
6. Shared-powers model
7. Michigan responsibility model
8. Corporate management model

chapter twelve

Institutional Security and Violence

Forty-three persons died in the 1971 uprising at the state prison in Attica, New York. This was one of the bloodiest one-day encounters between Americans since the Civil War.[1] The rioting inmates issued this statement of demands to the prison administration:

> **To the People of America**
>
> The incident that has erupted here at Attica is not a result of the dastardly bushwhacking of the two prisoners Sept. 8, 1971 but of the unmitigated oppression wrought by the racist administration network of the prison, throughout the year.
>
> We are MEN! We are not beasts and do not intend to be beaten or driven as such. The entire prison populace has set forth to change forever the ruthless brutalization and

disregard for the lives of the prisoners here and throughout the United States. What has happened here is but the sound before the fury of those who are oppressed.

We will not compromise on any terms except those that are agreeable to us. We call upon all the conscientious citizens of America to assist us in putting an end to this situation that threatens the lives of not only us, but each and everyone of us as well.

We have set forth demands that will bring closer to reality the demise of these prison institutions that serve no useful purpose to the People of America, but to those who would enslave and exploit the people of America.

Our Demands Are Such

1. We want Complete Amnesty. Meaning freedom for all and from all physical, mental and legal reprisals.
2. We want now speedy and safe transportation out of confinement, to a Non-Imperialistic country.
3. We demand that Fed. Government intervene, so that we will be under direct Fed. Jurisdiction.
4. We demand the reconstruction to Attica Prison to be done by Inmates and/or inmates supervision. . . .
5. We intensely demand that all Communications will be conducted in "Our" Domain "GUARANTEEING SAFE TRANSPORTATION TO AND FROM."

The Inmates Of Attica Prison[2]

CRITICAL THINKING QUESTIONS

If you were commissioner of correctional services and received this list of demands, what would you do? Do you believe that it would be a mistake to negotiate with rioting inmates?

The riot began on Friday 9 September 1971. By Friday evening, inmate leaders, realizing that their immediate demands were unrealistic, offered thirty-three proposals. In his weekend meetings and communications with inmates, Russell Osward, Commissioner of Correctional Services, was committed to bring the riot to a peaceful resolution. He indicated that he could accept twenty-eight of the inmates' proposals and would do everything in his power to implement them. But he insisted on one condition: The inmates had to release their hostages. On Monday morning, Oswald sent the inmates an ultimatum: Release the hostages, unharmed, within the hour. When no hostages were freed, an assault force retook the prison, killing thirty-nine individuals (twenty-nine inmates and ten hostages).[3]

A serious and perplexing problem, institutional violence manifests itself in a variety of forms—riots and other major disturbances, victimization of one inmate by another, staff brutality toward inmates, inmate assaults on staff, and self-inflicted violence by prisoners. Whatever form it takes, institutional violence is a severe indictment of the current policy of imprisonment. The more than three hundred prison riots since 1970 have established the dangers and the unstable character of contemporary prisons.[4]

Prison violence has been divided into two types of behavior—"interpersonal violence" and "collective violence."[5] What distinguishes these two categories is that collective violence brings with it a "significant breakdown in the normal patterns of social order in the institution."[6] Interpersonal violence, in contrast, refers to violent events that occur "within the everyday framework of the prison's social order."[7]

One lens through which institutional violence can be viewed is that of the correctional officers. Their perspective generally is that the social order of the prison has broken down because the inmates have all the power. Inmates see prison violence much differently. They are quick to say that if their needs were met, then institutional violence would dramatically decrease. Corrections experts who have analyzed the causes of institutional violence usually attribute it to personal and cultural characteristics of inmates and to organizational, social, and structural factors within the prison environment.

WHAT HAS HAPPENED TO SOCIAL ORDER WITHIN THE PRISON?

Order and control in the prison are similar but not the same. Order is a dynamic social equilibrium that can be defined negatively within the prison as "the absence of violence, overt conflict, or the imminent threat of the chaotic breakdown of social routines."[8] Control means "a set of strategies or tactics used by prison administrators to achieve order."[9]

In the orderly days of the past, convicts were told on their first day, both by staff and by other inmates, that they could do "easy time" or "hard time." The staff assured prisoners that troublemakers would lose whatever "good time" they had accumulated over the years. An unwritten but powerful **inmate code** was functional both to prison administrators and to the prisoners themselves.[10] The code promoted order by encouraging inmates to serve their sentences and not make trouble. Prisoners knew that disorder within the walls would mean the end of informal arrangements between inmate leaders and staff and the loss of privileges that it had taken them years to obtain.

Especially in the South, inmate trusties were widely used to control other inmates and performed many of the tasks ordinarily performed by custodial staff. Arkansas, Mississippi, and Louisiana permitted such inmates to carry firearms. Before the *Ruiz v. Estelle* (1987) decision rendered the **building tenders** system of the Texas Department of Corrections unconstitutional, inmate building tenders in Texas prisons had been given authority by prison administrators to discipline inmates who disturbed the social order.[11]

Today, order has given way to disorder. As will be discussed in Chapter 14, a thriving contraband market, frequent and serious violations of rules and procedures, and more inmates choosing protective custody are signs of the erosion of order. Riots, disturbances, and assaults, as well as ever-present abuses and indignities, are more serious manifestations of disorder within the walls.

Inmate gangs in forty states and the Federal Bureau of Prisons, the drug appetites of most prisoners, inmates serving longer sentences, and, most serious of all, overcrowded prisons do not make it easy to restore order within the walls. Correctional officers for the past decade have been quick to tell outsiders that the inmates are running the prison; today, in many prisons, that is more true than ever before. In Within The Walls 12.1, Denny Fitzpatrick, a correctional officer in New York at the time of the Attica riot, tells how the riot changed corrections in that state.

the walls   12.1

within

A Former New York Correctional Officer Speaks Out

"In 1970 I was on the job as a New York State Correctional Officer for only four weeks at the Green Haven maximum security prison when I had an encounter with Willie Sutton, the notorious safe cracker. Sutton once quipped he robbed banks because 'that's where the money is.'

"Sutton knew I was a new officer. He made it a point to tell me how to do the job, from when to ring the bell, to how to do a head count. He also offered a piece of advice; make sure you leave with everything you came with. I did not pay much attention to him as I went about performing my duties.

"At the end of the day, after I led the inmates through their daily routine, Sutton approached me and asked, 'Do you have everything you came with?' I checked my pockets and found my wallet was missing. Sutton handed over the wallet, grinned and promptly went back to his cell.

"I tell this fable because it illustrates a relationship between inmates and officers that rarely exists in New York's maximum-security prisons today. Thirty ago a mutual respect existed. Assaults by inmates on officers were rare.

"Finding an inmate in possession of a dangerous weapon or drugs was also rare. Today, there is no mutual respect between inmates and officers. Assaults by inmates upon officers are frequent. They are executed in the most despicable ways possible, including inmates throwing their human waste in an officer's face. Dangerous weapons and drugs are commonly found on inmates.

"In 1971, the bloody Attica riot left its mark on the Department of Corrections and the men and women who protect and serve the public. All the wannabe penologists came out of the woodwork and invoked their reasoning as to the cause of the riot and how to prevent another Attica. With this outside pressure came dramatic changes.

"The prevalence of gang activity is the most dramatic example of the changes that have taken place inside our facilities. Gang activity in 1970 could be described as *West Side Story* Sharks and Jets compared to today's violent prison gangs. The Bloods, Crips, Latin Kings, neo-Nazis' Aryan Nation, Neteas, and Amachateros are the most prominent gangs. Each one is extremely violent and willing to do almost anything to accomplish their criminal goals.

"Inmates prior to Attica were dressed in gray uniforms with their numbers on their back. The correction officer was dressed in police blue. After the riot, the inmates were dressed in green uniforms and the officers were dressed in grays. This was the beginning of erosion of an officer's authority and the role he or she would soon play.

"Prior to the Attica riot, the Department of Correctional Services emphasized the role of a correction officer to be care, control, and custody, and the inmate was almost totally dependent upon the officer for all his needs. The officer was also responsible for filing an evaluation to the Parole Board on the inmate's behavior under his care. This evaluation carried some weight at a Parole Board hearing, this giving an inmate an incentive to behave appropriately. Today counselors evaluate inmates' behavior and report to the Parole Board.

"The officers who observe and supervise inmates on a daily basis have no say at all. As a consequence, inmates no longer respect officers and only perceive them as the person who makes them obey rules and regulations. Therefore, the lines have been drawn in the sand. This may account for the 1,000 or more assaults on officers annually.

"Furthermore, the inmate can appear to be the model of propriety with a counselor who sees him once every three months, but consistently be a major problem to the officers.

"New York's correctional officers are high-quality law-enforcement professionals. There is no reason why we cannot entrust them with the responsibility to evaluate inmates. I strongly believe that returning to a system whereby correction officers file evaluations to the Parole Board will improve the officer–inmate relationship and lead to a safer prison environment.

"When I walked into Green Haven twenty-nine years ago, I did not feel the unrelenting tension that characterizes our prisons today. Something has to be done because there are no more Willie Suttons doing time."

> Today, there is no mutual respect between inmates and officers.

CRITICAL THINKING QUESTIONS

What does this former correctional officer say is the reason for the breakdown of order in New York's prisons? From what other perspectives might prison violence be explained?

Source: Denny Fitzpatrick, Director of Labor Relations for the New York State Correctional Officers and Benevolence Association (NYSCOPBA), Webpage, 28 November 2000.

WHAT ARE EXPRESSIONS OF PRISON VIOLENCE?

Correctional officers are very aware of the dangers present in their jobs, for they daily experience the hostility of inmates. Sometimes they receive verbal abuse; at other times they are physically assaulted. Officers, too, have been known to retaliate in abusive ways to inmates. The prison environment combines a number of factors that contribute to what can be called a controlled war among inmates. During imprisonment, many men and women lose hope and feel alienated from their families and other inmates. Of those who feel isolated, some break, direct their hostilities and frustrations toward themselves, and try to take their own lives.

Riots and Other Major Disturbances

Inmate disturbances are sometimes nonviolent and sometimes violent. Nonviolent disturbances include hunger strikes, sit-down strikes, work stoppages, voluntary lockdowns (staying in one's cell even when the cellblock is open), excessive numbers of inmates reporting for sick call, and the filing of grievances by nearly everyone in a cellblock or even in the entire institution. Violent inmate disturbances include crowding around a correctional officer and intimidating him or her so that a disciplinary ticket is not written, assaulting officers, sabotaging the electrical, plumbing, or heating systems, burning or destroying institutional property, and **riots**—attempts to take control, with or without hostages, of a cellblock, a yard, or an entire prison.

The riot at the New Mexico State Prison in Santa Fe began shortly after midnight on Saturday 2 February 1980. The savagery eventually cost thirty-three lives and hundreds of beaten, raped, and psychologically scarred prisoners. In Dormitory E-2, some of the men were watching the late movie on TV, and two boisterous prisoners were lying in their bunks drinking prison-made raisinjack. The noise attracted Captain Roybal, one of twenty-two officers on duty that night. When captain tried to confiscate the raisinjack, he was jumped by the intoxicated prisoners, taken hostage, and relieved of his keys—all the keys needed to gain entry to the corridor leading to the control room. Two officers who tried to assist Roybal were also taken hostage. All three were beaten and raped into unconsciousness. Dormitory E-2 and the corridor belonged to the prisoners within moments after the taking of the three hostages. Down the corridor they stormed. The control room was readily breached, and the supposedly shatterproof glass was shattered. The carnage began. Old inmate scores were settled. There was no inmate leadership or list of grievances. There was only unspeakable brutality.[12]

During the 1980s, numerous incidents of arson and vandalism took place in men's prisons. In 1981, five such disturbances erupted at Michigan prisons (State Prison, Southern Michigan; Michigan Reformatory; and Marquette) over a five-day period. In 1986, three more took place—at the West Virginia Penitentiary, South Carolina's Kirkland Correctional Institution, and Iowa State Penitentiary. Considerable damage was done in a 1987 riot at the Atlanta Federal Penitentiary that began when the government announced that twenty-five hundred Cuban inmates would be sent back to Cuba.[13] The riot at this federal penitentiary lasted eleven days and involved more than one hundred hostages.[14]

Prison riots continued to be a problem in the 1990s. A riot took place at the prison located in Lucasville, Ohio in 1993. In 1995, federal prisons at Talladega, Alabama; Allenwood, Pennsylvania; Memphis, Tennessee; and Greenville, Illinois, had disturbances apparently related to a congressional vote refusing to lower drug sentences. A survey found that 21 percent of state prison administrators reported that a riot had taken place in their facility during 1995.[15]

In 1998, a disturbance took place at Attica when seven inmates from Cellblock B refused to leave exercise yards reserved for the prison's most violent inmates. Fourteen correctional officers were injured.[16] In December 1999, a riot took place at the William G. McConnell Unit in Beeville, Texas. The disturbance started when an inmate pried his way out of his cell and made it through three security doors. He then stabbed a correctional officer and released eighty-three inmates from their cells. They were subdued by a tactical team an hour later.[17]

Riots may be spontaneous or planned to achieve some goal.[18] Planning a riot usually requires a degree of inmate solidarity. When prison riots break out today, they tend to be more like the New Mexico riot rather than the inmate revolt at Attica. In Attica, inmates had a high degree of organization, solidarity, and political consciousness. The New Mexico riot is notable for inmates' fragmentation, lack of effective leadership, and disorganization. Indeed, the 1980 New Mexico riot showed the extent to which relations between prisoners had fragmented during the 1970s. Political apathy and fighting among inmates had replaced the politicization and solidarity of earlier years.[19]

The hero of this chapter is Mark Colvin, professor of sociology at George Mason University in Virginia. His study of the Santa Fe riot and his other books have made him a widely respected criminologist and expert on institutional violence. Read what he wrote for *Invitation to Corrections* in 2001.

Inmate Assaults on Staff

The average number of assaults on staff increased throughout the 1990s. In 1990, the average number of assaults against staff was 239 per agency; in 1998, it was 304 per agency. Of the assaults committed by inmates during 1998, 35.4 percent were committed against staff members. Of the assaults for which medical attention was needed in 1998, 25.7 percent were against staff members.[20]

S. C. Light carried out a content analysis of official records dealing with nearly seven hundred prisoner–staff assaults in New York State.[21] He focused on the themes, or the immediate context, of the assaults and discovered that six themes accounted for over four-fifths of the cases. In decreasing order of frequency, these themes were:

- Officer's command: Assault followed explicit command to inmate.
- Protest: Assault occurred because victim considers himself victimized by unjust or inconsistent treatment by a staff member.
- Search: Assault occurred during search of an inmate's body or cell.
- Inmates' fighting: Assault resulted from officer intervening in fight between inmates.
- Movement: Assault took place during the movement of inmates from one part of the prison to another.
- Contraband: Assault followed a staff member suspecting an inmate of possessing contraband items.[22]

Officers in maximum-security prisons now generally prefer total lockup; they feel safer when inmates are in their cells twenty-four hours a day. Although tower positions are dead-end jobs, they are beginning to become desirable because they exclude contact with inmates. Thus, correctional officers, like inmates, serve time. The values they bring into the institution are reshaped by the necessities of institutional control and by nagging anxiety about their personal safety.

Correctional officers often express the conflict between inmates and officers with words of this nature: "They tell us that if we treated them like men, they would act like men. But we tell them that if they acted like men, we would treat them that way." They may go on to say, "Physical abuse follows verbal abuse, and we are getting a lot of verbal abuse."[23]

Staff Assaults on Inmates

Severe beatings of inmates by prison staff have occurred throughout much of U.S. corrections history.[24] All kinds of punitive and sadistic practices have taken place. James Marquart's examination of the maximum-security Eastham Unit in Texas in the 1980s found widespread staff brutality toward inmates. In explaining this abuse, Marquart concluded that physical coercion was deeply embedded in the guard subculture.[25]

Today, there is less evidence of staff's inappropriate use of force on inmates. Prisoners' rights organizations continue to accuse staffs of retaliating against rioting inmates after regaining control of the cellblock or prison.

h e r o e s   *Mark Colvin*

Professor of Sociology at George Mason University

"My interest in studying prisons began when I was an undergraduate student in a sociology of punishment and corrections class. This interest led me to seek employment in corrections after I graduated. I worked in the New Mexico Department of Corrections as a parole officer, prison education counselor, and correctional planner from 1975 to 1978. During that time I witnessed changes at the Penitentiary of New Mexico that had led to rising levels of violence by the time I left the prison in 1978. What I witnessed was similar to the organizational processes described in prison studies I had read as an undergraduate student. In 1979, I entered graduate school and wrote a class paper about the changes I had observed at the New Mexico prison from 1975 to 1978. I focused in the paper on the rapid changeover in top prison administrators, the disorganization in corrections management, the confusion in policies, and the greater reliance on coercive forms of control that preceded the rise in violence at this prison.

"When the riot broke out on February 2, 1980, the professor for whom I wrote the paper encouraged me to return to Santa Fe and get more information. I soon found myself in the office of the New Mexico attorney general, who was charged with investigating the causes of the riot. I had given him a copy of my student paper the previous day. After reading it, he offered me a position on the investigative team as a primary researcher into the causes of the riot. I then spent the next six months working with a highly dedicated team of investigators. We reviewed records and police evidence and conducted lengthy in-depth interviews with current and former staff members and inmates to reconstruct the gruesome events of the riot and the long-term history of the prison.

"In September 1980 we reported our findings, which were confirmed by independent investigations by several journalists and later by my own more in-depth study of the prison's history, contained in my book *From Accommodation to Riot: The Penitentiary of New Mexico in Crisis* (1992). The prison had gone through an enormous disruption of management from 1975 to 1980, with a rapid succession of five wardens and a turnover rate of correctional officers that reached 80 percent. Policy shifted away from an emphasis on rehabilitation programs, partly as a result of political shifts and a worsening economy outside the prison. Rehabilitation programs in the early 1970s had provided positive incentives for inmates to keep order in the prison because these programs gave a significant number of inmates something to lose by rebelling. Most of these programs had been eliminated by 1977. The lack of any coherent policy created a vacuum in which middle managers at the prison acted without guidance or accountability. They increasingly tried to maintain order with greater reliance on disciplinary lockdown and other coercive measures. They promoted a coercive "snitch" sys-

tem to force inmates to inform on each other. These coercive measures had the effects of creating heightened anger among inmates and of turning inmates against each other. Added to this, changes in sentencing policies led to overcrowded conditions, which only made tensions worse. As inmate anger grew and more and more inmates felt they had nothing to lose by rebelling, it was only a matter of time before this situation of turmoil and violence would be allowed (because of a series of security lapses) to explode into the most brutal riot in the U.S. prison history.

"The key lesson of this riot is that prisons are run most effectively when there is a stable and consistent correctional policy that provides a predictable set of positive incentives to gain inmate compliance. A degree of voluntary compliance is necessary for a safe prison environment, since staff members are greatly outnumbered by inmates and most inmate activities take place outside the surveillance of staff. Voluntary compliance is gained when inmates see that it is in their interest to help maintain order. Controlling inmate self-interest is the key to controlling prisons. A wide array of rehabilitation programs can provide a range of rewards and punishments that give inmates something to gain by conforming and something to lose by rebelling. Without this set of incentive controls, inmates perceive that they have nothing to lose by disrupting the prison.

"Recent get-tough policies make running prisons more difficult and the potential for violence more likely. Reductions in rehabilitation programs and prison overcrowding, which are the results of this effort to get tough, have reduced positive incentives that can be used to exercise effective inmate control. The reduction in positive incentives means that open displays of disorder (such as major riots) are only prevented with greater reliance on coercion, such as the growing trend toward super-max lockdown facilities. But super-max and other coercive controls are at best only a short-term, stopgap reaction. Even with super-max, inmate-on-inmate violence and attacks on correctional staff have remained at high levels in prisons. These coercive measures merely add more fuel to a potential explosion that may be temporarily contained by high-tech (and highly expensive) measures like super-max. But these measures do not eliminate the underlying causes of institutional violence that were highlighted in the investigation of the New Mexico prison riot. Effective control in prisons emerges from a coherent set of positive incentives that have their greatest effect when tied to a consistent and comprehensive program of inmate rehabilitation aimed at reintegrating offenders back into the community."

CRITICAL THINKING QUESTIONS

According to Mark Colvin, why did the New Mexico prison riot take place? What could have been done to prevent it? What does Colvin suggest would be helpful in preventing prison riots elsewhere?

This involuntary lockdown was a result of an inmate disturbance. What are the types of inmate disturbance, and how are they dealt with? What are some theories about the causes of inmate disturbances and prison riots? Has the incidence of prison riots increased or decreased since the 1970s? What factors might account for that trend? What factors affect prisons and prison life that, in turn, affect law and order in the prison?

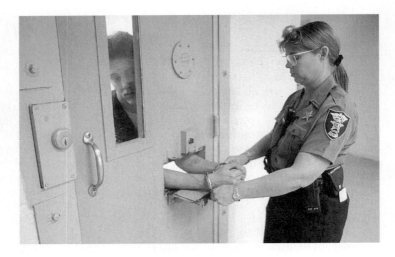

Most of the criticism of staffs' brutality against prisoners has come from those who have examined high-security unit or super-max prisons. Fay Dowker and Glenn Good document a number of instances of staffs' brutality in high security units or prisons. For example, in Missouri's Potosi Correctional Center, prison officials apply the "double-litter restraint" to difficult prisoners. The prisoner's hands are cuffed behind him; his ankles are cuffed, and he is forced to lie face down on a cot. A second cot is then tightly strapped upside-down over the inmate and the ends are strapped shut, which totally encloses and immobilized him.[26]

In recent years, as previously discussed, correctional officers in California's Corcoran and Pelican Bay Prisons have received the most attention for their use of force against inmates. From 1988 to 1996, correctional officers at Corcoran Prison shot and killed seven inmates and wounded about fifty others. Lieutenant Steve Riggs, who worked at Corcoran at the time, charged that "of all the shooting, right off the top of my head, I'd say about 80 percent of them are [inappropriate] shootings."[27]

Inmates versus Inmates

The prison environment combines a number of factors that contribute to inmates' assaults on each other. These factors include inadequate supervision by staff members, architectural designs that promote rather than inhibit victimization, the easy availability of deadly weapons, the housing of violence-prone inmates in close proximity to relatively defenseless victims, a high level of tension produced by close quarters and crosscutting conflicts among both individuals and groups of inmates, and feedback systems through which inmates feel the need to take revenge for real or imagined slights or past victimizations.[28]

In 1998, there were 27,169 inmate assaults on other inmates in U.S. correctional institutions. Of that number, 6,759 required medical attention and 1,350 were referred for prosecution. In California, there were 4,052 inmate assaults on inmates. Other states with large number of inmate-on-inmate assaults were Louisiana (2,809), New York (1,556), and Texas (1,510); and the Bureau of Prisons number was 1,382.[29]

Emotional harassment, physical assaults, rapes, stabbings, and homicides are part of prison life, especially in large maximum-security prisons. A misspoken word, a slight bump of another inmate, an unpaid gambling debt, a racial slur, or an invasion of an inmate's turf can provoke a violent attack. The failure of an expected visitor to appear, news about problems being experienced by a spouse or child, cancellation of a scheduled and looked-forward-to bit of entertainment, an unanticipated cell search, or an unusually hot and humid day also can produce explosive consequences.[30]

The divisions among inmates contribute to the unpredictable nature of prison violence. Some prison violence is gang and clique related. The cause of other violence lies in personal pathology, drug-induced hallucinations, or the danger of an accidental meeting. Most inmate violence appears to be of a situational nature, almost a chance occurrence—being in the wrong place at the wrong time.[31] Sylvester Sawyer and colleagues' national study found that the most frequent type of homicide (25 percent) had no apparent motive.[32] Research in California also found that the largest category of inmate-on-inmate assault (35 percent) fell into the category of "accidental, real or imagined insults combined with hypersensitivity."[33]

Understandably, inmates make every effort to protect themselves. Weaponry has replaced fists as the primary means of self-protection in male institutions. A variety of objects can be weapons: chisels, screwdrivers, sharpened shanks of spoons, broomsticks, baseball bats, clubs, chunks of concrete, stiff wire, heavy-gauge metal, metal from beds, boiler plate metal, and zip guns. Smuggled weapons also appear. Correctional officers collect barrelfuls of knives and other weapons during shakedowns in some institutions.

Sexual Victimization. Sex occurs in men's prisons in three contexts: consensual sex involving affection and sexual release; coercive sexual behavior that combines force and domination; and sex for hire, the purchase of sexual release at various levels of domination.[34] The violence and brutality of inmates toward other inmates is probably expressed more often in **sexual victimization** than in stabbings or slayings. Most first arrivals in prison, especially white males who have committed minor crimes, are "on trial." If they have the willingness and capacity to fight, they will usually pass the examination. If not, then prison time will indeed be "hard time."

The violent world of the prison remains a sexual jungle, especially in maximum-security prisons. "Sex and power go hand in hand in prison," C. Paul Phelps, former secretary of the Louisiana Department of Corrections, explains, "Deprived of the normal avenues, there are very few ways in prison for a man to show how powerful he is—and the best way to do so is for one to have a slave, another who is in total submission to him."[35] In Within the Walls 12.2, inmate Wilbert Rideau's prize-winning essay powerfully captures the importance of sex in prison.

within the walls 12.2

Sex in Prison

Man's greatest pain, whether in life or in prison, is the sense of personal insignificance, of being helpless and of no real value as a person, an individual—a man. Imprisoned and left without voice in or control over the things that affect him, his personal desires and feelings regarded with gracious indifference, and treated at best like a child and at worst like an animal by those having control of his life, a prisoner leads a life of acute deprivation and insignificance. The psychological pain involved in such an existence creates an urgent and terrible need for reinforcement of his sense of manhood and personal worth. Unfortunately, prison deprives those locked within of the normal avenues of pursuing gratification of their needs and leaves them no instruments but sex, violence, and conquest to validate their sense of manhood and individual worth. And they do, channeling all of their frustrated drives into the pursuit of power, finding gratification in the conquest and defeat, the domination, and subjugation of each other. Thus, the world of the prisoner is ruled by force, violence, and passions. Since the prison population consists of men whose sexuality, sense of masculinity, and sexual frame of reference are structured around women, weaker inmates are made to assume the role of "women," serving the strong, reinforcing their sense of manhood and personal importance, and providing them the gratification of their needs that would, in the normal world, be provided by women. Within the peculiar societal context, an exaggerated emphasis is placed on the status of "man," and the pursuit of power assumes overriding importance because power translates into security, prestige, physical and emotional gratification, wealth—survival.

> ...the world of the prisoner is ruled by force, violence, and passions.

CRITICAL THINKING QUESTIONS

How does Wilbert Rideau explain sexual exploitation in prison? Taking his argument a step further, what could be done to reduce sexual assaults in a prison setting?

Source: Reprinted from Wilbert Rideau, "The Sexual Jungle," in *Life Sentences: Rage and Survival behind Bars,* ed., Wilbert Rideau and Ron Wikberg (New York: Times Books, 1992), pp. 74–75.

Daniel Lockwood found that in the correctional settings he studied in New York State, violent sexual incidents among men in prison fell into two groups. In the first group, aggressors use violence to coerce their targets. The causes of this violence can be traced to subcultural values upholding the right to use force to gain sexual privileges. In the second group, targets react violently to propositions viewed as threatening. In other words, victims, or targets, have a tendency to answer sexual propositions with counterthreats.[36] Hans Toch adds that some prisoners use violence against those who make sexual approaches to them in order to get the predators to leave them alone.[37] Lockwood concluded that because violent incidents in prison appear to be divided about equally between these two categories, programs to reduce prison sexual violence should be aimed at both targets and aggressors.[38]

There is wide agreement that new inmates in maximum-security prison will be tested sexually, but there is disagreement about how frequently sexual victimization will take place in the prison. Regardless of whether sexual assaults are seen as epidemic or as relatively infrequent, few would deny that sexual victimization has many unfortunate effects. It curbs victims' freedom to act; indeed, many victims feel that their only viable alternative is to check into **protective custody.** Sexual victimization also leads to feelings of helplessness and depression, fear of AIDS, damaged self-esteem, possible self-destructive acts such as self-mutilation or suicide, lowered social status, psychosomatic illnesses, sometimes increased difficulty in adjusting to life after release, and possibly even increased risk of recidivism.[39]

Self-Inflicted Violence

Ex-offenders, in discussing prison suicides, frequently put it this way: "They couldn't handle it; prison was too much for them."[40] In 1996, there were 154 suicides in this nation's prisons.[41] However, cases clearly are missing from these official suicide counts because they were counted as something else. Some prison homicides are suicides, because inmates let themselves be murdered by violent inmates. Inmates have been known to charge the fence, knowing that guards will shoot them down. Furthermore, prisoners on death row who have lost their will to live may call off their appeals, letting the state carry out the suicidal act.[42]

There are several times as many attempted suicides as there are actual suicides. It is difficult to estimate accurately the number of genuinely self-destructive acts and to differentiate them from acts by inmates seeking attention or wishing to receive protection. What is common among inmates who engage in self-destructive acts is a sense of desperation or hopelessness.

The motivation for prison suicide seems to be fear or loss: fear of other prisoners or imprisonment, or the loss of a significant relationship. Most suicides take place by hanging and at night. They also are more likely to occur on weekends and during the summer months. In addition, a slightly disproportionate number occurs in special locations, such as in segregation, health care centers, and other areas of seclusion.[43]

Three types of inmates seem to be likely candidates for self-inflicted injuries in correctional institutions. First are the inmates who do not have a criminal history and are embarrassed because of the grief they have brought on themselves and their families. These persons generally inflict injury on themselves soon after admission to the prison. Second are the inmates who have been confined in prison for months or years and have developed feelings of hopelessness about the future. Third are antisocial persons who exhibit suicidal behavior in order to manipulate others; they tend to choose methods that will ensure their survival.[44]

Prison suicide is most common among young unmarried white males. Suicide generally occurs early in confinement, and hanging is the usual method. Inmates also use razor blades to mutilate themselves. If razor blades are not available, fragments of metal, glass, wire, or even eating utensils can be transformed into lethal instruments. Swallowing objects or toxic substances, such as mercury from a thermometer, is sometimes tried.[45]

WHAT ARE THE CAUSES OF PRISON VIOLENCE?

The violent characteristics of inmates, social factors, and structural and institutional factors are the main causes of violence within the walls. The most important social factors are racial unrest, the presence of organized gangs within the walls, and the use of drugs by the inmate population. Prison overcrowding is the main institutional factor contributing to violence.

Violent Characteristics of Inmates

Four personal factors seem directly related to violent behavior in prison: youth, lower-class attitudes, fear of humiliation, and a personal history of violent behavior.[46] Prisons are filled with men and women between the ages of 18 and 30. Generally, these young people seem less receptive than their elders to institutional control because they had few responsibilities before imprisonment, have spent less time in prison and therefore are less prepared to submit to discipline, and are not firmly established in an occupation.

Most offenders are lower-class males who carry with them subcultural values and attitudes that quickly erupt into violence. These inmates often regard superior strength as a criterion of maleness and retaliate quickly for any episode that they consider to be an attack on their manhood. Individuals unwilling to resort to physical combat are contemptible in their eyes. They prefer privately administered justice, taking punishment into their own hands. They have learned that survival on the streets and in prison depends on the intimidation of others, the exploitation of the weak, and the protection of oneself.

Fear of humiliation is an important underlying reason for cultivating an image as a "badass," someone whom other people do not dare confront. As inmates vie for violent reputations, confrontational incidents increase, especially among younger inmates. Winners in this violent competition for the "badass" role gain power in the inmate social structure. Losers become victims.[47] Inmates of the state penitentiary in New Mexico told Colvin that they placed a premium on gaining a reputation for violence.

> "The young ones, I don't know, I guess they're trying to think they are cool. They walk around pushing everybody around. They're just trying to get them a name, a reputation," said an inmate. "They want to be recognized as being real tough," added another inmate. "This new generation is very aggressive. . . . They're all out to build a reputation here quick. As quick as possible. . . . They don't care if they leave or not," said a third inmate.[48]

It does not take much for an interaction to erupt into a violent incident: sense of disrespect, a face-to-face conflict with a rival gang member, a desire for retaliation, or a feeling of intoxication. The propensity for violence also extends to those who feel powerless, mistreated, sexually frustrated, bored, and hopeless.[49]

Social Factors

The social factors most likely to contribute to prison violence are racial unrest, the presence of organized gangs, and drug use.

Racial Unrest.   In the traditional prison, African Americans were usually docile. Then in the late 1960s and early 1970s African American prisoners began to use the perspective of black power to integrate their role as prisoners in an oppressive and corrupt state.[50] Still, the debasement and degradation of being an inmate posed serious threats to self-esteem, and increasing numbers of African Americans began to conclude that one way to regain some sense of self-pride was to dominate and exploit whites in every possible way.[51] Leo Carroll quotes an African American inmate in Rhode Island who explained why African Americans exploited whites:

> To the general way of thinking it's cause they're confined and they got hard rocks. But that ain't it at all. It's a way for the black man to get back at the white man. It's one way he can assert his manhood. Anything white, even a defenseless punk, is part of what the black man hates. It's part of what he's had to fight all his life just to survive, just to have a hole to sleep in and some garbage to eat. . . . It's a new ego thing. He can show he's a man by making a white guy into a girl.[52]

In Texas prisons, whites grew increasingly fearful of African Americans in the 1980s. An African American inmate echoed the prisoner in Rhode Island: "Yeah, we got an attitude toward whites. Why not? The reason I say this is because the white inmates have always more or less run this farm [Eastham]. This place has always been a white boy's farm, so our attitude is kind of bitter."[53]

By the 1990s, prisons were more racially polarized than ever before. Within each group there was at least one leader. Racial tension and hostility became so intense that different racial and ethnic groups avoided each other as much as possible. They sat on different sides of the dining room and had their own "space" in the yard. They stayed apart when attending church and when assembling to watch movies or television. Even a slight disagreement among races—for example, over changing a television station— could quickly spark violence. If an inmate was stabbed and the stabbing did not appear to have racial overtones, there might not be any problems. But if a person from one racial or ethnic group stabbed an inmate from a different group, retaliation usually followed.

Inmate Gangs.   Prison gangs exist in forty states and in the Federal Bureau of Prisons (see Figure 12.1). In some states, especially California, Illinois, and Texas, prison gangs are the dominant force in inmate life. In nearly all of the other states that have prison gangs, they pose security problems and cause increased levels of violence.

Prison gangs vary from loosely organized to highly organized and structured groups. The gangs that reconstituted from the streets of cities in California and Illinois are particularly highly organized. For example, the Conservative Vice Lords, a Chicago-based

Figure 12.1
States with Prison Gangs

Source: Reprinted with permission from American Correctional Association, *Gangs in Correctional Institutions: A National Assessment* (Laurel, Md., ACA, 1993), pp. 8–9.

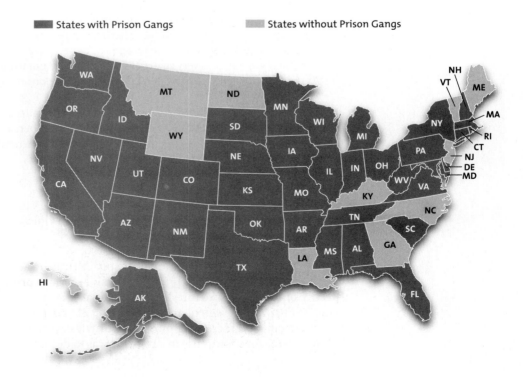

street gang, has eleven divisions. This gang, as well as other Chicago "supergangs," has a well-established leadership structure and clearly defined social norms. Violations of these social norms bring punishment ranging from a beating to death.[54]

Prison gangs spread from one state to another in several ways. Inmate gang members may be transferred to a federal or another state correctional institution, where they spread their gang's ideas. Gang members who move from one state to another and are then imprisoned for criminal activities may organize a gang in the prison. Also, the leaders of some street gangs send gang members to other states specifically to establish a gang organization, and those organizers end up in prison after committing a crime.

In California, the Mexican Mafia (chiefly from East Los Angeles) vies for power with the Nuestra Familia (consisting of rural Chicanos). Chicanos join gangs when it is necessary to fight the whites and the African Americans. African Americans in California are organized into the Black Guerrilla Family, the Black Muslims, the Black Panthers, and other groups; the Neo-Nazis and the Aryan Brotherhood are white gangs that have organized to provide protection against abuse and intimidation.

In the Illinois prison system, the Black P Stone Nations, the Black Gangster Disciple Nation, the Conservative Vice Lords, and the Latin Kings vie for control. James Jacobs claims that the most important factor contributing to violence at Stateville was the presence of these four Chicago street gangs.[55] All of these "supergangs" originated in the slums of Chicago, and many of the leading figures were gang leaders when in free society. Jacobs found that formal agreements among the gang leaders assured incarcerated members that members of other gangs would not molest them. Inmates unaffiliated with a gang—around 50 percent of the Stateville population—were fair game for thievery, intimidation, blackmail, assault, and sexual pressure.[56]

Prison gangs in Texas are also increasing their control over prison life. Formed in 1975 by a group of prisoners who had served time in the California prison system, the Texas Syndicate is the oldest and the second largest inmate gang in the Texas prison system. The Mexican Mafia, or MEXIKANEMI (Soldiers of Azthan), is only a few years old, but it is the largest inmate gang in Texas. The Aryan Brotherhood of Texas and the Texas Mafia are two other powerful inmate gangs. Figure 12.2 shows the tattoo insignia of these four gangs.

Texas Syndicate

Aryan Brotherhood of Texas

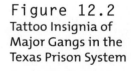

Figure 12.2
Tattoo Insignia of Major Gangs in the Texas Prison System

Source: Ben M. Crouch and James W. Marquart, *An Appeal to Justice: Litigated Reform of Texas Prisons* (Austin: University of Texas Press, 1989). p. 210.

Mexikanemi (Mexican Mafia)

Texas Mafia

Both the Texas Syndicate and the Mexican Mafia are organized along paramilitary lines. Regardless of rank, both inmate gangs require their members to abide by a strict code of conduct known as the "Constitution."[57]

The Bureau of Prisons identifies the Aryan Brotherhood, Mexican Mafia, Texas Syndicate, and Black Guerrilla Family as particularly troublesome for prison officials. In addition, the BOP has identified as "security threat groups" other gangs such as the Arizona Aryan Brotherhood, Black Gangster Disciples, Hells Angels, and Jamaican Posse.[58]

Prison gangs usually specialize in economic victimization. They typically force all independent operators out of business and either divide among themselves the spoils of drugs, gambling rackets, and prostitution rings, or they fight to the death to determine who will establish a monopoly within the prison.[59] High levels of violence may occur when gangs are in conflict with each other. Interracial conflict also disrupts institutional life when large gangs organized along racial and ethnic lines make it a deliberate policy to attack other racial and ethnic gangs.

The gangs from Chicago exemplify the problems that can exist when leaders of street gangs are sent to prison. One problem is that the incarcerated gang leader may continue to have some influence on what takes place in the community. He maintains his influence by phone and visits. In view of the fact that prison officials usually monitor phone calls, some gangs develop a code to communicate the wishes of the gang leader. Another problem is that imprisoned gang leaders usually have tight control over what takes place within the prison where they are confined and, sometimes, throughout the prison system. In the late 1980s, leaders of the two largest Chicago gangs, Larry Hoover of the Gangster Disciples and Willie Johnson of the Vice Lords, joined together to deescalate interpersonal violence among prisoners throughout the Illinois prison system. Prison officials quickly noticed that levels of violence fell dramatically. But imprisoned gang leaders also have incited prison disturbances, the taking of hostages, and inmates' refusal to work or come out of their cells.[60]

Use of Drugs. In examining the use of drugs by prisoners in 1996, the Bureau of Justice Statistics found that 42.6 percent had taken drugs on a daily basis in the month before the current offense, 35.3 percent were under the influence of drugs at the time of their offense, and 62.3 percent had used drugs on a regular basis.[61]

Colvin documented the relationship between drugs and violent behavior at the New Mexico State Prison. Drug consumption there increased dramatically from about 1971 to 1976, as did the number of inmate groups involved in trafficking. Staff toleration for, and in some cases collusion with, drug trafficking became an important feature of social control during these years. Inmates were willing to "keep the lid" on the prison, because they did not want drug connections jeopardized or "heat" brought on traffickers. But when a new administration took office in 1975, curtailment of drug use within the penitentiary became one of its major goals. More drug searches took place, and possible conduits by which drugs were brought into the institution were closed. The removal of incentives in drug trafficking disrupted inmate sources of nonviolent power, and a power vacuum developed, triggering a struggle for power among the inmates. As nonviolent sources of power diminished, power became increasingly based on violence. Violence begets violence, and, according to Colvin, "a reputation for violence became a necessary requisite for survival—and especially for protection from sexual assault."[62]

Structural and Institutional Factors

Prison violence also results from the double- and triple-celling of inmates; indefensible space; the frustration of living in a setting characterized by filth, lack of privacy, and enforced idleness from lack of jobs; the easy availability of violent weapons; a gener-

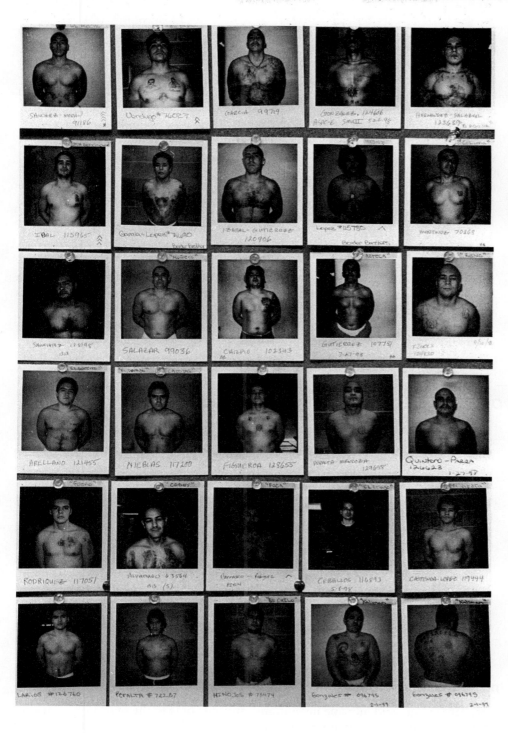

These Mexican American inmates were members of a prison gang called the Border Brothers. Gang activities account for much of the violence that plagues prisons. What are some examples of prison gang activities? What specific benefits and threats can gang membership confer on inmates? What causes gang violence, and what have been some effective measures for reducing prison violence?

ally high level of tension because of the deprivations of prison life; and a crisis of authority within the walls. Most of these structural factors relate to overcrowding.

Overcrowding contributes to the victimization of weak prisoners. When two or three inmates are placed in a cell, the weakest is clearly vulnerable to the demands of the strongest. In a cell housing three, it is usually two against one. The great amount of **indefensible space** in most prison compounds makes it difficult for staff to protect the weak from predatory peers. In the conventional prison, the weak have few places to go for protection.

Violence also arises from the lack of private space. Violence-prone people particularly need space, but, in prison they are placed with at least one other person in 6-by-9-foot cells. This arrangement increases tension and reduces the options in conflict resolution. The easy availability of weapons, usually made by the inmates themselves, provides a lethal means of striking out at others.

Overcrowding means that more inmates are idle and fewer inmates can participate in the institutional programs or receive the prison industry assignments they desire. Crowded conditions also mean a more stressful environment and possibly adverse effects on health.[63] Younger inmates tend to respond in more violent ways to crowded conditions than do older ones, and white inmates frequently have more problems with crowding than do minority inmates.[64]

In short, the prison is a violent environment because the characteristics of inmates combine with abnormal social factors and institutional imperfections to generate aggression and violence. The claim can be made, of course, that the prison is not as violent as some of the neighborhoods from which prisoners came, but this is difficult to substantiate. It does appear that institutional violence is tapering off as administrators regain some control. For example, the period from 1985 to 1995 was less violent than the decade before. Yet most prison staff, as well as inmates, continue to see violence as one of the most troubling problems of prison life.

HOW CAN PRISON VIOLENCE BE REDUCED?

Many factors leading to violence are beyond the control of prison officials. Among them are the size of prisons and the crowding of facilities; the enforced idleness of too many inmates; inadequate financial support from the state legislature; public indifference; and the increasing number of violent and aggressive criminals, including gang members from the streets, being sentenced to prison. Furthermore, prison officials cannot alter the belief of prisoners that the only way they can gain the public's attention and overcome public apathy is through institutional violence.

Institutional violence, which varies in seriousness and expression from state to state, may possibly be reduced by these methods: making the prison more humane, improving the quality of correctional leadership, improving the training of staff, better screening to identify the violent and vulnerable, making prison space defensible, denying recognition to inmate gangs, and incarceration in super-max prisons and high-security units.

More Humane Institutions

Smaller facilities and humane institutions can contribute to the reduction of institutional violence. Large, maximum-security prisons are the most likely to have frequent and violent inmate disturbances.[65] Large prisons have difficulty providing services to inmates, and the lack of services generates considerable animosity. Large institutions also find it more difficult to control the possession of weapons and drug trafficking.

Effective Correctional Administration

A breakdown in administrative control and operation is usually found in a riot-prone prison. Typical elements of this breakdown include scandals, escapes, inconsistent rules for inmates and guards, fragmentation, instability within the system, conflict between administration and guards, and the disruption of everyday routines for eating, work, and recreation. Poorly managed prisons, lacking stability and uniformity, perpetuate the feelings among inmates that they must do something about the inadequate conditions of their confinement.[66]

Line Staff and Defusing Violence

Correctional systems are beginning to discover that one of the most effective ways to defuse violence is by having well-trained line staff. California sends correctional staff to conflict-resolution training as a means of handling tension within the walls.[67] Most states are aware that the recruitment of staff members from minority groups is another helpful factor in controlling prison violence. A higher percentage of minority staff eliminates many of the problems created when a core group of white guards control predominantly African American inmates.

Correctional Ombudsmen

Ombudsmen are public officials who investigate complaints in the prison and recommend corrective action. Ombudsmen demonstrate integrity in their dealings with inmates and staff can often resolve some of the tension-producing prison problems that lead to violence. Ombudsmen also serve as a channel of information from inmates to administrators and can focus attention on conditions and situations appearing to be most conducive to victimization.[68]

Adequate Screening

Better **screening of the vulnerable** can reduce violence. Special programs and isolation cells can be provided for emotionally disturbed, disabled, or defenseless inmates. Another strategy is to remove the weak from the presence of the strong through a classification process that would prevent violent and nonviolent prisoners from being housed together. Some states protect inmates who are informants, delinquent debtors, or homosexual targets by assigning them to institutions restricted to those who could not survive in other correctional facilities.

Defensible Prison Space

Victimization rates tend to be high in areas of prisons that are hard for the staff to see. Thus violence can be reduced by making prison space defensible. For example, removing the roof from a covered walkway will give tower guards an open view of the walkway. A cul-de-sac in a hallway that precludes staff observation can be walled off or monitored with a remote television camera.[69]

Gang Control

The lockup, punitive segregation, institutional transfers, and denying recognition are the four most widely used methods to deal with gang control, and all four have shortcomings. Wardens and superintendents can always resort to the lockup to keep the lid on gang violence. Keeping gang members in their cells twenty-three hours a day may enable staff to regain control of the institution, but ultimately gang members must be released from their cells, and the repressed tension may create even greater problems. Institutional transfers, of course, permit prison administrators to send troublemaking inmates, including gang members, to other institutions, but this merely spreads the problem from one prison to another. Indeed, one of the reasons why gangs have spread throughout the nation is the policy of institutional transfers for troublemaking inmates. The best strategy to control gangs at the present time appears to be for the entire department of corrections to adopt a policy of denying recognition to gangs.

Super-Max Prisons and High-Security Units

A widely used strategy by departments of corrections and the Federal Bureau of Prisons is to send violence-prone inmates to newly created super-max prisons or high security units. Correctional administrators contend that such placements are deescalating violence within their correctional systems. For example, the Security Threat Group Management Unit in the Northern State Prison in Newark, New Jersey opened in March 1998 to stem a rise in gang membership. For the first ten months of 1999, the number of assaults on staff was down 30 percent from the same period two years before—from 578 to 405. The number of times that inmates were cited for group demonstration dropped by 85 percent since the unit was opened—from 352 to 53.[70]

SUMMARY

The abnormal social environment and institutional and structural imperfections combine to produce violent surroundings within the contemporary prison. Overcrowding, the drug appetites of prisoners, and racial and gang skirmishes seem to be the most important factors that create an incendiary situation. If inmates can be tough enough, they will turn themselves into the worst kind of predators, forcing themselves on the weak and enjoying the spoils of their predation. The background of prisoners suggests that there will always be some institutional violence, but violence, predation, and corruption need not have the upper hand. The fact remains that creating a lawful prison—in which compliance with the law and reasonable regulations prevail—will be no easy task. Prison violence can be reduced with such strategies as more humane institutions, effective correctional administration, adequate screening of inmates, and more secure placements of out-of-control inmates.

KEY TERMS

building tenders, p. 283
indefensible space, p. 295
inmate code, p. 283
inmate disturbance, p. 285

protective custody, p. 290
riot, p. 285
screening of the vulnerable, p. 297
sexual victimization, p. 289

CRITICAL THINKING QUESTIONS

1. Draw a mental picture of a prison. What security features will you include? What might you have forgotten?
2. Some observers say that prisoners applying for protective custody do so in order to enjoy "easy time." How would you make certain that a prisoner applying for protective custody really needed protection?
3. Gangs are the most powerful social units in some prisons. How do gangs escalate violence in the cellhouse?
4. Crowding, filth, deprivation, and enforced idleness—what effect do these conditions of prison life have on prison behavior?
5. Violence is not only other-directed. Which prisoners are most likely to be their own victims? Why?
6. Can prisoner violence be reduced? How? Will any one method do it?

WEB DESTINATIONS

Read an article on how a New Jersey prison responded to inmate violence by implementing a get-tough approach.
http://www.nj.com/jersey/ledger/e4992f.html

This is the story of Attica.
http://www.acsu.buffalo.edu/~bjackson/attica.htm

Read a government report on how eight federal and state prisons have dealt successfully with inmate riots.
http://www.soci.niu.edu/~critcrim/escapes/prisriot.txt

Read about innovations in prison security at the site of the National Law Enforcement and Corrections Technology Center.
http://www.nlectc.org/

This account describes and assesses the suicides of Native American women in a Canadian provincial prison.
http://nativenet.uthscsa.edu/archive/nl/9606/0007.html

FOR FURTHER READING

Attica: The Official Report of the New York State Special Commission on Attica. New York: Praeger, 1972. This official report on the Attica riot is required reading for the serious student of corrections.

Braswell, Michael C., Reid H. Montgomery Jr., and Lucien X. Lombardo, eds. *Prison Violence in America.* 2d ed. Cincinnati: Anderson, 1994. This reader provides a good overview of institutional violence.

Bottoms, Anthony E. "Interpersonal Violence and Social Order in prisons," in *Prisons,* ed. Michael Tonry and Joan Petersilia (Chicago: University of Chicago Press, 1999), pp. 205–281. The most current and comprehensive study of prison violence.

Carroll, Leo. *Hacks, Blacks, and Cons: Race Relations in a Maximum Security Prison.* Lexington, Mass.: Heath, 1974. Carroll portrays the growing racial conflict between blacks and whites in a prison in the Northeast.

Colvin, Mark. *From Accommodation to Riot: The Penitentiary of New Mexico in Crisis.* Albany: State University of New York Press, 1990. An excellent study of the 1980 riot at the state penitentiary of New Mexico.

Crouch, Ben M., and James W. Marquart. *An Appeal to Justice: Litigated Reform of Texas Prisons.* Austin: University of Texas Press, 1989. The authors depict the escalating violence in the state prisons of Texas with the *Ruiz* decision.

Fleisher, Mark S. *Warehousing Violence.* Newbury Park, Calif.: Sage, 1989. Fleisher examines the methods of social control used to maintain order at Lompoc, a federal institution in California.

Irwin, John. *Prisons in Turmoil.* Boston: Little, Brown, 1980. A lively account of the social factors behind the violence in today's prisons.

Liebling, Alison. "Prison Suicide and Prisoner Coping," in *Prison,* ed. Michael Tonry and Joan Petersilia (Chicago: University of Chicago Press, 1999), pp. 283–359. A up-to-date examination of prison suicide.

Useem, Bert, and Peter A. Kimball. *States of Siege: U.S. Prison Riots, 1971–1986.* New York: Oxford University Press, 1989. A first-rate study of the Attica, New Mexico, Michigan, Joliet, and West Virginia penitentiary riots.

NOTES

1. *Attica: The Official Report of the New York State Special Commission on Attica* (New York: Praeger, 1972), p. xi.
2. Appendix C in Bert Useem and Peter Kimball, *States of Siege: U.S. Prison Riots, 1971–1986* (New York: Oxford University Press, 1989), p. 238.
3. See ibid., Ch. 3.
4. Ibid., p. 3. Reid H. Montgomery Jr. and his colleagues' examination of prison riots documented two hundred riots between 1900 and 1970. See Montgomery, "American Prison Riots: 1774–1991," in *Prison Violence in America,* 2d ed., ed. Michael C. Braswell, Reid H. Montgomery Jr., and Lucien X. Lombardo (Cincinnati: Anderson, 1994), p. 227.
5. Braswell, Montgomery, and Lombardo divided prison violence into these two categories. See Braswell, Montgomery Jr., and Lombardo, *Prison Violence in America,* 2d ed.
6. Anthony E. Bottoms, "Interpersonal Violence and Social Order in Prisons," in *Prisons,* ed. Michael Tonry and Joan Petersilia (Chicago: University of Chicago Press, 1999), p. 206.
7. Ibid.
8. Ibid., p. 251
9. Ibid.
10. Gresham Sykes, *Society of Captives* (Princeton, N.J.: Princeton University Press, 1958.
11. *Ruiz v. Estelle,* 811 F.2d 856 (1987).
12. Simon Dinitz, "Are Safe and Humane Prisons Possible?" *Australia and New Zealand Journal of Criminology* 14 (March 1981), pp. 3–4.

13. Bert Useem et al., *Resolution of Prison Riots* (Washington, D.C.: National Institute of Justice, 1995).

14. Ibid.

15. George W. Knox, "Preliminary Results of the 1995 Adult Corrections Survey," *Journal of Gang Research* 3 (Winter 1996), p. 42.

16. *News-Journal Online,* 4 August 1998.

17. Jennifer Stump, "Unit Riots at Beeville Prison," *Caller* 21 December 1999.

18. Richard Hawkins and Geoffrey P. Alpert, *American Prison Systems: Punishment and Justice* (Englewood Cliffs, N.J.: Prentice-Hall, 1989), p. 254.

19. Mark Colvin, *From Accommodation to Riot: The Penitentiary of New Mexico in Crisis* (Albany: State University of New York Press, 1992).

20. Camille Graham Camp and George M. Camp, *The Corrections Yearbook 1999: Adult Corrections* (Middletown, Conn.: Criminal Justice Institute, 1999), p. 41.

21. S. C. Light, "Assaults on Prison Officers: Interactional Themes," *Justice Quarterly* 78 (1991), pp. 243–251.

22. Ibid.

23. Correctional officers have made such comments to the author on various occasions.

24. For a history of violent behavior by staff members, see Mark Fleisher, *Warehousing Violence* (Newbury Park, Calif.: Sage, 1989).

25. Ben M. Crouch and James W. Marquart, *An Appeal to Justice: Litigated Reform of Texas Prisons* (Austin: University of Texas Press, 1989).

26. Fay Dowker and Glenn Good, "The Proliferation of Control Unit Prisons in the United States," *Journal of Prisoners on Prisons* 4 (1993), pp. 95–110; Holly J. Buckhalter, "Torture in U.S. Prisons," *The Nation,* 3 July 1995, pp. 17–18.

27. Don Knapp, "California Prison at Center of Violence Accusations," *CNN Interactive,* 22 November 1996.

28. Colvin, *From Accomodation to Riot.*

29. Camp and Camp, *The Corrections Yearbook 1999,* p. 41.

30. Hawkins and Alpert, *American Prison Systems,* p. 268.

31. Sawyer Sylvester, John R. Reed, and David O. Nelson, *Prison Homicide* (New York: Spectrum, 1977), p. 80.

32. Ibid.

33. John J. Gibbs, "Violence in Prison," in *Critical Issues in Corrections,* ed. by R. R. Roberg and V. J. Webb (St. Paul, Minn.: West, 1981), pp. 121–122.

34. Hawkins and Alpert, *American Prison Systems,* p. 275.

35. Quoted in Wilbert Rideau, "The Sexual Jungle," in *Life Sentences: Rage and Survival behind Bars,* ed. by Wilbert Rideau and Ron Wikberg (New York: Times Books, 1992), p. 75.

36. Daniel Lockwood, "Reducing Prison Sexual Violence," in *The Pains of Imprisonment,* ed. by Robert Johnson and Hans Toch (Beverly Hills, Calif.: Sage, 1982), p. 257.

37. Hans Toch, "Institutional Violence Code, Tentative Code of the Classification of Inmate Assaults on Other Inmates" (report prepared for the California Department of Corrections Research Division, September 1965).

38. Lockwood, "Reducing Prison Sexual Violence," p. 257.

39. Lee H. Bowker, "Victimizers and Victims in American Correctional Institutions," in *The Pains of Imprisonment,* p. 64.

40. Interviewed correctional officers have made such statements.

41. Bureau of Justice Statistics, *Correctional Populations in the United States, 1996* (Washington, D.C.: U.S. Department of Justice, 1999), p. 95.

42. Hawkins and Alpert, *American Prison Systems,* p. 294.

43. Alison Liebling, "Prison Suicide and Prisoner Coping," in *Prisons,* p. 297.

44. Bruce L. Danto, "The Suicidal Inmate," in *Jail House Blues* (Orchard Lake, Mich.: Epic Publications, 1973), pp. 20–21.

45. Hawkins, *American Prison Systems,* pp. 295–296.

46. Albert K. Cohen, "Prison Violence: A Sociological Perspective," in *Prison Violence,* ed. by Albert K. Cohen, George F. Cole, and Robert C. Bailey (Lexington, Mass.: Heath, 1976), pp. 10–14. See also Bottoms "Interpersonal Violence and Social Order in Prisons" p. 227.

47. Colvin, *From Accommodation to Riot.*

48. Ibid.

49. Fleisher, *Warehousing Violence.*

50. Leo Carroll, *Hacks, Blacks, and Cons: Race Relations in a Maximum Security Prison* (Lexington, Mass.: Heath, 1974).

51. Leo Carroll, "Race, Ethnicity, and the Social Order of the Prison," in *The Pains of Imprisonment,* pp. 184–185.

52. Carroll, *Hacks, Blacks, and Cons,* pp. 184–185.

53. Crouch and Marquart, *An Appeal to Justice,* p. 193.

54. Information collected from interviews with leaders of the Conservative Vice Lords.

55. James B. Jacobs, *Stateville: The Penitentiary in Mass Society* (Chicago: University of Chicago Press, 1977), p. 146.

56. Ibid.

57. See Crouch and Marquart, *An Appeal to Justice.*

58. D. Orlando-Morningstar, *Prison Gangs* (Washington, D.C.: Federal Judicial Center, 1997).

59. Ibid., and Lee Bowker, *Prison Victimization* (New York: Elsevier, 1980).

60. Information derived from interviews with Hoover and Johnson.

61. Bureau of Justice Statistics, *Correctional Populations in the United States, 1996,* p. 95.

62. Colvin, *From Accommodation to Riot.*

63. James Bonta and Paul Gendreau, "Reexamining the Cruel and Unusual Punishment of Prison Life," in *Prison Violence in America,* pp. 39–68.

64. Ibid.

65. Peter Scharf, "Empty Bars: Violence and the Crisis of Meaning in Prison," in *Prison Violence in America,* p. 32.

66. Useem and Kimball, *States of Siege,* pp. 218–219.

67. Ibid., p. 220.

68. Lucien X. Lombardo, "Alleviating Inmate Stress: Contributions from Correctional Officers," in *The Pains of Imprisonment,* p. 287.

69. Bowker, "Victimizers and Victims in American Correctional Institutions," p. 72.

70. Brian Donohue, "Harsh Unit Is Prison's Answer to Violence," *The (Newark, N.J.) Star-Ledger,* 23 January 2000.

CHAPTER 12 / BUILT-IN STUDY GUIDE

Multiple Choice Questions

1. All of the following are forms of institutional violence except:

    A. Riots
    B. Victimization of one inmate by another
    C. Inmate assaults on staff
    D. Use of electronic stun guns on inmates by staff

2. What was the ruling of the *Ruiz v. Estelle* decision?

    A. The Texas Department of Correction's building tender system was unconstitutional
    B. The use of inmates in work detail assignments was protected by the Fourteenth Amendment
    C. Inmates were required to have minimal due process proceedings prior to having their good time credits taken
    D. Denying inmate visitation privileges was determined cruel and unusual punishment

3. In the Attica riot inmates had all of the following except:

    A. A high degree of organization
    B. Solidarity
    C. Political consciousness
    D. Dysfunctional leadership

4. Which of the following was the most brutal riot in U.S. prison history?

    A. Attica
    B. Santa Fe
    C. West Virginia Penitentiary
    D. Atlanta Federal Penitentiary

5. All of the following are factors that contribute to inmates' assaults on each other except:

    A. Inadequate supervision by staff
    B. Easy availability of deadly weapons
    C. Increase aging of the inmate population
    D. Architectural designs that promote rather than inhibit victimization

6. Identify the most significant structural factor that contributes to prison violence.

    A. Overcrowded conditions
    B. Social factors
    C. Racial unrest
    D. Presence of organized gangs

7. All of the following are widely used measures that address gang control except:

    A. Lockup
    B. Punitive segregation
    C. Interstate transfers
    D. Institutional transfers

8. Correctional systems have started to discover that one of the most effective ways to calm a potentially violent incident is:

    A. Staff who have military experience
    B. Well-trained staff
    C. Staff who are experts in physical force
    D. Staff who are young

9. All of the following are contexts in which sex occurs in prisons except:

    A. Consensual sex involving affection
    B. Coercive sexual behavior that combines force and domination
    C. Sex for hire
    D. Sex in the emotional development of male inmate families.

10. How is voluntary compliance from inmates gained in a prison environment?

    A. Through coercion
    B. Through exchange relationships
    C. When inmates see it is in their interest to help maintain order
    D. Through a military model of administration

11. According to Denny Fitzpatrick, what element of the correctional officer's roles and responsibilities has changed since the Attica riot that has influenced the relationship between staff and inmates as well as inmate behavior?

    A. Correctional officers no longer file an evaluation of inmate behavior report to the parole board
    B. Correctional officers are now required to file an evaluation of inmate behavior report to the parole board
    C. Correctional officers no longer serve as counselors to inmates
    D. Correctional officers now serve as counselors to inmates

True/False Questions

T F   1. According to the correctional officer, the break-down of social order that results with inmates having all the power is the cause of institutional violence.

T F   2. Recent get-tough policies make operating a prison easier and the potential for violence less likely.

T F   3. A level of voluntary compliance from inmates is necessary for a safe prison environment.

T F   4. The average number of inmate assaults on staff increased throughout the 1990s.

T F   5. Staff assaults on inmates have just recently been recorded and become a problem for U.S. correctional institutions.

T F   6. Prison gangs usually specialize in economic victimization.

T F   7. Inmate behavior resulting in self-injuries occurs among those who have developed a feeling of hopelessness and futility about the future.

T F   8. In the 1990s, prisons had become more racially polarized than at any time in the history of U.S. corrections.

T F   9. Controlling inmates' self-interest is not related to controlling prisons.

T F   10. The 1980 New Mexico riot showed a degree of improvement in the area of inmate relationships since the early 1970s.

T F   11. Recently, positive incentives that can be used to exercise effective inmate control have been affected by a reduction in rehabilitation programs.

Fill-in-the-Blank Questions   (based on key terms)

1. The _____ system gave authority and power to a select group of inmates to discipline other inmates who violated institutional rules and regulations.

2. Hunger strikes, sit-down strikes, work stoppages, and voluntary lockdowns are all examples of nonviolent _____.

3. Inmate violence directed toward other inmates is expressed most frequently through _____.

4. This type of _____, referred to as a violent uprising, has patterns of widespread arson and vandalism.

5. An area of the prison that is less visible to staff members is known as _____.

Essay Questions

1. Identify and explain the various ways institutional violence is expressed.

2. Compare the 1980 New Mexico riot with the 1971 Attica riot. Characterize inmate relationships as well as the degree of organization in each. What contributed to each riot?

3. What are the different types of prison violence? From a social perspective, identify and explain the different causes of prison violence.

4. From the early history of American corrections, how has prison order developed?

5. Identify and explain three ways prison violence can be reduced.

ANSWERS

Multiple Choice Questions

1.	D	7.	C
2.	A	8.	B
3.	D	9.	D
4.	B	10.	C
5.	C	11.	A
6.	A		

True/False Questions

1.	T	7.	T
2.	F	8.	T
3.	T	9.	F
4.	T	10.	F
5.	F	11.	F
6.	T		

Fill-in-the-Blank Questions

1. Building tenders
2. Inmate disturbance
3. Sexual victimization
4. Riot
5. Indefensible space

Correctional Programs
and Services

Correctional counselors perform the roles of a caseworker, a counselor, and an advocate for the inmates on their caseload. A correctional counselor in a male prison recalled the following situation:

> You have been a counselor for ten years, but this is one part of your job that has never gotten any easier.
>
> Doug, an inmate at the institution where you work, has just been turned down for parole for the second time in six years. The two of you are sitting at the hearing room table silently staring out the barred window. You can see the tears silently streaming down Doug's face. You can sense the anger and humiliation he is feeling and the explosion within himself that he is fighting to contain.
>
> Doug has a good prison record with respect to both his conduct and his commitment to rehabilitation programs. The problem is apparently a political one. The local judge simply does not want Doug released in his county. As the institutional counselor, you know

several other inmates who have been granted parole to that particular county. They were paroled despite having committed more serious offenses than Doug and having been much less receptive to the various institutional rehabilitation programs. Doug also knows of these paroles. To make matters worse, the parole board did not even give him a reason for rejecting his application, nor did they tell him what he could do to increase his chances for parole.

Doug spent weeks in preparation for his parole hearing. The letters of recommendation, the acquisition of his high school diploma, and other related material had in the end meant nothing. The board had convened less than ten minutes to make a parole decision based on six years of Doug's life. The chairman simply told you that Doug's parole had been denied and for you to pass the decision along to Doug. You had reluctantly done so, knowing that Doug could see the decision in your eyes before you even spoke. So here the two of you sit, bitter and disillusioned.[1]

CRITICAL THINKING QUESTIONS

How would you handle the situation with Doug if you were the counselor? What would you say? How would you keep yourself and Doug calm and centered?

Inmates who enter prison can often relate to the inscription on the gate of Dante's inferno: "Abandon hope, all ye who enter here." As inmates leave the life of a free citizen for the life of a confined felon, they are aware of what they have lost. But unless they have been in prison before, they can only imagine what experiences they will face.

The responsibility of the states, constitutionally mandated by federal and state courts, is to provide programs and services to prisoners placed in their care. The rehabilitation model brought therapy into the prison. Supporters wanted to turn the prison into a hospital and to treat the "disease" of criminality. Even with the present debunking of treatment, prison administrators are aware that increasing numbers of inmates have substance abuse and mental health problems and need appropriate programs.

In addition to treatment programs, the state is responsible for providing adequate, basic care of inmates. This care includes providing for inmates' medical and spiritual needs, ensuring that inmates have opportunities to visit with family and others, and furnishing a sufficient legal library.

Whether inmates lose all hope depends in part on the quality of programs and services available to them. The role of correctional counselors, whose title and job responsibilities vary from one correctional system to another, is to do what they can to make certain that adequate programs and services are provided to inmates. At times, counselors intervene with inmates when emotional support is needed or when they need an advocate within the institution or with the parole board.

What does it mean for the state to provide quality care to inmates? Should inmates have the same quality of medical care as individuals in the free community? How good does the food that the state serves inmates need to be? Does the state have any responsibilities for inmates' education beyond a GED? Does the state need to pay inmates for the work they do?

WHAT ABOUT CLASSIFICATION SYSTEMS?

Psychological systems started with the psychological evaluation of the inmate, and this evaluation was the first step in the treatment process. The reintegration model was incorporated into the classification process during the 1970s. According to this philosophy, offenders are processed through three stages: assessment, programming, and evaluation. Classification by the 1980s had become a management tool. Unit management was first used in the Federal Bureau of Prisons and then spread throughout state correctional systems. States also used inmate classification in order to avoid institutional problems. An early example of this was the California Department of Corrections' decision to send rival gang members to different institutions.

Classification and Treatment

The founders of the rehabilitation model in the late nineteenth and early twentieth century considered **classification** the first step of treatment. In the medical model, inmates were seen as sick and in need of treatment. Psychiatric evaluations and psychological workups were made, and special reception centers were built to assist in the process of diagnosis. The theory was that an inmate's psychological needs could be identified, and the inmate could be assigned to programs compatible with those needs. This use of the medical model in the classification process did not last many years. It soon became apparent to inmates and then to everyone else that it did not belong in a prison context.

Correctional institutions have experimented with psychological evaluation systems. The most widely administered test in adult prisons is the Minnesota Multiphasic Personality Inventory (MMPI), a standardized personality inventory of 556 true–false items. The MMPI has fourteen commonly scored scales: ten clinical scales that measure different personality dimensions and four validity scales that measure test-taking attitudes that could influence the validity of the scores on the clinical scales. The ten clinical scales measure hypochondriasis, depression, hysteria, psychopathic deviancy, masculinity–femininity, paranoia, psychasthenia, schizophrenia, hypomania, and social introversion.[2]

Classification and the Reintegration Model

In the 1970s, the reintegration model was incorporated into the classification process. The reintegration model asks the inmate to make choices among the opportunities available. The reintegration model is also concerned about the total needs of the prisoner—medical, vocational, educational, and religious. This model was widely used in American prisons during the 1970s but since then has lost much of its popularity.

Assessment. The first step is to discover inmates' total needs: Do they lack vocational skills? Are they deficient in reading ability? Do they have other educational needs? Do they need medical or dental care? Should they be placed in protective custody?

An inmate is first sent to a classification and reception center, which may be a separate facility or part of a larger institution. If the reception center is part of a larger prison, inmates are isolated from the prison population during the three weeks or so of their assessment. They are evaluated through a variety of techniques.

Programming. At the end of the assessment process, the correctional counselor goes over the basic classification findings with the inmate. The counselor then asks, "What are your goals and what type of program do you think will fulfill these goals?" If the preferred program has an opening and the institutional classification committee agrees, the inmate makes a program agreement with the counselor. If the first choice is not available, the inmate chooses another program or elects to begin an alternative program until the first choice becomes available.

Evaluation. The final process in the inmate management flow—evaluation—should take place every four to six weeks during the inmate's stay. If an inmate brings a request for a program change to his or her counselor, the counselor presents this request to the classification committee.[3]

Reality of Reintegration Classification.   Classification as a treatment tool, whether implemented in the medical or in the reintegration models, has had several problems in the contemporary American prison. Crowded institutions frequently reduce assessment to a rapid scan. The sole purpose of the classification that does take place may be to find a resident to fill a bed or to guarantee security. Also, many prisons cannot afford to hire the quality of staff needed to set up adequate classification programs.

Classification as a Management Tool

Skyrocketing prison populations, institutional violence, and inmate gangs convinced administrators that inmates had to be classified into proper security groups when they came into the corrections system. In the late 1970s and 1980s, the rising prison population made it difficult to handle the volume of inmates coming into the system, much less attempt to provide them treatment-oriented classification attention. The institutional violence that flared up in prison riots and assaults, as well as the spread of inmate gangs from Illinois and California to prisons in the majority of other states, were other reminders of the importance of classification to promote security and order.

Unit management, one of the most widely used efforts to use classification for security and control, was established in the Federal Bureau of Prisons in the 1970s. The basic philosophy behind unit management is to divide the prison into small units. The unit in some sense becomes a prison unto itself. The rationale behind this organizational structure is twofold: (1) Decentralizing authority in the institution will ensure maximum services to inmates. (2) Dividing the prison into small units will ensure better control of inmates.[4] Unit management is presently used in most of the federal correctional institutions.

In the late 1970s, administrators of Stateville Correctional Center in Illinois used unit management to regain control of the prison from three Chicago-based street gangs. The first step was to identify three categories of inmates: gang leaders who had been involved in aggressive and assaultive behavior during incarceration, inmates who were making an essentially normal adjustment to prison, and inmates who required separation from more aggressive inmates. Once all the inmates in the institution were divided into these three categories, inmates in each group were placed in a separate cellhouse, and a unit management system was established throughout the prison.[5]

WHAT ARE THE MOST WIDELY USED TREATMENT PROGRAMS?

The three main groups of treatment modalities used within the prison are psychological technologies, behavior therapy, and drug-related interventions. The psychological technologies are designed to help inmates develop insight about why they do what they do. The goal of behavior therapy is to reinforce positive behavior. Behavior therapies include behavior modification and cognitive–behavioral therapy. Drug-related programs are focused on helping inmates deal with addictive patterns of behavior. Drug-related treatment programs serve those in separate units or in special addiction groups and are found in more prisons than any other treatment modality.

Psychological Technologies

The insight-based psychological treatment technologies include psychotherapy, transactional analysis (TA), reality therapy, and the therapeutic community. The heyday of these programs was at the height of the rehabilitative ideal, when inmates wanted to impress parole boards that they were getting treatment.

Psychotherapy.   Psychiatrists, clinical psychologists, and psychiatric social workers have used various adaptations of **psychotherapy** in American prisons since the early twentieth century. Either in a one-to-one relationship with a therapist or in a group context, prisoners were encouraged to talk about past conflicts causing them to express emotional problems through aggressive or antisocial behavior. The insight that inmates gained from this individual or group psychotherapy supposedly helped them resolve the conflicts and unconscious needs that drove them to crime. As a final step of psychotherapy, inmates became responsible for their own behavior.

Psychotherapy has some fundamental limitations in a prison context. Inmates usually do not see themselves as having emotional problems and are reluctant to share their inner thoughts with a therapist. This is particularly true of street offenders, most of whom can relate a bad experience they had with a psychiatrist or psychologist in the system. Another limitation of psychotherapy is that psychiatrists and clinical psychologists have little time to conduct ongoing therapy sessions with inmates. Indeed, the few trained therapists in U.S. prisons are swamped with classification work and emergency cases. For the types of interventions used by psychiatrists, see Within the Walls 13.1, which describes problems that corrections officers in Ohio faced in 1999. Crisis intervention needs and other problems erode support for the use of psychotherapy in reducing recidivism. Yet, even when psychotherapy was more widely used in prison, it received few positive evaluations for its effect on recidivism.[6]

Transactional Analysis.   Based on interpreting and evaluating relationships among people, **transactional analysis** (TA) generated interest, especially in the 1960s and 1970s, because offenders, like their counterparts outside, could see its immediate value. TA used catchy language to promise people who feel "not OK" that several easy steps can make them feel "OK."

The TA leader and the inmate first do a "script analysis," in which they estimate the effect that negative "tapes" have on offenders' present behavior. If the offender decides to negotiate a treatment contract with both short- and long-range goals, treatment be-

the walls 13.1

within

Crisis Intervention Is Necessary

An inmate has cut both his wrists and is rushed to the infirmary in a state of shock from lacerations and loss of blood. He has a history of suicide attempts; in one, he was found hanging from a belt but was revived. Officers found a letter he wrote in his cell, documenting his various self-destructive attempts and including the statement "I'm trying to get out of the institution."

He is sent to the psychiatrist as soon as he has recovered. Correctional officers want to know how to handle the inmate. Should he be put on suicide watch? Or will close watch suffice? Is he simply manipulating the staff to be transferred to another institution?

Another inmate has been on a hunger strike for three days. He is angry, bitter, and frustrated. He says that he will stay on the hunger strike because of the unfair treatment he is now receiving on segregation. This inmate also poses problems for officers. How long should he be permitted to deny himself food? Does he need medications to improve his adjustment to the prison? Does he need to be taken off segregation?

> Will this inmate, who has killed before, . . . carry through on his threat?

Then there is the inmate who says that he has a nervous problem and does not like being around people. He claims that loud noises upset him and set him off. He has a history of explosive disorders and racism. When an African American inmate was placed in his cell, he quickly informed staff that he would cut his "cellie's" head off with a pair of scissors if he were not removed.

Staff know that policy is quite clear concerning this matter. Race is not a factor in the assignment of inmates to cells, but the officers are concerned about the possibility of a prison homicide. The officers want some questions answered from the psychiatrist. Will this inmate, who has killed before in the community and has been involved in several stabbing incidents in the institution, carry through on his threat? Would it be best to humor him and assign him to a single cell?

CRITICAL THINKING QUESTIONS

How would you respond to each of these incidents if you were the psychiatrist? How would you handle making a decision that resulted in the death of another person?

gins in a group. In a group, the goal is to help each offender use the adult ego state and to turn off the "not OK" feelings buried in the childhood tape.[7] Offenders undergoing TA also learn that four life positions describe the judgments they make about themselves and others: (1) "I'm OK—You're OK," (2) "I'm not OK—You're OK," (3) "I'm not OK—You're not OK," and (4) "I'm OK—You're not OK."[8]

TA has several advantages. It is easy to learn, offers hope, and provides a future job possibility for inmates who become highly skilled in its use. Administrators also profit because TA serves to reduce disciplinary problems in units where it is used. TA works less well for offenders who are not motivated to examine their own problems, who are evading personal change, and who have serious behavior problems. Adults with borderline intelligence, with sociopathic tendencies, and with immature personalities also tend not to profit from this modality. Therapeutic communities often used TA, along with other treatment modalities, but since the demise of these communities in U.S. prisons, the use of TA has declined.

Reality Therapy.   William Glasser and G. L. Harrington, two Los Angeles psychiatrists, developed reality therapy. This popular modality rests on the assumption that all persons have basic needs and act irresponsibly when they are unable to fulfill those needs. The basic human needs are relatedness and respect; they are satisfied by actions that are realistic, responsible, and right—the three R's of **reality therapy**.[9] Three steps are involved in reality therapy: (1) The inmate is expected to form an honest and real relationship with the therapist. (2) The therapist must then demonstrate that the inmate is accepted but his or her irresponsible behavior is not. (3) The therapist teaches the inmate better ways to fulfill his or her needs within the current situation.

Although no empirical evidence demonstrates the effectiveness of reality therapy in prison, reality therapy has been well received in some adult institutions, such as Rentz in Missouri, because its emphasis on behavior makes sense to inmates and staff who are unreceptive to other forms of insight therapy. Critics, however, charge that reality therapy is an oversimplification of human behavior, that ignoring the past is not necessarily wise, and that reality therapy can lead to paternalistic and authoritarian attitudes on the part of the therapist.

Therapeutic Communities.   The **therapeutic community**, focusing on the total environment and using all the experiences of that environment as the basic tools for therapeutic intervention has sometimes had marked success with drug abusers and hard-core offenders in prison. Evolving from the work of Maxwell Jones, this approach attempts to give persons within the therapeutic unit greater authority in the operation of their living units.[10]

The most widely hailed therapeutic community in adult institutions was developed by Dr. Martin Groder at the federal penitentiary at Marion, Illinois. Groder's program

These inmates are in a "therapeutic community." What are the characteristics of a therapeutic community, and what model of corrections does a therapeutic community serve? What three "psychological technologies" other than the therapeutic community are used in correctional treatment programs? What other types of treatment programs might prisons offer?

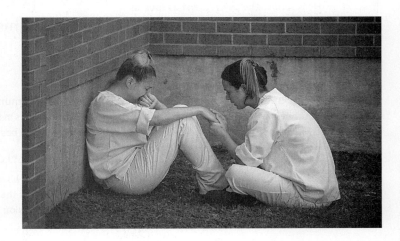

has been copied in correctional facilities at Terminal Island, California; Oxford, Wisconsin; Stillwater, Minnesota; and the Fort Grant Training Center, Arizona. Other therapeutic communities have been established at Niantic in Connecticut, Patuxent in Maryland, and St. Cloud in Minnesota, and through the prison systems of California and New York.

Influenced by transactional analysis as well as by Synanon in California, Groder managed to persuade institutional administrators to allow an inmate group of about twenty-five volunteers to devise their own treatment program. Inmates initially lived in a separate unit in the prison hospital, attended lectures on transactional analysis, and participated in Synanon-type confrontation groups. The basic rules—no physical violence or threats of violence, gambling, drugs, or homosexual behavior—were rigidly enforced; violation brought automatic expulsion from the group.[11]

Self-contained therapeutic communities are difficult to establish in institutional settings. Prison authorities are reluctant to delegate responsibility and authority to therapeutic communities and to change traditional rules to accommodate an atypical prison social system. Some drug programs in prison today, especially if they have their own units, may retain some elements of the therapeutic community.

The hero of this chapter is Martin Groder, M.D., who is presently a psychiatrist in Raleigh, North Carolina, but who spent many years working as a psychiatrist and later a prison warden for the Federal Bureau of Prisons. He is best known for the therapeutic

heroes | *Martin Groder, M.D.*

Advocate of Therapeutic Communities within the Walls

"In our original formulation, we discovered there was a culture that we called 'the convict culture.' This culture was actually made up of a combination of administrative, guard, and inmate cultures. The basic agreement was that the men who were incarcerated were bad. The rescuers, the bleeding hearts, and the do-gooders come into this closed culture. They tended to be driven off by the guards, through rejection and tyranny, and by the prisoners, through misuse. It does not take them long to be worn out and cast off.

"So, then comes the anti-Christ, that's me. I was basically saying that you are all wrong. The convicts are wrong, the helpers are wrong, and the staff is wrong. And I know how to do it.

"The therapeutic community that I developed at Marion and that was replicated in other settings was a separate culture. It was a culture that was not very different from American settler culture. We saw ourselves as a culture of opportunity, with severe sanctions against any type of improper behavior. We also had a tremendous spirit of community and cooperation where we saw ourselves as working together under adverse circumstances. We knew that the staff viewed themselves as the civilized people, but we saw them as the barbarians. They were unconscious, lacked psychological sophistication, and were part of the problem and not the solution. We knew that we had to provide them re-education in order to be useful, and we did. That clash of cultures meant that ultimately one would win out over the other or it would be necessary to live with some uneasy balance.

"For the fifteen years or so that the program existed, there was at best an uneasy balance. When I was in the prison system, we were able to get a mandate to continue the program. We were seen as legitimate enough, but there was still a tense balance. When I went away, the programs got isolated because there was no overall supportive structure. Each of the therapeutic communities got eliminated, not by conspiracy but by just the way things go. They were foreign bodies, and the barbarian immune system eliminated them one by one.

"I considered the option of continuing to fight with the barbarians, but I chose to go into private practice instead. It was a very conscious choice because I knew how history works. I knew it in 1975 with the publication of Robert Martinson's 'nothing works' article. It was very distorted and biased toward the negative and ignored or trivialized all positive results. I could see that the general American culture had turned against the notion of treatment for a variety of reasons.

"I find it interesting that the barbarians not only eliminated the hope for a resettlement culture, but that they just keep returning these people back into their exiled positions in their communities the same as when they went to prison. We have eliminated treatment, but, at the same time, the barbarian empire has quadrupled in size and gorged itself on the public money."

CRITICAL THINKING QUESTIONS

What can you find to agree with in Dr. Groder's sharp statement about the rejection of treatment in prison? Who are the "barbarians"? Where do you disagree with Dr. Groder

community that he developed at the maximum-security federal prison at Marion, Illinois, from 1968 to 1974. The community was named Asklepieion, after the temple of the Greek god of healing. Read what Dr. Groder said for *Invitation to Corrections* in 2000.

Behavior Therapy

Behavior therapy rests on the assumption that desirable behaviors that are rewarded immediately and systematically will increase and undesirable behaviors that are not rewarded will decrease. Behavior therapy uses positive and negative reinforcement to encourage desirable and extinguish undesirable behaviors. Positive reinforcers include attention, praise, money, food, and privileges. Negative reinforcers include threats, confinement, punishment, and ridicule.

Behavior modification is a behavior therapy technique. Formal programs of behavior modification appear to be on the decline in adult corrections, but the technique is still practiced informally in a great many correctional institutions. It works like this: Inmates receive additional privileges as they become more accepting of institutional rules and procedures and as they give evidence of more positive attitudes.

The Youthful Offender Center in Morganton, North Carolina, has used this principle. Offenders begin their orientation period in the Spartan setting of the fourteenth floor and progress to the relative luxury of the fifth floor. Movement to a lower floor is a reward for tractability. The reward consists of amenities, privileges, and improved living arrangements. By the time an offender reaches the fifth floor, he is ready for release and has a key to his room, comfortable furniture, attractive china on which to eat, and a wide range of options for recreation, visiting, eating, canteen use, and dress.[12]

Does the program at Morganton work? Does changing the external environment actually change the behavior of offenders?

In the past couple decades, behavior therapy has switched its emphasis from seeking outward compliance to obtain rewards and amenities to that of affecting behavior by changing the thinking patterns of offenders.

S. Yochelson and S. E. Samenow's research at St. Elizabeth Hospital in Washington D.C. with the criminally insane concluded that there exists a criminal personality that incorporates some fifty-two errors in thinking.[13] In the 1980s, this notion that offenders have certain personality characteristics leading to basic errors in thinking became popular as society's need to control and reform serious habitual offenders increased. This general approach became known as **cognitive-behavioral interventions** and has been increasingly used in correctional settings in the United States and elsewhere. The goal of these interventions is to identify cognitive deficits linked to criminality, such as impulsivity associated with poor verbal self-regulation, a concrete thinking style that impinges on the ability to appreciate the feelings and thoughts of others, impairments in means–end reasoning, conceptual rigidity that ties individuals to a repetitive pattern of self-defeating behavior, egocentricity, inability to reason critically, poor interpersonal problem-solving skills, and a preoccupation with self.[14]

Cognitive-behavioral interventions have been identified as the treatment program most likely to be associated with reductions in offender recidivism.[15] The most widely adopted of the cognitive-behavioral interventions is the **Cognitive Thinking Skills Program (CTSP)** developed by Robert Ross and Elizabeth Fabiano. It is a core program in the Canadian correctional system and has been implemented in the United States, Australia, New Zealand, and some European countries.[16]

CTSP was developed through a systematic review of all correctional programs published during the 1970s that were associated with reduced criminal recidivism. The researchers identified one hundred evaluations of effective programs and discovered that all applied techniques designed to target offenders' thinking. Ross and Fabiano then scanned the literature for interventions that addressed successfully each thinking deficit area. Impulsivity, they found, can be reduced by consequential thinking. Fatalistic thinking can be reduced by teaching participants meta-cognitive skills, which will enable them to assess how their thinking influences their actions. Antisocial behaviors can be reduced by teaching participants to replace them with prosocial behaviors. Rigid thinking can be minimized by teaching participants creative thinking skills, providing them with prosocial alternatives to use when responding to interpersonal problems. Critical thinking skills can modify illogical thinking. Egocentrism can be reduced by teaching offenders' values enhancement and social perspective taking. Teaching offenders techniques of self-control can improve social adjustment. These interventions are the core components of CTSP.[17]

Modest evidence exists that CTSP reduces criminal recidivism in general offender populations, but there is stronger evidence that positive results are more likely to take place among certain subgroups. For example, CTSP seems to be more effective with offenders over age 25 and with nonproperty offenders.[18]

Drug-Related Treatment Programs

Groups devoted to the drug problems of inmates have increased significantly since 1980. In 1979, an estimated 4.4 percent of inmates in the fifty state correctional systems were in drug treatment. By 1987, 11.1 percent of inmates were enrolled in treatment programs. On 1 January 1999, the Federal Bureau of Prisons, thirty-nine states, and the District of Columbia had 172,747 or 14.1 percent of inmates in drug programs. Thirty-five agencies reported that 40,213 prisoners were housed in a separate addiction unit, 100,152 were involved in addiction groups, and 21,324 received only counseling for their drug abuse. Alaska had the highest percentage of its inmates in drug programs (68.3 percent); Louisiana had the lowest percentage (0.8 percent) in drug treatment.[19]

The Cornerstone Program (Oregon), the Lantana Program (Florida), the Simon Fraser University Program (British Columbia), and the Stay'n Out Program (New York) are four promising programs that have reported relatively low rates of recidivism among participants. Among the noteworthy characteristics and features of those four programs are the following:

1. The programs have special sources of funds, earmarked for their use and administered separately from other correctional services.
2. The programs exist as guests of established host institutions; thus they can focus on program activities rather than on institutional matters such as housing and food preparation.
3. The programs use a comprehensive approach and offer a wide range of activities commonly found in free-standing residential programs rather than in traditional prison drug programs.
4. Program providers are likely to come from professions other than corrections, although they are sensitive to security regulations and willing to work within them.
5. Program participants typically were involved heavily in drug use and committed many serious crimes before incarceration.
6. In carrying out program activities, participants learn a range of practical life skills.
7. Program staff members maintain contact with participants after release and provide follow-up support.[20]

Other features shared by drug and alcohol treatment programs include clear statements of program rules and the consequences of breaking them, obvious concern by program staff about the welfare of participants, participant regard for staff members as persons worth imitating, and utilization of community resources.[21]

The Federal Bureau of Prisons operates forty-four residential drug treatment programs for the nearly 30 percent of the inmate population with histories of substance abuse. Residential programs allow inmates to live in housing units devoted to drug treatment activities. Nearly fifty thousand inmates have completed this residential program since 1990. An interim report from an ongoing evaluation of these programs showed that inmates who had been released to the community for a minimum of six months after completing residential treatment were 73 percent less likely to be arrested for a new offense and 44 percent less likely to test positive for drug use than similar inmates who did not complete such a program.[22]

Alcoholics Anonymous (AA), Narcotics Anonymous (NA), and other drug programs are also conducted in prisons. Some are brought into the prison by AA or NA members from the community. Others are conducted by staff members.

Given the ever-increasing drug abuse found among prison inmates, it is imperative that drug treatment programs continue to be increased. The replications of the characteristics and features of the four programs described here would do much to ensure the effectiveness of other drug treatment programs.

WHAT ARE THE MOST POPULAR SELF-HELP PROGRAMS?

Departments of corrections frequently encourage inmates to establish **self-help programs,** These are run primarily by the inmates themselves and often express ethnic and cultural goals. Self-help groups meet in the evenings or on weekends. They usually are required to have a staff sponsor and to establish governing bylaws and procedures. The following are some of the self-help groups that have met in California correctional institutions:

Seventh Step	Black Culture
Organization to Help Every Race	Toastmasters
Hillel	Narcotics Anonymous
People Builders	Community Awareness
Alcoholics Anonymous	Wives and Husbands in Prison
No Other Reason than Help	Mexican-American Culture
Winners (Placement)	Transactional Workshop
20 Psych Counseling	Asian Culture
Gamblers Anonymous	American Indian Culture
Inner Wisdom Study	

Other self-help programs offered in prisons are Jaycees, Lifers, Dale Carnegie, Checks Anonymous, Native American Spiritual and Cultural Awareness Group, Yoga, transcendental meditation, Tai Chi, Insight Incorporated, Positive Mental Attitude (P.M.A.), assertiveness training, anger management, moral development, and emotional maturity instruction.

A national service organization, Jaycees is probably the largest self-help group, having sixteen thousand inmate members in 420 chapters in state and federal prisons. Sponsored by Jaycee chapters in the community, Jaycee groups in prison raise money for charities, refurbish visiting rooms, donate toys to children's hospitals, sponsor entertainment and sport events for prisoners, and operate radio stations.

Lifers, an organization made up of individuals sentenced to prison for life, is a popular organization and usually has a waiting list. Yoga and transcendental meditation are both rapidly gaining recognition in correctional institutions; both have been established in more than twenty prisons. Teaching motivation for inmates—through programs such as Zzoom, P.M.A., and Guide for Better Living—is important in many institutions. Table 13.1 presents a self-help program on communication skills. Prison SMART Foundations, Inc., is a new self-help program that is offered in prisons across the United States (see Within the Walls 13.2).

°Table 13.1

Communication Skills

PARTICIPANTS: 15–20

TARGET POPULATION: Graduates of Self-Awareness Module

OBJECTIVE: To improve the participant's knowledge of what constitutes good communication skills; also, to have the participant exhibit appropriate communication skills.

GOAL: To provide participants with the information regarding good communication skills. To allow them to practice these skills with other group members and to use these skills with other individuals (staff and inmates).

1. *SESSION I*—Introduction to Communication Skills
   —Verbal
   —Nonverbal

2. *SESSION II*—Matching Behaviors
   —Voice Characteristics
   —Body Language

3. *SESSION III*—Nonverbal Listening Behavior
   —"SOLER Model"
   —Roadblocks to Communication

4. *SESSION IV*—Self-Expression, Model I
   —Thoughts, Feelings and Behaviors
   —Genuineness and Respect

5. *SESSION V*—Self-Expression, Model II
   —Explanation or Clarification
   —Desire or Preference

6. *SESSION VI*—Active Listening Skills, Model I
   —Content and Feeling

7. *SESSION VII*—Active Listening Skills, Model II
   —Encouraging Responses
   —Open Questions

8. *SESSION VIII*—Review and Summarization
   —The Use of Fantasy and Imagery

Source: Tennessee Department of Corrections.

the walls 13.2

within

Prison SMART Foundation, Inc.

The Prison SMART Foundation, Inc., was launched in 1992. This unique stress management program . . . was originally taught in the Barnstable County, Mass., House of Correction. This program assists prisoners in their personal rehabilitation, reducing violence and drug dependence, while teaching inmates to accept responsibility for past actions and future conduct. The 6- to 10-day program, which utilizes advanced yogic breathing practices, is based on the dynamic cleansing effects of the breath on the body and mind. Prison administrators have reported that inmates who have participated in the

> The 6- to 10-day program . . . is based on the dynamic cleansing effects of the breath on the body and mind.

program are easier to handle and exhibit less acting-out behavior in confrontational situations.

CRITICAL THINKING QUESTIONS

What type of inmate do you think is most likely to be interested in such a stress reduction program? Do you think that inmates who have issues with stress management would find such a self-help program helpful?

Source: Reprinted from the Prison SMART Foundation, Inc., Webpage, 2000.

ARE INMATES INTERESTED IN HELPING OTHERS?

Inmates seem increasingly eager to become involved in projects involving service. These projects may have both self-help and service aspects or may focus on a needed institutional or community service. Some **service projects** are ongoing; others arise because of a disaster or emergency in the community. Service projects include providing child care for prison visitors, fighting forest fires and floods, adopting war orphans, doing peer counseling, recording books for the blind, training Seeing Eye dogs, donating blood, participating as paramedics or in other lifesaving roles, and umpiring Little League games in the community.

WHAT ABOUT PRISON PROGRAMS?

A correctional institution is responsible for providing all the necessary services to care for the physical, educational, recreational, and spiritual needs of inmates. The questionable quality of these services in many U.S. prisons has resulted in the National Prison Project, the Osborne Association, and the John Howard Association pressing for reform. Since the 1970s the federal courts have also realized the need for change in many state and some federal prisons. The result has been programs focused on academic education, vocational training, and religion.

Academic Education

In adult institutions, academic education is usually available through Adult Basic Education (ABE) programs, secondary and general education studies, postsecondary education programs, and social education programs. In 1999, nearly 6,000 inmates in federal prisons received the general equivalency diploma (GED). Thousands of other inmates completed a variety of educational programs, as well as vocational training programs.[23] In 1999, 146,140, or 15.2 percent, of inmates in state correctional institutions were involved in full-time academic or vocational training.[24]

College courses have been provided through live instruction, correspondence courses, television hookups, and release time, which allows inmates to attend educational institutions in the community. For a time, community colleges offered inmates courses leading to a two-year degree. However, prisoners are no longer eligible to receive Pell Grants, federal grants that provide assistance to lower-income college students. This has led to the demise of the inmate college programs in most areas.

The improvement of inmates' educational skills may reduce recidivism through several mechanisms:

- Inmates who have attained sufficient reading and writing skills to attain functional literacy may increase the possibility of lawful employment after release from prison. The importance of postrelease employment is an importance consideration in staying crime free. Therefore, educational programming in prison may reduce recidivism by improving job opportunities.

- The educational process may be helpful in reducing recidivism by facilitating the conscientiousness, maturation, and dedication that educational achievement requires. This viewpoint proposes that education may equip inmates to evaluate their environments and their decisions more thoughtfully and, as a result, make decisions that will assist them in remaining out of prison when released.

- The educational setting within the prison enables inmates to have an opportunity to interact with civilian employees in the context of a goal-oriented and nonauthoritarian relationship.[25]

The research literature on the effectiveness of education in reducing recidivism is not well developed. Robert Martinson found that dynamic and effective instruction can help prisoners improve their academic skills, but he still concluded that "education and skill development have not reduced recidivism by rehabilitation criminals."[26] In contrast, three more recent surveys found that in most studies educational program participation was related to reduced rates of recidivism.[27]

Vocational Training

The need for vocational training has always been evident, because most inmates are educable and trainable but lack any regular work experience or any demonstrable skills in a trade. The basic purpose of vocational training, then, is to prepare inmates for jobs in the community.

The variety of vocational programs offered in men's prisons is impressive. There are programs in printing, barbering, welding, meat cutting, machine shop work, electronics, baking, plumbing, computer programming, television and radio repair, bus repair, air conditioning maintenance, automotive body and fender repair, sheet metal repair, sheet metal work, painting, blueprint reading, and furniture repair and upholstering. Fewer vocational programs exist for women in correctional institutions. Vocational programs for women typically include beauty culture, secretarial training, business machine operation, data processing, baking and food preparation, and child care. But recently this pattern has been changing in some women's prisons. For example, Bedford Hills in New York offers women training in auto mechanics, electronics, and video technology, and the women's prison in Nebraska provides a course in truck driving.

These prison inmates are in a vocational training program. What kinds of skills might prisoners learn? What are some of the diverse goals of correctional programs and services? What are some examples of self-help and service programs that prisons might offer? What are some examples of programs that focus on education and on religion?

A number of corrections institutions, especially in the Federal Bureau of Prisons and in Connecticut and Minnesota, have noteworthy vocational training programs. Honeywell, Inc., an electronics firm, provides volunteers and the equipment to teach prisoners to use computers; over one thousand prisoners have completed the course. Prisoners at a Connecticut prison have been trained to design, sell, and supervise the installation of residential and light commercial solar energy systems.

The participation in vocational programs is seen as a means of reducing recidivism, based on the premise that the acquisition of vocational skills such as goal-setting, motivation, commitment, and learning of technical and nontechnical knowledge increases ex-offenders' legitimate employment opportunities following release.[28] J. Gerber and E. J. Fritsch's examination of thirteen studies of vocational education programs in prisons revealed that participation in these programs was associated with reduced recidivism in nine studies.[29]

Religion

Religious instruction and services are always provided in federal, state, and private prisons. Full-time Protestant and Roman Catholic chaplains are available in most prisons. In some prisons, an imam, a Muslim leader of prayer, comes in from the outside community to conduct services. Religious services include Sunday Mass and morning worship, confession, baptism, instruction for church membership, choir, and religious counseling.

Religion traditionally is not popular within the walls. Prison officials generally agree that no more than 15 percent of inmates are committed to a faith. Yet several religious groups have had stirring impacts on prisoners. For example, the Black Muslims and the Moorish Science Temple of America have received a strong response from many African

American inmates. An inmate who was released in 2000 talks about how Islam has affected his life:

> The night I got there I met a brother, a beautiful brother. The first thing he said was, "Do you need anything? But I won't give you cigarettes or anything harmful." He introduced me to Islam. He showed me some notes he had taken from a book he had read. He gave me a copy of the book and it hooked me. I found in that book the thing I wanted to be as a man. After reading that book, he and I started studying together every day. We prayed three times a day. I began reading the Koran. I found such beauty in it that I'm still living it this day. I intend to be a Muslim the rest of my life.[30]

Bo and Sita Lozoff, founders of the Human Kindness Foundation, have been actively working with prisoners of all faiths for over twenty years in an effort to deepen their religious and spiritual journey. Stressing self-honesty, kindness, courage, a sense of humor, and a spirit of wonder, they encourage inmates to find peace within themselves in order to live more peacefully in prison and in the world when they are released from prison.

WHAT PRISON SERVICES ARE OFFERED?

The courts have mandated that medical services, visitation with family, and the use of a sufficient law library are constitutional rights of prisoners. Prisons also provide recreation programs.

Medical Services

Medical services have become one of the most important issues of corrections, because of infectious diseases (HIV, AIDs, hepatitis B, hepatitis C, tuberculosis), female health issues, mental health problems, and elderly prisoner medical concerns.

Prisoners have always been critical of medical care within the prison. They typically claim that the medical care is inadequate and physicians are incompetent, that requested treatment is denied, that special diets are not provided, that medical treatment and drugs are forced on them, and that they are forced to work when they are physically unable to do so.[31] Two lawsuits in Alabama, *Pugh v. Locke* (1976) and *Newman v. Alabama* (1977), were concerned with the gross inadequacy of medical services.[32] The trend toward contracting out medical service appears to be leading toward major improvements.[33]

Acquired immune deficiency syndrome (AIDS) is one of the most difficult public health issues facing the United States. AIDS also poses a challenge for corrections, especially for persons working and living in prisons. Inmate populations include high proportions of individuals in AIDS risk groups, particularly intravenous drug users. Table 13.2 indicates the numbers of state and federal prisoners known to be HIV-positive and confirmed AIDS cases. In 1996, there were 907 AIDS-related deaths among state prisoners, which represented nearly one-third of all prisoners' deaths.[34] The problem of AIDS is particularly serious in New York prisons, which have four times as many diagnosed cases as any other state prison system.[35]

Several approaches are being used with inmates with AIDS. Most prisons hospitalize them in the infirmary and return them to the general population when their condition stabilizes. California moves all patients with AIDS to a medical facility in Vacaville, to prevent the spread of the disease. Prison programs increasingly are informing inmates about the risks of unsafe sex and drug abuse. State laws make it mandatory to take blood from inmates to test for exposure to the HIV virus. But, whatever approach is used, prison personnel tend to be extremely cautious about having contact with and treating inmates with HIV/AIDS.

Table 13.2

State and Federal Prisoners Known to Be Positive for the Human Immunodeficiency Virus (HIV) and Confirmed AIDS Cases, by Region and Jurisdiction 1995, 1996, and 1997

Jurisdiction	Total Known to Be HIV Positive			HIV/AIDS Cases as a Percent of Total Custody Population[a]			Confirmed AIDS Cases for 1997
	1995	1996	1997	1995	1996	1997	
United States, Total	24,256	23,881	23,548	2.3%	2.2%	2.1%	6,184
Federal	822	947	1,030	0.9	1.0	1.0	368
State	23,434	23,934	22,518	2.4	2.3	2.2	5,816
Northeast	12,262	11,090	10,394	7.8	6.9	6.4	2,219
Connecticut	755	690	798	5.1	4.6	5.1	202
Maine	4	4	NA	0.3	0.3	—	NA
Massachusetts	409	393	402	3.9	3.6	3.7	137
New Hampshire	31	18	17	1.5	0.9	0.8	7
New Jersey	847	705	867	3.7	3.0	3.4	302
New York	9,500	8,500	7,500	13.9	12.2	10.8	1,301
Pennsylvania	590	652	697	1.8	1.9	2.0	221
Rhode Island	126	125	107	4.4	3.9	3.2	46
Vermont	0	3	6	—	0.3	0.5	3
Midwest	1,667	1,874	1,849	0.9	1.0	0.9	574
Illinois	583	634	655	1.5	1.6	1.6	201
Iowa	20	24	34	0.3	0.4	0.5	8
Kansas	24	16	4	0.3	0.2	0.1	1
Michigan	379	528	419	0.9	1.2	0.9	203
Minnesota	46	24	31	1.0	0.5	0.6	5
Missouri	173	190	227	0.9	0.9	0.9	37
Nebraska	19	17	22	0.6	0.5	0.7	3
North Dakota	2	3	7	0.3	0.4	0.9	1
Ohio	346	343	365	0.8	0.7	0.8	91
South Dakota	3	4	1	0.2	0.2	0.0	1
Wisconsin	72	91	84	0.6	0.7	0.6	23
South	7,870	8,162	8,291	1.9	1.9	2.0	2,614
Alabama	222	234	212	1.1	1.1	1.0	51
Arkansas	83	77	86	1.0	0.9	1.0	14

Note: These data were collected by the U.S. Department of Justice, Bureau of Justice Statistics through the National Prisoner Statistics (NPS) program. The NPS program provides year-end data for the prisoner populations of the fifty states, the District of Columbia, and the Federal Bureau of Prisons. These data represent the custody population, which includes only those prisoners housed in a jurisdiction's facilities. Indiana did not report the number of HIV/AIDS cases for 1995–1997.

Should patients with AIDS be hospitalized, segregated, or paroled? Should officers be notified when an inmate tests positive? How about notifying past or prospective sexual partners? Does educating inmates about safe sex and needle hygiene imply that the state condones sexual behavior and drug use in prison? Does this education obligate prison officials to provide the means for prisoners to practice safe sex and good needle hygiene while imprisoned?[36]

Tuberculosis (TB) also poses medical problems for prison inmates and staff. Because this disease is transmitted through the air, its spread could be initiated by nothing more than the cough of someone who is infected. Some strains of TB are resistant to medical

Jurisdiction	Total Known to Be HIV Positive			HIV/AIDS Cases as a Percent of Total Custody Population[a]			Confirmed AIDS Cases for 1997
	1995	1996	1997	1995	1996	1997	
Delaware	122	NA	NA	2.5	—	—	NA
District of Columbia	NA	NA	75	—	—	1.1	75
Florida	2,193	2,152	2,325	3.4	3.4	3.6	826
Georgia	858	814	861	2.5	2.3	2.4	NA
Kentucky	41	55	55	0.4	0.5	0.5	11
Louisiana	314	347	397	1.8	2.0	2.1	107
Maryland	724	832	766	3.4	3.8	3.5	274
Mississippi	138	135	189	1.4	1.3	1.8	38
North Carolina	526	589	519	1.9	2.0	1.7	170
Oklahoma	115	108	107	0.8	0.7	0.7	4
South Carolina	380	422	432	2.0	2.1	2.1	171
Tennessee	120	131	131	0.9	1.0	0.9	42
Texas	1,890	1,876	2,126	1.5	1.4	1.5	829
Virginia	134	383	NA	0.6	1.5	—	NA
West Virginia	10	7	10	0.4	0.3	0.4	2
West	1,635	1,808	1,984	0.8	0.8	0.8	409
Alaska	5	10	10	0.2	0.3	0.3	0
Arizona	140	205	105	0.7	0.9	0.4	46
California	1,042	1,136	1,328	0.8	0.8	0.9	157
Colorado	93	94	110	1.0	0.9	1.0	31
Hawaii	12	23	16	0.4	0.7	0.4	4
Idaho	11	17	10	0.4	0.5	0.3	3
Montana	4	6	8	0.2	0.4	0.4	7
Nevada	147	133	139	1.9	1.6	1.6	43
New Mexico	24	11	23	0.6	0.2	0.6	3
Oregon	29	39	54	0.4	0.5	0.7	7
Utah	31	31	60	0.8	0.7	1.2	16
Washington	92	99	119	0.8	0.8	0.9	92
Wyoming	5	4	2	0.4	0.3	0.1	0

[a]Percent calculations for the United States totals, the state totals, and the regional totals exclude prisoners in jurisdictions that did not report data for HIV/AIDS cases. Percentages for all years are based on year-end custody counts.

Source: U.S. Department of Justice, Bureau of Justice Statistics, *HIV in Prisons 1997*, Bulletin NCJ 178284 (Washington, D.C.: U.S. Department of Justice, November, 1999), pp. 2, 3.

treatment, and given the problem of prison crowding and poor ventilation in many facilities, it is not difficult to imagine how devastating TB could become in a prison setting.[37] All states except Vermont and West Virginia screen inmates at intake for TB. Illinois detected the highest number of inmates in corrections systems in the United States with TB infection at intake (4,233) during 1996, and Texas detected the highest number of inmates with active TB at times other than intake.[38]

As discussed in Chapter 20 on prisoners' rights, inmates continue to feel that medical care in prison is inadequate. They continue to address the courts for remedies in particular institutions and, at times, for liability for what they feel has been negligent health care.

Visitation

The quality of the visiting experience has improved in recent years. Visiting arrangements tend to fall into the following categories: (1) closed visits; (2) limited-contact visits; (3) informal-contact visits; (4) freedom of the grounds; and (5) conjugal or family visits. For a while, the general trend was to permit prisoners much more physical contact than they had been allowed in the past, but this trend began to change in the final years of the twentieth century.

Closed visits do not allow any physical contact between prisoner and visitor, who are separated by a partition extending from floor to ceiling. The limited-contact visit substitutes a long table with a center partition that extends from the floor to a few inches above the surface of the table. The informal-contact visit usually takes place in a visiting room furnished with chairs, small tables, and, often, food-vending machines. Some institutions also provide picnic and play areas for visiting during nice weather.

Conjugal visits, or family visitation, are permitted at a number of states for inmates who have earned the privilege. Mississippi instituted a program of conjugal visitation in the 1950s; in 1968, the California State Prison at Tehachapi instituted family visitation. More recently, Alabama, Alaska, Connecticut, Minnesota, New York, South Carolina, and Washington State began programs of family visitation.

Conjugal or family visitation usually means that prisoners enjoy twenty-four or forty-eight hours of privacy with their families. A trailer is frequently provided for the visit. The wife or family member brings food to prepare, and a correctional officer checks on the inmate once a day or so. These programs have been expanded in most participating states to include female prisoners.

The Library

In recent years prison libraries have been expanded and made available to all inmates. Inmates in most prisons are now permitted to obtain books from the state library if they are not available at the prison. In contrast to the days when law books were kept in the warden's office or in other inaccessible places, well-equipped law libraries generally are available for inmate use.

Recreation

Recreation is the most popular program in prison for a number of reasons. It alleviates the boredom of prison life, provides an outlet for pent-up emotions, and provides an opportunity for physical conditioning and body-building exercise.

In some prisons, organized sports thrive, and cellblocks compete in sports such as touch football, basketball, baseball, softball, and volleyball. Weight lifting, boxing, and jogging are also popular. Television, radio, movies, cards, chess, dominoes, and checkers help many inmates pass the time. A major form of recreation today is arts and crafts, often used in conjunction with therapy. There are also many forms of art and theater.

How about Prison Industries Today?

Prison industries began as forced labor imposed as punishment. Forcing inmates to break up rocks or to move coal from one pile to another was intended to break their spirits. Later, it was decided to use inmate labor to help pay the costs of imprisonment, and some prison systems at the end of the nineteenth century found themselves making considerable revenue from prison industries. However, resistance from labor unions and from local businesses resulted in the passage of state and federal laws early in the twentieth century that prohibit inmate-made goods from competition in the free market.

Prisoners have several responses to prison labor. In some correctional systems where they are required to work at a job, prisoners typically feel negative about the work, especially when they receive no or little compensation. Indeed, some prisoners go to nearly any extreme to avoid such required labor. More typically, inmates choose to become involved in a prison industry because it enables them to earn much-needed money, even though the hourly wage for most state inmates is pitifully low.

Federal Prison Industries (FPI) has consistently made a profit through the sale of goods to federal agencies; it is entirely self-sustaining and operates without any appropriated funds.[39] FPI pays prisoners reasonably well, at least in comparison with the pay they get in most state systems.

The Free Venture Model, a federal program that began in Connecticut, attempts to achieve productive labor with private-sector efficiency, wages, and relevance. The goal of the Free Venture Model is a realistic work environment with a full workday, inmate wages based on work output, and training for job skills that can be transferred to work in the community. Since 1980, more than half the states have adopted legislation providing for private-sector involvement in prison industries.[40]

Prison industry provides a variety of goods and services. Tennessee prisoners produce jeans for Kmart and JCPenney and wooden rocking ponies for trendy Eddie Bauer (list price $80). Oregon inmates make uniforms for McDonald's. Nevada inmates convert luxury cars into stretch limousines. Inmates also book rooms for motel chains and take reservations for Trans World Airlines. In Kansas, they process Social Security numbers. In Iowa, they work for the Department of Tourism's Information Bureau. Iowa and Nebraska are among the states that rent their inmates out as telemarketers.[41]

CRITICAL THINKING QUESTIONS

How do you feel about private businesses' involvements in prison labor? Are inmates providing unfair competition to outside society?

Research on prison labor, according to Gaes, et al., indicates that it produces better-behaved prisoners during confinement, lower recidivism rates following release, and higher rates of involvement in constructive community employment.[42]

HOW CAN CORRECTIONAL TREATMENT BECOME MORE EFFECTIVE?

A number of principles of correctional treatment were formulated in the late 1980s and 1990s that have the potential to make correctional treatment more effective. They are:

- Criminogenic needs: Intervention efforts must be linked to criminogenic characteristics.
- Multimodel programs: All criminogenic deficits should be treated.
- Responsivity: Treatment providers should match client learning styles with staff teaching styles.
- Risk differentiation: Higher-risk clients are more likely to benefit from treatment than are lower-risk clients; the higher level of treatment intensity should be used for the highest-risk clients.
- Skills-oriented and cognitive-behavioral treatments: Treatment providers should use programs that teach clients skills that allow them to understand and resist antisocial behavior.
- Program implementation and continuity of care: Clients should be treated in well-supported programs.
- Dosage: Interventions should be comprehensive and of sufficient duration (sufficient dosage).
- Researcher involvement: Researchers should be involved in both program development and evaluation.[43]

These principles not only form the basis of a model of behavioral change but outline a plan for a better future for correctional treatment. They propose that effective implementation of treatment ultimately depends on research to provide the information on who should get what treatment, when treatment is best given, and what frequency and intensity of treatment is necessary.

If offenders are placed in the right program at the optimal time for them to benefit from treatment, then program integrity becomes a matter of major importance. Program integrity requires that effective interventions deliver the services to offenders that they claim to deliver; that treatment has sufficient strength to accomplish its goals; that program personnel are equipped to deliver the specified services; and that treatment is not only matched to the interests and needs of offenders, but has the flexibility to be modified according to the changing interests and needs of offenders.[44]

SUMMARY

This chapter discusses and evaluates the basic purposes and services that are offered in correctional institutions. Larger institutions tend to have more treatment modalities and educational, vocational, and self-help programs than do smaller ones, but all institutions have some programming for inmates.

When treatment was under wide attack in the early 1970s, the number of treatment programs offered within correctional institutions was reduced. The treatment programs that are offered within prisons today tend to be more drug- and behavior-oriented than in the past and much less based on psychological models and insight.

The programs and services provided to prisoners at the end of the twentieth century were better for the most part than those offered earlier in the century. Prison libraries, especially law libraries, had significantly improved. Academic education and vocational training used more up-to-date methods and equipment. Medical care was better but still varied in quality from institution to institution. Prison labor provided a much greater variety of goods and services, sometimes to the free market, and a somewhat higher pay wage for prisoners. Visiting was more liberal than in the past but was becoming more security-oriented as the century drew to a close.

It is encouraging that the majority of 1980s and 1990s evaluation studies found that cognitive-treatment and drug-related treatment programs, academic education, vocational training, and prison labor had positive effects on reduced rates of recidivism for ex-offenders. It is discouraging that the climate in contemporary prisons is probably less favorable toward correctional treatment than it has been for decades.

KEY TERMS

behavior modification, p. 312
classification, p. 307
closed visits, p. 322
cognitive-behavioral interventions, p. 312
Cognitive Thinking Skills Program (CTSP), p. 312
conjugal visits, p. 322

psychotherapy, p. 308
reality therapy, p. 310
self-help program, p. 314
service project, p. 316
therapeutic community, p. 310
transactional analysis (TA), p. 309

CRITICAL THINKING QUESTIONS

1. Although it is generally agreed that treatment does not work in prison, treatment programs exist in nearly every American prison. Why?

2. In some prisons inmates receive excellent care. Is it fair for them to receive better medical care than many citizens in the community?

3. Do you think that prisoners should have to pay for their food, board, medical care, and other services? Why or why not?

4. You are inside. The parole board tells you to get some therapy. Every choice mentioned in this chapter is available to you. Which will you choose? Why?

WEB DESTINATIONS

Read a report on the most effective antidrug treatment programs in prisons today.
http://www.ncjrs.org/txtfiles/drugsupr.txt

This site describes the mission and resources of the Correctional Education Association.
http://www.ibiblio.org/icea/

Survey the products and services available through Unicor, the business name of Federal Prison Industries, Inc., which operates as part of the Federal Bureau of Prisons.
http://www.unicor.gov/about/index.htm

Survey products and services available through state prison industries, such as New Jersey's DeptCor and New Hampshire's Correctional Industries.

http://www.state.nj.us/deptcor/

http://www.state.nh.us/nhci/

Read about Florida's innovative Prison Industry Enhancement Program.
http://www.dc.state.fl.us/orginfo/pie/

Take Delaware's practice test for starting a career as a correctional counselor in that state. See what you would need to do to be a youth correctional counselor in California.
http://personnel.spo.state.de.us/jobs/sg/cocon.htm

http://www.cya.ca.gov/jobs/exams/webpages/ycc.htm

FOR FURTHER READING

Gaes, Gerald G., Timothy J. Flanagan, Laurence L. Motiuk, and Lynn Stewart. "Adult Correctional Treatment." In *Prisons,* Vol. 26, edited by Michael Tonry and Joan Petersilia, pp. 361–426. Chicago: University of Chicago Press, 1999.

McDonald, Douglas C. "Medical Care in Prisons." In *Prisons,* Vol. 26, edited by Michael Tonry and Joan Petersilia,

pp. 427–478. Chicago: University of Chicago Press, 1999.

Waxler, H. K., G. DeLeon, G. Thomas, D. Kressel, and J. Peters. "The Amity Prison TC Evaluation: Reincarceration Outcomes." New York: New York Center for Therapeutic Community Research at the National/Development and Research Institutes, n.d.

NOTES

1. This case is found in Michael C. Braswell, Reid H. Montgomery Jr., and Lucien X. Lombardo, eds., *Prison Violence in America,* 2d ed. (Cincinnati: Anderson, 1994), p. 360.

2. Edwin E. Megargee and Martin J. Bohn Jr., *Classifying Criminal Offenders: A New System Based on the MMPI* (Beverly Hills, Calif.: Sage, 1979), pp. 75–76.

3. The philosophy and procedures of reintegration classification were explained to the author by correctional counselors and their supervisors who used it in their institutions.

4. See Robert B. Levinson and Roy E. Gerard, "Functional Units: A Different Correctional Approach," *Federal Probation* 37 (December 1973), pp. 8–16.

5. Richard Gramley, at the time the director of classification for the Department of Corrections in Illinois, described this process to the author.

6. See Douglas Lipton, Robert Martinson, and Judith Wilks, *The Effectiveness of Correctional Treatment: A Survey of Treatment Evaluation Studies* (New York: Praeger, 1975), p. 210.

7. Eric Berne, *What Do You Say after You Say Hello?* (New York Grove Press, 1972).

8. Thomas A. Harris, *I'm OK—You're OK* (New York: Harper & Row, 1965).

9. William Glasser, *Reality Therapy* (New York: Harper & Row, 1965).

10. Maxwell Jones, *Social Psychiatry in Prison* (Baltimore: Penguin Books, 1968).

11. Martin Groder, "An Angry Resignation," *Corrections Magazine* 1 (July/August 1975), p. 33.

12. William G. Nagel, *The New Red Barn: A Critical Look at the Modern American Prison* (New York: Walker, 1973), p. 14.

13. S. Yochelson and S. E. Samenow, *The Criminal Personality: A Profile for Change,* Vol. 1 (New York: Aronson, 1976); and Y. Yochelson and S. E. Samenow, *The Criminal Personality: The Change Process,* Vol. 2 (New York: Aronson, 1977).

14. Gerald G. Gaes, Timothy J. Flanigan, Lawrence L. Motiuk, and Lynn Stewart, "Adult Correctional Treatment," in *Prisons* 26, ed. Michael Tonry and Joan Petersilia (Chicago: University of Chicago Press, 1999), pp. 374–375.

15. P. Gendreau and D. A. Andrews, "Tertiary Prevention: What the Meta-Analysis of the Offender Treatment Literature Tells Us about What Works," *Canadian Journal of Criminology* 32 (1990), pp. 173–184; R. L. Izzo and R. R. Ross, "Meta-Analysis of Rehabilitation Programs for Juvenile Delinquents," *Criminal Justice and Behavior* 17 (1990), pp. 134–142.

16. Gaes et al., "Adult Correctional Treatment," pp. 374–375.

17. Ibid., p. 375.

18. Ibid., p. 385.

19. Camille Graham Camp and George M. Camp, *The Corrections Yearbook 1999: Adult Corrections* (Middletown, Conn.: Criminal Justice Institute, 1999), pp. 118–119.

20. Marcia R. Chaiken, *Prison Programs for Drug-Involved Offenders* (Washington, D.C.: U.S. Department of Justice, 1989), p. 2.

21. Ibid.

22. Ibid. For Pelissier's evaluation of in-prison drug treatment programs administered in nineteen federal prisons, see B. Pelissier, "Triad Drug Treatment Evaluation Project: Six Month Interim Report," Unpublished manuscript (Washington, D.C.: Federal Bureau of Prisons, 1997).

23. Camp and Camp, *The Corrections Yearbook 1999*, p. 97.

24. Ibid.

25. Gaes et al., "Adult Correctional Treatment," p. 399.

26. Robert Martinson, "Works—Questions and Answers about Prison Reform," *Public Interest* 35 (Spring 1974), p. 28.

27. J. Gerber and E. J. Fritsch, "The Effects of Academic and Vocational Program Participation on Inmate Misconduct and Reincarceration," *Prison Education Research Report: Final Report* (Huntsville, Tex.: Sam Houston State University, 1994); S. L. Anderson, D. B. Anderson, and R. E. Schumacker, *Correctional Education: A Way to Stay Out* (Springfield: Illinois Council on Vocational Education, 1988; F. Porporino and D. Robinson, *Can Educating Adult Offenders Counteract Recidivism?* (Ottawa: Correctional Service of Canada, 1992).

28. Gaes et al., "Adult Correctional Treatment," p. 402.

29. Gerber and Fritsch, "The Effects of Academic and Vocational Program Participation on Inmate Misconduct and Reincarceration," p. 8.

30. Interviewed in January 2001.

31. Prisoners have made such comments to the author on a number of occasions.

32. *Pugh v. Locke,* 406 F.Supp. 318 (MD Ala. 1976); and *Newman v. Alabama,* 559 F.2d. 283 (5th Cir. 1977).

33. Douglas C. McDonald, "Medical Care in Prison," in *Prisons,* p. 455.

34. Bureau of Justice Statistics, *1996–1997 Update: HIV/AIDS, STDs and TB in Correctional Institutions* (Washington, D.C.: U.S. Department of Justice, 1999), pp. 7–8.

35. Alex Durham III, *Crisis and Reform: Current Issues in American Punishment* (Boston: Little, Brown, 1994), pp. 70–71.

36. Leo Carroll, "AIDS and Human Rights in the Prison: A Comment on the Ethics of Screening Segregation" (paper presented at the annual meeting of the American Society of Criminology, Reno, November 1989), p. 3.

37. McDonald, "Medical Care in Prison," pp. 427–478.

38. Camille Graham Camp and George M. Camp, *The Corrections Yearbook 1997* (South Salem, N.Y.: Criminal Justice Institute, 1997), p. 33.

39. Sawyer's statement to the Senate Judiciary Committee.

40. Connecticut Department of Corrections, *Free Venture Model in Corrections* (Hartford, Conn.: Department of Corrections, n.d.).

41. Steven Elbow, *Isthmus* (1995). http://www.TheDailyPage.com.

42. Gaes et al., "Adult Correctional Treatment," p. 404.

43. Gaes et al., "Adult Correctional Treatment," pp. 363–365. These researchers derived these principles from an examination of a number of research studies in the late 1980s and 1990s. For these studies, see ibid., p. 363.

44. Herbert C. Quay, "The Three Faces of Evaluation: What Can Be Expected to Work," *Criminal Justice and Behavior* 4 (December 1977), pp. 341–353.

CHAPTER 13 / BUILT-IN STUDY GUIDE

Multiple Choice Questions

1. All of the following are roles that correctional counselors perform except:

   A. Caseworker
   B. Counselor
   C. Advocate for inmates
   D. Developing parole release guidelines

2. What is the first step in the treatment process of inmates?

   A. Psychological evaluation
   B. Sociological evaluation
   C. Medical evaluation
   D. Criminal history

3. Which of the following is the most frequently administered test in adult correctional systems?

   A. National Multiphasic Personality Inventory
   B. Minnesota Multiphasic Personality Inventory
   C. Georgia Multiphasic Personality Inventory
   D. California Multiphasic Personality Inventory

4. According to the text, the three main groups of treatment modalities used within a prison are:

   A. Sociological therapy, social psychological therapy, drug therapy
   B. Sociological therapy, violence therapy, drug therapy
   C. Psychological technologies, behavior therapy programs, drug-related interventions
   D. Psychological technologies, milieu therapy, drug-related interventions

5. The basic philosophy behind unit management is:

   A. To divide the prison into smaller units that have authority and communication links
   B. To divide the prison into smaller units that report to a central unit
   C. To divide the prison into smaller units using a paramilitary approach
   D. To divide the prison into smaller units using an inmate grievance system

6. The advantages of Transactional Analysis Groups include all of the following except:

   A. It is easy to learn
   B. It reduces disciplinary problems
   C. It provides future opportunities for inmates who become skilled at it
   D. It is always effective because all offenders are motivated to examine their own problems

7. Which of the following is not an example of a positive reinforcer of behavior?

   A. Attention
   B. Praise
   C. Privileges
   D. Threats

8. Which of the following is the largest self-help group?

   A. Jaycees
   B. Gamblers Anonymous
   C. Hillel
   D. Toastmaster

9. Which of the following diseases is transmitted through the air?

   A. Measles
   B. AIDS
   C. Tuberculosis
   D. Hepatitis

10. Identify the most popular program in prison.

    A. Recreation
    B. Law library
    C. Academic education
    D. Vocational training

11. What type of prison program is designed for inmates who lack work experience or demonstrable skills or trades and has the basic purpose of preparing inmates for jobs in the community.

    A. Vocational training
    B. Academic training
    C. Occupational schools
    D. GED preparation

12. Beyond treatment programs, what does the state have to provide for inmates?

    A. Conjugal visits
    B. Adequate basic care
    C. Parole systems
    D. Counseling in legal issues

True/False Questions

T F   1. By the 1980s, classification had become a treatment tool.

T F   2. Prior to spreading to state correctional systems, unit management was first used in the Federal Bureau of Prisons.

T F   3. The goal of behavior therapy is to reinforce positive behavior in inmates.

T F   4. The goal of social work therapy is to assist inmates in developing insight on why they do what they do.

T F   5. A fundamental limitation of psychotherapy is that psychiatrists have little time to conduct ongoing therapy sessions with inmates.

T F   6. Drug-related treatment programs that address inmates with substance abuse problems have increased significantly over the past two decades.

T F   7. The use of behavior modification is increasing at a substantial rate in adult corrections.

T F   8. Cutbacks in federal grant money have led to the decline in the number of college courses being offered in prison.

T F   9. One of the criticisms of vocational programs offered in male prisons is their lack of variety.

T F   10. Traditionally, religion is popular inside a prison.

T F   11. The quality of the visiting experience has improved in recent years for the inmate.

T F   12. According to prison officials, no more than 20 percent of inmates are committed to a religious faith.

Fill-in-the-Blank Questions   (based on key terms)

1. Currently, _____ systems utilized in prisons are focused on security issues rather than treatment needs.

2. _____ encourages prisoners to talk about past conflicts that caused them to express emotional problems through aggressive or antisocial behavior.

3. A _____ focuses on the total environment and the experiences of that environment as instruments for treatment interventions into offenders.

4. The use of consequential thinking to reduce impulsivity is one of the core components of the _____.

5. To avoid boredom inmates are eager to participate in activities that focus on benefiting the institution and community. This type of activity is known as a _____.

6. The type of visit in which a partition extending from floor to ceiling is placed between the prisoner and visitor is known as a _____.

7. A treatment approach that operates with a therapist demonstrating to an inmate that his or her irresponsible behavior is not acceptable is known as _____.

8. _____ is a treatment approach based on interpreting and evaluating relationships among people.

9. _____ focus on identifying dysfunctional thinking patterns associated with criminal behavior such as impulsivity associated with poor verbal self-regulation and impairment in means–ends reasoning.

10. _____ such as Seventh Step are operated primarily by inmates and are designed to help inmates close to being released become successful in society.

Essay Questions

1. Explain the role of classification in the treatment process of criminal offenders.

2. Identify and describe the three main categories of treatment methods used within a prison.

3. Identify and explain the three categories of prison services that institutions are required to offer to comply with the constitutional rights of inmates.

4. During the late nineteenth and early twentieth century, how did the rehabilitation model affect the operation of the prison?

5. Describe the various academic educational, vocational training, and religious programs offered in prison. Are they effective?

ANSWERS

Multiple Choice Questions

1.	D	7.	D
2.	A	8.	A
3.	B	9.	C
4.	C	10.	A
5.	A	11.	A
6.	D	12.	B

True/False Questions

1.	F	7.	F
2.	T	8.	T
3.	T	9.	F
4.	F	10.	T
5.	T	11.	T
6.	T	12.	F

Fill-in-the-Blank Questions

1. Classification
2. Psychotherapy
3. Therapeutic community
4. Cognitive Thinking Skills Program
5. Service project
6. Closed visit
7. Reality therapy
8. Transactional analysis
9. Cognitive behavioral interventions
10. Self-help programs

chapter fourteen

The Male Prisoner

William, a long-term Pennsylvania inmate tells how he has learned to do time. He also gives some information on how he sells drugs in prison:

What I have to say may sound real strange to the individual on the outside. Let me start with the statement that time is time. Like I'm doing time, but I'm doing the best time possible. Even though I'm locked up away from society I can push society aside and live in this world. I don't even miss society; it's either that or I know it is senseless to think of what is not possible. So to save my sanity, I live where I am. I guess I'll survive, it's a mental process. To think about going home everyday would drive you nuts. Time would do you. I do time and enjoy it. That's deep, isn't it? . . .

I was thinking earlier that I know this world better than the outside world. I have more than a third of my life in here, and in seven years I'll have half of my life in here. Believe me I'm not proud of it. I have a son who is 14; he is coming to see me next week. I have not seen him since he was 18 months old. Do you realize the shock I'm in when I call him on the phone and he calls me Dad. It messes me up. All of a sudden I'm cast into fatherhood.

I'm here listening to soft music and thinking. I've been thinking about deals on the yard. I spend a lot of time in the corner where the card game is. I keep the book—who owes who. The only times I leave the area is when I am making a drug deal. While out, I scan the yard. We call it "prowling." I need to know who is doing what. If you sell a certain drug, you try to beat your competitor to the punch. Also, it's good to know who has been buying what, so you know how much the user owes out. If you let the drug user go too far, he will take lockup. He might give you up to get out of lockup, and then you are in lockup.[1]

CRITICAL THINKING QUESTIONS

How is this male prisoner doing time? How is being a father interfering with his doing time? What risks besides lockup does selling drugs in prison present?

In the movie *Shawshank Redemption,* Red has learned how to do time. He plays the social role of a "merchant"—he is able to locate what inmates desire, for a price. Red poses no problem for the prison staff and is eventually released. William also has learned how to do time, but his way is much different from Red's. He becomes the leader of a white gang, takes a hostage at one point (the hostage is released unarmed), and becomes one of the largest drug sellers within the prison. It is unlikely that William will ever be released.

All prisoners, male and female, experience many of the same feelings about and reactions to confinement. Usually far from home with little or no contact with loved ones, both men and women feel alienated. They must learn to adapt to a world of deprivation, doing without certain comforts and pleasures they enjoyed in the free world. Some pleasures, however, such as drugs, can be attained within the walls. Boredom is ever present. The experienced male or female convict eventually learns to do time but has to fight against going "stir crazy." Furthermore, the total impact of incarceration—one negative experience stacked on the next—hardens a person. Male inmates, especially, learn that the best way to avoid being hurt is to repress their emotions. An ex-offender talks about the consequences of repressing his emotions in prison: "It took me a long time after I got out before I could feel anything. I was so used to making sure that nobody 'messed' with me that I didn't trust nobody. I couldn't let anyone close to me. I didn't know what it felt like to love somebody. Man, I was dead."[2]

Major differences do exist in how male and female prisoners serve their prison sentences. The male must learn to coexist with larger numbers of peers because men's prisons are several times the size of women's prisons. Survival is less certain in men's prisons, so men are more likely to arm themselves for self-protection. In most state and federal prisons, the male prisoner also must deal with inmate gangs. As a gang member in a midwestern prison noted, "In here you can't fly alone; you've to join an organization if you want to survive."[3] Moreover, racial conflict is more acute in men's than in women's prisons. Racial tension sometimes erupts in sexual victimization, in stabbings and killings, and in mass disturbances. In women's prisons, African American inmates tend to adopt the dominant roles and to bring solidarity to the inmate culture (women in prison is the subject of Chapter 15).

HOW HAS THE INMATE WORLD CHANGED?

John Irwin's division of the recent history of the prison into three eras—those of the Big House, the correctional institution, and the contemporary prison—provides a helpful outline for examining changes in inmate culture in U.S. prisons—changes in social roles, informal behavior norms, and social solidarity.[4]

The so-called Big House dominated American correction from the early twentieth century through the 1950s. In the Big House, prison populations showed considerable homogeneity. Most of the inmates were white, were property offenders, and had spent several stints in prison during the course of their criminal careers.[5] "Convicts," as they were known then, developed a unified culture and kept their distance from the "hacks" or guards.

After World War II, correctional institutions replaced Big Houses in many states. The use of indeterminate sentencing, classification, and treatment represented the realization of the rehabilitative ideal.[6] But as most staff knew and new prisoners quickly learned, the main purpose of the correctional institution was to punish, control, and restrain prisoners, and treatment played only a minor role. The solidarity present among inmates of the Big House disappeared. Racial conflict developed, inmates saw themselves as political prisoners, and violence toward staff and other inmates took place on a regular basis.

Today, in the era of the contemporary prison, the social order often verges on collapse; in fact, at times, the social order does collapse. Over the long term, however, this fragmented, tense, and violent setting remains intact because inmates ultimately prefer order to disorder. As one gang leader stated, "We're in control around here. If we wanted to, we could take the prison apart, but we choose not to. We've too much to lose."[7]

The prison of the twenty-first century is a place of violence and disillusionment. Several factors account for the hopelessness that many inmates feel: the ever-increasing problem of idleness, longer sentences, tighter controls imposed by staff, overcrowding, the decline of political ideology, more lockdown time and fewer privileges, and the reduced possibility of relief through the judicial process.

The Big House

In the Big House, as movies of the 1930s suggest, old "cons" informed new prisoners that the guards were in control and the inmates had to make the best of it. To make their time easier in the Big House, convicts developed their own social roles, informal codes of behaviors, and language.[8] Gresham Sykes created a typology of their social roles:

Rats and center men, who hope to relieve their pains by betrayal of fellow prisoners

Gorillas and merchants, who relieve deprivation by preying on their fellow prisoners, taking their possessions by force or the threat of force

Wolves, punks, and fags, who engage in homosexual acts either voluntarily or under coercion to relieve the deprivation of heterosexuality

Real men, who endure the rigors of confinement with dignity, as opposed to ball busters who openly defy authority

Toughs, who are overtly violent, who will fight with anyone, strong or weak, and who "won't take anything from anybody"

Hipsters, who talk tough but are really "all wind and gumdrops"[9]

The social roles that prisoners, other than "real men," chose to play provided ways to reduce the rigors of prison life at the expense of fellow prisoners. Convicts fulfilling the social role of the "real man" were loyal and generous and tried to minimize friction among inmates. To the extent that they succeeded, they fostered social cohesion moving in the direction of inmate solidarity. Quoting Thomas Hobbes's famous account of society in a state of war, "where every man is an enemy to every man . . . and which is worst of all, [in] continual fear and danger of violent death," Sykes concluded that when cohesion was not achieved, and the rats, center men, gorillas, wolves, and toughs breached solidarity, prison life became "solitary, poor, nasty, brutish, and short."[10]

In the Big House, the informal inmate code of behavior was based on the following tenets:

1. Don't interfere with inmate interests.
2. Never rat on a con.
3. Do your own time.
4. Don't exploit fellow inmates.
5. Be tough; be a man; never back down from a fight.
6. Don't trust the "hacks" (guards) or the things they stand for.[11]

The **inmate code** was functional not only to prisoners but to prison administrators.[12] The code promoted order. It encouraged each prisoner to serve his sentence rather than creating problems. Prisoners understood that disorder within the walls would mean that informal arrangements between prisoner leaders and staff would be set aside and prisoners would lose privileges it had taken them years to attain. The code also protected the self-respect of inmates because they knew they were maintaining order not for the staff but for themselves. "Hacks" were the enemy, and a convict who was worthy of his role within the prison made his animosity toward the enemy very clear.

Nevertheless, inmates and guards in the Big House knew that they depended on each other. Inmates maintained order and performed many of the tasks of running the institution. In turn, guards permitted inmates to violate certain rules and to gain privileges that were contrary to policy. What took place was an exchange. Staff and inmates accommodated each other's needs while maintaining a hostile stance toward each other.

Donald Clemmer, who studied the Big House in his seminal study of Menard Prison in southern Illinois, claimed that the solidarity of the inmate world caused prisoners to become more criminalized than they already were. Clemmer coined the term **prisonization,** defining it as the "taking on in greater or lesser degree of the folkways, customs, and general culture of the penitentiary."[13] "Prisonization," he added, "is a process of assimilation, in which prisoners adopt a subordinate status, learn prison argot (language), take on the habits of other prisoners, engage in various forms of deviant behavior such as homosexual behavior and gambling, develop antagonistic attitudes toward guards, and become acquainted with inmate dogmas and mores."[14]

Clemmer's emphasis was on the unique situation of the prison as a half-closed community composed of unwilling members under the coercive control of state employees. The prison was viewed as a closed system, despite the fact that staff and the prisoners themselves were bringing in the outside culture and its values. Clemmer thought that all convicts are prisonized to some extent and possibly as many as 20 percent are completely prisonized. It appeared that upon release the highly prisonized offenders were likely to return to crime. Just as an immigrant coming to the United States would be "Americanized" to a greater or lesser degree, so would a convict entering prison be more or less prisonized. See Within the Walls 14.1 for an analysis of how order was maintained in the Big House.

The Correctional Institution

Michel Foucault has argued that the rehabilitative ideal offers the ultimate means of promoting order within the correctional institution.[15] The indeterminate sentence and the parole board represented a direct means of promoting order, or control, because they communicated the clear message to the inmate that conformity was necessary for release. What also promoted peace and stability was the fact that most prisoners were busy at work or at school, whether or not they believed in the rehabilitative ideal.

Yet at the time the rehabilitative ideal was being attempted in prison—in the 1960s—American society was experiencing social and political unrest. The Black Power movement developed on the West Coast and soon spread throughout the nation and into

According to Gresham Sykes, by what process did these convicts become "prisonized"? What is "prisonization," and how did it come to be associated with the concept of the Big House? What are some characteristics of the Big House values, norms, and sanctions that are involved in "prisonization"?

the walls   14.1

Structural–Functional Perspective on Imprisonment

According to Gresham Sykes, the structural–functional approach to the prison, rested on a set of basic insights:

1. It was recognized that prison, like any other complex social system persisting through time, could not be run by the use of force alone, that some degree of voluntary cooperation on the part of those who were ruled was necessary. The problem then was how this cooperation could be obtained.

2. The rewards and punishments legally available to the prison authorities were generally inadequate, as far as securing cooperation was concerned....

3. Some degree of cooperation could be obtained—and usually was—by a system of illegal or forbidden rewards, such as guards ignoring the infraction of prison rules by inmates. Prisoners were allowed to engage in various forms of deviant behavior—ostensibly—of a minor sort—in exchange for a quiet institution. This pattern of the custodians breaking the rules for the sake of peace and quiet was part of an extensive pattern of "corruption" based on friendship and the innocuous encroachment on the guards' duties on the part of inmates.

4. Imprisonment involved a set of deprivations that went far beyond the loss of liberty or material comfort. Prisoners were faced with a number of psychological threats to their self-conception or sense of worth, such as being reduced to childhood's dependence or being forced into homosexual liaisons.

5. Much of the behavior of inmates could be interpreted as attempts, conscious or unconscious, to meet and

> ...custodians breaking the rules for the sake of peace and quiet was part of an extensive pattern of "corruption" based on friendship...

counter the problems posed by the deprivations of prison life, including the potent threats to the ego....

6. It was claimed that the behavior patterns of inmates sprang from a set of values, attitudes, and beliefs that found expression in the so-called inmate code couched in prison argot. The code held forth a pattern of approved conduct, but as Shelly Messinger and I tried to make clear, it was an ideal rather than a description of how inmates behaved....

These ideas came to be labeled "the structural–functional perspective on the prison," and I suppose that designation was appropriate, in the sense that interest in the prison centered on (1) the social structure of the prison as a whole, and (2) the ways in which beliefs, norms, and behavior of both inmates and guards functioned to maintain the prison as an ongoing system.

CRITICAL THINKING QUESTIONS

What are the dangers in the types of accommodations that took place between staff and inmates in the Big House? Do you think correctional officers would go back to such an arrangement if it meant cooperative inmates?

Source: Gresham M. Sykes, "The Structural–Functional Perspective on Imprisonment," in *Punishment and Social Control: Essays in Honor of Sheldon L. Messinger,* ed. Thomas G. Blomberg and Stanley Cohen (New York: Aldine de Gruyter, 1985), pp. 81–82.

---

the prisons. As the number of African American inmates began to increase in the 1960s, the Black Power movement contributed to the racial unrest and hostility that would become a major source of disruption within correctional institutions. Racial unrest followed the desegregation of housing units, jobs, classrooms, and recreational programs in the prison. Racial unrest toppled the social order in many prisons, but as it fell, inmates tried to stop the disintegration, mend the cracks, and pull the pieces back together.[16]

The social reintegration of prisoners began in the late 1960s, as inmates began to redefine, in a newly political fashion, their relationships with one another, the prison administration, the criminal justice system, and society. The politicization of prisoners contributed to an outbreak of prison riots totally different from the riots of past eras. The riots were more organized, supported from the outside, led by prisoners who defined themselves as political activists, and intended to make far-reaching changes in the prison and justice system, if not in society itself.[17]

Inmates' responses to imprisonment received some examination during the era of the correctional institution. In a study of the Washington State Reformatory, Stanton Wheeler found strong support for Clemmer's concept of prisonization. But Wheeler found that the degree of prisonization varied according to the phase of an inmate's institutional stay: An inmate was most strongly influenced by the norms of the inmate subculture during the middle stage of his or her prison stay (with more than six months remaining).[18]

Further examination of the process of prisonization led to the development of the deprivation model and the importation model. The **deprivation model,** according to Gresham Sykes, views the losses experienced by an inmate during incarceration as part of the costs of imprisonment. The model describes the prisoner's attempt to adapt to the deprivations imposed by incarceration.[19] But John Irwin and Donald R. Cressey, among others, contended that patterns of behavior are brought to, or imported into the prison, rather than developed within the walls. The **importation model** suggests that the influences that prisoners bring into the prison affect their process of imprisonment.[20] Charles W. Thomas, in a study of a maximum-security prison in a southeastern state, concluded that integration of the deprivation and importation models was needed to understand the impact of the prison culture on an inmate. Thomas found that the greater the degree of similarity between a person's preprison activities and the norms of the prison subculture, the greater was the person's receptivity to the influences of prisonization. He also found that the inmates who had the greatest degree of contact with the outside world had the lowest degree of prisonization.[21]

James B. Jacobs's study of the Stateville Penitentiary in Illinois examines how much the external society influences what takes place within the prison. Jacobs describes the various external groups that entered Stateville and sought to participate in the decision-making process. In the 1960s and 1970s, Jacobs highlights the penetration of the prison by the Black Muslims, by street gangs from Chicago, and by civil liberty and legal groups. But he saw the basis of real transformation as coming from the judicial review of prison administration and prison procedures.

In the late 1960s, the courts started to apply their definition of due process and to extend to the prisoner the essential aspects of the rights of citizenship. What emerged was a new set of legalistic and bureaucratic rules and procedures for guiding the day-to-day activities of prison administrators and staffs. Understandably, under these conditions, the unionization of the guards took place because they also were searching for a set of rules and procedures to defend their position in the prison system. Thus, Jacobs's analysis of Stateville contends that the social organization and moral values, as well as the major societal changes, of the larger society are found in the microsociety within the walls.[22] In Within the Walls 14.2, a conflict view of imprisonment is found in the radicalization of prisoners movement.

The Contemporary Prison

Support for inmate codes eroded in the 1960s and 1970s and seems to be disappearing from the contemporary prison. The only solidarity evident in the inmate culture today exists within prison gangs and within racial groups. However, there are signs that the solidarity of inmate gangs may be breaking down. Drug-addicted street "punks" typically do not follow any inmate or gang norms and thus incur the disapproval of gang leaders. Also, in the late 1990s, increasing numbers of gang members were "turning" **state's evidence,** providing prosecution attorneys with evidence resulting in the conviction of several top gang leaders.[23]

Administrative controls, especially in super-max facilities and high-security units, and stiffer penalties for criminal behavior have increased hopelessness within the walls. The increased number of habitual offender statutes has led to the graying of the prison population. The prevailing political attitude seems to favor making confinement as stressful as possible. Indeed, confinement is a disorienting experience for nearly all inmates. In *The Society of Captives,* Gresham Sykes describes the causes of what he calls the pains of imprisonment: (1) the deprivation of liberty, (2) the deprivation of goods and services, (3) the deprivation of heterosexual relationships, (4) the deprivation of au-

the walls   14.2

within

Radicalization of Prisoners Movement

Leaders of the radicalization of prisoners movement included Malcolm X, Eldridge Cleaver, and George Jackson. In radical and revolutionary inmate organizations, members of the lower class were perceived as political prisoners—victims of an unjust system of social control and economic relationships that "force" the poor into antisocial behavior. *Soledad Brother,* the prison letters of the late George Jackson, was a sacred document for the movement. In one of his most widely quoted statements, Jackson warned:

> There are still some blacks here who consider themselves criminals—but not many. . . . Believe me, my friend, study and think, you will find no class or category more aware, more embittered, desperate or dedicated to the ultimate remedy—revolution. The most dedicated, the best of our kind—you'll find in the Folsoms, San Quentins, and Soledads.

The prisoner radicalization movement extended far beyond California's African American inmates. Russell Oswald, commissioner of corrections in New York State, claimed that revolutionary activity at Attica was one of the chief causes of the inmate rebellion there. John Faine

> . . . a majority of inmates . . . perceived impoverished offenders to be the unwilling victims of an oppressive social system.

and Edward Bohlander investigated the extent of a radical worldview nurtured by the prison environment in a large correctional facility in Kentucky. They concluded that a majority of inmates, both white and African American, perceived impoverished offenders to be the unwilling victims of an oppressive social system. Moreover, a propensity for extreme radicalism and violence was exhibited in different degrees by one-half to two-thirds of the inmate population.

CRITICAL THINKING QUESTIONS

Do you think that most prisoners in the 1960s and 1970s considered themselves political prisoners? Do you think that this notion of being a political prisoner is widespread in the twenty-first century?

Source: George Jackson, *Soledad Brother: The Prison Letters of George Jackson* (New York: Coward-McCann, 1970), p. 26; Russell G. Oswald, *My Story* (Garden City, N.Y.: Doubleday, 1972), p. 26; and John R. Faine and Edward Bohlander Jr., "The Genesis of Disorder: Oppression, Confinement, and Prisoner Politicization," in *Issues in Contemporary Corrections*, ed. C. Ronald Huff (Beverly Hills, Calif.: Sage, 1977), pp. 54–77.

tonomy, and (5) the deprivation of security. Each deprivation, according to Sykes, is serious, and in combination they have a pathological effect on the prison environment and on the inmate.[24] The pains, or stresses, of confinement are greatest for those who have no links with or supportive networks in the outside world; who live in overcrowded prisons where no personal space is available; who must struggle with various forms of victimization, especially sexual; who are mentally ill and are totally baffled by the prison environment; who face long sentences; or who are living under the sentence of death.[25]

Lynne Goodstein's study of three state correctional institutions for adult males in two northeastern states provides a serious critique of this nation's policy of imprisonment. Goodstein found that the inmates who adjusted most successfully to a prison environment encountered the most difficulty making the transition from institutional life to freedom. She concluded that the inmates who were least able to adjust to the formal institutional culture seemed to make the smoothest transition to community life. "It is ironic," she remarks, "that . . . inmates who accepted the basic structure of the prison, who were well adjusted to the routine, and who held more desirable prison jobs . . . had the most difficulty adjusting to the outside world."[26]

The hero in this chapter is James B. Jacobs, professor of law and sociology at New York University Law School and author of *Stateville.* Because of that work and his subsequent analyses of prisoners' rights and the guard culture, he is considered one of the most perceptive experts on corrections in the United States. Read what he said for *Invitation to Corrections* in 2000.

h e r o e s

James B. Jacobs

Professor of Law at New York University Law School

"We must always be wary of sweeping generalizations about 'the American prison,' the 'American prisoner,' and so forth. No matter how many times we remind ourselves that ours is an enormous country with a massive penal infrastructure populated by some 2 million inmates, it is easy to fall into the trap of imagining that all prisons and prisoners conform to one's own small sample. Like everything about American crime and criminal justice and, for that matter, about America itself, there is great diversity. Super-max prisons are completely different from minimum-security work camps. Prisons carrying on the remnants of the plantation culture in Mississippi are completely different from prisons in New York. To some extent the Federal Bureau of Prisons is a world in itself. A 22-year-old armed robber will have a very different prison experience than a 55-year-old judge convicted of corruption.

" 'Doing time' at Stateville in the early 1970s was dominated by the power of prison gangs, by racial tension and avoidance, and by the relative weakness of prison management during an era of major transition. In the mid-1970s, at least at Stateville, there was much uncertainty in the daily life of the prison. What could the correctional officers do and not do under the rapidly evolving prisoners' rights law? To what extent would the prisons continue to be penetrated by outside reform groups grounded in treatment philosophy? What kind of living conditions, medical care, and 'services' were inmates entitled to?

"No doubt, some of these issues are still relevant, but they probably look different today. Race is still a major factor in how inmates do time. There is still a great deal of voluntary racial separation, although the picture may be complicated by the presence of more ethnicities. Interracial conflict continues to be a fact of prison life and hard-core racist gangs continue to flourish in some prisons. Still, the kind of horrendous prison race riots and race wars that characterized some prisons (whole prison systems) of the 1960s and 1970s does not seem to characterize American prisons in the last decades of the twentieth century.

"Prison management has become much better, more savvy and more sophisticated than it was in the early 1970s. Prison officials have learned how to organize their agencies as modern bureaucracies and to live with the courts. There is less uncertainty. There is less expectation that the next day will bring some new and sweeping court decision that will send the prison officials on their heels.

"This does not necessarily mean that prisons are more comfortable or safer today than they were in the early 1970s. The massive increase in prison population has strained almost all our state prison systems. Day-to-day living conditions in many prisons are not good.

"Inmates serve more time for the same offense today than they did three decades ago. And far more inmates carry life sentences, frequently reinforced by no-parole guarantees. That means that there are many more old prisoners today than in the early 1970s, and their numbers will continue to increase.

"The prison, like all social institutions, is always a product of its society. If that society devotes no resources or shows no concern for its prisoners, by taking that position, of course, it influences and shapes what happens inside. In *Stateville,* I argued that in the 1960s the Stateville warden lost control of his organization's boundaries. It would no longer be possible to operate an American prison in the style of the autocrats of old. The courts, for one, would no longer give prison officials that kind of carte blanche. In addition, in many states public employee unions brought another powerful actor into the prisons and interfered with the warden's historical dominance of his staff.

"The world, of course, is never still. New laws, political waves, cultural styles, all shape the prison world. Very few prison officials or prison scholars in the early 1970s would have anticipated that within a decade or two a substantial fraction of the correctional officers in men's prisons would be females. That revolutionary change was a consequence of Title VII rather than any kind of penal policy or reform. Other laws, like the Americans with Disabilities Act and the Freedom Reformation Act have also sent shock waves through the prisons.

"The Prison Litigation Reform Act (PLRA) is the most important federal law affecting prisons of the last quarter century, perhaps of all time. It represents an omnibus attack on every aspect of the prisoners' rights movement and the federal judicial authority to monitor state prisons. It has put an end to an entire phase of American penal reform characterized by activist judges and court-appointed masters.

"American politics turned to the right in the 1980s, with enormous consequences for prisons and jails. The renewed commitment to law and order and to being tough on crime led to a massive increase in the number of penal institutions and inmates. Those same political impulses led to the elimination of some progressive prison programs, like Pell Grants for inmates pursuing college degrees. Time served increased, and parole was more quickly revoked.

"We learned in the 1980s and 1990s that prisons are not spared the ravages of health epidemics. Indeed, because of close and unsanitary living conditions and the unhealthy lifestyles of many of the prisoners, prison populations were especially vulnerable to AIDS and tuberculosis, which, in retrospect, will probably be seen as the most important prison issues of the last decades of the twentieth century."

CRITICAL THINKING QUESTIONS

According to James Jacobs, what are the shortcomings of generalizations about U.S. corrections? How have prisons changed in the past three decades? How are prisons a product of their society?

WHAT ARE SPECIAL GROUPS OF MALE PRISONERS?

Within the social world of the prison, members of different races barely tolerate each other, interpersonal violence is increasing, and inmate gangs vie for control. Certain groups of male inmates deserve a close examination because imprisonment poses a particularly difficult challenge for them.

The sex offender, especially if he has victimized children, knows that he will not be well received in this inmate society. In the midst of all their conflicting norms, inmates in nearly every prison find the violator of children repulsive.

Individuals with AIDS also have an especially difficult time in inmate society. They are gravely ill and usually anxious about whether proper medical care will be available. Instead of being concerned about exploitation from fellow inmates, prisoners with AIDS experience rejection by fellow inmates in a number of ways. Long-term prisoners, like prisoners with AIDS, must deal with survival in the prison context. Someone who has a sentence of life without parole or who believes that he will never be paroled faces the prospect of dying in prison.

An elderly prisoner may have been imprisoned for years or may be relatively new to the prison experience. Because he is likely to spend his final days in the correctional environment, he deals with the same types of issues as the long-term prisoner and the inmate with AIDS. He may be receiving various forms of medical care and may have been moved into an institution or unit with other elderly prisoners.

Sex Offenders

Increased prosecution and conviction, as well as longer and harsher sentences, have contributed significantly to increased numbers of sex offenders in prison.[27] *Corrections Compendium* reported that in 1988 federal and state prisons held 62,000 sex offenders—9.8 percent of the inmate population. In 1992, these facilities held 98,000 sex offenders—11.5 percent of the prison population. California had the largest number of prisoners convicted of sex offenses (16,000); North Dakota, the smallest (93).[28]

Other signs of the get-tough attitude toward sex offenders are laws permitting the indefinite confinement of rapists and child molesters who are viewed as too dangerous for release at the end of their court-imposed sentences. The state of Washington had the first such law, but Kansas, New Jersey, and Wisconsin have adopted similar laws.[29] With their release, sex offenders, especially those convicted of offenses against children, are faced with Megan's Law and the National Sex Offender Registry.

The major categories of sex offenders received in prison are the rapist and the child molester. The rapist has traditionally not had his offense held against him in prison. The crime of rape is viewed as a violent offense against women, and inmates can usually make sense of or at least accept this type of criminal behavior. Prisoners view much more negatively an inmate who raped several women or who has a history of raping juvenile girls.

The child molester has long had difficulty with his prison adjustment. There may no longer be "honor among thieves" in prison, but there certainly appears to be a desire to make a child molester pay for his crimes. Unless these offenders are placed in protective custody, they are likely to be raped—brutally. They also are likely victims of prison homicides, as another inmate takes a "shank" (home-made knife) to them.

Prisoners with AIDS

Chapter 13 discusses the response of the corrections system to inmates with acquired immune deficiency syndrome (AIDS). Some corrections systems have many more inmates with AIDS than do other systems. New York, for example, has nearly 40 percent of the inmates with AIDS.[30]

Chapter 13 also lists the difficult questions posed by the threat of AIDS in prison.[31] How those questions are answered determines in large part the quality of care that AIDS inmates receive in prison. What those questions do not consider is how other inmates and staff will respond to AIDS inmates. With some exceptions, an inmate with AIDS is treated as if he has the plague and is avoided whenever possible. Relationships, other than relationships with other inmates with AIDS (if any are present and are receptive to a relationship), are scarce. AIDS in prison is a lonely and frightening journey. It is especially hard for an inmate with AIDS to face dying in a prison setting.

Long-Term Prisoners

Some long-term prisoners are inmates who have been given a life sentence but retain some hopes of parole. Some have been given a life sentence without the possibility of parole. Some have spent years on death row and expect to remain on death row until they are executed by the state. There are more long-term prisoners today than in the past, because sentencing structures require inmates to serve more of their sentences.

Lifers, individuals serving a life sentence, have always organized themselves into a strong group. In the era of the Big House, lifers did service projects around the penitentiary and helped maintain prison order. During the era of the correctional institution, lifers in several facilities across the nation began working with juvenile groups who were brought into the institution. Their task was to stage a horror show about prison life, including the likelihood of sexual exploitation, and to scare the juveniles out of crime. The ineffectiveness of these "Scared Straight" programs led to their being terminated.[32] In the 1990s lifers turned to new projects—recording books for the blind, donating blood, and preparing clothing and canned goods for victims of floods and other natural disasters.

There are always a few long-term prisoners who spend their time becoming proficient jailhouse lawyers; writing short stories, poetry, and either fiction or nonfiction books; painting; or working on various arts and crafts. Alva E. Campbell, Jr., who has been in prison for most of his life, writes about prison life in Within the Walls 14.3.

Elderly Prisoners

Traditionally, elderly prisoners, much fewer in number than today, were appointed trusties on the prison farm, did chores at the warden's guest house or home, took care of the flower gardens around the prison, or grew their own vegetable gardens. Today,

What challenges do prisons face in dealing with aging prison populations? What are the characteristics of older inmates that affect their adjustment to prison life? What realities do elderly inmates face? What are some other special populations among prison inmates, and how do prisons accommodate them?

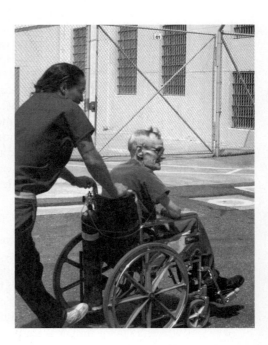

the walls   14.3

within

Serving Time

Serving time in prison is a very weary task. Most outsiders know, or think they know, what the real prison is, but there is no way one can truthfully comprehend prison unless they have experienced prison.

Prison is loneliness that sinks its teeth into the souls of men, an emptiness that leaves a sick feeling inside. It is uncertainty that smothers and stifles; it is a memory that comes in the night, its cry like the screams of a trumpet; it is frustration, futility, despair, and indifference.

Prison is where men struggle fervently to find the answer to themselves. The prison of routine where, at times, merely living is a very tiresome task. It is the mute dream of men who have been paying a debt for five, ten, twenty years and more, and who don't know if their debt will ever be paid in full. Prison is the bitterness in the hearts of many who became a part of it only because they were ignorant of the laws, or because they were without money. It is a place where everyday the crowd of men's tired faces reflect their acceptance of the system, or find proof of man's inadequacy as they drag out their days.

Prison is men who no longer know the love of a woman, their children, and the clean fresh air of a spring night. Prison is where men hope when hope seems futile.

Prison is walking in the visiting-room to see the worried, careworn face of the mother who anxiously studies the face of her son; still the same loved son, her pride and

> Prison is loneliness that sinks its teeth into the souls of men . . .

joy, who only now wears a prison number. Also in the visiting-room is the presence of the man who remembers the past warmth of love and tenderness as he talks softly to his wife, now separated by the crime he committed; and the face of his kids as they try to understand why their daddy can't go home with them.

Prison is the feeling that tears a man apart because that letter or visit anxiously awaited never comes. It is also the anguish that swells inside a man who knew it might happen, but could not really believe his wife would divorce him. Prison can only be understood by those who live within its walls!!!

Dwell hard on these thoughts, all who think that prison is like the movies, "glamorous and swashbuckling," because prison is time spent needlessly, wasted years gone by that can never be brought back at any price. It is futility, loss, and frustration. You will never be the same again.

CRITICAL THINKING QUESTIONS

What is your response to this statement? If you work with male offenders, you will encounter this feeling that the prison violates them in countless ways. What will you say?

Source: Written by Alva E. Campbell Jr., death row inmate in the state of Ohio, and used with permission.

---

there are nearly fifty thousand elderly prisoners (age 55 and older) in state and federal correctional institutions. The elderly prisoner is vulnerable to victimization and requires special attention when it comes to medical treatment, housing, nutrition, and institutional activities.

There are different adjustment rates for elderly inmates. The longer the amount of time remaining to be served, the harder it usually is for an elderly person to deal with confinement. Background factors, such as level of education and marital status, can also affect the adjustment of the elderly. Evidence indicates that individuals with more education have a greater difficulty dealing with confinement.[33] Some inmates, especially those imprisoned early in life, are more institutionally dependent than others. Some have higher morale and are more involved in programs and prison life than others.

Why might a relatively well-educated elderly inmate have difficulty dealing with prison life?

Because of the increasing numbers of elderly inmates, the adjustment of individuals in this group may be eased by the presence of age-mates and by programs that the correctional system provides especially to meet their needs. Nevertheless, like the long-term inmate and the inmate on death row, many elderly inmates face the prospect of dying in prison.

HOW DO MEN COPE WITH PRISON LIFE?

Prisoners do not experience prison in the same way. Every prisoner approaches his sentence with his own fears and expectations, preparations and emotions, and problems and solutions.[34] Inmates, then, must socially construct what the prison experience will mean for them.

Richard S. Jones and Thomas J. Schmid's case study of how inmates did time in a midwestern prison found that inmates progressed from viewing the prison as a world that was dominated by the themes of violence and uncertainty, to viewing it as a world dominated by the themes of boredom and predictability, to viewing the prison as an obstacle to a continued participation in the outside world.[35]

Nevertheless, interpersonal violence, racial conflict, and the presence of inmate gangs make survival from one day to the next difficult. Within this setting, there are at least six general strategies for making it in prison: aggressive reaction, collective reaction, self-satisfying reaction, legalistic reaction, withdrawal reaction, and positive reaction (see Table 14.1). At the beginning of a sentence, an inmate might use one coping strategy and in the course of confinement change strategies several times. It is also possible to use more than one strategy at a time.

Aggressive Reaction

One way to deal with prison life is to fight the system and not give an inch. This strategy is most frequently tried by inmates newly arrived in prison. They want to prove that they are tough and believe that the best way to appear tough is to fight the "Man" at every opportunity.

Table 14.1

Strategies for Coping with Prison Life

Type of Response	Characteristics	Outcomes
Aggressive reaction	Fights the system by disobeying the rules.	Prolonged imprisonment and considerable time in segregation.
Collective reaction	Fights the system through rebellion and protest.	Prolonged imprisonment, perhaps brutality from staff and some improvement in living conditions.
Self-satisfying reaction	Makes the best of the prison experience by satisfying himself in every way possible.	Reduction of the pain of imprisonment.
Legalistic reaction	Fights the system through the courts.	Possible reduction of time or even release from imprisonment.
Withdrawal reaction	Escapes from the painfulness of prison life.	Depends on the withdrawal-coping mechanism.
Drug use	Escapes through chemicals ranging from alcohol to hard drugs.	No negative outcome unless inmate is caught.
Protective custody	Requests segregation.	Safety from prison violence, but if the choice is later made to return to the general population, increased vulnerability to victimization is possible.
Mental disturbance	Escapes through mental illness.	May be permanently affected, which may result in transfer to hospital for the criminally insane.
Suicide	Choice is to end one's life because of the meaninglessness and pain of prison life.	Death.
Positive reaction	Uses the prison experience for self-development.	Depends on the permanence of the positive reaction; if the offender can sustain it in the community, he may be able to turn his life around.

They soon realize the problems this strategy: An aggressive inmate will receive disciplinary reports, or tickets, and might spend much of his time in segregation, and parole boards take a dim view of poor conduct reports. Most aggressive inmates rather quickly come to the conclusion that personal defiance has no real impact on the system, that it is self-destructive, and that it will result in a prolonged institutional stay. Some inmates, however, remain embittered about their imprisonment and resist prison rules and procedures for years.

Inmates of the state penitentiary of New Mexico told Mark Colvin that they placed a premium on gaining a reputation for violence. "The young ones, I don't know, I guess they're trying to get them a name, a reputation," said an inmate. "They want to be recognized as being real tough," added another inmate. Said a third, "This new generation is very aggressive. . . . They're all out to build a reputation here quick. As quick as possible. . . . They don't care if they leave or not."[36] Aggressive inmates are as much a threat to staff as they are to other inmates. Mindful of the fact that they may explode at any time, staff are usually quick to find reasons to put them in prolonged lockup. These inmates also are transferred to high-security prisons in the state or federal systems. In high-security prisons, they can be placed in permanent lockup status and are unable to attack other inmates or staff.

Over the life course, will the rage of aggressive inmates burn out? Will the prolonged years of confinement finally break their spirits?

Although this question lacks empirical examination, most enraged inmates do seem to be ultimately beaten by the institutional process. About one such inmate, recently released, it was said, "You should see him now. Man, the system broke him. He's pitiful. He just mopes around. There is nothing left of him."[37]

Collective Reaction

In the late 1970s, inmates who referred to themselves as political prisoners viewed themselves as victims of an oppressive social system and claimed that they were in prison because of their race and class rather than for their crimes. They were quite willing to join with others to express violence toward the system. In 1971, riots at Attica in New York State and at San Quentin and Folsom in California were led by inmates who identified themselves as political prisoners.

Today, inmates who choose this collective reaction to imprisonment can be divided into three groups. One group consists of individuals who become radicals and attempt to incite large-scale institutional riots and other forms of institutional disturbance. They hope to draw the public's attention to the oppressive conditions of the prison so that some of their conditions of confinement will be changed. Another group consists of those who go along with collective violence once it begins. Usually, a riot begins in a spontaneous way. For example, in the New Mexico riot, a guard was jumped by intoxicated inmates. Once a riot starts, an inmate has the choice of either hiding or becoming a participant. In the excitement of the moment, it is difficult not to become a participant.

The largest group of political prisoners consists of those who "talk the talk" of being a political prisoner but are not foolish enough to become involved in violence toward the staff or the institution. They usually are members of a gang and believe that the collective force of the gang provides some protection against the tyranny of staff and the state. They see themselves as "slaves to support the economy of the state," and as "cannon fodder and propaganda policy."[38]

Self-Satisfying Reaction

Instead of fighting the system, the majority of inmates try to make the best of prison life. They want to do easy time. They may choose to make up for the sexual deprivation of prison life by taking a young inmate under their wing. They may steal food from the dining hall so that they will have food in their cells when they want a snack. They may purchase food at the commissary so that they do not have to eat prison food all the time. They may have the inmates who work in the laundry press their prison clothes, a small but satisfying luxury. Furthermore, they may fix up their cells to contain any amenities that are permitted in prison.

The self-satisfied adaptation to prison life does require capital. It may be the capital of money to purchase what is desired, or it may be having the power to persuade others to do what you want (provide sexual favors, do your laundry, or give you food or cigarettes). Most of the inmates who attain a high degree of self-satisfaction are drug dealers. One drug dealer in prison bragged about his financial success:

> I made $5,600 last month. I live in a jungle and every once in a while another predator is going to try me. Why don't I get out of the game? Since January, I made over $32,000. I need big money for expert witnesses and attorneys. I will never get out if I just wait for them to let me out. I'm maxing out on my first 20-year sentence. I have life after that. Money means nothing to me if I can't get out of prison.[39]

An example of inmates' success with this coping strategy is their highly developed contraband market. In examining the contraband market at the State Prison of Southern Michigan (SPSM), David B. Kalinich found that the flow of contraband through the prison was extensive. **Contraband** is any unauthorized substance or material possessed by inmates—for example, weapons, drugs, alcoholic beverages, prohibited appliances, and clothing. Contraband has always been found in American prisons, but the drug appetites and addictions of today's inmates have encouraged the expansion of this market. Kalinich found that the most visible and widely used drug was marijuana, but large amounts of heroin, some cocaine, and an assortment of amphetamines and tranquilizers also were available.[40]

Legalistic Reaction

More and more, inmates try to fight the system through the federal courts. Supported by jailhouse lawyers and by lawyers from the free community, many inmates devote all their energy to studying criminal law, preparing civil suits, and writing legal briefs to appeal their cases or to ask for new trials. Some inmates have won release through the appeals process. Some have been given new trials; others have been awarded damages by the courts. Because of inmates' suits, some correctional systems have been charged by the federal courts to either institute major reforms or close their facilities. Thus, it is easy to see why prisoners with long sentences become so involved with the law. Within the Walls 14.4 is a statement written by Ernest F. Walters, a jailhouse lawyer at the Iowa State Penitentiary, written for *Invitation to Corrections* in 2000.

An even more widely used legalistic response when inmates disagree with a disciplinary committee decision or with an ordered institutional transfer is to turn to the formal grievance process. In using the institutional appeals process, inmates are saying that they will not passively accept the decision made against them without challenging it before a grievance committee. It is possible in some state correctional systems for an inmate to protest a decision all the way to officials in the department of corrections.

Withdrawal Reaction

Many prisoners cope by withdrawing in ways ranging from using narcotics and alcohol, invoking protective custody, and becoming mentally ill, to attempting escape or suicide. Escape from work-release or home-furlough programs is easy. It is extremely difficult from high- and medium-security facilities. In 1998, there were 7,179 escapes/walkaways: 6,519 (90.8 percent) from work-release or furlough programs, 553 (7.7 percent) from low- or minimum-security prisons, and 107 (1.5 percent) from high- or medium-security facilities.[41]

The methods that inmates use to escape from maximum-security institutions are legendary: placing dummies in their bunks and scaling the wall; using a smuggled gun

the walls 14.4

within

A Jailhouse Lawyer Speaks

"Besides many prisoners' rights cases, this writer has been involved in over three hundred criminal appeals, including postconviction relief actions and federal habeas corpus actions. In context of the criminal law jurisdiction, this writer has assisted more prisoners on a personal basis than most practicing lawyers holding themselves out to be advocates in this area of the law.

"By necessity, more than by design, I have honed my skills in the field of criminal law as a writer and researcher. This area encompasses state and federal appellate work, as well as habeas corpus and state postconviction work. Typically, a jailhouse lawyer files initial motions and writs that trigger the court's jurisdiction over the person (prisoner) and the subject matter (the issues at law). Seldom does one see the complete jailhouse lawyer: the one who can do it all, from start to finish. This jailhouse lawyer, despite vehement objections from the state attorney general, has personally represented prisoners in federal habeas corpus proceedings. Oftentimes it is imperative to allow this nonstandard representation, especially in those cases where the lawyers refuse to do anything for the prisoner.

"The most important form of assistance I provide to other prisoners is that of common ol' advice. Advising a

> The most important form of assistance I provide to other prisoners is that of common ol' advice.

prisoner as to his rights doesn't entail filing lawsuits for them. Most often I play a central background role as a liaison between disgruntled prisoners and their court-appointed attorneys. In many other instances I actually perform all of the legal research and writing for lawyers appointed to represent prisoners, but who carelessly neglect them because, in the lawyer's viewpoint, the money isn't good enough and they have other big paying clients whose interests and concerns are placed ahead of the prisoners'. This area of assistance is the most troubling to me. It's this area that causes me to complain about the system being broken. The indigent prisoners receive the bulk of my attention. Because if I didn't focus on these, then they would fall completely through the cracks of our so-called criminal justice system. My biggest role as a jailhouse lawyer is that of a fiercely loyal advocate."

CRITICAL THINKING QUESTIONS

What do you think about the role of a jailhouse lawyer? How competent do you think Ernest Walters is at what he does?

to take hostages and to demand release; commandeering a prison garbage truck and ramming the gate; hiding in the garbage or in a container taken out of the prison. In one escape, inmates used smuggled guns to blast their way out of a prison bowling alley. Eleven inmates who escaped from the New Mexico State Penitentiary cut their way through a window, used knotted sheets first to climb down to the ground and then to climb over the roof of the penitentiary's central corridor, crossed the lighted yard in full view of the tower, and cut their way through a chain-link fence. In Florida in the late 1990s, seven inmates escaped into an alligator-infested swamp after stabbing a correctional officer and climbing over two fences topped with razor wire. In a Texas prison escape in December 2000, seven inmates used knives made from scrap materials or filed down spoons and an ax handle to threaten and overpower guards. Other escapes illustrate the impact of modern technology. Helicopters were used in escape attempts at the State Prison of Southern Michigan and at the Federal Penitentiary at Marion, Illinois. In another incident at Marion, four inmates opened electrically controlled gates with a computer they had made.[42]

Withdrawal becomes an attractive strategy for inmates who have lost hope of ever getting out of prison or of anything positive happening to them. Narcotics probably offers the most common means of withdrawing from the stresses and pressures of prison life. Its popularity is explained by the plentifulness of drugs and by the high percentage of inmates who have developed an appetite for drugs on the streets.

Protective custody is the preference of more and more inmates. Although no nationwide or recent statistics on protective custody are available, the demand for it is so great that the available space is generally filled and there is a waiting list. Sometimes inmates who seem strong and capable of taking care of themselves opt for protective custody. More commonly, those who choose protective custody want to get away from the general population because they fear for their safety, they have a gambling or drug debt they cannot pay, or there is a "hit" on them because they offended another inmate or have been accused of being a "snitch."

Some inmates are overwhelmed by the totality of the prison environment. They may withdraw into a world of their own or become so depressed that they are dysfunctional. Suicide is chosen by inmates who would rather be dead than live in prison.

Positive Reaction

Some inmates cope in prison by viewing the prison experience as an opportunity to develop a strong mind. Inmates who are attracted to this strategy want to prevent the dehumanizing prison experience from permanently damaging their self-respect. They are determined to come out of prison better and stronger than they were when they went in.

Some Black Muslims, for example, subject themselves to rigorous mental and physical discipline, sleeping on the floor and spending much of their time in meditation. Other inmates work on empowering themselves by making individual sacrifices, such as limiting the amount they eat, so they can purify their bodies. Still others use rigorous exercise, running marathon distances or lifting enormous weights. A few become involved in religion as a means of developing a strong mind. Other prisoners turn to working on creative projects, such as writing, painting or sculpting, designing jewelry, or working at handicrafts of some kind.

Victoria R. DeRosia found that those inmates with more effective coping skills adjust easier to prison and are more likely to have a positive response. In contrast, other inmates find prison difficult and have a variety of negative experiences. They are far less likely to have a positive response to imprisonment.[43] Others have documented that long-term inmates are more likely to pursue a positive response. They are older and more mature and tend to use their time profitably, such as pursuing opportunities for self-improvement, skill development, and education.[44]

SUMMARY

The era of the Big House, as featured in the movies of the 1930s, is no more. Also in the past is the era of the correctional institution. The contemporary prison is a violent and unpredictable environment in which to do time. Violence between inmates and between inmates and staff occurs on a regular basis within the walls. The presence of inmate gangs makes the prison especially dangerous for individuals who are not gang members. That gangs are present in so many states and have so much support within contemporary prisons is one reason why prison order is likely to crumble at any time.

A number of subjects related to the sociology of the prison are given attention in this chapter. They include the inmate code, the deprivation model and importation model, the pains or stresses of confinement, and the various ways of adapting to the prison environment. Inmates construct their own ways or means of making it in prison, and this social construction varies from one inmate to another.

Other than the death penalty, the most severe punishment society can inflict on a criminal is imprisonment. Today, prison time is hard time. Many male prisoners seek protective custody rather than dealing with the tensions and conflicts of prison life. A male prisoner who is strong and knows the score is likely to survive in prison. But for a person who is not streetwise or is easily intimidated, incarceration may have an entirely different outcome.

KEY TERMS

contraband, p. 344
deprivation model, p. 336
importation model, p. 336
inmate code, p. 333

lifer, p. 340
prisonization, p. 334
state's evidence, p. 336

CRITICAL THINKING QUESTIONS

1. You are in prison. Which coping strategy will you choose? Why?
2. How painful should the prison experience be? If inmates can afford to purchase televisions and stereos, should this equipment be permitted in their rooms? If outsiders will accept collect calls, should prisoners be allowed to make unlimited phone calls to the community? If prisoners are married and incident-free, should they be permitted conjugal visits in facilities (trailers) on institutional grounds?
3. You are the warden of a correctional facility that has extremely high rates of violence among racial and ethnic groups. What will your strategy be for defusing the racial and ethnic tension?
4. Should an inmate on death row have the same rights as inmates elsewhere in the prison?

WEB DESTINATIONS

Go to this site for Bureau of Justice statistics on prison inmates.
http://www.ojp.usdoj.gov/bjs/prisons.htm

This site describes prison gangs and their history in some detail.
http://www.gangsorus.com/gangs/gangprison.html

White supremacist gangs in prison are the subject of this article.
http://www.adl.org/frames/front_behind_bars.html

Follow links at this site for information and resources regarding prisoners with HIV/AIDS.
http://www.thebody.com/whatis/prison.html

Prison New Links summarizes current news article on prison inmates in the United States and in other countries.
http://userwww.sfsu.edu/~tamamail/wire.html

FOR FURTHER READING

Brady, Malcolm. *On the Yard.* Boston: Little, Brown, 1967. One of the best and most interesting accounts of inmate life.

Clemmer, Donald. *The Prison Community.* New York: Holt, Rinehart, & Winston, 1958. A classic examination of prison culture and how it affects prisoners.

Crouch, Ben M., and James W. Marquart. *An Appeal to Justice: Litigated Reform of Texas Prisons.* Austin: University of Texas Press, 1989. The authors document the breakdown of order in Texas prisons in the 1980s and inmates' response to this disorder.

Earley, Pete. *The Hot House: Life Inside Leavenworth Prison* (New York: Bantam Books, 1992. The case studies in this book provide a glimpse into the worldviews and adaptations of 1980s inmates in a secure federal facility.

Evans, Jeff, ed. *Undoing Time: American Prisons in Their Own Worlds.* Boston: Northeastern University Press, 2001. Contains an anthology of autobiographical prison writings that bring the reader to the hidden world of the prison.

Irwin, John. *Prisons in Turmoil.* Boston, Little, Brown, 1980. Irwin, an ex-con, traces the development of the twentieth-century prison to its present form.

Jones, Richard S. and Schmid, Thomas J. *Doing Time: Prison Experiences and Identity among First-Time Inmates.* Stamford, Conn.: JAI Press, 2000. An ethnographic study of the various ways of adjusting to prison for first-time inmates.

Rideau, Wilbert, and Ron Wikberg, eds. *Life Sentences: Rage and Survival behind Bars.* New York: Times Books, 1992. Two inmates at the Louisiana State Penitentiary at Angola write about the life of a long-term inmate in a southern prison long acknowledged as one of the most brutal in the nation.

Sykes, Gresham M. *The Society of Captives.* Princeton, N.J.: Princeton University Press, 1971. This analysis of prison life at the Trenton State Prison has become one of the most popular studies of the prison.

NOTES

1. Interviewed by the author in 1995.
2. Interviewed by the author in June 1985.
3. John Irwin, *Prisons in Turmoil* (Boston: Little, Brown, 1980).
4. Ibid.
5. Ibid., pp. 37, 40.
6. Ibid.
7. Interviewed by the author in May 1981.
8. Gresham M. Sykes, *The Society of Captives* (Princeton, N.J.: Princeton University Press, 1958.
9. Ibid., pp. 64–108.
10. Ibid.
11. Adapted from Gresham M. Sykes and Seldon L. Messinger, "The Inmate Social System," in *Theoretical Studies in the Social Organization of the Prison,* ed. Richard A. Cloward, Donald R. Cressey, George H. Grosser, Richard McCleery, Lloyd E. Ohlin, Gresham M. Sykes, and Sheldon L. Messinger (New York: Social Science Research Council, 1960), pp. 6–8.
12. Sykes, *The Society of Captives;* and Sykes and Messinger, "The Inmate Social System."
13. Donald Clemmer, *Prison Community* (New York: Holt, Rinehart & Winston, 1958), p. 299.
14. Ibid., pp. 299–300.
15. Michel Foucault, *Discipline and Punishment: The Birth of the Prison,* trans. Alan Sheridan (New York: Pantheon Books, 1977).
16. Irwin, *Prisons in Turmoil,* p. 75.
17. Ibid., pp. 76–77.
18. Stanton Wheeler, "Socialization in Correctional Communities," *American Sociological Review* 26 (October 1961), pp. 697–712.
19. Sykes, *The Society of Captives.*
20. John Irwin and Donald R. Cressey, "Thieves, Convicts and the Inmate Culture," *Social Problems* 10 (Fall 1962), p. 143.
21. Charles W. Thomas, "Prisonization or Resocialization: A Study of External Factors Associated with the Impact of Imprisonment," *Journal of Research in Crime and Delinquency* 10 (January 1975), pp. 13–21; and Charles W. Thomas, "Toward a More Inclusive Model of the Inmate Contraculture," *Criminology* 8 (November 1970), pp. 251–262.
22. Morris Janowitz, foreword to James B. Jacobs, *Stateville: The Penitentiary in Mass Society* (Chicago: University of Chicago Press, 1977), pp. x–xi.
23. The author observed several ranking members of gangs turn state's evidence against their gang leader to avoid maximum penalties in their own cases.
24. Sykes, *The Society of Captives,* pp. 70–77.
25. For an excellent overview of the pains of imprisonment, see Robert Johnson and Hans Toch, *The Pains of Imprisonment* (Beverly Hills, Calif.: Sage, 1982).
26. Lynne Goodstein, "Prisonization and the Transition to Community Life," *Journal of Research in Crime and Delinquency* 16 (July 1979), pp. 265–266.

27. William M. DiMascio, *Seeking Justice: Crime and Punishment in America* (New York: Edna McConnell Clark Foundation, 1995), p. 21.
28. "Incarcerated Sex Offenders Total Nearly 100,000," *Corrections Compendium* (Lincoln, Neb.: CEGA Services, November 1993).
29. DiMascio, *Seeking Justice,* p. 22.
30. Bureau of Justice Statistics and U.S. Department of Health and Human Services, Centers for Disease Control and Prevention, *1966–1997 Update: HIV/AIDS, STDs, and TB in Correctional Facilities* (Washington, D.C.: U.S. Department of Justice, 1999), pp. 7, 8
31. Leo Carroll, "AIDS and Human Rights in the Prison: A Comment on the Ethics of Screening and Segregation" (paper presented at the annual meeting of the American Society of Criminology, Reno, November 1989), p. 3.
32. See James Finckenauer, *Scared Straight* (Englewood Cliffs, N.J.: Prentice-Hall, 1981).
33. Michael J. Sabath and Ernest L. Cowles, "Factors Affecting the Adjustment of Elderly Inmates to Prison," in *Older Offenders: Perspectives in Criminology and Criminal Justice,* ed. Belinda McCarthy and Robert Langworthy (New York: Praeger, 1988), p. 178–195.
34. Richard S. Jones and Thomas J. Schmid, *Doing Time: Prison Experience and Identity Among First-Time Inmates* (Stamford, Conn.: JAI Press, 2000), p. 21.
35. Ibid., p. 22.
36. Mark Colvin, *From Accommodation to Riot: The Penitentiary of New Mexico in Crisis* (Albany: State University of New York Press, 1991), p. 306.
37. Comment made to the author in 1998 about a notorious inmate in his fifties recently released after serving thirty years in prison.
38. Inmates who view themselves as political prisoners have made these statements to the author.
39. Letter received by the author in March 1992.
40. David B. Kalinich, *Power, Stability, and Contraband: The Inmate Economy* (Prospect Heights, Ill.: Waveland Press, 1986), p. 42.
41. Camille Graham Camp and George M. Camp, *The Corrections Yearbook 1999: Adult Corrections* (Middletown, Conn.: Criminal Justice Institute, 1999), p. 23.
42. See Bert Useem and Peter Kimball, *Stages of Siege: U.S. Prison Riots, 1971–1986* (New York: Oxford University Press, 1986); and "4 Inmates at Large in Florida Prison Escape," *Chicago Tribune,* 8 August 1994, p. 11; Guillermo X. Garcia, "Prison Break Unfolded Like a TV Script," *USA Today,* 12 January 2001, p. 3A.
43. Victoria R. DeRosia, *Living Inside Prison Walls: Adjustment Behavior* (Westport, Conn.: Praeger, 1998), p. 71.
44. Timothy Flanagan, "Dealing with Long-Term Confinement: Adaptive Strategies and Perspective Among Long-Term Prisoners," *Criminal Justice and Behavior* 8 (1981), pp. 201–222; and Hans Toch and Kenneth Adams, *Coping: Maladaption in Prisons* (New Brunswick, N.J.: Transaction Publishers, 1989).

CHAPTER 14 / BUILT-IN STUDY GUIDE

Multiple Choice Questions

1. Which of the following statements is accurate?

   A. Male inmates form networks that resemble families for emotional support
   B. Male inmates are more likely than female inmates to arm themselves for self-protection
   C. Male inmates do not hide their emotions
   D. Male inmates are less violent than female inmates

2. The hopelessness experienced by many prison inmates can be explained by all of the following except:

   A. Longer sentences
   B. Tighter controls imposed by staff
   C. Overcrowded institutions
   D. The initiation of boot-camp programs

3. According to Gresham Sykes, which of the following inmate social roles was characterized by inmates relieving the restrictions imposed on them in the prison environment by preying on fellow prisoners, taking their possessions by force or the threat of force?

   A. Wolves and punks
   B. Toughs
   C. Gorillas and merchants
   D. Real men

4. How did the politicization of prisons influence the prison environment?

   A. Outbreak of a series of prison riots
   B. Increase in prisoners' rights
   C. Decrease in prisoners' rights
   D. More control for correctional officers

5. How does the indeterminate sentence and parole board promote order in a prison?

   A. Communicates to the inmate the need for treatment
   B. Good time credits influence parole officers on the parole board
   C. Communicates the clear message to the inmate that conformity is necessary for release
   D. Earned release by program participation alone

6. The only solidarity in the inmate culture exists with:

   A. Prison gangs and religious groups
   B. Prison gangs and racial groups
   C. Religious groups and ethnic groups
   D. Ethnic groups and prison gangs

7. According to Stanton Wheeler's study, when was the inmate most strongly influenced by the norms of the inmate subculture?

   A. During the reception stage
   B. During the beginning stage (with less than 6 months in the prison)
   C. During the middle stage (with more than 6 months remaining in the prison)
   D. During the final stage (with less than 6 months remaining in the prison)

8. Identify the most important federal law effecting prisons in the last quarter century.

   A. Prison Litigation Reform Act
   B. Crime Control Act of 1994
   C. Truth in Sentencing Act
   D. Americans with Disabilities Act

9. According to the text, all of the following are ways to make it in prison except:

   A. Aggressive reaction
   B. Withdrawal reaction
   C. Legalistic reaction
   D. Colonization reaction

10. Inmate radicals who attempt to incite large-scale institutional riots and other forms of institutional disturbances have adopted which means of adapting to prisons?

    A. Positive reaction
    B. Political reaction
    C. Collective reaction
    D. Aggressive reaction

11. All of the following are areas in which the elderly inmate presents special needs for the correctional institution except:

    A. Medical treatment
    B. Housing
    C. Nutrition
    D. Processing Social Security checks

12. When did the social reintegration of prisoners begin?

    A. The late 1940s
    B. The late 1950s
    C. The late 1960s
    D. The late 1970s

True/False Questions

T F   1. In male prisons, correctional officers and inmates form supportive networks.

T F   2. Foucault believed the rehabilitative ideal is the ultimate means of promoting order in the correctional institution.

T F   3. Donald Clemmer believed that only weak inmates with no support system became prisonized.

T F   4. The increased number of habitual offender statutes has led to an increasingly older prison population.

T F   5. Laws exist that permit the indefinite confinement of rapists and child molesters who are viewed as too dangerous for release at the end of their court-imposed sentence.

T F   6. The most common method of withdrawal from prison life is suicide.

T F   7. One reason inmate may choose protective custody pertains to a gambling or drug debt he or she cannot pay.

T F   8. Inmates who want to make the best of prison life and do easy time are practicing the self-satisfying reaction to prison.

T F   9. The prison race riots that were prevalent in the 1960s and 1970s did not seem to characterize U.S. prisons in the last decade of the twentieth century.

T F 10. Lynne Goodstein's study found that inmates who adjusted most successfully to a prison environment encountered less difficulty making the transition from institutional life to freedom.

T F 11. Male prisons are larger than female prisons.

T F 12. The elderly inmate population does not present any special needs to the prison.

Fill-in-the-Blank Questions   (based on key terms)

1. Unauthorized substances or material such as weapons or drugs are known as _____.

2. Inmates who have been given a life sentence but retain some hope for parole fall into the category of a _____.

3. The _____ explains inmate behavior as a reflection of what occurs on the streets of society.

4. For prison administrators, _____ is functional because it encourages inmates to do their own time and not cause problems.

5. The _____ explains deviant and violent behavior as well as the development of an inmate subculture as a result of the restrictions placed on inmates by prison officials.

6. The process whereby new inmates become socialized to the institutional environment is referred to as _____.

Essay Questions

1. Using Irwin's historical framework, explain how the inmate world has changed from the era of the big house, to the correctional institution, and finally to the contemporary prison.

2. How do the deprivation and the importation models influence the process of prisonization?

3. Identify and explain the problems that the long-term and elderly prisoner has in prison. Additionally, describe the problems the elderly present to the prison system.

4. Explain the inmate code and identify four elements of it. What purpose did the inmate code serve for prisoners and staff members?

5. Identify and explain the basic elements of Syke's structural–functional approach to prisons.

ANSWERS

Multiple Choice Questions

1.	B	7.	C
2.	D	8.	A
3.	C	9.	D
4.	A	10.	C
5.	C	11.	D
6.	B	12.	C

True/False Questions

1.	F	7.	T
2.	T	8.	T
3.	F	9.	T
4.	T	10.	F
5.	T	11.	T
6.	F	12.	F

Fill-in-the-Blank Questions

1. Contraband
2. Lifer
3. Importation model
4. Inmate code
5. Deprivation model
6. Prisonization

chapter fifteen

The Female Prisoner

An empowerment approach is one lens through which women in prison can be viewed. Ellen H. McWhirter captures the essence of what empowerment means in her inclusive definition:

> Empowerment is the process by which people, organizations, or groups who are powerless (a) become aware of the power dynamics at work in their life context, (b) develop the skills and capacity for gaining some reasonable control over their lives, (c) exercise this control without infringing upon rights of others, and (d) support the empowerment of others in their community.[1]

CRITICAL THINKING QUESTIONS

Why might empowerment provide an interesting viewpoint from which to study women who go to prison? How could prison staff empower female inmates?

Empowerment theory, with its focus on personal, social, educational, and political factors, offers a useful framework for addressing the needs of women at all levels of the criminal justice system. From the empowerment perspective, individual problems arise not from personal deficits but from the failure of society to meet the needs of all the people.[2] This perspective builds on women's strengths rather than their faults and failures. It focuses on solutions rather than problems and renews emphasis on rehabilitation rather than punishment. The view of humanity underlying this approach is that humans are unique and multidimensional beings with the potential to make contributions to their communities.[3]

A second lens through which women in prison can be viewed is the correctional one. Those who support this perspective are committed to helping imprisoned women find purpose and healing, so that they can leave prison and live responsible and productive lives. They try to approach incarcerated women in sensitive and supportive ways. The statement supplied by Elaine Lord, the hero in this chapter, describes how this position has been implemented at the Bedford Hills Correctional Center, where Lord has been superintendent since 1984.

Women in prison also can be viewed through the punishment lens. Instead of using words like *empowered* or *helped,* proponents of this perspective contend that women are responsible for their actions and must pay for the consequences of their behavior. They are particularly disturbed by the number of women who are abusing drugs, assisting in the trafficking of drugs, harming unborn children by their drug habits, and abusing and harming their own children. They believe that these women are bad and deserve long prison sentences.[4] Today, proponents of punishment insist that the purpose of prison is to punish, not to provide incarcerated females (or males) a lot of programs and services.

Women in prison are sometimes called the "forgotten offenders." There are several reasons for the relative lack of interest in the female prisoner:

1. Few women are incarcerated. Women were 4 percent of the incarcerated population in 1980, and today they account for 6.4 percent.[5]
2. Women's prisons are smaller than most men's prisons, and there are fewer of them.[6]
3. Until recently, reform groups ignored the plight of confined women because female prisoners called so little attention to themselves.
4. Typically, female offenders are not involved in organized crime, in crimes involving large property losses, or in crimes that endanger large groups.[7]

The literature on women's prisons began to be published almost thirty years after research began to be conducted in men's prisons. Eugenia H. Lekkerkerker's examination of women's prisons in the United States was published in 1931.[8] In the 1960s, Rose Giallombardo and David A. Ward and Gene G. Kassebaum pioneered the present-day works describing women's prisons.[9] In the 1970s, Esther Heffernan and Arlene E. Mitchell examined subcultures within women's prisons.[10] Alice Propper later published a study exploring homosexuality within women's correctional institutions.[11] In the 1980s, Estelle B. Freedman and Nicole H. Rafter published books on the history of women's prisons.[12] Joycelyn M. Pollock-Byrne's 1990 study of women's prisons shows that aspects of the prisoner subculture, other than homosexuality, must be explored to understand the woman prisoner's adaptation to confinement.[13] In the mid-1990s, Karlene Faith and Kathryn Watterson, as well as Meda Chesney-Lind, examined women's responses to incarceration and the effects of incarceration on women.[14]

As Chapter 14 describes in greater detail, Donald Clemmer found that prisoners become assimilated to the antisocial culture within the walls and, to varying degrees, become committed to criminality. He called this process *prisonization.* Clemmer suggested that the more imprisonment deepens inmates' criminality, the more difficult it will be for them to reenter free society.[15] Studies of women prisoners are beginning to examine the negative effects of imprisonment on them. Phyllis J. Baunach suggested that "the lack of autonomy, powerlessness, and the loss of identity create for incarcerated women an exaggerated dependency upon those in authority" and reactions to this environment may result in despondency, frustrations, heightened tensions, anxiety, and apathy.[16]

This chapter considers several questions about the imprisonment of women. *How does the social structure of women's prisons differ from that of men's prisons? Do women cope with prison life any differently than do men? What are the main issues involved with women in prison?*

WHAT IS THE HISTORY OF WOMEN'S PRISONS?

In the early days of prison history, women were confined in separate quarters in men's prisons and, like men, suffered from filth, overcrowding, and hard conditions.[17] Women lodged at Auburn Penitentiary in New York were subject to beating and sexual abuse by the male guards. African American and poor women were disproportionately incarcerated in all parts of the United States.

The roots of feminism lie deep within the prison reform movement. Even before the end of slavery, Quaker abolitionists and suffragists were at the forefront of this movement. Elizabeth Fry of England helped organize the women confined at London's Newgate Gaol in the early 1800s. Her brave and innovative work at Newgate with incarcerated women and their children was testimony to the fact that, with decent treatment, women convicts were redeemable. Fry challenged the rampant sexual abuse of institutionalized women and advocated that they be under the authority of other women and confined in their own institution. She also sought to substitute for the Quaker system of absolute silence a system that permitted inmates to communicate with each other and help each other reform. Fry was able to instill hope and dignity where there had been only despair. Today, Elizabeth Fry associations in Canada play an active role in exposing abuses in women's prisons.[18]

The Indiana Woman's Prison, the first separate prison for women, was founded by a Quaker couple and opened in 1873. Four years later, Massachusetts built an all-female state reformatory. Another American Quaker helped found the progressive women's reformatory at Bedford Hills. Other states gradually followed, and separate institutions for men and women became the norm, although there were still exceptions. Fry's program, which emphasized women helping women, rehabilitation, religious education, and obedience, was instituted throughout North America.[19]

Many significant aspects of contemporary corrections were pioneered by female administrators in charge of institutions for female offenders—for example, educational instruction, work release, and vocational activities. Samuel Walker observes that women's prisons became a testing ground for new ideas. Prison reformers regarded women as good candidates for rehabilitation, partly because they were considered less dangerous than their male counterparts.[20] See the Timeline for the establishment of women's prisons in each state.

During the Progressive era cottage-style reformatories were developed as an alternative to the harsh custodial institutions.[21] Inmates of the custodial prisons, mostly African American women, suffered from the filthy conditions and violence inflicted by male guards. The new "reformatories" were usually staffed by women and aimed to correct women's moral behavior. Women were sentenced to these reformatories for various sexual offenses, including pregnancies outside marriage and unlawful sexual intercourse. By 1935, the Progressive era was over, and the reformatories and custodial prisons were merged. The legacy of the "cottage system" is evident at the women's federal prison at Alderson, West Virginia, and in many state prisons, such as Bedford Hills in New York State.

The 1960s and 1970s, a period of civil rights awareness and protest by various oppressed groups—minorities, women, gays and lesbians—was also a time of feminist reformist zeal concerning women in prison. Compassion was expressed for women who killed their husbands in self-defense and were charged with murder. There was also a huge outcry over prisoners such as Angela Davis and Joan Little. Davis was charged with abetting the escape of a violent prisoner, and Little was tried for killing her jailer during the act of rape.

The period of retrenchment of social services and the War on Drugs, which got under way in the 1980s and was continuing at the beginning of the twenty-first century, parallels a mass media campaign dramatizing crimes of violence. Women of color have been the most adversely affected by the new mandatory drug-sentencing laws, namely, the harsh sentencing for crack cocaine. Another factor affecting all prisoners is the vested interests of major corporations—the prison industrial complex—and many local communities in the building and maintaining of prisons for their economic well-being.[22]

timeline

Establishment of Women's Prisons in Each State

State	Title at Opening	Date at Opening	State	Title at Opening	Date at Opening
Indiana	Woman's Prison	1873	Illinois	State Reformatory for Women	1930
Massachusetts	Reformatory Prison for Women	1877	Virginia	State Industrial Farm for Women	1932
New York	House of Refuge for Women	1887	North Carolina	Correctional Center for Women	1934
New Jersey	State Reformatory for Women	1913	California	California Institution for Women	1938
Maine	Reformatory for Women	1916	Kentucky	Correctional Institution for Women	1938
Ohio	Reformatory for Women	1916	South Carolina	Harbison Correctional Institution for Women	1938
Kansas	State Industrial Farm for Women	1917	Maryland	Correctional Institution for Women	1940
Michigan	State Training School for Women	1917	Alabama	Julia Tutwiler Prison for Women	1942
Connecticut	State Farm for Women	1918	West Virginia	State Prison for Women	1948
Iowa	Women's Reformatory	1918	Puerto Rico	Industrial School for Women	1954
Arkansas	State Farm for Women	1920	Georgia	Rehabilitation Center for Women	1957
California	Industrial Farm for Women	1920	Missouri	State Correctional Center for Women	1960
Minnesota	State Reformatory for Women	1920	Louisiana	Correctional Institute for Women	1961
Nebraska	State Reformatory for Women	1920	Nevada	Women's Correctional Center	1964
Pennsylvania	State Industrial Home for Women	1920	Oregon	Women's Correctional Center	1965
Wisconsin	Industrial Home for Women	1921	Tennessee	Prison for Women	1966
United States	Industrial Institution for Women (now Federal Reformatory for Women in Alderson, West Virginia)	1927	Colorado	Women's Correctional Institute	1968
Delaware	Correctional Institution for Women	1929	Washington	Purdy Treatment Center for Women	1970
Connecticut	Correctional Institution for Women	1930	Oklahoma	Women's Treatment Facility	1973

Source: Estelle B. Freedman, *Their Sister's Keepers: Women's Prison Reform in America, 1830–1930* (Ann Arbor: University of Michigan Press, 1981), p. 302

When the dividends of crimes are so profitable to outside interest groups, supporters of the empowerment perspective are quick to say, it is difficult to alter priorities by putting money into substance abuse treatment and subsidized housing in order to prevent crime.

WHAT IS THE SOCIAL STRUCTURE IN WOMEN'S PRISONS?

The formal structure of the women's prison in many ways belies the informal treatment women receive within the prison walls. Typically, women are treated not as adult offenders, but as children. They are **infantilized.** In Within the Walls 15.1, Jean Harris, a former school headmistress who was in prison for murder, presents a snapshot of how women in prison are sometimes treated.

Prison officials encourage "good" passive behavior. Punishments are dealt out for cursing, disrespect, and other minor violations.[23] Independent thinking, much less grassroots organizing for social change, is punished. Appropriately, Kathryn Watterson refers to women's prison as "inside the concrete womb," a phrase that serves as the subtitle for her book.[24]

The complex and diverse histories of incarcerated women produce a prison culture that is itself complex and diverse.[25] In this section we consider three aspects of that culture: the social and cultural backgrounds of the women themselves, the cliques or family-like groups that form in prison, and sexuality.

within the walls   15.1

Rules in Women's Prisons

A lieutenant pulled me aside tonight as I was on my way to medication, and said in a very serious tone, "Mrs. Harris, we're having a good deal of trouble with several of your packages."

I said, "Why? What's the matter?"

He said, "Some of them have no address on the outside so they have to be returned to the sender without opening them."

"How do you do that?"

"Return them to the sender without opening them? Just stamp 'return to sender'! I'm just telling you, you better tell your friends to be sure to put an address on the outside, because, by law, we cannot open them if they don't have an address."

"But how will the mail know where to return them to if there isn't any address on the outside?"

"I've just told you, Mrs. Harris, the law says you can't open a package that doesn't have an address on the outside."

Finally, I said, "OK, just do whatever you have to do with it." God alone knows what was in the packages, or who sent them, or where they ended up.

> "Mrs. Harris, we're having a good deal of trouble with several of your packages."

The lieutenant must be a cousin of the C.O. who refuses to let me alphabetize the many names of my visiting list to make it easier for the C.O.s at the gate to find the names when the people come to visit me.

"Mrs. Harris," he said, in the sort of tone one uses with a not very bright child after you explained something simple to them at least five times, "it ain't gonna do no good to put 'em in alphabetical order. Those people don't visit you in alphabetical order."

CRITICAL THINKING QUESTIONS

How do you respond to Jean Harris's comments about the intelligence of correctional officers? Do you believe that the incidents she describes actually took place?

Source: Reprinted from Jean Harris, *Strangers in Two Worlds* (New York: Kensington, 1986), pp. 452–454.

The Social World of Women's Prisons

Any attempt to comprehend the social organization of the prison must address the contemporary prisoner experience in light of what John Irwin calls the "cultural baggage" that inmates bring into the prison setting with them.[26] Today, much of this cultural baggage is the end product of the drug wars on the streets and the War on Drugs in society. Caught up in the drug wars are minority women (Latina and African American) involved with male gang members, foreigners arrested at airports as "couriers" for international drug syndicates, and violent and nonviolent offenders arrested for crime indirectly related to drug use. Race and class intersect in predictable ways to ensure that the persons most feared and resented by society are those who are shut away. Today, as Meda Chesney-Lind suggests, "street crime" has become a code word for "race." And racial tensions in the free community lay the groundwork for ethnic differences and resentments behind prison bars.[27]

Sometimes the resentments, as Jean Harris reports, get taken out on "honkie" or white correctional officers.[28] Sometimes prisoners take them out on each other. In at least one prison, as reported by Clarice Feinman, overt problems occur more often between African American and Hispanic women than between white and black women.[29] More studies are needed to confirm this phenomenon throughout the prison system. What research does tell us is that the race wars and gang warfare so common in men's prisons seem to have no counterpart in women's institutions.[30]

Prison "Families"

Often located in rural areas miles away from inmates' own families and inaccessible in any case because of financial and legal constraints, women's prisons tend to develop networks of family-like ties. In sharp contrast with the male prison society, which is organized around power, women prisoners in the United States often replicate the family relationships they knew on the outside. "Married" couples may head such families, which occasionally also include a father figure. Prison "mamas" keep their "children" in line and provide emotional support.[31] Although these women generally live in a world characterized by pettiness, gossip, and regressive behavior, they give and receive a lot of love and nurturing. Care and respect for the elderly and mothering of the young or retarded are common.

There is considerable controversy today over the viability of these family-like forms and even over whether they actually exist. As Joycelyn Pollock suggests, "Although it seems clear that women do form affectional ties that have some similarity to familial relationships, it is not clear that the extensive **kinship networks** are anywhere near as defined as one might believe reading the early studies."[32] Karlene Faith concurs with the view that early researchers exaggerated the centrality of familial forms.[33] See Within the Walls 15.2 for an account of early studies describing pseudo-families in women's prisons.

Juanita Diaz-Cotto argues that Latina prisoners' active involvement in fictive families and their tremendous emotional investment in these relationships are consistent with descriptions in the classic studies.[34] A difference is the ethnic cliquishness of these bondings. The fact that Latina inmates come from families with strong extended kinship ties and the fact that many of these women are incarcerated in a foreign country would seem to increase the need to re-create familiar role relationships.[35]

The argument can be made that as long as women are shut away from the outside world and from the close caring (and scolding) relationships to which they are accustomed, the traditional, familiar pattern will be replayed with a different cast. The functions of these fictive families are many. They offer support and protection in a strange and often bewildering environment. They provide a mutual aid network in an atmosphere of deprivation. They often are encouraged by the prison administration because of their social control aspect—keeping family members out of trouble. Above all, they create situations for fun and laughter.[36]

the walls   15.2

within

Pseudo-Families in Women's Prisons

In their 1965 study of the Frontera Correctional Institution in California, Ward and Kassebaum found that women attempted to deal with the painful conditions of confinement by establishing homosexual alliances. The researchers described these prison love affairs as appearing to be unstable, short-lived, explosive, and involving strict differentiation between the roles of "butch" and "femme." **Butch** is the dominant, or male, role. **Femme** is the docile, or female, role. The person in the butch role is expected to to be strong, in control, and independent and to pursue the femme.

However, Giallombardo's 1966 study of the Federal Reformatory for Women at Alderson, West Virginia, indicated a major difference between male and female prisons. Among female inmates, membership in **fictive families** was more common than participation in homosexual activity and occurred earlier than sexual involvement. Giallombardo reported that the women at Alderston established familiar relationships similar to their relationships in the free world. A sort of family life—with "mothers and fathers," "grandparents," and "aunts and uncles"—was at the very center of inmate life at Alderson and provided a sense of belonging and identification that enabled inmates involved in "family affairs" to do easy time. Unlike male prisoners, the women at Alderson did not design a social system to combat the social and physical deprivations of prison.

LeShanna's 1969 investigation at the Maryville Correctional Institution in Ohio also discovered the presence of the fictive family. Unlike the families in Giallombardo's study, most of the families studied by LeShanna were matricentric—centered on the maternal role. They did not center around a "mother" and "father" united in a homosexual marriage. LeShanna further observed that "mother" was the most frequently reported and most influential role at Maryville.

The 1972 research of Heffernan at the District of Columbia Women's Reformatory in Occoquan, Virginia, also

> ... family life—with "mothers and fathers," "grandparents," and "aunts and uncles"—was at the very center of inmate life at Alderson ...

supported the hypothesis that fictive kinship structures are present in women's prisons. Heffernan, along with Giallombardo, emphasized the concept of latent cultural identity as a factor leading to the formation of the fictive family. By this she meant the preinstitutional identity that the female offender brings with her into the prison setting. Heffernan argued that women construct the kinship structure because females are socialized to conceive of themselves, their needs, and their peer relations primarily in terms of family roles and situations.

Owen's 1998 study conducted at the Central California Women's Facility (CCWF), the world's largest female facility, supports in large part the findings of the earlier studies. She found the play family and the intimate dyad forming the basis of prison social structure. She did find that there were many women who "do not play" or become involved with another prisoner in a physically intimate relationship. Women's adaptation to prison, she adds, depended on the stage of their confinement.

CRITICAL THINKING QUESTIONS

What do these studies, most of which are classics, suggest about the interpersonal relationships of women in prison? Why do women form these relationships?

Source: Rose Giallombardo, *Society of Women: A Study of a Women's Prison* (New York: Wiley, 1966); Esther Heffernan, *Making It in Prison: The Square, the Cool, and the Life* (New York: Wiley, 1972); Richard S. Jones, "Coping with Separation: Adaptive Responses of Women Prisoners," *Women and Criminal Justice* 5 (1993), pp. 71–97; Linda L. LeShanna, "Family Participation: Functional Responses of Incarcerated Females" (master's thesis, Bowling Green State University, 1969); David A. Ward and Gene G. Kassebaum, *Women's Prison: Sex and Social Structure* (Chicago: Aldine, 1965), and Barbara Owen, *"In the Mix": Struggle and Survival in a Woman's Prison* (Albany: State University of New York, 1998).

Another possible advantage of the clearly defined family roles for women living in close quarters is that relationships can become very intimate and include touching and hugging without taking on sexual connotations. In same-sex institutions, where sexual tensions often get played out as homophobia, a clarification of one's relationship in terms of sister-to-sister and mother-to-daughter ties can serve to legitimize the bonding between unrelated women.[37]

In what sense are female inmates the "forgotten offenders"? How might women respond to incarceration differently than men? Why might this group of Latina inmates resemble a family both in organization and in behavior? How does this group reflect the findings of classic studies of the interpersonal relationships of women in prison?

Sexuality

In men's prisons, homophobia gets played out in a different vein. A men's prison is a world of untempered masculinity where the strong preserve their sense of manhood through sexual conquest. Sexual threats, taunting, and assault dominate the scene into which the new inmate is initiated.

Women behind bars re-create a world of the familiar. Many seek out strong types of women with whom to relate and to play their accustomed roles. Butches usually assume the role of father or brother. These women are not necessarily lesbians but are simply women playing at being men. Their popularity in a house of femmes exceeds all expectations. Referred to by masculine pronouns, butches are sought after by male-starved women, who provide them with cigarettes and other enticements.

Butches tend disproportionately to be African American women, and those who play the femme role are usually white. Jean Harris described the role playing at the facility in which she was imprisoned:

> Many of the butches make a concentrated effort to emulate the behavior of young black males, the hip-walking, cool-talking model of masculinity. Some cut their hair short or shave their heads. . . . I've watched many a woman wash, iron, and cook for her "butch," "dike," "bulldagger," and I've heard one stand outside a cell door, begging forgiveness for some wrongdoing she couldn't identify. Inside, as well as outside, it's the woman who pays.[38]

Even though sex role playing in prison says more about female heterosexuality than about homosexuality, it probably worsens homophobia by increasing sexual tension in a crowded institution. Thus, as we have seen, in some women's prisons women define themselves as kin—as sisters, mainly, or as mother and daughters. As kin, women can maintain a certain closeness while avoiding the gossip that would flow from a less clearly defined relationship.

HOW ABOUT WOMEN ON DEATH ROW?

In February 1998, entreaties from all over the world and from the pope failed to gain clemency for Karla Faye Tucker, the first woman executed in Texas since 1863. Despite the fact that she was an admitted ax murderer who had killed strangers in a drug-induced rage, Tucker galvanized the sympathy of the world. Like Velma Barfield before her, Tucker was a born-again Christian whose good works in prison and femininity endeared her to people. A month after Tucker's execution, but without much fanfare, Judias Buenoano, an unrepentant woman prisoner known as the "Black Widow," was executed in Florida's electric

more difficult to manage.[46] Louisa D. Brown, warden of the Women's Correctional Center in Columbia, South Carolina, observed in the late 1980s: "The needs of a woman are different. Women tend to be more emotional. You have to be very cautious about everything you do because their emotions are more on the surface."[47]

Nevertheless, much less violence is reported in women's prisons than in men's prisons. One reason for this difference is that women are less likely to manufacture and carry weapons than are men, because women's prisons generally do not have metal shops or other industries that provide materials for weapons. Even when women carry weapons, the weapons tend to be less lethal than weapons found in men's prisons. During an altercation, women generally pick up nearby objects—chairs, brooms, irons—or they fight without weapons. The result is that women prisoners typically do not suffer serious injuries from violence.[48]

Another reason for reduced violence in women's prisons is the lack of gangs. Owen found that the social power of the older prisoners, especially those known as "Original Gangsters," or "OGs," would not tolerate the challenges to their authority that gangs would bring. Nor would they tolerate the exploitation that gangs would bring to prison life.[49]

Further, inmates typically advise new inmates in women's prisons to stay out of trouble. In Owen's study, this advice was expressed, "Stay out of the mix." The mix referred to any behavior that can bring trouble and conflict with staff and other prisoners.[50]

Nevertheless, women prisoners are capable of committing violent acts behind bars. In South Carolina, correctional officers were attacked on two different occasions; during one of the attacks, two inmates tried to castrate a male correctional officer. In Illinois, a woman officer was seriously injured when she was hit on the head by two women inmates during an escape. In Missouri, a superintendent was stabbed and seriously wounded by angry female prisoners.[51]

Withdrawal Reaction

Prescription drugs are widely used to control the institutional behaviors of women prisoners.[52] A correctional officer commented on the tendency of prison officials to use prescription drugs to control women prisoners:

> I don't see as much drunkenness, for example, among women in prison. . . . An awful lot of people will tell you that psychotropic drugs are used more and they're used probably legally perhaps because the medical staff are more prone to give out Valium, probably the same way, you know, if you went into everybody's pocketbook on this floor you'd find a lot of Valium. Doctors seem to give it to the women and it's a drug that's very easily abused.[53]

Women, however, have less contraband, including drugs, than men prisoners. Women have fewer street drugs because they lack the outside community contacts, have fewer financial resources, and do not have gang organizations within the walls to develop narcotics-trafficking rackets.[54]

Legalistic Reaction

Women prisoners in the 1980s and 1990s were no longer content to form family-like alliances and to complain among themselves about the conflicts and emotional hurts resulting from fractured relationships. Instead, they began to see themselves as aggrieved citizens of the state. Less afraid to express their grievances toward the institution, women began to file more federal lawsuits and to use these lawsuits to strike out at staff.

Nevertheless, Anna Aylward and Jim Thomas's comparison of women's and men's prisons revealed that women were still much less likely to bring lawsuits than men. In examining the summary decisions of all federal civil rights complaints filed in the Illinois Northern Division under 42 U.S.C. section 1983 between August 1977 and December 1983, they found that women inmates constituted 13 percent of the population but represented only 6 percent of the cases brought to the courts.[55] In surveying several women's prisons to determine why women initiate less litigation than men, Katherine Gabel found that women prisoners cited jail credit or "good time" and child custody issues as reasons why they did not use the court process to have their needs met.[56]

Gabel also concluded that the women prisoners most likely to use the legal process were better educated, had some history of employment in the community, and were serving long sentences.[57] Jim Fox predicted that more legal action would be forthcoming from women prisoners as younger and more aggressive females are imprisoned.[58] Both Gabel and Fox also found that institutional variables such as legal resources, outsider legal volunteers, and communication among prisoners influenced women's rate of litigation.

Positive Reaction

Most inmates, men as well as women, want to do their time and get out of prison. Some women renew their commitment to motherhood while in prison, and those involved

h e r o e s | *Elaine A. Lord*
Superintendent of Bedford Hills Correctional Center

"When I began college, I was a pre-med major, but in order to satisfy one of my elective requirements, I took an introduction to sociology course; I had heard it would be easy. In fact, it turned out to be a very tough course, but I struggled through it and even decided to take a criminology course because it was being taught by the same professor. He later arranged for me to spend a summer working at a training facility for juvenile delinquents. I loved working with the kids there, and I felt effective. The next semester, I switched my major to sociology, and I have been studying and working in the field of corrections ever since.

"Bedford Hills is New York State's only maximum-security facility for women; we house approximately 820 women. Sentences range from eight years to life, with an average of twenty years. For this type of population, my staff and I always have to be thinking creatively, willing to try new things, developing programs that are meaningful for women who are serving long sentences, often for committing violent crimes, who have left families—particularly children—behind.

"We must always be careful to identify and recognize the differences between the needs of women and men as prisoners, and this is a particular challenge to us because in many cases, our officers have been trained and have gained their experience in men's facilities. Many controversial and difficult issues arise from this: cross-gender pat-frisking, a woman's need for more privacy; a woman's tendency to talk about problems—this is sometimes interpreted by officers as being insubordinate.'

"Our facility is known for its programs, and that is something we are very proud of. We get the inmates involved in the development of these programs, with some outside help. In this way, the inmates feel empowered and responsible for the success of the program, but even more important, I believe that it is the inmates who are in the best position to recognize and articulate the need for a particular program. The model for this philosophy came from Sister Elaine Roulet, a Sister of St. Joseph who began working at the prison thirty years ago and who has earned international recognition for her compassion and insight into the needs of incarcerated women and their children.

"The inmates conceive of a program and then connect with a civilian professional in that area: sometimes a college professor, a retired social worker, a professional in a particular field—people find us or we find them. As word of our program spreads, it becomes easier to find the support we need. Some of the women are now able to develop programs on their own, without outside help, and they serve as well as mentors to other women who are trying to develop programs. Each program is the direct result of the needs of the women. From a 'correctional' point of view, if we want the women to make proper choices, they really have to have the opportunity to do so in a meaningful way. The women have developed programs to deal with issues such as helping teens cope with prison life, parenting from a distance, AIDS counseling and education, an AIDS walk-a-thon, bringing college back into the facility, family violence, spiritual and religious enrichment, peer-tutoring for ABE and GED, and pre- and postnatal workshops.

"When I first arrived in 1984, I was not sure how the prison could connect to the community. Bedford Hills is one of the most affluent towns in the United States; many wealthy and influential people are our neighbors. Therefore we needed to find a way to make connections. In that way, we could draw on the resources around us, but more importantly, the people in our community could see the women not only as inmates but as neighbors, as mothers, as sisters, as daughters.

"Sister Elaine suggested that the best way to make connections is through children, so we began to think of ways to have the community help us find ways for the inmates to maintain contact with their children. We developed the summer host family program in which people from the community open their homes to the inmates' children for a week or two. They bring them to the facility each morning and pick them up each afternoon. Thus, the children get to visit their mothers every day for a week or two, providing an opportunity for mother/child relationships to grow stronger, to supplement the weekly or monthly visits that occur throughout the year.

"In 1996, when an inmate committee formed to bring college back into the facility, we reached out to the com-in institutions with family visitation programs are able to develop more positive relationships with their children. Other women become involved in drug counseling programs and other forms of empowering group processes. Women prisoners find it much easier to have a positive response when they are offered the type of programming that is found in the Bedford Hills Correctional Center.

The hero in this chapter is Elaine A. Lord, superintendent of Bedford Hills Correctional Facility in Westchester County, New York, since 1984. In this women's prison, Lord and her staff have designed and implemented many innovative programs, some of which have been used as models in prisons around the world. She is currently completing the dissertation requirements for her Ph.D. in criminal justice at the State University of New York at Albany. Read what she had to say for *Invitation to Corrections* in 2000.

munity yet again: One of our long-time volunteers helped the women contact the president of Marymount Manhattan College, who in turn offered to find other academics to administer and teach college courses. Other community members raised substantial funds, and within a year, we had a thriving college program in place, with almost two hundred women participating. When it became apparent that we needed a precollege program to help prepare the women for their college courses, volunteers again helped by procuring a grant from the Reader's Digest Fund and from Mercy College to implement such a program.

"In the future, I believe the issue of mental illness in prison will be a major challenge not only to our resources but to our ability to run safe, progressive prisons. As more mental institutions are downsized and as social services are reduced, more and more mentally ill women wind up in prison—abandoned by society. Our challenge is to provide the services they need while maintaining services to the rest of the population. Approximately 50 percent of the inmates at Bedford Hills are on psychotropic medication, and about 40 percent are under psychiatric care. While we do our best to treat these women with compassion and dignity, they are very often the ones who cause the most serious disruptions, placing a strain on officers, on other inmates, on the facility's budget.

"Another issue we are dealing with is inmates receiving longer sentences, and many of these inmates are teenagers. It is very difficult for a 17-year old to understand what a fifty-year sentence means; we need to provide services and counseling for these women; their well-being and the well being of the facility depends on our ability to help the women make this transition and to use their time productively, to see that imprisonment does not mean that their lives are over or at a standstill; that is why we concentrate on program development; they are vital to the women.

"The officers face many challenges as well: How can they remain creative, innovative, fair, and responsive to the myriad of issues facing us in the field of corrections given the 'lock-them-up-and-throw-away-the-key' men-

tality that seems to be so pervasive? And it is sometimes very difficult for officers to make the transition to a female facility, given that most of their training has occurred in a male facility: cross-gender pat-searches, the women's need for more privacy, the women's tendency to form very close ties to each other. And it pains me to still hear, in the year 2001, that in order to advance in corrections, you have to come up through the ranks in a *male* facility because women's facilities aren't *tough* enough. I believe that there is much to be learned from female facilities, the most important of which is the value of dialogue, of discussion, of consensus building. It is no coincidence that the relatives of my officers often come up to me at social events and tell me they feel safe knowing their spouse or son or daughter is working at Bedford.

"I think that the women at Bedford Hills have taught me and the other members of the staff that prison is not just about punishment; it can be about transformation as well. I have learned that if I do the best I can, if I continue to see the women as complex human beings who have much to offer themselves, each other, and society, if we can talk and commiserate and laugh, then we have formed a community. We have formed a place where the women can *choose* to change and grow—a safe place—away from the drugs and the abuse and the family violence and the poverty that often influenced their choices. Most of the women in Bedford Hills will leave some day. When they leave, my hope for them, and the thing that I work so hard to accomplish, is that they will have gained something valuable as a result of having been here—a sense of self, a sense of worth, a sense of dignity, a sense that they can do something on the outside as a result of what they learned in prison. And most important of all, I want them to never ever return to this place.'"

CRITICAL THINKING QUESTIONS

Would you like to be a staff member at Bedford Hills? How does Elaine Lord treat inmates? What might other women's prisons learn from Bedford Hills?

WHAT SPECIAL ISSUES ARE RAISED BY THE INCARCERATION OF WOMEN?

Superintendent Lord mentioned the increasing number of mentally ill women being confined in prison and the difficulty of caring for them in a correctional context. Another issue, previously mentioned, is that men's prisons offer many more educational and vocational programs than do women's prisons and most of the vocational programs available for women aim to prepare them for stereotypical "feminine" occupations. Another serious issue is **sexual abuse** of female prisoners by male guards. Also, the problems posed by motherhood while a person is incarcerated constitute an issue in every women's prison.

Sexual Abuse in Prison

All rape is an exercise of power, but some rapists have an edge that is more than physical: They operate within an institutionalized setting.[59] Rape in slavery, rape in the military, and rape in prison are three examples.

The scandal involving sexual harassment of women in the military has been highlighted in the mass media. Until recently, relatively little attention has been paid to the sexual assaults on female prisoners by their male guards. In 1996, extensive documentation was provided by the Women's Rights Project of Human Rights Watch, an international nongovernmental organization, that revealed that the extent of guard-on-inmate abuse behind the closed doors of prison is staggering. The 347-page report drawn from firsthand interviews, court records, and records of guards' disciplinary hearings is astonishing in the graphic detail provided of everyday experiences of women in state prisons. Within the Walls 15.3 summarized the report's findings.

the walls   15.3

within

Sexual Victimization in Women's Prisons

The custodial sexual misconduct documented in this report takes many forms. We found that male correctional employees have vaginally, anally, and orally raped female prisoners and sexually assaulted and abused them. We found that in the course of committing such gross misconduct, male officers have not only used actual or threatened physical force, but have also used their near total authority to provide or deny goods and privileges to female prisoners to compel them to have sex or, in other cases, to reward them for having done so. In other cases, male officers have violated their most basic professional duty and engaged in sexual contact with female prisoners absent the use of threat of force or any material exchange. In addition to engaging in sexual relations with prisoners, male officers have used mandatory pat-frisks or room searches to grope women's breasts, buttocks, and vaginal areas and to view them

... male officers have not only used actual or threatened force, but have also used their ... authority to provide or deny goods and privileges to female prisoners to compel them to have sex ...

inappropriately while in a state of undress in the housing or bathroom areas. Male correctional officers and staff have also engaged in regular verbal degradation and harassment of female prisoners, thus contributing to a custodial environment in the state prisons for women which is often highly sexualized and excessively hostile.

CRITICAL THINKING QUESTIONS

Do you believe that these statements are accurate? If they are accurate, why are these sorts of behaviors permitted in prisons in the twenty-first century?

Source: Reprinted from Human Rights Watch Women's Rights Project, *All Too Familiar: Sexual Abuse of Women in U.S. State Prisons* (New York: Human Rights Watch, 1996), p. 1.

Table 15.2

History of Physical or Sexual Abuse

Forty-two percent of women under correctional authority reported that they were physically or sexually assaulted at some time during their lives. Sixty-nine percent of women reporting an assault said that it had occurred before age 18.

	Women		
	Probation	Local Jails	State Prisons
Ever physically or sexually abused	42%	48%	57%
Before age 18	16	21	12
After age 18	13	11	20
Both periods	13	16	25
Ever abused			
Physically	15%	10%	18%
Sexually	7	10	11
Both	18	27	28

Source: Bureau of Justice Statistics, *Women Offenders* (Washington, D.C.: U.S. Department of Justice, 1999), p. 8.

Human Rights Watch takes the U.S. government to task for failing to protect the women who are subjected to institutionalized rape by prison authorities. The placing of male officers in contact positions over female prisoners is in violation of the United Nations Standard Minimum Rules for the Treatment of Prisoners.[60] The persons who are most vulnerable to sexual abuse are first-time offenders, the young or mentally ill, and lesbian and transgendered persons. One of the most poignant tragedies of the sexual victimization of women in prison is that so many of them have a history of physical or sexual abuse (see Table 15.2).

Prisoners, such as those in Georgia who are not given a stipend for their work, have no means of purchasing the many supplies they need. Many times female inmates willingly trade sex for favors. In many instances, women have been impregnated as a result of sexual misconduct, placed in segregation if they filed a complaint, and sometimes pressured to get an abortion.[61] The gripping Hollywood prison drama *Love Child,* produced in 1982, tells the true story of an inmate who became pregnant by a guard in Florida and fought for her right to keep the baby. Male guards who have been involved in sexual relations with female inmates are transferred to men's prisons instead of being fired.

According to Louis Rothenstein, a psychologist who worked for six years in the federal prison in Dublin, California, it was not uncommon for guards to go into women's cells and have sex.[62] Complaints by women inmates and their advocates were ignored. "You would be blackballed if you were thought of as an advocate for the inmates," Rothenstein said.[63] An internal code of silence shields the prison industry from public scrutiny, he added. In 1998, at the U.S. District Court in San Francisco, a settlement was reached providing $500,000 for three female inmates who filed a grievance after being raped by male inmates while housed at the male facility at Dublin, California.[64] The inmates reportedly had been given access to the women after bribing a male officer.

The public got a rare look at the racist and sexist brutality in the women's federal prison when the Canadian Broadcasting Company aired a videotape of male guards roughing up crying women in a forced strip search. The outcry that ensued and the resulting follow-up investigations have done a lot to force the prison to take remedial action and to get the women transferred to regional institutions.[65]

The events at the notorious women's prison in Georgia are even more scandalous. Women there sued the prison for sexual abuse in 1984 but had to wait eight years to win their case, in November 1992. In the end, fourteen former employees—ten men including the deputy warden and four women—were indicted on sexual abuse charges including rape, sexual assault, and sodomy in "one of the worst episodes of its kind in the history of the nation's women's prisons."[66] The incidents took place in the warden's house, in a prison rest room, and in other areas.

Those indictments were only the tip of the iceberg at the Georgia penitentiary. Whether brought about through trade-offs or coerced through violence between male guards and female inmates, sexual involvement was not deviant behavior in that setting; it was the norm. Even female staff members were implicated in sexually abusive behavior, according to court records cited in the Human Rights Watch report. There is no way to begin to estimate the number of inmates involved before the lawsuit was filed in 1992. Between 1992 and 1996, when record keeping improved because of the investigations taking place, attorney Bob Cullen told Human Rights Watch that he had learned of approximately 370 reported incidents during this period. Some of the cases have been publicized in the media.[67]

Not surprisingly, there is extensive litigation concerning the sexual mistreatment of female inmates. According to Chesney-Lind, scandals have erupted in California, Georgia, Hawaii, Ohio, Louisiana, Michigan, Tennessee, New York, and New Mexico.[68] Most of them came to light only because of publicity surrounding legal suits.

Motherhood

The separation of women prisoners from their children can be traumatic for all. Prisons, and especially women's prisons, generally are located in remote, rural areas. Family ties, over time, are broken. Yet prisoners' family relationships are very important not only for mental health reasons but for postrelease success.[69] For the number of children of women under correctional supervision in 1998, see Table 15.3.

Some inmate-mothers are concerned about the custody and care of their children during their confinement. Mary Martin's examination of mothers who were incarcerated in the Minnesota Correctional Facility at Shakopee in 1985 established that their commitment to parenthood was deep.[70] When these mothers were followed up five years later, most of them had sustained continuous and primary parenting from within prison and had reunited with their children when released from prison. Nevertheless, internal prison policies as well as traditional public policies provide minimal support for the maintenance of family relationships by individuals involved in the criminal justice system.

Children most frequently stay with maternal grandmothers, but other caretakers include a child's father or other relatives. Imprisoned women express the most satisfaction

Table 15.3			
Children of Women under Correctional Supervision, 1998			
	Estimated Number		
	Women Offenders	**Women Offenders with Minor Children**	**Minor Children**
Total	869,600	615,500	1,300,800
Probation	721,400	516,200	1,067,200
Jail	63,800	44,700	105,300
State prisons	75,200	49,200	117,100
Federal prisons	9,200	5,400	11,200

Note: Only children under age 18 are counted.

Source: Bureau of Justice Statistics, *Women Offenders* (Washington, D.C.: U.S. Department of Justice, 1999), p. 7.

when children are placed with their maternal grandmothers, and when they have participated in the decision about where their children will live. In placing children with their maternal grandmothers, inmates feel relatively confident that they will encounter minimal difficulties when taking the children back upon release. If no suitable family alternatives are available, children may be placed in foster homes or put up for adoption. Those placements make it very difficult for mothers to regain custody of after release.[71]

Imprisoned women are burdened with the knowledge that their own behavior has caused their separation from children. This separation generates feelings of emptiness, helplessness, guilt, anger, and bitterness, and fear of loss or rejection by the children. With prolonged separation, mothers fear children might establish stronger bonds of affection with caretakers than with mothers. Furthermore, mothers fear that teenage children staying with maternal grandparents may be arrested because of inadequate supervision.[72]

Even more problems await women who are pregnant at the time they are imprisoned or who become pregnant during their sentence. During imprisonment, the likelihood of pregnancy is high because of coed prisons, home furloughs and work release, conjugal visits, and even the possibility of sexual intercourse or rape by prison staff. On the one hand, the termination of prison pregnancy may not be possible even if the inmate desires it. On the other hand, the inmate may be forced to have an abortion by prison officials.[73]

Several states and other countries have innovative programs for mothers of young children (see Within the Walls 15.4). In contrast, the Department of Corrections in Florida takes responsibility for the newborn child and arranges a custody hearing for placement of the child. Other states fall in between these extremes, but the fact of the matter is that mothers stand a high risk of losing children they bear in prison.[74]

within the walls 15.4

Innovative Family Programs

California has a 1978 statute mandating the creation of a Mother-Infant-Care program, an alternative-sentencing project that allows one hundred women with infants who are 6 months old or younger to live in one of the seven community-based facilities with their children and take parenting classes. Several hundred women have graduated from the program.

The program at Bedford Hills in New York State is the one most written about. The Bedford Hills program provides a nursery where babies up to 18 months old can live with their mothers. A playroom is available for older children, who are encouraged to come and visit with their moms. The mother–child bonding has been excellent in this program, and the women learn child care skills.

The Nebraska Correctional Center for Women, similarly, has a prison nursery and overnight visits for older children to maintain the bonds between mother and child. Children can stay up to five days a month. According to the male warden, the presence of children has a harmonizing effect on the whole population.

> The mother–child bonding has been excellent in this program, and the women learn child care skills.

In Australia, inmate mothers usually care for their children until they reach age 2 or 3. In western Europe, except for Norway (which makes extensive use of long-term foster care), children are kept at the prison for up to several years. Germany has, perhaps, the most outstanding prison nursery system. In the German program, teachers and social workers help women learn how to be good mothers.

CRITICAL THINKING QUESTIONS

How do you think that a prison should handle prisoners who have children and want extended visitation times with their children? What are the advantages and disadvantage for children of extended visits with their mothers in prison?

Source: K. Boudin, "Lessons from a Mother's Program in Prison: A Psychosocial Approach Supports Women and Their Children," *Women and Therapy* 21 (1998), pp. 103–125; and Claudia G. Dowling, "Women Behind Bars," *Life*, October (1997), pp. 76–83.

Baunach explored attitudes of inmates toward allowing children to stay in the prison for short periods of time—all day or over night—and found that women in prison, regardless of whether they had children of their own, tend to respond favorably to the presence of children. Many women responded that they try to "clean up their language and behavior" when children are present and enjoy watching or playing with children. No research, however, has been done on the effects on the children of being in prison with mothers for short or long periods.[75]

SUMMARY

The "forgotten criminal" is coming into her own. A few violent, sensationalized crimes by women in the mid-1970s generated considerable interest in the woman offender. The law-and-order emphasis in the mid-1970s also resulted in greater numbers of women being incarcerated. Several states found it necessary to build new prisons to house the increasing number of women prisoners. The South has long been notorious for incarcerating large numbers of women, but all sections of the nation are now incarcerating increasing numbers.

Women, like men, must learn how to cope with imprisonment. Whereas the prison for men brings to mind a jungle where the strong survive at the expense of the weak, the prison for women is marked by small pockets of friendship and allegiance. Women prisoners must be alert against exploitation, both from other inmates and staff, but there is less reason to fear and more opportunity to create bonds of love.

In the 1980s, equality for women was the word. In the field of corrections, the focus was on equality of opportunity for female correctional officers in men's prisons. In light of some unintended consequences of the bid for equality—namely, the widespread sexual harassment of female prisoners by male correctional officers (the counterpart of female officers working without restriction in men's prisons) and the mandatory harsh minimum sentences for drug possession and dealing—women's advocates are arguing for an empowering feminist approach geared toward women's special needs.

Before women's prisons can be improved, several questions must be considered: What effect does imprisonment have on women? What prison programs will be most helpful to those who have a history of drug abuse? Why is the imprisoned female offender becoming more difficult to handle? What can be done to prepare women more effectively for release to the community? What can be done to better handle the problem of the separation of the confined female from her children? What can be done to reduce the stigma of being processed through the criminal justice system? What correctional policy is needed to respond to confined women with understanding and respect? Confusion abounds, but the answers to these question are crucial—both to the female offender and to society.

KEY TERMS

butch, p. 359
femme, p. 359
fictive families, p. 359

infantilized, p. 357
kinship networks, p. 358
sexual abuse, p 366

CRITICAL THINKING QUESTIONS

1. Women are committing more crimes, but the real increase shows up in drug-related crimes against property rather than against people. Explain this pattern.
2. The typical woman offender has children. How does motherhood affect her "doing time"?
3. "Women's inmate society establishes a substitute group in which women can identify or construct family patterns similar to those in the free world." Describe the family structure in a women's prison.
4. Sexual abuse of women prisoners is a major problem in U.S. corrections. What can be done about it?
5. How do the subcultures of men's and women's prisons differ?
6. Do you support a separate but equal women's criminal justice system? Why or why not?

WEB DESTINATIONS

Refer to the Canadian Association of Elizabeth Fry Societies for various efforts to reform women's prisons.
www.elizabethfry.ca/

Read about women on death row.
www.whateverdesign.com/com/speakout/html/death-row.htm
Newsletter, Sisterko@aol.com

This site describe substance abuse treatment of women in prison.
www.harmreduction.org, www.jointogether.org

California now has the uncertain distinction of having the most women prisoners in the nation, as well as the world's largest women's prison.
www.prisonactivist.org/women/women-in-prison.html

Women represent the fastest growing population in prison.
www.unix.oit.umass.edu/

Read how sexual misconduct is alleged at a women's prison.
www.concordmonitor.com/stories/front

FOR FURTHER READING

Barfield, Velma. *Woman on Death Row.* Minneapolis: World Wide Publications, 1985. Barfield provides a glimpse of what death row is like for a female prisoner.

Chesney-Lind, Meda. "Rethinking Women's Imprisonment: A Critical Examination of Trends in Female Incarceration." In *The Criminal Justice System and Women: Offenders, Victims, and Workers,* 2d ed., edited by Barbara Raffel Price and Natalie J. Sokoloff, pp. 105–117. New York: McGraw-Hill, 1995. Chesney-Lind provides one of the most critical analyses of women's imprisonment in the 1990s.

Chesney-Lind, Meda. *The Female Offender: Girls, Women, and Crime.* Thousand Oaks, Calif.: Sage, 1997. Chesney-Lind expands her coverage of women in prison in this volume.

Diaz-Cotto, Juanita. *Gender, Ethnicity, and the State: Latina and Latino Prison Politics.* Albany: State University of New York Press, 1996. A helpful examination of how Latina women adjust to imprisonment.

Giallombardo, Rose. *Society of Women: A Study of a Women's Prison.* New York: Wiley, 1966. An interesting study of inmates at the Federal Correctional Prison for Women at Alderson, West Virginia.

Heffernan, Esther. *Making It in Prison: The Square, the Cool, and the Life.* New York: Wiley, 1972. This classic study of the District of Columbia Women's Reformatory in Occoquan, Virginia, identifies the three dominant social roles in this institution.

Human Rights Watch Women's Rights Project. *All Too Familiar: Sexual Abuse of Women in U.S. State Prisons.* New York: Human Rights Watch, 1996. Documentation of sexual abuse in women's prisons in the United States.

O'Shea, Kathleen. *Women and the Death Penalty in the United States, 1900–1998.* Westport, Conn.: Greenwood Press, 1999. A helpful view of the history of capital punishment in women's prisons in the twentieth century.

Owen, Barbara. *In the Mix: Struggle and Survival in a Women's Prison.* Albany: State University of New York Press, 1998. An analysis of how imprisoned women cope with confinement.

Pollock, Joycelyn. M. *Counseling Women in Prison.* Thousand Oaks, Calif.: Sage, 1998. In a first-rate book, Pollock surveys how women are treated in prison and the programs they are offered.

Pollock-Byrne, Joycelyn M. *Women, Prison and Crime.* Pacific Grove, Calif.: Brooks/Cole, 1990. A comprehensive look at women's prisons, especially helpful in identifying the inmate subculture.

Rierden, Andi. *The Farm: Life Inside a Women's Prison.* Boston: University of Massachusetts Press, 2000. Written by a journalist, this book depicts the daily struggles of women inmates at the Connecticut Correctional Institution in Niantic.

Ward, David A., and Gene G. Kassebaum. *Women's Prison: Sex and Social Structure.* Chicago: Aldine-Atherton, 1965. These authors, like Giallombardo, discuss the specific roles women play in the fictive-family structure.

NOTES

1. Ellen H. McWhirter, "Empowerment in Counseling," *Journal of Counseling and Development* 69 (1991), pp. 222–227.
2. Lorraine Gutierrez, "Empowering Women of Color: A Feminist Model," in *Feminist Social Work Practice in Clinical Settings,* ed. Nancy R. Hooyman and Naomi Gottlieb (Newbury Park, Calif.: Sage, 1991), pp. 271–303.
3. Pat Kelley, "Narrative Theory and Social Work Treatment," in *Social Work Treatment: Interlocking Theoretical Approaches,* ed. Frances Turner (New York: Free Press, 1996), pp. 461–479.
4. Ania Wilczynski, "Images of Women Who Kill Their Infants: The Mad and the Bad," *Women and Criminal Justice* 2 (1991), pp. 78–80.

5. Bureau of Justice Statistics, *Prisoners, 1999* (Washington, D.C.: U.S. Government Printing Office, 2000).

6. Joycelyn M. Pollock-Byrne, *Women, Prison and Crime* (Pacific Grove, Calif.: Brooks/Cole, 1990), p. 1.

7. Rita James Simon, *Women and Crime* (Lexington, Mass.: Heath, 1975), pp. 69–70.

8. Eugenia Lekkerkerker, *Reformatories for Women in the U.S.* (Gronigen, Netherlands: J. B. Wolters, 1931).

9. Rose Giallombardo, *Society of Women: A Study of a Women's Prison* (New York: Wiley, 1966); David A. Ward and Gene G. Kassebaum, *Women's Prison: Sex and Social Structure* (Chicago: Aldine-Atherton, 1965).

10. Esther Heffernan, *Making It in Prison: The Square, the Cool, and the Life* (New York: Wiley, 1972); Arlene E. Mitchell, *Informal Inmate Social Structure in Prisons for Women: A Comparative Study* (San Francisco: R & E Research Associates, 1975).

11. Alice Propper, "Importation and Deprivation Perspectives on Homosexuality in Correctional Institutions: An Empirical Test of their Relative Efficacy" (Ph.D. diss., University of Michigan, Ann Arbor, 1976).

12. Estelle B. Freedman, *Their Sister's Keepers: Women's Prison Reform in America, 1830–1930* (Ann Arbor: University of Michigan Press, 1981); Nicole H. Rafter, *Partial Justice: State Prisons and Their Inmates, 1800–1935* (Boston: Northeastern University Press, 1985).

13. Pollock-Byrne, *Women, Prison and Crime.*

14. Karlene Faith, *Unruly Women: The Politics of Confinement and Resistance* (Vancouver, British Columbia: Press Gang Publishing, 1993); Kathryn Watterson, *Women in Prison: Inside the Concrete Womb* (Boston: Northeastern University Press, 1996); Meda Chesney-Lind, *The Female Offender: Girls, Women, and Crime* (Thousand Oaks, Calif.: Sage, 1997); and Meda Chesney-Lind, "Rethinking Women's Imprisonment: A Critical Examination of Trends in Female Incarceration," in *The Criminal Justice System and Women: Offenders, Victims and Workers,* 2d ed., ed. Barbara Raffel Price and Natalie J. Sokoloff (New York: McGraw-Hill, 1995), pp. 105–117.

15. Donald Clemmer, *The Prison Community* (New York: Holt, Rinehart & Winston, 1958).

16. Phyllis Jo Baunach, "Critical Problems of Women in Prison," in *The Changing Roles of Women in the Criminal Justice System,* ed. Imogene L. Moyer (Prospect Heights, Ill.: Waveland Press, 1985), p. 96.

17. Nancy Kurshan, "Behind the Walls: The History and Current Reality of Women's Imprisonment," in *Criminal Justice: Confronting the Prison Crisis,* ed. Ellen Rosenblatt (Boston: South End Press, 1996).

18. American Friends Service Committee, *Struggle for Justice: A Report on Crime and Punishment in America* (New York: Hill & Wang, 1971), p. 16.

19. Clarice Feinman, *Women in the Criminal Justice System,* 3d ed. (Westport, Conn.: Praeger, 1994), 44.

20. Samuel Walker, *Popular Justice: A History of American Criminal Justice* (New York: Oxford University Press, 1980), p. 21.

21. W. David Lewis, *From Newgate to Dannemora* (Ithaca, N.Y.: Cornell University Press, 1965).

22. Chesney-Lind, "Rethinking Women's Imprisonment."

23. Joycelyn M. Pollock, *Counseling Women in Prison,* (Thousand Oaks, Calif.: Sage, 1998).

24. Watterson, *Women in Prison.*

25. B. Owen, *In the Mix: Struggle and Survival in a Women's Prison* (Albany: State University of New York Press, 1998).

26. John Irwin, *Prisons in Turmoil* (Boston: Little, Brown, 1980).

27. Chesney-Lind, *The Female Offender.*

28. Jean Harris, *They Always Call Us Ladies: Stories from Prison* (New York: Zebra Books, 1988).

29. Feinman, *Women in the Criminal Justice System.*

30. Pollock, *Counseling Women in Prison.*

31. Giallombardo, *Society of Women;* and Kathryn van Wormer, "Female Prison Families: How Are They Dysfunctional?" *International Journal of Comparative and Applied Criminal Justice* 11 (1987), pp. 263–271.

32. Pollock, *Counseling Women in Prison.*

33. Faith, *Unruly Women.*

34. Juanita Diaz-Cotto, *Gender, Ethnicity, and the State: Latina and Latino Prison Politics* (Albany: State University of New York Press, 1996).

35. Ibid.

36. C. B. Hart, "Gender Differences in Social Support among Inmates," *Women and Criminal Justice* 6 (1995), pp. 67–68.

37. See van Wormer, "Female Prison Families."

38. Harris, *They Always Call Us Ladies,* pp. 136, 139.

39. Bureau of Justice Statistics, *Capital Punishment 1999* (Washington, D.C.: U.S. Department of Justice, 2000).

40. Feinman, *Women in the Criminal Justice System.*

41. Velma Barfield, *Women on Death Row* (Minneapolis: World Wide Publications, 1985), p. 106.

42. Cathy Thompson, "The Invisibility of Women on Death Row: A Personal View," *Lifelines Ireland* 3 (1997), p. 3.

43. Kathleen O'Shea, *Women on the Row* (special issue based on an online discussion, 25 May 1998), pp. 1–18.

44. Kathleen O'Shea, *Women and the Death Penalty in the United States, 1900–1998* (Westport, Conn.: Greenwood Press, 1999).

45. Barbara Owen, *"In the Mix": Struggle and Survival in a Women's Prison* (Albany: State University of New York Press, 1998), p. 175.

46. Kathryn Watterson Burkhart, *Women in Prison* (New York: Popular Library edition, 1976).

47. Interviewed by the author in October 1978.

48. Pollock-Byrne, *Women, Prison and Crime,* p. 153.

49. Owen, *"In the Mix,"* p. 170.

50. Ibid., p. 179.

51. Information gained by the author during interviews with administrators of women prisoners during the late 1970s and the 1980s.

52. Sheila Balkan, Ronald J. Berger, and Janet Schmidt, *Crime and Deviance in America* (Belmont, Calif.: Wadsworth, 1980).

53. Pollock's 1981 interview with correctional officers. In Pollock-Byrne, *Women, Prison and Crime.*

54. Pollock-Byrne, *Women, Prison and Crime,* p. 153.

55. Anna Aylward and Jim Thomas, "Quiescence in Women's Prisons Litigation: Some Exploratory Issues," *Justice Quarterly* 1 (1984), pp. 253–276.

56. Katherine Gabel, *Legal Issues of Female Inmates* (Northampton, Mass.: Smith College School for Social Work, 1984).
57. Ibid.
58. J. Fox, "Women's Prison Policy, Prisoner Activism, and the Impact of the Contemporary Feminist Movement: A Case Study," *The Prison Journal* 64 (1984), pp. 15–36.
59. Susan Brownmiller, *Against Our Wills: Men, Women, and Rape* (New York: Bantam Books, 1975).
60. Human Rights Watch Women's Rights Project, *All Too Familiar: Sexual Abuse of Women in U.S. State Prisons* (New York: Human Rights Watch, 1996).
61. Ibid.
62. See B. Stein, "Life in Prison: Sexual Abuse," *The Progressive* (1996), pp. 23–24. See also Nina Siegal, "Stopping Abuse in Prison," *The Progressive* (April 1999), pp. 31–33.
63. Ibid., p. 24.
64. "Bureau of Prisons Sexual Abuse Suit Settled for $500,000," *Prison Legal News* (1998), p. 9.
65. Sharon Doyle Driedger, "Showdown of P4W; Women Are Being Moved into Men's Prisons," *Maclean's*, 27 January 1997), p. 4.
66. *New York Times*, 14 November 1992, pp. 1, 7.
67. Human Rights Watch Women's Rights Project, *All Too Familiar*.
68. Meda Chesney-Lind, *The Female Offender*. Iowa is another state in which prison officials have been sued. For information on these six suits, see William Petroski, "Sex in Prisons Costs Taxpayers," *Des Moines Sunday Register*, 21 May 2000, pp. 1A, 5A.
69. Creasle Finney Hairston, "Family Views in Correctional Programs," in *Encyclopedia of Social Work*, 19th ed. (Washington, D.C.: NASW Press, 1995), pp. 991–996.
70. Mary Martin, "Connected Mothers: A Follow-Up Study of Incarcerated Women and Their Children," *Women and Criminal Justice* 8 (1997), pp. 1–23.
71. Baunach, "Critical Problems of Women in Prison," pp. 97–98.
72. Ibid.
73. Karen E. Holt, "Nine Months to Life—The Law and the Pregnant Inmate," *Journal of Family Law* 20 (1982), pp. 524–525.
74. Ibid., p. 537.
75. Baunach, "Critical Problems of Women in Prison."

Multiple Choice Questions

1. According to the text, empowerment theory focuses on all of the following dimensions accept:
   A. Social
   B. Education
   C. Political
   D. Religious

2. Which of the following perspectives takes the position that women are responsible for their actions and must pay for their behavior.
   A. Empowerment
   B. Correctional
   C. Punishment
   D. Reintegrative

3. According to the text, currently women account for what percentage of the total incarcerated population?
   A. 4.4%
   B. 5.4%
   C. 6.4%
   D. 7.4%

4. Which of the following was the first separate prison for women?
   A. Indiana Women's Prison
   B. New York Women's Prison
   C. Massachusetts Women's Prison
   D. Philadelphia Women's Prison

5. All of the following are functions of prison families except:
   A. Offer mutual support and protection
   B. Have a social control aspect
   C. Create situations for fun and laughter
   D. They control the spread of HIV & AIDS from high risk behavior

6. The degree to which a female inmate participates in the prison culture is influenced by all of the following factors accept:

   A. Time spent in prisons
   B. State of confinement
   C. Social and cultural background
   D. Degree of commitment to a deviant, lawbreaking lifestyle

7. Female inmates have always
   A. Been treated as equal to male prisoners
   B. Been incarcerated in separate correctional institutions
   C. Been more violent then males
   D. Accounted for a lower amount of the incarcerated population then males

8. Which of the following characteristics has been prevalent throughout the history of women's prisons?
   A. The treatment of female prisoners as children
   B. The treatment of female prisoners with punitive punishment
   C. The treatment of female prisoners with shock incarcerations
   D. The treatment of the majority of female prisoners with psychotropic drugs

9. Which of the following have the new mandatory drug-sentencing laws most adversely affected?
   A. White women
   B. Jewish women
   C. Colored Women
   D. Asian Women

10. According to the text, which of the following is not the most vulnerable to sexual abuse?
    A. First time offenders
    B. Mentally ill offenders
    C. Young inmates
    D. Violent inmates

True/False Questions

T F   1. The empowerment perspective focuses on solutions with emphasis on renewed rehabilitation.

T F   2. In the early history of American prisons, women were incarcerated in separate prisons from men.

T F   3. Women of color have been most adversely affected by the new mandatory drug-sentencing laws.

T F   4. Similar to male prison society, female prison culture is organized around power and violence.

T F 5. Female prisoners commit suicide more than male prisoners.

T F 6. During the 1980s and 1990s female prisoners began to file more federal suits.

T F 7. Vocational programs in female prisons tend to prepare females for stereotypical "feminine" occupations.

T F 8. According to the text, prescription drugs are rarely used with female prisoners to control their institutional behavior.

T F 9. In a female prison, the father's role in the family is usually assumed by a butch, who tends to be an African American woman.

Fill-in-the-Blank Questions

(based on key terms)

1. The docile, or female, role is known as the _____ role

2. Among female inmates, membership in _____ is more common than participation in homosexual activity.

Essay Questions

1. Compare the empowerment, correctional and punishment approaches for examining women in prisons.

2. Describe the history of the female prison experience from the early nineteenth century to the contemporary era.

3. Explain the development and purpose of kinship networks in female prisons. Identify and explain the roles that make up these groups.

4. Describe the female inmate's social world by using the social and cultural background of the woman, the families female inmates develop in prison and prison sexuality.

5. Identify and explain three challenging issues that confront female prisons.

ANSWERS

Multiple Choice Questions

1. D	6. B
2. C	7. D
3. C	8. A
4. A	9. C
5. D	10. D

True/False Questions

1. T	6. T
2. F	7. T
3. T	8. F
4. F	9. T
5. F	

Fill-in-the-Blank Questions

1. Femme
2. Fictive families

chapter sixteen

The Juvenile Offender

School shootings have alerted the whole nation that juvenile crime is a serious problem. The 1 October 1997, shooting in Pearl, Mississippi, was one in a long line of shootings in schoolyards in the United States. Here is what took place in the courtroom:

> HATTIESBURG, Miss.—Sobbing repeatedly and proclaiming that he loved the girl he killed after she jilted him, Luke Woodham said Thursday that he felt like a "total reject" when he opened fire at his high school last October, killing two classmates and wounding seven.
>
> Woodham, 17, took the witness stand apparently against the advice of his attorneys. He described himself as an outcast and a loner who found a sense of belonging in a satanic cult that worshiped demons and cast magic spells. But he said it was a broken heart—after his girlfriend, Christina Menafee, broke up with him—that made him snap.
>
> The breakup "destroyed me," he said, his voice breaking into heavy, racking sobs. "There's no way you people can understand what it did to me. It's just not fair. I tried to do everything I could. She didn't love me. But I loved her."
>
> Several jurors recoiled in horror and looked into their laps as they listened to [psychologist Richard] Jepsen read an entry Woodham made in his diary last April about five months before the school shooting. In the account, Woodham said he and Boyette [the

alleged leader of the satanic group] had beaten and tortured Woodham's pet dog, Sparkle, wrapping it in a sack and setting it afire, then laughing as the burning dog tried to escape.

Woodham described it as his "first kill," and after writing gruesome details, concluded, "It was true beauty."

Jepsen also read from a letter Woodham handed to a friend and alleged fellow Kroth member [satanic group] minutes before he opened fire at Pearl High School.

"All through my life I've been ridiculed," he wrote. "I was always beat on and hated. I am malicious because I am miserable." He also proclaimed, "Murder is gutsy."[1]

CRITICAL THINKING QUESTIONS

Why does the public react so strongly to school shootings? Why do you think shootings occurred as frequently as they did in the 1990s? Do you believe that there will be as many in the next decade?

There were school shootings in the 1990s both before and after the one at Pearl, Mississippi (see Table 16.1). The most horrific took place at Columbine High in Littleton, Colorado, on Tuesday 20 April 1999. On that long tragic day, Dylan Klebold and Eric Harris, armed with guns, bombs, and a relentless fury, laid a brutal siege. By the time the terror ended with the killers' own suicides, twelve students and a teacher were dead and twenty-three students were wounded. The arsenal the shooters used included a double-barrel shotgun, a TEC 9 semiautomatic rifle, a pump shotgun, a 9-mm semiautomatic rifle, a propane tank, and more than 30 pipe bombs. It took days for police to find and defuse the pipe bombs that they had planted in the school. They intended to get the last laugh.[2]

The school shootings, usually by middle-class white students, spotlighted one type of juvenile offender in the 1990s. In the early- to mid-1990s, the nation's newspapers tes-

Table 16.1

School Shootings in the 1990s

Date	School Location	What Happened
Early- to mid 1990s	Amityville, New York	One dead, one wounded
	Redland, California	One dead, one wounded
	Blackville, South Carolina	Two dead, one wounded
	Lynnville, Tennessee	Two dead, one wounded
	Mises Lakes, Washington	Three dead, one wounded
	Bethel, Alaska	Two dead, two wounded
	Grayson, Kentucky	A teacher and a custodian killed
1 October 1997	Pearl, Mississippi	Two students killed, seven wounded
1 December 1997	West Paducah, Kentucky	Three students killed, five wounded
March 1998	Jonesboro, Arkansas	Five students killed, ten wounded
21 May 1998	Springfield, Oregon	Two students killed, twenty-four wounded
20 April 1999	Littleton, Colorado	Twelve students, a teacher, and two gunmen killed; twenty-three wounded

Source: Adapted from Clemens Bartollas, *Juvenile Delinquency* (Boston: Allyn & Bacon, 2000), pp. 269–270.

tified nearly daily to the senseless killings and rapes committed by violent and hard-core juvenile criminals. This new breed of juvenile criminal was blamed for the epidemic of youth homicide that had begun in the mid-1980s. At the time, these juveniles were called "superpredators" or "monsters," and the increase in violence was attributed to character changes in these youths resulting from economic and emotional deprivation.[3] However, in 1994 youth homicides began a decline that continued through the end of the decade, and the notion of juvenile "superpredators" seemed to have been laid to rest as the twentieth century came to a close.

From the end of the 1980s through the 1990s, youth gang members received considerable public attention. As discussed later in this chapter, the youth gang seemed to spring from nowhere and within a two- or three-year period spread throughout the nation. Accounts appeared describing how communities that had never before had serious problems with youth were struggling with youth gangs that were selling drugs and terrifying the community.

The mission of juvenile corrections in the United States is to control the behavior of law-violating juveniles. This has never been an easy task; perhaps, it is more difficult today than ever before. Although nearly everyone agrees that juvenile corrections must change, there are various opinions about what the new form of the system should be.

Some contend that the *parens patriae* **doctrine,** which allows the juvenile court to assume parental responsibility over wayward children, with its rehabilitative emphasis, offers the best approach to handling children in trouble.[4] Others argue that the ineffectiveness of juvenile corrections requires that the basic goal of juvenile corrections be changed from rehabilitation to the justice model and that punishments be commensurate with the seriousness of the offense or harm done ("just deserts").[6] Still others are so dissatisfied with the juvenile justice system that they want to dismantle it and let the adult system handle juvenile offenders.[6]

Today, all three of these positions are well represented. For minor offenses, as well as for **status offenses** (offenses that would not be crimes if perpetrated by adults) in most states, the "best interest of the child" is the guiding standard of decision making in juvenile court. For offenders who commit more serious delinquent acts, the principles of the justice model are increasingly applied in adjudicatory and dispositional hearings. Repetitive or violent youthful offenders are more commonly transferred to the adult court and handled as adults.

What is the history of juvenile justice? How does the system process juveniles in community-based programs as well as in short- and long-term institutional care? How do juveniles cope in an adult prison? What are the basic issues in juvenile corrections?

WHAT IS THE HISTORY OF JUVENILE JUSTICE?

The way law-violating juveniles have been dealt with in the past is an important consideration in understanding how youthful offenders are handled today. The history of juvenile justice begins in the colonies. The colonists looked to the family to control children, but children who were still recalcitrant after whipping and other parental punishment could be turned over to community officials for public whippings, the stocks, dunkings, or even capital punishment.[7]

Reformers soon became disillusioned with the family as the main source of juvenile control and looked for an alternative that would provide an orderly, disciplined environment similar to that of the "ideal" Puritan family. **Houses of refuge** were proposed as the solution.[8] These institutions represented a new direction in juvenile justice. They were the first institutions to offer vocational training and to emphasize the priority of participating in work. They were also intended to protect children from corrupting home environments. Thus, no longer were parents the first line of control for children. The authority of the family was replaced by that of the state, and wayward children were placed in institutions presumably better equipped to reform them.

Reformers discovered by the middle of the first half of the nineteenth century that houses of refuge were not dealing adequately with youth crime. Some of these houses had grown unwieldy in size, and order and discipline had disappeared from most. Furthermore, many youths were still being confined with adults in jails and prisons, which were filthy, dangerous, and ill equipped to meet the needs of children.

A change was in order, and during the final decades of the nineteenth century the juvenile court emerged. An important legal factor was the *parens patriae* doctrine, which justified governmental intervention in family matters when a child's welfare was threatened. It guided the development of the court. *Parens patriae* satisfied the interests of middle-class groups who were concerned about "saving" or properly socializing lower-class immigrant children.[9] In 1899, the first juvenile court were created, in Cook County (Chicago), Illinois; soon thereafter one was set up in Denver, Colorado.

Advocates of juvenile court promised that the informational setting of the court and the parental role of the judge would enable children in trouble to be "saved" or "rescued" from a life of crime. However, the juvenile courts did not produce radical changes in the philosophy of juvenile justice, for the family continued to be subservient to the state and children in trouble could still be institutionalized. The creation of the juvenile court as an official agency to control wayward children was the only new factor. The children were to remain under the control of the state until they were rehabilitated or too old to be under the jurisdiction of the court.

Criticism of the juvenile court continued to mount until, by the 1960s, the court was widely accused of capricious and arbitrary justice. The U.S. Supreme Court responded to this criticism in a series of decisions that changed the course of juvenile justice.[10] The intent of these decisions was to establish the due-process rights of young offenders in the juvenile justice system. The 1967 *In re Gault* decision stated that juveniles have the right to due-process safeguards in proceedings where a finding of delinquency could lead to confinement, and that juveniles have the rights to notice of charges, to counsel, to confrontation and cross-examination of witnesses, and to privilege against self-incrimination (see Outside the Walls 16.1).

Three other important cases at this time were *In re Winship* (1970), *McKeiver v. Pennsylvania* (1971), and *Breed v. Jones* (1975). In *Winship* the U.S. Supreme Court decided that juveniles are entitled to proof beyond a reasonable doubt during the adjudication proceedings.[11] The decision that was issued in *McKeiver v. Pennsylvania* (1971) denied the right of juveniles to have jury trials.[12] In *Breed* the Supreme Court ruled that a juvenile court cannot adjudicate a case and then transfer the case over to the criminal court for adult processing on the same offense.[13]

outside the walls   16.1

In re Gault

Gerald Gault, a 15-year-old Arizona boy, and his friend, Ronald Lewis, were taken into custody on 8 June 1964, on a verbal complaint made by a neighbor. The neighbor accused the boys of making lewd and indecent remarks to her over the phone.

Gault's parents were not notified that he had been taken into custody. Gault was not advised of his right to counsel; neither was he advised that he could remain silent; and no notice of charges was made to Gault or his parents. In addition, the complainant was not present at either of two hearings.

In spite of considerable confusion about whether Gault had made the phone call, what he had said over the phone, and what he had said to the judge during the course of the two hearings, the judge committed him to the State Industrial School "for the period of his minority (that is, until twenty-one) unless sooner discharged by due process of law."

CRITICAL THINKING QUESTIONS

If you were the parents of Gerald Gault, would you have been troubled by how the case was handled in the juvenile court? Why?

Source: In re Gault, 387 U.S. 1, 18 L. Ed. 2d 527, 87 S. Ct. 1428 (1967).

The reform agenda of the mid- to late 1970s emphasized reducing the use of juvenile correctional institutions, diverting minor offenders and status offenders from the juvenile justice system, and reforming the juvenile justice system. The major thrust of this reform agenda was to divert status offenses (offenses defined as criminal only because they were committed by minors) from a criminal to a noncriminal setting. The reason for the focus on status offenders was that the federal Juvenile Justice and Delinquency Prevention Act (1973) stressed the need for the diversion and deinstitutionalization of status offenders as a means to initiate juvenile court reforms.[14]

At the same time that the spirit of reform was so pronounced, there was an emerging philosophy of crime control in juvenile corrections. This philosophy was especially critical of the fact that so little consideration was given to the violent juvenile offender. In 1978, Lloyd Ohlin predicted that failure to give attention to violent youth crime and repeat offenders could prove to be "the Achilles heel of a reform process."[15] The inability of reformers during the 1970s to provide meaningful programs and policies aimed at serious youth offenders did contribute to the wave of get-tough legislation that swept through the United States during the late 1970s.[16]

Alerted by the media to the chilling realities of youth crime, the public became increasingly alarmed in the early 1980s and wanted something done to curb juvenile crime in U.S. society. Ronald Reagan was in the White House, and the formerly muted voices of the hard-liners suddenly became public policy. The new federal agenda attacked the Juvenile Justice and Delinquency Prevention Act as being "antifamily" and called for cracking down on juvenile law violators.

In 1984, the National Advisory Committee for Juvenile Justice and Delinquency Prevention also stated that "the time comes for a major departure from the existing philosophy and activity of the federal government in the juvenile justice field."[17] The National Advisory Committee recommended that the "federal effort in the area of juvenile delinquency should focus primarily on the serious, violent, or chronic offender."[18]

During the mid- to late 1980s, as if to reinforce the need to get tough on juveniles, the rates of homicides among juveniles began to increase rather dramatically. Juveniles also began to carry and use guns and were increasingly involved in drug trafficking. Then, in the late 1980s, juvenile gangs began to appear across the nation. Unlike the gangs in urban settings, in which juveniles are a minority of gang membership, juveniles established and made up the leadership and membership of these gangs (youth gangs are discussed in detail later in this chapter).

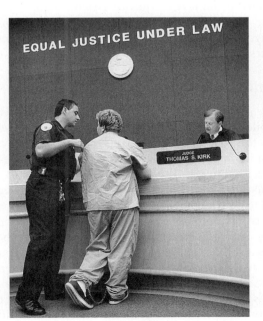

In what ways will this juvenile be handled in court that will be a direct result of the landmark case *In re Gault* and cases of the 1970s regarding juvenile justice? What is a "status offender"? How would the adjudication of this juvenile be affected if he had committed a status offense? What are the trends in juvenile justice today in terms of trial and sentencing?

timeline

History of Juvenile Justice

Date	Event
1899	Development of juvenile courts in Cook County (Chicago)
1966	*Kent v. United States*
1967	*In re Gault*
1970	*In re Winship*
1971	*McKeiver v. Pennsylvania*
1974	Juvenile Justice and Delinquent Prevention Act
1975	*Breed v. Jones*
1984	National Advisory Committee for Juvenile Justice and Delinquency Protection
1988	Amendment of 1973 Juvenile Justice and Delinquency Prevention Act (required that states address the issue of disproportionate minority confinement (DMC)
1992	Amendments of 1974 Juvenile Justice and Delinquency Act (addressed the issue of gender bias in the juvenile justice system and made DMC a core requirement)

Reagan's crime control policies for juveniles led to the development of five trends throughout the nation: (1) preventive detention, (2) transfer of violent juveniles to the adult court, (3) mandatory and determinate sentencing for violent juveniles, (4) increased imprisonment of juveniles, and (5) enforcement of the death penalty for juveniles who commit brutal and senseless murders.[19] See the Timeline for the history of juvenile justice.

HOW DOES THE JUVENILE JUSTICE SYSTEM FUNCTION?

The variations in the juvenile justice systems across the nation make it difficult to describe the process by which juvenile offenders are processed by juvenile justice agencies. Figure 16.1 is a flowchart that shows the common elements of the juvenile justice process.

Stages in the Juvenile Justice System

The juvenile justice process begins when the juvenile is referred to the intake division of the juvenile court. In some jurisdictions a variety of agents can refer the juvenile; in others, only the police are charged with this responsibility. More commonly, the juvenile is taken into custody by the police officers who investigated the crime and have made the decision to refer the youth to the juvenile court.

The intake division of the juvenile court, usually operated by a probation officer, must decide what to do with the referral. A decision is made on whether the youth should remain in the community or be placed in a shelter or detention facility. The intake officer has a variety of choices in determining what to do with the juvenile lawbreaker, but in more serious cases, the youth usually receives a petition to appear before the juvenile court.

The juvenile court judge or, in many jurisdictions, the referee hears the cases of those youths who receive a petition to the juvenile court. The first stage of the juvenile court proceeding is a **detention hearing,** in which the court must decide whether to return the child to his or her parents or to place the child in a detention facility. In serious cases, a

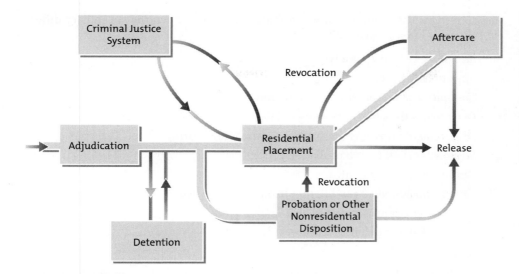

Figure 16.1
Flowchart of the
Juvenile Justice System

Source: Howard N. Snyder
and Melissa Sickmund, *Juvenile Offenders and Victims:
A National Report* (Washington, D.C.: Office of Juvenile
Justice and Delinquency
Prevention, 1995), p. 77.

transfer hearing may be held to determine whether the juvenile's case will be heard in the juvenile court or whether the juvenile should be transferred to adult court.

The next stage of the juvenile court proceedings is an **adjudicatory hearing.** The primary purpose of this hearing is to determine whether the youth is guilty of the delinquent acts alleged in the petition (indictment), and the court hears evidence on these allegations. The rights guaranteed to juveniles in *In re Gualt* include the right to representation by counsel, freedom from self-incrimination, the right to confrontation and cross-examination of witnesses, and, in some states, the right to a jury trial. Plea bargaining is increasingly taking place at this time, especially in urban courts, between the prosecutor and the defense attorney.

A **dispositional hearing** is held when a youth has been found delinquent in the adjudicatory stage or has waived his or her right to an adjudicatory hearing. Most juvenile court codes now require that the adjudicatory and dispositional hearings be held at different times. The wide discretion of the juvenile judge permits him or her to warn and release juveniles, place them on probation, place them in a day treatment or residential program, or place them in the care of the department of corrections, the youth authority, or the youth commission. In some jurisdictions, the judge has the authority to send a youth to a particular correctional facility, but in most jurisdictions, delinquents are adjudicated to the care of the state department of youth corrections.

In small states that have only one institution for males and one for females, the youth committed to a long-term juvenile correctional institution is sent directly to a training school. But in larger states that have several facilities for males and perhaps more than one for females, delinquents must undergo a classification process in which the decision is made about the most appropriate placement for them. Juveniles today do not spend as long in training school as they did in the past and usually are recommended for release within a year. The institutional staff normally recommends a youth for release, and this recommendation must be approved by the youth commission or youth authority. If the state has an established program of **aftercare,** the youth released from the training school is placed on aftercare status. He or she must fulfill the rules of aftercare, or parole, and must avoid unlawful behavior to be released from supervision.

Comparison of the Juvenile and Adult Justice Systems

The juvenile and adult justice systems have much in common. Both systems are made up of three basic subsystems, and the agencies are interrelated so that the flow of justice ideally follows the same sequence: from law violation to police apprehension, judicial process, judicial disposition, and rehabilitation in correctional agencies. Both justice systems use the same basic vocabulary, and even when the vocabulary differs, no change of intent is involved:

Adjudicatory hearing is a trial.

Aftercare is parole.

Commitment is a sentence to imprisonment.

Detention is the same as holding in jail.

Dispositional hearing is the same as a sentencing hearing.

Juvenile court officer is a probation officer.

Petition is an indictment.

Taking into custody is no different from being arrested.

A *petitioner* is a prosecutor.

A *respondent* is a defense attorney.

A *minor* is a defendant.

Furthermore, both systems are under pressure from society to get tough on crime, especially when dealing with offenders who commit violent crimes. Both systems must deal with overload, must operate on a fiscal shoestring, and must deal with ongoing problems of staff recruitment, training, and burnout. Finally, both the juvenile and the adult justice systems are faced with problems of violent and inhumane institutions and of the unlawful activities that take place in these facilities.

WHAT EARLY PROCESSING IS AVAILABLE IN THE JUVENILE JUSTICE SYSTEM?

Diversion, probation, and community-based programs are the forms of early processing of juvenile offenders. Diversion takes place in conflict-resolution and drug prevention programs in the public schools and in alternative schools, in gang prevention programs in the community, in drug court programs and youth shelters, and from agencies outside the juvenile justice system. Probation, similar to adult justice, is the most widely judicial disposition in juvenile justice. It also includes intensive supervision and, occasionally, house arrest and electronic monitoring. Community-based juvenile corrections consists of residential and day treatment and survival programs.

Diversionary Programs

There are some exciting prevention and diversionary programs for juveniles today. In public schools across the nation, conflict-resolution training is conducted as early as middle school (fifth and sixth grades) and even more in junior high school (seventh through ninth grades). These programs focus on teaching young people to resolve their conflicts in nonaggressive or nonviolent ways.

G.R.E.A.T. (Gang Resistance Education and Training) is a popular prevention program. As of June 1997, more than twenty-four hundred officers from forty-seven states and the District of Columbia had completed G.R.E.A.T. training. In at least forty-two school jurisdictions police officers teach the nine-week curriculum to middle school students. A 1995 evaluation that was based on a cross-sectional survey of 5,935 eighth graders from the forty-two schools where G.R.E.A.T. is taught found "that students who completed the G.R.E.A.T. lessons reported more prosocial behaviors and attitudes than their peers who did not finish the programs or failed to participate in the first place."[20]

The need for substance abuse prevention programs demands creativity and involvement by the police. The D.A.R.E. program (Drug Abuse Resistance Education) is a well-received effort by the police to prevent substance abuse. Project D.A.R.E. is designed to equip elementary school children with skills for resisting peer pressure to experiment with tobacco, drugs, and alcohol. Using a core curriculum consisting of seventeen hour-long weekly lessons, D.A.R.E. gives special attention to fifth and sixth graders to prepare them for entry into junior high, where they are likely to encounter pressures to use drugs. Since it was founded, D.A.R.E. has expanded to encompass programs for middle and high school students, gang prevention, conflict resolution, parent education, and after-school recreation and learning.[21] As the most popular school-based drug education program in the United States, it is administered in about 70 percent of this nation's school districts, reaching 25 million students in 1996. It has also been adopted in forty-four foreign countries.[22]

Several evaluations done in the 1980s and early 1990s were positive about the effectiveness of the D.A.R.E. program.[23] However, D.A.R.E. began to be more critically evaluated in the 1990s, and reservations about its effectiveness appear to be gathering momentum. Dennis P. Rosenbaum and colleagues' 1994 longitudinal evaluation was critical of D.A.R.E.'s effectiveness. In this randomized experiment conducted with 1,584 students in the year following exposure to the program, they found that "DARE had no statistically significant main effects on drug use behaviors and had few effects on attitudes or beliefs about drugs."[24]

Probation

Probation in juvenile corrections has always been more treatment oriented than in adult probation. During the 1990s, the balanced and restorative justice project was developed and implemented in juvenile probation. The major theme of this model is that "offenders should leave the juvenile justice system most capable of participating in conventional society."[25] The three basic goals of this approach are accountability, competency development, and community protection.

The probation officer is ordered by the juvenile judge to explain to the probationer how frequently he or she will report to the officer and the importance of complying with the conditions of probation. The most widely used conditions of probation are restitution of victims, community service, school attendance, participation in a drug abuse program, avoidance of drinking or drug abuse, and living at home and obeying parents.

The juvenile probation officer, like the adult probation officer, has been accused of being too soft and permissive. Thus, now more than ever before, the probation officer is expected to make certain that probationers comply with the conditions of their probation and that they do not break the law. This get-tough approach has led to an emphasis on risk control and crime reduction. Probation officers like restitution because it counters the criticism that probation is too soft and provides no justice to victims in society.

Juvenile probation is also following adult probation in implementing intensive supervision programs. Alabama, Georgia, New Jersey, North Carolina, Ohio, Oregon, and Pennsylvania are experimenting with or have implemented statewide intensive supervision programs for juveniles.[26] House arrest, or home confinement, is infrequently called upon in juvenile justice, and electronic monitoring equipment rarely monitors juveniles' presence at home.[27] Boot camps, which emphasize military discipline, physical training, and regimented activity for up to 180 days, are increasingly used in juvenile corrections. Juvenile probationers are sometimes given the option of a boot camp rather than the standard training school program.[28] There are currently twenty-four programs in operation across the nation.[29]

Community-Based Programs

Group homes, day treatment programs, and wilderness programs are the main types of community-based programs. Private agencies are frequently contracted for services to juveniles in these settings. Local institutions, psychiatric and mental health services, and alcohol and drug treatment programs are also included in some jurisdictions' network of community-based programs.

Such terms as *group residence, halfway house, group home,* and *attention home* are used in various parts of the United States to identify a small facility serving about thirteen to twenty-five youths. Group homes fulfill several purposes: They provide an alternative to institutionalization; they serve as a short-term community placement, wherein probation and aftercare officers can deal with youths' community problems; and they serve as a "halfway-in" setting for youths having difficulty adjusting to probation or as a "halfway-out" placement for delinquents who are returning to the community on aftercare but lack an adequate home placement.

The House of Umoja is one of the best known group homes in the nation. Each House of Umoja serves fifteen youths in a program that creates intensive family feelings within a framework of African-inspired consciousness. Headed by Sister Falaska Fattah, the House of Umoja deals almost entirely with gang delinquents. She has re-created an African-style extended family in which members of the gangs could find alternative values to those of their street life culture. Since the House of Umoja was established in the early 1970s, it has sheltered more than three hundred boys belonging to seventy-three different street gangs.[30]

Day treatment programs usually serve male juveniles, although California operates two such programs for girls and several coeducational programs. These nonresidential programs have been used widely by the California Community Treatment Project. The New York State Division for Youth also has established several nonresidential programs, called STAY, which expose youths to a guided group interaction experience.

Another day treatment program is conducted by Associated Marine Institutes (AMI). Twenty-five of its forty schools or institutes are nonresidential. Funded by state and private donations, this privately operated program tailors its institutes to the geographical strengths of each community, using the ocean, wilderness, rivers, and lakes to stimulate productive behavior in juvenile delinquents. In the treatment programs, which include both males and females, ages 14 to 18, the trainees live at home or in foster homes. Youths are referred to this program either by the courts or by the state division of youth services (see Outside the Walls 16.2).[31]

Outward Bound is the most widely used wilderness program. The main goals of Outward Bound are to use the "overcoming of a seemingly impossible task" to build self-reliance, to demonstrate one's worth, and to define one's personhood. An Outward Bound program usually includes rock climbing, rappelling, mountain walking, backpacking, high altitude camping, and survival alone. The wilderness experience generally lasts three or four weeks and has four phases: training in basic skills, a long expedition, a solo, and a final testing period. The locations of these programs include forests, high mountains, canoe country, the sea, and the desert.

How is juvenile probation like and unlike adult probation and supervision in the community? What are the three main types of community-based programs in which these youths might participate? What are the main types of short-term and long-term public and private correctional institutions for juveniles, and how do they operate?

outside the walls   16.2

The Programs of Associated Marine Institutes

Since 1969, Associated Marine Institutes has been working with juvenile delinquents. Over the years, new institutes were started throughout the United States and in the Cayman Islands.

AMI's main objectives are to develop in the youths its serves attitudes that will help them meet their responsibilities, develop employable skills, increase self-confidence, and encourage further education. After attending the program, each youth is placed in school, a job, or the armed forces. Aftercare coordinators monitor youths for three years after they graduate to offer assistance.

In September 1993, Attorney General Janet Reno and President Bill Clinton visited the Pinellas Marine Institute in St. Petersburg, Florida, one of the forty schools of AMI. In a nationally televised program where he announced his crime bill, the president said, "These programs are giving young people a chance to take their future back, a chance to understand that there is good inside them."

One of the ingredients of AMI's programs is a strong commitment to meaningful work. AMI looks upon work as one of the most beneficial forms of therapy and teaches that nothing worthwhile is achieved without hard work.

Academic success is also emphasized. The AMI programs aim to motivate students and to give them the right tools and opportunities so that they can succeed in school. Indeed, the goal of the AMI teaching staff is to prepare youths to take their GED exam and then attend vocational school, community college, or a four-year college.

A further important ingredient of this program is modeling. AMI staff support the belief that what they do is more important than what they say. Their philosophy on modeling is: Tell me, I'll forget. Show me, I may remember. Involve me, I'll be committed.

CRITICAL THINKING QUESTIONS

What is your initial evaluation of the AMI day treatment programs? Why do you think juveniles respond so well to them?

Source: "The Programs of the Associated Marine Institutes" (mimeographed, n.d.).

WHAT HAPPENS WHEN A JUVENILE IS SENT TO JUVENILE CORRECTIONAL INSTITUTIONS?

Juvenile institutionalization takes place in short-term and long-term facilities. Detention centers are found in the community, and juveniles have a relatively short stay in these facilities. Juveniles are usually sent to a detention center before the adjudication of their case. If they are found delinquent by the juvenile court, they can be sent to the department of youth services or youth commission for long-term correctional care. The juvenile generally first goes to a reception center and then is sent to a honor camp, forestry camp, or training school.

Detention Centers

Detention homes, also called juvenile halls and detention centers, were established at the end of the nineteenth century as an alternative to jail for juveniles. Their purpose is to serve as temporary holding centers for juvenile offenders who need detention either for their own safety or to ensure public safety. According to a 1991 survey of juvenile detention and corrections facilities, there were 355 public and 28 private detention centers. These 383 detention centers admitted 569,902 youths in 1990 for an average stay of fifteen days. The typical youth admitted to a detention center was a male, age 16, charged with a serious property offense.[32]

State and Private Institutions

Reception centers, ranches and forestry camps, and public and private training schools are the main forms of juvenile correctional institutions. There are over 3,100 short-term and long-term juvenile facilities in the United States. Although the 1,076 public facilities are nearly equally divided between state and locally operated facilities and between short-term and long-term, nearly 75 percent of the 2,032 private facilities are halfway houses.

Reception and Diagnostic Centers.

The purpose of reception and diagnostic centers, which are under the sponsorship of either public or private jurisdictions, is to determine which treatment plan suits each adjudicated youth and which training school is the best placement. The evaluation of each resident used to take from four to six weeks, but the process has been condensed today because the average length of stay is thirty-four days.[33] A case conference is held on each resident to summarize the needs and attitudes of the youth and recommend the best institutional placement.

Ranches and Forestry Camps.

Ranches and forestry camps and other minimum-security institutions are typically reserved for youths who have committed minor crimes and for those who have been committed to the youth authority or private corrections for the first time. Forestry camps are popular in a number of states. Of the sixty-four camps in the United States in 1992, sixteen were in Florida; fourteen in New York; six in South Carolina; five each in Alabama, California, Missouri, and North Carolina; and four each in Maryland and Oregon.[34] Residents usually do conservation work in a state park—cleaning up, cutting grass and weeds, and doing general maintenance. Treatment programs usually consist of group therapy, individual contacts with social workers and the child care staff, and one or two home visits a month. Residents also may be taken to a nearby town on a regular basis to make purchases and to attend community events. Escapes are a constant problem because of the nonsecure nature of these facilities.

Public and Private Training Schools.

Training schools, the end-of-the-line placement for the juvenile delinquent, are being used more today than they were in the 1970s and 1980s. A survey of the Office of Juvenile Justice and Delinquency Prevention found that 26 percent more juveniles were confined in training schools in 1991 than in 1979.[35]

Juvenile training schools represent an extremely expensive way for a state to handle delinquent youth. Some place the cost as low as $34,000 per person per year.[36] Others suggest that the figure is somewhere between $35,000 and $64,000 a year.[37] New York and Minnesota are known as states that spend $60,000 or more a year for the confinement of each delinquent youth.

A census of public and private juvenile facilities reports that in 1991 males represented 82 percent of those confined in these facilities. The proportions of African American and white youth who were confined on a one-day count were fairly equal (40 and 43 percent, respectively). However, the percentage of African American youth confined in juvenile facilities increased between 1985 and 1991 (11 and 5 percent, respectively), while the percentage of white juveniles decreased in both public (18 percent) and private (7 percent) facilities.[38]

Thirty-two percent of the population confined in public juvenile facilities in 1991 were being held for offenses against persons, 36 percent for property offenses, and 10 percent for drug-related offenses. Of juveniles confined in private training schools in 1991, 23 percent were being held for offenses against persons, 35 percent for property offenses, and 21 percent for drug-related offenses.[39]

The physical structure of training schools ranges from the homelike atmosphere of small cottages to open dormitories that provide little privacy, to fortress-like facilities that have individual cells and are surrounded by high fences. In 1990, the majority of juveniles (46 percent) were admitted to maximum-security facilities, while 32 percent were admitted to medium- and 15 percent to minimum-security facilities.[40]

The programs that public and private training schools offer are superior to those of other juvenile institutions. The medical and dental services that residents receive tend to be quite adequate. Most larger training schools have a full-time nurse on duty during the day and a physician who visits one or more days a week. Although institutionalized delinquents typically are unhappy with the medical and dental care they receive, most youths still receive far better medical and dental care than they did before they were confined.

The educational program is usually accredited by the state and is able to grant a high school diploma. According to the 1991 survey of juvenile facilities across the nation, the majority of training schools offer classes to prepare residents for the general equivalency diploma (GED). Classes for preparation for college are also provided in an increasing number of training schools (19 percent). Furthermore, basic education classes are usually available, consisting of a review of the necessary skills in reading, writing, and mathematics (95 percent). Special education (81 percent) and literacy or remedial reading (84 percent) are also provided in most of this nation's training schools.[41] Classes tend to be small, and individuals are permitted to progress at the rate that is most satisfactory to them.

According to the 1991 survey of juvenile facilities, vocational training provided by training schools consists of courses such as auto shop/engine repair (54 percent), carpentry/building trades (67 percent), cosmetology (12 percent), computer training (39 percent), food services (55 percent), electrical trades (21 percent), secretarial trades (18 percent), retail/sales (10 percent), printing (30 percent), forestry/agriculture (35 percent), and laundry services (17 percent).[42] Vocational training is generally not helpful for finding future employment. Residents have difficulty being admitted to the necessary labor unions after release, but a few residents do leave the institution and find excellent jobs with the skills they have learned.

The rehabilitation of juvenile delinquents remains the established purpose of most training schools. In the twentieth century, every conceivable method was used in the effort to rehabilitate residents so that they would refrain from unlawful behavior. The **treatment technologies** that are still in use include classification systems, treatment modalities, skill development, and prerelease programs. The most widely used treatment modalities are transactional analysis, reality therapy, psychotherapy, behavior modification, guided group interaction, positive peer culture, and drug and alcohol treatment. The errors-in-thinking modality, a new treatment modality in juvenile corrections, has recently been implemented in a number of private and public training schools across the nation.

One of the serious shortcomings of programming in many training schools is lack of attention to the needs of adjudicated female offenders. A comparative study of 348 violent juvenile females and a similar number of males found that half of the males were admitted to rehabilitative or alternative programs but only 29.5 percent of the females received treatment in any form.[43] The 1992 amendment to the Juvenile Justice and Delinquency Prevention Act addressed the issue of gender bias and required states to analyze the need, types, and delivery of gender-specific services.

Recreation has always been emphasized in training schools. Male residents are usually offered competitive sports such as softball, volleyball, flag football, basketball, and sometimes boxing or wrestling. Religious instruction and services are always provided in state training schools. A full-time Protestant chaplain and a part-time Roman Catholic chaplain are available in most schools. Religious services that are offered include Sunday Mass and morning worship, confession, baptism, instruction for church membership, choir, and religious counseling. Usually, few residents respond to these religious services—unless attendance is compulsory, in which case residents respond with considerable resistance.

The punishment that is administered to misbehaving residents varies from training school to training school. Fortunately, blatant staff brutality has disappeared from most schools. Adult correctional systems have had enough problems with the federal courts that state governments do not want confinement conditions in their juvenile institutions to be declared unconstitutional. The amount of time residents spend in solitary confinement, or maximum isolation, is also generally less than it was a decade ago.[44] However, mechanical restraints are more frequently used in training schools than they were in the past.[45]

One of the debates that has raged for years concerns the comparison between private and public training schools. Privately administered training schools are usually better known to the public than are state institutions because private institutions' soliciting of funds has kept them in the public eye. Proponents of private institutions claim that they are more effective than public training schools for several reasons: They have a limited intake policy, which means that they choose whom they want to admit. They have more professional staff. They have better staff–client ratios. They are smaller. They are more flexible and innovative.

One of the real problems of evaluating private juvenile placements is that few studies have examined the accuracy of the claims or the effects of institutional life on residents. Peter W. Greenwood, Susan Turner, and Kathy Rosenblatt's evaluation of the Paint Creek Youth Center (PCYC) in southern Ohio is probably the most positive evaluation of a private institutional placement for juveniles.[46] The researchers claimed that this program is different from the traditional training school because it is small (thirty-three beds); because it features a comprehensive and integrated therapeutic approach emphasizing accountability, social learning, and positive peer culture; and because it has been able to implement family therapy and intensive aftercare services.[47] In contrast, David Shichor and Clemens Bartollas's examination of the patterns of public and private juvenile placements in one of the larger probation departments in southern California revealed that there were relatively few differences between juveniles who were sent to private and those sent to public placements. Several of the other claims made by advocates of private placements also were not documented by this study, especially the claims that private placements provide more professional and treatment services to juveniles than do public placements and that private placements have lower staff–client ratios than do public placements. Furthermore, this study found that hard-core delinquents in private placements were not separated from those who had committed more minor offenses.[48]

A fair assessment of private placements is that with some glaring exceptions, private training schools are usually more flexible and innovative than state facilities. The smaller size of private training schools is somewhat balanced by the fact that one-half of them still house one hundred or more residents, numbers that are too large for effective work with institutionalized juveniles. Yet it is a matter of some concern that the length of stay at private facilities, which averages nearly as long as state training school commitments, seems unduly long in many cases and that those who are in charge of private placements sometimes make claims that are exaggerated or even untrue.[49] Perhaps, the adage is right after all: The best institutions are private ones, and the worst juvenile institutional placements are also private ones.

The hero in this chapter is Jerry Miller, president of Alternatives to Institutions. Dr. Miller was probably one of the most influential persons in the twentieth century in juvenile corrections. As commissioner of youth services in Massachusetts, he closed all the state's training schools. Later as commissioner of youth services in Pennsylvania, he brought social reform to juvenile corrections to that state. More recently, he has continued to advocate the diversion of juveniles from the system. Read what he had to say for *Introduction to Corrections* in 2000.

h e r o e s

Jerome Miller

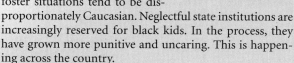

President of Alternatives to Institutions

"I think that what we are seeing today is a movement back to institutions. It is a system now driven by race. Teenagers who are diverted from institutions to smaller programs or specialized foster situations tend to be disproportionately Caucasian. Neglectful state institutions are increasingly reserved for black kids. In the process, they have grown more punitive and uncaring. This is happening across the country.

"I am afraid that as politicians demand getting tough on 'predatory' juveniles, their constituents see a black or brown face in their mind's eye. It is a way to be very racist without mentioning race. And race is never mentioned. It is fascinating for me to go to conferences and hear all the discussion of prisons and problems with training schools. They seldom mention race, when it is in fact what the system is all about.

"I think we have really betrayed the promise of the original juvenile court. In a marvelous article published in 1917, George Herbert Mead outlined the original promise of the juvenile court. He saw it as an opportunity to bring into the formal court deliberations all those hitherto 'irrelevant' factors that were so influential on a juvenile: the family, history of abuse, exposure to violence, economic factors, and so on. Then, according to Mead, we would try to develop policies to address those factors to help kids. That is now gone. Today, we are more concerned with defining the 'delinquent' and going after him or her.

"When I was in Massachusetts, I remember that we tried to keep and understand most kids under a 'child welfare,' rather than a 'correctional,' rubric. That seemed to me the proper way to go. I believe that we demonstrated that one could handle kids with care and concern and be successful while being decent. There was never anything that appeared in that experience suggesting that we needed to follow correctional, punitive, deterrent, or 'consequences' models. I don't believe that correctional models work particularly well with kids who have frequently been so damaged early in their young lives. One more strike across their back doesn't mean much.

"I do worry today about things getting inexorably more punitive. Even so-called helping professionals, when they become wedded to the current correctional industry, have begun to model the coercive language, rejection, and the ersatz 'help' that deny a basic respect to individual lives. Too many 'therapists' manipulate their charges. The behavioral approaches are particularly prone to be tied to law-enforcement models. There was a time when you went into the courts expecting the helper (social worker, counselor, psychologist, or psychiatrist) to argue for the well-being of the kid. You don't hear that very much anymore. They seem to be there to validate a system that is not particularly healthy for its clients. Neither is it going to be ultimately healthy for a democratic society.

"If we continue the way we are going, we will reach the point where virtually every minority family will have a son or daughter who will be touched by the system. As that starts to happen, I can only hope that we will pause, take a good breath, and decide to go back and reevaluate what we are doing. How soon will that be? I don't know. I guess that it won't be for quite some time, if ever. As long as the system is peopled by the very poor and minorities, I don't have much hope for productive change."

CRITICAL THINKING QUESTIONS

What do you agree with in Miller's statement? Where do you disagree with his comments?

WHAT ABOUT THE PLACEMENT OF JUVENILES IN ADULT PRISONS?

Adult prisons are a world apart from most training schools. They are much larger. Some have several thousand inmates and cover many acres. Life on the inside is typically austere, crowded, and dangerous. The crowded, violent, and exploitative relationships that exist in adult correctional institutions make this disposition very hard for juveniles. Institutionalized juveniles are particularly subject to sexual victimization and physical assault.

A 1996 national survey found that 5,599 juveniles were admitted that year to state and federal adult correctional facilities. The states that imprisoned the most juveniles were New York (624, under 15), Illinois (460, under 16), and Florida (773, under 17). The states that imprisoned the fewest juveniles were West Virginia (0), Hawaii (0), Maine (1), Oklahoma (5), and North Dakota (5). In twenty-three states, judges use the life-without-

outside the walls 16.3

What Would You Say?

The juvenile walks into your office and expresses the following concerns:

"I want to talk with you. I just came off orientation, and I'm already receiving pressure for sex from inmates on the cellblock. I don't want to go that way. I don't know whether I can make it in the general population. Do you think I can make it?"

What would you say?

"I have thought about going to PC, but I don't know about spending the rest of my life locked-up twenty-three or twenty-four hours a day. I think I would go crazy. What do you think?"

What would you say?

"There is another thing I want to talk with you about. I have been thinking about whether I want to go on living. All I have to look forward to is my mother coming a couple times a month. But you never knew whether she is going to show up or not. I am thinking about killing myself."

What would you say?

Source: Based on the author's conversations with juveniles who were either in or going to adult prison.

---

parole sentencing option that their states offer to incarcerate juveniles for the rest of their natural lives.

Some variations on the practice of confining juveniles in adult institutions do exist among the states. In some jurisdictions, states have no alternative but to place juveniles in adult institutions if the courts require incarceration. Under special circumstances, some states can place youths in either juvenile or adult institutions, and other states can refer juveniles back to juvenile court for their disposition. In some instances, youthful offenders are sent to juvenile facilities but are then transferred to adult institutions when they come of age.[51]

Kelly Dedel found that thirteen states permit the transfer of juveniles to adult facilities: California, Colorado, Hawaii, Indiana, Kentucky, Massachusetts, New Jersey, New York, Rhode Island, South Carolina, Texas, Washington, and Wisconsin. The court has the authority to make such transfer in one-third of these states, the committing agency has this authority in one-third, and the transfer decision is a joint decision between authorities (e.g., agency and court or juvenile agency and adult agency) in one-third. The reasons for such transfer include the age of the offender, seriousness of the offense, failure to benefit from the program, and poor institutional adjustment.[52] A violent attack on a staff member by an older resident with a serious committing offense would be the type of case most likely leading to a transfer from a juvenile facility to an adult program.

The juvenile, especially one who is not a member of a street gang or has relatives or family members already at the prison, faces several critical questions: Can I survive in the prison population without becoming someone's kid [prostitute]? If I lockup in PC [protective custody], can I survive twenty-four hours a day there? Is it worth staying alive when I am going to die in here anyway? Outside the Walls 16.3 lets you imagine yourself as a correctional counselor with a juvenile on your caseload who has just arrived in prison and has received a sentence of life without parole.

WHAT ARE THE ISSUES OF JUVENILE CORRECTIONS?

Racial inequality in institutional placements, the spread of juvenile drug-trafficking gangs, and the impact of juvenile institutions are three important issues in juvenile corrections.

Racial Inequality

Increased attention has been given in the past three decades to the effects of racial unfairness and disparity in processing a minority youth through the juvenile justice system. This disparity was brought to national attention by the Coalition for Juvenile Justice in its 1988 annual report to Congress. Subsequently, the 1988 amendments to the Juvenile Justice and Delinquency Prevention Act of 1974, Congress required that states address the issue of disproportionate minority confinement (DMC). In the 1992 amendments to the act, DMC was elevated to a core requirement, and future funding eligibility was tied to the issue of whether minority youths are disproportionately arrested or detained.[53]

Studies that examined the likelihood of juveniles being confined in a juvenile correctional facility before the age of 18 were conducted in sixteen states. In fifteen of the sixteen, African American youths had the highest prevalence rates of all segments of the population.[54] They represented 68 percent of the youth population in secure detention and 68 percent of those confined in training schools.[55] See Table 16.2 for a summary of states' compliance with DMC core requirements as of December 1997.

Carl E. Pope and William Feyerherm's review of the literature identified forty-six studies that considered the importance of minority status. From their review of these studies, they concluded that "the effects of race may be felt at various decision points, they may be direct or indirect, and they may accumulate as youth continue through the system."[56] Other current research concurred with Pope and Feyerherm's disturbing indictment of racial disparity.[57]

The Spread of Drug-Trafficking Gangs

Juveniles' participation in street gangs has received attention because the recent spread of gangs across the nation has resulted in increased trafficking of drugs, conflicts at school and in the community, and drive-by shootings. For example, a 1996 survey estimated that 4,825 U.S. cities may be experiencing gang problems and that there may be as many as 31,000 street gangs, with a membership of 848,000.[58]

The nationwide expansion of drug-trafficking gangs began in the late 1980s. It appears to be fueled in four different ways. First, ghetto-based gangs send ranking gang members into various communities for the purpose of persuading local juveniles to sell crack cocaine. Second, gang-related individuals, operating independently, establish drug-trafficking networks among community youth. Third, urban gang members whose families have migrated to these communities are instrumental in developing local chapters of the urban gang. Fourth, juveniles in communities with little or no intervention from outsiders develop their own versions of a gang.

In the late 1980s, urban gang chiefs realized that they needed to find new markets for crack cocaine, especially markets where it would command a higher price than it did in the inner cities. They began to map out a plan to spread their criminal operations. The goal was to develop a drug-trafficking network throughout the United States to sell crack cocaine.

Juveniles who belong to youth gangs are involved in more serious delinquent acts than are youths who do not belong to gangs.[59] Juveniles' participation in gangs also usually increases their involvement in drug use and drug trafficking. Furthermore, juvenile gang members are more likely than non–gang members to carry guns.

The 1997 National Youth Gang Survey revealed that the percentage of jurisdictions reporting active youth gangs decreased from 1996. Some 816,000 gang members were active in some 30,500 youth gangs in 1997, a modest decrease from the 1996 figures of 846,000 and 31,000, respectively. Yet, despite these declines, serious problems still remain with youth gangs—both drug trafficking and non–drug trafficking. For example, every city with a population of 250,000 or greater indicated the presence of youth gangs. In addition, small cities and rural counties reported increased numbers of gang members.[60]

Table 16.2

Summary of State Compliance with DMC Core Requirement[1] (as of December 1997)

- States that have completed the identification and assessment phases and are implementing the intervention phase:

Alaska	Kansas	North Dakota
Arizona	Maryland	Ohio
Arkansas	Massachusetts	Oklahoma
California	Michigan	Oregon
Colorado	Minnesota	Pennsylvania
Connecticut	Mississippi	Rhode Island
Florida	Missouri	South Carolina
Georgia	Montana	Tennessee
Hawaii	Nevada	Texas
Idaho	New Jersey	Virginia
Illinois	New Mexico	Washington
Indiana	New York	Wisconsin
Iowa	North Carolina	Utah

- States that have completed the identification and assessment phases and are formulating a time-limited plan of action for completing the intervention phase.

Alabama	South Dakota	West Virginia

- States (and the District of Columbia) that have completed the identification phase, submitted a time-limited plan of action for the assessment phase, and agreed to submit a time-limited plan for addressing the intervention phase:

Delaware	Louisiana
District of Columbia	Nebraska

- Territories that have completed the identification phase (it has been determined that minority juveniles are not disproportionately arrested or detained in the following territories):

American Samoa	Republic of Patau
Guam	Virgin Islands
Northern Mariana Islands	

- States that have completed the identification phase and are exempt from the DMC requirement because the minority juvenile population in the states does not exceed 1 percent of the total juvenile population:

Maine	Vermont

- State that has now reached 1 percent minority population (statewide) and will begin conducting the identification phase:

  New Hampshire

- Territory that is exempt from complying with the DMC requirement (as it has been exempted by the U.S. Census Bureau form reporting racial statistics due to the homogeneity of the population):

  Puerto Rico

- States that were not participating in the Formula Grants Program in FY 1997:

Kentucky	Wyoming

[1]Pursuant to Section 31.303(j) of the OJJDP Formula Grants Regulation (28 C.F.R. Part 31).

Source: Heida M. Hsia and Donna Hamparian, *Disproportionate Minority Confinement: 1997 Update* (Washington, D.C.: Office of Juvenile Justice and Delinquency Prevention, 1998), p. 4.

The Impact of Institutionalization

Juvenile institutionalization is a painful process for most youthful offenders, though it is clearly more painful for some than for others. The residential social system and juvenile victimization are especially troubling. Together, they call into question the quality of the long-term institutional care that this nation provides for juveniles in trouble.

The social roles in training schools for girls generally reflect a family or kinship social structure.[61] This social structure has much in common with the social roles within women's prisons. The social roles in training school for boys call for behavior that is aggressive, manipulative, or passive. As in prisons for adult men, aggressive behavior is the norm in most training schools.[62]

With the dominance of aggressive social roles in training schools for boys comes the possibility of some juveniles being forced into lowly social positions. Although they are aware that they must avoid victimization, some youths find it difficult to protect themselves against predatory peers. The degradation of victim status presents nearly overwhelming stress to some youths. In some institutions, juveniles create a brutal system of exploitation in which brute force, manipulation, and institutional sophistication carry the day and set the standards that ultimately prevail.

SUMMARY

The basic mission of juvenile corrections is to control and correct the behavior of law-violating juveniles. The *parens patriae* doctrine provides a rationale for the state's providing care for juveniles in trouble. Recently, there has been an attempt to get tough with juvenile offenders who commit serious property and violent crimes.

Juvenile and adult corrections have much in common. The processing of offenders, as well as the vocabularies to describe this processing, are similar much of the time. The tendency to go through cycles of reform and retrenchment is also much the same. The law-and-order attitude so popular in adult corrections is now also found in juvenile corrections. The issues of crowding, violence, and victimization faced in adult prisons are issues confronting training schools as well.

Some juveniles are transferred from juvenile court to adult court. If they are found guilty in adult court, they enter the adult system. They may be placed on probation, or they may be sentenced to an adult prison. Spending time in an adult prison is not easy for a juvenile; it is even more difficult if the juvenile is placed on death row.

KEY TERMS

adjudicatory hearing, p. 383
aftercare, p. 383
detention hearing, p. 382
dispositional hearing, p. 383

houses of refuge, p. 379
parens patriae doctrine, p. 379
status offense, p. 379
treatment technologies, p. 389

CRITICAL THINKING QUESTIONS

1. What due-process rights do juveniles have?
2. What should be done with the hard-core juvenile offender?
3. Do you think the structure of the juvenile court should be changed? Why or why not?

4. After reading this chapter, do you feel encouraged or discouraged about the ability of society to deal effectively with youth crime? Why?

WEB DESTINATIONS

Read the 1999 national report on juvenile offenders and their victims.
http://www.ncjrs.org/html/ojjdp/nationalreport99/toc.html

This government report describes the characteristics of chronic and violent juvenile offenders.
http://www.ncjfcj.unr.edu/homepage/g5.html

Read an "Indiana Close Up" that summarizes issues surrounding the legal and constitutional rights of juvenile offenders.
http://www.statelib.lib.in.us/WWW/ihb/cluprjo6.html

This 2000 PBS special focuses on "Kids and Crime."
http://www.pbs.org/newshour/forum/january00/kids_crime3.html

Read opinions on the question of whether juveniles should be tried and sentenced as adults, and express your opinions in an online poll.
http://www.publicdebate.com.au/is/213/

This site describes the success of correctional reform for juvenile offenders participating in a program called Criminon.
http://www.criminon.org/html/juvenile.htm

Follow links on the Koch Crime Institute's Guide to Community-Based Alternatives for Low-Risk Juvenile Offenders.
http://www.kci.org/publication/sji/index.htm

FOR FURTHER READING

Jankowski, Martin Sanchez. *Islands in the Street: Gangs and American Urban Society.* Berkeley: University of California Press, 1991. A comprehensive examination of street gangs in various parts of the nation.

Miller, Jerome G. *Last One over the Wall: The Massachusetts Experiment in Closing Reform Schools.* Columbus: Ohio State University Press, 1991. Miller presents a biting criticism of placing juveniles in long-term training schools.

Schwartz, Ira M. *(In)justice for Juveniles: Rethinking the Best Interests of the Child.* Lexington, Mass.: Lexington Books, 1989. The author is a serious critic of the juvenile justice system, and his book deserves serious attention.

Streib, Victor L. "Moratorium on the Death Penalty for Juveniles." *Law and Contemporary Problems* 61 (1998), pp. 55–87. Streib offers probably the best review of where the death penalty and juveniles has been in the past and is today.

NOTES

1. Carol Morello, "Sobbing Miss. School Killer Proclaims Love for Victim," *USA Today,* 12 June 1998, p. 4A.
2. "Anatomy of a Massacre," *Newsweek,* 3 May 1999, pp. 25–26.
3. Philip Cook, "The Epidemic of Youth Gun Violence," in *Perspectives on Crime and Justice: 1997–1998 Lecture Series* (Washington, D.C.: National Institute of Justice, 1998), pp. 107–116.
4. Leonard P. Edwards, "The Juvenile Court and the Role of the Juvenile Court Judge," *National Council of Juvenile Court and Family Court Judges* 43 (1992), p. 4.
5. For the application of the justice model to juveniles, see Charles E. Springer, *Justice for Juveniles* (Washington, D.C.: U.S. Department of Justice, 1986)
6. See Barry Feld, "The Transformation of the Juvenile Court," *Minnesota Law Review* 75 (February 1991), p. 578.
7. David J. Rothman, *The Discovery of the Asylum* (Boston: Little, Brown, 1971), pp. 46–53.
8. Ibid.
9. Anthony Platt, *The Child Savers* (Chicago: University of Chicago Press, 1967).
10. *Kent v. United States,* 383 U.S. 541, 86 S. Ct. 1045, 16 L. Ed. 2d 84 (1966); *In re Gault,* 387 U.S. 1, 18 L. Ed. 2d 527, 87 S. Ct. 1428 (1967); *In re Winship,* 397 U.S. 358, 90 S. Ct. 1968, 25 L. Ed. 2d 368 (1970); *McKeiver v. Pennsylvania,* 403 U.S. 528, 535 (1971); *In re Barbara Burrus,* 275 N.C. 517, 169 S.E. 2d 879 (1969); and *Breed v. Jones,* 421 U.S. 519, 95 S. Ct. 1779 (1975).
11. *In re Winship,* 397 U.S. 358, 90 S. Ct. 1968, 25 L. Ed. 2d 368 (1970).
12. *McKeiver v. Pennsylvania,* 403 U.S. 528, 535 (1971); *In re Barbara Burrus,* 275 N.C. 517, 169 S.E. 2d 879 (1969).
13. *Breed v. Jones,* 421 U.S. 519, 95 S. Ct. 1779 (1975).
14. U.S. Congress, Senate, Committee on the Judiciary, Subcommittee to Investigate Juvenile Delinquency, 1973, *The Juvenile Justice and Delinquency Prevention Act,* S.3148 and S.821., 92d Cong., 2d sess.; 93d Cong., 1st sess.
15. R. B. Coates, A. D. Miller, and L. E. Ohlin, *Diversity in a Youth Correctional System: Handling Deliquents in Massachusetts* (Cambridge: Ballinger, 1978), p. 190.
16. Barry Krisberg et al., "The Watershed of Juvenile Justice Reform," *Crime and Delinquency* 32 (January 1986), p. 30.

17. National Advisory Committee for Juvenile Justice and Delinquency Prevention, *Serious Juvenile Crime: A Redirected Federal Effort* (Washington, D.C.: Office of Juvenile Justice and Delinquency Prevention, 1984), p. iii.

18. Ibid., p. 9.

19. For a discussion of these emerging trends in juvenile justice, see Krisberg et al., "The Watershed of Juvenile Justice Reform."

20. Finn-Aage Esbensen and D. Wayne Osgood, *National Evaluation of G.R.E.A.T.* (Washington, D.C.: National Institute of Justice, 1997), p. 1.

21. National Institute of Justice, *The D.A.R.E. Program: A Review of Prevalence, User Satisfaction, and Effectiveness* (Washington, D.C.: U.S. Department of Justice, 1994), p. 1.

22. D. P. Rosenbaum and Gordon S. Hanson, "Assessing the Effects of School-Based Drug Education: A Six-Year Multilevel Analysis of Project D.A.R.E.," *Journal of Research in Crime and Delinquency* 35 (November 1998), pp. 381–412.

23. Of these evaluations, the most positive is probably W. DeJong "A Short-Term Evaluation of D.A.R.E.: Preliminary Indications of Effectiveness," *Journal of Drug Education* 17 (1987), pp. 279–294. For other positive evaluations, see R. R. Clayton, A. Cattarello, and K. P. Walden, "Sensation Seeking as a Potential Mediating Variable for School-Based Prevention Interventions: A Two-Year Follow-Up of DARE," *Journal of Health Communications* 3 (1991), pp. 229–239; and C. L. Ringwalt, T. R. Curtin, and D. P. Rosenbaum, *A First-Year Evaluation of D.A.R.E. in Illinois* (report to the Illinois State Police, 1990).

24. National Institute of Justice. *The D.A.R.E. Program: A Review of Prevalence, User Satisfaction, and Effectiveness.*

25. Rosenbaum and Hanson, "Assessing the Effects of School-Based Drug Education," p. 381.

26. Emily Walker, "The Community Intensive Treatment for Youth Program: A Specialized-Based Program for High-Risk Youth in Alabama," *Law and Psychology Review* 13 (1989), pp. 175–199.

27. Joan Petersilia, *Expanding Options for Criminal Sentencing* (Santa Monica, Calif.: Rand, 1987), p. 32.

28. Roberta C. Cronin, *Boot Camps for Adults and Juvenile Offenders: Overview and Update* (final summary report presented to the National Institute of Justice, 1994), p. 37.

29. Ibid.

30. For a statement on the House of Umoja, see Robert L. Woodson, *A Summons to Life: Mediating Structure and the Prevention of Youth Crime* (Cambridge: Ballinger, 1981),

31. Information on Associated Marine Institutes was supplied by Ms. Magie Valdés in a phone conversation with the author.

32. Dale G. Parent et al., *Conditions of Confinement: Juvenile Detention and Corrections Facilities* (Washington, D.C.: Office of Juvenile Justice and Delinquency Prevention, 1994), pp. 29–30.

33. Ibid., p. 21.

34. *Corrections Compendium* (Lincoln, Neb.: CEGA Services, July 1992), pp. 12–14.

35. This was a one-day population figure. See Parent, *Conditions of Confinement,* p. 36.

36. M. A. Cohen, *The Monetary Value of Saving a High-Risk Youth* (Washington, D.C.: Urban Institute, 1994).

37. George M. Camp and Camille Graham Camp, *Corrections Yearbook: Juvenile Corrections* (South Salem, N.Y.: Criminal Justice Institute, 1990).

38. James Austin, Barry Krisberg, Robert DeComo, Sonya Rudenstine, and Dominic Del Rosario, *Juveniles Taken into Custody: Fiscal Year 1993* (Washington, D.C.: U.S. Government Printing Office, 1995), pp. 1–2.

39. Kathleen Maguire and Ann L. Pastore, eds., *Sourcebook of Criminal Justice Statistics, 1993* (Washington, D.C.: U.S. Government Printing Office, 1994), p. 586.

40. Austin et al., *Juveniles Taken into Custody,* p. 21.

41. Parent et al., *Conditions of Confinement,* p. 134.

42. Ibid., p. 138.

43. R. G. Sheldon and S. Tracey, "Violent Female Juvenile Offender: An Ignored Minority within the Juvenile Justice System," *Juvenile and Family Court Journal* 43 (1992), pp. 33–40.

44. Ibid., p. 182. The present author's experience with confined youth indicates that few can tolerate isolation for more than a couple weeks.

45. The author testified in a 1993 case in which a juvenile was placed in mechanical constraints for nearly twenty-four hours. The Department of Human Services brought a child abuse charge against the supervisor of the institution's residential cottage where the incident occurred.

46. Peter W. Greenwood, Susan Turner, and Kathy Rosenblatt, *Evaluation of Paint Creek Youth Center: Preliminary Results* (Santa Monica, Calif.: Rand, 1989).

47. Ibid., p. 3.

48. David Shichor and Clemens Bartollas, "Private and Public Placements: Is There a Difference?" *Crime and Delinquency* 36 (April 1990), pp. 286–299.

49. See Clemens Bartollas and David Shichor, "Juvenile Privatization: The Expected and the Unexpected" (paper presented to the annual meeting of the American Society of Criminology, Baltimore, November 1990. See also Clemens Bartollas, "Little Girls Grown Up: The Perils of Institutionalization," in *Female Criminality: The State of the Art,* ed. Concetta Culliver (New York: Garland, 1993), pp. 469–482.

50. Snyder and Sickmund, Juvenile Offenders and Victims, p. 210.

51. Donna M. Hamparian et al., "Youth in Adult Court: Between Two Worlds," *Major Issues in Juvenile Justice Information and Training* (Columbus, Ohio: Academy for Contemporary Problems, 1981).

52. Kelly Dedel, "National Profile of the Organization of State Juvenile Corrections System," *Crime and Delinquency* 44 (October 1998), p. 515.

53. Heida M. Hsia and Donna Hamparian, *Disproportionate Minority Confinement: 1997 Update* (Washington, D.C.: Office of Juvenile Justice and Delinquency Prevention, 1998), p. 1.

54. R. E. DeComo, *Juveniles Taken into Custody Research Program: Estimating the Prevalence of Juvenile Custody by Race and Gender* (San Francisco: National Council on Crime and Delinquency, 1993).

55. Hsia and Hamparian, *Disproportionate Minority Confinement.*

56. See also Carl E. Pope, "Blacks and Juvenile Justice: A Review," in *The Criminal Justice System and Blacks,* ed. D. E.

Georges-Abeyie (New York: Clark Bordman, 1984); and Carl E. Pope and William Feyerherm, "Minority Status and Juvenile Justice Processing," *Criminal Justice Abstracts* 22 (1990), pp. 237–336 (part I), 527–542 (part II).

57. See Donna M. Bishop and Charles E. Frazier, *A Study of Race and Juvenile Processing in Florida* (report submitted to the Florida Supreme Court Racial and Ethnic Bias Study Commission, 1990).

58. John P. Moore and Craig P. Terrett, "Highlights of the 1996 National Youth Gang Survey," *OJJDP Fact Sheet* (Washington, D.C.: Office of Juvenile Justice and Delinquency Prevention, 1998), p. 1.

59. Terence P. Thornberry, "Membership in Youth Gangs and Involvement in Serious and Violent Offending," in *Serious and Violent Offenders: Risk Factors and Successful Intervention,* ed. R. Loeber and D. P. Farrington (Thousand Oaks, Calif.: Sage, pp. 147–166.

60. National Youth Gang Center, *1997 National Youth Gang Survey: Summary* (Washington, D.C.: U.S. Department of Justice, 1999), p. iii.

61. For a review of these studies, see Clemens Bartollas, *Juvenile Delinquency* 5th ed. (Boston: Allyn & Bacon, 2000), pp. 542–544.

62. For a review of these studies, see ibid., pp. 540–542.

Multiple Choice Questions

1. Which of the following positions is the guiding standard of juvenile court decision making?

   A. Best interest of the child
   B. Best interest of society
   C. Least restrictive alternative
   D. Best treatment approach

2. During the colonial era, what was the primary means of social control for children?

   A. Community
   B. Bow Street runners
   C. Religion
   D. Family

3. When and where was the first juvenile court created?

   A. 1888 in Philadelphia, Pennsylvania
   B. 1899 in Cook County, Illinois
   C. 1899 in Boston, Massachusetts
   D. 1899 in St. Louis, Missouri

4. Identify the first institution designed for juveniles that offered vocational training and emphasized the priority of participating in work.

   A. House of Reformatory
   B. Halfway House
   C. House of Refuge
   D. House of Reform

5. What U.S. Supreme Court decision resulted in juvenile cases having the standard of proof, beyond a reasonable doubt apply during adjudication proceedings?

   A. *In re Winship*
   B. *In re Gault*
   C. *McKeiver v. Pennsylvania*
   D. *Breed v. Jones*

6. Identify the most widely used judicial disposition in the juvenile justice system.

   A. Boot camps
   B. Probation
   C. Juvenile facilities
   D. Diversion

7. The criminal justice system and juvenile justice system have all of the following traits in common except:

   A. Operating on tight budgets
   B. Ongoing problems of staff burnout
   C. Problems of violence and inhumane institutions
   D. Problems with status offenders

8. The first stage of the juvenile court proceeding is a:

   A. Detention hearing
   B. Bail hearing
   C. Curfew hearing
   D. Adjudicatory hearing

9. Identify the U.S. Supreme Court decision that resulted in juveniles having the right to due-process safeguards in proceedings in which a finding of delinquency could lead to confinement.

   A. *In re Gault*
   B. *In re Winship*
   C. *McKeiver v. Pennsylvania*
   D. *Breed v. Jones*

10. All of the following are the main types of community-based programs except:

   A. Group homes
   B. Day treatment centers
   C. Work furloughs
   D. Wilderness programs

11. According to a study by Kelly Dedel, the reasons for transferring juveniles to adult facilities include all of the following except:

   A. Mental illness of the offender
   B. Age of the offender
   C. Seriousness of the offense
   D. Poor institutional adjustment and failure to benefit from the program

12. What occurs after a youth has been found delinquent at the adjudicatory stage or has waived their right to an adjudicatory hearing.

   A. Preliminary hearing
   B. Disposition hearing
   C. Postadjudicatory hearing
   D. Treatment hearing

True/False Questions

T F   1. Throughout the history of corrections juveniles have never been confined in the same facility as adults.

T F   2. A case can be adjudicated through the juvenile court and then can be transferred to criminal court for adult processing on the same offense.

T F   3. Throughout every jurisdiction in the United States, only the police can refer juveniles to the intake division of the juvenile court.

T F   4. One of the serious shortcomings of programming in many training schools is the lack of attention given to the needs of adjudicated female offenders.

T F   5. Security and treatment assessment are basic roles of the balanced and restorative justice project.

T F   6. It was not until the 1960s that youth involved in the juvenile court process began getting some of the due-process rights afforded to adults in the criminal justice system.

T F   7. A juvenile who steals property valued under $1,000 is known as a status offender.

T F   8. According to the text, a group home is one of the main types of community-based programs.

T F   9. Boot camp is the most widely used form of judicial disposition in the juvenile justice process.

T F   10. Diversion is one of the variety of sanctions used in the juvenile justice system.

Fill-in-the-Blank Questions   (based on key terms)

1. A _____ would not be a crime if it were committed by an adult.

2. Parole in the adult criminal justice system is referred to as _____ in the juvenile justice system.

3. A trial in the adult criminal justice system is referred to as a _____ in the juvenile justice system.

4. The philosophy in which the juvenile court accepts parental responsibility over delinquent, neglected, or abused children is known as _____.

5. Based on the "ideal" Puritan family, _____ were designed to provide an orderly and disciplined environment to control juveniles.

6. A juvenile will receive a sentence at a _____.

Essay Questions

1. Throughout the history of American society, how have juvenile lawbreakers been handled?

2. Explain how the U.S. Supreme Court decisions in *In re Gault, In re Winship,* and *Breed v. Jones* influenced the operation of the juvenile justice system?

3. Identify and explain the steps of the juvenile justice process.

4. What is the purpose of diversion in the juvenile justice system? Identify and explain two types of diversion programs that are in use today.

5. Describe community-based programs such as group homes, day treatment, and wilderness programs.

ANSWERS

Multiple Choice Questions

1. A	7. D
2. D	8. A
3. B	9. A
4. C	10. C
5. A	11. A
6. B	12. B

Fill-in-the-Blank Questions

1. Status offense
2. Aftercare
3. Adjudicatory hearing
4. *Parens patriae*
5. Houses of refuge
6. Dispositional hearing

True/False Questions

1. F	6. T
2. F	7. F
3. F	8. T
4. T	9. F
5. F	10. F

The Death Penalty

One of the most vocal groups opposing capital punishment is the American Civil Liberties Union (ACLU). This 2000 ACLU brochure was intended to promote opposition to the death penalty:

> *THANKS TO MODERN SCIENCE*
> 17 Innocent People Have Been Removed from Death Row.
>
> *THANKS TO MODERN POLITICS*
> 23 Innocent People Have Been Removed from the Living.

On April 15, 1999, Ronald Keith Williamson walked away from Oklahoma State Prison a free man. An innocent man. He had spent the last eleven years behind bars. "I did not rape or kill Debra Sue Carter," he would shout day and night from his death row cell. His voice was so torn and raspy from his pleas for justice that he could barely speak. DNA evidence would eventually end his nightmare and prove his innocence. He came within five days of being put to death for a crime he did not commit.

Williamson's plight is not an isolated one. Nor is it even unusual.

Anthony Porter also came within days of being executed. The state of Illinois halted his execution as it questioned whether or not Porter was mentally competent. Porter has an I.Q. of fifty-one. As the state questioned his competence, a journalism class at Northwestern University questioned his guilt. With a small amount of investigating, they managed to produce the real killer. After sixteen years on death row, Anthony Porter would find his freedom. He was lucky. He escaped with his life. A fate not shared by twenty-three other innocent men. . . .[1]

CRITICAL THINKING QUESTIONS

How serious a challenge do releases of death row inmates due to DNA evidence pose to the death penalty? Do you believe that the state is obligated to review cases to make certain that the men and women living on death row are in fact guilty?

Advances in DNA technology are raising questions about the guilt of some residents of death row and the legal procedures that gave them the death penalty. On 31 January 2000, George Ryan, governor of Illinois, imposed a moratorium on his state's death penalty. He wanted all lethal injections to be postponed indefinitely pending an investigation into why more executions had been overturned than carried out since Illinois reinstated capital punishment in 1977. Ryan told CNN, "We have now freed more people than we have put to death under our system—thirteen have been exonerated and twelve have been put to death. There is a flaw in the system, without question, and it needs to be studied." Ryan planned to create a special panel to study the state's capital punishment system as well as what happened in the thirteen specific cases in which men were wrongly convicted. He added, "I still believe the death penalty is a proper response to heinous crimes, but I want to make sure . . . that the person who is put to death is absolutely guilty."[2]

Thus, the death penalty can be viewed through the lens of fairness. Those holding this perspective, such as Governor Ryan, may continue to support the death penalty, but they are sensitive to the possibility of putting innocent persons to death. The fairness perspective seems to be gaining ground as increasing numbers of inmates are released from death row because they were found to be innocent.

The pro–death penalty perspective of the victim's family, as well as of people in the community who knew and respected the victim, offers another view. Capital punishment is a topic that stirs deep emotional reactions from opponents of the death penalty, but it elicits even deeper reactions from those who have had a loved one murdered. With some exceptions, they want the killer to be executed by the state. They claim that the right of this person to continue living ended when he or she took a life. In Outside the Walls 17.1 a prosecutor offers a glimpse of the horror that some victims have experienced.

It has been widely held that the death penalty is the only just ending for the poison planted by Timothy McVeigh, who killed 168 people—149 adults and 19 children—in the 1995 bombing of Oklahoma City's Murrah Federal Building. McVeigh saw the bombing as a retaliatory strike against the government and the government employees within the building who represented the government. McVeigh further drew the wrath of the American public by his referral to the children killed in the blast as "collateral damage" and by his lack of remorse for the pain that he had inflicted on so many families. He was executed in the death chamber of the U.S. Penitentiary in Terre Haute, Indiana, on Monday 11 June 2001.

outside the walls   17.1

The Death Penalty Is an Affirmation of Life

A 2½-year-old girl was kidnapped, raped, sodomized, tortured, and mutilated with vise grips over six hours. Then she was strangled to death. Her assailant, Theodore Frank, according to court records and his own admissions, had already molested more than 100 children during a 20-year period.

A sentence to death is the only appropriate punishment for such a serial assailant committing such an extraordinarily heinous crime. Two separate juries agreed, but now, 23 years after this horrendous murder, legal proceedings still continue in federal court. As district attorney of Ventura County since 1978 and prosecutor since 1967, I am convinced that there are some crimes that demand a sentence of death, despite recent publicity attacking the death penalty and calling for outright abolition or at least a "moratorium" until further studies are completed.

There have been 12 defendants sentenced to death in Ventura County while I have been district attorney. Their crimes included multiple murders and murders committed during the course of kidnappings and sexual assaults. These cases uniformly involve violent predators who attack the weakest, most defenseless members of our society. In one case, the defendant not only kidnapped and strangled the victim, but then committed a sex act on

her dead body. In another case, 8-year-old boy was kidnapped, sexually assaulted, strangled and then set afire. In yet another horrific murder, an elderly husband and wife were bludgeoned in their own home during a robbery.

A decision to seek the death penalty is never made lightly. We thoroughly investigate both the crime and the defendant's background. I then make the final decision after considering the results of this exhaustive investigation and meeting with the assigned attorneys, investigators, and other staff members. The defendant's attorneys are invited to appear at this meeting to present any information they consider relevant to the decision.

> . . . I am convinced that there are some crimes that demand a sentence of death . . .

CRITICAL THINKING QUESTIONS

Do you feel that the perspective of the victim's family has been given proper recognition? What do you think would be the response of an opponent to the death penalty to the heinous crimes described by this district attorney?

Source: Reprinted from Michael D. Bradbury, Ventura County District Attorney, "The Death Penalty Is an Affirmation of the Sanctity of Life," cited at www.prodeathpenalty.com/affirmation.htm.

WHAT ARE THE ROOTS OF CAPITAL PUNISHMENT?

The survival of capital punishment in the United States has been debated since the earliest days of the Republic. In 1787, Dr. Benjamin Rush (1745–1813) of Philadelphia, the most famous physician of his time and a signer of the Declaration of Independence, delivered an oration on the subject that set forth a position taken by religious liberals, especially Quakers, throughout American history. His essential rationale rests on the assumption that "the punishment of murder by death is contrary to reason and to the order and happiness of society."[3] Famous and revered though Rush was, he could not persuade the Commonwealth of Pennsylvania to outlaw the death penalty for homicide. He did succeed, however, in eliminating capital punishment as a sanction for lesser felonies.

Edward Livingston (1764–1836), a New York lawyer, was also opposed to the death penalty. He abruptly left New York in 1803 as a result of a scandal in his law office for which he felt responsible. He settled in New Orleans and in 1820 was elected to the Louisiana Assembly. Because of his influential advocacy of criminal justice law reform, he was commissioned by the legislature to draft a revision of the state's criminal code. When he presented his draft to the legislators, he accompanied it with an essay entitled

"The Crime of Employing the Punishment of Death."[4] His argument depended less on religious and moral precepts than on his view that capital punishment was an ineffectual and needless deterrent to crime and that imprisonment could better serve the aims of justice.

Rush and Livingston were among the first in a long line of famous Americans who vigorously opposed the death penalty. Perhaps the most powerful rhetoric favoring the death penalty came from England, where Sir James Fitzjames Stephen (1829–1894), a lawyer and judge, propounded uncompromising views on the need for severe punishment of all criminals:

> No other punishment deters men so effectually from committing crimes as the punishment of death. . . . [T]his is one of those propositions which it is difficult to prove, simply because they are in themselves more obvious than any proof can make them. It is possible to display ingenuity in arguing against it, but that is all. The whole experience of mankind is in the other direction. The threat of instant death is one to which resort has always been made when there was an absolute necessity for producing some result. . . ."All that a man has he will give for his life." In any secondary punishment however terrible, there is hope; but death is death; its terrors cannot be described more forcibly.[5]

Sir James's contact with murderers was frequent but only in the courtroom. His assumption that the terror of death could be a factor in a killer's calculations when deciding whether to engage in homicide must have been drawn from an estimate of his own probable behavior in the unlikely event that he would be faced with such a decision. It seems never to have entered his mind that criminals acting on the spur of the moment and with imperfect powers to calculate the risk might behave differently than he would. If capital punishment did not deter potential criminals, he believed that it at least satisfied society's justifiable demand for vengeance. He put it this way, "The criminal law stands to the passion of revenge in much the same relation as marriage to the sexual appetite."[6]

WHERE IS THE DEATH PENALTY TODAY?

The death penalty, as suggested in Chapter 2, has become an institution. Two driving forces in this institution are public opinions about capital punishment and political support for the death penalty. Another important dimension of the death penalty today is the profiles of the men and women who receive this sentence.

American public opinion on the death penalty shifted dramatically during the twentieth century. In the last two decades of the twentieth century, the public became highly supportive of it. Politicians tended to view support of the death penalty much as they viewed the public's preference for being tough on crime: Those who felt any reservations about the death penalty were typically reluctant to voice their misgivings.

The profile of the men and women who receive the death penalty consists of several social and demographic variables. It includes the frequency of persons placed under the sentence of death; the number of executions that take place in a given year; and the gender and the racial, social, and economic background of those who are executed. Other important considerations are the identification of the states that have death statutes, how often these states execute, and the methods of execution that they use.

Public Opinion

Ever since 1939, the Gallup Poll has asked the public, "Do you favor or oppose the death penalty for persons convicted of murder?" For several decades in the twentieth century, support for the death penalty gradually declined. As recently as 1978 a Roper poll found that 66 percent of the population opposed the death penalty. The reported increase in violent street crime during the late 1970s and 1980s reversed public opinion. Polls taken in the late 1980s found that as many as 80 percent of Americans favored the death penalty. In a Gallup Poll conducted on 8 and 9 February 1999, 71 percent polled favored capital punishment. A *Newsweek* poll taken in June 2000 found 73 percent supported the death penalty.[7]

Some evidence indicates that when the public is presented with the alternative of life imprisonment without the possibility of parole (LWOP), there is less support for the death penalty.[8] Mark Costanzo believes that if the public were assured that murderers would never be released on parole, they would be far less supportive of the death penalty.[9]

There has always been some concern that erroneous convictions take place in capital cases. In *In Spite of Innocence,* a widely cited examination of the death penalty, Michael L. Radelet, Hugo Adam Bedau, and Constance E. Putnam concluded that twenty-three individuals in the twentieth century had been wrongly accused and executed.[10] Scholarly books, however, have had little effect on public opinion. What appears to have more impact are newspaper and news magazine accounts about people released from death row because they were found to be innocent (see Outside the Walls 17.2).

outside the walls 17.2

How Many Innocent Death Row Inmates Will Be Killed?

Michael Ross states, "The most conclusive evidence that innocent persons have been condemned to death comes from examining the large number of people who were sentenced to death and later were able to prove their innocence and gain release from death row."

- Walter McMillian was released from Alabama's death row after spending six years there because of perjured testimony and withheld evidence that indicated his innocence.

- Federico Marcias was sentenced to death in the state of Texas for a murder that he did not commit. His conviction was overturned when a federal court found that Marcias's original attorney not only was grossly ineffective but had missed considerable evidence pointing to Marcias's innocence.

- Kirk Bloodsworth was sentenced to death for the 1984 rape and murder of a 9-year-old girl in Maryland. A volunteer lawyer later had the girl's underwear tested with a new DNA-testing technique not available at the original trial. The tests showed that the semen stains on the underwear could not have come from Bloodsworth. On 28 June 1993, Kirk Bloodsworth was released after the FBI's DNA testing confirmed that he was innocent.

- Clarence Brandley was convicted and sentenced to death for the murder of a high school student in 1981. In 1990, he was awarded a new trial when evidence

was uncovered that showed that the prosecutor had withheld evidence pointing to Brandley's innocence and prosecution witnesses had committed perjury. All charges were subsequently dropped, and Brandley was freed.

- Randall Dale Adams was convicted and sentenced to death for the murder of a police officer. In 1989, an appeals court judge set aside the conviction, stating, "[the] state was guilty of suppressing evidence favorable to the accused, deceiving the trial court . . . and knowingly using perjured testimony."

Since the mid-1990s, a host of other inmates were taken off death row and released from prison. They included Sabrina Butler (1995), Verneal Jimerson (1996), Troy Lee Jones (1996), Dennis Williamson (1996), Gary Gauger (1996), Donald Jones (1996), Anthony Porter (1999), and Steve Manning (2000).

> . . . Kirk Bloodsworth was released after the FBI's DNA testing confirmed that he was innocent.

CRITICAL THINKING QUESTIONS

How many innocent men and women do you believe are still on death row? What should a state do when DNA evidence reveals that an inmate was wrongly convicted and executed?

Source: Michael Ross, "How Many Innocent Men Will be Killed?" *Human Rights* 23 (Summer 1996), p. 1; and Jonathan Alter, "The Death Penalty of Trial," *Newsweek,* 12 June 2000, pp. 24–25.

Political Support

Politicians seem to be in three camps when it comes to the death penalty. One group regards opposition to the death penalty as political suicide. Politicians running for national office typically strongly support or at least defend the death penalty. Southern politicians also seem to be strongly supportive of the death penalty. Another group consists of politicians in the twelve states that do not have the death penalty. Active debate is taking place among these politicians, some of whom strongly oppose the death penalty. Indeed, in these states one or two powerful politicians are able to sustain the necessary support to withstand attempts to pass a death penalty statute. Opponents of the death penalty in these states fear that the balance of power might shift, as it recently did in New York State, and the death penalty might be passed during a legislative session. The third group consists of politicians in those death penalty statute states in which active debate is now taking place about this form of sentencing. The recent releases from death row due to DNA technology and faulty legal procedures have sparked this debate. Early signs of concern are moratoriums on the death penalty in Illinois and Kentucky.

Death Penalty Profile

The high numbers of persons under sentence of death in the 1930s gradually decreased until the early 1950s; then the numbers began to rise again. In 1976, the U.S. Supreme Court upheld state capital punishment laws, and the numbers of those under the sentence of death began a sharp rise that persists to this day (see Figure 17.1). On 31 December 1999, 37 states and the Federal Bureau of Prisons held a total of 3,527 prisoners under sentence of death (see Table 17.1).[11]

The death penalty remains a poor man's punishment. Indeed, as the adage puts it, "Only those without capital get capital punishment." The average inmate under sentence of death has less than a high school diploma (62 percent); the percentage of death row inmates who have not gone beyond eighth grade (14 percent) is larger than the per-

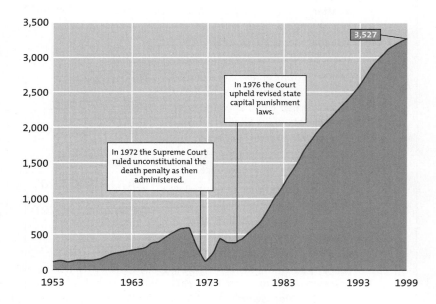

Figure 17.1 Persons under Sentence of Death, 1953–1999

Source: Bureau of Justice Statistics Bulletin, *Capital Punishment 1999*
(Washington, D.C.: U.S. Government Printing Office, 1999), p. 5.

Table 17.1

Status of the Death Penalty, 31 December 1999

Executions during 1999		Number of Prisoners under Sentence of Death		Jurisdictions without a Death Penalty
Texas	35	California	553	Alaska
Virginia	14	Texas	460	District of Columbia
Missouri	9	Florida	365	Hawaii
Arizona	7	Pennsylvania	230	Iowa
Oklahoma	6	North Carolina	202	Maine
Arkansas	4	Ohio	199	Massachusetts
North Carolina	4	Alabama	180	Michigan
South Carolina	4	Illinois	156	Minnesota
Alabama	2	Oklahoma	139	North Dakota
California	2	Georgia	116	Rhode Island
Delaware	2	Arizona	116	Vermont
Florida	1	Tennessee	100	West Virginia
Illinois	1	Nevada	86	Wisconsin
Indiana	1	Louisiana	85	
Kentucky	1	Missouri	83	
Louisiana	1	South Carolina	65	
Nevada	1	Mississippi	60	
Ohio	1			
Pennsylvania	1	21 other jurisdictions	332	
Utah	1	Total	3,527	
Total	98			

- At year-end 1999, thirty-seven states and the federal prison system held 3,527 prisoners under sentence of death, 2 percent more than in 1998.

Persons under Sentence of Death, by Race

	1990	1999
White	1,379	1,948
Black	945	1,514
American Indian	25	28
Asian	15	24
Other	1	13

- The 325 Hispanic inmates under sentence of death accounted for 10 percent of inmates with a known ethnicity.

- Fifty women were under a sentence of death in 1999, up from thirty-five in 1990.

- Among persons for whom arrest information was available, the average age at time of arrest was 28; 2 percent of inmates were age 17 or younger at arrest.

- At year-end the youngest inmate was 18; the oldest was 84.

- Of the 6,365 people under sentence of death between 1977 and 1999, 9 percent were executed, 3 percent died by causes other than execution, and 32 percent received other dispositions.

- The number of states authorizing lethal injection increased from twenty in 1989 to thirty-four in 1999. In 1999, 96 percent of all executions were by lethal injection, compared to 44 percent in 1989.

Source: Bureau of Justice Statistics Bulletin, *Capital Punishment* (Washington, D.C.: U.S. Government Printing Office, 2000), p. 1.

centage of those who attended some college (10 percent). Slightly over half of these inmates are white (55 percent). A disproportionate number are African American (43 percent). About one of five prisoners under sentence of death is married (23 percent); over half were never married (53 percent). Half of all inmates under sentence of death were age 20 to 29 at the time of arrest for their capital offense; the average age at time of arrest was 28 years. The oldest prisoner under sentence of death was 84, and the youngest was 18.[12]

Twelve states and the District of Columbia do not impose the death penalty for any crime. Alaska, Hawaii, Iowa, Maine, Massachusetts, Michigan, Minnesota, North Dakota, Rhode Island, Vermont, West Virginia, Wisconsin, and the District of Columbia are the jurisdictions without capital punishment. Of the thirty-eight states with death penalty statutes, New Hampshire has no imposed death sentences, and Connecticut, Kansas, New Jersey, New York, South Dakota, and Tennessee have not carried out an execution since 1976. States in the South have imposed far more sentences of death than states in any other region of the nation. From 1 January 2000 through 31 December 2000, Texas had 40 executions; Oklahoma, 11; Virginia, 8; Florida, 6; Missouri, 5; Alabama, 4; Arizona, 4; Arkansas 2; Delaware, 1; Louisiana, 1; North Carolina, 1; South Carolina, 1; Tennessee, 1; and California, 1.[13] For the number of executions/commutations by state since 1976, see Table 17.2.

Table 17.3 shows methods of execution used in each state where the law allows capital punishment. As of 31 December 1999, lethal injection had become the predominant method of execution (34 states). Eleven states still used the electric chair; four states, the gas chamber; three states, hanging; and three states, a firing squad. In seventeen states, more than one method was authorized—lethal injection and an alternative method. Twelve of those states permitted the condemned prisoner to choose the method that would be used.

Table 17.2

Executions/Commutations by State since 1976

State	Number	State	Number
Texas	221/37*	Indiana	7/0
Virginia	76/11**	Utah	6/0
Florida	48/6	Mississippi	4/0
Missouri	42/2	Maryland	3/1
Oklahoma	28/0	Washington	3/0
Louisiana	26/1	Nebraska	3/0
South Carolina	24/0	Oregon	2/0
Georgia	23/4	Pennsylvania	3/0
Alabama	23/1	Kentucky	2/0
Arkansas	22/1	Montana	2/1
Arizona	21/0	Idaho	1/1
North Carolina	15/2	Colorado	1/0
Illinois	12/1	Ohio	1/8
Delaware	10/0	Wyoming	1/0
Nevada	8/0	New Mexico	0/5
California	8/0	Tennessee	1/0

*36 commutations granted for judicial expediency.
**5 commutations granted for judicial expediency.

Source: National Coalition to Abolish the Death Penalty, Webpage, 2000.

Table 17.3

Method of Execution, by State, 1999

Lethal Injection		Electrocution	Lethal Gas	Hanging	Firing Squad
Arizona[a,b]	New Hampshire[a]	Alabama	Arizona[a,b]	Delaware[a,c]	Idaho[a]
Arkansas[a,d]	New Jersey	Arkansas[a,d]	California[a]	New Hampshire[a,e]	Oklahoma[f]
California[a]	New Mexico	Florida	Missouri[a]	Washington[a]	Utah[a]
Colorado	New York	Georgia	Wyoming[a,g]		
Connecticut	North Carolina	Kentucky[a,h]			
Delaware[a,c]	Ohio[a]	Nebraska			
Idaho[a]	Oklahoma[a]	Ohio[a]			
Illinois	Oregon	Oklahoma[f]			
Indiana	Pennsylvania	South Carolina[a]			
Kansas	South Carolina[a]	Tennessee[a,i]			
Kentucky[a,g]	South Dakota	Virginia[a]			
Louisiana	Tennessee[a,i]				
Maryland	Texas				
Mississippi	Utah[a]				
Missouri[a]	Virginia[a]				
Montana	Washington[a]				
Nevada	Wyoming[a]				

Note: The method of execution of federal prisoners is lethal injection, pursuant to 28 CFR, Part 26. For offenses under the Violent Crime Control and Law Enforcement Act of 1994, the method is that of the state in which the conviction took place, pursuant to 18 U.S.C. 3596.

[a]Authorizes two methods of execution.

[b]Arizona authorizes lethal injection for persons whose capital sentence was received after 11/15/92; for those sentenced before that date, the condemned may select lethal injection or lethal gas.

[c]Delaware authorizes lethal injection for those whose capital offense occurred after 6/13/86; for those whose offense occurred before that date, the condemned may select lethal injection or hanging.

[d]Arkansas authorizes lethal injection for those whose capital offense occurred on or after 7/4/83; for those whose offense occurred before that date, the condemned may select lethal injection or electrocution.

[e]New Hampshire authorizes hanging only if lethal injection cannot be given.

[f]Oklahoma authorizes electrocution if lethal injection is ever held to be unconstitutional, and firing squad if both lethal injection and electrocution are held unconstitutional.

[g]Wyoming authorizes lethal gas if lethal injection is ever held to be unconstitutional.

[h]Kentucky authorizes lethal injection for persons whose capital sentence was received on or after 3/31/98; for those sentenced before that date, the condemned may select lethal injection or electrocution.

[i]Tennessee authorizes lethal injection for those whose capital offense occurred after 12/31/98; those whose offense occurred before that date may select lethal injection of electrocution.

Source: Bureau of Justice Statistics Bulletin, *Capital Punishment 1999* (Washington, D.C.: U.S. Government Printing Office, 1999), p. 5.

HOW HAVE THE COURTS RULED ON THE DEATH PENALTY?

Lawyers have debated in the federal courts whether capital punishment is cruel and unusual within the meaning of the **Eighth Amendment** of the Constitution. Whether it is cruel depends on one's perspective, but it certainly is unusual.[14] During the late 1990s, there were about 19,000 homicides in the United States, a decrease of nearly 2,000 from the 1980s. The percentage of reported homicides cleared with an arrest is high—more than 70 percent. The percentage of death sentences pronounced is minute, and, even with the increase of executions in the 1990s, there has been a clear-cut decline in the annual numbers of executions from the peak of 199 in 1933.[15]

Important U.S. Supreme Court Decisions

In 1972, in one grand gesture, the U.S. Supreme court in *Furman v. Georgia* swept away the death penalty in every state and spared the lives of men and women on death row.[16] The *Furman* case was the climax of a long battle against the death penalty. One of the campaigners was the NAACP, acutely sensitive to the fact that African Americans have been disproportionately given the death penalty.[17] (See the Timeline for a list of significant Supreme Court cases on the death penalty.)

Furman v. Georgia was the case of an African American man accused and convicted of murder and rape. In a 5-to-4 decision that elicited five differing opinions for the majority and four for the minority, the Supreme Court relied on the "equal protection of the laws" provision of the **Fourteenth Amendment** to overturn the sentence as well as the "cruel and unusual punishment" provision of the Eighth Amendment. In his opinion, Justice William O. Douglas wrote,

> The high service rendered by the "cruel and unusual" clause is to require legislatures to write penal laws that are even-handed, non-selective, and non-arbitrary, and to require judges to see to it that general laws are not applied sparsely, selectively, and spottily to unpopular groups.[18]

Douglas went on to hold that the Georgia law violated the Fourteenth Amendment because, like the laws of the other states authorizing the death penalty, it provided trial courts with such discretionary freedom that it was imposed only on the poor, the unpopular, and the unstable.

After intense national controversy, the Supreme Court arrived at a resolution of the ambiguities and cast the death penalty into a moratorium. Hundreds of prisoners occupying death-row cells had their sentences commuted to life imprisonment. Legislatures across the land responded to the chief justice's invitation to reevaluate the role of capital punishment in criminal justice.

timeline
Significant Supreme Court Decisions on the Death Penalty

Case	Date	Decision
Furman v. Georgia	1972	Overturned death penalty in Georgia.
Gregg v. Georgia	1976	Declared death penalty in Georgia is constitutional.
Ford v. Wainwright	1986	Prohibited the state from executing the insane.
McCleskey v. Kemp	1987	Rejected racial injustice of the death penalty.
Thompson v. Oklahoma	1988	Prohibits execution of juveniles under age 16.
Penry v. Lynch	1989	Mental retardation is no bar to capital punishment.
Stanford v. Kentucky	1989	Seventeen-year-old can be executed.
Wilkins v. Missouri	1989	Sixteen-year-old can be executed.

The case that ended the moratorium was *Gregg v. Georgia,* decided in 1976. By a 7-to-2 margin, the Court concluded that capital punishment was a justifiable expression of outrage at the commission of a heinous crime, that it was a deterrent to persons who might otherwise commit such a crime, and that it is not disproportionate to the gravity of the offense. The Georgia legislature had carefully drafted a statute ensuring that the sentencing judge would be furnished adequate information and guidance in deciding to impose this ultimate penalty. The Supreme Court found that "no longer can a jury wantonly and freakishly impose the death sentence; it is always circumscribed by legislative guidelines."[19]

After all this deliberation, the constitutional questions were settled. Capital punishment is constitutional if the statutes clearly provide that, during the sentencing process, these conditions are met:

1. The court is informed about the defendant's background and criminal history.
2. Mitigating factors affecting culpability are brought to the attention of the court.
3. There are standards to guide trial courts in making the sentencing decision.
4. Every death sentence will be reviewed by a state appellate court.[20]

In the 1980s, the U.S. Supreme Court handed down several important decisions concerning the death penalty. One was *Barefoot v. Estelle* (1983).[21] Barefoot, a recidivist, had been found guilty in a Texas court of murder in the first degree. Texas law says that capital punishment may be imposed only if in the opinion of the jury certain criteria are met. One such criterion is that the defendant is a dangerous person who is likely to commit more serious crimes if allowed to survive. At Barefoot's trial two psychiatrists, neither of whom had interviewed Barefoot, testified that Barefoot posed such a danger. Barefoot's attorneys argued that psychiatrists are not competent to make such a prediction. In support of that contention they submitted a statement by the American Psychiatric Association that "the unreliability of predictions of dangerousness is by now an established fact within the Psychiatric profession." The Association's best estimate was that two out of three predictions of long-term future violence made by psychiatrists are wrong.

Justice Byron White, who delivered the opinion of the Supreme Court majority, dismissed this point as "without merit," saying that the decision as to dangerousness is up to the jury: "To accept the defendant's argument would call into question predictions of dangerousness that are constantly made." Justice Harry A. Blackmun, in a vigorous dissent, held that the authority of a professional psychiatrist would inevitably carry great weight with a jury, especially when both psychiatric experts felt themselves qualified to make predictions of dangerousness with a very high degree of accuracy.[22]

In *Pulley v. Harris* (1984), the question was whether California law was inconsistent with U.S. constitutional requirements by not requiring that the California court compare the facts of the case with the disposition of other similar cases in order to ensure that the sentence was proportional to the seriousness of the crime.[23] The Supreme Court decided that California's death penalty law could be imposed if the California court could find that one or more of seven "special circumstances," as spelled out in the California statute, obtained. Those circumstances are (1) murder for profit, (2) murder perpetrated by an explosion, (3) murder of a police officer on active duty, (4) murder of a victim who was a witness to a crime, (5) murder committed in a robbery, (6) murder with torture, and (7) murder by a person with one or more previous convictions of murder. In *Pulley v. Harris,* the murder was committed in the course of a robbery. The Supreme Court was satisfied that the California statute met the constitutional requirement of proportionality and that Harris was eligible for execution.[24]

The Georgia case of *McCleskey v. Kemp* (1987) has been through the federal courts several times.[25] McCleskey was an African American man who was convicted in 1978 of the murder of a white police officer during an armed robbery. He contended that the imposition of the death penalty was cruel and unusual because African American men killing white victims are sentenced to death with greater frequency than white men killing white victims.

This mentally retarded inmate was on death row. In 2001, the Supreme Court commuted his sentence to life in prison due to his mental retardation. What are the arguments and precedents for executing people with mental retardation in the United States? What are the characteristics of death row inmates generally? How has the U.S. Supreme Court ruled on questions of the constitutionality of the death penalty? How does constitutionality figure in the execution of the mentally ill and juveniles?

In support of this contention, McCleskey presented to the Supreme Court a study by Professor David Baldus showing the following: In Georgia, 22 percent of African American defendants with white victims received the death penalty, but only 8 percent of white defendants with white victims received the death penalty. Only 3 percent of white defendants charged with killing African American victims were sentenced to death. Prosecutors sought the death penalty in the cases of 70 percent of African American defendants killing white victims, but capital punishment was sought for only 32 percent of white defendants killing African American victims. It was argued that these figures showed that Georgia courts and prosecutors were discriminatory in their application of the laws.

Justice Lewis Powell, writing for a 5-to-4 Supreme Court majority, rejected this argument. He held that the statistics did not prove that race entered into the decision of the Georgia court in this case. Further, following the defendant's line of reasoning, any penalty could be challenged on the basis of unexplained discrepancies correlating to membership in minority groups or even to gender.[26]

McCleskey returned to the Supreme Court for another attempt to overturn his sentence. In a decision announced on 15 April 1991, Justice Anthony Kennedy wrote for a 6-to-3 majority rejecting McCleskey's contention and went on to pronounce a new rule on such appeals. Henceforth "a failure to press at the outset a claim of constitutional defect will be excused only if the inmate can show that something actually prevented raising that issue and can prove that the claimed defect made a difference in the outcome of the verdict or sentence."[27] This decision will have the effect of reducing the number of habeas corpus appeals to the federal courts. A writ of **habeas corpus** calls on the custodian of any person detained to produce the body of the prisoner at a designated time and place, to do, to submit to, and receive whatever the court shall consider in that behalf. Prisoners on death row argue in such a writ that their detention as condemned persons is based on some error in the administration of the law.

On 22 February 1994, Supreme Court Justice Harry A. Blackmun used the Supreme Court's denial of an appeal by Bruce Edwin Callins, a Texas death row inmate, to explain why he would forever be opposed to the death penalty (see Outside the Walls 17.3). In his dissent, Justice Blackmun protested what he considered to be the arbitrariness with which the death penalty is imposed.

outside the walls   17.3

Justice Harry A. Blackmun's Pronouncement on the Death Penalty

From this day forward, I no longer shall tinker with the machinery of death. For more than 20 years I have endeavored—indeed, I have struggled—along with a majority of this Court, to develop procedural and substantive rules that would lend more than the mere appearance of fairness to the death penalty endeavor. Rather than continue to coddle the Court's delusion that the desired level of fairness has been achieved and the need for regulation eviscerated, I feel morally and intellectually obligated simply to concede that the death penalty experiment has failed. It is virtually self-evident to me now that no combination of procedural rules or substantive regulations ever can save the death penalty from its inherent constitutional deficiencies. The basic question—does the system accurately and consistently determine which defendants "deserve" to die?—cannot be answered in the affirmative. . . . The problem is that the inevitability of factual, legal, and moral error gives us a system that we know must wrongly kill some defendants, a system that fails to deliver the fair, consistent, and reliable sentences of death required by the Constitution.

It is the decision to sentence a defendant to death—not merely the decision to make a defendant eligible for death—that may not be arbitrary. While one might hope that providing the sentencer with as much relevant mitigating evidence as possible will lead to more rational

> . . . I feel morally and intellectually obligated simply to concede that the death penalty experiment has failed.

and consistent sentences, experience has taught otherwise. It seems that the decision whether a human being should live or die is so inherently subjective—rife with all of life's understandings, experiences, prejudices, and passion—that it inevitably defies the rationality and consistency required by the Constitution.

Perhaps one day this Court will develop procedural rules or verbal formulas that actually will provide consistency, fairness, and reliability in a capital-sentencing scheme. I am not optimistic that such a day will come. I am more optimistic, though, that this Court eventually will conclude that the effort to eliminate arbitrariness while preserving fairness "in the infliction of [death] is so plainly doomed to failure that it—and the death penalty—must abandoned together. . . ."
I may not live to see the day, but I have faith that eventually it will arrive. The path the Court has chosen lessens us all. I dissent.

CRITICAL THINKING QUESTIONS

Do you think that the death penalty is as arbitrary as Justice Blackmun believes it to be? Do you believe that the U.S. Supreme Court eventually will abandon the death penalty? Why or why not?

Source: Reprinted from *Callins v. Collins,* 510 U.S. 1141 (1994).

Execution of Mentally Ill Persons

According to Amnesty International, an organization dedicated to avoiding human rights violations, since 1983 over sixty inmates diagnosed with mental illness or mental impairment have been executed in U.S. prisons. Amnesty International argues that executing these inmates who cannot understand the nature of or reason for their punishment serves no deterrent or retributive purpose. In addition, common law has traditionally maintained that persons with mental illness may be incapable of pursuing available appeals or preparing themselves, in keeping with humanitarian or religious principles, for death.[28]

In 1986, in *Ford v. Wainwright,* the Supreme Court heard the case of a person who became mentally deficient after receiving a death sentence.[29] In prison, Ford began to exhibit extremely delusional behavior. He claimed that the Ku Klux Klan was part of a conspiracy forcing him to commit suicide and that his female relatives were being tortured and sexually abused elsewhere in the prison.

Writing for the majority, Justice Thurgood Marshall, ruled that the Eighth Amendment prohibits the state from executing persons with mental illness because the accused person must understand that he or she has been sentenced to death and the reasoning behind this decision. Marshall found the alternative offensive to humanity.[30]

In Arkansas in 1991 this issue arose again. Rickey Ray Rector had killed a police officer and another citizen and then shot himself in the temple, lifting three inches off his brain and leaving himself with the competence of a small child. Rector was convicted at trial and given the death penalty. In prison, he howled day and night, jumping around and giving no indication that he realized he was on death row and would be executed. The Supreme Court rejected his appeal, and Governor Bill Clinton refused to halt his execution, which took place on 24 January 1991.[31]

Christopher Burger was another mentally ill person who was executed. Burger and an accomplice were convicted of murdering a man in 1977. Burger was diagnosed as schizophrenic, suffering from organic brain impairment, and having severe trauma to the central nervous system. These factors were not presented at Burger's sentencing hearing. In 1993, when the state of Georgia electrocuted him at age 33, he had the intellectual capacity of a 12-year-old.[32]

Execution of Mentally Impaired Persons

Amnesty International contends that humanitarian standards require that people with mental impairment not be subjected to the death penalty. Amnesty International cites a 1988 recommendation by the United Nations Committee on Crime Prevention and Control that "persons suffering from mental retardation or extremely limited mental competence should not be executed for their acts." In 1989, the United Nations Economic and Social Council adapted a similar resolution.[33]

In *Penry v. Lynch* (1989), Penry had been convicted of rape and murder by a Texas court. On psychological examination he was found to have an IQ of 54 and a mental age of 6. The Supreme Court ruled in 1989 that his death sentence was unconstitutional because Texas law did not permit jurors to take into account such factors as retardation and child abuse when deliberating in a capital case.[34] Penry was eventually retried by a Texas court and again given the death penalty. On Monday, 4 June 2001, the Supreme Court ruled that the judge's instructions to the jury were still inadequate and that Penry is entitled to a new sentencing hearing.[35]

On 16 August 2000, John Satterwhite, a 53-year-old who had been diagnosed as having both mental impairment and paranoid schizophrenia, died by lethal injection by the state of Texas. Satterwhite had been sentenced to death for the 1979 murder of Mary Francis Davis during the robbery of a shop in San Antonio.[36]

Execution of Juveniles

One disadvantage of juveniles being waived to adult court is that they are eligible to stand trial for murder and be convicted of a capital offense. According to Victor L. Streib, the United States has put approximately 350 juveniles to death since the seventeenth century. These juveniles account for 1.8 percent of the 19,000 executions carried out in the United States since that time. The first juvenile execution occurred in 1642 in Plymouth Colony, Massachusetts, when 16-year-old Thomas Graunger was put to death for sodomizing a horse and a cow.[37] Amnesty International and the United Nations General Assembly are among the many organizations that have expressed their strong disapproval of the juvenile death penalty.

Of the thirty-eight states that permit capital punishment, twenty-four allow it for individuals who were under the age of 18 when they committed the crime (see

Table 17.4

Minimum Death Penalty Ages by American Jurisdiction

Age 18	Age 17	Age 16
California*	Georgia*	Alabama*
Colorado*	New Hampshire*	Arizona**
Connecticut*	North Carolina*	Arkansas**
Illinois*	Texas*	Delaware**
Kansas*	————	Florida***
Maryland*		Idaho**
Nebraska*	4 states	Indiana*
New Jersey*		Kentucky*
New Mexico*		Louisiana*
New York*		Mississippi**
Ohio*		Missouri*
Oregon*		Montana**
Tennessee*		Nevada*
Washington*		Oklahoma*
Federal*		Pennsylvania**
————		South Carolina**
		South Dakota**
14 states		Utah**
and federal		Virginia**
		Wyoming*
		————
		20 states

*Express minimum age in statute.
**Minimum age required by U.S. Constitution per U.S. Supreme Court in *Thompson v. Oklahoma*, 487 U.S. 815 (1988).
***Minimum age required by Florida Constitution per Florida Supreme Court in *Allen v. State*, 636 So.2d 494 (Fla 1994).
[Thirteen American jurisdictions without the death penalty: Alaska, District of Columbia, Hawaii, Iowa, Maine, Massachusetts, Michigan, Minnesota, North Dakota, Rhode Island, Vermont, West Virginia, and Wisconsin]

Source: Victor L. Streib, "Moratorium on the Death Penalty for Juveniles," *Law and Contemporary Problems* 61 (1998), p. 63.

Table 17.4). Since 1973, 172 juvenile death sentences have been imposed—2.7 of the total of almost 6,300 death sentences imposed on offenders of all ages. No death sentences have been imposed on offenders age 14 or younger at the time of their crimes, one-third have been imposed on offenders ages 15 and 16, and over two-thirds have been imposed on 17-year-old offenders.[38]

Of the 172 juvenile death sentences, only 69 (40 percent) remain in force. Ninety-eighty percent of the juveniles sentenced to death have been males. Four female juveniles were sentenced—in Alabama, Georgia, Indiana, and Mississippi. The 172 juvenile death sentences have been imposed in twenty-two states. Texas and Florida each have imposed twice as many as any other jurisdiction. Five states have imposed ten or more such sentences. Up until the execution of Gary Graham, who allegedly committed his crime at age 17, eleven death penalty cases had resulted in execution, and ninety-two had been reversed. The eleven executions (now twelve with Graham) resulting from juvenile death sentences translate into an execution rate of 6.4 percent.[39] Table 17.5 lists the executions of juvenile offenders from 1 January 1973 through 1 June 1998.

Table 17.5

Executions of Juvenile Offenders from 1 January 1973 through 1 June 1998

Name	Date of Execution	Place of Execution	Race	Age at Crime	Age at Execution
Charles Rumbaugh	9–11–1985	Texas	White	17	28
J. Terry Roach	1–10–1986	South Carolina	White	17	25
Jay Pinkerton	5–15–1986	Texas	White	17	24
Dalton Prejean	5–18–1990	Louisiana	Black	17	30
Johnny Garrett	2–11–1992	Texas	White	17	28
Curtis Harris	7–1–1993	Texas	Black	17	31
Frederick Lashley	7–28–1993	Missouri	Black	17	29
Ruben Cantu	8–24–1993	Texas	Latino	17	26
Chris Burger	12–7–1993	Georgia	White	17	33
Joseph John Cannon	4–22–1998	Texas	White	17	38
Robert A. Carter	5–18–1998	Texas	Black	17	34

Source: Victor L. Streib, "Moratorium on the Death Penalty for Juveniles," *Law and Contemporary Problems* 61 (1998), p. 66.

In 1982, in *Eddings v. Oklahoma,* the Supreme Court was able to avoid directly addressing the constitutionality of the juvenile death penalty by ruling that "the chronological age of a minor is itself a relevant mitigating factor of great weight."[40] Monty Lee Eddings was 16 when he shot and killed an Oklahoma State Highway Patrol officer; his execution sentence was reversed in 1982 because of his age.[41] Then, in 1988, the Supreme Court heard the case of **Thompson v. Oklahoma.**[42] Wayne Thompson was 15 when he was arrested along with his half brother—then age 27—for the shooting and stabbing to death of Charles Keene, Thompson's former brother-in-law. The Court ruled by a 5-to-3 vote that "the Eighth and Fourteenth Amendments prohibit the execution of a person who was under sixteen years of age at the time of his or her offense."[43]

In **Stanford v. Kentucky** (1989), the question had to do with the eligibility of a murderer for execution when the crime was committed while he was a minor.[44] Stanford was 17 years and 4 months old when he was sentenced to death. Writing for a divided court, Justice Antonin Scalia ruled that inasmuch as common law prescribed 14 as the minimum age for execution, the sentence of a 17-year-old did not violate the Eighth Amendment proscription against "cruel and unusual punishment."[45]

In the related case of *Wilkins v. Missouri* (1989), the defendant, Wilkins, was 16 years and 6 months old when he killed a woman clerk at a convenience store he was robbing.[46] He was arrested, pled guilty, and declined counsel. He wanted to be executed, saying that he feared life imprisonment more than death. The Supreme Court heard his case because of his age and his apparent mental disturbance. Writing for a 5-to-4 majority, Justice Scalia rejected the argument that Wilkins's age disqualified him for execution and pointed out that the question of his mental disturbance had been duly considered in court and could not be raised on appeal.[47]

WHAT ARE THE ARGUMENTS FAVORING THE DEATH PENALTY?

Defenders of the death penalty make several arguments supporting their position. They claim that this punishment is a deterrent to murder. They assert that individuals who commit heinous crimes deserve the death penalty and that in too many cases life imprisonment does not protect society because of parole eligibility.

Deterrent Value

Supporters have long justified the death penalty by claiming that it has deterrent value. They contend that crime is a rational process and that it stands to reason that the possibility of a death sentence will deter some individuals who are contemplating murder.[48]

A prolific defender of the death penalty is Ernest van den Haag, a professor of social philosophy and jurisprudence who expressed views about crime and punishment in his book *Punishing Criminals: Concerning a Very Old and Painful Question*,[49] in articles for law reviews and philosophical journals, and in a series of debates with John P. Conrad.[50] Van den Haag is certain that common sense supports the deterrent effect of capital punishment:

> Our experience shows that the greater the threatened penalty, the more it deters. . . . [T]he threat of fifty lashes deters more than the threat of five. . . . [T]en years in prison deter more than one year in prison. . . . [T]he threat of life in prison deters more than any other term of imprisonment.
>
>   The threat of death may deter even more. . . . [D]eath differs significantly, in kind, from any other penalty.[51]

Capital punishment also gained substantial support from the publication of an article by economist Isaac Ehrlich showing that the deterrence effect of the death penalty was far from negligible or nonexistent.[52] Using the complex statistical methodology of regression analysis, Ehrlich arrived at the conclusion that every execution deters eight homicides. His article was the first empirical study showing that capital punishment might be a very substantial deterrent.[53] The U.S. solicitor general cited it to the Supreme Court to show that capital punishment was an effective deterrent.[54] Even though Ehrlich's fellow economists, as well as sociologists, challenged his study on many counts, Ehrlich continues to be cited by those who claim deterrence in the death penalty.

Retribution for Brutal Crimes

Supporters of the death penalty maintain that fairness dictates that cold-blooded killers pay for their crimes with their own lives. In Outside the Walls 17.4, the political scientist Walter Berns draws on humanity's anger against Nazi war criminals to justify capital punishment as retribution. Van den Haag also adopts a retributivist position when he says, "To refuse to punish any crime with death, then, is to avow that the negative weight of a crime can never exceed the positive value of the life of the person who committed it. I find that proposition implausible."[55]

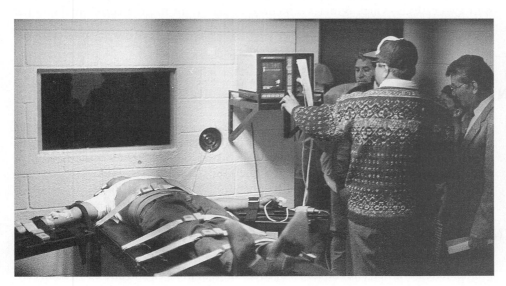

Is lethal injection more humane than electrocution? For what other reasons are methods of execution a concern? To what extent do methods of execution serve as deterrents against capital crimes? Does the system have enough safeguards against executing individuals who are innocent of the crimes for which they are being executed? How has technological change challenged capital punishment in the United States?

outside the walls   17.4

Walter Berns on the Need for Revenge

I . . . reflect on the work of Simon Wiesenthal, who has devoted himself exclusively since 1945 to the task of hunting down the Nazis who survived the war and escaped into the world. . . . What did he hope to accomplish by finding them? . . . Punish them, of course. But why? To rehabilitate them? The very idea is absurd. To incapacitate them? But they present no present danger. To deter others from doing what they did? That is a hope too extravagant to be indulged. The answer—to me and, I suspect, everyone else who agrees that they should be punished—was clear: to pay them back. And how do you pay back SS Obersturmbann-fuhrer Franz Stangl, SS Untersturmfuhrer Wilhelm Rosenbaum, SS Obersturmbannfuhrer Adolf Eichmann,

> . . . Eichmann was executed, and . . . this was the only way he could be paid back.

or someday—who knows?—Reichsleiter Martin Bormann? As the world knows, Eichmann was executed, and I suspect that most of the decent, civilized world agrees that this was the only way he could be paid back.

CRITICAL THINKING QUESTIONS

Are there crimes so monstrous that the perpetrators deserve death even if other criminals do not? If so, what are these crimes against humanity?

Source: Reprinted from Walter Berns, *For Capital Punishment* (New York: Basic Books, 1979), p. 8.

Life Imprisonment Does Not Protect Society

Defenders of the death penalty charge that life imprisonment does not protect society, because prisoners who have committed murder are usually eligible for parole after thirteen or fourteen years. It is rare, they add, for a murderer to remain in prison for the remainder of his or her life. Thus, the person who has already victimized society once by taking a life probably will have an opportunity to do so again. And, say these advocates, a murderer who receives a sentence of life without parole still has the opportunity to hurt or even kill again—during incarceration.

This argument supporting the death penalty is compelling. Murders by inmates occasionally do take place in U.S. prisons; it is not that unusual for a person sentenced to prison for murder to commit another murder in prison. In 1999, in Ohio prisons, there were two cases in which inmates sentenced to prison for murder committed another murder in prison.[56]

WHAT ARE THE ARGUMENTS OPPOSING THE DEATH PENALTY?

Contemporary opposition to capital punishment is generally based on beliefs about the immoral nature of state-administered homicide, and on pragmatic criticisms. Moralists who reject the death penalty as a response even to murder hold that it is state-administered homicide.[57] Leaving aside the moral question, all of which boil down to questions of right and wrong, supporters are left with the difficulties of administering the death penalty under the conditions required by the Constitution and public opinion.

Immoral Nature of State-Administered Homicides

In killing the criminal, opponents of capital punishment charge, the state engages in premeditated murder, and the solemn proceedings of prosecution and conviction cannot disguise it as anything else. Opponents hold that the lesson that killing people is wrong cannot be taught by killing people, even murderers. Instead, the punishment of criminals must be limited to confinement, not harming or destroying their bodies.

The American Civil Liberty Union, in formulating its objections to the death penalty, suggests that "capital punishment is cruel and unusual. It is cruel because it is a relic of the earliest days of penology, when slavery, branding, and other corporal punishments were commonplace." The ACLU adds that "a society that respects life does not deliberately kill human beings."[58]

Nearly everyone agrees that the death penalty is cruel when an innocent person is put to death. One study found that since 1900, on average, four innocent people each year have been convicted of murder. This study documented twenty-three cases in which individuals wrongly accused were executed.[59] A report by the House Subcommittee on Civil and Constitutional Rights in October 1993 listed forty-eight inmates who had been freed from death row since 1972. The report concluded: "Judging by past experience, a substantial number of death row inmates are indeed innocent, and there is a high risk that some of them will be executed."[60] Research done for a *Newsweek* article in June 2000 turned up eighty-seven who had been freed from death row by DNA and other evidence.[61]

Furthermore, opponents of the death penalty have always made the point that the majority of men and women executed have been African American or Hispanic, despite all the precautions against prejudice that have been built into the judicial process. A General Accounting Office review of the literature of racial discrimination in sentencing turned up twenty-eight statistical studies of the topic. Of these studies, 82 percent showed that the race of the victim determined the decision to sentence the convicted defendant to death. Individuals who murdered whites were more likely to be sentenced to death than those who murdered African Americans.[62]

Pragmatic Criticisms

Several pragmatic criticisms are made of the death penalty. One has to do with the deficiencies of the fallible human institutions that make up the criminal justice system. The police may have used illegal methods to obtain evidence. A confession may have been induced without cautioning the arrested person about the right to remain silent. A search may have been conducted without a proper warrant. There may have been a mistake in identifying the person responsible for the murder. The police may have overlooked or withheld important evidence.

Once a case is in the hands of a prosecutor, more mistakes may be made. The evidence against the defendant may not have been disclosed to the defense attorney in time to prepare for rebuttal. The defense lawyer may have been incompetent or negligent. Inflammatory or misleading statements may have been made in the presence of the jury. The pool of jurors may not have represented all elements of the community in which the crime was committed. The judge may have erred in discussing the evidence against the defendant, or by minimizing the evidence in his or her favor. The application of the law defining first-degree murder to the facts in the case may have been incorrectly interpreted to the jury. When all the possible sources of error are considered, it is no wonder that so many inmates have been freed from death row because of problems or errors in the legal process or that DNA testing has occasionally shown that someone else committed the crime.

Opponents of the death penalty also denounce capital punishment as failing to deter capital crimes. Capital punishment is not a deterrent, according to this position, for three basic reasons. First, "a punishment can be an effective deterrent only if it is consistently and promptly employed," and the administration of capital punishment does not meet these conditions. Another reason is that "most capital crimes are committed in the heat of the moment" and are not acts of premeditation. Finally, if severe punishment can deter crime, it is reasonable to assume that "long-term imprisonment is severe enough to deter any rational person from committing a violent crime."[63]

A final pragmatic argument made by those who wish to abolish the death penalty is that capital punishment costs more than incarceration. It is impossible to arrive at an estimate of the costs of capital punishment litigation. Some famous cases have incurred

h e r o e s | *Sister Helen Prejean*

Spiritual Adviser to Death Row Inmates

Sister Helen talked about the fundamental unfairness of capital punishment: "The death penalty is a symbol that is riddled with race and class. . . . You never find a rich person on death row." She added that the racial injustice of the death penalty is that more value is placed on a white life than on the life of an African American. Those minorities who have been executed are those who have killed whites. Another fatal flaw concerning the fairness of the death penalty is that innocent people are put to death. Indeed, she noted that "within recent months 82 innocent people came off death row."

Sister Helen talked about how difficult it is for those whose loved ones have been murdered. Even if the murderer is found and convicted, years will pass before his or her execution takes place. She acknowledged that wanting revenge is a normal process but reminded her listeners that there is no way to exact enough revenge to satisfy the loss that victims have experienced. She quoted the father of one victim, who, after the execution, remarked to the press, "You know he died too quick." Instead of a vengeful spirit, she urged that victims must somehow come to the point of forgiveness if they are to get on with their lives.

In the final part of her lecture Sister Helen dealt with the role of the state and its citizens in capital punishment. She challenged the United States to uphold human rights and to become a moral leader of the world. According to Prejean, "it is sad that we're one of five countries of the world to kill juveniles and mentally retarded." She reported that increasing numbers of politicians are against capital punishment, but, as one member of a legislature reported to her, "I am against capital punishment, but you can't get reelected without voting for it." She closed her lecture by saying that Illinois, Kentucky, and Nebraska now have moratoriums on the death penalty. She urged her listeners to put their names on a petition for a death penalty moratorium as they left the auditorium.

CRITICAL THINKING QUESTIONS

Sister Helen sees a rising tide of opinion against the death penalty. Is she correct? Do you agree with her that unless a victim's family forgives the murderer of their loved one they will be unable to move on with their lives?

costs ranging in the millions of dollars. The Kansas legislature voted against reinstating the death penalty in 1988 when it was informed that reintroduction would involve a first-year cost of "more than $11 million."[64] Texas is spending an average of $2.3 million on each execution; lifetime imprisonment costs range from $800,000 to $1 million. With one of the nation's most populous death rows, Florida has estimated that the true cost of each execution is approximately $3.2 million, "approximately six times the cost of a life-imprisonment sentence."[65]

Sister Helen Prejean was the spiritual adviser of Patrick Sonnier, the convicted killer of two adolescents who was sentenced to die in the electric chair of the Angola State Prison in Louisiana. She walked with him to the electric chair and was spiritual adviser to four other inmates subsequently executed by the state. She has come to know the families of victims as well as those who carry out the orders of execution. The movie *Dead Man Walking*, starring Susan Sarandon and Sean Penn, is a film adaptation of the book she wrote about her experiences. She is the hero in this chapter. The Heroes box contains some comments taken from a lecture she gave at the University of Northern Iowa in November 1999.

SUMMARY

Individuals have been executed for their crimes since the beginning of recorded history. In more recent history, the state has assumed responsibility for executing criminals. In the late nineteenth and early twentieth centuries, executions took place not in public but within the walls of state institutions.

In the twentieth century, public opinion varied on the use of the death penalty. In the past couple decades, with 60 to 70 percent of the population of the United States in support, the use of the death penalty occurred more frequently, especially in southern states. Lethal injection has become the predominant method of execution; thirty-four states have adopted it.

The death penalty, which has a culture of its own, is receiving increased support from the U.S. Supreme Court. But as we begin a new century, because of the increasing numbers of individuals being released from their death sentence because of DNA testimony and other errors during the legal process, public opinion has slowly started to change. Due to increased concern about putting the innocent to death, a few states with death penalty statutes decided to have a moratorium on capital punishment. Whether this uneasiness will grow and affect the numbers being placed on death row will be seen in the years to come.

KEY TERMS

Eighth Amendment, p. 411
Fourteenth Amendment, p. 412
Furman v. Georgia, p. 412
Gregg v. Georgia, p. 413

habeas corpus, p. 414
McCleskey v. Kemp, p. 413
Stanford v. Kentucky, p. 418
Thompson v. Oklahoma, p. 418

CRITICAL THINKING QUESTIONS

1. Is Sir James Fitzjames Stephen correct? Do we need the death penalty to satisfy our need for revenge? Is it possible for society to give up the death penalty?
2. What is the purpose of taking the life of a person who is mentally ill or mentally impaired and is not aware of what is taking place? Is there some more appropriate punishment for such a person?
3. Is it as scandalous as some make it out to be to execute inmates who committed capital crime when they were juveniles? What does it say about U.S. society that the United States is one of very few countries to execute persons who committed crimes as juveniles?
4. What do you think is the most persuasive argument for the death penalty?
5. What do you think is the most persuasive argument against the death penalty?
6. What does the recent stance of the U.S. Supreme Court suggest will be the future of the death penalty in this nation?

WEB DESTINATIONS

Yahoo's comprehensive news coverage on the death penalty includes current and archived stories and photos in news media nationwide.
http://fullcoverage.yahoo.com/fc/US/Death_Penalty

The University of Alaska's comprehensive information site on death rows in the United States. Includes history, U.S. Supreme Court cases, statistics, the international context, and both sides of the death penalty debate.
http://www.uaa.alaska.edu/just/death/deathrow.html

Texas Department of Criminal Justice: Death Row Statistics. Includes names of Texas death row inmates and schedules of execution.
http://www.tdcj.state.tx.us/statistics/stats-home.htm

American Civil Liberties Union Death Penalty Page. Includes summaries and analysis of ethical, legal, and political issues relating to capital punishment.
http://www.aclu.org/issues/death/hmdp.html

Frontline: The Execution. A documentary that examines in depth the 1998 execution of Clifford Boggess and evaluates the use of the death penalty in the United States.
http://www.pbs.org/wgbh/pages/frontline/shows/execution/

FOR FURTHER READING

Bedau, Hugo Adam, ed. *The Death Penalty in America.* 3d ed. New York: Oxford University Press, 1982. Bedau is a convinced and consistent abolitionist, but in this collection he scrupulously includes articles by articulate retentionists such as Walter Berns and Ernest van den Haag, as well as abolitionist articles by Anthony Amsterdam, Charles Black, and Hans Zeisel, among others.

Johnson, Robert. *Death Work: A Study of the Modern Execution Process.* 2d ed. Pacific Grove, Calif.: Brooks/Cole, 1998. Johnson has compiled an account of the actual processes of execution in the United States, together with its effects on executioners, witnesses, and the men and women executed.

Marquart, James W., Sheldon Ekland-Olson, and Jonathan R. Sorensen. *The Rope, the Chair, and the Needle: Capital Punishment in Texas, 1923–1990.* Austin: University of Texas Press, 1994. Marquart and colleagues' examination of the relationship among culture, inclusion, and the death penalty in Texas addresses why the South has such high rates of execution.

Prejean, Helen. *Dead Man Walking.* New York: Random House, 1993. Sister Helen, in her book and as portrayed in the movie, presents an emotional and insightful glimpse into the minds of death penalty prisoners, their families, and the victims of their crimes.

Van den Haag, Ernest, and John P. Conrad. *The Death Penalty: A Debate.* New York: Plenum Press, 1983. An extended exchange of views between an uncompromising supporter and an equally uncompromising opponent of the death penalty. Most of the significant policy and scholarly issues are examined vigorously.

NOTES

1. Statement from a brochure of the American Civil Liberties Union, Webpage, 2000.
2. "Illinois Suspends Death Penalty," 31 January 2000, para. 5, http://www.cnn.com.
3. Dagobert D. Runes, ed., *The Selected Writings of Benjamin Rush* (New York: Philosophical Library, 1947).
4. Philip English Mackey, ed., *Voices against Death* (New York: Burt Franklin, 1976), pp. 14–33.
5. Sir James Fitzjames Stephen, "Capital Punishment," *Frazer's Magazine* (1864), quoted in Franklin E. Zimring and Gordon Hawkins, *Capital Punishment and the American Agenda* (Cambridge, England: Cambridge University Press, 1986), p. 159.
6. Sir James Fitzjames Stephen, *A General View of the Criminal Law of England* (London: Macmillan, 1963), p. 99.
7. Jonathan Alter, "The Death Penalty on Trial," *Newsweek,* 12 June 2000, p. 26. Mark Gillespie, "Public Opinion Supports Death Penalty," 24 February 1999. The Gallup Organization Webpage, http://www.gallup.com.
8. Mark Costanzo, *Just Revenge* (New York: St. Martin's Press, 1997), pp. 123–128. See also Gillespie, "Public Opinion Supports Death Penalty."
9. Ibid., p. 124.
10. Michael L. Radelet, Hugo Adam Bedau, and Constance E. Putnam, *In Spite of Innocence: Erroneous Convictions in Capital Cases* (Boston: Northeastern University Press, 1992).
11. Bureau of Justice Statistics Bulletin, *Capital Punishment 1999* (Washington, D.C.: U.S. Department of Justice, 2000) p. 1.
12. Ibid., pp. 8–9.
13. Ibid., p. 12.
14. David C. Baldus, Charles A. Pulaski Jr., and George Woodworth, "Arbitrariness and Discrimination in the Administration of the Death Penalty: A Challenge to State Supreme Courts," *Stetson Law Review* 15, no. 2 (Spring 1986), pp. 146–149.
15. Lawrence M. Friedman, *Crime and Punishment in American History* (New York: Basic Books, 1993), p. 316.
16. *Furman v. Georgia,* 408 U.S. 238 (1972).
17. Friedman, *Crime and Punishment in American History,* p. 316.
18. *Furman v. Georgia.*
19. *Gregg v. Georgia,* 428 U.S. 153 (1976).
20. Ibid.
21. *Barefoot v. Estelle,* 103 S.Ct. 3383 (1983).
22. Ibid.
23. *Pulley v. Harris,* 104 S.Ct. 881 (1984).
24. Ibid.
25. *McCleskey v. Kemp,* 107 S.Ct. 1756 (1987).
26. Ibid.
27. Ibid.
28. Amnesty International, Webpage, 1 September 2000.
29. *Ford v. Wainwright,* 477 U.S. 399 (1986).
30. Ibid.
31. Marshall Frady, "Death in Arkansas," *New York Times,* 23 February 1993, p. 105.
32. Amnesty International, Webpage, 1 September 2000.
33. Ibid.
34. *Penry v. Lynch,* 45 Cr.L.Rptr. 3188 (1989).
35. Thomas Healy, "Retarded Man's Death Sentence Overturned," *The Des Moines Register,* 5 June 2001, p. 4 A.
36. Amnesty International, Webpage, 1 September 2000.
37. Victor L. Streib, "Moratorium on the Death Penalty for Juveniles," *Law and Contemporary Problems* 61 (1998).
38. Ibid.
39. Ibid.
40. *Eddings v. Oklahoma,* 102 S.Ct. (1982).
41. Ibid.
42. *Thompson v. Oklahoma,* 102 S.Ct. (1982).

43. Ibid.

44. *Stanford v. Kentucky,* 109 S.Ct. 2969 (1989).

45. Ibid.

46. *Wilkins v. Missouri,* 109 S.Ct. 2969 (1989).

47. Ibid.

48. James Q. Wilson, *Thinking about Crime,* rev. ed. (New York: Basic Books, 1963).

49. Ernest van den Haag, *Punishing Criminals: Concerning a Very Old and Painful Question* (New York: Basic Books, 1975).

50. Ernest van den Haag and John P. Conrad, *The Death Penalty: A Debate* (New York: Plenum Press, 1983).

51. Ibid., p. 68.

52. Isaac Ehrlich, "The Deterrent Effect of Capital Punishment: A Question of Life and Death," *American Economic Review* 65 (1975), p. 397. This article was followed by more elaborate studies focusing on capital punishment. For a full bibliography of Ehrlich's numerous articles defending his methodology and the articles of others supporting him and opposing him, see Deryck Beyleveid, "Ehrlich's Analysis of Deterrence," *British Journal of Criminology* 22 (April 1982), pp. 101–123.

53. *Fowler v. North Carolina,* 428 U.S. 904 (1976).

54. Ibid.

55. Ernest van den Haag, "In Defense of the Death Penalty: A Practical and Moral Analysis," in *The Death Penalty in America,* 3d ed., ed. Hugo Adam Bedau (New York: Oxford University Press, 1982), pp. 332–333.

56. The author served as an expert witness in these cases.

57. Keep in mind that supporters of the death penalty also claim that their arguments are based on profoundly moral considerations. This chapter aims to summarize the opposing views impartially.

58. National Coalition to Abolish the Death Penalty, Webpage, 24 June 2000, pp. 2–3.

59. Radelet, Bedau, and Putnam, *In Spite of Innocence.*

60. Amnesty International, Webpage, 1 September 2000.

61. Alter, "The Death Penalty on Trial," p. 25.

62. U.S. General Accounting Office, *Death Penalty Sentencing* (Washington, D.C., U.S. Government Printing Office, February 1990). However, the federal courts have rejected discrimination as grounds for reversal of the sentence of death. See *McCleskey v. Kemp,* 753 E.2d 877 (1989).

63. Bedau, *The Case against the Death Penalty* (Wye-Mill, Md.: American Civil Liberties Union, 1997) pp. 4–5.

64. Cited ibid., p. 13.

65. Amnesty International, Webpage, 1 September 2000.

Multiple Choice Questions

1. During the late 1970s and 1980s, what trend influenced public opinion about the death penalty?

   A. Increase in violent street crime
   B. Increase in violent corporate crime
   C. Increase in juvenile delinquency
   D. Increase in lethal injection

2. According to the text, as of 31 December 1999, how many prisoners were under a sentence of death in the thirty-seven states and the Federal Bureau of Prisons?

   A. More than 3,000
   B. More than 3,500
   C. More than 4,000
   D. More than 4,500

3. How many states have death penalty statutes?

   A. 34
   B. 36
   C. 37
   D. 38

4. What has been the most frequently used method of execution used since 31 December 1998?

   A. Electric chair
   B. Lethal injection
   C. Gas chamber
   D. Firing squad

5. According to Victor L. Streib, how many juveniles have been executed since the seventeenth century?

   A. 250
   B. 350
   C. 450
   D. 550

6. What type of legal document do prisoners on death row use to argue that their detention is based on some error in the administration of the law?

   A. Writ of habeas corpus
   B. Writ of certuria
   C. Writ of amicus curiae
   D. Writ of justina

7. Identify the U.S. Supreme Court Case that concluded that the Eighth Amendment forbids the state from executing the mentally ill.

   A. *Penry v. Lenough*
   B. *Stanford v. Oklahoma*
   C. *Ford v. Wainwright*
   D. *Breed v. Jones*

8. The legitimacy of capital punishment depends upon the interpretation of what two constitutional amendments?

   A. Eighth and First
   B. First and Fourteenth
   C. Fifth and Fourteenth
   D. Eighth and Fourteenth

9. What percentage of inmates who have been sentenced to death are African Americans?

   A. 33%
   B. 43%
   C. 53%
   D. 63%

10. What 1992 U.S. Supreme Court case ruled, "the chronological age of a minor is itself a relevant mitigating factor of great weight."

    A. *Eddings v. Oklahoma*
    B. *Breed v. Oklahoma*
    C. *Stanford v. Oklahoma*
    D. *Wilkins v. Missouri*

True/False Questions

T F   1. Public opinion is a driving force that supports capital punishment.

T F   2. The average inmate under a sentence of death has at least a high school diploma.

T F   3. There is some evidence that suggests when the public is presented with the alternative of life imprisonment without parole, there is less support for the death penalty.

T F   4. According to Radelet, Bedau, and Putnam's death penalty study, there have been twenty-three cases in the twentieth century in which the defendant has been wrongly accused and executed.

T F   5. Since 1973, offenders who have been age 14 at the time of their crime have been eligible to be executed.

T F   6. Defenders of the death penalty further charge that life imprisonment does not protect society because prisoners who have committed murder are usually eligible for parole after thirteen or fourteen years.

T F   7. Political support is a driving force that supports capital punishment.

T F   8. The decision in *McCleskey v. Kemp* prevents the state from executing the mentally ill.

T F   9. According to the Baldus study, the combination of a white defendant and minority victim results in a disproportionate amount of executions.

T F   10. *Furman v. Georgia* ruled that the death penalty violates the Eighth Amendment's cruel and unusual punishment clause no matter how it is administered.

Fill-in-the-Blank Questions

(based on key terms)

1. The U.S. Supreme Court ruled in _____ that the sentence of a 17-year-old did not violate the Eighth Amendment's proscription against cruel and unusual punishment.

2. The U.S. Supreme Court decision in _____ used the equal protection of laws clause found in the Fourteenth Amendment to abolish death penalty statues in every state.

3. _____ ruled that the death penalty is constitutional as long as there are guidelines to decide upon the sentence of the death penalty.

4. _____ ruled that the Eighth and Fourteenth Amendments prohibit the execution of a person who was under 16 years of age at the time of his or her offense.

Essay Questions

1. Identify and explain three perspectives used to examine capital punishment.

2. Describe the history of capital punishment in the United States.

3. What were the results of the United States Supreme Court decisions in *Furman v. Georgia, Gregg v. Georgia, Ford v. Wainwright,* and *McCloskey v. Kemp?* How did the results from these landmark cases influence capital punishment?

4. Describe the demographic characteristics of the inmate population sentenced to death in this country.

5. Identify and describe two arguments supporting and two arguments opposing capital punishment in this country.

ANSWERS

Multiple Choice Questions

1.	A	6.	A
2.	B	7.	C
3.	D	8.	D
4.	B	9.	B
5.	B	10.	A

True/False Questions

1.	T	6.	T
2.	F	7.	T
3.	T	8.	F
4.	T	9.	F
5.	F	10.	F

Fill-in-the-Blank Questions

1. *Stanford v. Kentucky*
2. *Furman v. Georgia*
3. *Gregg v. Georgia*
4. *Thompson v. Oklahoma*

Incarceration Trends:
Race, Gender, and Class

Who goes to prison is one of the major issues of corrections. Do incarceration rates reflect criminal behaviors or discriminatory actions by the criminal justice system? Mumia Abu-Jamal begins our discussion by telling of an experience on death row in the Huntington Correctional Center in Pennsylvania.

> Long-termers on the row, those here since 1984, recall a small but seemingly significant event that took place back then. Maintenance and construction staff, forced by a state court order and state statute to provide men with a minimum of two hours daily outside exercise, rather than the customary fifteen minutes every other day, erected a number of steel, cyclone-fenced boxes, which strikingly resemble dog runs or pet pens. Although staff assured inmates that the pens would be used only for disciplinary cases, the construction ended and the assurances were put to the test. The first day after completion of the cages, death cases, all free of any disciplinary infractions, were marched out to the pens for daily exercise outdoors. Only when the cages were full did full recognition dawn that all the caged men were African.
>
> Where were the white cons of death row?
>
> A few moments of silent observation proved the obvious. The death row block offered direct access to two yards: one composed of cages, the other "free" space, water fountains, full-court basketball spaces and hoops, and an area for running. The cages were for the blacks on death row. The open yards were for the whites on the row. The blacks, due to racial insensitivity and sheer hatred, were condemned to awaiting death in indignity. The event provided an excellent view, in microcosm, of the mentality of the criminal system of injustice, suffused by the toxin of racism.[1]

CRITICAL THINKING QUESTIONS

Do you believe that this is an accurate representation of what took place? To what extent do you think racial injustice of this nature still exists?

Mumia Abu-Jamal, regarded as a political prisoner by his supporters, charges that the overrepresentation of African Americans in prisons and on death row is due to racism.[2] He and others make the case that the disproportionate rates of minority confinement reflect the prevalence of racial profiling by law-enforcement, officers, the unfair sentencing of minority defendants, especially drug offenders, and social policy.[3] Feminist theorists likewise argue that troublesome women are subjected to discrimination, exploitation, and criminalization.[4] These forms of oppression, they add, are expressions of sexism, racism, and classism and are resulting in the imprisonment of females growing at a faster rate than that of males.[5] Imprisonment, according to Jeffrey Reiman, is primarily reserved for the lower-class offender.[6] He and others contend that sentencing policies are unfair. White-collar criminals who do far more social harm than street criminals represent a very small minority of the prison population.

Others challenge these accusations of oppression. To those charging racism, they respond that African Americans are overrepresented in prison because they commit so many violent offenses and serious property crimes. Women, others insist, benefit from the leniency of the system, which reduces rather than increases their incarceration rates. In response to the charge that the crimes of the poor are less likely than the crimes of the rich to be excused, the claim is made that white-collar criminals do not harm and rob citizens as street criminals do.

What is the truth of these conflicting claims? What factors account for incarceration trends in the United States? What roles do race, gender, and class really play?

WHAT IS THE RELATIONSHIP BETWEEN RACE AND INCARCERATION TRENDS?

A serious correctional issue is the disproportionate number of minorities confined in correctional facilities. The skyrocketing growth of the correctional population since the early 1970s has disproportionately affected this population. According to Samuel Walker, Cassia Spohn, and Miriam DeLone, "nearly every problem related to criminal justice issues involves matters of race and ethnicity":

- Half of all prisoners in the United States (49.4 percent in 1996) are African American, despite the fact that blacks represent only 12 percent of the U.S. population. Even more alarming, the incarceration *rate* for African American men is seven times the rate for white men (3,250 per 100,000 compared with 461 per 100,000).
- Hispanics were 17.5 percent of all prisoners in 1996, up from only 10.9 percent in 1995.
- About 40 percent of the people currently on death row and 53 percent of all the people executed since 1930 are African American.[7]

How do these statistics compare with official rates of criminal offending? What else is involved in the overrepresentation of minorities in correctional settings?

Race and Criminal Offending

The argument that African American men and women are more likely than white men and women to commit serious property offenses and violent crimes has strong support.[8] Michael Hindelang's classic analysis of victimization data from a 1970s survey of eight cities found no evidence of bias against African Americans.[9] In his analysis of data from the National Crime Victimization Data, Hindelang found that "by far, most of the arrest percentage appears to be attributable to the substantially greater involvement of blacks than whites in these crimes."[10]

Alfred Blumstein's analysis of racial arrest and imprisonment patterns in the 1980s also concluded that differential involvement in arrests explains a large amount of the racial disproportion in prison populations. Blumstein's analysis revealed that arrests explained 80 percent of the racial disproportion in prison.[11]

Patrick Langan used national victimization data from 1973 to 1982 in an attempt to build on Hindelang's and Blumstein's analyses. His findings offer even less support for claims of wholesale racial discrimination in sentencing than did Blumstein's. According to Langan, the data revealed that the percentage of serious crimes perpetrated by African Americans was essentially stable from 1972 to 1982, which is consistent with arrest data for 1976 to 1982 from the FBI's *Uniform Crime Reports.* He concluded that rather than suggesting that disproportionate imprisonment results from racial bias, the data strongly support differential involvement in crime.[12]

Blumstein's 1993 analysis replicated his earlier study but softened its finding. Blumstein concluded that arrests explained 76 percent of the racial disproportion in prison. He found that the arrest data could explain the high numbers of African Americans who are confined for homicide and robbery. Yet arrest data appeared to have a lower reliability in explaining the disproportionate confinement of African Americans for drugs and other less serious crimes.[13]

Michael Tonry's discussion of racial disproportion in the criminal justice system and criminal behavior identifies two patterns in the arrest data.[14] First, at least since 1976, the proportion of African Americans among persons arrested for offenses has greatly exceeded their 12 to 13 percent presence in the general population.[15] Second, the relative proportions of African Americans and whites among persons arrested for imprisonable crimes have held steady for nearly two decades. Tonry points out that this fact contradicts the idea that there has been a dramatic increase of African Americans among prison admissions and prison and jail populations since the early 1980s.[16]

Hispanics and Native Americans are also overrepresented in federal and state prisons but not to the degree that African American males and females are. Hispanics, who constitute 9 percent of the U.S. population, make up 18 percent of federal and state prisoners. Native Americans constitute less than 0.7 percent of the general population and Asian Americans make up 3.0 percent of the general population but both groups comprise about 1 percent of federal and state inmates.[17] See Figure 18.1 for minority representation in federal and state prison populations.

Nearly everyone agrees that drug offenses demonstrate the greatest disparity in offending rates and incarceration. Although government surveys reveal that drug use cuts across class and racial lines, law-enforcement priorities have been concentrated on

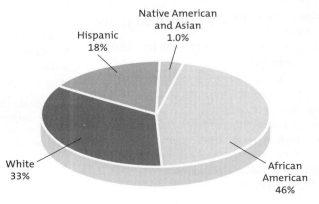

Figure 18.1
Representation of Racial and Ethnic Groups in U.S. Prisons, 1999

Source: Bureau of Justice Statistics, *Prisoners in 1999* (Washington, D.C.: U.S. Department of Justice, 2000), p 9.

Native American and Asian 1.0%

Hispanic 18%

White 33%

African American 46%

inner-city communities where there are large concentrations of African Americans and drug use and selling often occur in "open-air" drug markets. Not surprisingly, African Americans made up 38 percent of all those arrested for drug offenses in 1996 and 58 percent of those incarcerated in state prisons on drug offenses. Within Bureau of Prisons institutions from 1990 to 1996, drug offenses accounted for an even greater share of the increase among African American inmates (82 percent) than for either whites (65 percent) or Hispanics (67 percent).[18]

Federal sentencing guidelines for drug offenses differentiate between crack and powder cocaine. In fact, the guidelines treat crack cocaine as being one hundred times worse than powder cocaine. Possession of 500 grams of powder cocaine, but only 5 grams of crack, results in a mandatory minimum sentence of ten years. Critics charge that this policy, which purports to be racially neutral, actually discriminates against African American drug users, who prefer the less expensive crack cocaine to powder cocaine. Over 90 percent of the offenders sentenced for crack in federal courts are African Americans.[19] See Outside the Walls 18.1.

Race and Differential Processing

The presence of racial discrimination during the processing of minorities in the criminal justice system has been a matter of extensive examination. Studies have mixed findings on whether racial discrimination takes place during arrests of minorities.[20] Few or no reliable data are available that demonstrate systematic discrimination, suggesting that the much higher arrest rate of African Americans for serious crimes is not the re-

outside the walls   18.1

Penalties for Crack and Powder Cocaine

In 1993 Judge Lyle Strom, the chief judge of the U.S. District Court in Nebraska, sentenced four African American crack dealers to significantly shorter prison terms than were called by federal sentencing guidelines. In explanation, Strom wrote in a letter to the *Omaha World Herald*, "Members of the African American race are being treated unfairly in receiving substantially longer sentences than Caucasian males who traditionally deal in powder cocaine."

The Eighth Circuit Court of Appeals overturned Strom's decision in 1994. The three-judge panel ruled that even if the guidelines are unfair to African Americans, that is not reason enough to justify a more lenient sentence than called for by the guidelines. Other federal appellate courts have upheld the hundred-to-one rule, holding that the rule does not violate the equal protection clause of the Fourteenth Amendment (see, for example, *U.S. v. Thomas*, 900 F.2d 37 [4th Cir. 1990]; *U.S. v. Frazier*, 981 F.2d 92 [3rd Cir. 1992]; and *U.S. v. Lattimore*, 974 F.2d 971 [8th Cir. 1992]).

> . . . even if the guidelines are unfair to African Americans, that is not reason enough to justify a more lenient sentence than called for . . .

In May 1994, the U.S. House of Representatives voted 424 to 9 to ask the U.S. Sentencing Commission to develop a proposal for equalizing penalties for the use of crack and powder cocaine. In April 1995, the U.S. Sentencing Commission recommended that the hundred-to-one ratio for crack versus powder cocaine be changed to a one-to-one ratio. By 2001, the movement to equalize crack and powder cocaine was still stalled.

CRITICAL THINKING QUESTIONS

How do you think the hundred-to-one ratio came about? Why did it become part of the federal sentencing guidelines? How do you think other federal judges reacted to Judge Strom's ruling?

Source: Omaha World Herald, 17 April 1993, p. 1. See also Samuel Walker, Cassia Spohn, and Miriam DeLone, *The Color of Justice: Race, Ethnicity, and Crime in America* (Belmont, Calif.: Wadsworth, 1996), p. 159.

What are the various explanations and theories regarding the relationship between race and ethnicity and justice in corrections and at other stages of the criminal justice process? Which explanations do you find most persuasive, and why?

sult of bias. One study found that in cases of assault, race appears to have little effect on the probability of arrest. This study also found that neither does the racial composition of the neighborhood have a significant impact on whether police make an arrest.[21]

Coramae Richey Mann claims that racial differences at early stages of the criminal justice process (pretrial) are detrimental to minority defendants.[22] Defendants' demeanor and appearance affect pretrial release decisions. Mann notes that "keeping up a front" or being "macho" is part of the minority cultural facade. If an African American male is lucky enough to have made bail while his case is pending, his luck may end when he strolls up to the bench showing what the judge interprets as "black insolence."[23]

The discrimination found during the sentencing stage depends on the political climate of the times in which a study was conducted. Studies from the pre–civil rights era clearly demonstrated bias against minorities brought before the hall of justice, but the conclusion of most current studies is that "comparatively little systematic difference in contemporary sentencing outcomes appears to be attributable to race."[24] Yet, as one study aptly put it, "After fifty years of research on whether or not there are racial or ethnic disparities in sentencing, there is only one generalizable finding: sometimes judges discriminate and sometimes they don't."[25]

More evidence exists that discrimination takes place against minorities in correctional institutions. Minorities appear to be shortchanged in receiving placements in good work assignments and desirable programs. Further, they receive more severe penalties for disciplinary offenses, such as more time in segregation units.[26] They compose a disproportionate number of prisoners in maximum-security facilities and in super-max prisons. For example, 283 of the 288 inmates in the super-max Maryland Correctional Adjustment Center are black. Inmates are sent to this prison from other correctional institutions where they have been deemed dangerous to corrections staffs or to other inmates.[27]

In examining charges of racism in the treatment of minority inmates, William Wilbanks concludes that it is true that these inmates receive more rule infractions, segregation placements, and institutional transfers than white inmates. Guards rationalize the differences, according to Wilbanks, by saying that African American inmates show more negative attitudes and engage in more negative behaviors than do white inmates. These negative attitudes and behaviors make African American inmates seem more aggressive or dangerous than whites and thus deserving of more negative sanctions than whites.[28]

the walls 18.2

outside

The Myth of a Racist Criminal Justice System

I take the position that the perception of the criminal justice system as racist is a myth. Since this assertion can be interpreted in many ways, it is necessary to specify what it means and what it does not mean.

First, I believe that there is racial prejudice and discrimination *within* the criminal justice system, in that there are individuals, both white and black, who make decisions, at least in part, on the basis of race. I do not believe that *the system* is characterized by racial prejudice or discrimination against black; that is, prejudice and discrimination are not "systematic." . . .

Second, the question of whether the criminal justice system is "racist" cannot be discussed until the term *racist* is defined. . . . If one defines racism as a conscious attitude or conscious behavior by individuals that discriminates against blacks, however, there is little or no evidence that most individuals in the system make decisions on the basis of race. In short, the definition of racism often predetermines the answer to the question, "Is the criminal justice system racist?" . . .

Third, the assertion that the criminal justice system is not racist does not address the reasons why blacks appear to offend at higher rates than whites even before coming into contact with the criminal justice system. It may be that racial discrimination in American society has been responsible for conditions that lead to higher rates of offending by blacks, but that possibility does not bear on

> . . . there is insufficient evidence to support the charge that the system is racist today.

the question of whether the criminal justice system discriminates against blacks. . . .

Fourth, the assertion that the criminal justice system is not racist does not deny that racial prejudice and discrimination have existed in or even been the dominant force in the design and operation of the criminal justice system in the past. . . . But the question today concerns whether the operation of the system *at this time* is characterized by racial prejudice and discrimination. I believe that there is insufficient evidence to support the charge that the system is racist today. . . .

Fifth, I am not suggesting that the nondiscrimination thesis has been proven by the existing literature. But surely the burden of proof rests on those who hold that the system is racist. . . . The belief that the criminal justice system is racist is a myth in the sense that there is insufficient evidence to support this position.

CRITICAL THINKING QUESTIONS

Do you believe that Wilbanks adequately supports his basic contention that it is a myth that the criminal justice system is racist? Where do you agree or disagree with what he has to say?

Source: Reprinted from William Wilbanks, *The Myth of a Racist Criminal Justice System* (Monterey, Calif.: Brooks/Cole, 1987), pp. 5–8.

Wilbanks challenges the charges of racism in the criminal justice system throughout his book, *The Myth of a Criminal Justice System.* For the basis of his argument, which has generated a great deal of debate, see Outside the Walls 18.2.

Marjorie S. Zatz brings some clarity to this discussion of whether there is racism in the justice system when she suggests that overt bias should be differentiated from subtle bias. Overt bias is evident when race directly affects court outcomes. Subtle bias is evident when race interacts with other factors or indirectly affects the outcome of court decisions.[29] According to Zatz, overt bias is easier to detect and was more common in the past.

Darrell F. Hawkins and Kenneth A. Hardy, in their investigation of the possibilities of regional differences in sentencing, examined state-specific imprisonment rates.[30] Across the fifty states, they found wide variation in African American imprisonment rates in relation to African American arrest rates. Some regions, such as the South, had much higher imprisonment rates in relation to arrest rates than did other regions.[31]

Several researchers feel that **contextual discrimination** better explains the comparatively higher incarceration rates of African Americans.[32] Contextual discrimination is discrimination that is evident in specific social contexts. For example, researchers have begun to examine the racial composition of incarceration in light of social contexts such as unemployment and regional culture. One study found that high African American male unemployment rates at the county level are predictive of high African American incarceration rates.[33] Hawkins and Hardy's analysis revealed that states and regions with smaller percentages of African American residents have greater racial overrepresentation in the prison population than could be accounted for by arrest rates.[34]

Walker, Spohn, and DeLone draw the following conclusions: Most decision makers in the criminal justice system make every attempt to "wash out" all means of overt bias and discrimination against minorities. Subtle influences on decision making—such as the personal fears, attitudes, and prejudices of decision makers—to some degree affect overall levels of discrimination toward minorities. Furthermore, discrimination at a particular stage of decision making may appear to be minor, but the total cumulative effects of discrimination at all stages may be significant.[35]

WHAT IS THE RELATIONSHIP BETWEEN GENDER AND INCARCERATION TRENDS?

The effects of cultural values, such as chivalry, on the sentencing of female offenders to prison, are examined in this section, as well as the influence of sexism, racism, and classism on female offenders. It could be argued that these two sets of social values cancel each other out—that the norms of chivalry protect certain female offenders from being treated as harshly as male offenders. However, sexism, racism, and classism give rise to forms of oppression that increase the punishment of female offenders.

Chivalry and the Protection of Female Offenders

Overlooking, excusing, and letting go have traditionally characterized the handling of the adult female in the criminal justice system. The female offender has been less visible in the criminal justice system than the male because of old-fashioned notions of **chivalry,** such as women are harmless beings who must be sheltered from life's harsh blows and society has nothing to fear from the "fair sex," the "weaker vessel," and so on. In many instances, victims of female violators and witnesses to their crimes have been reluctant to take action against them. Police have been unwilling to arrest women or to hold them for court action. Courts have gone easy on women because they were women, and especially when their children were depending on them for emotional and financial support. Women have been treated more leniently than men because criminal justice officials have viewed women as less dangerous, less culpable, and less likely to relapse than men, and, accordingly, requiring less punitive treatment.[36]

In the 1960s, police attitudes and behavior toward women started to change. "If it's equality these women want, we'll see to it that they get it," one officer said.[37] But if chivalry was less evident at the arrest stage, it was still very much alive at other stages of the correctional process. Not only were women less likely than men to remain in custody during the pretrial period, but they were also less likely to be convicted when they came to trial. A woman who was convicted was likely to receive lighter sentence than would a man convicted of the same crime. Only in parole decisions did gender appear to make little difference.[38]

Research in the 1970s discovered that the greatest discrepancy between the treatment of males and females occurred in sentencing. Judges seemed less inclined to send females to prison, because females usually posed a lesser threat than males to the community. Females committed less violent crimes, and the violent crimes that females committed usually involved family members or lovers. Few of these violent crimes were premeditated, and most were the outcome of frustration and abuse, motives that judges and society find easy to excuse. In addition, the secondary or accomplice role that many women played in their crimes made it easy for judges to be lenient. A survey of thirty judges and state's attorneys (prosecutors) confirmed that most female offenders neither planned nor managed the crimes for which they were arrested.[39] Furthermore, a judge could not avoid considering who would take care of a woman's children if she were sent to prison. A superintendent of the California Institution for Women explained this dilemma:

> If a man goes to prison, the wife stays home and he usually has the family to return to and the household is there when he gets out. Very few men are going to sit around and take care of the children and be there when she gets back. So to send a woman to prison means you are virtually going to disrupt her family.[40]

Social scientists analyzing the handling of male and female defendants in the 1990s reached somewhat contradictory conclusions.[41] Some found women to be more likely than men to be released on their own recognizance or on bail and to have their cases dismissed before trial. In these studies, women are less likely than men to be convicted, to receive sentences, or to be incarcerated. Other researchers, however, found that females are treated no differently from males, especially with respect to decisions to prosecute, to plea-bargain, or to convict.[42]

In examining the differences in felony court processing, Margaret Farnworth and R. H. C. Teske Jr. describe the three most often claimed hypotheses concerning women offenders and chivalry: (1) The "typicality" hypothesis holds that "women are treated with chivalry in criminal processing, but only when their charges are consistent with stereotypes of female offenders." (2) The "selective chivalry" hypothesis is based on the belief that "decision makers extend chivalry disproportionately to white females." (3) The "differential discretion" hypothesis suggests that disparity is "most likely in informal decisions such as charge reductions rather than in formal decisions at final sentencing."[43]

Data from 9,966 felony theft cases and 18,176 felony assault cases disposed of in California in 1988 indicated that females with no prior record were more likely than similar males to receive charge reductions. This disparity, in turn, enhanced females' chances of receiving probation. The only selective chivalry that Farnworth and Teske found was a tendency to change charges of assault to nonassault more frequently among white female defendants than among minority females. They further found that pivotal decisions concerning charge reduction provided some support for the notion of differential discretion, but their findings provided no clear support for the "typicality" hypothesis.[44]

Today, the effects of chivalry are less evident in the justice system than before the 1970s. Nevertheless, the bulk of the evidence still indicates more lenient treatment of female defendants, especially at the sentencing stage.

Sexism, Racism, and Classism

Feminists would challenge the preceding discussion because it ignores two pivotal questions: Why were more women in the 1990s being sent to prison? Do race and class variables influence which women are sent to prison? Feminists would answer these questions by saying that racism and classism explain why more women are sent to prison.

Eileen Leonard contends that efforts to understand women's crime must include analysis of the links among gender, race, class, and culture.[45] It is through examining sexism, classism, and racism, according to E. V. Spelman, that discrimination against women can be clearly grasped and understood.[46] She notes, "It isn't easy to think about gender, race, and class in ways that don't obscure or underplay their effects on one another."[47] When gender, race, and class are combined, Leonard, Spelman, and others would add, the effect is greater than its parts. Thus, multiple forms of discrimination for women offenders have more negative consequences than one form of discrimination.[48]

Gender discrimination is evident in the intolerance for certain types of female offenders. Females who are involved in prostitution receive little, if any, protection from chivalry. Women who abuse their children are looked on as bad and deserving of pun-

Of persons convicted of crimes, why are proportionally fewer women in prison than men? What are the intersections of gender, race, and class in corrections? How might conflict and feminist theorists explain how race, gender, class, and age determine who are in the corrections system and what happens to them?

ishment, and women who kill their children are looked on as evil and deserving of harsh punishment. Also considered bad are women who harm their unborn children through drug use.[49]

Class discrimination is another aspect of marginality experienced by many women in U.S. society. In a number of ways, powerful and serious problems of childhood and adolescence related to poverty set the stage for females' entry into homelessness, unemployment, drug use, survival sex, and prostitution, and, ultimately, more serious criminal acts. Social class also affects adult women's experiences within the system. Middle-class women who commit crimes are more likely than lower-class female offenders to be given respect at the time of arrest, to be given mental health placements, to spend less time in jail, and to be given probation more frequently than lower-class offenders. Moreover, they are sentenced to prison much less frequently than lower-class offenders.[50]

Racial discrimination seems to contribute more marginality for minority women than does gender or class. D. K. Lewis has noted that "black women . . . tended to see racism as a more powerful cause of their subordinate position than sexism and to view the women's liberation movement with considerable mistrust."[51] The increased frequency with which minority women are sent to prison is a vivid reminder to these women of racism and sexism. Research seems to be supportive of the finding that white rather than minority female offenders are the ones who receive the protection of chivalry.

In the 1990s, Meda Chesney-Lind extended this argument when she said that adolescent females and women are victims of **multiple marginality** because their gender, class, and race have placed them at the economic periphery of society.[52] To be labeled a delinquent takes place in a world, Chesney-Lind charges, "where gender still shapes the lives of young people in very powerful ways. This means that gender matters in girls' lives and that the way gender works varies by the community and the culture into which the girl is born."[53] Chesney-Lind also makes the point that the social context of this world is not fair to women and girls, especially to those of color and those of low incomes.[54]

The effects of multiple marginality can be seen in the lives of the majority of women prisoners, especially if they are women of color. Many are sexually victimized by fathers, stepfathers, or mothers' boyfriends and turn to the streets where drugs, prostitution, and other forms of crime are available to relieve their impoverished lives. It is not long before a drug habit and a life of prostitution become new forms of oppression. They soon find themselves in the criminal justice system, especially if they have picked up a crack cocaine habit and must find the means to support it. Then, like other poor women, they do their time and return to the streets. Unless they have a strong support system in the community, they can swing back and forth between the community and prison for most of their lives.

In sum, there seems to be sufficient evidence that women who commit certain crimes are disproportionately imprisoned, that lower-class women experience more discrimination during justice system processing than do middle- and upper-class women, and that women of color sometimes receive less benefit from chivalry than do white women. In addition, the argument has been made that women experiencing multiple marginality are more likely to receive discriminatory treatment by the justice system.

Our hero in this chapter is Coramae Richey Mann, a retired professor of criminal justice. She spent her career at the Florida State University School of Criminology and the University of Indiana. She is the author of three important books on race and gender injustice in the United States—*Female Crime and Delinquency, Unequal Justice: A Question of Color,* and *When Women Kill*—and coauthor, with Marjoire S. Zatz, of *Images of Color, Images of Crime.* Read what she said for *Invitation to Corrections* in 2000.

h e r o e s | *Coramae Richey Mann*

Retired Professor of Criminal Justice

"The point that I was trying to make in my book *Unequal Justice* is that not just African Americans but all people of color are discriminated against in the criminal justice and juvenile justice systems of the United States. The fact is that because it happens to every person of color, not just one group, it becomes **institutionalized racism.**

Unequal Justice was very favorably received. A lot of people contacted me and said that they agreed. I believe it was well received because I included all minorities and not just African Americans. There was not a whole lot of research compiled on other racial/ethnic groups at that time. I think that another fallout from my book is that people of color have become more conscious of their own background and contributions. For example, Native Americans are now studying Native American crime, and Latinos are studying their crime. So the book has really served as a catalyst to get more information about how the system treats people of color.

"My book *When Women Kill* came out in 1996. This book was based on research that I did in six U.S. cities and secondary data where I compared two time periods. I did a lot of cross-calculations that related to race, victimization, and use of weapons. My sample consisted of cleared homicide cases. What I found was that the usual arrestee and person charged with murder was a woman of color. Homicide detectives would tell me that white women were rarely charged with first-degree murder. It was always self-defense with them. It also became apparent that if there were better medical assistance in the poor communities of color, a lot of the cases would not have been murder. So once again the shabby treatment of people of color leads to women of color being charged with homicide that would have been an assault if it were white women. Or if it were a white woman, it would have been self-defense. When it got down to the final charge, white women had a reduction in the charge more frequently than women of color.

"The corrections system is the end product of the whole system. It has a number of problems that lead to discrimination, like what work assignments people are given, what prison people are sent to, and whether people of color can practice their religion. For example, now some prisons are letting Native Americans practice their religion, but for many years they wouldn't allow them to.

"The super-max prisons are probably the most racist of all. From what I understand about them, the vast majority, 90 percent, are people of color. How does that happen? You can't tell me that something isn't biased when the majority that end up there are people of color. And when you get out of there, these super-prisons are turning out people of color who are worse off than when they went in. The public may be clamoring for everybody to be locked up, but they don't seem to think that eventually they *do* get out.

"Discrimination has become so subtle and so covert that people in the system don't even recognize it. I have talked to corrections staff, ranging from wardens to correctional officers, who say that they are not prejudiced, but yet they are supporting a prejudiced structure. They said that they don't have any problems about color, but they are still enforcing a system that does. What makes it institutionalized is when even the employees aren't aware of how frightening it is.

"It seems like the politicians are getting the public so wrapped up in putting people in prison that they are not figuring the cost of the prison industry. They also are not considering the fact that prisons are producing more violent people. There are people who could have been turned around in the community, but when they are sent to prison, they come out angrier and more violent."

CRITICAL THINKING QUESTIONS

What does Coramae Richey Mann mean by institutionalized racism? How pervasive do you believe institutionalized racism is in the criminal justice system?

WHAT IS THE RELATIONSHIP BETWEEN CLASS AND INCARCERATION TRENDS?

Few people would challenge the statement that prisons are filled with poor people. Part of the reason for their overwhelming presence in prison is that historically the poor have been feared by people who are better-off and who view the poor as threats to their lifestyle. Consequences of this fear include placing greater surveillance on the poor, tolerating less deviancy from them, and punishing them in ways that prevent them from infringing on the lives of the better-off. Despite legal protections, class has become an important determinant of how individuals are treated by the justice system. People who are poor do not fare nearly as well as people who have financial means. Nor are the crimes of the rich—white-collar and corporate crimes—considered to be as serious as the crimes of poor, or street criminals.

The Threat of the "Dangerous Poor"

Throughout U.S. history, crime has been blamed on the so-called dangerous poor, especially newcomers with different cultural, ethnic, and religious backgrounds. It was viewed that institutions were needed to protect society against the behavior of these people.[55] Until the late nineteenth century, waves of immigration brought impoverished newcomers who were seen as threatening a new crime wave. Many children and adults who had recently come to America found themselves embroiled with the justice system. Anthony Platt partly explains why this took place when he points out that members of the middle and upper classes who saw themselves as preservers of the social order and pillars of the community selected behaviors found primarily among lower-class children to be penalized—sexual license, roaming the streets, drinking, begging, fighting, frequenting dance halls and movies, and staying out late at night.[56]

The association of poverty with dangerousness persists. It is expressed, especially, in the fear of violence and gang behaviors by African American and Hispanic underclass children. Elijah Anderson describes the fear that young African American males inspire in others:

> An overwhelming number of young black males in the Village [in Philadelphia] are committed to civility and law-abiding behavior. They often have a hard time convincing others of this, however, because of the stigma attached to their skin color, age, gender, appearance, and general style of self-presentation. Moreover, most residents ascribe criminality, incivility, toughness, and street smartness to the anonymous black male, who must work hard to make others trust his common decency. . . .
>
> When young black men appear, women (especially white women) sometimes clutch their pocketbooks. They may edge up against their companions or begin to walk stiffly and deliberately. On spotting black males from a distance, other pedestrians often cross the street or give them a wide berth as they pass.[57]

One of the defenses of law-and-order imprisonment policies is that sympathy for inmates is misplaced because the majority of them are dangerous people who committed serious crimes. John DiIulio wrote in a 26 January 1994 article in the *Wall Street Journal,* "More than 95 percent of state prisoners are violent criminals, repeat criminals (with two or more felony convictions), or violent repeat criminals."[58] Official crime statistics, however, paint a much different picture. They indicate that in any given year about one-quarter of the persons arrested in the United States had committed a violent crime.[59]

Class and Criminal Justice Processing

Marxist criminologists contend that certain acts are termed *criminal* because it is the interest of the ruling class to so define them. Marxist theorists view law as an oppressive force that is used to promote and stabilize existing socioeconomic relations. The

outside the walls 18.3

Social Injustice in the Justice System

The criminal justice system does not simply weed the peace-loving from the dangerous, the law-abiding from the criminal. At every stage, starting with the very definitions of crime and progressing through the stages of investigation, arrest, charging, conviction, and sentencing, the system *weeds out the wealthy*. It refuses to define as "crimes" or as serious crimes the dangerous and predatory acts of the well-to-do—acts that, as we have seen, result in the loss of thousands of lives and billions of dollars. Instead, the system focuses its attention on those crimes likely to be committed by members of the lower classes. Thus, it is no surprise to find that so many of the people behind bars are from the lower classes. The people we see in our jails and prisons are no doubt dangerous to society,

> ...the system weeds out the wealthy.

but they are not *the* danger to society, not *the greatest danger* to society. Individuals who pose equal or greater threats to our well-being walk the streets with impunity. [Reiman's italics]

CRITICAL THINKING QUESTIONS

Do you agree or disagree with Jeffrey Reiman's statement? Why? Do you believe that the criminal justice process intentionally weeds out the wealthy? Do the privileged classes intentionally discriminate against the lower classes?

Source: Reprinted from Jeffrey Reiman, *The Rich Get Richer and the Poor Get Prison: Ideology, Class, and Criminal Justice*, 5th ed. (Boston: Allyn & Bacon, 1999), p. 102.

---

law maintains order, Marxists admit, but it is an order that the privileged and powerful impose on the poor and powerless.

Marxist theorists argue that crime must be seen as part of the larger problem of class inequality, which leads to alienation and economic exploitation of the lower classes. Economic exploitation, according to Marxist criminologists, affects the poor in many ways, including higher rates of crime. Three aspects of class inequality seem strongly related to street crime: forced employment or unemployment, poverty, and income inequality. The thrust of the Marxist argument is that the criminal justice system is biased in favor of the middle and ruling classes and that bias is the reason why the vast majority of prison inmates come from the lower classes. Jeffrey Reiman notes this bias in his book *The Rich Get Richer and the Poor Get Prison* (see Outside the Walls 18.3).

The variable of class has taken a strange twist in both federal and state sentencing guidelines. In an attempt to eliminate considerations from sentencing that favor middle-class offenders, policymakers make it difficult or impossible for judges to make allowances for disadvantaged offenders. Judges are forbidden by most sentencing guidelines to consider employment, education, or family status. This notion of **class neutrality,** however, rests on the false empirical premise that middle-class offenders are present in felony court. The fact is that very few defendants in urban court have anything but deeply disadvantaged backgrounds, and the failure to consider personal or adverse factors reduces the chances that they will receive some mitigation in sentencing.[60]

SUMMARY

An examination of incarceration must consider the issue of whether people are sent to prison because of what they have done or because of other social factors. Some critics claim that disproportionate numbers of minorities are being sent to prison because of the racism of criminal justice decision makers. Others argue that the recent increase in women's imprisonment is due to sexism, racism, and classism. Another position is that the crimes of the lower classes result in imprisonment more often than the crimes of the privileged classes. However, there are those who challenge these charges of social injustice. They claim that disproportionate numbers of minorities are being sent to prison because of their serious personal and property crimes. It is also claimed that the system protects rather than oppresses women and that class neutrality is found among decision makers.

Although there is little debate about whether discrimination and inequality influenced justice officials' decision making in the past, there is great debate how much social injustice affects incarceration rates today.

There seems to be support for three conclusions: (1) Bias when it exists among decision makers is more subtle than overt. (2) The total cumulative effects of discrimination may be significant although discrimination at a particular stage may appear to be minor. (3) Bias varies from one criminal justice official to another and from one region and state to another.

KEY TERMS

chivalry, p. 435
class neutrality, p. 440
contextual discrimination, p. 434

institutionalized racism, p. 438
multiple marginality, p. 437
Uniform Crime Reports, p. 431

CRITICAL THINKING QUESTIONS

1. How would you respond to this statement: The criminal justice system is racist.
2. Can female offenders be both leniently treated and oppressed at the same time? How can that take place?
3. How might the criminal justice system become more class-neutral in its processing of cases? Would that be desirable?

4. Are you troubled by the fact that youthful offenders constitute such a large segment of prison populations? How might this situation be changed?

WEB DESTINATIONS

This news article provides a comprehensive case study for understanding issues of who goes to jail in the American criminal justice system.
http://www.auschron.com/issues/dispatch/2000-07-28/pols_feature3.html

Read facts concerning race and prison.
http://www.drugwarfacts.org/racepris.htm

This data-based article examines the question of who goes to prison for drug offenses.
http://www.igc.org/hrw/campaigns/drugs/ny-drugs.htm

Read a classic Shaffer Library on Drug Policy article on inequities affecting the "The Dollar Cost of Punishment."
http://www.druglibrary.org/schaffer/LIBRARY/dolrcost.htm

Read "Mexican Americans in Texas Prisons: Insights Concerning a Texas Therapeutic Community."
http://www.io.com/~ellie/eval.html

FOR FURTHER READING

Free, Marvin D. *African Americans and the Criminal Justice System.* New York: Garland, 1996. A well-documented and unbiased account of the treatment of minorities in the criminal justice system.

Mann, Coramae Richey. *Unequal Justice: A Question of Color.* Bloomington: Indiana University Press, 1993. Richey contends that all persons of color receive discriminatory treatment by the justice system.

Mann, Coramae Richey, and Marjorie S. Zatz, eds. *Images of Color, Images of Crime.* Los Angeles: Roxbury, 1998. A fascinating collection of essays written by people of color.

Reiman, Jeffrey. *The Rich Get Richer and the Poor Get Prison: Ideology, Class, and Criminal Justice.* 5th ed. Boston: Allyn & Bacon, 1999. Reiman forcefully presents the thesis of class inequality in the justice system.

Tonry, Michael. *Malign Neglect: Race, Crime, and Punishment in America.* New York: Oxford University Press, 1995. A classic examination of how the relationship between race and crime in the United States has been handled.

Walker, Samuel, Cassia Spohn, and Miriam DeLone. *Race and Ethnicity and Crime in America: The Color of Justice.* 2d ed. Belmont, Calif.: Wadsworth, 2000. A helpful examination of the processing of minorities in the justice system.

NOTES

1. Mumia Abu-Jamal, *Live from Death Row* (Reading, Mass.: Addison-Wesley, 1995), pp. 33–34.
2. Ibid. Also see the statements Mumia Abu-Jamal has written for posting on the Internet.
3. Samuel Walker, Cassia Spohn, and Miriam DeLone, *Race and Ethnicity and Crime in America: The Color of Justice,* 2d ed. (Belmont, Calif.: Wadsworth, 2000), p. 1.
4. E. V. Spelman, *Inessential Women* (Boston: Beacon Press, 1989).
5. Ibid.
6. Jeffrey Reiman, *The Rich Get Richer and the Poor Get Prison: Ideology, Class, and Criminal Justice,* 5th ed. (Boston: Allyn & Bacon, 1999).
7. Walker, Spohn, and DeLone, *Race and Ethnicity and Crime in America,* p. 233.
8. Michael Tonry, *Malign Neglect: Race, Crime and Punishment in America* (New York: Oxford University Press, 1995), p. 3.
9. Michael Hindelang, *Criminal Victimization in Eight American Communities: A Descriptive Analysis of Common Theft and Assault* (Washington, D.C.: Law Enforcement Assistance Administration, 1976).
10. Michael Hindelang, "Race and Involvement in Common Law Personal Crimes," *American Sociological Review* 43 (1978), pp. 93–109.
11. Alfred Blumstein, "On the Racial Disproportionality of United States' Prison Populations," *Journal of Criminal Law and Criminology* 73 (1982), pp. 1259–1281.
12. Patrick A. Langan, "Racism on Trial: New Evidence to Explain the Racial Composition of Prisons in the United States," *Journal of Criminal Law and Criminology* 76 (1985), pp. 666–683.
13. Alfred Blumstein, "Racial Disproportionality of U.S. Prison Population Revisited," *University of Colorado Law Review* 64 (1993), pp. 743–760.
14. Tonry, *Malign Neglect,* p. 65.
15. Ibid., pp. 67–68.
16. Ibid.
17. Bureau of Justice Statistics, *Prisoners in 1998* (Washington, D.C.: U.S. Department of Justice, 1999), p. 3.
18. Walker, Spohn, and DeLone, *Race and Ethnicity and Crime in America,* p. 205.
19. Ibid.
20. See Michael J. Lynch and E. Britt Patterson, *Race and Criminal Justice* (New York: Harrow & Heston, 1991).
21. Tonry, *Malign Neglect,* p. 71.
22. Coramae Richey Mann, *Unequal Justice: A Question of Color* (Bloomington: Indiana University Press, 1993), p. 212.
23. Ibid.
24. Tonry, *Malign Neglect,* p. 68.
25. J. D. Unnever and L. A. Hembroff, "The Prediction of Racial/Ethnic Sentencing Disparities: An Expectation States Approach," *Journal of Research in Crime and Delinquency* 25 (1987), pp. 69–92.
26. Mann, *Unequal Justice.*
27. William J. Chambliss, "Crime Control and Ethnic Minorities: Legitimizing Racial Oppression by Creating Moral Panics," in *Ethnicity, Race, and Crime: Perspectives across Time and Place,* ed. Darnell F. Hawkins (Albany: State University of New York Press, 1995), pp. 253–254.
28. William Wilbanks, *The Myth of a Racist Criminal Justice System* (Monterey, Calif.: Brooks/Cole, 1987), p. 133.
29. M. S. Zatz, "The Changing Forms of Racial/Ethnic Biases in Sentencing," *Journal of Research in Crime and Delinquency* 25 (1988), pp. 53–82.
30. Darrell F. Hawkins and Kenneth A. Hardy, "Black–White Imprisonment Rates: A State-by-State Analysis," *Social Justice* 16 (1989), pp. 79–94.
31. Ibid., p. 79.
32. Walker, Spohn, and DeLone, *Race and Ethnicity and Crime in America,* p. 215.
33. Miriam A. DeLone and Theodore G. Chiricos, "Young Black Males and Incarceration: A Contextual Analysis of Racial Compositions" (paper presented at the annual meeting of the American Society of Criminology, Miami, 1994).
34. Hawkins and Hardy, "Black–White Imprisonment Rates," pp. 75–94.
35. Walker, Spohn, and DeLone, *Race and Ethnicity, and Crime in America.*
36. Mann, *Unequal Justice;* Coramae Richey Mann, *When Women Kill* (Albany: State University of New York Press, 1996); Coramae Richey Mann, *Female Crime and Delinquency* (Tuscaloosa: University of Alabama Press, 1984); and Coramae Richey Mann and Marjorie S. Zatz, eds., *Images of Color, Images of Crime* (Los Angeles: Roxbury, 1998).
37. Rita James Simon, *Women and Crime* (Lexington, Mass.: Heath, 1975), p. 18.
38. Ibid., p. 49.
39. Ibid., pp. 69–70.
40. Ibid.
41. C. C. Spohn and J. W. Spears, "Gender and Case Processing Decisions: A Comparison of Outcomes for Male and Female Defendants Charged with Violent Felonies," *Women and Criminal Justice* 8 (1997), pp. 29–59.
42. Ibid., pp. 30–31.
43. M. Farnworth and R. H. C. Teske Jr., "Gender Differences in Felony Court Processing: Three Hypotheses of Disparity," *Women and Criminal Justice* 6 (1995), p. 23.
44. Ibid., pp. 23–24.

45. Eileen Leonard, "Theoretical Criminology and Gender," in *The Criminal Justice System and Women: Offenders, Victims, and Workers,* ed. B. R. Price and N. J. Sokoloff (New York: McGraw-Hill, 1995), pp. 54–70.

46. Spelman, *Inessential Woman,* p. 115.

47. Ibid.

48. Kathleen Daly, "Class-Gender-Gender: Sloganeering in Search of Meaning, *Social Justice* 20 (1993), pp. 56–71.

49. A. Wilczynski, "Images of Women Who Kill Their Infants: The Mad and the Bad," *Women and Criminal Justice* 2 (1991), pp. 71–88.

50. Kathleen Daly and Michael Tonry, "Gender, Race, and Sentencing," *Crime and Justice: A Review of Research* 23, ed. Michael Tonry (Chicago: University of Chicago Press, 1997), p. 203.

51. D. K. Lewis, "A Response to Inequality: Black Women, Racism, and Sexism," *Signs: Journal of Women in Culture and Society* 3 (1977), p. 339.

52. Meda Chesney-Lind, *The Female Offender: Girls, Women, and Crime* (Thousand Oaks, Calif.: Sage, 1997), p. 4.

53. Ibid., p. 121.

54. Ibid., p. 133.

55. David J. Rothman, *The Discovery of the Asylum: Social Order and Disorder in the New Republic* (Boston: Little, Brown, 1971).

56. Anthony M. Platt, *The Child Saver* (Chicago: University of Chicago Press, 1969).

57. Elijah Anderson, *Street Wise: Race, Classism, and Change in an Urban Community* (Chicago: University of Chicago Press, 1990), pp. 163–164.

58. Cited in Tonry, *Malign Neglect,* p. 26.

59. Federal Bureau of Investigation, *Uniform Crime Reports* (Washington, D.C.: U.S. Government Printing Office, 1999), pp. 220–221.

60. Tonry, *Malign Neglect,* p. 167.

CHAPTER 18 / BUILT-IN STUDY GUIDE

Multiple Choice Questions

1. Approximately what percentage of the incarcerated population did African American males represent as of 1996?

   A. 10%
   B. 20%
   C. 50%
   D. 80%

2. What percentage of the incarcerated population in the United States is made up of young men and women who are between the ages 16 and 24?

   A. 16%
   B. 26%
   C. 36%
   D. 46%

3. According to Hawkin's and Hardy's analysis, states and regions with smaller percentages of African American residents have:

   A. Greater racial overrepresentation in the prison population than could be accounted for by arrest rates
   B. Greater racial overrepresentation in the prison population than could be accounted for by prosecutorial discretion
   C. Greater racial overrepresentation in sentencing decisions than could be accounted for by judicial discretion
   D. Greater racial overrepresentation in charging decisions than could be accounted for by arrest rates

4. Middle-class women who commit crimes are more likely then lower-class female offenders to be:

   A. Given drug tests at the time of arrest
   B. Given the right to counsel during the arrest phase
   C. Given the opportunity enter a boot camp program
   D. Given probation

5. What segment of the population was blamed for crime in the early history of this nation?

   A. Slaves
   B. Nonreligious observers
   C. Poor
   D. Native Americans

6. Which of the following statement does not have sufficient evidence to support it?

   A. Women who commit certain crimes are disproportionately imprisoned
   B. Lower-class women receive more discrimination by justice system processing than do middle- and upper-class women
   C. Women of color sometimes receive less benefit from chivalry than do white women
   D. Females involved in prostitution receive protection from chivalry

7. According to the text, all of the following aspects of class inequality are strongly related to street crime except:

   A. Forced unemployment
   B. Social status inequality
   C. Poverty
   D. Income inequality

8. What type of criminology supports the position that certain acts are termed crime because it is in the interest of the ruling class to define them as crimes?

   A. Marxist criminology
   B. Positivist criminology
   C. Biological criminology
   D. Organic criminology

9. Eileen Leonard suggests that efforts to understand women's crime must include an analysis of the links among all of the following categories except:

   A. Gender
   B. Race
   C. Class
   D. Religion

10. Mumia Abu-Jamal and many others suggest that the disproportionate rates of minorities confined on death row relate to all of the following except:

    A. Increase in violent crime by minorities
    B. Social policy
    C. Unfair sentencing of minority defendants
    D. Law enforcement practices of racial profiling

True/False Questions

T F 1. According to Jeffrey Reiman, imprisonment is primarily reserved for lower-class offenders.

T F 2. Immigrants in the early nineteenth century were welcome to the United States and not viewed as a threat to crime.

T F 3. The association of poverty with dangerousness ended in the early twentieth century.

T F 4. Despite legal protections, class has become an important variable in how individuals are treated by the justice system.

T F 5. Criminal penalties for using crack and powder cocaine are equal in this country.

T F 6. Research studies strongly support the position that systematic racial discrimination takes place during arrests of minorities.

T F 7. There is strong support for the premise that drug offenses demonstrate the greatest disparity in offending and incarceration rates among African Americans.

T F 8. According to Reiman, white-collar criminals do far more social harm than street criminals.

Fill-in-the-Blank Questions   (based on key terms)

1. A study at the county level that finds high African American male unemployment rates are predictive of higher African American incarceration rates is an example of _____.

2. The cultural value of _____ supposedly protects certain female offenders from being treated as harshly as male offenders.

3. According to Chesney-Lind's analysis, as a result of gender, class, and race, adolescents are victims of _____ and are on the economic border of society.

4. Sentencing guidelines that prevent judges from considering the offender's employment, education, or family status in determining a sentence support the premise of _____.

5. Coramae Richey Mann's position that the structure of the criminal justice system is prejudiced against all people of color is known as _____.

Essay Questions

1. What explains the disproportionate numbers of minorities confined to correctional facilities? How severe is this disproportionality for African American males?

2. How would a feminist explain why more women in the 1990s are being sent to prison?

3. How would a Marxist criminologist explain the problem of crime?

4. Explain the significance of the relationship between class and incarceration rates.

ANSWERS

Multiple Choice Questions

1. C	6. D
2. C	7. B
3. A	8. A
4. D	9. D
5. C	10. A

True/False Questions

1. T	5. F
2. F	6. F
3. F	7. T
4. T	8. T

Fill-in-the-Blank Questions

1. Contextual discrimination
2. Chivalry
3. Multiple marginality
4. Class neutrality
5. Institutional racism

chapter nineteen

Politics, Law, and
Prison Crowding

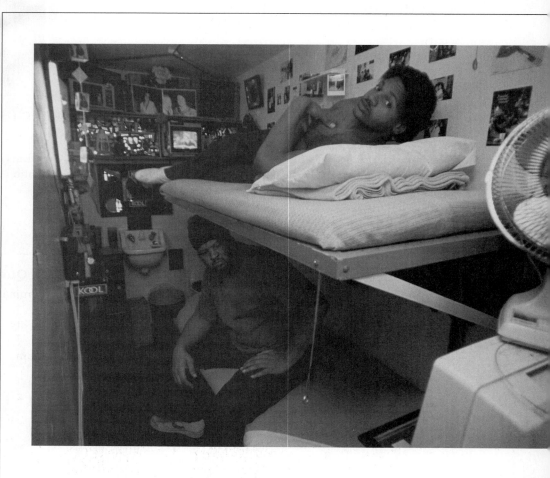

W. L. Kautzky, director of the Iowa Department of Corrections, speaks about crowding in correctional institutions in Iowa and explains why Iowa is forced to deal with prison crowding:

After building three new 750-bed institutions at Clarinda, Newton, and Ft. Dodge, crowding is still an issue. Prison bed space demand requires nearly 8,000 beds and [court-imposed] capacity remains static at 6,772. A record 4,920 admissions in FY 2000 included 2,203 new court commitments. The balance of admissions were [probation and parole] revocations that exceeded all expectations despite a reduction of felony filings statewide.

State courts have played a significant role in shaping demand for prison beds. Truth-in-sentencing and a national drug control policy are driving local policymakers. From a policy perspective the significant growth in drug offenses stands in stark contrast to the stable conviction rate for violent and sex offenses. Although Iowa experienced a definable drop in violent and property offenses, drug convictions represent 22 percent of the offender population compared with only 13 percent in 1995. In addition to new court commitments, revoked probation and parole sentences account for 45 percent of Iowa's new admissions.

The federal courts have impacted conditions of confinement by requiring the Iowa correctional system to reduce crowding to court-imposed levels. Inmates have successfully litigated issues related to crowding at the Iowa State Penitentiary.

A careful analysis by the Criminal and Juvenile Justice Planning Division suggests that prison bed demand will require 12,400 beds in 2010. If the state revenues remain static, Iowa will follow California's lead in reducing expenditure for higher education, health care, and other essential state services to fund an increasingly costly correctional system.[1]

447

CRITICAL THINKING QUESTIONS

How does Director Kautzky account for prison crowding in Iowa? What does he see as the consequences of this problem?

Other interviewed directors of federal and state correctional agencies are quick to agree that their most serious problem is prison crowding. They can list many ways in which crowding undermines their correctional mission. These administrators often talk about the prison construction projects that their governmental jurisdictions have been involved in during the past two decades and the troubling problem of financing them. They may discuss a strategy or plan of their own to overcome prison crowding, or they may reflect on political factors that affect prison crowding. Generally, they go on to predict the size of the prison population and what overcrowding will be like in five, ten, or more years.[2]

The corrections literature conveys a sense of dismay about the dramatic and continued growth and expense of U.S. prisons. Among corrections professionals there is little support for the public and political majorities that favor the building and filling of prisons. Concern is expressed about the folly of attempts to control increasing numbers of inmates with fewer resources. Furthermore, it is argued that as prison populations continue to grow, the disproportionate incarceration of minorities, the increasing numbers of females, and the rise of geriatric inmates will pose new challenges.[3]

Why are prisons overcrowded? What can be done to relieve prison crowding? How does politics enter in?

HOW SERIOUS IS THE PROBLEM OF PRISON CROWDING?

Since the mid-1970s, the dizzying rise in prison population and incarceration rates has reflected the growing public impatience with and fear of crime.[4] By the 1990s the prison population crisis was attracting the attention of most administrators almost to the exclusion of other problems. Between 1970 and the late 1990s, the population of this nation's prisons increased from 196,479 to 1,366,721 and resulted in crowded conditions.

This crowding has adverse consequences for the Federal Bureau of Prisons and for state departments of corrections. **Prison crowding** also has serious consequences for a state's economy, such as when a lawsuit leads to court-ordered changes such as the rebuilding or remodeling of correctional facilities. Moreover, both staff and inmates are adversely affected by prison crowding. Staff must work in a more volatile environment, and inmates must live in facilities in which they are jammed and crammed with other inmates.

Extent of Prison Crowding

On 31 December 1999, 1,366,721 prisoners were under the jurisdiction of federal or state adult correctional authorities. During that year, the states and District of Columbia added 31,591 prisoners and the federal system added 12,205. Thus, the inmate population of state and federal authorities increased by 43,796 during 1999, significantly less than the 58,420 increase in 1998. The prison population has grown an average of 65,867 per year since 1990, an increase of more than half a million people in nine years. The rate of incarceration increased from 292 sentenced inmates per 100,000 in 1990 to 476 sentenced inmates per 100,000 in 1999. On 31 December 1999, federal prisons were operating at 32 percent above capacity, and state prisons were operating at from 1 to 17 percent above capacity.[5] (See Table 19.1 for federal and state prison capacities on 31 December 1999).

Table 19.1

Reported Federal and State Prison Capacities, Year-End 1999

Region and Jurisdiction	1999			Custody Population as a Percent of —	
	Rated	Operational	Design	Highest Capacity[a]	Lowest Capacity[a]
Federal	90,075	...	...	132%	132%
Northeast					
Connecticut[b]	...	...	...	...	...
Maine	1,460	1,639	1,460	100%	112%
Massachusetts	...	...	9,162	116	116
New Hampshire	2,036	2,064	1,944	109	116
New Jersey	...	...	17,282	143	143
New York	61,265	66,384	53,815	108	133
Pennsylvania	25,228	32,384	25,228	113	145
Rhode Island	3,724	3,724	3,862	76	79
Vermont	1,140	1,200	1,023	95	111
Midwest					
Illinois	32,313	32,313	27,529	138%	162%
Indiana	15,383	17,944	...	96	111
Iowa	6,219	6,219	6,219	116	116
Kansas	8,860	...	...	97	97
Michigan	...	47,178	...	98	98
Minnesota	5,664	5,786	5,786	98	100
Missouri	...	27,416	...	95	95
Nebraska	...	2,963	2,371	120	150
North Dakota	1,005	952	1,005	91	96
Ohio	37,245	...	...	125	125
South Dakota	...	2,545	...	96	96
Wisconsin	...	10,951	...	139	139
South					
Alabama	21,800	21,800	21,800	97%	97%
Arkansas[c]	10,426	10,426	10,426	100	100
Delaware	...	4,206	3,192	—	—
District of Columbia	5,424	5,424	...	85	85
Florida	80,491	73,325	52,252	82	121
Georgia	...	43,808	...	89	89
Kentucky	11,947	11,707	7,421	93	150
Louisiana	19,174	19,363	...	83	84
Maryland	...	23,213	...	97	97
Mississippi[c]	...	17,827	...	102	102
North Carolina	27,145	...	27,145	109	109
Oklahoma[c]	...	22,594	...	99	99
South Carolina	...	23,565	22,177	89	95
Tennessee[c]	17,522	17,127	...	96	98
Texas[c,d]	155,924	152,805	155,924	97	99
Virginia	31,767	31,787	31,787	91	91
West Virginia	3,059	2,880	2,950	94	100
West					
Alaska	2,603	2,691	2,603	94%	97%
Arizona	...	24,310	24,310	101	101
California	...	154,467	80,272	101	194
Colorado	...	11,230	9,424	116	138
Hawaii	...	3,406	2,481	102	141
Idaho	3,182	3,956	3,182	97	120
Montana	...	1,400	896	100	156
Nevada[c]	9,379	...	6,948	99	134
New Mexico[c]	...	5,592	5,504	92	93
Oregon	...	9,550	...	99	99
Utah	...	4,418	4,584	115	119
Washington	8,862	12,036	12,036	119	161
Wyoming	1,231	1,243	1,047	101	120

... Data not available
— Not calculated.
[a] Population counts are based on the number of inmates held in facilities operated by the jurisdiction. Excludes inmates held in local jails, in other states, or in private facilities.

[b] Connecticut no longer reports capacity because of a law passed in 1995.

[c] Includes capacity of private and contract facilities and inmates housed in them.
[d] Excludes capacity of county facilities and inmates housed in them.

Source: Bureau of Justice Statistics, *Prisoners in 1999* (Washington D.C.: U.S. Department of Justice, 2000), p. 8.

Figure 19.1
Sentenced Prisoners in State Institutions per 100,000 civilians, 31 December 1997

Source: U.S. Department of Justice, Bureau of Justice Statistics. *Bulletin* (Washington, D.C.: U.S. Government Printing Office, August 1998). p. 3.

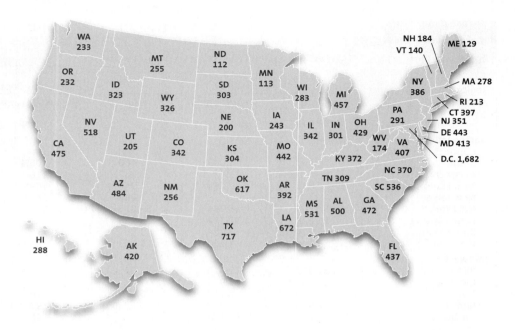

In 1999, Texas (163,290), California (163,067), and the Bureau of Prisons (135,246) together held one in every three prisoners in the United States. Two jurisdictions had increases of 10 percent in 1998, led by Idaho (12.9 percent) and Wisconsin (10.9 percent). Nine jurisdictions experienced decreases; Rhode Island was down 12.8 percent, the District of Columbia 12.0.[6]

Analyses of imprisonment rates from 1990 to 1999 revealed a 60 percent increase among male inmates and an 84 percent increase among female inmates under the jurisdiction of state or federal prison authorities. A similar analysis revealed widespread disparities by race and ethnicity. In 1999, the rate among African American males in their late twenties reached 8,300 prisoners per 100,000 residents of the United States, compared to 2,703 among Hispanic males and 868 among white males. Nearly one in four African American men ages 20 to 29 in the United States was under the supervision of the criminal justice system—on probation or parole or in jail or prison.[7]

A closer examination of prison crowding reveals that the rate varies significantly from one region to another and from one state to another. The South has the highest rates of imprisonment. On 31 December 1999 the seventeen southern states and the District of Columbia had an incarceration rate of 543 per 100,000 U.S. residents, which was considerably higher than the western rate of 421, the midwestern rate of 367, and the northeastern rate of 330.[8] States that border each other sometimes show wide variation in levels of imprisonment (see Figure 19.1).

Why do some states have much higher rates of imprisonment than other states even though they have similar crime rates?

Consequences of Prison Crowding

One consequence of prison overcrowding is that the fundamental expectations and ideals of the system fall more and more by the wayside. Under the stress of overcrowding, consider what has to be done for the system to operate at all. First is the practical problem of finding room for prisoners within existing facilities. Two or more prisoners must be crammed into cells designed for single occupancy. Double bunks are installed in dormitories so that a hundred prisoners can be accommodated in space intended for fifty. In some cases day rooms and industrial facilities are vacated to convert the floors into dormitories. Even then, some prisoners may find themselves sleeping on mattresses spread out in corridors.

States have begun to transfer prisoners from state prisons to county jails in other states. In 1996, 2,500 prisoners were taken from jammed penitentiaries in Colorado, Missouri, North Carolina, Utah, and Virginia and sent to Texas jails. As tough new sentencing guidelines packed prisons beyond their limits, state governments paid to send their inmate overflow out of state. For example, Oregon planned to move 1,700 inmates out of its penitentiary system at a cost of $27 million.[9]

The obvious problems of control that crowding presents have been brought to the attention of the federal courts, which have intervened to mandate strict population ceilings for individual prisons and, in some cases, for entire state systems. These rulings often lead to the overcrowding of county jails, where convicted felons wait for vacant cells in a state prison.

The problems posed by crowded prisons include the difficulty of controlling large inmate populations, feelings of anxiety and stress among inmates, and increased levels of stress among all who work within the walls.[10] When the prison population increases, correctional officers are required to keep track of too many inmates, have inadequate space to separate troublemakers, and deal with unending daily problems. A crowded prison tends to be a violent prison, which means that both inmates and staff are more likely to be injured or killed. For example, inmates who took hostages during the 1986 riot at the Moundsville, West Virginia, penitentiary petitioned for the reduction of the prison's population because they believed that crowding increased the probability of confrontations and violence among inmates.[11] In crowded prisons, correctional officers may be unwilling to permit inmates to participate in programs when they are having difficulty with basic security duties. Moreover, individuals who live or work in a crowded prison experience high levels of psychological stress and physical illnesses.[12] In Within the Walls 19.1, an inmate describes the impact of crowding on inmates.

By what means has the correctional system tried to accommodate ever greater numbers of convicted offenders sentenced to incarceration? What are some negative outcomes of prison overcrowding for prisoners? For correctional officers? For correctional institutions and jurisdictions? For communities and society? What might be some solutions to the problem of prison overcrowding?

the walls   19.1

within

Surviving in a Crowded Concrete Tomb

In here, the cells are the size of the average living room closet, with one sink and toilet connected to each other and two people living in them; if one is to get around, the other has to lie down.

Prisons have what are called galleries, which is exactly like the porches in projects. Human flesh—prisoners—are stacked on top of each other, each having their own problems. This is an implosion, and from every implosion, it is always simply a matter of time before an explosion comes about.

With no space at all, we are thrown together with other inmates. Imagine being in a community of murderers, robbers, rapists, dope fiends, drug dealers, snitches, homosexuals, and any other form of degrading behavior that the human mind can concoct; a community where there is no security, no real form of protection.

> Imagine being in a community of murderers, robbers, rapists, dope fiends, drug dealers, snitches, homosexuals, and any other form of degrading behavior . . .

There are no rules, and the only standards are survival of the fittest. You immediately realize you are all alone. The only person that you can trust, talk to, or confide in is "yourself." In this world you cannot cry, tears are a sure sign of weakness, and somebody, somewhere is always looking for someone to exploit. You have to be strong, tough, and wise if you are to survive.

CRITICAL THINKING QUESTIONS

Why does this Illinois inmate call the prison "a crowded concrete tomb"? What does he mean by "you have to be strong, tough, and wise to survive."?

Source: Reprinted from Herron Lewiel "Prison Life: From the Womb to the Tomb," (unpublished manuscript), p. 31. Used with permission.

HOW CAN INCREASES IN PRISON CROWDING BE EXPLAINED?

Prison crowding can be explained in a number of ways. There is the perspective of crime rates. High rates of violence and sex crimes and the spread of drug-trafficking gangs are evidence that more, rather than fewer, offenders require long-term incarceration. There is the perspective of sentencing practices and laws: mandatory sentencing, three-strikes laws, truth-in-sentencing laws, antidrug laws, and sentencing guidelines. There is the perspective of criminal justice practices: Tough parole policies are probably the most influential, but the increasing numbers of sex offenders and people with mental illness sent to prison also contribute to crowding. There is the perspective of law-and-order politics. And, last, there is the multidimensional perspective: No one explanation suffices to explain prison crowding.[13]

Crime Rates

The old idea that incarceration rates are an outgrowth of crime rates is still widely believed. Émile Durkheim's writings on crime and punishment are based on the rational assumption that increased levels of crime will result in increased levels of punishment.[14] Alfred Blumstein and colleagues' "hypothesis of the stability of punishment" is an extension of Durkheim's notion that punishment is directly related to the rates of crime in a society.[15] According to that hypothesis, during a stable period, rates of punishment and incarceration remain constant, but when crime rates go up, the rates of imprisonment likewise rise. Blumstein ultimately concluded that his thinking on the stability of punishment was incorrect, but his primary assertion of the direct relationship between crime and imprisonment still receives wide support.[16]

The idea that rates of imprisonment rise and fall with increases and decreases in crime rates seems to make sense.[17] However, research on the relationship between the rise of crime and crowded prison conditions offers little support for the "crime-causes-overcrowding hypothesis."[18] The fact is that states that lock up the most offenders continue to have the highest crime rate and states that incarcerate the fewest offenders have the lowest crime rate.[19] Also significant is the fact that imprisonment rates continued to rise in the past decade even though the levels of crime leveled off or decreased.

Law and Sentencing Practices

The idea that crowding in large part is due to more punitive laws and sentencing practices has wide support.[20] Mandatory sentencing laws require imprisonment for certain offenses, and most specify a minimum number of years an offender must spend in prison. The enormous appeal of mandatory sentencing laws as a cause of overcrowding is that all fifty states have these laws for violent and gun-related crimes, drug offenses, and drunk driving.[21] Moreover, thirty-four states have "habitual offender" laws that require enhanced prison terms for repeat felony offenders, in some cases regardless of the seriousness of the offense.[22]

Three-strikes laws had been adopted by fourteen states and the federal government by the end of 1994. Georgia went further and passed a two-strikes law. California's three-strikes law doubles the sentence on a second felony conviction.[23] California is expecting huge increases in its prison rates because its three-strikes law requires a sentence of twenty-five years to life for a person convicted of a third felony. An analysis of the California law during the first eight months of its implementation found that in 70 percent of the cases the final strike involved a nonviolent offense.[24] For example, Jerry Williams of Redondo Beach, California, was convicted of a third strike when he stole a slice of pizza. The 27-year-old had two prior robbery convictions and received a sentence of twenty-five years to life for his third strike.[25]

Truth-in-sentencing practices have been enacted in response to the public's concern that offenders are being released before serving their full sentences. These practices generally require that the actual sentence served by the inmate be a substantial percentage, often 85 percent, of the maximum time imposed by the sentencing judge. This percentage of sentence served is a considerable increase from the average 48 percent of a sentence served by violent offenders in 1992.[26]

Changes in drug laws also are widely considered to contribute to prison crowding. Michael Tonry and others have pointed out that drug policies have greatly increased the numbers of African Americans in prison (see Chapter 18). Yet, as Joseph Dillon Davey states, "there are more factors involved in the rise of imprisonment than the disproportionate imprisoning of African Americans." He goes on to say that since "drug offenders presently account for less than one-fourth of the total prison population, we cannot explain the quadrupling of the rate of imprisonment as an outgrowth of drug policy alone."[27] Davey suggests that drug laws provide only part of the explanation for prison crowding.

Sentencing guidelines are in use in at least fourteen states and the federal courts. Those who have examined guidelines contend that they can lead to more or to less imprisonment. Where policymakers have addressed concerns about the growth of prison populations, states have been able to control prison growth. The 1988 federal sentencing guidelines do not take prison capacity into consideration, and this failure has contributed to the dramatic increase of federal inmates.[28]

There is support for the view that the increasingly harsh sentencing statutes, both federal and state, have contributed to a rise of imprisonment. In mandatory sentences, for example, certain offenses require the imposition of a prison sentence. In addition, legislatures have adopted get-tough laws concerning gun crimes, crimes committed by repeat offenders and habitual criminals, and certain categories of drug crimes. All these laws are designed to keep inmates in prison longer and thus would seem to contribute to prison overcrowding.[29] However, Zimring and Hawkins argue that legislative changes in the law may be increasing the lengths of imprisonment but that does not explain why so many more inmates are sent to prisons than in the past.[30]

Criminal Justice Practices

Previous chapters have mentioned the return of large numbers of offenders to prison for probation and parole revocations. W. L. Kautzky's comments at the beginning of this chapter suggest that probation and parole revocations constitute 45 percent of Iowa's new prison admissions. In California and other states, technical violations of parole mean even higher numbers of returnees to prison.

The increased numbers of persons with mental illness sent to jail and prison also have been mentioned. According to the National Coalition for the Mentally Ill in the Criminal Justice System, there are 33 percent more mentally ill persons in jails than are found in mental hospitals.[31] A 1994 California study found that 8 percent of the state prison population had one of four major mental disorders and that another 17 percent had less severe but still serious mental illnesses.[32]

Sex offenders, as previously discussed, have been prosecuted and convicted in much greater numbers than before. They have been given longer and harsher sentences. Four states have passed "sexual predator" laws that provide for indefinite confinement of child molesters and rapists.[33]

It is difficult to refute the argument that changes in criminal justice policy have contributed to a rise in prison populations. The most influential of these changes would appear to be the high rates of probation and parole revocations. What makes the probation and parole revocation position a little less convincing is that probation and parole returnees tend to receive short sentences and then are released to the community.

Public fear of violent crime against persons and property is one of the reasons given for the belief that incarceration rates in the U.S. are a direct outgrowth of crime rates. What evidence tends to contradict this belief? What are some other explanations for high incarceration rates in this country?

outside the walls   19.2

The Politicization of Crime

In the 1970s, politicians began to overdramatize the social damage that crime was doing to American society. Criminals were identified as persons fundamentally different in character from law-abiding members of society. Political rhetoric tended to oversimplify crime as a conflict between good and evil. Criminals were portrayed as bad people who make the world a dangerous and violent place. Criminals were described as predators awaiting their opportunity to attack persons and property. This political rhetoric fostered a fear of crime.

> The wars on crime and drugs were fought from the White House . . .

The public was assured that a get-tough approach to crime was all that was needed to return to the stability of the past. At all levels of government, a no-nonsense approach was advocated as the only way to restore order to American society. The public seemed receptive to the issue of crime and punishment. It not only united the public, because of strong opposition to crime, especially street crime, but also aroused strong feelings of fear and outrage. Punishment was said to be the only appropriate moral and practical response to criminals.

The **politicization of crime** took place as federal, state, and local governments waged war on crime and drugs in the 1970s and 1980s. The wars on crime and drugs were fought from the White House, especially by Presidents Richard Nixon, Gerald Ford, and Ronald Reagan. Their administrations repeatedly called for tougher penalties, more prisons, mandatory sentences, death penalties, and reduced rights for prisoners. Supporters claimed that these tougher measures would make America safe. The wars on crime and drugs were also carried on in state legislatures and governors' offices: criminal codes were revised, the death penalty was restored, and mandatory and determinate sentences were enacted for certain crimes. The survival of this crime control approach depends on the public's continuing belief that only harsher and harsher punishment will work.

CRITICAL THINKING QUESTIONS

Is the notion that criminals are bad people still attractive to the American public? Is the politicization of crime as popular today as it was in the 1970s? Is it different in any way?

Source: See Stuart A. Scheingold, *The Politics of Law and Order: Street Crime and Public Policy* (New York: Longman, 1984).

Politics and Recent Crime Control Policies

There are those who claim that the most persuasive explanation for prison crowding is the get-tough agenda of politicians at all levels of government. In the late 1960s and early 1970s, politicians made crime the scapegoat for the social disorder apparent in the larger society. This law-and-order agenda led to a **War on Crime** and late in the 1980s to a **War on Drugs.** See Outside the Walls 19.2 for the social construction of a crime control model.

The War on Crime and the War on Drugs escalated in the 1990s to a different political platform based on increasing the dosages of punishment on offender populations. It seemed that everyone had gotten into this get-tough approach to offenders. Indeed, as Todd Clear notes, "In the collective work of these officials—judges, elected executives, legislators, and line criminal justice workers—to increase punitiveness, no single actor stands out as primary. At times, the punishment experiment seemed to take on the appearance of a kind of contest—who can advocate the most serious punitiveness."[34]

According to Clear, believing that the solution to crime involves being nasty to criminals, the nation finds itself in a cycle of escalation.[35] Clear makes the point that in this social context, a rise of imprisonment is to be expected. Yet, although the interaction between crime and politics may explain policy changes, it has not provided tangible evidence of a direct relationship between law and order politics and prison crowding. For that, we look to the states.

Do Governors Influence Prison Crowding?   Davey argues that the governor of a state with a strong law-and-order platform can directly influence the rise of imprisonment:

> It is my argument that the political views of U.S. governors concerning the proper reaction to criminal offenders should be considered one of the most significant factors in determining interstate variations in the rate of imprisonment. A governor who wants to encourage a Draconian approach to the problem of crime can send out a law-and-order message to participants in the state criminal justice system and expect a quick response."[36]

For example, police officers can respond by using discretion to make a formal arrest rather than giving a warning. Parole officers can return more parolees to prison for minor violations. District attorneys can take a harder line in plea negotiations. Judges can opt for harsher sentencing options and send more defendants to prison.[37]

Davey examined the rates of imprisonment in all fifty states. The seven states with law-and-order governors had the largest rise in imprisonment. In nearby states where the governors espoused less punitive policies, rates of imprisonment did not increase. Davey concluded that both formal and informal processes are at work in the states led by governors with a strong law-and-order political platform but informal get-tough messages sent to participants in the criminal justice system may have a more immediate effect on prison expansion.[38]

Multidimensional Explanations

A final perspective on why prisons are so crowded is that there is no single answer. Zimring and Hawkins argue that none of the legislative changes or criminal justice initiatives in the 1970s and 1980s was widespread enough to account for the large increase in prison population that occurred in the United States.[39] They agree that law-and-order politics clearly had an effect, but to specify why policies vary from state to state and to determine the degree of each of the influences is currently beyond the scope of research that has been done or the knowledge we have.

Theodore Caplow and Jonathan Simon explain the rise in incarceration by saying that there is "a bias toward complexity."[40] They state that the rise in incarceration is a result of three independent but interactive factors: First, crime control has become a privileged function of government. The rhetoric of punishment is presently being drawn on to resolve basic administrative problems. Second, the intensification of the war on drugs in the 1980s took place at the same time as the introduction of crack cocaine and produced a virtually limitless supply of candidates for prison. Third, the penal system has become more responsive since the 1960s to political pressures for growth and has been capable of handling such growth.[41]

Caplow and Simon agree with David Garland who has argued that it is a mistake to reduce our tendencies to punish in society to singular social processes or forces.[42] According to Caplow and Simon, this is so because punishment "serves so many different functions, involves the life choices of so many people, and bears on so many other social institutions that reductionist explanations are necessarily misleading."[43]

The hero in this chapter is Michael Tonry, director of the Institute of Criminology at Cambridge University and Sonosky Professor of Law and Public Policy at the University of Minnesota Law School. Tonry is one of the most highly respected scholars today in the areas of criminal sentencing, race relations and corrections, and intermediate sentencing. He subscribes to the idea of multidimensional explanations of prison crowding. Read what he wrote for *Invitation to Corrections* in 2000.

h e r o e s

Michael Tonry

Director of the Institute of Criminology at Cambridge University

"What we see depends both on where we stand and when we look, and this is no less true of punishment than anything else.

"Seen from the perspectives of America in the 1950s and 1960s or Europe today, American policies are extraordinarily harsh, inhumane, and costly, and they are based much more on symbolic than on substantive foundations. The harshness is clear. In the 1960s, the incarceration rate was around 150 per 100,000 residents, about the same as the highest rates in other Western countries today (most are between 60 to 100 per 100,000). The current U.S. rate exceeds 700 per 100,000. In the 1960s, capital punishment appeared to be on its way out. It has been abolished in every European or other English-speaking country. Nearly 4,000 people live on American death rows and the number of executions per year is steadily increasing. The United States also executes mentally retarded and minor offenders, practices forbidden by all international human rights conventions.

"Finally, offenders in America are commonly sentenced to terms of life without possibility of parole or to fixed terms measured in decades. Such sentences were unheard of in 1960s America, where parole release was always a possibility. In most European countries today, sentences over a year are uncommon and human rights norms make sentences longer than 12 or 14 years unconstitutional.

"The inhumanity of U.S. practice is also plain to see. Lengthy prison sentences take away large fractions of people's lives and take parents away from millions of children. Although crime is known to be powerfully associated with economic and social disadvantage, blighted childhoods, drug dependence, and inadequate education, little effort is made in prisons or community programs to provide adequate treatment and skills training. In recent years, no-frills regimes have eliminated programs and self-improvement opportunities. Justification of current practice is made harder when notice is taken that prisoners disproportionately come from minority backgrounds.

"The costs of current American practice are staggering. The annual costs of imprisonment at $35,000 per prison bed per year exceed $70 billions. The more important costs, however, are in the diminution of the lives of offenders and their communities, families, partners, and children. Only recently have scholars begun to examine the collateral effects of imprisonment and harsh crime policies generally. They are at least as substantial and as important as any direct effects on crime rates or prevention.

"How are American practices to be explained or understood? One kind of explanation focuses on the civil rights movement. The Democratic Party lost its dominant role in southern politics, and Republicans soon recognized that crime and welfare could be used as code words to appeal to antiblack sentiments. It worked, and it also soon became evident that emotional appeals about toughness could galvanize electoral support. By the 1990s, many Democrats abandoned rational argument and competed with their opponents to demonstrate their toughness. By this account, crime policy became primarily symbolic, and its harshness, inhumanity, and cost became almost irrelevant.

"Another kind of explanation focuses on the social and economic turbulence of the past quarter-century. People are fearful of change and instability. Blacks, welfare recipients, and foreigners became scapegoats, and policies directed at them were a way for politicians to acknowledge the anxieties and fears of many ordinary people.

"Another kind of explanation focuses narrowly on the increased crime rates of the 1960s and 1970s and argues that harsher policies were needed to control crime and reduce victimization. Zero-tolerance policing, three-strikes laws, and harsher sentences in the 1990s are believed to have worked.

"Most scholars, and officials and practitioners in most Western countries, disagree. Crime, they argue, is the product of the inadequate socialization of individuals and of changing social and economic conditions. Short-term policy changes can affect none of those causal forces. What is needed are modulated policies, fairly and consistently applied and backed up by treatment and social programs that address the deficiencies in people's lives that make crime an attractive opportunity.

"From outside the United States the belief that current harsh policies have played a major role in reducing crime rates looks naive. Crime rates have fallen abruptly in nearly every Western country in the 1990s, and no other has adopted U.S.-style toughness policies. Looking inside the United States, crime rates have fallen in every state and in most large cities, but states vary enormously in their crime control and punishment policies and cities vary enormously in their policing policies.

"Whether responsibility for the current American crime policies should be laid at the feet of cynical politicians or attributed to the fears and prejudices of the American public remains to be decided. Historians will tell us. It is striking though that, were the United States in Europe, the courts would strike down many current policies and practices as violative of the European Convention on Human Rights."

CRITICAL THINKING QUESTIONS

What evidence does Tonry offer for the view that crime policies in the United States are not related to crime rates? Which explanation of U.S. crime policies do you favor, and why? How might you defend U.S. crime policies in comparison with European crime policies?

WHAT CAN BE DONE TO REDUCE PRISON CROWDING?

In the early 1970s, the National Council on Crime and Delinquency (NCCD) issued policy statements that defined the function of imprisonment as "incapacitation" and specified the amount of prison space required to perform that function. "Confinement," said the NCCD, "is necessary for the offender who, if not confined, would be a serious danger to the public. For all others, who are not dangerous and who constitute the great majority of offenders, the sentence of choice should be one or another of the wide variety of non-institutional dispositions." With this benchmark of "dangerousness," the NCCD drew the conclusion that "only a small percentage of offenders in penal institutions today" require incarceration. Indeed, "in any state no more than one hundred persons would have to be confined in a single maximum-security institution."[44]

In contrast, James Q. Wilson drew a much different conclusion concerning the function of the prison: "We would view the correctional system as having [this] function—namely, to isolate and to punish. . . . [The] purpose of isolating—or more accurately closely supervising—offenders is obvious. Whatever they may do when they are released, they cannot harm society while confined or closely supervised. The gains from merely incapacitating convicted criminals may be very large."[45]

Wilson's point of view is predominant today. If the NCCD program had been accepted, the total prison population would have been only around five thousand. Instead, the prison population has about doubled each decade. Emphasizing imprisonment as a punishment deserved by increasing numbers of offenders has proven politically satisfying to the electorate. It also has created a system that has grown larger and larger.[46]

What can be done to reduce prison crowding is a critical question today. Crowding decreased slightly from 1998 to 1999 in state prisons, but this change did not affect the overall trend of crowding. The solution to the problem of crowded prisons may be even more elusive than the question of why we have prison crowding.

Prison construction is one proposal, but the problem with building new prisons is that they tend to fill very quickly. It is not unusual for prison construction to increase rather than to decrease prison crowding. Judges sometimes sentence to new facilities defendants who otherwise would have received community-based corrections. In addition, putting state prisoners in county jails tends to shift crowding from one location to another. Leasing private prison space relieves state and federal crowded prisons, but, as indicated in Chapter 10, major issues remain to be resolved about the privatization of corrections. The proposal that has had the greatest effect on reducing prison crowding is the expansion of community-based alternatives to imprisonment. Outside the Walls 19.3 describes a strategy developed by Democrats in the Oklahoma House of Representatives in 1996 to deal with the problem of crowded prisons in their state.

Long-Term Objectives

The long-term objectives point in two directions, and at this time neither objective seems likely to be achieved. One long-term objective is to deal with the reasons why disproportionate numbers of African Americans, members of other minority groups, and the poor are in prison. Their overrepresentation is related in part to their high rates of poverty, underemployment, racial bias, illiteracy, lack of education, and drug abuse.[47] Few would disagree that criminogenic forces are strongest in inner-city areas of concentrated poverty. Crime and poverty have always marched together. African Americans experience material conditions that are far worse, on average, than conditions experienced by white Americans. They are more likely to be born to unwed mothers, to be part of families with incomes below the poverty line, to be dependent on welfare, and to live in inner-city neighborhoods. Comparable racial statistics for African Americans and whites seem to understate the disadvantages of

outside the walls   19.3

A Comprehensive Strategy for Addressing the Problem of Crowded Prisons in Oklahoma

OKLAHOMA CITY—A coordinated strategy incorporating myriad variables to resolve Oklahoma's long-term prison dilemma has been developed by Democrats in the House of Representatives, Speaker Glen D. Johnson announced Friday.

"For years we've coped with prison problems through crisis management, lurching from one unmanageable situation to another," the Okemah Democrat said, "We need a logical long-term, coordinated plan to deal with this complex issue." . . .

Oklahoma Attorney General Drew Edmondson reviewed the coordinated strategy proposed by the House Democrats and found it "to be comprehensive, innovative, and effective, not only in its approach toward managing Oklahoma's prison dilemma, but toward a more dependable and meaningful administration of justice."

The House Democrats' blueprint identifies several elements that can be used by the legislature to initiate a plan to alleviate prison crowding and simultaneously ensure that justice is administered. Those elements are a combination of:

- New prison construction
- Leasing private prison space and utilizing available bed space in county jails throughout Oklahoma
- Policy options such as truth-in-sentencing, which would require convicted felons to serve at least 85 percent of their prison sentence

> We need a logical long-term, coordinated plan to deal with this complex issue.

- Community-based correctional work programs and other alternatives to incarceration
- Program options, particularly educational courses, job skills training and rehabilitation to lower the rate of repeat offenders returning to prison
- Funding options, such as appropriations from the state's General Revenue Fund versus tapping the "rainy day" Constitutional Reserve Fund

"A sound corrections policy will need to include key elements such as additional medium-security bed space, sentencing reform, alternative sentencing policies, innovative inmate programs, involvement of local-government jurisdictions and a comprehensive funding plan," House Democrats declare in their corrections road map.

CRITICAL THINKING QUESTIONS

What do you think of the Oklahoma Democrats' plan to relieve prison crowding? What would need to be added to address prison crowding across the nation? Why do you think this plan was defeated in the Oklahoma House of Representatives?

Source: Reprinted from Oklahoma House of Representatives Media Division Webpage.

---

inner-city blacks. Data on the worst-off third of African Americans would be even more disturbing.[48]

Another long-term objective—which would have the most immediate effect on reducing prison crowding—is a change in the political climate away from a crime control model to community-based and rehabilitative models. The law-and-order policies see crowding as an inevitable part of corrections because of the necessity of incarcerating the criminal element. Until the politics of crime change, state and federal prisons will remain crowded.

Short-Term Strategies

Michael Sherman and Gordon Hawkins have argued that prison construction can do much to improve the quality of institutional care, if construction is used to replace existing facilities or to improve the care they provide. Sherman and Hawkins state that decisions about building new prisons, as well as funding them, should be based on the condition that prison capacities do not increase.[49] They go on to say that the short-term effects of sentencing reform would probably be greater if reform made the system less harsh and increased the likelihood that offenders would be assigned to community-based programs. Instead, sentencing reform in recent years has increased the number of offenders eligible to go to prison and lengthened sentences of those sent to prison.[50]

In *America's Imprisonment Binge* John Irwin and James Austin argue that a major reason why we imprison so many is that there are too many people in prison who do not belong there.[51] They conducted interviews with 154 male prisoners randomly selected from the intake populations of Washington, Nevada, and Illinois and concluded: "Rather than being vicious predators, most were disorganized, unskilled, undisciplined petty criminals who very seldom engaged in violence or made any significant amount of money from their criminal acts."[52]

Irwin and Austin also state that the single most direct solution to the imprisonment binge is to shorten prison terms. They argue that this can be done through a number of existing mechanisms, such as increasing use of existing good-time credit statutes, accelerating parole eligibility, developing reentry programs for prisoners, and altering existing parole revocation policies.[53]

In addition, the following strategies have been of some help in alleviating crowded conditions in U.S. prisons:

- The increased use of intermediate sanctions and private prisons
- "Capping" legislation, which establishes a population limit and provides for emergency release measures to maintain a desired population level
- Extended parole, which directs the parole board to use risk assessments when establishing durations of parole supervision
- Community corrections acts, which keep in the community certain offenders who otherwise would be sent to prison
- Emergency powers acts, which permit governors to release state inmates up to ninety days early when prison populations exceed operating capacity.[54]

Perhaps, as Davey proposed, the best strategy for achieving short- and long-term reductions in prison populations would be to examine the states that manage crowding better than others. What types of governors do they usually have? What are their sentencing structures? How are their networks of community programs developed? What other factors are present that affect the numbers of offenders sentenced to prison?[55]

SUMMARY

Prison crowding is one of the most serious problems facing corrections today. It undermines the ability of correctional systems to provide adequately for the care, protection, and security of inmates, and it forces correctional officers and other prison staff to work in an environment in which they must keep track of too many inmates, have inadequate space to separate troublemakers, and deal with unending daily problems. Violence among inmates and between inmates and staff is more likely to occur in crowded prisons, and they are more likely to explode in a major riot or disturbance.

The causes of prison crowding are not easily explained. There are several schools of thought. Some observers attribute prison crowding to crime rates. There is more support for the idea that current laws and sentencing practice are a major contributor to prison crowding. Criminal justice practices, too, contribute to prison crowding. The crowding problem also can be related to the politics of law and order and to the effect on incarceration rates of the War on Crime and War on Drugs. The complexity of the issue and the apparent inadequacy of any single answer have led to multidimensional explanations.

Nor is the issue of how to reduce crowding any less complex. Prison construction, intermediate sentencing, early release, and other strategies have been attempted, but prison populations continue to increase. Some states have fewer problems with crowding than other states do, and it may be that an examination of how those states manage the issue of crowding might provide helpful directions for other states.

KEY TERMS

politicization of crime, p. 455
prison crowding, p. 448

War on Crime, p. 455
War on Drugs, p. 455

CRITICAL THINKING QUESTIONS

1. Can you think of any other explanations for prison crowding besides those mentioned in this chapter?

2. What do you think generated the harsh crime control policies toward offenders in the 1990s? How long do you think that approach will last? Support your answer.

WEB DESTINATIONS

Read articles from the Office of International Criminal Justice on remedies for prison overcrowding.
http://www.oicj.org/public/story.cfm?story=9FD2986B-F6AC-11D3-AA9E-00C04F409AD4

Study the graph and follow the links at this Public Agenda Online site for an analysis of prison overcrowding in the United States.
http://www.publicagenda.org/issues/factfiles_detail.cfm?issue_type=crime&list=8

Read about the effects of mandatory minimum sentences on prison overcrowding and other problems in the criminal justice system.

http://www.famm.org/famm-test/what3.html

This in-depth news story explores the relationship between prison overcrowding and the privatization of corrections.
http://www.abcnews.go.com/sections/us/prison/prison_business.html

Evaluate a specific plan for relieving prison overcrowding in Illinois.
http://venus.soci.niu.edu/~sociclass/JJ/jjprop.html

FOR FURTHER READING

Caplow, Theodore and Jonathan Simon. "Understanding Prison Policy and Population Trends." In *Prisons,* ed. Michael Tonry and Joan Petersilia. Chicago: University of Chicago Press, 1999: 63–120. One of the most perceptive articles explaining the rise of incarceration in U.S. society. They define prison crowding as arising from several interactive factors.

Davey, Joseph Dillon. *The Politics of Prison Expansion: Winning Elections by Waging War on Crime.* Westport, Conn.: Praeger, 1998. Davey examines the role that governors have played concerning the issue of prison crowding.

Irwin, John and James Austin. *It's About Time: America's Imprisonment Binge.* 2d ed. Belmont, Calif.: Wadsworth, 1997. This book offers a powerful response to those who would have us continue a "lock them up" strategy. After making their case how costly incarceration is in human and monetary terms, they offer some solutions to reducing the numbers of those in prison.

Tonry, Michael. *Malign Neglect: Race, Crime, and Punishment in America.* New York: Oxford University Press, 1995. Tonry offers a strong indictment of politicians and the decisions they made in the 1980s concerning drug laws that strongly affected African Americans.

Zimring, Franklin E., and Gordon Hawkins. *The Scale of Imprisonment.* Chicago: University of Chicago Press, 1991. The authors examine the various factors that contribute to the rise of imprisonment in the United States.

NOTES

1. Statement provided to the author in November 2000.

2. In the past two decades, the author has interviewed forty directors and commissioners of state systems and the past three directors of the Federal Bureau of Corrections. These statements represent a summary of their comments about prison crowding.

3. Alan T. Harland, "Editorial Introduction," *The Prison Journal* 76 (December 1996), p. 381.

4. Franklin E. Zimring and Gordon Hawkins, *The Scale of Imprisonment* (Chicago: University of Chicago Press, 1991).

5. Bureau of Justice Statistics, *Prisoners in 1999* (Washington, D.C.: U.S. Department of Justice, 2000), pp. 1–2.

6. Ibid., p. 1,

7. Ibid., pp. 1, 9.

8. Ibid., p. 3

9. Lee Hochberg, "Cells for Rent," *News Hour Online*, 3 January 1996.

10. For the effects of crowding, see Matthew Silberman, *A World of Violence: Corrections in America* (Belmont, Calif.: Wadsworth, 1995), p. 206.

11. Ibid., p. 63. For an article that challenges whether overcrowding is associated with violence, see Gerald G. Gaes, "Prison Crowding Research Reexamined," *Prison Journal* 74 (September 1994), p. 329.

12. F. E. Cheek and M. D. S. Miller, "The Experience of Stress for Corrections Officers: A Double-Bind Theory of Correctional Stress," *Journal of Criminal Justice* 11 (1983), pp. 105–120.

13. Zimring and Hawkins, *The Scale of Imprisonment,* p. 20.

14. Émile Durkheim, "The Evolution of Punishment," in *Durkheim and the Law,* ed. S. Lukes and A. Scull (New York: St. Martin's Press, 1983), p. 121; originally published in 1900.

15. Alfred Blumstein and Jacqueline Cohen, "A Theory of the Stability of Punishment," *Journal of Criminal Law and Criminology* 64 (1973), pp. 198–207.

16. Joseph Dillon Davey, *The Politics of Prison Expansion: Winning Elections by Waging War on Crime* (Westport, Conn.: Praeger, 1998), p. 19. See also Alfred Blumstein, "Prisons," in *Crime,* ed. James Q. Wilson and Joan Petersilia (San Francisco: ICS Press, 1995), p. 388.

17. Zimring and Hawkins, *The Scale of Imprisonment,* p. 121.

18. See Federal Bureau of Investigation, *Uniform Crime Reports* (Washington, D.C.: U.S. Government Printing Office, 1998.

19. William M. DiMascio, *Seeking Justice: Crime and Punishment in America* (New York: Edna McConnell Clark Foundation, 1995), p. 17.

20. The material in this section is adapted from DiMascio, *Seeking Justice,* pp. 19–23.

21. National Council on Crime and Delinquency, "National Assessment of Structured Sentencing Final Report" (Oakland, Calif.: National Council on Crime and Delinquency, January 1995).

22. The Sentencing Project, *Why "3 Strikes and You're Out" Won't Reduce Crime* (Washington, D.C.: The Sentencing Project, 1994).

23. Alan Karpelowitz, "Three Strikes Sentencing Legislation Update" (paper presented at the annual meeting of the National Conference of State Legislatures, New York, November 1994).

24. California Legislative Analyst's Office, "The 'Three Strikes and You're Out' Laws: A Preliminary Assessment," Sacramento, Calif.: Legislative Branch of Government, January 6, 1995).

25. Eric Slater, "Pizza Thief Gets 25 Years to Life," *Los Angeles Times,* 3 March 1995.

26. Bureau of Justice Statistics, *Prison Sentences and Time Served for Violence* (Washington, D.C.: U.S. Department of Justice, 1995).

27. Davey, *The Politics of Prison Expansion,* p. 20.

28. DiMascio, *Seeking Justice,* p. 23.

29. Zimring and Hawkins, *The Scale of Imprisonment,* p. 168.

30. Ibid., p. 173.

31. National Coalition for the Mentally Ill in the Criminal Justice System. Cited in DiMascio, *Seeking Justice,* p. 22.

32. Donald Specter, "Mentally Ill in Prison: A Cruel and Unusual Punishment," *Forum* (December 1994).

33. Barry Meier, "Sexual Predators' Finding Sentence May Last Past Jail," *New York Times,* 27 February 1995.

34. Todd R. Clear, *Harm in American Penology: Offenders, Victims, and Their Communities* (Albany: State University of New York Press, 1994), p. 56.

35. Ibid.

36. Davey, *The Politics of Prison Expansion,* p. 7.

37. Ibid., p. 47.

38. Ibid., p. 111.

39. Zimring and Hawkins, *The Scale of Imprisonment,* p. 173.

40. Theodore Caplow and Jonathan Simon, "Understanding Prison Policy and Population Trends," in *Prisons* ed. Michael Tonry and Joan Petersilia (Chicago: University of Chicago Press, 1999), p. 66.

41. Ibid, pp. 110–111.

42. David Garland, *Punishment and Modern Society* (Chicago: University of Chicago Press, 1990).

43. Caplow and Simon, "Understanding Prison Policy and Population Trends," p. 67.

44. Cited in Zimring and Hawkins, *The Scale of Punishment,* p. 87.

45. James Q. Wilson, "The Political Feasibility of Punishment," in *Justice and Punishment,* ed. J. B. Cederblom and William L. Blizen (Cambridge: Ballinger, 1977), pp. 193–194.

46. Zimring and Hawkins, *The Scale of Imprisonment,* p. 121.

47. See Michael Tonry, *Malign Neglect: Race, Crime, and Punishment in America* (New York: Oxford University Press, 1995), p. 133.

48. Ibid.

49. Michael Sherman and Gordon Hawkins, *Imprisonment in America: Choosing the Future* (Chicago: University of Chicago Press, 1981), p. 101.

50. Ibid., p. 58.

51. John Irwin and James Austin, *It's About Time: America's Imprisonment Binge,* 2d ed. (Belmont, Calif.: Wadsworth, 1997).

52. Ibid., p. 41.

53. Ibid., p. 246.

54. Ibid.

55. Davey, *The Politics of Prison Expansion.*

CHAPTER 19 BUILT-IN STUDY GUIDE

Multiple Choice Questions

1. What happened to the size of the U.S. prison population in this country between 1970 and the late 1990s?
   A. Nearly doubled
   B. Increased six times
   C. Decreased by one-half
   D. Decreased by one-fourth

2. From 1990 to 1999 imprisonment rates for male inmates
   A. Increased by 30%
   B. Increased by 60%
   C. Increased by 84%
   D. Increased by 10%

3. What region of this country has the highest rate of imprisonment?
   A. South
   B. Northeast
   C. Midwest
   D. Northwest

4. All of the following sentencing practices contribute to the explanation of overcrowding except:
   A. Three-strikes laws
   B. Truth-in-sentencing laws
   C. Antidrug laws
   D. Indeterminate sentencing laws

5. Sentencing laws that generally require that the actual sentence served by the inmate be a substantial percentage, often 85 percent, of the maximum time imposed by the sentencing judge are known as:
   A. Truth-in-sentencing laws
   B. Presumptive sentencing laws

C. Indeterminate sentencing laws
   D. Judicial sentencing laws

6. What 1988 White House antidrug policy meant that society would not tolerate drug-related crimes?
   A. Nil tolerance
   B. Abolish tolerance
   C. Zero tolerance
   D. No tolerance

7. All of the following strategies have been of some help in overcoming crowded conditions is U.S. prisons except:
   A. The increased use of private prisons
   B. Capping legislation designed to establish a population limit
   C. Emergency powers act
   D. Mandatory sentencing strategies

8. What happened to the incarceration rate in this country between the 1970s and the late 1990s?
   A. More than doubled
   B. More than tripled
   C. Decreased by one-half
   D. Decreased by one-fourth

9. According to the text, the problems of crowded prisons include all of the following except:
   A. Difficulty in controlling large inmate populations
   B. Mandatory parole and work furlough programs in all states
   C. Feelings of anxiety and stress among inmates
   D. Increased stress among all workers inside the walls

True/False Questions

T F   1. Prison crowding has little impact on a state's economy.

T F   2. There were 1,100,000 prisoners under the jurisdiction of federal and state correctional authorities as of 31 December 1999.

T F   3. As a result of prison crowding, some states have begun to transfer prisoners from state prisons to county jails in other states.

T F   4. Research on the relationship between the rise of crime and crowded prison conditions widely

supports the crime-causes-overcrowding hypothesis.

T F   5. Mandatory sentencing laws require imprisonment for certain offenses and must require a minimum number of years an inmate must spend in prison.

T F   6. Technology has no significant impact on the War on Drugs.

T F   7. James Q. Wilson believed the function of prisons was to isolate and punish offenders.

T F 8. According to Clear, the solution to crime involves being nasty to criminals.

T F 9. Sherman and Hawkins have argued that prison construction will not do much to improve the quality of institutional care.

T F 10. In 1999, Texas, California, and the Bureau of Prisons held one in every three prisoners in the United States.

Essay Questions

1. Explain how prison crowding affects the prison system.

2. Identify and explain how sentencing practices influence prison crowding.

3. How severe of a problem is prison crowding in America? How much did the prison population increased during 1999? From 1990 to 1999 how much has the prison population grown?

4. Identify and explain three strategies for reducing prison crowding.

ANSWERS

Multiple Choice Questions

1. B		6. C	
2. B		7. D	
3. A		8. A	
4. D		9. B	
5. A			

True/False Questions

1. F		6. F	
2. F		7. T	
3. T		8. F	
4. F		9. T	
5. T		10. T	

Prisoners' Rights

Chris LeGear, an Iowa inmate convicted of murder, is seeking assistance on his case:

I'm writing here to discuss the possibility of obtaining your services in regard to a legal matter I'm pursuing. At present I'm in the process of bringing my criminal case back into state court. I've already run the gauntlet of state and federal remedies as a matter of course, but was unable to obtain justice/relief. I've discovered that my host of prior attorneys provided less than acceptable representation, in that all of them in tandem, failed to recognize and raise a proper claim resting on grounds of insanity/temporary insanity.

My trial attorney raised a limited defense of diminished capacity. However, the defense neither fit the predicate facts attending my biological/psychological condition, nor fit the predicate facts underlying the state's charge of first-degree murder. In 1981 I was charged, tried, and convicted of killing my girlfriend. I was seen by two personal defense experts, a psychiatrist and psychologist, who provided scant diagnostics—the drug histories on both counts were terribly insufficient. It is my feeling, based upon some research, that a reevaluation, based on proper diagnostic methods, will generate a report with conclusions indicating a substantial question as to criminal responsibility.

Careful research has shown that my trial attorney did not fully investigate the complete defense of insanity, a legal theory, because he, and his selected defense experts, failed to subject me to a full and proper evaluation. The best resolution to this matter is to reevaluate me based on the same facts made available to the expert witnesses.

The evaluation/reevaluation on me I'm seeking would be based on information, namely, having to do with the mixing of alcohol, Nembutal, and Elavil. I can provide you with specifics regarding the amounts of drugs and alcohol consumed within a given time window, as well as background history regarding illegal drug use, all of which must be factored into a proper diagnostic approach.

In addition, I've teamed up with recognized jailhouse lawyer, Ernest Walters, and together we've done some exhaustive research on the effects of low serotonin levels on human behavior, e.g., aggression, impulsivity, to name a few. We've become immersed in the study of neuro-transmitters, among which norepinephrine and serotonin rank highest in priority. Past studies on serotonin, coupled with more recent controlled studies, have spotlighted a principal biological connection between my past drug and alcohol abuse and serotonin depletion. The gist of where I'm going with this thing is somewhat obvious to the trained medical professional who has had some experience in forensic pathologies, in particular psychology and psychiatry.[1]

CRITICAL THINKING QUESTIONS

What might make it difficult for this inmate to get relief from the courts for his murder conviction? Why would an inmate seek every possible avenue in order to attain a reversal of his or her conviction?

This inmate is arguing that his conviction for murder should be reversed because his constitutional rights were violated at trial. Having served many years in prison, he has spent considerable time studying his court transcript and has developed some degree of sophistication in the areas of law, psychology, and human physiology. In spite of previous disappointments in state and federal courts, he continues to seek all possible avenues so that his rights will finally be honored.

Several perspectives on the issue of prisoners' rights are presented in this chapter. The inmate's viewpoint is contained in Chris LeGear's letter. The courts' viewpoint, both the U.S. Supreme Court and state courts, is contained in many court rulings on the individual rights of prisoners. Another perspective is offered by this chapter's hero, Vincent Nathan, a highly respected legal expert involved in the area of prisoners' rights. At odds with his opinions are advocates of the crime control perspective. They argue that inmates have been given too many rights within the walls and that many of their lawsuits are frivolous and are a waste of the courts' time.

Any discussion of rights must begin with a definition of the term. We open with our own formulation: A *right* is a claim by an individual or group of individuals that another individual, a corporation, or the state has a duty to fulfill. Philosophers and jurists have written volumes about the source of rights. Legal positivists claim that the only rights anyone possesses are the rights that are conferred by law. Many other philosophers disagree, asserting that all human beings possess "natural" rights—from which legal rights are derived—necessary for survival in human society. According to this view, laws that are inconsistent with natural rights cannot and should not survive. Examples would be the race laws of Nazi Germany and the apartheid laws of South Africa.

Convicted felons do not have rights other than those conferred on them by law. In the United States, those rights are derived by the courts from the Constitution of the United States, from the state constitutions, and from the laws that Congress and the state legislatures enact.

WHAT HAS BEEN THE RESPONSE OF THE U.S. SUPREME COURT TO THE ISSUE OF PRISONERS' RIGHTS?

Since the 1970s prisoners have appealed to the federal courts in civil rights suits challenging every aspect of prison programs and practices (see Table 20.1). The courts have become a battlefield where prisoners and corrections officials spar over a variety of issues. Corrections officials charge that the demands of litigation and court orders are pressing their staffs and limited resources to the verge of collapse. Prisoners and their advocates claim that recent unfavorable court rulings, especially by the U.S. Supreme Court, spell the demise of the prisoners' rights movement.[2]

An examination of judges' actions over the years makes it possible to distinguish three phases of the prisoners' rights movement: (1) the convicted-felon-as-slave-of-the-state phase, (2) the high-water mark of the prisoners' rights movement, and (3) the crime control response of the federal and state courts.

Convicted Felons as Slaves of the State

Until well into the twentieth century, the laws assumed that a convicted felon was "civilly dead." There were centuries of precedent. The philosopher Immanuel Kant (1724–1804), a liberal moralist in most respects, thought that an incarcerated robber or thief enjoyed no rights: "He has nothing and can also acquire nothing, but he still wants to live, and this is not possible unless others provide him with nourishment." Kant added that "the state will not support him gratis," and, therefore, he must do whatever kind of work the state may wish to use him for, "and so he becomes a slave, either for a certain period of time or indefinitely, as the case may be."[3]

For most of the history of the United States, the prisoner has been a slave of state corrections—that is, prisoners lost all their rights when sentenced to prison. An 1871 case, *Ruffin v. the Commonwealth of Virginia*, expressed it this way: "[The prisoner] has, as a consequence of his crime, not only forfeited his liberty, but all his personal rights except those which the law in its humanity accords to him. He is for the time being the slave of the state."[4]

For many years, the courts avoided the issue of prisoners' rights, for at least three reasons: (1) Judges wished to maintain the separation of powers and looked on the administration of prisons as a state executive branch function. (2) Judges acknowledged their lack of expertise in corrections. (3) Judges feared that judicial intervention would subvert prison discipline.[5]

High-Water Mark of the Prisoners' Rights Movement

From 1966 to 1976, judges did a 180-degree reversal and became extensively involved in rulings on prisoners' rights. This about-face took place at the same time as the civil rights movement and the rise of the women's movement. It was a time of reform in American society, a time in which social wrongs identified by African Americans, women, prisoners, and other groups were addressed.

Table 20.1

Petitions Filed in U.S. District Courts by Federal and State Prisoners, by Type of Petition, 1977–1998

	Total	Petitions by Federal Prisoners					
		Total	Motions to Vacate Sentence	Habeas Corpus	Mandamus, etc.	Civil Rights	Prison Conditions
1977	19,537	4,691	1,921	1,745	542	483	✕
1978	21,924	4,955	1,924	1,851	544	636	✕
1979	23,001	4,499	1,907	1,664	340	588	✕
1980	23,287	3,713	1,322	1,465	323	603	✕
1981	27,711	4,104	1,248	1,680	342	834	✕
1982	29,303	4,328	1,186	1,927	381	834	✕
1983	30,775	4,354	1,311	1,914	339	790	✕
1984	31,107	4,526	1,427	1,905	372	822	✕
1985	33,468	6,262	1,527	3,405	373	957	✕
1986	33,765	4,432	1,556	1,679	427	770	✕
1987	37,316	4,519	1,669	1,812	313	725	✕
1988	38,839	5,130	2,071	1,867	330	862	✕
1989	41,481	5,577	2,526	1,818	315	918	✕
1990	42,630	6,611	2,970	1,967	525	1,149	✕
1991	42,462	6,817	3,328	2,112	378	999	✕
1992	48,423	6,997	3,983	1,507	597	910	✕
1993	53,451	8,456	5,379	1,467	695	915	✕
1994	57,940	7,700	4,628	1,441	491	1,140	✕
1995	63,550	8,951	5,988	1,343	510	1,110	✕
1996	68,235	13,095	9,729	1,703	444	1,219	✕
1997	62,966	14,952	11,675	1,902	401	974	✕
1998	54,715	9,937	6,287	2,321	346	641	342
Percent change 1998 over 1997	−13.1%	−34.0%	−46.1%	22.0%	−13.7%	−34.2%	✕

Note: Petitions by federal prisoners are suits brought against the federal government. Petitions by state prisoners are those petitions in which the state or its representative(s) is (are) named as the defendant(s). "Habeas corpus" is a writ whose object is to bring a party before a court or judge. "Mandamus" is a writ from a superior court to an inferior court or to a public official, a corporation, etc., commanding that a specified action be taken. Data for 1977–1991 are reported for the twelve-month period ending 30 June. Beginning in 1992, data are reported for the federal fiscal year, which is the twelve-month period ending 30 September.

In the 1960s, a number of cases held that the Black Muslim faith was an established religion and that members of the Nation of Islam were entitled to the same rights as members of other established religious groups.[6] The federal courts have generally held that the religious rights granted to one religious group must be accorded to all such groups within a correctional facility.

Prisoners also won important rights concerning personal correspondence, their rights during disciplinary procedures, and their rights concerning quality medical care. No area of correctional law has attracted as much litigation as prisoner correspondence, largely because personal correspondence usually also involves an individual in the free community who is protected by the First Amendment. In an important 1974 case, *Procunier v. Martinez,* the U.S. Supreme Court ruled that "Censorship of prison mail works as a consequential restriction on the First and Fourteenth Amendment rights of those who are not prisoners."[7] What this means is that citizens in the outside community have

		Petitions by State Prisoners			
	Total	**Habeas Corpus**	**Mandamus, etc.**	**Civil Rights**	**Prison Conditions**
1977	14,846	6,866	228	7,752	X
1978	16,969	7,033	206	9,730	X
1979	18,502	7,123	184	11,195	X
1980	19,574	7,031	146	12,397	X
1981	23,607	7,790	178	15,639	X
1982	24,975	8,059	175	16,741	X
1983	26,421	8,532	202	17,687	X
1984	26,581	8,349	198	18,034	X
1985	27,206	8,534	181	18,491	X
1986	29,333	9,045	216	20,072	X
1987	32,797[a]	9,542	276	22,972	X
1988	33,709	9,880	270	23,559	X
1989	35,904	10,554	311	25,039	X
1990	36,019	10,823	353	24,843	X
1991	35,645	10,331	268	25,046	X
1992	41,426	11,299	481	29,646	X
1993	44,995	11,587	390	33,018	X
1994	50,240	11,918	397	37,925	X
1995	54,599	13,632	398	40,569	X
1996	55,140	14,726	418	39,996	X
1997	48,014	19,956	397	27,661	X
1998	44,778	18,838	461	13,115	12,364
Percent change 1998 over 1997	−6.7%	−5.6%	16.1%	−52.6%	X

[a]Includes 7 motions to vacate sentence.

Source: Kathleen Maguire and Ann L. Pastore, *Bureau of Justice Statistics: Sourcebook of Criminal Justice Statistics—1998* (Washington, D.C.: U.S. Department of Justice, 1999), p. 442.

the right to correspond with prisoners without censorship of their mail. More recent Court rulings (see the section on First Amendment rights later in this chapter) have extended the right of prison officials to censor inmate mail.

The high-water mark of the prisoners' rights movement was the *Wolff v. McDonnell* decision in 1974.[8] McDonnell, a prisoner, had filed a class-action suit against the state of Nebraska, claiming that its disciplinary procedures, especially those pertaining to the loss of "good time" (time subtracted from a sentence for good behavior), were unconstitutional. The state court ruled that the defendant had not received the minimum requirements for disciplinary proceedings. He petitioned the U.S. Supreme Court to restore the "good time" he had lost and to assess damages against corrections officials. The Supreme Court ruled that the state of Nebraska had properly enacted laws pertaining to the granting and revoking of "good time." Nevertheless, the procedure used to revoke "good time" was found to be in violation of the due-process rights granted in the Fourteenth Amendment.[9]

Since the *Wolff* decision, prisoners have won other important victories in the Supreme Court. In *Estelle v. Gamble* (1976), the Court ruled that deliberate interference with serious medical needs constitutes cruel and unusual punishment.[10] Significantly, this suit also demonstrated that a complaint of systemwide deprivation of medical care receives a more sympathetic hearing than do complaints alleging inadequate medical treatment for an individual.

Crime Control Response by the Court

By 1976, court opinions had shifted slightly toward a more balanced position between prisoners' rights and legitimate institutional interests. This so-called restrained-hands doctrine of the U.S. Supreme Court was obvious in four decisions made during the spring of 1976: *Baxter v. Palmigiano*,[11] *Enomota v. Clutchette*,[12] *Meachum v. Fano*,[13] and *Montanye v. Haymes*.[14] The *Meachum v. Fano* decision most clearly expressed the restrained-hands doctrine because of its ruling that the prisoner is subject to the rules of the prison system: "Given a valid conviction, the criminal defendant has been constitutionally deprived of his liberty to the extent that the state may confine him and subject him to the rules of its prison system so long as the conditions of confinement do not otherwise violate the constitution."[15]

The 1981 *Rhodes v. Chapman* case, which held that the Southern Ohio Correctional Facility (SOCF) was not in violation of the Eighth Amendment for double-celling inmates, was an even greater victory for prison officials.[16] Pointing to the fact that SOCF had cells of the most modern design, the Court majority downgraded the "expert" opinion that double-celling in these conditions would lead to the evils predicted from overcrowded conditions generally. The Court's insistence on the judiciary's deferring to administrators on matters such as celling arrangements to meet problems of overcrowding also gave warning that future decisions of the Court would be decidedly less inmate oriented.[17]

Other victories for prison officials in upholding institutional security over prisoners' rights occurred in *Hewitt v. Helms* (1983),[18] *Ponte v. Real* (1985),[19] and *Whitney v. Albers* (1986).[20] Another major victory occurred when a federal judge ruled against prisoners in *Bruscino v. Carlson* (1987), upholding the use of long-term, near-total lockdown of prisoners at the out-of-control federal prison at Marion, Illinois.[21] A federal appeals court upheld this decision.[22]

Rudolf Alexander suggests that the crime control trend of the U.S. Supreme Court is continuing. He cites Supreme Court decisions against prisoners' lawsuits concerning (1) the Eighth Amendment prohibition against cruel and unusual punishment (e.g., *Wilson v. Seiter*, 1981[23]); (2) habeas corpus relief (*Coleman v. Thompson*, 1991[24]); and (3) the deprivation of constitutional rights (*Washington v. Harper*, 1990[25]). Alexander concludes that a clandestine **hands-off doctrine** may be reemerging that leaves prisoners essentially at the mercy of the states.[26]

Several reasons explain this more restrained posture of the courts toward prisoners' rights. The increasingly conservative political philosophy of the 1980s and 1990s has dampened judicial interest in questioning prison authorities. The most conservative wing of the Court, made up of Chief Justice William Rehnquist and Justices Antonin Scalia and Clarence Thomas, have been the most vocal to limit judicial supervision of criminal punishment.[27] This reduced court activism also appears to reflect the fact that there are fewer younger lawyers interested in prisoners' right as well as less money to support their efforts. Furthermore, there are fewer violations of constitutional rights by prisons than there have been the past.[28]

The Prison Litigation Reform Act (PLRA), which was passed by Congress and signed by President Clinton in 1996, has further limited the ability of prisoners to complain about conditions of confinement and to allege violation of their constitutional

Historically, how has the Supreme Court attempted to achieve a balance between the rights of prisoners as citizens of the United States with the needs of correctional institutions and rights of states? In particular, what are the perennial constitutional issues that prisoners and prisoner advocacy groups raise? What are the present trends in deciding those issues?

rights. The PLRA requires prisoners to either pay the full fee when filing a complaint ($150 in 1998) or to make an initial down payment followed by periodic installment payments. A three-strikes provision of this act prohibits an indigent prisoner from filing new lawsuits when the prisoner has previously filed frivolous or meritless claims. The PLRA appears to have had the greatest impact on civil rights prisoners, from whom the number of petitions filed dropped 20 percent from 1996 to 1997 and another 11 precent from 1997 to 1998.[29]

Those cases, as well as other decisions since the mid-1970s, have made it clear that although prisoners are not "slaves of the state" they are not "fully enfranchised citizens" either. Prisoners retain basic human rights, but they are not entitled to the same degree of protection they enjoyed before conviction.

The hero in this chapter is Vincent M. Nathan. He has worked as a court monitor or special master for a number of courts. The two largest cases he was involved in were the *Ruiz* case, which related to the entire Texas Department of Corrections and the suit against the Puerto Rico correctional system, which dealt with some thirty institutions on the island. Read what he said for *Invitation to Corrections* in 2000.

h e r o e s | *Vincent M. Nathan*

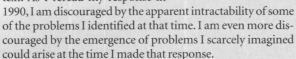

Court Monitor of Several State Correctional Systems

"More than ten years ago, Professor Bartollas and John Conrad interviewed me on the subject of 'problems in turning prisons around,' and they published my response in an earlier corrections text. As I reread my response in 1990, I am discouraged by the apparent intractability of some of the problems I identified at that time. I am even more discouraged by the emergence of problems I scarcely imagined could arise at the time I made that response.

"Although the rate of growth of the incarcerated population in the United States is slowing from the alarming rates we experienced during the 1990s, and prison construction has added untold thousands of new beds in state and federal correctional systems, our country's rate of incarceration has remained the highest in the industrialized world. Double-celling and other forms of crowding have become the norm in American corrections, increasing the dangers of prison life, limiting access to programs and services, making staff's job harder.

"Even more than ten years ago, the extensive expansion of prison systems—Texas and California are extreme examples—has placed an enormous strain on administrative and executive capability. Megasystems of more than one hundred facilities challenge central office managers beyond the capability of the most skilled administrators, and the pool of qualified candidates to become wardens and to fill midmanagement positions falls far short of what is needed. Moreover, many systems today, in the face of growing economy and low unemployment, are finding it impossible to meet their fast-growing needs for line security and non-uniformed staff.

"Thus, prisons continue to be crowded, prison systems continue to grow almost exponentially, and the pool of qualified managers and employees has not kept up with that growth. This, in the context of what I am about to describe, is a prescription for disaster.

"Two developments during the last decade are contributing to the difficulty of 'turning prisons around.' The first of these is the spate of decisions by the United States Supreme Court and lower federal courts that have redefined the concept of prisoners' rights. It would be hyperbolic to assert that the federal courts have entirely resumed their former hands-off policy, but any observer must acknowledge that it is in this direction that courts have been moving. Many rights—such as that of due process prior to placement in disciplinary segregation for a violation of institutional rules—have ceased to enjoy judicial recognition. Indeed, the most conservative justices on the Supreme Court have questioned whether the Eighth Amendment even applies to the conditions inmates encounter in prisons and have asserted that the right to be free from cruel or unusual punishment terminates at the point of sentencing.

"Along with increasing judicial conservatism, the legislative enactment of the Prison Reform Litigation Act (PLRA) has made the maintenance of effective litigation challenging conditions of confinement much more difficult to sustain. Although the PLRA itself does not raise the substantive bar of prisoners' rights from the level the Supreme Court has established, the law—passed by Congress and signed by the president in 1996—has provided a basis to vacate virtually all consent decrees in effect at that time, has imposed unrealistic limitations on professional fees an attorney can earn following a successful action under Section 1983, and has deprived courts of the benefits of a court monitor or special master for any purpose other than conducting formal hearings. These and other facets of this federal legislation guarantee that fewer courts and attorneys will be able to become engaged effectively in maintenance even of the diluted standards of constitutionality the Supreme Court continues to recognize.

"One may ask whether these developments reflect the fact that over the past several decades the courts have accomplished their purpose in bringing reasonable standards of decency to our country's jails and prisons. The short answer to this question is no. Despite the effectiveness of judicial intervention since the mid-1970s, our jails and prisons are far from a reflection of the society we strive to be. In large part because of the problems of crowding, administration, and staffing that I have described, there is a dearth of programming in many systems, and the provision of essential services such as those relating to medical care and mental health treatment is substandard. The increasing sway of violent inmate gangs, combined with the dearth of security staff, has rendered the correctional environment an exceptionally dangerous one for prisoners and for staff. Despite the accomplishments of the past, our penal facilities are far from the lawful, safe, industrious, and hopeful institutions for which John Conrad argued when I first met him two and a half decades ago.

"One legacy of the period of reform offers some hope. Without question, the attitude of many directors of correctional systems and wardens toward prisoners' rights has changed in response to judicial intervention. Today, most correctional professionals with whom I come into contact acknowledge that prisoners enjoy basic constitutional rights and that the rule of law is an appropriate fixture in the institutional setting. As legislators and governors continue to enact legislation that guarantees that more persons will go to prison and serve longer sentences but—as they inevitably will—simultaneously go about the business of restructuring their fiscal priorities in response to recent Supreme Court decisions and the enactment of the PLRA, one must question how much effect this new breed of correctional professional will have on the future of American corrections."

CRITICAL THINKING QUESTIONS

What does Vincent M. Nathan say is the status of prisoners' rights today? What decisions have courts made that make it more difficult for prisoners' rights advocates? Does Nathan believe that the courts have accomplished their mission of bringing reasonable standards of decency to this nation's jails and prisons?

WHAT INDIVIDUAL RIGHTS DO PRISONERS HAVE?

Prisoners have sued to establish rights in four areas: (1) the right to physical security and the minimum conditions necessary to sustain life, (2) the right to receive their constitutionally guaranteed safeguards, (3) the right to challenge the legality of their convictions through the courts, and (4) the right to receive the benefit of reasonable standards and procedural protections.

First Amendment Rights

Congress shall make no law respecting an establishment of religion, or prohibiting the free exercise thereof; or abridging the freedom of speech, or of the press; or the right of the people peaceably to assemble, and to petition the government for a redress of grievances.

—First Amendment to the Constitution

The rights of prisoners under the **First Amendment**—freedom of religion, speech, the press, and assembly—have been widely ruled upon.

Religion.   As previously mentioned, in the 1960s federal courts ordered prison officials to allow Black Muslim ministers to conduct services and to permit Muslim prisoners access to the Koran and other religious materials. The courts have also applied the freedom of religion clause to other religious groups, such as Buddhists.[30] However, the Fifth Circuit Court of Appeals, in a ruling on the "Church of the New Song" movement, decided that it was inappropriate to give First Amendment protection to "so called religions which tend to mock established institutions and are obviously shams and absurdities and whose members are patently void of religious sincerity."[31] Harry Theriault originated the Church of New Song (so named because it created the acronym CONS) while serving time in a federal prison. This "religion" called for porterhouse steaks and sherry to be served to its members.

Congress passed the Religious Freedom Restoration Act (RFRA) in 1993 as a reaction to concerns about restraining free exercise of religion. Congress rejected corrections officials' request to exclude jail and prison inmates from aspects of the act. Prior to this act, the inmate's exercise of religion could be restricted by prison officials if the restrictions were reasonably related to the maintenance of institutional security and discipline. The RFRA shifted the burden of proof from the prisoner to prison officials who had to show that the restriction was necessary because of a compelling government interest.[32] In a 1997 case, the Supreme Court ruled that the RFRA was unconstitutional except for the Federal Bureau of Prisons, which must still abide by the RFRA provisions.[33]

What First Amendment rights have prisoners won and lost? What are the limits of freedom of religion, for example, and why have inmate publications of books, articles, and interviews proved so controversial? How do the Fourth, Eighth, and Fourteenth Amendments affect prison inmates? Why are suits against the totality of correctional institutions so difficult to rule on and enforce?

In 1999, the U.S. District Court was asked to determine if Lord Natural Self-Allah, a member of the Five Percenters (a Harlem-born offshoot of the Black Muslims) and a prisoner in New York, was denied his First and Fourteenth Amendment rights when prison officials withheld delivery of his subscription to *The Five Percenter,* a religious publication of the Five Percent Nation of Islam. Prison authorities argued that the Five Percenters functioned as a violent prison gang, participating in robbery, assaults, and drug trafficking, and therefore allowing access to the Five Percenter literature encouraged disruptive behavior. The U.S. District Court judge ruled in favor of prison officials. The judge explained that Five Percenterism in its pure form may not encourage violence but that the prison version appears to do so.[34]

In general, the federal courts have consistently held that the religious rights granted to one religious group must be accorded to all such groups within a correctional institution. Religious freedom has been looked upon as a preferred freedom; thus, the burden of proof is on institutional administrators when they wish to limit religious practices.[35] However, the courts usually have not required prison administrators to provide special diets, nor are they willing to allow the free exercise of religion to jeopardize the security and safety of the institution.

Censorship of Personal Correspondence.   Correctional officials have always felt that there is strong reason to place stringent limitations on inmate correspondence. Censorship of incoming mail is necessary, prison officials say, to detect contraband—including instruments of escape, pornographic materials, and narcotics or drugs. Censorship of outgoing correspondence is also necessary, they say, to protect the public from insulting, obscene, and threatening letters; to avoid defaming the prison; and to detect escape or riot plans.

In *Procunier v. Martinez* (1974), the U.S. Supreme Court defined the criteria for determining when the regulation of inmate correspondence constitutes a violation of First Amendment liberties. According to the Court, prison officials may not censor inmate correspondence simply to eliminate unflattering or unwelcome opinions or factually inaccurate statements. Rather, they must show that a regulation authorizing mail censorship furthers one or more of the substantial governmental interests of security, order, and rehabilitation. Second, the limitation of First Amendment freedoms must be no greater than is necessary or essential to the protection of the particular governmental interest involved.[36] This decision disappointed prison managers who wanted greater procedural restrictions on inmate correspondence, for the Supreme Court placed a relatively heavy burden of proof on prison censors.

In *Pell v. Procunier* (1974), California inmates challenged prison rules that prohibited them from conducting interviews with the press. The Supreme Court ruled that prisoners do not have an automatic right to meet the press, because the legitimate state interest in security, order, and rehabilitation has to be considered.[37] The *Pell* decision solidified the balance test established in *Martinez,* but it also gave corrections officials the major role in determining when the interests of security, order, and rehabilitation were involved.

Freedom of Speech.   Most court decisions have rejected the argument that prisoners should be able to express their views freely. The courts have been dubious about giving prisoners the right to speak when such speech may create an institutional problem or disturbance. In one case, the court upheld the punishment of a prisoner who circulated materials calling for a collective protest against the administration.[38]

Censorship of Publications and Manuscripts.   The extent to which prison officials can censor the publications prisoners receive and can restrict the freedom of prisoners to publish articles and books while in prison has been the subject of much litigation. Although the courts have cautiously advised a broadening of these rights, they have reserved discretionary responsibility to prison administrators. The need for lawsuits is seen in Within the Walls 20.1.

the walls   20.1

within

The Right to Write

The Federal Penitentiary at Lompoc is a maximum-security prison holding many men who are serving long terms. Among them was Dannie Martin, a middle-aged bank robber serving a thirty-three-year term, who discovered a talent for narrative in a creative writing class. In 1986 he submitted an article about AIDS in prison to the *San Francisco Chronicle*. It was accepted and published with a byline. There followed a series of thirty articles, which the *Chronicle* published and for which it paid fees to Martin's lawyer.

The articles were mostly about prison life: "What's it like in there? How do the days go by?" The contributions to the *Chronicle*'s "Sunday Punch" section were widely read and continued until June 1988, when an article appeared to which the newspaper editor had given this headline: "The Gulag Mentality: Some Wardens Know How to Make Hell Burn a Little Hotter." The headline was the *Chronicle*'s idea, not Martin's. This article caught the attention of the Lompoc staff.

Martin had recounted the actions of a new warden, Richard Rison, who had begun his tenure by closing down the exercise yard in the mornings, thereby denying night workers the opportunity to exercise. This action provoked a good deal of annoyance, and one prisoner remarked to Martin that the warden was trying to provoke a riot. Later, without warning, the guards descended on the TV room and confiscated the old-timers' chairs. Martin had written:

> For as long as most of us can remember, we've had our own chairs in the TV rooms as well as in our cells. There's little enough in here for a man to call his own, and over the years these chairs have been modified and customized to an amazing degree—legs bent to suit the occupant, arm rests glued on, pads knitted for comfort. The final personal touch is always the printing of the name on the back. . . . Shorty Blue, Big Red, Monster Mack and Mukilteo Slim. Names that run from somber identification of the occupants to bizarre sobriquets. But whatever the name on the back or the condition of the chairs, those chairs were ours.

Those prized possessions were replaced by metal folding chairs, which certainly were not as comfortable or capable of personalization. A memorandum was posted to the effect that defacing a chair in any way would be an of-fense subject to disciplinary action. No advance notice of the change, no explanations.

All that was written up with the concluding sentences: "We wait and watch for the next move. Many of us older convicts feel that if the lids stay on until our next 'landlord' arrives it will be a small miracle."

When Warden Rison read the article, he ordered Martin into segregation. His writing materials were taken from him, and Martin was told that he was being segregated for his protection because other prisoners might attack him. Why? Because they might think that the article would bring about a lockdown. Martin was instructed not to write any more articles.

On 16 July 1979, seven years before Martin began writing his articles, the Bureau of Prisons had issued Rule 540.62b: "An inmate currently confined in an institution may not be employed or act as a reporter or publish under a byline." However, the rule explicitly allowed an inmate to write a letter to the editor of a newspaper, signing his or her name, or to write a book.

The problem for the Bureau was to prevent prisoners from conducting a business—for example, selling stocks and bonds—and writing articles for pay constituted a business by the Bureau's definition. Further, writing with a byline was making Martin a "big wheel" among his fellow prisoners, and that was undesirable. There was no explanation of why Martin's articles had been published for two years without interference from the warden or other officials of the Bureau of Prisons.

Martin was released from segregation after two days. Later, he wrote an article about his experience, making it sound like a session in "the Hole" rather than the relatively benign conditions of protective segregation. A week later, Martin was transferred to the Federal Correctional Institution at Phoenix, Arizona.

Martin sued the Bureau of Prisons on the ground that his First Amendment right to free speech had been infringed. The suit was joined by the *San Francisco Chronicle*. A federal court issued a preliminary injunction, ruling that "there's been substantial showing that the acts against Mr. Martin were indeed retaliation." Martin's articles continued to be published until June 1990, when the court, after an extended hearing, dissolved the pre-

... writing with a byline was making Martin a "big wheel" among his fellow prisoners, and that was undesirable.

(continued)

liminary injunction and entered judgment for the Bureau of Prisons. In his opinion, Judge Charles Legge ruled that "the penological interest of prison security was invoked by Martin writing and the *Chronicle* publishing the 'Gulag' article. The fact that there was a genuine concern for security was established by a preponderance of evidence."

Martin continues to write for the *Chronicle,* but anonymously. As of the late-1990s, the case was on appeal.

CRITICAL THINKING QUESTIONS

Do you believe inmates have the right to write for publication? Should they profit from their writings? If they do not receive any financial compensation for their writings, what censorship from prison officials do you believe is constitutional?

Source: Clemens Bartollas and John P. Conrad, *Introduction to Corrections* (New York: HarperCollins, 1992), pp. 444–445.

Right to Assemble. Prisoners' right to assemble is also restricted. The emergence of prisoner unions in ten states in the early 1970s brought about litigation on this subject.[39] *Goodwin v. Oswald* (1972) brought a decision upholding the right to prisoners to form unions. The Supreme Court stated that nowhere in state or federal law is the formation of prisoner unions outlawed or prohibited.[40] However, in *Jones v. North Carolina Prisoners' Union* (1977), the Supreme Court overruled a favorable decision and held that a state regulation prohibiting prisoners from soliciting others to join a union and barring union meetings did not violate the First Amendment.[41]

The *Jones* decision represented another setback for prisoners' rights. On the one hand, the Supreme Court extended the position in *Pell,* in which prison officials were looked to as the party that would decide when institutional security and order were threatened. On the other hand, the *Jones* decision extended the power of prison officials to limit First Amendment rights if they believed the potential existed for disruption of order.[42]

Fourth Amendment Rights

The right of the people to be secure in their persons, houses, papers, and effects, against unreasonable searches and seizures, shall not be violated, and no warrants shall issue but upon probable cause, supported by oath or affirmation, and particularly describing the place to be searched, and the persons or things to be seized.

—Fourth Amendment to the Constitution

The basic issue in the **Fourth Amendment** is proper search and seizure. The courts have consistently held that the protection the Fourth Amendment provides against unreasonable searches and seizures does not extend to prison. For example, *Moore v. People* (1970) concluded that searches conducted by prison officials "are not unreasonable as long as they are not for the purpose of harassing or humiliating the inmate in a cruel or unusual manner."[43]

Cell searches have raised the privacy issue. In *Bell v. Wolfish* (1979) the Supreme Court made it clear that unannounced cell searches, or "shakedowns," were necessary for security and order.[44] *Hudson v. Palmer* (1984) further shattered any hope that the Fourth Amendment would limit cell searches. The Court ruled that "the Fourth Amendment has no applicability to a prison cell."[45] Strip searches also have been allowed by the courts, which generally have permitted prison officials to conduct pat searches and body-cavity examinations in the name of institutional order and security.[46]

Eighth Amendment Rights

Excessive bail shall not be required, nor excessive fines imposed, nor cruel and unusual punishments inflicted.

—Eighth Amendment to the Constitution

In the prison setting, the **Eighth Amendment** has been applied to living conditions, painful executions, excessive corporal punishment, medical experimentation, and abuse of labor. The three principal tests of conformance with the Eighth Amendment deal with these questions: Does the punishment shock the conscience of a civilized society? Is the punishment unnecessarily cruel? Does the punishment go beyond legitimate penal aims? Considerable case law concerns violation of the Eighth Amendment by means of solitary confinement, physical abuse, deadly force, the death penalty, denial of access to medical treatment and services, and segregation.

Solitary Confinement.   The courts have generally supported the separation of troublesome prisoners from the general prison population. They have ruled that separation is necessary to protect the inmate, other prisoners, and the staff, and to prevent escapes. Although several courts have ordered the release of inmates from harsh solitary confinement, most courts have been unwilling to interfere unless the conditions were clearly "shocking," "barbarous," "disgusting," or "debasing." Court decisions often disagree whether cruel and unusual punishment existed when prisoners were denuded, exposed to the winter cold, and deprived of such basic necessities of hygiene as soap and toilet paper. For example, a federal district court in *Knop v. Johnson* (1987) ruled that cruel and unusual punishment existed when the state of Michigan failed to provide inmates with winter coats, hats, and gloves.[47] In *Harris v. Fleming* (1988), the federal court found that cruel and unusual punishment did not exist when an Illinois inmates was deprived of toilet paper for five days and soap, toothpaste, or a toothbrush for ten days.[48]

Physical Abuse.   Not until the mid-1960s did a court decide that the disciplinary measure of whipping a prisoner with a leather strap constituted "cruel and unusual punishment."[49] More recently, the court ruled in the *Madrid v. Gomez* decision (1995) that excessive and unnecessary force was used at the Pelican Bay State Prison in a variety of ways and circumstances.[50]

The courts have generally been unwilling to impose liability on prison officials for failing to protect prisoners from physical abuse and sexual assault from other inmates. The courts have ruled that prison officials are liable for damages if they display indifference to attacks on inmates occurring inside the prison. As Within the Walls 20.2 describes, in the early 1970s the Supreme Court found that the conditions in Arkansas prisons constituted a violation of the Eighth Amendment.

Deadly Force.   The courts have ruled that the use of deadly force is permissible to prevent the commission of a felony or the infliction of severe bodily harm.[51] These rulings permit the use of deadly force to prevent an inmate from escaping if a state has classified escape as a felony. Nevertheless, the courts have ruled that to avoid civil and criminal liability, deadly force must be used only as a last resort—after all other reasonable means have failed. The use of deadly force at Corcoran Prison in California is one that will likely bring several lawsuits from prisoners and their families.[52] Between 1988 and 1997, 2,000 shooting incidents took place, in which hundreds of inmates were wounded and five were killed.[53]

Medical Treatment and Services.   A convict serving time in a correctional facility in the United States has had reason to be concerned about his or her access to medical care. One of the principal grievances underlying the destructive and lethal 1971 riot at Attica State Penitentiary in New York was the inmates' belief that medical care was inadequate and indifferently administered by physicians whose competence was in question. The *Official Report of the New York State Special Commission on Attica* noted that medical staff conducted the daily sick call from behind a wire mesh screen—hardly a setting to inspire a confident doctor–patient relationship. The report went on to conclude that "the purpose of medical care at Attica was limited to providing relief from

the walls   20.2

within

An Unconstitutional Correctional System

Judicial decisions in Arkansas reversed at least to some degree the levels of overcrowding, brutality, and outright corruption that were found in the state correctional system. A breakthrough came in 1970 with the class-action case of *Holt v. Sarver*. The plaintiffs were prisoners in the Cummins Farm Unit and the Tucker Intermediate Reformatory of the Arkansas Penitentiary System. Their complaints were that their "forced, uncompensated labor" violated the Thirteenth Amendment to the Constitution and that the conditions and practices within the system were such that their confinement was cruel and unusual punishment within the meaning of the Eighth Amendment. They also contended that racial segregation in these facilities violated the Fourteenth Amendment.

Prisoners assigned to solitary confinement for disciplinary offenses were jammed into windowless 8-by-10-foot cells with no facilities other than a water tap and a toilet that could be flushed only from outside the cell. Four men usually occupied a cell, but as many as eleven were sometimes so accommodated. At night filthy mattresses were spread on the floor. The diet consisted of gruel—a mixture of meat, potatoes, margarine, and syrup mashed together and baked. The caloric value was less than 1,000 calories a day.

This attempt to sharpen the meaning of the Eighth Amendment necessarily relies on subjective terms—as does "cruel and unusual"—but it was accepted. The final

> . . . conditions and practices within the system were such that their confinement was cruel and unusual punishment . . .

determination was that "confinement in a given institution may amount to cruel and unusual punishment prohibited by the Constitution where the confinement is characterized by conditions so bad as to be shocking to the conscience of reasonably civilized people." Based on this definition, the Supreme Court specified that measures had to be taken to remedy the trusty system and the barracks conditions, to provide for inmate safety, and to clean up the filthy isolation cells. It ordered the state to submit a report and plan to show what would be done to accomplish these ends and when it would be done. Four hearings and continued supervision by the Court eventually resulted in the elimination of the conditions on which the original complaint had been based. New and modern facilities were built, and personnel were recruited and trained to manage the system in a manner consistent with modern correctional standards.

CRITICAL THINKING QUESTIONS

Why were the conditions in the Arkansas correctional system ruled to be cruel and unusual? If this class-action suit came before the Supreme Court today, how do you believe the Court would rule?

Source: *Holt v. Sarver*, 309 F. Supp. 362 (E.D. Arkansas, 1970). Affirmed, 442 F.2d 304 (8th Cir. 1971).

pain or acute anguish, correcting pathological processes that may have developed before or while the inmates were serving their terms, and preventing the transmittal of sickness among the prison population."[54] Chronic disabilities, whether correctable or not, were not assessed or treated. "Part of this . . . was due to lack of personnel and time, but much reflected a lack of commitment to attempt restorative efforts."[55] Prompted by this report, the state took, without court intervention, remedial action in the improvement of medical care.

Elsewhere, intervention by the courts has been called for, but their remedies have been cautious. In Texas, a prisoner's complaint that the medical staff had failed to treat him competently for an injury received when a bale of cotton fell on him while he was unloading a truck brought the Department of Corrections into court.[56] Many treatments had been administered, but the patient's condition had gotten worse. Both the medical and the custodial staffs decided that the plaintiff was malingering. The case found its way to the Supreme Court, which ruled that the state could not be held liable for medical malpractice—a misfortune that could befall anyone, prisoner or free individual. The Supreme Court would not decide against the state because its physicians' treatment was ineffective, but it made clear that "deliberate indifference to serious medical needs" constituted "unnecessary and wanton infliction of pain" within the meaning of cruel and unusual punishment.

Racial Segregation.   Until well into the 1960s, racial segregation in prisons, in both North and South, was general. Cellblocks were either black or white, and so were mess-hall lines. The good jobs went to deserving white prisoners; black prisoners had to be specially deserving to be assigned as runners, clerks, or other desirable positions. That began to change in a few states in the 1950s, but wardens and custodial staffs are naturally conservative. Apprehensions of riots and other violence if the traditional segregation was disturbed inspired stubborn resistance to change. The right to equal opportunity for minority prisoners had to be adjudicated. But the initial court to hear arguments on this matter was presided over by a judge whose primary concern was avoiding the appearance of any type of judicial activism.

The Alabama case of *Washington v. Lee* (1966) was the first judicial intervention on the desegregation of prisons.[57] Federal Judge Frank Johnson, who later was to preside over *Pugh v. Locke* (1976), held that "this court can conceive of no consideration of prison security or discipline which will sustain the constitutionality of state statutes that on their face require complete and permanent segregation of the races in all Alabama penal facilities." The state was therefore ordered to provide for the total desegregation of all the prisons within one year. This was done. There were no riots and no other unpleasant consequences. Throughout the nation, desegregation of the prisons has been achieved with remarkably little difficulty, even though the anxieties of many wardens had seemed to be self-fulfilling prophecies.[58]

Fourteenth Amendment Rights

> *Section I.* All persons born or naturalized in the United States, and subject to the jurisdiction thereof, are citizens of the United States and of the State wherein they reside. No State shall make or enforce any law which shall abridge the privileges or immunities of citizens of the United States; nor shall any State deprive any person of life, liberty, or property, without due process of law; nor deny to any person within its jurisdiction the equal protection of the laws.
>
> —Fourteenth Amendment to the Constitution

Due process is the major issue in the **Fourteenth Amendment,** especially related to disciplinary hearings and inmates helping each other to prepare their cases for appeal.

Due-Process Rights in Disciplinary Hearings.   The 1974 *Wolff v. McDonnell* decision has been heralded as a landmark because of its impact on correctional administration and prisoners' rights.[59] In reviewing disciplinary procedures, the Supreme Court held that they were not equivalent to criminal prosecution and that during disciplinary hearings prisoners do not have the full due-process rights of a defendant on trial. Nevertheless, the Court specified certain minimum requirements for disciplinary proceedings:

1. The inmate must receive advanced written notice of the alleged rules infraction.
2. The prisoner must be allowed sufficient time to prepare a defense against the charges.
3. The prisoner must be allowed to present documentary evidence on his or her own behalf and therefore may call witnesses, as long as the security of the institution is not jeopardized.
4. The prisoner is permitted to seek counsel from another inmate or a staff member when the circumstances of the disciplinary infraction are complex or the prisoner is illiterate.
5. The prisoner is to be provided with a written statement of the findings of the committee, the evidence relied upon, and the rationale for the action. A written record of the proceedings must also be maintained.[60]

The Court left to the discretion of correctional administrators the question of whether a witness could be confronted and cross-examined by the prisoner. The Court further ruled that a prisoner's incoming mail from his or her attorney can be opened in the presence of the inmate to check for contraband but cannot be read by institutional staff.

Wolff v. McDonnell was significant because it standardized certain rights and freedoms within correctional facilities. Although inmates received some procedural safeguards to protect them against the notorious abuses of disciplinary meetings, they did not receive all the due-process rights of a criminal trial. Nor did the Court question the right of correctional officials to revoke the "good time" of inmates.

Legal Assistance to Inmates.   Until well past the time when the hands-off doctrine passed into obsolescence, correctional authorities were obsessed by their belief that prisoners should not trouble the courts with their complaints. Particularly discouraged were "writ-writers," who prepared complaints for themselves and other prisoners. In many states, the preparation of writs was a disciplinary offense, calling for a session of punitive isolation.[61] Access to the courts was vigorously prevented. In 1941 the Supreme Court took notice of the obstacles to writs of habeas corpus in *Ex Parte Hull*.[62]

Hull had filed for a writ of habeas corpus, only to have the papers he filed returned to him by prison officials without submission to the court. When ordered by the Supreme Court to show cause why Hull's petition for a writ should not be granted, the warden replied that he had issued a regulation that all such petitions had to be referred to the legal investigator for the parole board. The regulation went on to say that "documents submitted to [the investigator], if in his opinion are properly drawn, will be directed to the court designated or will be referred back to the inmate." Justice Frank Murphy's opinion pronounced this regulation invalid: "The state and its officers may not abridge or impair petitioner's right to . . . apply for writ of habeas corpus."

The principle is clear and has consistently been upheld. However, as one commentator has pointed out, "The problem . . . —as with any 'right' possessed by prisoners— is not with the principle but with the implementation."[63] After all, it is one thing to allow a prisoner to petition the court but quite another to equip him or her to submit such a petition in a form that will allow the court to proceed. The solution should be to create a modest law library in which prisoners could assemble the information and authorities they might need to make an intelligible case.

The Supreme Court took notice of this problem in *Bounds v. Smith* (1977).[64] In a 5-to-4 decision, the Court ruled that the state of North Carolina had a duty to provide adequate law libraries in each of its correctional facilities. Although the state's proposal for a standard library is rather generous in its content, including the standard legal references, the Supreme Court Reports, and the North Carolina court reports as well as federal and state statutes, other states have gone far beyond North Carolina in the provision of law libraries, some of them so extensive as to be the envy of practicing attorneys.

In *Johnson v. Avery* (1969), the Supreme Court ruled that institutional officials may not prohibit inmates from assisting one another with legal work unless the institution provides reasonable legal assistance to inmates.[65] This decision denied the constitutionality of a Tennessee prison regulation that provided: "No inmate will advise, assist or otherwise contract to aid another, either with or without a fee, to prepare Writs or other legal matters. . . . Inmates are forbidden to set themselves up as practitioners for the purpose of promoting a business of writing Writs." The Court ruled that inmates have the right to receive assistance from jailhouse lawyers. The Court also stated that the activities of the jailhouse lawyer could be restricted as to time and place and that jailhouse lawyers could be prohibited from receiving fees for their services.[66]

Some prisons have avoided the use of jailhouse lawyers by establishing their own legal assistance programs. Although they vary from prison to prison, these programs generally use lawyers or law students to represent inmates in postconviction proceedings. The Correctional Institution at Graterford in Pennsylvania developed a paraprofessional law clinic to provide legal assistance to inmates.[67]

timeline
Significant U.S. Supreme Court Decisions on Prisoners' Rights

Date	Case	Decision
1974	*Procunier v. Martinez*	Censorship of inmate mail is subject to some restrictions.
1974	*Wolff v. McDonnell*	Disciplinary procedures are necessary to lose "good time"
1975	*Ruiz v. Estelle*	Texas's correctional system is unconstitutional.
1976	*Estelle v. Gamble*	Lack of proper medical care by the state is cruel and unusual punishment.
1976	*Meachum v. Fano*	Inmate is subject to rules of prison system.
1977	*Theriault v. Carlson*	The First Amendment does not protect religions that are shams and are void of religious sincerity.
1979	*Bell v. Wolfish*	Unannounced cell searches are necessary for security and order.
1981	*Rhodes v. Chapman*	Double-celling is not unconstitutional.
1984	*Hudson v. Palmer*	Fourth Amendment does not apply to cell searches.
1986	*Whitley v. Albers*	A prisoner shot during a riot does not suffer cruel and unusual punishment if the actions was taken to maintain discipline rather than causing harm.
1987	*Bruscino v. Carlson*	Long-term lockdown is constitutional.
1987	*Turner v. Safley*	Prison regulations that infringe on prisoners' rights are valid as long as they are reasonably related to the security and safety of the institution.
1991	*Wilson v. Seiter*	Prisoners must prove that cruel and unusual prison conditions exist because of the indifference of officials.

WHY HAS CORRECTIONAL REFORM THROUGH THE COURTS BEEN DIFFICULT?

The hands-off doctrine allowed correctional systems to abide by the standards, or lack of them, that state governments would tolerate. In some states, progressive commissioners managed prisons with reasonably humane policies. The best that could be said for most states was that without professional administration, without trained personnel, and without public interest in correctional policy and practice, conditions in the prisons did not descend to the levels of brutality and outright corruption that were to be found in the worst of them. In this section are two brief case studies documenting how Judge Frank Johnson in Alabama and Judge William Wayne Justice in Texas attempted to bring reform to what they ruled were unconstitutional correctional systems.

Reform in Alabama

The case of *Pugh v. Locke* (1976) was brought in the federal district court for Alabama before Judge Frank Johnson. It was a class-action suit complaining of the conditions of confinement in Alabama prisons and demonstrates the difficulties confronting the courts when the state resists the decrees requiring remedies.[68] It also illustrates the procedures that a determined judge can adopt to enforce his orders.

In *Pugh,* the court found that the state of Alabama had not met constitutional standards for the administration of its prison. To provide for relief from these deficiencies, the court enjoined the governor and other officers of the state government from failing to implement its statement of "Minimum Constitutional Standards of the Alabama Prison System," contained in its decrees. These standards comprised eleven categories of requirements, ranging from the overcrowding of facilities to the installation of a modern system of prisoner classification. Each category was laid out with a great deal of specificity about which officials would be held accountable. Deadlines for compliance were established in the decree, to all of which the state consented.

The decree met with a furious response from Governor George C. Wallace, who proclaimed that "thugs and judges" had taken charge of Alabama's prisons. Despite strong public support for prison reform, Wallace denied the court's right to intervene and heaped scorn on those who sympathized with prisoners living in foul conditions nearly identical to those that had prevailed in Arkansas before *Holt v. Sarver.* His opposition softened over the years, but many influential politicians found it expedient to advocate measures that amounted to maximum resistance.

The state appealed *Pugh v. Locke.* On review by the Circuit Court of Appeals, the orders were upheld with the exception that the committee was dissolved because supervision should have been placed in the hands of a monitor rather than a large and unwieldy committee. The court held that such a committee, largely composed of persons with no experience in the administration of prisons, placed an unfair burden on the state's administrators as defendants. The task of reviewing the adequacy of plans to implement the decree would be better assigned to a **special master,** a judicial officer appointed by the court to hear testimony and develop a plan for the implementation of the changes ordered by the court.[69]

Prison reform came slowly in Alabama. Governor Wallace was reelected in 1982 and dragged his feet. Judge Robert Varner replaced Judge Johnson and appointed a special implementation committee to supervise the final stages of compliance. This committee met from 1983 to the end of 1988, observing, prodding, making recommendations, and reporting periodically to the court. The committee was finally dissolved in late 1988 when measures taken by the parole board to reduce the population of the prisons brought about a balance between the numbers of prisoners and the number of beds.

Reform in Texas

The process of legal reform in Texas started in a quite unusual way.[70] George Beto, Director of the Texas Department of Corrections, barred an attorney, Frances Jalet, from visiting or corresponding with inmates in the Texas prison system. When his action was challenged by the courts, Beto transferred all of Jalet's inmates clients to one wing of the Wynne Unit, creating what became known as the "eight-hoe squad." A hoe squad in Texas was a work detail of prisoners assigned to fields where they did all the work by hand, using implements such as hoes, shovels, and hand saws. Jalet and twelve of the twenty-seven inmates assigned to the "eight-hoe squad" filed suit against Beto. In *Cruz v. Bette II* (1979), they claimed that he had unlawfully barred Jalet and at the same time confined her inmate clients to a segregation cellblock, denying them privileges that they previously had enjoyed in the general population. Segregated from the general population, they were routinely subjected to "unusually and discriminatorily harsh conditions and practices."[71]

The segregated inmates became deeply dedicated to reform through litigation. Isolated and harassed, they developed a "brotherhood with a single cause—litigated reform."[72] Their single-mindedness transcended racial and cultural barriers, and they "spent countless hours during the eleven months of confinement improving their legal skills, strategizing and coordinating their efforts, and assisting one another in the drafting of petitions."[73] These prisoners became the "who's who" of Texas Department of Corrections writ-writers. They produced nearly all the reform litigation and kept the Texas Corrections department under court supervision for the next two decades.[74]

The fourth of the class-action suits filed by "eight-hoe" prisoners, *Ruiz v. Estelle* (1972), placed almost the entire system in ligitation and became the most massive prisoners' rights suit in the history of U.S. jurisprudence. On 29 June 1972, David Ruiz filed his handwritten petition, which was later consolidated with petitions from two other prisoners of the "eight-hoe squad."

Led by Director W. J. Estelle, Texas prison officials were determined; they were convinced that they had right on their side. For years they fought the decisions of federal judge William Wayne Justice tooth and nail. One of their many defeats came when they attempted unsuccessfully to have Justice's special master, Vincent Nathan, removed. In 1987, the final judicial order was issued in the *Ruiz* case. As a result, the repressive Texas model of corrections came to an end; it was totally dismantled.

With the demise of the Texas model came a period of social disorder in the late 1980s and 1990s. Inmate assaults against other inmates and staff dramatically rose. Inmate gangs began to intimidate other inmates as well as staff. A number of seasoned wardens and guards left the prison, and the new prison administrators and guards were overwhelmed by the situation. Only in the late 1990s, more than a decade after Judge Justice's final ruling, was there some sense that prison officials had regained control over the Texas prisons.[75]

Pugh v. Locke and *Ruiz v. Estelle* demonstrate the difficulties confronting the courts when the state resists decrees requiring remedies. They also illustrate the procedures that committed judges can adopt to enforce their orders. Usually the intervention of the court is resented by the government and by the penal establishment. Funds required to make the mandated changes are scarce and may not be appropriated by the legislature, which usually ranks prison reform low on its list of priorities. Conditions are improved grudgingly or not at all. If relief must be granted, the court assumes a burden that may remain on the docket for months and sometimes—as in *Holt v. Sarver, Pugh v. Locke,* and *Ruiz v. Estelle*—for years.

The court is faced with a limited number of unattractive options for the enforcement of its orders. It may undertake a wholesale release of prisoners to reduce the population. It may hold prison officials in contempt and impose fines for their noncompliance—an action taken by the court at one point in the *Pugh* litigation. Some courts have entertained the possibility of committing one or more officials to jail for criminal contempt, but so far this option has not been put into effect. The court may even elect to close a prison down entirely, another option that no court has yet adopted.

WHAT HAS BEEN THE IMPACT OF THE PRISONERS' RIGHTS MOVEMENT?

As we begin a new century, there is both good news about prisoners' rights—the enormous gains that have been made—and bad news—the reluctance of federal and state courts to correct the remaining human rights violations.

The Good News

The good news is that the bad conditions of the worst prisons and correctional systems in the 1970s have been corrected and prisoners have made gains in several areas. The improvements are undeniable and would not have been achieved without judicial intervention. In addition, two-thirds or more of the state prison systems are still operating, in whole or in part, under court decrees that deal with issues such as disciplinary procedures and conditions, food services, transfer, sewage, ventilation, fire safety, lighting, recreation opportunities and facilities, cell size and assignment, and guard training.[76] Thus, it is likely that more court-mandated reforms will be forthcoming.

Prisoners have made the greatest gains in the right to send and receive letters, but they also have made strides in their right to communicate with lawyers and the courts.

Furthermore, the courts have permitted the right of religious freedom as long as it does not jeopardize institutional security. Courts also have been willing to rule on the totality of conditions in a prison setting when prisoners appeared to be undergoing severe dehumanization and deterioration in their mental and physical well-being. It can be argued that many of these improvements are probably irreversible and that the states can be trusted to maintain constitutionally acceptable prisons.

The Bad News

The bad news is that overcrowding and its associated evils are reappearing and will be difficult to correct. Further bad news is that in the 1990s prisoners were expected to do "hard time" and not to enjoy the amenities that they were given in the past. With this social and political context, it has been more difficult for prisoners to win cruel and unusual punishment suits. Another source of bad news is that federal courts, which were actively involved in prisoners' rights from the 1960s on, withdrew their receptivity to inmate suits in the 1990s.[77] A final source of bad news is that the Prison Litigations Reform Act (PLRA) passed by Congress and signed by President Clinton in 1996 has limited the ability of prisoners to allege violations of their constitutional rights.

Prisoners may retain basic human rights, but they are not entitled to the same degree of constitutional protections that they enjoyed before conviction. The conditions of confinement can never satisfy prisoners. Convicts and their plight attract little public sympathy, so action to correct intolerable conditions is usually delayed until a crisis occurs. At that point, remedies must be drastic and thus costly, far more so than would be the case if farsighted planning, development, and fiscal support were available to implement changes as soon as they were needed.

SUMMARY

The prisoners' right movement has gone through three stages. The first stage was one in which convicted felons were regarded as slaves of the state. The U.S. Supreme Court and most other courts avoided judicial intervention in corrections. In the second stage, which lasted from about 1966 to 1976, judges became extensively involved in rulings on prisoners' rights. During the stage, prisoners won several important victories in the Supreme Court. In the third stage, which has taken place since 1976, the Supreme Court has had a so-called restrained-hands approach to prisoner's rights. Most of the decisions during the stage have represented victories for prison officials in upholding institutional security over prisoners' rights.

Despite the difficulties confronting the courts in rectifying unconstitutional conditions of confinement, much has been accomplished since the 1960s. Courts

have been willing to rule on the totality of prison conditions when inmates appeared to be undergoing deterioration. Prisoners also have made gains in sending and receiving letters, in communicating with lawyers and the courts, and in receiving the right of religious freedom. But the gains prisoners have made still leave them far short of the constitutional protections that they enjoyed before conviction.

Courageous judges and public officials have changed the nature and quality of corrections beyond the reasonable expectations of reformers early in the twentieth century. Much remains to be done, but there has been solid constitutional support for decency in corrections. Judges have provided that support. Capable corrections administrators are increasingly on hand to carry out their orders.

KEY TERMS

Eighth Amendment, p. 479
First Amendment, p. 475
Fourteenth Amendment, p. 481

Fourth Amendment, p. 478
hands-off doctrine, p. 472
special master, p. 484

CRITICAL THINKING QUESTIONS

1. What did it mean to say that a convicted felon was "civilly dead"?
2. Summarize the most important cases establishing the hands-off doctrine.
3. Why is the right to due process so difficult to disentangle from institutional priorities?
4. What led to the restrained-hands doctrine of the courts?
5. Why has the implementation of prisoners' rights been so difficult for the courts?

WEB DESTINATIONS

Read a government report on conflict between states seeking to reduce the high cost of medical care and prisoners' rights to adequate, appropriate health care.
http://www.window.state.tx.us/comptrol/fnotes/jan96fn.txt

The ethics of end-of-life care for ill or elderly prisoners is the subject of this article.
http://www.aslme.org/pub_jlme/27.3b.html

Read a comprehensive report on the laws and precedents that govern the complex issue of freedom of religion in prison.
http://www.fac.org/publicat/prison/done.htm

Follow links at these prisoners' rights advocacy sites to learn more about the movement's background and the present status of prison law.
http://www.facts1.com/reasons/harm.htm
http://www.prisonwall.org/links.htm

Take a test on the application of correctional law in Oregon.
http://www.open.org/~hawley/law.htm

Read a comprehensive summary of the recent history of correctional reform in the United States.
http://www.ojp.usdoj.gov/reports/98Guides/lblf/panel5c.htm

FOR FURTHER READING

Chilton, Bradley. *Prisons under the Gavel: The Federal Court Takeover of Georgia Prisons.* Columbus: Ohio State University Press, 1991. Chilton reviews the intervention of the courts in the Georgia prison system and the judge's response to resistance from state officials to court-mandated reform.

Crouch, Ben M., and James W. Marquart. *An Appeal to Justice: Litigated Reform of Texas Prisons.* Austin: University of Texas Press, 1989. An examination of what went on in the Texas prison system before, during, and after the *Ruiz v. Estelle* decision.

Jacobs, James B. "The Prisoners' Rights Movement and Its Impacts, 1960–1980." In *Crime and Justice: An Annual Review of Research.* Vol. 2, edited by Norval Morris and Michael Tonry. Chicago: University of Chicago Press, 1980. Jacobs, whose writings on the prisoners' rights movement are highly respected, provides perspective on the accomplishments of this movement.

Jacobs, James B. "Judicial Impact on Prison Reform." In *Punishment and Social Control: Essays in Honor of Sheldon L. Messinger,* edited by Thomas G. Blomberg and Stanley Cohen, pp. 61–75. New York: Aldine de Gruyter, 1995. Jacobs debates Gerald Rosenberg's thesis that the courts have had a limited role in producing prison reform. Jacobs argues that Rosenberg's thesis is naive, because every prison has changed its practices, partly because of court-mandated reform.

Martin, Steven J., and Sheldon Eklund-Olson. *Texas Prisons: The Walls Came Tumbling Down.* Austin: Texas Monthly Press, 1987. This book provides fascinating documentation of the history of *Ruiz v. Estelle.*

NOTES

1. Letter received by the author in June 2000. Used with permission.
2. James B. Jacobs, "The Prisoners' Rights Movement and Its Impacts, 1960–1980," in *Crime and Justice: An Annual Review of Research* 2, ed. Norval Morris and Michael Tonry (Chicago: University of Chicago Press, 1980), pp. 429–430.
3. Immanuel Kant, *The Metaphysical Elements of Justice,* trans. John Ladd (Indianapolis: Bobbs-Merrill, 1965), p. 102.
4. *Ruffin v. Commonwealth,* 62 Va. 790, at 796 (1871).
5. John P. Palmer, *Constitutional Rights of Prisoners,* 2d ed. (Cincinnati: Anderson, 1977), p. 211.

6. *Cooper v. Pate*, 378 U.S. 546 (1964), was the first major case.

7. *Procunier v. Martinez*, 416 U.S. 396 (1974).

8. *Wolff v. McDonnell*, 418 U.S. 539 (1974).

9. Ibid.

10. *Estelle v. Gamble*, 429 U.S. 97 (1976).

11. *Baxter v. Palmigiano*, 425 U.S. 308 (1976).

12. *Enomota v. Clutchette*, 425 U.S. 308 (1976).

13. *Meachum v. Fano*, 427 U.S. (1976).

14. *Montanye v. Haymes*, 96 S. Ct. 2543 (1976).

15. *Meachum v. Farro*.

16. *Rhodes v. Chapman*, 29 Cr. L. Rptr. 3061 (1981).

17. Ibid.

18. *Hewitt v. Helms*, 459 U.S. 460 (1983).

19. *Ponte v. Real*, 471 U.S. 491 (1985).

20. *Whitney v. Albers*, 475 U.S. 312 (1986).

21. *Bruscino v. Carlson* (Civil Action No. 84–4320), D.C.S.D. III (1987).

22. On 22 July 1988, the U.S. Court of Appeals for the Seventh Circuit affirmed *Bruscino*.

23. *Wilson v. Seiter*, 501 U.S. 294 (1991).

24. *Coleman v. Thompson*, 501 U.S. 722 (1991).

25. *Washington v. Harper*, 494 U.S. 210 (1990).

26. Rudolf Alexander Jr., "Slamming the Federal Courthouse Door on Inmates," *Journal of Criminal Justice* 21 (1992), pp. 103–117.

27. Christopher E. Smith, "The Constitution and Criminal Punishment: The Emerging Visions of Justices Scalia and Thomas," *Drake Law Review* 43 (1995), pp. 610–612.

28. Ben M. Crouch and James W. Marquart, "Ruiz: Intervention and Emergent Order in Texas Prisons," in *Courts, Corrections, and the Constitution: The Impact of Judicial Intervention on Prisons and Jails*, ed. John J. DiIulio Jr. (New York: Oxford University Press, 1990), p. 109.

29. "Legislation Has Mixed Effect on Petitions," *The Third Branch* 31 (April 1999).

30. *Cruz v. Beto*, 405 U.S. 319 (1972).

31. *Theriault v. Silber*, 391 F. Supp. 578 (W.D. Texas, 1975).

32. Philip L. Reichel, *Corrections: Philosophies, Practices, and Procedures* (Boston: Allyn & Bacon, 2001), p. 528.

33. *Boerne v. Flores*, 521 U.S. 507 (1997).

34. *Lord Natural Self-Allah v. Annucci*, W.D.N.Y., No. 97-CV-607 (H) (1999).

35. See Christopher E. Smith, *Law and Contemporary Corrections* (Belmont, CA: Wadsworth, 1999).

36. *Procunier v. Martinez*.

37. *Pell v. Procunier* 417 U.S. 817 (1974).

38. *Roberts v. Papersack*, 256 F. Supp. 415 (M.D. 1966).

39. Ronald Huff, "Unionization Behind the Walls," *Criminology* 12 (August 1974), pp. 184–185.

40. *Goodwin v. Oswald*, 462 F.2d 1245–46 (3d Cir. 1972).

41. *Jones v. North Carolina Prisoners' Union*, 433 U.S. (1977).

42. C. Ronald Huff, "The Discovery of Prisoners' Rights: A Sociological Analysis," in *Legal Rights of Prisoners*, ed. G. P. Alpert (Beverly Hills, Calif.: Sage, 1980), pp. 60–61.

43. *Moore v. People*, 171 Colorado 338, 467 P.2d (1970).

44. *Bell v. Wolfish*, 441 U.S. 520 (1979).

45. *Hudson v. Palmer*, 82 L. Ed.2d 393 (1984).

46. See *Bell v. Wolfish*.

47. *Knop v. Johnson*, 667 F.Supp. 467 (1987).

48. *Harris v. Fleming*, 839 F.2d 1223 (1988).

49. *Jackson v. Bishop*, 404 F.2d 571 (8th cir. 1968).

50. *Madrid v. Gomez*, 889 F.Supp. 1146 (N.D. Cal 1995).

51. *Beard v. Stephens*, 372 F.2d 685 (5th Cir. 1967).

52. A wrongful death lawsuit was brought on behalf of the last prisoner fatally shot on the yards. See Corey Weinstein, "Even Dogs Confined to Cages for Long Periods of Time Go Berserk," in *Building Violence: How America's Rush to Incarcerate Creates More Violence*, ed. John P May and Khalid R. Pitts (Thousand Oaks, Calif.: Sage Publications, Inc., 2000), p. 116.

53. Ibid.

54. *Attica: The Official Report of the New York State Special Commission on Attica* (New York: Praeger, 1972), pp. 60–62.

55. Ibid.

56. *Estelle v. Gamble*, 429 U.S. 97 (1976).

57. *Washington v. Lee*, 263 F. Supp. 27 (M.D. Alabama 1966). Affirmed, *Lee v. Washington*, 390 U.S. 333 (1968).

58. Ibid.

59. *Wolff v. McDonell*.

60. *Prisoner Law Reporter*, "Prison Discipline Must Include Notice," hearing, Commission on Correctional Facilities and Services of the American Bar Association, vol. 3 (July 1975), pp. 51–53.

61. For examples of the measures taken to stamp out such activities, see Steve J. Martin and Sheldon Ekland-Olson, *Texas Prisons: The Walls Came Tumbling Down* (Austin: Texas Monthly Press, 1987), pp. 32–45, 50–58.

62. *Ex Parte Hull*, 312 U.S. 546. Rehearing denied, 312 U.S. 716 (1941).

63. Ibid.

64. *Bounds v. Smith*, 430 U.S. 817 (1977).

65. *Johnson v. Avery*, 393 U.S. 483 (1969).

66. Smith, *Law and Contemporary Corrections*.

67. David Rudovsky, Alvin J. Bronstein, and Edward I. Koren, *The Rights of Prisoners: The Basic ACLU Guide to a Prisoner's Rights* (New York: Avon, 1977), pp. 51–52.

68. *Pugh v. Locke*, 406 F. Supp. 318 (M.D. Alabama, 1976). A longer account of this litigation, which lasted for fifteen years, is found in Larry W. Yackle, *Reform and Regret: The Story of Federal Judicial Involvement in the Alabama Prison System* (New York: Oxford University Press, 1989).

69. *Newman v. Alabama*, 559 F.Supp 283 (1977).

70. The following account of the reform in Texas is derived from Martin and Ekland-Olson, *Texas Prisons*.

71. *Cruz v. Beto II*, 603 F.2d 1178, 1180 (1979).

72. Martin and Ekland-Olson, *Texas Prisons*, p. 53.

73. Ibid., p. 53.

74. Ibid., p. 54.

75. Ibid.

76. James B. Jacobs, "Judicial Impact on Prison Reform," in *Punishment and Social Control: Essays in Honor of Sheldon L. Messinger*, ed. Thomas G. Blomberg and Stanley Cohen (New York: Aldine de Gruyter, 1995), p. 71.

77. Ibid.

Multiple Choice Questions

1. A claim by an individual or group of individuals that another individual, a corporation, or the state has a duty to fulfill is referred to as a:

   A. Entitlement
   B. Right
   C. Privilege
   D. Law

2. What was the significance of the 1871 case *Ruffin v. the Commonwealth of Virginia*?

   A. Individuals lost all their rights and were slaves of the state when they were sentenced to prison
   B. Individuals lost one-half of their rights when they were sentenced to prison
   C. Individuals lost minimal rights when they were sentenced to prison
   D. Individuals did not lose any rights when they were sentenced to prison

3. Identify the U.S. Supreme Court case that resulted in the finding that deliberate indifference to the medical needs of inmates resulted in cruel and unusual punishment.

   A. *Wolff v. McDonnell*
   B. *Procunier v. Martinez*
   C. *Estelle v. Gamble*
   D. *Bell v. Wolfish*

4. Which of the following is not a minimal due-process right a prisoner has during a disciplinary proceeding?

   A. Inmates must receive advance notice of the alleged rule infraction
   B. Inmates must be allowed to present documentary evidence on their behalf if this presentation does not jeopardize the safety and security of the facility
   C. Inmates must be allowed to call witnesses on their behalf as long as the safety and security of the facility is not jeopardized
   D. Inmates must be allowed to have counsel from a trained attorney

5. Identify the first U.S. Supreme Court case that ruled on the desegregation of prisoners.

   A. *Pugh v. Locke*
   B. *Bell v. Wolfish*
   C. *Washington v. Lee*
   D. *Pell v. Procunier*

6. All of the following are reasons why the court avoided becoming involved in the area of prisoners' rights except:

   A. Judges wished to maintain the separation of powers among the branches of government
   B. Judges acknowledged their lack of expertise in corrections
   C. Judges feared that judicial intervention would subvert prison discipline
   D. Judges feared challenges from the federal government

7. Which of the following cases challenged the constitutionality of prison disciplinary proceedings pertaining to the loss of good time?

   A. *Wolff v. McDonnell*
   B. *Procunier v. Martinez*
   C. *Estelle v. Gamble*
   D. *Bell v. Wolfish*

8. Identify the U.S. Supreme Court case that defined the criteria for determining when the regulation of inmate correspondence constitutes a violation of an inmate's First Amendment liberties.

   A. *Wolff v. McDonnell*
   B. *Procunier v. Martinez*
   C. *Bell v. Wolfish*
   D. *Washington v. Harper*

9. What was the result of *Hudson v. Palmer*?

   A. The Fourth Amendment has no applicability to prison officials searching inmate's mail
   B. The Fourth Amendment has no applicability to prison officials searching pretrial detainees
   C. The Fourth Amendment has no applicability to prison officials searching visitors
   D. The Fourth Amendment has no applicability to prison officials searching a prison cell

10. According to the text, the three principle tests of conformity to the Eigth Amendment address all of the following questions except:

    A. Does the punishment shock the conscience of a civilized society?
    B. Is the punishment unnecessarily cruel?
    C. Does the punishment go beyond legitimate penal aims?
    D. Does the punishment apply to pretrial detainees?

True/False Questions

T F   1. Throughout the history of American corrections, racial segregation was deemed unconstitutional.

T F   2. An inmate's right to access to the courts can be satisfied only through the use of a law library in a correctional institution.

T F   3. Convicted felons have rights that are conferred on them by law.

T F   4. No area of correctional law has attracted as much litigation as prisoners' rights to practice religion.

T F   5. Double-celling of inmates in cells designed for one inmate is a violation of the Eighth Amendment's cruel and unusual punishment clause.

T F   6. From 1966 to 1976 courts became extensively involved in cases addressing prisoners' rights.

T F   7. Prisoners are not allowed to organize or join unions.

T F   8. Traditionally, courts have required prison administrators to allow religious groups the right to free exercise of their religion.

T F   9. Throughout history, the prisoner has enjoyed minimal legal rights in state corrections systems.

T F 10. Various court cases from the 1960s held that the Black Muslim faith was an established religion and its followers were entitled to the same rights as those of more conventional faiths.

Fill-in-the-Blank Questions   (based on key terms)

1. When a court mandates a correctional institution to make changes within a prison or jail, the _____ must develop a plan to implement these changes.

2. The _____ to the Consitution grants freedom of religion, speech, the press, and assembly.

Essay Questions

1. Identify and explain the areas in which inmates have pursued civil litigation to gain legal rights.

2. Explain how the Eighth Amendment has influenced prisons in the area of solitary confinement, deadly force, and medical treatment services.

3. Identify and describe the due-process rights an inmate has during prison disciplinary proceedings in which the loss of good time credits may occur.

4. Identify and explain what rights are afforded to inmates under the First Amendment of the Constitution. What are the limitations to these rights?

5. Identify and explain the positive aspects that the prisoners' rights movement has had on correctional institutions. Also, describe the areas in which shortcomings still exist.

ANSWERS

Multiple Choice Questions

1. B	6. D
2. A	7. A
3. C	8. B
4. D	9. D
5. C	10. D

True/False Questions

1. F	3. T
2. F	4. F
5. F	8. F
6. T	9. F
7. F	10. T

Fill-in-the-Blank Questions

1. Special master
2. First Amendment

Glossary

adjudicatory hearing a hearing held in juvenile court to determine whether a juvenile is guilty of the delinquency alleged against him or her.

aftercare supervision of adults and juveniles who are released from correctional institutions so that they can make an optimal adjustment to community living.

Auburn Silent System a system, first used in the prison in Auburn, New York, that demanded silence from all prisoners at all times, even when they were eating or working together.

autocratic warden a warden who is clearly the boss and who uses negative and punitive means in an attempt to control staff and inmates.

bail bonds generally a cash deposit but sometimes property or other valuables.

behavior modification a technique in which rewards or punishments are used to alter or change a person's behavior.

boot camp a military-style facility used as an alternative to prison in order to deal with prison crowding and public demands for severe treatment.

bridewells houses of corrections run by local authorities to teach habits of industry to vagrants and idlers.

building tenders inmates in Texas prisoners who were given authority by prison administration to discipline inmates who disturbed the social order.

bureaucratization of corrections the process after World War II in which state corrections were organized around a bureaucratic model.

butch the dominant, or male, role in a homosexual relationship.

California consensual model a participatory approach to prison management in which prison administrators in California surrendered so much control that they were accused of negotiating with prison gangs.

campus style open prison design that allows some freedom of movement; the units of the prison are housed in a complex of buildings surrounded by a fence.

chivalry old-fashioned notions about the "fair sex" that result in letting female offenders go or overlooking their offenses.

classification the process of assigning inmates to types of custody or treatment programs appropriate to their needs.

class neutrality the absence of class-related factors, such as employment, education, and family status, from sentencing guidelines.

closed visit a visit during which no physical contact is permitted between prisoner and visitor, who are separated by a partition extending from floor to ceiling.

Code of Draco exceedingly harsh law code issued in Athens by Draco in 621 B.C.E.; death was the punishment for nearly every offense.

Code of Hammurabi law code issued during the reign of Hammurabi of Babylon. The law of talion makes its appearance in this code, one of the first comprehensive views of the law.

cognitive-behavioral interventions interventions that attempt to identify cognitive deficits linked to criminality.

Cognitive Thinking Skills Program (CTSP) the most widely adopted of the cognitive-behavioral interventions.

community-based assistance program a reentry program designed to help ease the transition from prison to the community, especially in terms of employment and housing.

Community Corrections Acts state-based acts through which counties who participate receive subsidies for diverting minor offenders from state prisons.

community service order a court order that requires an offender to perform a certain number of work hours at a private nonprofit or government agency.

concurrent sentences prison terms for more than one crime that are served simultaneously.

conflict perspective the view that conflict is a permanent feature of society, that the source of conflict is the unequal distribution of the things that people most desire; that those who control scarce resources protect their own interests at other people's expense, and, consequently, that social order is maintained by force or by the implied threat of force.

conjugal visit a visit lasting one or two days during which prisoners can enjoy private visitation with their families.

consecutive sentences prison terms for more than one crime that are served one after the other.

contextual discrimination discrimination that is evident in specific social contexts.

contraband any unauthorized substance or material possessed by inmates.

corporate management model A version of participatory management that emphasizes modern management techniques.

corrections programs, services, and institutions that are responsible for individuals who are accused and convicted of criminal offenses.

courtyard style a prison design in which a corridor surrounds a courtyard; housing, educational, vocational, recreational, and dining areas face the courtyard.

criminal justice system an integrated system that is concerned with the apprehension, prosecution, conviction, sentencing, and correction of criminals.

day fine a fine the amount of which is determined by the offender's daily income.

day reporting center a facility where an offender, usually on probation, must report every day to participate in counseling, social skills training, and other rehabilitative activities

Declaration of Principles principles developed by the Correctional Congress that met in Cincinnati in 1870 to guide the reformation of prisons in the United States and abroad.

deferred sentence a sentence that delays conviction on a guilty plea until the sentenced offender has successfully served his or her probation term.

deinstitutionalization a strategy that focuses on keeping offenders in the community rather than placing them in prison.

deprivation model a model that views the losses experienced by an inmate during incarceration as one of the costs of imprisonment.

detention hearing a hearing in which the court decides whether to temporarily hold a juvenile in a secure facility, because he or she is acknowledged to be dangerous either to self or to others, or to return the person to his or her parents.

determinate sentencing sentencing that imposes a sentence for a definite term. Its main forms are flat-time sentences, mandatory sentences, and presumptive sentences.

deterrence crime control strategy that uses punishment to prevent others from committing similar crimes.

direct supervision a form of supervision in jail that gives staff members the ability to see and speak with inmates throughout the day.

dispositional hearing a hearing in which the juvenile court judge decides the most appropriate placement for a juvenile who has been adjudicated a delinquent, a status offender, or a dependent.

diversionary programs alternatives to confinement in a prison, such as deferred prosecution, resolution of citizen disputes, and placement in a therapeutic community.

drug courts courts designed for nonviolent offenders with substance abuse problems who require integrated sanctions and services such as mandatory drug testing, substance abuse treatment, supervised release, and aftercare.

due process a constitutional guarantee of fair and proper treatment by the government.

Eastern State Penitentiary a fortress-like prison consisting of seven wings radiating from a central control hub. Prisoners were kept in solitary confinement. It became a model for prisons in several European countries.

Eighth Amendment U.S. constitutional amendment forbidding excessive bail, excessive fines, and cruel and unusual punishments.

electronic monitoring the use of electronic equipment to verify that an offender is at home or in a community correctional center during specified hours.

femme the docile, or female, role in a homosexual relationship.

fictive family a grouping of unrelated individuals who have assumed the traditional family roles of mother, father, grandparents, and so on.

financial restitution payment of a sum of money by an offender either to the victim or to a public fund for victims of crime.

First Amendment U.S. constitutional amendment guaranteeing four freedoms: religion, speech, press, and assembly.

flat-time sentencing a form of determinate sentencing specifying that the offender will serve the entire sentence, no more and no less.

Fourth Amendment U.S. constitutional amendment that protects citizens against unreasonable searches and seizures by the government.

Fourteenth Amendment U.S. constitutional amendment that protects against deprivation of life, liberty, or property without due process and ensures equal protection of the laws.

functionalist perspective the view that societies are held together by their members' shared beliefs and values.

Furman v. Georgia (1972) U.S. Supreme Court decision that declared the death penalty unconstitutional.

galley service forced rowing of large ships called galleys, an example of punishment as a source of labor.

general deterrence The idea that punishing one person for his or her criminal acts will discourage others from committing similar acts.

"good time" a period of good behavior that entitles an inmate to a reduction on the length of time served.

graduated sanctions community-based sanctions that become more and more punitive as the seriousness of the criminal behavior increases.

Gregg v. Georgia (1976) U.S. Supreme Court decision that superseded *Furman v. Georgia* and declared the death penalty constitutional if certain conditions are met.

habeas corpus a Latin expression meaning "you have the body"; a writ of habeas corpus brings a person before a court or judge to determine the legality of his or her restraint in custody.

halfway house a residential center in which offenders are placed. Offenders leave the halfway house during the day for work, school, or therapy and on weekends to visit families.

hands-off doctrine the idea that persons sentenced to prison are not entitled to the same constitutional protections they enjoyed before conviction.

home furlough a home visit or temporary leave that usually lasts from 48 to 72 hours and is given on weekends.

house arrest a court-imposed sentence that orders an offender to remain confined in his or her own residence for the duration or remainder of the sentence.

house of refuge the first type of juvenile correctional facility in the United States; its goals were discipline and reform, vocational training, and protection from corrupting home environments.

importation model a model that suggests that the influences prisoners bring into the prison affect their process of imprisonment.

incapacitation isolating offenders to protect society.

indefensible space space within a prison that staff are unable to control.

indeterminate sentencing sentencing that permits early release from a correctional institution after the offender has served a required minimum portion of his or her sentence.

inmate code an unwritten but powerful code regulating inmates' behavior; inmate codes are functional to both inmates and prison administrators because they promote order within the walls.

inmate disturbance disorderly behavior by inmates that is violent (assaults, sabotage) or nonviolent (sit-down strike, hunger strike).

institutionalized racism racism that is so pervasive throughout a system that participants in the system may be unaware of its presence.

intensive probation supervision that is far stricter than standard probationary supervision.

intensive supervision of probation supervision based on the belief that increased contact and referral result in more positive adjustments to society, such as higher employment rates and lower rates of involvement in crime.

interactionalist perspective the view that emphasizes social interaction.

intermediate sanctions punishments, such as house arrest, electronic monitoring, and boot camp experience, that are more restrictive than traditional probation but less so than incarceration.

jail crowding the situation that exists when a jail has more inmates than it was built to hold.

just deserts punishment that is commensurate with the seriousness of the offense or the harm done.

justice model a model of corrections based on the belief that individuals have free will and are responsible for their decisions and thus deserve to be punished if they violate the law, and the punishment they receive should be proportionate to the offense or the harm done.

Justinian Code law code compiled by order of the Roman emperor Justinian in the sixth century; it revised, reorganized, and updated Roman law.

law of talion the principle of "an eye for an eye," embodied in the Code of Hammurabi.

Laws of Solon laws that replaced the Code of Draco in Athens in 594 B.C.E. Solon attempted to make laws that applied equally to all citizens and to make punishment proportionate to the severity of the crime.

Law Enforcement Assistance Administration federal agency created in 1967 to distribute funds to local governments for improved crime control.

lifer a prisoner who is serving a life sentence.

mandatory sentencing a form of determinate sentencing that sets a required period of incarceration for specific crimes.

mark system a system in which prisoners received "marks of commendation" for completing assigned tasks. They could use the marks to buy food and clothing. Prisoners who accumulated enough marks received a ticket of leave.

maximum-security prison a prison in which the complete control of any and all prisoners can be applied at any time.

medical model the idea that criminality is a sickness that can be cured through psychological intervention.

medium-security prison a prison with single or double fencing, guarded towers, or closed-circuit television monitoring, sally-port entrances, and zonal security systems to control inmate movement within the institution.

McCleskey v. Kemp (1978) U.S. Supreme Court decision that rejected the idea that the death penalty is racially unjust.

Michigan responsibility model a participatory approach to prison management that aims to make inmates responsible for their own actions.

minimum-security prison a prison with relaxed perimeter security, sometimes without fences or any means of external security.

multiple marginality marginality resulting from several factors, such as race, gender, and class.

"New Generation" jail a popular architectural design that foster the interaction of inmates and staff.

Panopticon A circular prison, in which guards could keep prisoners under constant observation.

paramilitary model a military-style operation featuring uniforms, a hierarchy of officers, and military nomenclature.

parens patriae doctrine a medieval English doctrine that today allows the state to intervene into family relations when a child's welfare is threatened.

parole the conditional release from confinement of an offender serving an indeterminate sentence.

parole board an official panel that determines whether an inmate serving an indeterminate sentence is ready for release.

parole guidelines actuarial devices predicting the risk of recidivism based on information about the offender and the crime.

participatory management a management style based on a team approach and on involving employees throughout the organization in decision making.

penal system a system consisting of local jails and police lockups; state and federal correctional institutions; state, county, and federal probation; state parole departments; and community-based agencies.

penitentiary a prison in which persons found guilty of a felony are isolated from normal society.

penitence model a system that provides offenders with an environment structured to convince them to repent their wrongdoings and become useful citizens upon their return to the community.

Pennsylvania model a penal system based on the belief that most prisoners would benefit from the experience of incarceration.

politicization of crime blaming crime for the social disorder perceived in the larger society.

positivism the belief that human behavior is caused by specific factors and that it is possible to know what these factors are.

prerelease instruction a reentry program that aims to help inmates make the transition from prison to life in the community by teaching inmates a number of skills.

presentence investigation an investigation whose main purposes are to help the court decide whether to grant probation, to determine the condition of probation, to determine the length of the sentence, and to decide on community-based or institutional placement for the defendant.

presumptive sentencing a form of determinate sentencing in which the judge follows sentencing guidelines that describe "typical" sentences or sentence ranges for particular categories of offenses and offenders

pretrial detention see *preventive detention.*

pretrial release release from jail or a pretrial detention center pending adjudication of the case.

preventive detention retaining in jail defendants who are deemed dangerous or likely to commit crimes while awaiting trial.

prisonization the process by which inmates learn and internalize the customs and culture of prison.

probation a form of punishment that permits a convicted offender to remain in the community, under the supervision of a probation officer and subject to certain conditions set by the court.

probation subsidy state funds paid to counties that divert adult and juvenile offenders away from incarceration in state prisons and into probation instead.

protective custody a specific area of the prison in which vulnerable inmates are isolated from the general population.

psychotherapy treatment of a mental disorder that involves any means of communication between a patient and a trained person.

radial design a wheel-like prison design with the control center at the hub and the "spokes" extending outward from this central core.

reality therapy psychological therapy that aims to teach an inmate ways to fulfill his or her needs for relatedness and respect through actions that are realistic, responsible, and right.

reformatory model a penal system for youthful offenders featuring indeterminate sentencing and parole, classification of prisoners, educational and vocational training, and increased privileges for positive behavior.

rehabilitation changing an offender's character, attitudes, or behavior patterns so as to diminish his or her criminal propensities.

reintegration model the idea that offenders' problems must be solved in the community in which they occur and community-based organizations can help offenders readjust to community life.

reintegrative philosophy the idea that every effort should be made to return offenders to the community as law-abiding citizens.

release on own recognizance (ROR) the release without bail of defendants who appear to have stable ties in the community and are a good risk to appear for trial.

reparation something done or paid to make amends for harm or loss.

residential programs community-based programs offered in residential facilities to probationers and parolees.

restorative justice making amends to the victim or to society for the harm resulting from a criminal offense.

retribution something given or demanded as repayment for wrongdoing; "getting even" for violating the social contract on which the law is based.

revocation of parole a formal procedure that takes place when a parole board, after listening to both the parolee and his or her parole officer and their witnesses, decides that parole must end because the offender committed a new crime or violated the conditions of parole.

revocation of probation a judicial procedure that takes place when a probation officer recommends to the court that probation should end because a probationer committed a new crime or violated the conditions of probation.

riot a violent inmate disturbance in which inmates attempt to take control of a cellblock or some other part of the prison.

screening of the vulnerable efforts by prison staff to identify vulnerable inmates and protect them from sexual or physical victimization.

selective incapacitation identifying high-rate offenders and providing for their long-term incarceration.

self-help program a program from which inmates seek self-improvement, such as anger management, or express ethnic and cultural goals.

sentencing guidelines federal and state guidelines intended to ensure fair sentencing by ending the reduction of terms in prison by grants of parole, ensuring that persons committing similar crimes serve similar terms, and ensuring that sentences reflect the severity of the criminal conduct.

service project a worthy cause, such as disaster relief or peer counseling, in which inmates willingly participate.

sexual victimization forcing an inmate to submit sexually to one or more inmates.

shared-powers model a version of participatory management that involved not only staff but also inmates in the governance of the prison.

social construction a human creation based on people's expectations of social life. Corrections is a social construct, a human creation rather than a fact of nature.

sociologically mindful able "to see more deeply into the process of world-making and to appreciate the nature of the social world as a human accomplishment" (Michael Schwalbe, *The Sociologically Examined Life* [Mountain View, Calif.: Mayfield, 1998], p. 79).

special deterrence the idea that an individual offender will decide against repeating an offense after experiencing the painfulness of punishment for that offense.

special master a judicial officer appointed by the court to hear testimony and make reports that become the decision of the court.

split sentence a sentence requiring an offender to spend a period of time in jail before being placed on probation in the community.

Stanford v. Kentucky (1989) U.S. Supreme Court decision allowing the execution of murderers who were age 17 at the time of the crime.

state's evidence evidence that an accomplice to a crime voluntarily provides to the prosecutors against other defendants.

status offense an act that would not be a crime if perpetrated by an adult but is considered a crime when perpetrated by a minor.

study release release of an inmate from prison to attend school in the community.

supervisory mandatory release a conditional release that occurs when an offender has served the original sentence minus time off for good behavior.

systems approach an approach to criminal justice that is based on the assumption that effective handling of the crime problem depends on the coordination and cooperation of all components of the criminal justice system.

telephone-pole design a prison design characterized by a long central corridor serving as the means for prisoners to go from one part of the prison to another.

Texas control model an approach to prison management in which corrections staff exercises strong control of inmates.

therapeutic community a community treatment group designed to divert drug abusers from the criminal justice system; therapeutic communities are sometimes allowed within prisons.

Thompson v. Oklahoma (1988) U.S. Supreme Court decision that prohibits execution of juveniles under age 16 at the time of their offense.

ticket of leave permission granted in Australia to a convict with good behavior to seek paid employment anywhere in the colony, subject to restrictions and the possibility of revocation.

transactional analysis (TA) a form of psychotherapy that tries to bring into balance the three states of the ego: "parent," "adult," and "child."

transportation banishment of criminals to colonies abroad.

treatment technologies rehabilitative programs used in correctional institutions—for example, treatment modalities, skill development, and prerelease programs.

Twelve Tables the foundation of Roman civil and criminal law, legislated in 450 B.C.E. by a commission of both patricians and plebians.

unconditional prison release a release that occurs when an offender's obligation to serve a sentence has been satisfied.

Uniform Crime Reports a national compilation of crime statistics based on information that local and state police agencies provide to the FBI.

utilitarianism the belief that punishment will yield some socially beneficial outcome.

victims' rights movement a grassroots movement asserting that the rights of victims of crime must be considered in the sentencing process.

War on Crime a federal get-tough response to crime that began in the 1960s and continues to the present.

War on Drugs a federal get-tough response to drugs that began in the 1970s and continues to the present.

Wisconsin classification system a system for classifying probationers by required level of supervision—intensive, medium, or minimum—and assigning them to appropriate casework groups.

work release release of an inmate from a prison or jail during the day so that the inmate can work in the community in a job that he or she can keep after confinement ends.

Name Index

Subject Index

Photo Credits

Ch.1 Opener: Joel Gordon; p. 5: North Wind Picture Archives; p. 8: Federal Bureau of Prisons; p. 11: Bettmann/Corbis; **Ch. 2** Opener: North Wind Picture Archive; p. 28: North Wind Picture Archive; p. 35, left: North Wind Picture Archives; p. 35, right: Eastcott/The Image Works; p. 36: North Wind Picture Archives; **Ch. 3** Opener: William C. Erickson/New Wave Photography; p. 56: Corbis; p. 61: courtesy of Richard A. McGee; **Ch. 4** Opener: Joel Gordon; p. 73: Zefa Visual Media/Index Stock Imagery; p. 78: A. Ramey/PhotoEdit; p. 83: courtesy of Norval Morris; **Ch. 5** Opener: Spencer Grant/PhotoEdit; p. 101: Larry Downing/Corbis Sygma; p. 105: courtesy of Kenneth F. Schoen; p. 112: AP/Wide World Photos; **Ch. 6** Opener: Kevin Horan/Stock, Boston; p. 133: John Boykin/PhotoEdit; p. 142: courtesy of Samantha J. O'Hara; **Ch. 7** Opener: A. Ramey/PhotoEdit; p. 161: AP/Wide World Photos; p. 163: AP/Wide World Photos; p. 168: courtesy of Doris L. MacKenzie; **Ch. 8** Opener: Gary Wagner/Stock, Boston; p. 184: AP/Wide World Photos; p. 191: State of California Department of Corrections; p. 195: courtesy of Joanne Page; **Ch. 9** Opener: Spencer Grant/PhotoEdit; p. 209: Joel Gordon; p. 215: Reuters/Mark Wilson/Archive Photos; **Ch. 10** Opener: Mikael Karlsson; p. 233: Minnesota Department of Corrections File Photo; p. 237: courtesy of Kathleen Hawk Sawyer; p. 241: Courtesy of the Corrections Corporation of America; **Ch. 11** Opener: AP/Wide World Photos; p. 261: AP/Wide World Photos; p. 265: courtesy of Frank Wood; p. 270: Mikael Karlsson; **Ch. 12** Opener: Santi Visalli Inc./Archive Photos; p. 287: courtesy of Mark Colvin; p. 288: Joel Gordon; p. 295: Mike Fiala/Getty Images; **Ch. 13** Opener: AP/Wide World Photos; p. 310: Richard Lord/The Image Works; p. 311: courtesy of Martin Groder; p. 318: Bob Daemmrich/The Image Works; **Ch. 14** Opener: Joel Gordon; p. 334: Bettmann/Corbis; p. 338: courtesy of James B. Jacobs; p. 340: Sean Cayton/The Image Works; **Ch. 15** Opener: Joel Gordon; p. 360: A. Ramey/PhotoEdit; p. 362: AP/Wide World Photos; **Ch. 16** Opener: Reuters New Media Inc./Corbis; p. 381: Joel Gordon; p. 386: A. Ramey/PhotoEdit; p. 391: courtesy of Jerome Miller; **Ch. 17** Opener: Mike Simons/Getty Images; p. 414: Shelly Katz /Time Pix; p. 419: AP/Wide World Photos; p. 422: courtesy of Sister Helen Prejean ; **Ch. 18** Opener: Reuters/Archive Photos; p. 433: Joel Gordon; p. 437: Joel Gordon; ; p. 438: courtesy of Coramae Richey Mann; **Ch. 19** Opener: Ed Kashi/Corbis; p. 451: Frank Pedrick/The Image Works; p. 454: AP/Wide World Photos; p. 457: courtesy of Michael Tonry; **Ch. 20** Opener: Joe Sohm/The Image Works; p. 473: Pearson Education; p. 474: courtesy of Vincent M. Nathan; p. 475: David McNew/Getty Images.